The Impact of Privatization with Foreign Involvement on the Restructuring Process of the Sugar Industry in Poland

European University Studies
Europäische Hochschulschriften
Publications Universitaires Européennes

Series V
Economics and Management

Reihe V Série V
Volks- und Betriebswirtschaft
Sciences économiques, gestion d'entreprise

Vol./Bd. 3239

PETER LANG
Frankfurt am Main · Berlin · Bern · Bruxelles · New York · Oxford · Wien

Cezary Iwan

The Impact of Privatization with Foreign Involvement on the Restructuring Process of the Sugar Industry in Poland

PETER LANG
Europäischer Verlag der Wissenschaften

Bibliographic Information published by the Deutsche Nationalbibliothek
The Deutsche Nationalbibliothek lists this publication in the Deutsche Nationalbibliografie; detailed bibliographic data is available in the internet at <http://www.d-nb.de>.

Zugl.: Frankfurt (Oder), Europa-Univ., Diss., 2006

521
ISSN 0531-7339
ISBN-10: 3-631-56023-0
ISBN-13: 978-3-631-56023-5
US-ISBN 0-8204-8768-6

www.peterlang.de

Table of Contents

List of Acronyms

ABF	Associated British Foods
BCC	Business Consulting Center
BSO	British Sugar Overseas
CAP	Common Agricultural Policy
CBOS	Centrum Badania Opinii Społecznej (Public Opinion Research Center)
CEECs	Central and Eastern European Countries
CEFS	European Committee of Sugar Manufacturers
CMO	Common Market Organization
COMECON	Council for Mutual Economic Assistance
EBIT	Earnings Before Interest and Tax
EBRD	European Bank for Reconstruction and Development
EDI	electronic data interchange
FDI	foreign direct investment
f.o.b.	free on board
FDPA	Foundation for the Development of Polish Agriculture
FPI	foreign portfolio investment
GATT	General Agreement on Tariffs and Trade
GDP	gross domestic product
GDR	German Democratic Republic
GHP	Good Hygienic Practice
GNP	Good Manufacturing Practice
GUS	Główny Urząd Statystyczny (Central Statisitical Office)
HACCP	Hazard Analysis and Critical Control Point
IAF	International Accreditation Forum
IERiGŻ	Instytut Ekonomiki Rolnictwa i Gospodarki Żywnościowej (Institute of Agricultural and Food Economics)
IHAR	Instytut Hodowli i Aklimatyzacji Roślin (Plant Breeding and Acclimatization Institute)
IMF	International Monetary Fund
IPC	Instytut Przemysłu Cukrowniczego (Institute of the Sugar Industry)
ISO	International Organization for Standardization
KRS	Krajowa Rada Narodowa (National Homeland Council)
KSC	Krajowa Spółka Cukrowa (National Sugar Corporation)
LIZ	Landwirtschaftlicher Informationsdienst Zuckerrübe
M&As	mergers and acquisitions
MNC	multinational corporation
MST	Ministry of State Treasury
mt	metric tonne

NAFTA	North American Free Trade Agreement
NBP	Narodowy Bank Polski (National Bank of Poland)
NATO	North Atlantic Treaty Organization
NIK	Najwyższa Izba Kontroli (Supreme Chamber of Control)
OECD	Organization for Economic Cooperation and Development
OHSAS	Occupational Health and Safety Assessment Series
PAI	Polska Agencja Informacyjna (Polish Information Agency)
PAIiIZ	Polska Agencji Informacji i Inwestycji Zagranicznych (Polish Information and Foreign Investment Agency
PAIZ	Polska Agencja Inwestycji Zagranicznych (Polish Agency for Foreign Investment)
PGRs	Powszechne Gospodarstwa Rolne (State Agricultural Enterprises)
P&L	Pfeifer & Langen
PKWN	Polski Komitet Wyzwolenia Narodowego (Polish Committee of National Liberation)
PLN	Polish zloty
PWE	Polskie Wydawnictwo Ekonomiczne
R&D	research and development
REI	regional economic integration
TNC	transnational corporation
TQM	total quality management
UNCTAD	United Nations Conference on Trade and Development
USDA	United States Department of Agriculture
USSR	United Soviet Socialist Republics
SAPARD	Special Accession Program for Agriculture and Rural Development
STC	Stowarzyszenie Techników Cukrowników (Association of Technicians of the Sugar Industry
ŚSC	Śląska Spółka Cukrowa (Silesian Sugar Company)
SZVG	Süddeutsche Zuckerrübenverwertungs-Genossenschaft eG
VAT	value added tax
VSZ	Verband Süddeutscher Zuckerrübenanbauer
WGK	Warszawska Grupa Konsultingowa (Warsaw Consulting Group)
WTO	World Trade Organization
ZPBC	Związek Plantatorów Buraka Cukrowego (Association of Sugarbeet Growers)

List of Tables

List of Figures

Preface

The production of sugar has a long history in Poland. The first beet-sugar manufacturing complex in the world was constructed by Franz Carl Achard (1753-1821) in Konary, a small village in Silesia, in 1802. The evolution of the Polish sugar industry during the following two centuries has constituted a fascinating field of study for economists and historians, as well as for all types of observers of social and political transformations in Poland. The present research focuses on the most recent developments in this sector of the Polish economy, namely, the privatization and restructuring process of sugar factories, initiated in the beginning of the 1990s.

At the end of 2002, I realized that despite the considerable involvement of foreign capital in the privatization of the sugar industry in Poland, and the frequent discussions in the media about the participation of foreign investors in this process, a comprehensive study examining the results of post-privatization restructuring activities at privatized sugar factories did not yet exist and decided to attempt to fill this gap. As somebody who has been observing the developments in the sugar industry in Poland for many years, I was convinced that the above problem was worth exploring.

My interest in the privatization and restructuring process of the sugar sector in Poland is due predominantly to my family background. Both my parents spent their entire professional careers working at several sugar factories for more than 30 years. Already at the age of nine I was accompanying often my father during the beet-processing season (campaign) on his daily rounds through all stations of the sugar factory in *Gryfice* to make sure that everything was working properly. Many years later, after enrollment as a full-time student of International Business Administration at the European University Viadrina in Frankfurt (Oder), Germany, I became fascinated by micro- and macroeconomic aspects of transition in Central and Eastern Europe, while at the same time, the situation in the sugar industry in my home country was becoming more and more interesting.

The primary concern of this research is to explore and evaluate how privatization of the sugar sector in Poland has influenced its restructuring up to the season 2004/05, inclusively. Apart from seeking to provide an answer to this primary research question, the present study constitutes a compendium of information on the evolution of the Polish sugar industry since 1945, in particular on the course of ownership transformations as well as the causes, direction and scope of restructuring processes in this sector in the 1990-2004 time period.

Cezary Iwan,

Słubice, 11.08.2006

Acknowledgements

I could have not completed this study without the generous help of many people to whom I would like express here my gratitude.

First, I would like to thank Prof. Dr. Hans-Jürgen Wagener for his willingness to take on the supervision of this project, for providing me with continuous support and encouragement, and a thoughtful critique of draft materials, as well as guidance in the writing of this book.

I am also deeply grateful to Prof. Dr. Alfred Kötzle, my second academic advisor, for valuable comments regarding the structure and contents of this study.

I am, of course, indebted to the *Bundesministerium für Bildung und Forschung* (Federal Ministry of Education and Research) for providing funds for this project under the framework of the *Europa-Fellows 2 (EF2)* program.

I thank Dr. Barbara Breysach, the Head Coordinator of the *EF2* program for her willingness to provide financial resources for field research.

Ms. Elżbieta Skiba from the Coordination Office of the *EF2* program deserves special recognition for prompt and extremely competent help in the handling of innumerable formalities.

I am infinitely grateful to the organizers of the *EF2* program, the Adam Mickiewicz University in Poznań and the European University Viadrina in Frankfurt (Oder), for the creation of excellent working conditions at Collegium Polonicum in Słubice as well as for providing me with accommodation in *Dom Doktoranta* (also in Słubice) throughout the entire length of my doctoral studies.

I thank the employees of sugar companies operating in Poland as well as all other persons interviewed for the purpose of this study (full list at the end of the References section), for their hospitality and willingness to provide me with necessary information. My special thanks go to Dr. Thomas Kirchberg, Dr. Stanisław Dziedzic, Rafał Wereszczaka, Dr. Gerd Jung, Dr. Henrik Einfeld, Dr. Adam Koziołek, Janusz Pierun, Dr. Łucja Chudoba and Dr. Marian Brzeziński.

I also thank my colleagues: Aleksandra Sznajder, Vera Trappmann, Onno Hoffmeister, Frank Bönker and Jan Wielgohs for helpful comments and suggestions.

I would like to thank Barty Begley for the proofreading of the original manuscript of this book.

I am grateful to Magda Jarmużewska for the design of several maps included in this book.

My thanks also to Ms. Ute Winkelkötter (Peter Lang Publishing) for instructions on the formatting of the manuscript of this book for publication.

Finally, I wish to thank my father, Stanisław Iwan, for his invaluable help in data collection and for frequent discussions on the technology and economics of sugar production as well as on the history of the Polish sugar industry.

1 Introduction

Between 1945 and 1989 all sugarbeet-processing plants in Poland were under strict governmental control and formed one large state enterprise with all activities being subject to administrative directives. After Poland's transition to a market economy in 1990, the state monopoly in sugar production was removed and the 78 sugar factories existing at that time in the country became individual economic units. The vast majority of them remained initially under state ownership. In the following years, 49 plants were privatized, two went bankrupt and 26 entered into a national sugar corporation.[1] All of the privatized sugar factories were transferred into the hands of foreign investors, in the vast majority of cases through a primary ownership transfer.

The central concern of this research is to critically explore and evaluate how privatization of the sugar sector in Poland has influenced the process of its restructuring up to and including the season 2004/05. In other words, the major aim of the study is to analyze restructuring activities introduced by foreign investors in sugar factories taken over in Poland and to find out to what extent these activities brought about a change in the productive efficiency and competitiveness of privatized plants.

Under pressure from various groups hostile to privatization of the sugar industry with foreign participation, the Polish government withdrew from the process in the middle of 2001 and made a decision about the formation of a national sugar company from all non-privatized sugarbeet-processing plants. On September 30, 2003, the district court in Toruń confirmed the merger of 22 of them to form the largest sugar corporation in Poland, *Krajowa Spółka Cukrowa "Polski Cukier"* (National Sugar Corporation "Polish Sugar") (in short *KSC*). Another 4 plants were incorporated into *KSC* until May 2005. 30% of the share capital of *KSC* is to be distributed free of charge to sugarbeet growers (15%) and employees (15%) of sugar factories incorporated in the company. The rest of the share capital is to be transferred into their hands in return for a payment at a later time.

Developments of the last 14 years in the sugar industry in Poland provide a very good ground for various analyses and comparisons. Which is restructuring more effectively, the state or foreign investors? What are the actual and potential consequences of the halting of privatization in the sugar sector? What is the optimal structure of the sugar industry in Poland? What are the most important achievements and failures in the restructuring process of the sugar industry in Poland? And finally, what does the 2004 EU enlargement mean for sugar produ-

[1] One sugar factory, *Leśmierz*, is owned by the state but for the time being it remains an independent economic unit.

cers, consumers and sugarbeet growers in Poland? These issues are also addressed in the present study in addition to the main research question.

1.1 Statement of the Problem

After the breakdown of socialism in Poland in 1989, the need was enormous for a thorough restructuring of the country's industrial enterprises. The local sugar industry was not an exception. Labor productivity, sugar and sugarbeet yields as well as other indicators of productive efficiency in this sector were much below western European standards. Whereas the economies-of-scale effect is strongly pronounced in the production of beet sugar, the sugar industry in Poland was highly fragmented and local beet-processing plants were very small compared with factories in Western Europe. In 1989, the average processing capacity of a Polish sugar factory amounted to 2,100 tonnes of beet throughput per day. Sugarbeet-processing plants in France, Italy, the German Federal Republic and the Netherlands started the campaign 1989/90 with an average daily processing capacity of 8,600, 7,220, 7,000 and 10,500 tonnes respectively (Sugar Economy Europe 1990/91).

The location of the sugar factory also has a significant impact on the cost efficiency of sugarbeet processing. Sugarbeets are bulky and heavy which makes their transport very expensive. Therefore, it is highly desirable that the distance between a sugar factory and its beet-procurement area is as little as possible. Unfortunately, a lot of sugar factories in Poland were constructed for political reasons in areas with unfavorable conditions for sugarbeet cultivation. Other features typifying the sugar industry in Poland at the time of the country's transition to a market economy included technological obsolescence of most sugar factories, overcapacity, excessive use of resources, serious environmental problems and lack of finance for investment.

Given the above facts, the major challenge after Poland's transition to a market economy was a consolidation of the 78 sugar factories into larger and more productive units, located in the vicinity of large beet-growing regions. Another necessary requirement for an improvement in the cost efficiency and overall competitiveness of sugar producers in Poland was an increase in the productivity and quality of the beet harvest.

The principal purpose of the present study is to explore and evaluate critically how privatization of the sugar sector in Poland has influenced the process of its restructuring up to and including the season 2004/05.

The most important microeconomic goal of privatization from above is the improvement in productive efficiency and competitiveness of privatized enterprises through their thorough restructuring.[2] This research aims to provide an answer to the question of to what extent the above goal has been achieved with regard to the sugar industry in Poland. It will explore what kind of restructuring activities were introduced by foreign investors in the post-privatization period and how these activities contributed to the improvement in the efficiency of beet-sugar production in a particular group of plants. The analysis covers the time period 1990 to 2004 (including results of the campaign 2004/05).

On the basis of the results of existing empirical studies examining the relationship between ownership form and restructuring efficiency (see Review of the Literature) as well as theoretical considerations on the potential microeconomic benefits and costs of the privatization to foreign investors of state-owned enterprises in CEECs (see section 12.4), the following three **hypotheses** have been formulated in order to give this research a testable form:

1) A takeover of sugar factories in Poland by foreign investors is followed by consistent institution of strategic restructuring activities aimed at the improvement in the overall efficiency of sugar production.

2) Sugar factories taken over by foreign investors benefit in the post-privatization period from appreciable transfer of capital and technology as well as technical and managerial know-how.

3) Restructuring activities conducted by individual foreign investors lead to a considerable improvement in the key indicators of productive efficiency and competitiveness at acquired groups of sugar factories.

In order to carry out the tasks specified above, it is essential to familiarize oneself first with the fundamentals of the technology and economics of sugarbeet processing as well as the specificity of the organization of the sugar market in Poland before and after the country's EU accession. It constitutes a necessary precondition for the determination of the desired direction of restructuring processes in the sugar sector and for the understanding of the significance of individual restructuring activities. For this reason, a lot of attention is devoted in the theoretical part of this study to the description and explanation of the above issues in an accessible way.

Furthermore, the present study follows the approach proposed by Djankov/Murrell (2000, 2002) and Johnson/Loveman (1995, p. 19), among others, who claim that in order to understand the challenges facing reformers in former Soviet-type economies and, which is of crucial importance, considering the scope of the present research, in order to define the term *restructuring*, it is essential to be thoroughly acquainted with the typical features of the socialist economy and the characteristics of its enterprises. Therefore, developments in governmental policy and the way state-owned enterprises, particularly sugar factories, were functioning

---

2 See for example Wagener 1994, pp. 13-16; Marinov et al. 1998, p. 29; Bałtowski 1998, pp. 33-38; Olesiński 2000, p. 46; Bałtowski 2002a, p. 27.

in Poland as the country entered the path of socialism and central planning in 1945 are delineated in the first few sections of this study.

The assessment of the effectiveness of restructuring activities implemented by individual sugar producers required also the identification of the key indicators of productive efficiency in sugar production and the major determinants of competitiveness in the sugar industry.

In this way, apart from its core function of providing an answer to the main research question, this book constitutes a compendium of information about the evolution of the Polish sugar industry from 1945 onwards, about the technology and economics of beet processing as well as factors influencing the competitiveness of sugar producers.

1.2 Review of the Literature

The political and economic transition processes initiated in Central and Eastern Europe in the beginning of the 1990s were accompanied by a proliferation of literature on privatization and restructuring challenges in countries of the region. Initially, this literature was dominated by books containing theoretical considerations regarding the above issues (discussion of problems and difficulties connected with microeconomic adjustment, description of the economic and legal environment in individual countries, policy recommendations, etc.), overviews of privatization programs introduced in individual countries as well as case studies portraying the course and results of post-privatization restructuring at selected enterprises.[3] The authors of many of these early publications pointed to the sale of state-owned companies to strategic foreign investors as the correct position to take in order to ensure effective restructuring and proper corporate governance. By the same token, they advised governments in CEECs to adopt policies attracting the inflow of privatization-related FDI.[4]

As time went by, the economic literature was systematically enriched by empirical studies examining the effects of ownership transformations in CEECs. Many of them, e.g. EBRD (1999, 2005), examine the impact of ownership form on restructuring efficiency and economic performance of firms on the basis of research embracing a large number of companies in different CEECs. Most of the studies find that enterprises controlled by foreign investors perform better than companies privatized domestically and those remaining in state hands. They show that foreign-owned companies are especially better able to cope with stra-

---

3 See for example Lipton/Sachs 1990a; Blanchard et al. 1991; Tirole 1991; Earle et al. 1993; Frydman et al. 1993; Sachs 1993; McDonald 1993; Pinto et al. 1993; Schmidt/Schnitzer 1993; Amsden et al. 1994; Roland 1994; Johnson/Loveman 1995; Brada 1996, Bornstein 1999.

4 See for example McDonald 1993; Megyery/Sader 1996.

tegic restructuring requiring strong managerial expertise and considerable financial outlays.[5]

Similar conclusions stem from the vast majority of empirical studies focusing on the case of Poland. They show that restructuring activities at enterprises privatized to foreign investors are carried out faster and more efficiently than at firms privatized domestically and at state-owned companies. They find that foreign-owned enterprises engage more in strategic restructuring, are more productive, profitable and export-oriented than indigenous firms. Their investment expenditures significantly exceed those of firms privatized domestically and state-owned companies.[6]

In the second half of the 1990s, a number of books were published on privatization in Poland and other CEECs, written by Polish authors.

The macro- and microeconomic goals of privatization from above as well as various privatization paths and problems connected with this aspect of economic transition have been defined and described thoroughly, *inter alia*, in Surdykowska (1997); Bałtowski (1998); PWE (1998); Olesiński (2000) and Bałtowski et al. (2002).

Since at the time of the publication of the books privatization and restructuring processes in Poland were already at an advanced stage, they contain in-depth overviews of the implemented reforms, reconsiderations of adopted policies as well as case studies showing the effects of selected privatization projects. Moreover, they offer an insight on the role and participation of foreign capital in the privatization of the Polish economy.

As far as the problems of industrial restructuring as well as the types and measurement methods of this process are concerned, one of the best-known and most influential textbooks on restructuring that has been published in Poland is entitled *Restructuring of enterprises: Change management process* (*Restrukturyzacja przedsiębiorstw: Proces zarządzania zmianami*). It was written by Cezary Suszyński, a professor of economics at the Warsaw School of Economics (*Szkoła Główna Handlowa w Warszawie*). The book has served since its publication in 1999 as a basis for the development of several restructuring programs in Poland, for the development of a restructuring plan for *KSC "Polski Cukier" inter alia*. The most important theoretical concepts included in the book were incorporated later in Suszyński's *Restructuring, consolidation, globalization of enterprises* (*Restrukturyzacja, konsolidacja, globalizacja przedsiębiorstw*), published in 2003 and containing an analysis of the successes and failures of industrial restructuring in Poland, an overview of new restructuring trends as well as future challenges standing in front of local enterprises.

---

5 See for example Carlin et al. 1995; Estrin et al. 1995; Pohl et al. 1997 ; EBRD 1999, 2005; Djankjov/Murrell 2000, 2002.

6 See for example Jarosz 1997; Jensen 2000; Kamiński/Smarzyńska 2001; Konings 2000; MST 2002; MST 2005; Żukowska-Gagelmann 2001.

In both the theoretical and empirical part of the present study, restructuring methods and restructuring activities have been divided, classified and weighted mainly on the basis of concepts presented in the above two books. Other theoretical and/or mixed studies on restructuring to which the present author refers repeatedly in the theoretical part of this research include: Carlin et al. (1995), Estrin et al. (1995), Grosfeld/Roland (1995); Ernst et al. (1996); Pohl et al. (1997); Djankov/Murrell (2000, 2002) and Hare (2003).

Of direct relevance to the present research are also studies explaining the determinants of competitiveness of economic units in today's marketplace. As in the case of the literature on restructuring, several publications on competitiveness exist that are very useful in the development of theoretical models enabling a meaningful interpretation of results of an empirical study, regardless of the type of industry under investigation. These publications include Flejterski (1984); Krugman (1994); Upton (1995); Porter (1998); Porter (1998a); Skawińska (2002); Stankiewicz (2002) and Wziątek-Kubiak (2003).

The evolution of the Polish sugar industry and its functioning in the 1945-1989 time period has been well documented by Łuczak (1981); Jaworowski (1995, 2001); Wykrętowicz (1997); Gierszewski (2001) and Waleriańczyk (2001). An analysis of these records greatly facilitates the understanding of restructuring challenges facing the sugar industry in Poland after the end of the communist period in the country. It constitutes, therefore, a perfect supplement to the aforementioned books presenting various definitions and theoretical concepts of industrial restructuring in former Soviet-type economies.

To the knowledge of the present author, there are only two publications where challenges facing the sugar industry in Poland after the country's transition to a market economy are discussed in a complex manner. The first of the two books, *Restructuring the Sugar Industry in Poland: Transition from State Socialism to the Common Agricultural Policy*, was written by Peter Walkenhorst. The primary concern of that study was the determination of the optimal structure of the sugar industry in Poland with the help of a mathematical programming model. Despite its topicality and direct relevance to the present research, the study was completed in 1995 and therefore it does not relate to many vital issues that emerged since that point in time. At the end of 2000, Walkenhorst complemented his earlier analyses in an article published in 2001 in the *European Review of Agricultural Economics*.[7] In the face of Poland's endeavors to join the EU, the determination of the optimal structure of the sugar sector in the country was extended in the above article by the simulation of several pre-accession and accession scenarios.

---

7 See Walkenhorst 2001.

The active participation of foreign investors in the privatization of the sugar industry in Poland, a sudden shift in governmental policy in 2001 resulting in the establishment of a national sugar corporation, adverse effects of an unsound regulation of the sugar market in the 1995-2003 time period on the financial situation of sugar factories, and finally, Poland's EU accession, call for a reflection and a reconsideration of the restructuring process of the sugar sector in the country.

One of the issues that remain to be discussed in the economic literature is the impact of ownership transformations in the Polish sugar industry on the restructuring of the sector. Such an analysis has not been carried out in Kondrakiewicz's *Holdings in the sugar industry* (*Holdingi w przemyśle cukrowniczym*), the second of the two major studies on sugar industry restructuring in Poland, published in 2000. Nonetheless, the book constitutes an important and well-known contribution to the literature about transformations in the Polish sugar sector after 1990. It analyses the establishment process and functioning of four sugar holdings brought into existence in 1994 and charged with the restructuring and privatization of state-owned sugar factories.

Information about major post-privatization restructuring activities conducted hitherto by foreign investors at sugar factories acquired in Poland can be found in a number of short reports published in three specialist periodicals available on the Polish market (*Gazeta Cukrownicza*, *Nowe Cukrownictwo* and *Burak Cukrowy*).[8] Several articles on the activity of foreign investors in Poland and on the situation in the local sugar sector have been published within the last 14 years also in foreign journals like the German *Zuckerindustrie/Sugar Industry*, *Zuckerrübe* and *Deutsche Zuckerrübenzeitung* as well as in the *International Sugar Journal*.[9] All these reports constitute a valuable source of information about restructuring activities implemented by individual investors at privatized sugar factories and about the resultant changes in the productivity and efficiency of sugarbeet processing and sugarbeet growing. Nevertheless, they are quite limited in scope. The purpose of the articles is rather to inform the readers about major investment projects implemented at a particular factory or a group of factories and/or to demonstrate the change of selected indicators of productivity over a short period of time. This allows one to assess to a certain extent whether there is a positive relationship between privatization and restructuring efficiency but information provided in the reports is insufficient to make a definite judgment on the issue.

Information concerning the relationship between ownership form and restructuring efficiency with regard to the sugar industry in Poland can also be derived from several short studies conducted by Łucja Chudoba from the Institute of Agri-

---

8 See for example Warnes/Thompson 1993; Antkowiak 1995, Nikiel 1999; Marjankowska 2002; Kleta 2003; Marjankowska 2003; Węgrzynowski 2003; Burak Cukrowy 2004; Marjankowska 2004; Pawełek 2004; Wojnarowska/Igras 2004; Kuczyński 2005.

9 See for example Farrow et al. 1993; Kirchberg 2003; Bücherl 2004; Wawro/Küster 2004.

cultural and Food Economics in Warsaw. The studies were published within the last few years in *Nowe Cukrownictwo*.[10] Chudoba compares in her analyses selected indicators of productive efficiency and competitiveness at five groups of sugar factories controlled by five sugar companies competing on the sugar market in Poland. Regrettably, the comparisons refer to one particular point in time and do not show how the selected indicators were changing over time at a particular group of plants. Assessment of the impact of privatization on productivity and changes in competitiveness with regard to a given group of factories is in this situation impossible.

With the exception of the aforementioned two studies conducted by Walkenhorst, there are no comprehensive publications analyzing the desired direction of structural changes in the sugar industry in Poland.

1.3 Methodology and Structure

The present study begins with a presentation of the basic information on the evolution of sugarbeet processing in Poland and other countries, and with a delineation of the most significant characteristics of the Polish sugar industry under the previous state-socialist system (**sections 2 and 3**). It is portrayed, *inter alia*, how selected indicators of productive efficiency developed between 1945 and 1989 in the Polish sugar industry and sugar industries in other European countries. This should facilitate the understanding of the restructuring challenges at the beginning of Poland's transition to a market economy and of the definition of the term *restructuring* with regard to the sugar sector.

Section 4 of the study contains a review of basic information on the technology and economics of sugarbeet processing. The main purpose of this section is to present the structure of costs in the production of beet sugar and to identify possible ways to reduce them.

In order to verify theoretical considerations included in section 4, **section 5** contains an analysis of the structural changes that took place in the European sugar industry within the last few decades. Another aim of this section it to reveal differences and similarities between sugar producers in Poland and the rest of Europe, particularly highly developed countries in the West.

In **sections 6 and 7**, developments in the world sugar market and in the sugar market in Poland in the 1990-2004 time period are portrayed and discussed. Furthermore, changes in selected indicators of productive efficiency in the Polish sugar sector in the above time period are presented.

Subsequently, in **chapter 8**, the development of the financial and economic condition of the sugar industry in Poland in the 1990-2004 time period is analyzed.

[10] See for example Chudoba 2003.

Section 9 presents the roots and seeds of the organization of the sugar market in the EU as well as the key features of regulation of the sugar market in Poland before the country's EU accession. Moreover, it contains an analysis of potential short-term implications of Poland's EU entry for local sugar producers, consumers and beet growers. It also portrays developments in the sugar market in Poland during the first few months of the country's EU membership. In the last subsection of section 9, possible consequences are discussed of the introduction of a planned overhaul of the EU sugar regime for sugar producers, consumers and sugarbeet growers in Poland.

In **section 10,** determinants of competitiveness in the sugar industry as well as the key indicators of productive efficiency in the production of beet sugar are defined.

In **section 11** the goals of privatization, determinants of enterprise restructuring as well as types and measurement methods of this process are precisely defined with reference to economic literature. Additionally, privatization paths that were used in the transfer into private hands of sugar factories in Poland are described. Section 11 also contains a discussion of social problems connected with industrial restructuring in transition economies.

Section 12 contains a definition of the term *foreign direct investment* (FDI) and a short overview of the development of possibilities of undertaking this form of business activity in Poland. Moreover, selected theories are presented that explain what prompts firms to move their operations abroad and why they choose a particular region or country for this purpose. In the last subsection of section 12, potential microeconomic benefits and costs of privatization-related FDI inflow to a given country are discussed.

In **section 13** the privatization process of the sugar industry in Poland and its current framework are presented.

In the last section of the theoretical part of the present study, **section 14**, the desired direction of structural changes in the sugar industry in Poland is specified. The section contains, *inter alia*, an analysis of the results of mathematical modeling conducted by Peter Walkenhorst in order to determine the optimal structure of the sugar industry in Poland. Moreover, the restructuring process of the sugar industry in Poland and the restructuring process of the sugar industry in East Germany are compared.

In **section 15,** the empirical part of the present study, the types and effectiveness of restructuring activities introduced at Polish sugar factories taken over by foreign investors as well as at plants incorporated into *KSC "Polski Cukier"* are analyzed and evaluated.

A combination of qualitative and quantitative research techniques was used to address hypotheses formulated in subsection 1.1. Greater emphasis was placed, however, on quantitative methods. Since each of the five sugar companies operating in Poland manufactures sugar at several locations, a case-study method was used to analyze systematically the process of enterprise adjustment.

Qualitative research was employed to test **hypothesis 1**. Each of the foreign sugar companies controlling a number of sugar factories in Poland was researched by carrying out in-depth, structured interviews with selected staff. The interview questions included open-ended, contingency (filter) and dichotomous questions divided into four areas: operational restructuring, organizational restructuring, raw-material management and financial restructuring. Interviewees were selected on the basis of personal contact and the willingness to participate in the research project. Most of the interviewed persons carried out at the time of the interview the functions of chief executive officers, members of the boards of directors and/or functional managers at individual sugar companies. All interviews were conducted in the interviewee's own language in the time period June 2003-May 2005. The full list of persons interviewed for the purpose of this study is presented at the end of the **References** section.

Apart from the collection of primary data during interviews, secondary information on restructuring activities introduced by individual sugar companies was gathered and used to test hypothesis 1 (articles, reports).

The test of **hypothesis 2** included both qualitative and quantitative research methods. It has been examined, for example, how much money was invested in the modernization of a given group of factories (collection of primary and secondary information). Subsequently, open-ended questions were asked during interviews with selected staff of individual sugar companies to derive a richer understanding about the functional nature of individual investment projects.

Quantitative research methods were used to test **hypothesis 3**. As a precondition for the carrying-out of the test, in section 10 of the present study the key indicators of productive efficiency and competitiveness in the sugar industry were defined and weighted according to their relative importance. In section 15 it has been examined how these indicators have changed with regard to a given group of sugar factories from the moment of their privatization up to and including the campaign 2004/05. The number of variables analyzed to test hypothesis 3 is not equal for all sugar companies. It varies depending on the availability of secondary numerical data and the willingness on the part of individual producers to provide primary data.

The prevailing opinion among representatives of the sugar industry is that the effects of complex post-privatization restructuring activities in the sugar sector should be evaluated no sooner than three years after the privatization. This is partly because of the fact that results of certain restructuring measures, e.g. those aimed at the increase in agricultural yields, need a considerable amount of time to materialize. Furthermore, privatization deals in the Polish sugar sector were often accompanied by the signature of the so-called *privatization packages*. In some cases, these packages obliged investors, *inter alia*, to keep the employment level at acquired sugar factories unchanged for a particular period of time. Therefore, the possibilities of labor-productivity improvement after privatization were, at least initially, heavily constrained.

Given the above facts, only sugar factories acquired by individual foreign investors before the beginning of the campaign 2002/03 were taken into account by the test of hypothesis 3. Moreover, factories at which sugarbeet processing ceased until the campaign 2004/05 were excluded from the test of hypothesis 3. Raw numerical data used to test hypothesis 3 was collected from two sources:

1) Brochures compiled after every campaign by the Institute of the Sugar Industry (*Instytut Przemysłu Cukrowniczego*) and Association of Technicians of the Sugar Industry (*Stowarzyszenie Techników Cukrowników*), both based in Warsaw;[11]
2) Questionnaires sent to individual sugar companies after the campaign 2004/05.

Analysis and interpretation of obtained results was carried out with the help of descriptive statistics.

In addition to the test of the above three hypotheses with regard to sugar factories privatized to foreign investors, the types and effectiveness of restructuring activities implemented up to the season 2004/05 at the group of state-owned plants which, since 2003, make up *KSC "Polski Cukier"* were described and analyzed in the last part of section 15. The purpose of this analysis is to compare restructuring efficiency at privatized and state-owned sugar factories.

[11] See IPC; STC.

2 Evolution of Sugarbeet Processing in Poland and Other Countries

The production of sugar from beets has its origins in the current territory of Poland. In 1802, in Konary, a small village in Silesia, Franz Carl Achard (1753-1821), physicist, chemist and botanist, initiated production of this type in a self-constructed factory. It was preceded by the discovery of sugar (sucrose) in beets by Andreas Sigismund Marggraf (1709-1782), member of the Royal Academy of Sciences in Berlin and Achard's teacher, in 1747.[12] European countries in those days depended entirely on the supply of raw cane sugar imported from their tropical colonies and subsequently processed in refineries located in the major ports of England, Germany and the Netherlands. The introduction of "a continental blockade" by Napoleon Bonaparte in late 1806 as an element of his struggle with England thwarted the import of cane sugar to Europe. Its rocketing price, added to by an earlier slaves' revolt on the French island of San Domingo[13], from where large quantities of raw cane sugar were procured, offered a strong incentive to look for new methods and sources of sugar extraction. Achard's method thus begun to spread throughout the Continent, especially in France where the process was strongly supported by the Emperor. Over time, the "white crystals" were transformed from an expensive luxury good into a commodity used in most European households. Sadly, the pioneering sugar factory in Konary was completely consumed by fire in March 1807. The demise of Napoleon, only a few years later, was followed by the revival of the import of cheap cane sugar into Europe, which led to the collapse of sugarbeet processing in most regions. It began to recover again in the 1830s, when an increasing number of European countries started to impose high tariffs on imported cane sugar. In the following years, production of sugar from beets gained increasingly in importance and flourished. Productive facilities where beet-sugar production took place increased in number while the aforementioned refineries designed for raw cane-sugar processing were disappearing apace. The originally small and, by today's standards,

[12] Two remarks have to be made here. Firstly, it has to be pointed out that unlike Marggraf, who was an indigenous German, F. C. Achard had French roots. His father, Guillaume, was a descendant of French Huguenots while his mother, Marguerite Elisabeth Henriette Roupert, came from Kassel. Nevertheless, since the architect of the first beet-sugar manufacturing complex in the world was born, brought up and educated in Berlin, it would not be mistaken to consider him a German. Secondly, at the time when the aforementioned factory was being built, the site of Achard's factory was called Cunern and the lands where it is located were part of Prussia. In 1945 the name Cunern was changed for Konary.

[13] In 1804, after a bloody uprising, San Domingo had become Haiti, the first independent nation in the Caribbean. Among the ranks of Napoleon's armed forces fighting for many months against the rebels in San Domingo there were several thousands of Polish soldiers. In 1844, a partition of Haiti was decided upon, and a large part of the island became the Dominican Republic.

primitive beet-sugar manufacturing units were gradually modernized and replaced by larger and more cost-efficient plants which together formed significant industries in numerous countries.[14] Today, sugarbeets are processed in nearly 800 plants in over fifty states worldwide. With an annual output of roughly 35 million tonnes of sugar they cover about 30% of world demand for this good. The rest is supplied by manufacturers extracting sugar from cane. Almost 80% of production based on sugarbeets is located in Europe (Bruhns, G. 2000; Zuckerwirtschaft 2003).

The establishment of the sugar factory in *Częstocice* in 1826 is officially recognized as the beginning of industrial production of sugar in Poland.[15] Evolution of the Polish sugar industry has since then been accompanied by alternate periods of destruction and slump during succeeding wars and occupations, followed by strenuous reconstruction and gradual rebirth. It is worth emphasizing that the development of this sector has contributed in many ways to the economic advancement of the whole country. Sugar factories served in Poland as early providers of electricity and various social services to neighboring households and local communities. They backed the development of transport infrastructure, gave financial support to the government in 1918 and pioneered the use of chemical engineering (Waleriańczyk 2001, p.52; Dmitrzak 1981, p. 354).[16] It would not be an exaggeration to say that until recently the sugar industry constituted one of the flagships of the Polish economy. Unfortunately, the institution of central planning after the Second World War gave rise to the emergence of a considerable gap in technological advancement and productivity between Polish and West European sugar factories, widening continuously to the disadvantage of the former, especially from the 1960s. The radical change in political and economic system introduced thirty years later made it clear that in order to sustain itself in the new, market-oriented environment and to make up for the deficiencies of the past, the sugar industry, like many other sectors of the economy, requires a comprehensive and careful restructuring.

This study follows the approach proposed, among others, by Djankov/Murrell (2000, 2002) and Johnson/Loveman (1995, p. 19) who claim that to understand the challenges facing reformers in former Soviet-type economies and, which is of crucial importance considering the scope of the present research, in order to define the term *restructuring*, it is essential that one be thoroughly acquainted with the typical features of the socialist economy and the characteristics of its enterprises. The vast majority of sugar factories that have been privatized in Poland

[14] The above historical overview is based on Łuczak 1981; Kowalewski 1992; Bruhns 1997, 2000; Wilk 2002 and Wężowska 2004.

[15] This still functioning sugarbeet-processing plant is the place where the 175th anniversary of the Polish sugar industry was celebrated in June 2001.

[16] For more detailed information concerning the history of the Polish sugar industry see Łuczak 1981 and/or Waleriańczyk 2001.

had to wait several years for the transfer into private hands after the country's sudden "leap to a market economy" in 1990. Hence, some may argue that before privatization occurred, most sugarbeet-processing plants had been already operating in the new system for a long time and there is no longer any need to discuss the communist past but to concentrate on the challenges of the present day instead. Unfortunately, regardless of the structure of that economic sector and of current ownership, industrial enterprises with a "communist ancestry" still suffer the consequences of their socialist legacy. And in most cases, those that will survive have a long way to go before being completely rid of problems attributable solely to the old heritage. Therefore, the next section portrays developments in governmental policy and the way state-owned enterprises, particularly sugar factories, were functioning in Poland as the country entered the path of socialism and central planning in 1945.

3 The Polish Sugar Industry under Communist Rule

The end of World War II marked the beginning of profound changes and the introduction of a new order in Poland. The Soviet Union quickly became the key provider of assistance in the reconstruction of Polish cities and the Polish economy, mainly as a source of capital and imports. The result was an increasing dependence on Moscow authorities. This position was soon sealed by the Yalta agreements, which made clear that in the foreseeable future Poland would remain under the influence of the USSR. This facilitated the gradual transformation of the country into a socialist economic system with all activities organized in compliance with the needs and ideology of the Soviets. Their leader, Josef Stalin, obsessed with the eventuality of a military offensive supposedly being plotted by the United States, was eliminating any kind of opposition and, with an iron hand, strove to model the political and economic framework in Poland according to his will. This included the establishment of large and powerful military forces, an economic structure favoring heavy industry and autarky, control by a single communist party, strict censorship of mass media, collective ownership of basic means of production and a command economy based on central planning (Zonis/Semler 1992, pp. 14-17; Lavigne 1999, pp. 3-14).

3.1 Agricultural Reforms and their Effect on the Economic Efficiency of Sugar Production

One of the early decisions made by the first, provisional post-war government in Poland, the Polish Committee of National Liberation (PKWN)- nominated by and subordinated to the Soviets- concerned agriculture as a whole, but from the point of view of economic efficiency turned out to be particularly unfavorable for the sugar industry. On the basis of a decree of September 6, 1944, large private farms were expropriated and parceled out into thousands of much smaller lots (Gierszewski 2001, p. 29; Wykrętowicz 1997, p. 22). In other words, all big plantations were compulsorily divided into smaller lots and distributed to local people. The fact that some landowners possessed 50 hectares of land and more while others had little or nothing was contradictory to the tenets of the new political system, as was private property. Therefore, parts of arable areas of land were entered into the composition of State Agricultural Enterprises (PGRs). Nevertheless, it never came to a large-scale collectivization of agriculture in Poland. Two major attempts to achieve this met with the resistance of peasants, coincided with general economic crises in the country, and turned out to be complete failures. These attempts were abandoned in 1956 and then again in the second half of the 1970s.[17] The result of the aforementioned division of land was that the number of sugarbeet growers and small farms increased dramatically. In 1938 the number of sugarbeet growers in Poland amounted to 40,000 and in 1946 the corresponding number was 376,000. In the following years it was still rising and reached over one million growers in 1952 (See Table 1). Many of them were confronted with sugarbeet growing for the first time and did not possess the necessary skills, experience and equipment. The engagement of large numbers of additional workforce in the sugar industry became necessary in order to instruct new beet growers, arrange beet deliveries and cope with spreading bureaucracy (Wykrętowicz op. cit., p. 39).

Table 1. Number of sugarbeet growers and average area per grower in Poland, 1946-1989

	1946	1950	1955	1960	1965	1970	1975	1980	1985	1989
Number of growers (in 1000)	375.9	819.8	906.2	755.6	723.9	548.6	554.7	450.0	425.1	358.8
Average area per grower (in ha)	0.45	0.35	0.43	0.56	0.66	0.74	0.89	0.98	1.04	1.18

Source: Wykrętowicz 1997, p. 111; Cukier i Skrobia.

The increasing dispersion of small plantations and the growing number of individual farmers were accompanied by the establishment of regional sugarbeet-purchasing centers throughout the country. Their task was the storage of sugar-beets delivered by local growers who were unable to bring them directly to sugar factories. The creation of such centers was favored by the fact that, especially up until the 1960s, the answer to a low beet yield per hectare was the expansion of the harvested area and not the improvement of farming techniques. After 1956 more than a half of sugarbeets processed in Polish factories were delivered to hundreds of regional purchasing centers (Łuczak 1981, p.262). From there, they were transported by trains and trucks to nearby plants. The running of each center

[17] The share of collectivized lands where beets were grown in the overall beet-harvested area amounted at its peak to about 30% (in the middle of the 1950s and 1970s). In other years this share fluctuated between 14% and 20 % (Łuczak op. cit, p. 255).

required an adequate workforce, equipment and coordination. It is noteworthy that in the early years of the existence of the regional purchasing centers, the unloading of beets was carried out manually and it was not until the middle of the 1970s that this process became almost fully mechanized. In 1960 the number of the aforementioned centers reached nearly 2000. In the following years, it started to gradually decrease due to the fact that their maintenance was very costly for sugar factories. Consequently, more and more beets were delivered directly from the fields to the processing facilities.[18] Nevertheless, in 1989, about 60% of beets procured by Polish sugar factories were still being conveyed from 903 regional purchasing centers (Wykrętowicz op. cit., p. 145).

The negative effects of the agricultural reform were reflected most visibly in poor quality of sugarbeets and low sugarbeet yields per hectare. The aforementioned lack of experience in growing techniques on the part of a large number of new planters as well as a shortage of fertilizers had the effect that during the entire period under consideration the sugarbeet yield per hectare in Poland was considerably lower than in Western Europe. In the time period 1965-69, for example, it amounted to 45.2 t in France, 42.6 t in the German Federal Republic, 36.0 t in Italy and 37.9 t in Great Britain (F.O. Licht's World Sugar Statistics). As presented in Table 2, the average beet yield per hectare in Poland in the first half of the 1960s was equal to a mere 31.3 t. In the following five-year periods, the relative under-performance of Polish agriculture increased even further. A low sugarbeet yield per hectare was accompanied by a comparatively low sugar yield per hectare, calculated as a quotient of total sugar production and the beet harvested area.[19] It was influenced, among other things, by the fact that the then authorities dictated for a long time the use of sugarbeet seeds bringing profits to farmers but at the cost of sugar factories (Jaworowski 1995, p. 35). Such seeds, used widely, especially in the 1960-1975 time period, grew into big, heavy beets with a lot of leaves (nourishment for farm animals) but had lower sugar content than beets from other seed types, preferred by the manufacturers of sugar. Additionally, beet growers were paid according to the weight of beets delivered to factories and not according to the sugar content. It gave an incentive to grow a lot of beets but without taking any special care of their quality.

Sugar yield per hectare constitutes a very valuable indicator reflecting accurately the overall productive efficiency in sugarbeet growing and, to a lesser extent, beet processing, in a particular region or country (ibid., p. 56). In the 1965-69 time period, it reached, for instance, 6.9 t in France, 6.5 t in the German Federal Re-

---

[18] The coordination of such deliveries left much room for improvement. The general rule was that the decision regarding the date and time of delivery of contracted beets to factories was left to the growers. The result were long queues of tractors waiting in front of factories during the campaign and mountains of sugarbeets accumulated in storage areas designed for this purpose.

[19] According to the methodology adopted by F.O. Licht.

public, 5.5 t in Great Britain, 7.1 t in the Netherlands and 7.2 t in Austria (F.O. Licht's World Sugar Statistics). A comparison of the above results with those achieved at the same time in Poland (Table 2) offers an equally unflattering picture as the sugarbeet yield per hectare. Unfortunately, with regard to sugar yield per hectare, the superior performance of West European countries was assuming ever greater proportions right up to the end of the time period discussed in this section.[20]

Table 2. Sugarbeet and sugar yield per hectare, Poland, 1945-1989 (five-year periods average, in tonnes)

	1945-49	1950-54	1955-59	1960-64	1965-69	1970-74	1975-79	1980-84	1985-89
Sugarbeet yield/ha	16.8	18.8	19.6	24.5	31.3	30.8	29.1	30.1	33.3
Sugar yield/ha	2.4	2.8	2.6	3.3	3.5	3.6	3.1	3.5	4.0

Source: Calculations by the author, based on Cukier i Skrobia; Łuczak 1981, pp. 342-344.

As concerns the sugar factories, their effectiveness in sugar extraction is measured with the help of an indicator called "recovery of sugar". This can be calculated as a quotient of the sugar yield in percent of the raw sugar value on beet and the polarization of cossettes (the content of sugar in sliced beet roots expressed as percentage). In 1989, for example, the average sugar content in sliced beet roots delivered to factories in Poland amounted at the industry level to 15.79%. In the production process factories obtained from those beets, on average, 12.25% raw sugar value on beet, giving a recovery of sugar for the entire industry in 1989 of 77.58%. This is not very good, considering the fact that in the years 1945-49 this figure came to, on average, 82%. The results achieved in other five-year periods between 1945 and 1989 are presented in Table 3, portraying also the average polarization and sugar yield in percent of raw sugar value on beet in those time periods.

The poor quality of sugarbeets processed at many Polish factories was influenced also by their transportation over very long distances, from the Eastern regions of Poland to the West and South of the country. The fact that industrialization of the economy in the East was not as intense as elsewhere meant that a lot of people living there continued or started to work in agriculture, while many farmers from other regions found employment in other industries.

---

[20] In order to get a more transparent picture of how the gap between Poland and the aforementioned West European countries developed over time, it is important to note that in the 1945-50 time period sugarbeet yield per hectare in Poland constituted on average about 70% of the level recorded in Western Europe. Sugar yield per hectare in Poland amounted at that time to about 80% of the West European average. In the second half of the 1980s the above relations looked much worse from the point of view of Poland. The average sugarbeet yield and sugar yield per hectare in this country in the 1985-89 time period constituted, respectively, only 60% and 50% of the results achieved by most West European states (F.O. Licht's World Sugar Statistics).

Table 3. Sugar yield (in % of raw sugar value on beet), polarization of cossettes and recovery of sugar (in %), Poland, 1945-89 (five-year periods average)

	1945-49	1950-54	1955-59	1960-64	1965-69	1970-74	1975-79	1980-84	1985-89
Sugar yield	14.08	15.06	13.84	13.18	11.66	12.00	11.05	11.56	12.18
Polarization	17.16	18.07	17.27	16.51	15.04	15.51	14.74	15.26	15.57
Recovery of sugar	81.98	83.32	80.05	79.84	77.46	77.35	74.96	75.70	78.23

Source: Calculations by the author, based on Łuczak 1981, pp. 342-44; Wykrętowicz 1997, p. 268.

Consequently, more sugarbeets were grown in the Eastern regions than the local factories were able to process. At the same time, managers of sugar factories in other parts of the country complained about the shortage of beets. In the first half of the 1960s, long-distance transports of beets in Poland fluctuated between 1.4 and 2 million t (Łuczak op. cit., p. 261). Unfortunately, sugarbeets tolerate neither too much travel nor long storage periods. Exposed to such conditions they quickly lose on quality. Last, but not least, the degrading of beets was brought about by the long duration of campaigns at many factories, noticeable especially from 1960 onwards. Production facilities which were extending their production until January were often compelled to process beets that had already lost much of their original sugar content and had started to go rotten.[21] The result of all these developments was that from the middle of the 1950s, both polarization and sugar yield in % of raw sugar value on beet decreased considerably and remained at this low level until the end of the totalitarian era in Poland (See Table 3). Logically, this was accompanied by a significant increase in total production costs for sugar factories. The fact that, for instance, between 1950 and 1954 sugar yield in % of raw sugar value on beet amounted on average to 15.06% while in the 1965-69 time period the corresponding number was 11.66% means that in the first half of the 1950s sugar factories in Poland had to process 6.6 t of beets in order to obtain one tonne of sugar and in the second half of the 1960s, the amount rose to 8.6 t. It needs to be added that the payment for sugarbeets (excluding transport costs) has always represented the largest part in the overall structure of the production costs of one tonne of sugar. In 1955 and 1985 this share amounted to 62% and 52%, respectively (Wykrętowicz op. cit., pp. 318-319).

The availability of large amounts of sugarbeets in the vicinity of *Lublin* and *Zamość* was one of the major reasons why the government decided to build five

[21] The average duration of a campaign, starting usually in late September or early October, amounted to 112 days in 1965, 110 in 1975, 91.5 in 1985 and 83.5 in 1989 (Wykrętowicz, op. cit., p.183). At the same time, a considerable differentiation between individual sugar factories could be observed. For instance, during the season 1984/85, there were 18 factories in Poland where the length of a campaign did not exceed 90 days and there were 16 factories where it was longer than 115 days. The processing campaign at three plants, *Chełmża*, *Brześć Kujawski* and *Dobre* lasted more than 130 days (STC 1985, p. 7).

new factories in the East. The construction of the first, *Werbkowice*, with a daily processing capacity of 3,400 t, was completed in 1963. Another motive for the expansion of the processing capacity at the industry-level through construction of new plants and modernization of the existing ones was that the latter could hardly cope with the increasing beet harvest in the country and manage the implementation of larger and larger production targets dictated from above.[22] In this way the aforementioned long-distance transportation of beets was reduced in the following years but only to a certain amount, and they were to continue until 1989 (ibid., p. 49). It is important to note that during the entire time period under discussion the costs of beet transport placed a huge burden on the sugar factories, with farmers often growing beets in areas located tens of miles from the nearest factory or regional beet-purchasing center. Until the late 1960s, about 51% of beets were shipped to sugar factories on trains, nearly 27% by trucks and the rest, from nearby plantations, was delivered by farmers or collected by factories with their own means of transport. In the following years, the share of railway in the above structure decreased, so in 1974 it amounted to 23% and it was the transport on trucks that became the dominant form of beet delivery (Łuczak op. cit., p. 249; Wykrętowicz op. cit., p. 129).

In the 1960s the sugarbeet yield per hectare increased significantly in comparison with previous years. This was mainly due to increasing use of fertilizers and various chemicals protecting beets from diseases and reducing the growth of weeds on the fields. Nevertheless, the quantitative usage of such agents was still much less than in Western Europe. The sugar yield per hectare was also slowly improving owing to the gradual replacement of low sugar sugarbeet seeds by a different sort, producing beets containing more sugar.

From the middle of the 1950s, the number of beet growers began to fall with the average harvested area per grower rising at the same time. The reduction in the number of beet growers applied predominantly to small farms, characterized by poor soil quality. It has to be mentioned here that up to the early 1950s sugar constituted the dominant form of compensation for delivered beets. Therefore, in the first years of the post-war period many farmers entered into beet growing with the sole purpose of obtaining sugar that was scarce at that time. They could subsequently use part of the sugar they received for their own use and sell the rest on the market at a good price (Wykrętowicz, op. cit., p. 125; Łuczak, op. cit, p. 258). Later, when sugar became easily available and relatively cheap, this group of farmers ceased growing beet, an activity that still paid but was also labor-intensive. Other reasons for the shrinking number of beet growers included: shortage of labor on farms; increasing competitiveness of other crops; and the rise in prices for services connected with field-crop production. Despite the above

[22] The construction of new plants was accompanied by the closure of three small and obsolete sugar factories: *Stare Pole* in 1967, *Ząbkowice* in 1984 and *Izabelin* in 1986 (Jaworowski op. cit., pp. 41-42).

developments, in 1989 the average number of beet growers per sugar factory was still enormous, at 4,600 (IERiGŻ 1992, p. 5).

All in all, the above structural changes in the raw-material base of sugar factories entailed great expenditures and had a negative effect on the economic efficiency of sugar production. Unfortunately, experience has shown that a reversion of those reforms has been extremely difficult. Most sugar producers in Poland are today still going to great lengths to influence the process of increasing the area of individual sugar plantations while reducing the number of plantations. This will be discussed in more detail later in this study.

3.2 Structure, Organization and Functioning of the Sugar Industry between 1945 and 1989

Apart from significant changes in agriculture, there began in 1946 the implementation of policies adherent to the communist dogma, including the nationalization of large industrial enterprises. The legal foundation for this 'ownership reform' was constituted by the law of January 3, 1946, on the nationalization of key sectors of the national economy, passed by the National Homeland Council (KRN). The process applied also to the sugar industry, which was just being raised from the post-war ruins. As Waleriańczyk (2001, p. 47) recalls: "*In the majesty of law, owners of sugar factories were deprived of their lives' fortunes and dispossessed of private property. For the next fifty years, sugarbeet-processing plants in Poland did not have an owner since an official administering real-estate on the behalf of the government is not an owner. As we clearly see today, it was one of the worst decisions made after 1945*".

It has to be mentioned at this point that apart from the general, and extremely serious, war damage that affected the Polish sugar industry, the most severe losses were recorded among employees of sugar factories.[23] Transport infrastructure was also destroyed with many sugar factories completely cut off from the world. Nonetheless, the reconstruction and repair of sugar factories was managed in a quite short period of time. After the completion of the process in 1948, the restored structure of the sugar sector in Poland comprised 76 factories.[24] Figure 1 displays their location and includes also the five aforementioned plants constructed at a later period of time: *Werbkowice* (1963, with a nominal processing capacity of 3,400 t of beet throughput per day), *Łapy* (1974,

[23] According to Łuczak 1981, pp. 218-219, from the overall number of about 800 employees of the sugar industry who did not survive the war, nearly 350 belonged to highly qualified and experienced staff. This amounted to 10% and 25% of full-time employees, respectively.

[24] 101 factories found themselves within the borders of post-war Poland but production was resumed in 76 (Łuczak 1981, p. 221).

Figure 1. The sugar industry in Poland, 1945-1989

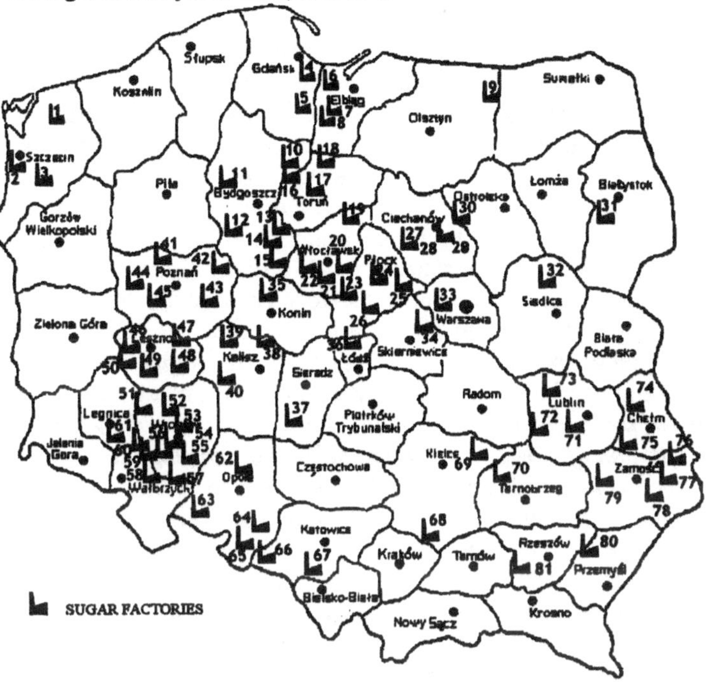

1. GRYFICE 1898
2. SZCZECIN 1884
3. KLUCZEWO 1884
4. PRUSZCZ GDAŃSKI 1881
5. PELPLIN 1879
6. NOWY STAW 1877
7. STARE POLE 1880-1967
8. MALBORK 1880
9. KĘTRZYN 1882
10. ŚWIECIE 1863
11. NAKŁO 1881
12. ŻNIN 1894
13. TUCZNO 1883
14. JANIKOWO 1875
15. KRUSZWICA 1880
16. UNISŁAW 1883
17. CHEŁMŻA 1882
18. MEŁNO 1883
19. OSTROWITE 1900
20. CHEŁMICA 1899
21. BRZEŚĆ KUJAWSKI 1884
22. DOBRE 1907
23. OSTROWY 1847
24. BOROWICZKI 1900
25. MAŁA WIEŚ 1899
26. DOBRZELIN 1850
27. GLINOJECK 1986
28. IZABELIN 1859-1986
29. CIECHANÓW 1882
30. KRASINIEC 1866
31. ŁAPY 1974
32. SOKOŁÓW 1846
33. MICHAŁÓW 1852
34. GUZÓW 1830
35. GOSŁAWICE 1911
36. LEŚMIERZ 1838
37. WIELUŃ 1912
38. ZBIERSK 1852
39. WITASZYCE 1897
40. ZDUNY 1881
41. SZAMOTUŁY 1895
42. GNIEZNO 1882
43. ŚRODA WLKP. 1880
44. OPALENICA 1881
45. KOŚCIAN 1882
46. WSCHOWA 1880
47. GOSTYŃ 1897
48. MIEJSKA GÓRKA 1884
49. GÓRA ŚLĄSKA 1889
50. GŁOGÓW 1897
51. MAŁOSZYN 1897
52. SUŁKOWICE 1890
53. KLECINA 1839
54. PUSTKÓW 1898
55. STRZELIN 1871
56. ŁAGIEWNIKI 1859
57. ZIĘBICE 1883
58. ZĄBKOWICE 1884-1984
59. ŚWIDNICA 1848
60. PASTUCHÓW 1838
61. JAWOR 1871
62. WRÓBLIN 1882
63. OTMUCHÓW 1880
64. CEREKIEW 1870
65. BABORÓW 1873
66. RACIBÓRZ 1870
67. CHYBIE 1884
68. ŁUBNA 1845
69. CZĘSTOCICE 1826
70. WŁOSTÓW 1913
71. LUBLIN 1895
72. OPOLE 1883
73. GARBÓW 1908
74. REJOWIEC 1899
75. KRASNYSTAW 1976
76. STRZYŻÓW 1900
77. WERBKOWICE 1963
78. WOŻUCZYN 1912
79. KLEMENSÓW 1895
80. PRZEWORSK 1895
81. ROPCZYCE 1979

Source: Illustration by the author, based on Łuczak 1981, pp. 226-227 and Wykrętowicz 1997, p. 53.

4,800 t/d), *Krasnystaw* (1976, 4,800 t/d), *Ropczyce* (1979, 6,000 t/d) and *Glinojeck* (1986, 6,000 t/d).

Concentration on the build-up of an industrial-military complex constituted the primary issue for the communist establishment, which resulted in the sugar industry and the whole agricultural sector being undervalued. Financial resources allocated to the modernization and technological upgrading of sugar factories did not meet the actual needs of the industry. Ironically, the revenues from the exportation of sugar as well as direct and indirect taxes imposed on this good constituted, especially up to the 1960s, a significant resource within the national budget (Wykrętowicz, p. 298; Łuczak, p. 325). Expenditures for the development of the agro-food sector were most severely reduced in the beginning of the 1950s, when the world stood on the brink of a nuclear conflict and all funds were redirected to the expansion of heavy industry. Industries like mining and mechanical engineering gained primary importance at that time.

"*In Cracow, the ancient university city was overshadowed by the construction and the pollution of Nowa Huta, a new suburb supporting the Lenin Steelworks, the largest of its kind in the country*" (Davies 1981, p. 579).

Shipbuilding, the manufacture of automobiles and airplanes were other target sectors that soon evolved into pillars of the economy. Unfortunately, this tremendous growth was accompanied by extensive and systematic increase in the use of production factors without any technological improvements. Raw material shortages were inevitable while over-employment was already in place. Interestingly, sugar factories were regular purchasers of goods provided by the heavy industry like coal and limestone, which were used in large quantities in the production process. It is worth adding here that specialization on heavy industry in selected regions was completely dictated by governmental policy and did not take comparative advantages into account (Meyer 1998, p. 9).

For the sugar industry, the above developments were tantamount to stagnancy in technological advancement and sluggish expansion of processing capacities. In 1955, the cumulative daily beet throughput per day at 76 Polish sugar factories amounted to 100.5 t, which was still slightly below the 1938 level (Wykrętowicz op. cit., p. 46). It was not before the middle of the 1960s that the processing capacity of the sugar industry reached 120 t per day and was slowly increasing from year to year. This was influenced by the already mentioned construction of several new factories as well as by the modernization and enlargement of the existing ones.

In the last five-year period before the collapse of communism in Poland, the average daily beet throughput per day of the 78 sugar factories functioning in the country amounted to 164 t. Regrettably, the vast majority of Polish plants were already at that time much smaller than average-sized sugar factories in Western Europe. In Poland, during the campaign 1989/90, the nominal processing capacity of 43 of the 78 factories was smaller than 2,000 t of beet throughput per day, at 31 plants it was between 2,000 and 4,000 t, and only in four cases was it greater than 4,000 t (ibid., p. 182). By comparison, sugarbeet-processing plants in France, Italy, the German Federal Republic and the Netherlands started the campaign 1989/90 with an average daily processing capacity of 8,600, 7,220, 7,000 and 10,500 t, respectively (Sugar Economy 1990/91). This was mainly the result of considerable structural changes in the sugar industries of West European countries and the consolidation of their productive facilities, taking place especially from the 1960s onwards. In Poland such changes were almost non-existent (See chapter 5).

The employment level in the Polish sugar industry between 1945 and 1989 was kept constantly high till the 1970s. Only when the automation of technological processes and the mechanization of labor-intensive activities were introduced, did employment begin to fall. Since beet sugar production has a seasonal character, it is important to distinguish between employment levels during and after a campaign in order to get a comprehensive picture of any changes and to understand their implications. Figures presented in Table 4 clearly show that it was the reduction of the workforce employed during the campaign what accounted for the general decrease in employment in the Polish sugar industry after 1965. The average number of people working in this sector during the entire year remained more or less at the same level.

Table 4. Employment in the Polish sugar industry, 1946-1986

	1946	1950	1955	1960	1965	1970	1975	1980	1986
Campaign (total)	78,100	84,900	90,800	80,600	91,420	62,950	56,700	51,700	48,400
Campaign (per factory)	1,100	1,117	1,194	1,060	1,202	828	736	660	620
Annual average (total)	38,768	39,790	37,905	39,401	43,143	34,310	36,072	29,200	29,900
Annual average (per factory)	546	523	498	518	560	451	468	374	383

Source: Łuczak 1981, p. 295; Wykrętowicz 1997, p. 223.

Since the processing campaign lasts only about three months, the figure expressing average annual employment is shaped predominantly by the regular workforce. This group is made up of 'hoarded' blue-collar workers and administrative staff, which includes a large number of people responsible for collaboration with beet growers and all those dealing with a complicated system of bureaucracy encompassing a wide range of procedures. An important development that could be observed especially in the 1970s was an intensive build-up of welfare facilities for employees of the sugar industry. Their maintenance and management necessitated the engagement of additional employees. Soon, such non-productive facilities of sugar factories included: 32 holiday centers and 77 health centers, 74 hotels for workers and 64 kindergartens for their children, 1240 blocks or individual houses, 61 community centers and 13 cultural centers (Łuczak, op. cit., p. 311; Wykrętowicz, op. cit., p. 258). Involvement in numerous non-core activities, overwhelming bureaucracy, poor organization of work and other factors had the effect that in 1989 the average number of employees per factory in Poland, with reference to both campaign and annual employment, was still much higher than in Western Europe.

The nationalization of the key sectors of the Polish economy was accompanied by the introduction of a new administrative system for enterprises taken over by the state. Their entrepreneurial sovereignty was soon considerably restricted and management strictly centralized. The organizational structure of the sugar industry consisted of three levels with almost all activities and decisions subordinated to the top level. At the top of this hierarchy stood a central administrative office, which defined strategic objectives for the whole sugar sector and assigned the coordination of their execution to several regional agencies. These agencies constituted the second level in the organizational ladder. Each of them controlled a particular group of sugar factories (the third level) and supervised the implementation of directives from above. Despite several reorganizations aimed at making this structure flatter and giving more decision-making freedom to the lower level, in practice, the three-level structure existed until 1989. The modifications introduced in 1959, 1968 and 1982 were of a more or less cosmetic character. In reality, they were limited to a change in the names of the individual levels of the structure, a regrouping of regional agencies and sugar factories and a transfer of various functions from one level to another. For the purpose of the present study it is important to give the reader an insight into the shape of the organizational structure of the Polish sugar industry from the end of the time period discussed in this section. After 1982 the functioning of this sector of the Polish economy was in the hands of the Association of the Sugar Industry "Cukropol" (*Zrzeszenie Przemysłu Cukrowniczego "Cukropol"*) comprising 13 grouped enterprises. The enterprises, in turn, controlled the activity of 78 sugar factories (See Appendix 1).[25] The most important centers of sugar production in Poland included the following six grouped enterprises: *Cukrownie Lubelskie*, *Cukrownie Bydgoskie*, *Cukrownie Toruńskie*, *Cukrownie Poznańskie*, *Cukrownie Dolnośląskie* and *Cukrownie Mazowieckie*. In the late 1980s sugar manufactured in factories located within the territories of these groups amounted to about 70% of total sugar production in the country. This should not come as a surprise since regions where the enterprises were situated accounted at the same time for nearly 73% of the total beet-harvested area in Poland (Wykrętowicz, op. cit., p. 141, 279). The share of the beet-harvested area in the overall harvested area was largest in provinces with the following capital cities: *Zamość* (more than 9%), *Wrocław*, *Leszno*, *Legnica*, *Włocławek*, *Płock* (7-9%), *Poznań*, *Bydgoszcz*, *Toruń*, *Wałbrzych*,

[25] The sugar factory in *Ropczyce* on its own constituted one of the 13 grouped enterprises.

Opole, Lublin, Przemyśl (5-7%). In other provinces this share amounted to less than 5% (ibid., p. 158). As with all its predecessors, under the above organizational structure the mechanism of central planning remained to a large extent untouched and a firm hand was kept on market forces. The volume and assortment of production, prices of sugarbeets and materials used in the production process as well as investment outlays and employment levels were scrupulously determined in advance by state administration with the help of an all-embracing bureaucracy. The selling price for sugar was specified on the basis of average production costs of one tonne of sugar at the industry-level. The average production costs augmented by a "planned profit", amounting to about five percent of the production costs, formed the so-called "manufacturing price". This price plus turnover tax constituted the actual selling price of sugar. The reliance on average production costs in the industry had the effect that differences between regions and individual sugar factories regarding access to raw material, transport infrastructure, as well as many other factors, were completely ignored (ibid., p. 325). There were many factories at which the actual production costs were either much below or much above the average. This in turn implied that while plants belonging to the first group made profits, the second group generated substantial losses. The problem was solved with the help of a system ensuring financial support for sugar factories that found themselves in a parlous economic situation, provided for by those achieving relatively good results. Transfer of financial resources from profitable to unprofitable plants guaranteed that the latter continued to work without suffering any consequences of their under-performance. Another form of putting unprofitable productive facilities on a financial 'drip' was the paternalistic protection by the government in the form of generously allocated subsidies. This procedure had become common especially since the mid-1970s when the Polish sugar industry as a whole started to generate losses (ibid., p. 338). Sugar factories at which costs of production exceeded revenues from sales were supplied either with direct subsidies or interest-free bank loans—a typical phenomenon of the socialist system which Kornai (1998) named "soft budget constraint". The above mechanisms ensured an artificial maintenance of numerous unprofitable plants for many years and secured incomes for thousands of workers and farmers.

Lack of competition hindered the improvement in productive efficiency and to a great extent eliminated innovation. It was conducive to low productivity, and the profligate use of capital, energy, water and other supplementary materials utilized in the production process (such as coal, coke, limestone and others). Workers were paid according to salary levels set by the state, which gave no incentive to make efforts to become more productive. On the contrary, lounging on the job was commonplace. At the same time, strong official trade unions opposed redundancies and in this way strengthened job security (Lavigne, op. cit., p. 7). Plan-fulfillment predominated above all other objectives, regardless of the impact on operating costs and general economic efficiency. The role of managers of sugar factories was limited to the fulfillment of directives from above and to the coordination of the production process.

When sketching the most significant characteristics typifying industrial production in socialist Poland, it is important to mention that enterprises in general showed little concern for environmental issues. Sugar factories were no exception. A good example was offered by an executive working at one of them: "We took water from the nearby river and after using it in the production process, we pumped it, polluted with all kind of toxic waste, back into the river. Some of our employees called it, sarcastically, 'a closed circuit'." A similar by-product was the impressive amounts of black smoke billowing from sugar factories' chimneys during the campaigns. The scale and intensity of such negative externalities differed depending on time and place. It does not change the fact, however, that they were quite common during the entire period of time discussed here.

3.3 The Production, Consumption, Export and Import of Sugar

The production of sugar in Poland developed most dynamically during the first fifteen years after the war (See Figure 2). It was favored by the advancing industrialization and urbanization of the country. This in turn resulted in increasing incomes for the working class, which was reflected in, among other things, increasing consumption of sugar per head (See Table 5).

Table 5. Production and Consumption of Sugar (in kg per head), Poland, Selected years

	1947	1950	1955	1960	1965	1970	1975	1980	1985	1989
Production	20.4	38.5	36.0	46.5	43.0	42.3	51.1	29.2	44.6	45.1
Consumption	12.5	21.0	24.0	27.9	32.6	39.2	43.2	41.4	41.0	46.9

Source: Łuczak 1981, p. 325; Jaworowski 1995, p. 48; Wykrętowicz 1997, p. 293, GUS (Central Statistical Office).

The demanding economic plans dictated by the communist authorities had a great impact on the dynamically expanding levels of sugar production (Jaworowski, op. cit., p. 48). Since sugarbeet yield per hectare was improving very slowly, the amount of beets needed to achieve ambitious production targets was obtained through the expansion of the beet-harvested area (See Figure 3).

Farmers were eager to get involved in sugarbeet growing due to the fact that, of all arable crops, it was the sugarbeet that brought them the greatest profits (Łuczak, op. cit., p. 249). In the early 1960s, Poland had the second largest beet-harvested area in Europe, just behind the Soviet Union. At the same time, it was the fourth largest sugar manufacturer after the Soviet Union, France and the German Federal Republic, with its share of European sugar production slightly exceeding 7 percent (Zuckerwirtschaft). As Wykrętowicz (op. cit., p. 274) rightly observes, it was yet another indicator of the low productivity and a generally poor condition of Polish agriculture by comparison with developed countries in Western Europe.

Figure 2. Production and export of sugar, Poland, 1945-1989 (five-year periods average, in 1000 t)

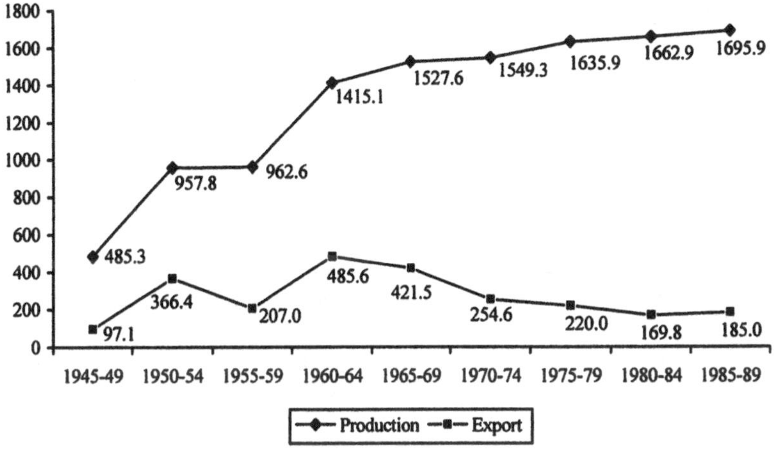

Source: Calculations by the author, based on Łuczak 1981, p. 327, 315; Wykrętowicz 1997, p. 299, Cukier i Skrobia.

Figure 3. Sugarbeet harvested area, Poland, 1945-1989 (five-year periods average, in 1000 ha)

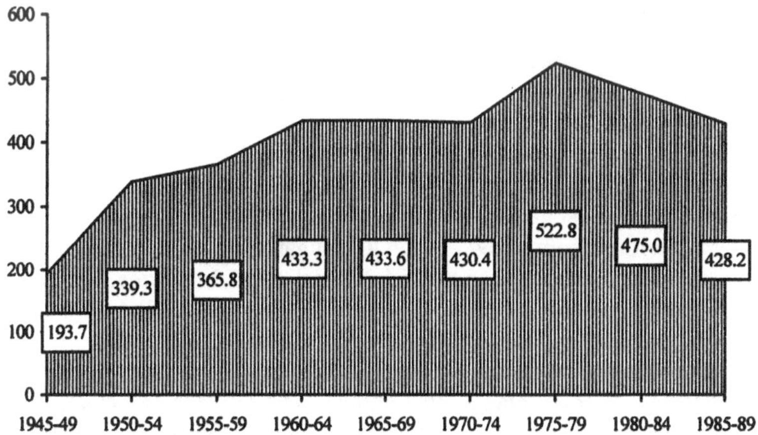

Source: Calculations by the author, based on Łuczak 1981, p. 254; Cukier i Skrobia.

After stabilization of the beet-harvested area in the 1965-1970 time period at about 430,000 hectares, a significant expansion could be observed once again in the second half of the 1970s. This was mainly a result of increasing consumption of sugar and of the breeding of farm animals for which the side products of sugar extraction, beet pulp and leaves, constitute valuable nourishment. In 1975, large-scale mechanization of sugarbeet growing was introduced. The first combine harvesters and other farm machines appeared on the fields. As well as this, seeds which produced sugarbeets with higher sugar content became widely used, which was followed in the 1980s by increasing polarization and sugar yield in % of raw sugar value on beet (See Table 3). These developments led to a richer harvest than in previous five-year periods and contributed to the reduction in the following years of the area where sugarbeets were grown (Figure 3).

Due to a shortage of sugar on the world market in the early post-war period, selling it abroad was at that time very remunerative and guaranteed access to foreign currency (Łuczak op. cit., pp. 328-329). Logically, this constituted an important incentive to the expansion of production of this good. In Figure 2, the curve portraying export of sugar from Poland in the 1945-1989 time period shows that the greatest quantities were shipped abroad during the first twenty years after the end of World War II.

This contributed to the fact that, as was mentioned earlier, the sugar industry financed to a large extent the build-up of other sectors of the Polish economy and the reconstruction of the country. The amount of exported sugar increased dynamically in the post-war period from 100,000 t in 1947 to 372,000 t in 1954. After a short but serious slump in the years 1955 and 1956, it started to climb again and reached its peak in 1962 with 734,000 t (60% of overall production).

The average share of exported sugar in total production between 1945 and 1989 amounted to about 20%. It is worth mentioning that the exportation of sugar was accompanied by the exportation of sugar factories. In the years 1954-75, 37 plants designed for production of sugar from sugarbeets and 8 facilities tailored to cane sugar production were constructed in Poland and shipped to the Soviet Union, Iran and many other countries around the world. Moreover, Polish specialists oversaw the modernization of over 40 plants in the German Democratic Republic and other countries from the former Eastern block (ibid., pp. 290-291).

The distribution of sugar on the domestic market was administered, as with most other activities, from above. Individual sugar factories received, irregularly, ordinances stating the exact amount and destination of deliveries. The remaining reserves, stored in depots, were sold abroad. This was handled by state-owned foreign trade agencies, principally "Rolimpex" (Gierszewski op. cit., p. 31). This mechanism ensured that depots at sugar factories were always empty and the management of individual plants did not have to do much to achieve this.

The United Kingdom, France, the German Federal Republic and the Soviet Union were the major importers of sugar from Poland. Apart from the above top four destinations, large amounts of sugar were shipped to Switzerland, former Yugoslavia, Norway, Finland, and Sweden, as well as to several North African states and to the Near East (International Sugar Organization). In the middle of the 1960s, both the quantity of exported sugar as well as its share in total production started to fall systematically and this trend persisted until the end of the period of time discussed in this section. This was caused mainly by increasing competitiveness from cheap cane sugar which was gradually dislodging beet sugar from the world market. At the same time, the productive efficiency of beet sugar factories in Western Europe was improving much faster than in Poland. This was accompanied by a considerable decrease in production costs at the former and, consequently, their increasing international competitiveness. Throughout the most part of the 1980s, the exportation of sugar from Poland was unprofitable and took place only because of sizeable surpluses of this good on the domestic market (Wykrętowicz op. cit., p. 309).

As regards imports, from the middle of the 1960s, small amounts of sugar were sent to Poland from Cuba and refined by several local factories after the regular campaign. This was not economically viable but took place for political reasons. In the 1980s, Poland also imported white sugar which during the 1980-89 time period amounted on average to 128 t per year (ibid., p. 310).

3.4 On the Verge of Transition to a Market Economy

In the late 1980s, the technological gap between Polish and Western sugar factories as well as overall under-performance of the former was judged to be one of fifteen to twenty years (Chudoba 1991, p. 57). This state of affairs was brought about by long-lasting underinvestment of the Polish sugar industry and agriculture, reflected in an outdated technological base and poor economic effectiveness. It was also the result of irrational decision-making and the intransigence of communist authorities sticking stubbornly to the assumptions of an ossified political system and concentrating on production growth achieved through extensive use of resources. As Wykrętowicz (op. cit., p. 318) aptly recapitulates: "*The focus on high output and full employment did not go hand in hand with improvement in quality, reduction in costs and sparing use of labor and capital. At the end of the day, all this led to the ultimate defeat of the socialist order by a free market economy.*" Despite several experiments undertaken by successive communist leaders, aimed at the introduction of elements of a market economy, socialism continually retained many of its original characteristics. An effort to reinvigorate the Polish economy through imports of Western technology initiated in the early 1970s ended in failure. No significant increase in exports to the West occurred. Therefore, the huge amounts of money borrowed from Western governments for new machinery could not be repaid. A worsening economic situation, manifesting itself in hyperinflation, chronic shortages and increasing resentment of the public, led to the collapse of communism in Poland at the end of the 1980s. The ineffective attempts to depart from real socialism with the help of half measures have been summarized very accurately and succinctly by Lavigne (op. cit., p. 12):

"*Only after the collapse of the system was it clearly understood that the system was not reformable*".

Notwithstanding the general backwardness of the Polish sugar industry in relation to developed countries, which emerged during forty years of central planning, it would be unfair not to appreciate several significant achievements of that period. These include the electrification of sugar factories, the mechanization of arduous manual tasks, especially loading and unloading of beets, improvements regarding the economizing of energy use as well as a twofold increase in the daily processing capacity of the sugar industry and a fourfold increase in sugar production. The greatest achievement was the introduction of an automated, permanent diffusion (extraction) which displaced periodical diffusion up to the end of the 1980s. It was accompanied by a tenfold reduction in staff working in this phase of the technological process. Furthermore, the introduction of permanent extraction was accompanied by a more economical use of fresh water and considerable reduction in the damage done to the environment, due to reduced production of industrial wastes (Wykrętowicz op. cit., pp. 49-349).

Nevertheless, in spite of the above accomplishments, the years 1945-89 constitute, in the recent history of the Polish sugar industry, a squandered period during which sugar manufacturers and beet growers from Western Europe outdistanced their Polish counterparts in productive efficiency and in the application of innovative solutions. It is worth recalling that between 1928 and 1939 Polish sugar factories excelled in Europe with regard to technology and overall performance. Apart from Ukraine, where many Polish specialists had worked since 1920, other European countries, including Germany and France, modelled their sugarbeet-processing plants on the example of Poland (Waleriańczyk 2001, p. 46). Unfortunately, forty years of communist control in Central and Eastern Europe led to a reversal of roles. While benefits stemming from economies of scale are of central importance in the manufacturing of sugar, most plants in Poland were very small compared with factories in Western Europe. Due to the high transportation costs of sugarbeets, the location of a sugar factory has also a significant impact on the cost efficiency of sugar production. Unfortunately, many sugar factories in Poland were constructed for political reasons in regions that are unsuitable for sugarbeet cultivation. Another feature typifying the sugar industry in Poland by the end of the 1980s was the usage of obsolete and unproductive equipment at most plants. The energy and heating systems in particular were in a poor state of repair. Their utilization in the production process was accompanied by an excessive use of energy. This, in turn, contributed to a significant increase in production costs. The automation of the technological process of sugar extraction at Polish sugar factories was not as widespread and advanced as in Western Europe. Finally, the majority of sugarbeet-processing plants in Poland was burdened with serious environmental problems and lacked financial resources for investment.

The comparison of three selected indices of productive efficiency in eight countries, presented in Figures 4, 5 and 6, reveals unequivocally a serious relative underdevelopment of the Polish sugar industry and agriculture on the cusp of Poland's leap to a market economy in 1990.

In conjunction with the previous considerations of the present chapter, the above juxtaposition partly provides an answer to one of the central questions of this study—about the desired direction of change. The purpose of the following sections is, *inter alia*, to state this direction as precisely and comprehensively as possible.

Figures 4, 5, 6. Average sugarbeet yield, sugar yield per hectare and sugar yield in % of raw sugar value on beet, 1985-89, selected countries

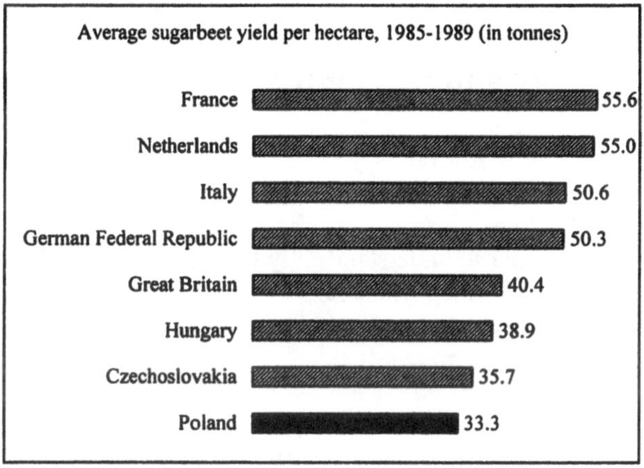

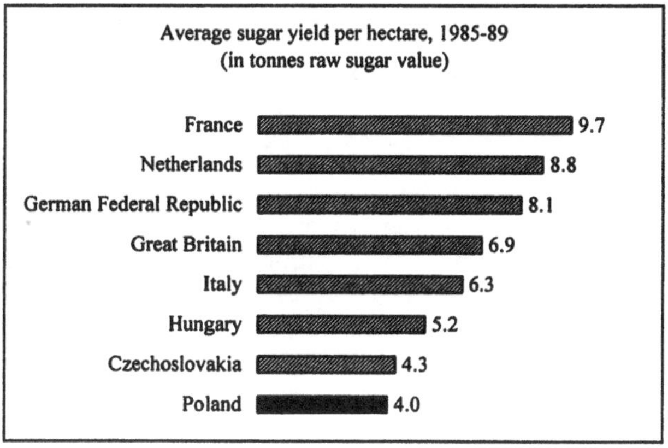

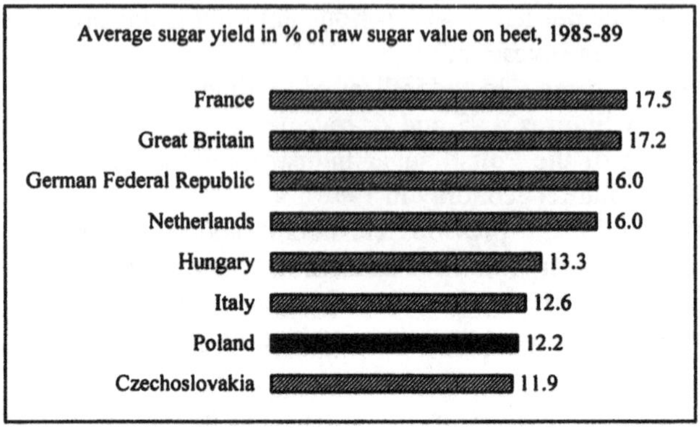

Source: F.O. Licht's World Sugar Statistics; Cukier i Skrobia; Łuczak 1981, pp. 342-344; Wykrętowicz 1997, p. 268.

4 The Technology and Economics of Sugarbeet Processing

In simplified terms, the cost efficiency of beet-sugar production depends on three factors: production and purchasing costs of sugarbeets; the costs of their procurement (contracting and transportation); and the overall costs of processing (Walkenhorst 1998, p.19). In order to understand fully the extent to which the above components influence the economic efficiency of beet sugar production, it is necessary to take a closer look at selected aspects of sugarbeet cultivation and the technological process of sugarbeet processing.
The purpose of the present section is thus to analyze and illustrate how sugar finds its way from the field to a labeled bag. It should facilitate further reasoning and indicate the potential role of certain activities in the restructuring process of the sugar industry in Poland.

4.1 Basic Information about Cultivation and Processing of Sugarbeets

Sugar is the conventional name for sucrose, which may be extracted either from sugar cane or sugarbeet. The former is grown in tropical climate conditions and the latter in temperate. In both cases the extracted sugar has the same sweet taste and is chemically identical. It is made up of almost pure, 99.9 percent sucrose (Blume et al. 2002, p. 33-34). Nonetheless, production costs of beet sugar are, on average, about three and a half times higher than the production costs of raw cane sugar.[26] Sugarbeet is a root crop consisting of about 75-80% of water. Its

[26] For details, see for example Knapp/Talks 2004, p. 10; Oxfam International 2004, p. 7.

weight at the time of harvest reaches 700-1000 grams. The sugar content in beet amounts to 15-20% of the total mass. Sugarbeet is a demanding crop as regards climate and soil quality. The most suitable conditions for sugarbeet growing include mild temperature, rainfall of about 500 millimeter per year and fertile soil supplemented with minerals and other nutrients. Moreover, sugarbeets are vulnerable to numerous diseases and weed infestation. Therefore, apart from nitrogen fertilizers, it is important to provide them with an adequate quantity of herbicides and pesticides. In the past, sugarbeet growers and their family members removed weeds from the soil using a hoe. This gave rise to the saying, "You have to hoe the sugar into the beets" (Bruhns 1997, p. 34). Today, this process is fully mechanized with manual labor being substituted by modern farming equipment. Not long ago the beet sugar industry was described as both labor-intensive and capital-intensive. At the present time, beet sugar production is becoming a more and more capital-intensive business due to progressing automation of most processes including the sugarbeet harvest.[27]

Natural conditions, as listed above, have a crucial impact on the profitability of sugarbeet cultivation and processing in a given region. Combined with appropriate fertilization and application of plant-protection products, they are decisive for the content of sugar in beets delivered to sugar factories (polarization). Other determinants of the technological value of sugarbeets are the appropriate choice of seeds, the mechanization level of the beet harvest and cultivation, as well as the tradition of sugarbeet growing in a particular region (Łuczak op. cit., p. 250; Jaworowski 2001, p. 163; Gierszewski 2002, p. 312). Although the list of necessary requirements for an effective sugarbeet growing is quite long, meeting them is financially rewarding. Sugarbeet is one of the crops that brings the greatest profits to farmers (Kondrakiewicz 2000, p. 74; Malec 2002, p. 229). Moreover, cultivation of sugarbeets positively influences the quality of soil and increases the farming skills of people employed in agriculture.[28]

It was mentioned already in the previous section that sugarbeets are quite sensitive to long-distance transportation and long storage periods. Hence, sugar factories employees say that the time interval between the harvest, the delivery of beets to a factory and their subsequent processing should be as short as possible. This greatly minimizes the "loss" of sugar content in beets, between the field and the beginning of the technological process of sugar extraction at the factory. Not only for this reason is it highly desirable that the distance between a manufacturing facility and its beet-procurement area is not too great. Sugarbeets are bulky and heavy, which makes their transport very expensive. At first glance at a map displaying beet-harvested areas and the location of sugar factories in France or Germany it becomes apparent that beet-processing plants in these countries are

---

[27] See for example Schröder 1998, pp. 1068-1069.

[28] For more information on sugarbeet, in particular its environmental impact, see for example IIBR 2005.

attached like leeches to large beet-growing regions. According to analyses recently carried out by a consortium of two consultancy companies, *Warszawska Grupa Konsultingowa* and *Pro-Invest International*, in the optimal situation, the beet-procurement area in Poland should be located within a 35-kilometer radius of a factory. At the same time, the authors of the above investigations emphasize that, in long-term restructuring programs, distances of up to 100 kilometers are tolerable (WGK and Pro-Invest International 2003, p. 70).

In Poland, sugarbeets are usually sown from late March until the end of April. The harvesting period starts in late September, when the sugar content in beets reaches its highest level, and usually lasts two to three months. It is also the time at which sugar factories work round the clock (usually with three eight-hour shifts) at top speed, processing the contracted and purchased beets. In the course of this short season, called a campaign, sugar companies manufacture sugar within the limits of quotas assigned to them by an authorized institution.

It is important to note at this point that interruption of a campaign for a few hours or days is highly problematic and expensive. One of the reasons for this is that it is quite laborious to bring some of the pieces of equipment and technological processes involved in the production of beet sugar to a standstill and to set them in motion again. Moreover, a detailed schedule of beet deliveries is nowadays specified long before the beginning of each campaign, in order to avoid the storage of large amounts of beets. Therefore, managers of sugar factories describe the scenario of interrupting a campaign for a couple of days (e. g. during Christmas) as "economically and technically unthinkable". Revenues from the sale of sugar produced in a short campaign have to suffice for the coverage of costs borne during the entire year, including the repayment of credits raised by sugar factories before each processing season. Of course, the sale of sugar is also meant to bring a profit which will allow for investments and development.

The length of a campaign constitutes a significant factor influencing the productive and economic efficiency of sugarbeet processing. Due to the considerable amount of fixed capital in sugar factories, a high level of capacity utilization is very desirable (Walkenhorst op. cit., p. 22). On the other hand, prolongation of sugar production until the end of December or early January is usually connected with deterioration of the technological quality of the processed raw material owing to a damaging impact of winter frost. This manifests itself in lower sugar content in delivered beets and, consequently, worse sugar yield in percent of raw sugar value on beet. In Poland, the optimal length of a campaign starting in late September is judged to be 85-90 days (Jaworowski 2001, p. 153; Wykrętowicz, op. cit., p. 221). Nevertheless, the actual duration of a campaign can match the theoretical optimum only if a sufficient amount of sugarbeets is provided. If, for some reason, this condition cannot be met, the optimal length of a campaign automatically becomes shorter. This leads, however, to an increase in average fixed costs, which is accompanied by an increase in unit costs (Mahler 1991, p. 95).

Waleriańczyk (1993, p. 94) places duration of a campaign among the four most important criteria by which the economic efficiency of sugar production at a given factory should be judged.[29]

On account of the seasonal character of sugar production, employment levels at sugar factories change during the year. Despite the trend towards mechanization of most phases of the technological process, the demand for additional workforce during a campaign is still considerable. The beginning of a campaign is usually connected with a substantial increase in the number of employees compared to employment levels during the rest of the year—the so-called *refurbishment period*. It is thus important to distinguish between the regular and seasonal workforce. In economic analyses, the average annual employment level is also often used as a benchmark (Wykrętowicz, op. cit., p. 221). One of the most popular measures of productivity in the sugar industry is the amount of sugar produced per one employee of a given factory. Depending on the choice of methodology, either the total number of employees or solely the 'industrial group' dealing directly with the production process can be taken into account.

Although slight differences in the technological process of sugarbeet processing between individual producers may exist, in general, beet sugar is manufactured using the same basic process. When sugarbeets arrive at a factory, they are weighed, cleaned of any dirt attached to them and chopped into thin strips called *cossettes*. In this form they are transported on conveyor belts to the extraction station where they are mixed with water heated to about 70 degrees Celsius. In this phase of the technological process, called *diffusion*, sugar is exuded from the cells of beets, forming a dark (almost black) raw juice. The juice is subsequently purified by mixing it with lime milk and carbon dioxide. Then it is filtered and repeatedly evaporated to become a viscous syrup in which crystals start to appear. At this stage small particles of sugar are often added to the syrup to stimulate crystallization. Sugar crystals formed in this way are separated from the thick juice in a centrifuge. After drying, segregation and cooling, they are bagged or conveyed to large storage silos and are ready to be marketed. The remaining by-product, a liquid called *molasses* has a wide range of applications in agriculture and industry. It can be used either as a fodder containing mineral salts and microelements or as a useful raw material, used, for instance, by distilleries or in the pharmaceutical industry. Another by-product of sugarbeet processing, *carbonation lime*, constitutes a very valuable fertilizer. Strips of beets that have been used in the production process, called *beet pulp*, are commonly used as nourishment for farm animals. A product obtained after enriching beet pulp with molasses, drying it and pressing is called *pellets*. It is used as a fodder given to cows, pigs and horses. In terms of calorific and energy value it is

[29] The three remaining criteria include the total amount of sugar production at a given plant, average transport distance of beets to a factory, and sugar production per employee (Waleriańczyk, ibid., p. 93).

comparable to barley (www.suedzucker.de). Last but not least, leaves of sugarbeets, cut off during the harvest, constitute a valuable animal feed for cattle. They are also often ploughed back into the soil and serve as natural fertilizer (Miedziak 2003, pp. 50-51).

Apart from sugarbeets, factories use large quantities of supplementary materials in the technological process of sugar production. These include limestone, coal, coke, water, filter materials, laboratory chemicals as well as antifoaming and acidification agents, only to mention the most significant ones. Furthermore, the sugar industry is an important partner of numerous small and medium-sized companies providing it with a variety of ancillary services and equipment. In this way, the sugar sector contributes indirectly to the prosperity and development of other branches of the Polish economy (Kondrakiewicz 2000, p. 75).

4.2 Costs Structure in the Production of Beet Sugar in Poland and the Possibilities for Their Reduction

The overall production costs of one tonne of sugar constitute the most significant determinant of competitiveness in the sugar industry. Considering the scope of this study, it is thus vitally important to analyze thoroughly the make-up of the production costs of sugar in Poland and to identify ways in which they can be reduced.

As portrayed in Table 6, the purchase of sugarbeets accounts for on average more than 40% of total production costs of sugar in the country under consideration. Sugarbeet-procurement costs (maintenance of regional purchasing centers, contracting and transportation of beets) add up to another 7-8%. In practical terms, this means that simply the payment for beets, their storage and the activities associated with their delivery to the sugar factory constitute together nearly 50% of total production costs. In this situation, activities aimed at the improvement in the productivity and quality of the harvest may lead to substantial cost savings for sugar producers. By the same token, the location of a sugar factory in close proximity to a large beet-growing region characterized by a high quality of soil, a high density of large plantations, and a good transport infrastructure constitutes a significant competitive advantage.

Apart from efforts aimed at increasing the sugar content in beets before the harvest, it would seem also to be highly desirable to try to achieve better extractability of sugar at the factory. The higher the sugar content in procured beet roots (polarization) and the more effective the extraction process at a factory (recovery of sugar/extraction efficiency), the smaller is the volume of beets needed to produce a given amount of sugar.

Once sugarbeets have been delivered to the factories, sugar companies have the possibility to improve the extractability of sugar by minimizing sugar losses during the technological process of beet processing. Nonetheless, if the sugar content in purchased beet roots amounts to 13% or 14%, which is very low by international standards, even the most efficient factory will not achieve a higher sugar yield in % of raw sugar value on beet.

Table 6. The structure of costs in the production of one t of beet sugar in Poland (in %)*

	1997/98	1998/99	1999/00	2000/01	2001/02	2002/03 (b)	2003/04 (c)
1. Variable costs	**67.1**	**67.8**	**60.3**	**62.8**	**63.5**	**67.6**	**64.0**
1.1 Raw material (sugarbeets)	44.4	36.3	40.9	40.3	42.8	45.0	38.7
1.2 Raw material procurement	8.0	7.1	6.5	7.2	6.4	6.8	6.5
1.3 Direct inputs and packaging	11.1	9.9	10.0	5.7	5.1	4.2	2.5 (d)
1.4 Energy and steam (a)	-	-	-	6.2	6.2	7.1	6.5
1.5 Direct salaries	1.5	1.1	1.0	1.4	1.2	1.2	-
1.6 Sale	2.1	13.4	1.9	2.0	1.8	3.3	-
2. Fixed costs	**25.7**	**23.4**	**28.7**	**29.9**	**30.0**	**29.3**	**36.0**
2.1 Individual factory departments	12.9	11.2	13.2	13.9	14.7	14.1	-
2.2 General administration	12.8	12.2	15.5	16.0	15.3	15.2	-
3. Financial costs	**7.2**	**8.8**	**11.0**	**7.3**	**6.5**	**3.1**	**4.9**
4. Total costs (PLN/t)	**1632**	**1928**	**1811**	**1679**	**1986**	**1741**	**2000**

*) The portrayed structure of costs in campaigns 1997/98, 1998/99, 1999/00, 2000/01 and 2002/03 is based on average technical production cost of one tonne of sugar (A, B and C sugar) and other costs **borne** by sugar factories in Poland up to September 30, 1998, 1999, 2000, 2001, 2003 and 2004 respectively. The structure of costs in the campaign 2001/02 is based on average technical production cost of one tonne of sugar and other costs **predicted** up to September 30, 2002. Sampling units comprise a representative sample of 13 sugar factories in the campaigns 1997/98 and 1998/99, 12 sugar factories in the campaign 1999/00, 10 sugar factories in the campaigns 2000/01 and 2001/02, and 5 factories in the campaign 2002/03. Information about the sampling unit in 2003/04 is not available.

a) In the campaigns 1997/98-1999/00, the category "Energy and steam" was included in the category "Direct inputs and packaging"; b) Calculations by the author, based on data published in Chudoba 2004, p. 7 (Table 3); c) Calculations by the author, based on data published in Urban et al. 2005, p. 19 (Table 5); d) Direct inputs only.

Source: Chudoba 1999-2004; Urban et al. 2005, p. 19.

Therefore, it is of primary importance for sugar companies to work in close co-operation with sugarbeet growers in order to achieve as high a sugar content in beets as possible. This collaboration may take various forms. One possibility is the organization of training courses and workshops for beet growers as well as providing them with professional advice in the choice of seeds, plant protection products and fertilizers. Sugar producers in Western Europe introduced a system many years ago, in which the payment for beets depends on the content of sugar and not, as had previously been the case, on the weight of delivered raw material. Sugar factories in Poland have recently been gradually adopting the same method.

The next item in the structure of sugar production costs in Poland is made up of those costs falling under the category "direct inputs and packaging". Their share in overall production costs amounts to about 10% (including energy and steam). It has been mentioned already in the previous subsection that apart from sugarbeets a lot of supplements and ancillary materials are used in the production of beet sugar. A particularly significant role is played here by costs connected with heating and the use of energy. Rationalization measures in these two fields have constituted one of the greatest challenges of operational restructuring at sugar factories in Poland. At the beginning of the 1990s, energy and heating systems were among the most outdated and inefficient apparatuses to be found in Polish beet-processing plants (Kondrakiewicz 2000, p. 112). In such a situation, investment in modern technology, e.g. the installation of evaporators allowing a more economical use of steam, constitutes a necessary undertaking on the road to better cost-efficiency. Innovations leading to a reduction in the use of coal, coke and limestone are also highly desirable. Unfortunately, the introduction of effective changes in these areas, especially the upgrading of the energy and heating systems, requires substantial financial resources.

As far as the packaging of sugar is concerned, a very convenient solution leading in the long run to appreciable cost savings is the storage of sugar in silos. It allows sugar producers to meet the wishes of customers at any time and to provide them with sugar in many different forms (e. g. loose or in 1 kg, 25 kg, 50 kg bags). While in Western Europe this method of storing sugar became standard a long time ago, only a small number of sugar factories in Poland keep their sugar in silos. The remaining ones fill sugar produced during a campaign into 50kg bags and place them in storehouses. If later a customer places a large order for sugar in, let's say, 25 kg bags, the 50 kg bags are torn, the content is removed and the packing changed. Obviously, such an operation is time-consuming and quite costly. It is worth adding that sugar can be stored in silos for an unlimited period of time without loosing on quality if appropriate air temperature (about 20 degrees Celsius) and humidity (65%) are guaranteed. The biggest if not the only problem in the construction of sugar silos is the expenditure connected with such an undertaking. Construction costs of a silo with a storage capacity of 30,000 t of sugar come to about PLN 16 million (Łękawski 2001, p. 113).

Of all cost categories listed in Table 6, the category "direct salaries" has the smallest share in the total production costs of one tonne of sugar in Poland. In the marketing years 1997/98-2002/03, it amounted on average to 1.2 percent. Regardless of this fact, there is still potential for its further reduction. Employment levels at most sugar factories in Poland are higher than in Western Europe despite the fact that sugarbeet-processing plants in, e.g. Germany and France, produce on average three times more sugar. Expenditure on direct salaries can be cut by automation and computerization of production, which allow for a reduction in workforce employed during a campaign. Cutbacks in direct salaries can be also achieved by slimming down regular staff.

The costs of the activities associated with the distribution and marketing of sugar have been put together and displayed in Table 6 under the category "Sale".

They represent a relatively small share in total production costs of sugar in Poland and have amounted normally to about 2% within the last few years. An exception was the season 1998/99 when this share reached 13.4%. This was brought about by considerable surpluses of sugar on the Polish domestic market and by the fact that producers were not allowed to sell it below the administrative minimal price set at that time at PLN 1.71. In order to evade this regulatory obstacle, sugar producers added to the actual sale costs various discounts and charges benefiting the purchasers of sugar. For example, a given sugar factory sold sugar to a hypermarket at PLN 1.71/kg but at the same time it paid the supermarket PLN 0.21/kg for advertising. In this way, the actual selling price was PLN 1.50/kg. In the following season, the share of sale costs in total production costs returned to the level of previous years owing to a temporary removal of sugar surpluses from the market. Shortly before the beginning of the 1999/2000 campaign, the A-quota[30] was reduced from 1,630,000 t to 1,222,500 t of sugar (Chudoba 2000, p. 40; Cukier i Skrobia 2003, p. 35).[31] In consequence, the market price of sugar soon rose above the administrative minimal selling price of PLN 1.71 and most sugar producers refrained from the 'artificial' augmentation of sale costs.[32] Not unexpectedly, the practices described above placed a number of sugar factories in difficulties later on. Plants at which state controllers detected suspicious methods of sale-costs increase were hit with enormous penalty fees or additional income and/or value added tax (NIK 2000, p. 11). Virtually all penalized sugar producers appealed against these decisions, explaining that a very low market price of sugar and their poor economic situation compelled them to sell below the administrative minimal price. Luckily for the sugar producers, the State Treasury has not been very eager to enforce the penalty payments, since this would be tantamount to forcing bankruptcy on many sugar factories.

In order to reduce the costs of sale, many sugar factories in Poland invite customers to collect purchased sugar directly from the factory with their own means of transport. An increasing number of producers who delivered sugar in the past to a location specified by the customer, e. g. the border with Ukraine, are unwilling to do so anymore and during negotiations ask clients to organize transport themselves.

Fixed costs account on average for nearly 30% of total production costs of sugar in Poland. These are costs borne by individual factory departments regardless of the volume of sugar production, along with the administrative costs connected with running an industrial unit (general administration). The former include expenses associated with the maintenance of the entire factory infrastructure

---

[30] A-quota is a sugar production quota destined for sale on the domestic market. For more information about sugar quotas see chapter 9.

[31] In 1999, consumption of sugar in Poland amounted to 1,580,000 tonnes (IERiGŻ).

[32] The average selling price for sugar rose at that time to about PLN 2.30/kg (NIK 2000, p. 11).

(buildings, storehouses, means of transport, machinery, grounds, etc.). The costs of general administration comprise, *inter alia*, expenditure connected with the work carried out by managerial staff (offices, business trips, meetings, secretaries, assistants, personal computers and other equipment, etc.). The financing of non-core activities such as canteens, kindergartens and holiday centers also falls under this category.

A reduction in fixed costs can be achieved through outsourcing of certain activities and the sale of all unnecessary, non-productive assets. Another way of keeping these costs within reasonable limits is the prevention of profligacy. The most efficient solution in the long run is, however, the expansion of the processing capacity of the sugar factory and the prolongation of the length of the campaign to the optimum. Given the significance of this issue, it has been analyzed and discussed separately in the next subsection of the present study.

The cost category "financial costs" includes costs incurred in consequence of raising and repaying bank loans, payment of insurance, taxes, etc. The seasonal character of beet-sugar production forces sugar companies to borrow considerable sums of money for the purchase of sugarbeets as well as for the organization and successful completion of the campaign. Interest paid on these loans, bank commissions and other charges account on average for about 8 percent of total production costs of beet sugar in Poland. The minimization of financial costs can be achieved through regular payment of installments and negotiation of loans on favorable terms.

As illustrated in the last line of Table 6, the total production costs of one tonne of sugar in Poland between the campaigns 1997/98 and 2002/03 were not stable. A considerable escalation of these costs was caused in the marketing year 1998/99 by an almost eightfold increase in the average sale costs from PLN 33/t in 1997/98 to PLN 259/t in 1998/99. The reasons for this development were discussed earlier in this subsection. Such an enormous rise in sale costs completely overshadowed cost advantages obtained thanks to a high sugar yield in % of raw sugar value on beet in the season 1998/99. On the industry level, it amounted to 13.97%, which means that 7.16 t of beets were needed to produce one tonne of sugar. In the previous year, sugar yield reached only 13.27% of raw sugar value on beet, which meant 7.54 t of beets were needed to produce one tonne of sugar (Chudoba 1999, pp. 37-40).

In the marketing year 1999/00 total production costs of one tonne of sugar declined to PLN 1811/t. This change was a result of a fall in average sale costs from PLN 259/t to PLN 35/t. This was achieved through the aforementioned removal of sugar surpluses from the domestic market, which led to a significant increase in sugar market-price. A significant drop in sale costs in the marketing year 1999/2000 was accompanied by a high sugar yield in % of raw sugar value on beet amounting, on the industry level, to 14.54%. In this situation, only 6.88 t on beets were needed for the production of one tonne of sugar. Since the amount of supplementary materials used in the production of beet sugar depends mainly on the volume of processed beets, a high sugar yield contributed to the reduction in costs associated with the use of limestone, coal, coke, and other direct inputs. As well as all these positive developments, however, the season 1999/2000 was characterized by a slight increase in average fixed costs due to a decline in sugar production in comparison with the previous year (Chudoba 2000, pp. 39-42).

A significant fall in the total production costs of one tonne of sugar in Poland in the marketing year 2000/01 was the result of an extraordinarily high sugar yield. It amounted on the industry level to 15.38% of raw sugar value on beet and led to a substantial reduction in the purchasing cost of sugarbeets as well as in costs connected with the use of supplementary materials. Moreover, the financial costs of sugar production were cut considerably by comparison with the previous season (Chudoba 2001, pp. 39-42).

The most important feature of the campaign 2001/02 was a dramatically low sugar yield in % of raw sugar value on beet (13.68%), caused by drought. As might be expected, this resulted in a significant increase in the purchasing and procurement costs of sugarbeets by comparison with the marketing year 2000/01. Furthermore, the rise in the amount of beets needed for the production of one tonne of sugar from 6.5 t in the campaign 2000/01 to 7.3 t in the campaign 2001/02 compelled sugar factories to use more ancillary materials in the technological process of sugar production. Finally, a drop in sugar production in 2001/02, despite an unchanged processing capacity in relation to the previous year, resulted in a noticeable rise in average fixed costs. Sugar production in the campaign 2001/02 was limited almost exclusively to A-quota sugar due to the extraordinary drought. This fact needs to be taken into account in the comparison of total production costs of one tonne of sugar in the campaigns considered in Table 6 since the production of A-quota sugar is more expensive than the production of B-quota sugar (designed for export with subsidies) and the so-called C-sugar (non-quota sugar which must be exported without any subsidies).[33] All these developments had the effect that overall production costs of one tonne of sugar in Poland rose from PLN 1679 in the marketing year 2000/01 to PLN 1986 in 2001/02 (Chudoba 2002, pp. 39-42).

In the season 2002/03, the average unit costs in the production of sugar in Poland were considerably lower and amounted to about PLN 1741. This was mainly a result of a much better average sugar yield in % of raw sugar value on beet than in the previous year. On the industry level, it reached 14.46% that year. Consequently, the amount of beets needed for the production of one tonne of sugar decreased by comparison with the campaign 2001/02 by 0.4 t, which meant a significant reduction in raw material costs. The marketing year 2002/03

[33] The price of beets designed for the production of A-quota sugar is higher than the price of beets from which B-quota sugar and C-sugar are produced.

was also characterized by an appreciable fall in financial costs in comparison with 2001/02. It should also be emphasized that in the campaign 2002/03 sugar factories in Poland produced much more B-quota sugar and C-sugar than in the previous year. Therefore, the share in overall costs of the relatively low costs connected with the production of B-sugar and C-sugar was much greater than in the campaign 2001/02.

In the marketing year 2003/04, the production costs of sugar increased to PLN 2,000/t. This came about due to a considerable increase in fixed and financial costs by comparison with the previous year and the fact that the share of A-quota sugar in total sugar production came back to its 'normal' level.

The above analysis of the development of sugar production costs in Poland in the marketing years 1997/98-2003/04 demonstrates, *inter alia*, the impact of the sugar yield in % of raw sugar value on beet on the economic efficiency of sugarbeet processing. The value of this indicator in a particular season not only decides about the purchasing costs of raw material, but has also a major effect on the scale of other variable costs (beet procurement, use of supplementary materials, etc.). This means that actions aimed at constant improvement in the sugar content in beets and at the minimization of overall sugar losses are a matter of central importance for all sugar producers. It has to be added, however, that as far as the productivity and quality of the harvest are concerned, the joint efforts of beet growers and sugar companies can produce results only if they are accompanied by favorable weather conditions. Drought, torrential rains, floods and other climatic misfortunes can lead to a substantial reduction in both beet and sugar yields in a particular year. It is estimated that even given all the factors that have an impact on the sugar yield per hectare in a given season, weather conditions determine the value of this indicator of productivity to a degree of about 30% (Świetlicki 2004, p. 38).

Among the various ways of reducing the costs of beet-sugar production, many of which have been discussed above, the most effective strategy for permanent cost savings is the expansion of sugar production at the factory and prolongation of the length of a campaign to its optimum. This results in a considerable reduction in labor costs and fixed costs per one tonne of sugar. This, in turn, contributes to the fall in total unit costs. Due to the tremendous significance of appropriate processing capacity of a sugar factory for the cost efficiency of beet sugar production, the next section is devoted to the analysis of the correlation between the size of a sugar factory and costs of sugar production.

4.3 The Relationship Between Size of a Sugar Factory and the Economic Efficiency of Beet Sugar Production

Whereas the purchasing costs of one tonne of beets are independent of the volume of sugar production, transportation and processing costs are subject to factory size. The economies of scale play a significant role in the production of beet sugar since unit costs decrease with increasing sugar production at the sugar factory (Konieczka 2002, pp. 295-296). This is due mainly to the fact that fixed costs constitute a large share of total production costs of beet sugar (See Table 6). The short period of time within which sugarbeet processing takes place provides another reason to produce sugar in factories with large capacities. According to Render (1989, p. 50), the expansion of the processing capacity of a sugar factory from 3,000 t/d to 10,000 t/d is accompanied by a reduction of 33% in the overall production costs per one tonne of sugar. Render emphasizes at the same time that further enlargement of daily processing capacity, from 10,000 t/d to 20,000 t/d, leads to only 10% additional cost savings in the production of one tonne of sugar.[34] This is a consequence of rising beet-procurement costs after any significant expansion of sugar production at a given plant. The larger the processing capacity of a sugar factory, the greater the amount of sugarbeets needed for its full utilization. This means that expansion of the processing capacity compels a sugar producer to procure beets from more distant locations, which means an increase in transportation costs.

The determination of the point at which diseconomies of scale resulting from increasing beet-procurement costs begin to dominate the economies of scale in processing depends on several factors, which differ between countries and regions. Such factors include the transport infrastructure and topography of a given region, the average size and density of beet plantations, or the number of beet growers. In a region with a fragmented beet-growing structure and an under-developed road system, the diseconomies of scale resulting from rising beet-procurement costs are much more pronounced than in an area characterized by large beet plantations and a well-organized transport infrastructure. The fragmentation of sugarbeet plantations and their low density mean a substantial increase in beet-procurement costs, especially at factories with a daily processing capacity exceeding 6,000 t of beet throughput per day (ibid., p. 58).

The size of farms where sugarbeets are grown has a considerable influence on labor costs. Referring to research carried out by agricultural scientists from the Technical University of Munich (Germany), Schröder (1998, p. 1068) points out that the annual labor input (measured in working hours per ha) at large sugarbeet plantations (more than 20 ha) is only a third of the labor input recorded at small plantations (below 2 ha).[35] This is due mainly to the fact that the mechanization of farm work increases with the increased area of the plantation (ibid., p. 1068).

Apart from the above factors, there are several other details that have to be taken into account in determining the optimal size of a sugar factory. As is the case for the optimal length of a campaign, the optimal size of a factory depends

[34] Render's calculations refer to West Germany.

[35] The results of the aforementioned research are based on investigations conducted in Southern Germany.

on the possibilities for beet procurement in a particular region (Mahler 1991, p. 93). It makes little sense to construct a sugar factory with a processing capacity of 8,000 or 10,000 t of beet throughput per day in a place where the amount of available beets would allow it to carry out a campaign lasting only a few weeks (assuming full utilization of the processing capacity). In such a situation, the average fixed costs would rise to a level making production of sugar at the factory economically inefficient. It is important to mention at this point that if the processing capacity of a plant cannot be fully utilized, the accompanying increase in unit costs is greater at a small factory than at a large facility due to larger fixed costs per one tonne of sugar at the former. On the other hand, the minimum utilization level of processing capacity required for the reduction in production costs per one tonne of sugar, following the expansion of the capacity, rises together with the size of a factory (Render op. cit., p. 53).

Another factor that needs to be considered in determining the optimal size of a sugar factory is the market potential. This is particularly important in countries where several sugar companies compete in the market and where regulators allocate production quotas to individual sugar producers. The structure of the sugar market in such a country constitutes a significant determinant of the optimum factory size (Mahler op. cit., pp. 93-102). The production quota allocated to a particular sugar company may be insufficient for the expansion of its plants' processing capacities to the theoretical optimum. The possibility for capacity adjustment is also limited when several small factories belonging to different sugar companies are located near one another (ibid., p. 81). In practice, any considerable enlargement of the processing capacity of one of the plants can be achieved in such a case only to the detriment of the neighboring competitors. One possible solution in such a situation is a merger of two or more sugar companies with processing facilities in the same region. This would pave the way for consolidation of the plants. In general, one of two approaches can be taken in the consolidation of sugar factories in a given region. One is the closure of all plants and the construction of one large and modern unit in the immediate vicinity of a large beet-growing area. The construction costs of a new plant are estimated at €15,000-25,000 per one tonne of daily processing capacity. Another policy option is the modernization and enlargement of a selected factory (or factories) and the closure of the others. In this case, the costs of each additional tonne of daily processing capacity amount to about €20,000-30,000 (Schröder 1998, p. 1082; Kobza 1999, p. 233, Łękawski 2001, p. 105).

Analysts from the consultancy companies *Warszawska Grupa Konsultingowa* and *Pro-Invest International* calculated in a report cited earlier in this study that after the consolidation of the Polish sugar factories incorporated into the national sugar corporation (*Krajowa Spółka Cukrowa "Polski Cukier"*) in 2003, the economically optimal volume of sugar production at one plant, in a campaign lasting 85 days, should amount to 86,275 t (WGK and Pro-Invest International op. cit., p. 64). Assuming an average sugar yield of 15% raw sugar value on beet, it implies that the optimal processing capacity of such a target factory should be around 6,800 t of beet throughput per day.

Existing studies relating to the case of West Germany indicate a much larger optimal size for a sugar factory. Mahler (1991, p.100) has shown that the daily processing capacity at which total costs in the production of one tonne of sugar are minimized is around 20,000 t in that region. It has to be emphasized, however, that this optimum capacity has been derived assuming a high density of beet plantations surrounding a factory. Mahler has shown also that fragmentation and low density of beet production (in tonnes of beets per square kilometer) contribute to the increase in transportation costs, which means that the optimal size of a factory decreases. Investigations concerning the optimal size of a factory in West Germany conducted by Render and cited earlier in this section yielded similar results to those obtained by Mahler. It is evident from the studies of both authors that the greatest cost savings can be obtained after the expansion of the processing capacity of a sugar factory from 3,000 to 10,000 t of beet throughput per day. Another common observation of these two studies is that further enlargement of the processing capacity, above 10,000 t, leads to diminutive additional cost savings (See Figure 7).

Figure 7. Sugar production costs in relation to processing plant size* (ECU/t)

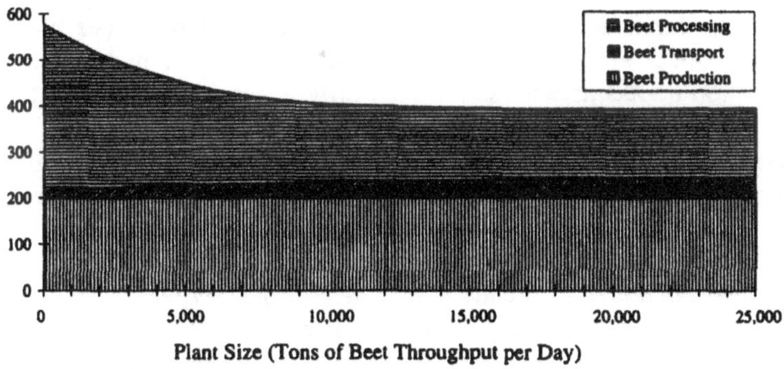

*) Assuming a Discount Rate of 5 Percent, a Processing Campaign Length of 90 days, and a Circular Beet Procurement Area with a Beet Production Density of 150 tons per Square Kilometer.

Source: Walkenhorst 1998, p.21.

The validity of these findings was reassessed and confirmed not long ago by Walkenhorst (1998, p. 21) and Janz (2002, pp. 217-224).

Several factors imply that there must be a difference in the optimal factory size between developed countries of the West and Poland. Firstly, agricultural yields in countries like Germany, France or the Netherlands are considerably higher than in countries from the former Eastern bloc. In a situation when sugarbeet yield per hectare, e.g. in France, is almost twice as great as in Poland, the beet-harvested area needed to satisfy the raw-material needs of a factory with identical processing capacity is much smaller in France. Consequently, distances of beet procurement are shorter and transport cheaper. According to the research carried out by Render (op. cit., p. 57), the concentration of beet-growing areas has an immense effect on the reduction of beet-procurement costs. Render's analyses showed that the larger the processing capacity of a sugar factory, the greater the cost savings obtained due to a high density of beet production in a given region. Secondly, the poor state of the transport infrastructure in Poland has the effect that diseconomies of scale generated by increasing transportation costs are, from a certain point, more pronounced than in Western Europe. And thirdly, the amount of fragmented sugarbeet plantations and the number of beet growers in Poland are much larger than in the West. All these facts lead one to think that the curve portraying the development of beet transportation costs according to factory size, depicted in Figure 7, would have a considerably steeper gradient when applied to the majority of districts in Poland than in the case of Western European countries. By the same token, it can be assumed that the economically optimal size of a sugar factory in most regions of Poland is at the present time smaller than in the highly developed countries of Western Europe.

The above considerations imply also that determination of the optimal size of a sugar factory on the industry level, in a country with such a differentiated transportation infrastructure and high fragmentation of beet plantations as Poland is fraught with opportunities for miscalculation. Even if one does not take into account in such an analysis the current structure of the sugar market, the existence of production quotas as well as regional differences in the quality of beets, the optimal processing capacity of a sugar factory will still vary substantially between regions. Another obstacle to exact specification of the optimum size of a factory in Poland is the fact that the number of sugarbeet growers, the sugarbeet-growing area and the structure of sugarbeet plantations in this country had been changing quite dynamically in the last 14 years. Between the seasons 1990/91 and 2004/05, the beet-harvested area in Poland was reduced from 437,000 to 297,000 ha. The number of sugarbeet growers declined in the same period of time from 383,700 to only 77,900, and the average size of sugarbeet plantations rose from 1.15 to 3.75 ha (IERiGŻ; IPC (Several Issues)). Although structural changes regarding the raw-material base in Poland slowed down considerably in the last few years, they are still in progress.

A thorough analysis of the actual production costs of one tonne of sugar at 44 working sugar factories in Poland in the campaign 2000/01, carried out by Brzeziński (2002), substantiates to a large extent the existence of the economies of scale effect in sugarbeet processing. Moreover, as far as the correlation between sugar-production costs and factory size is concerned, there is a clear parallel between the results obtained by Render and Mahler, and the results of the research conducted by Brzeziński. As portrayed in Figure 8, the production costs of one tonne of sugar in Poland at sugar factories with a processing capacity between 2,000 and 3,000 t of beet throughput per day in the season 2000/01 were higher than at plants with a nominal capacity amounting to 1,100-1,700 t. Nevertheless, it is also evident that the more the processing capacity of sugar factories exceeded 3,000 t of beet throughput per day, the lower were the production costs of one tonne of sugar. Unfortunately, during the campaign 2000/01, there were no sugar factories in Poland with a processing capacity larger than 6,000 t of beet throughput per day. Referring to the studies of Mahler and Render, it can be assumed, however, that unit costs at such plants would be, on average, lower than at factories included in the last size category in Figure 8.

Figure 8. Production costs of one tonne of sugar according to factory size, Poland, Campaign 2000/01

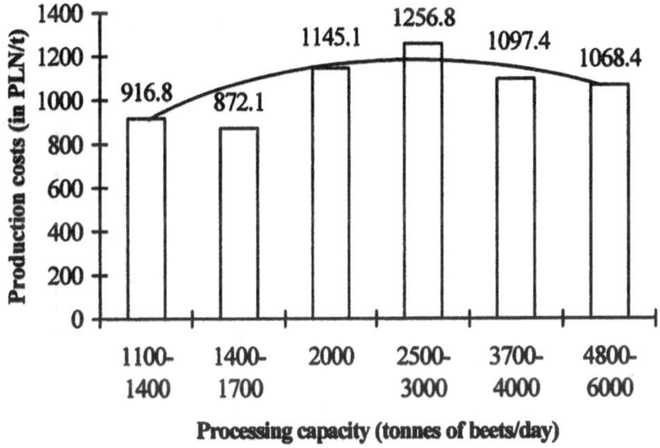

Source: Brzeziński 2002, p. 11.

It must pointed out at this point that analyses of the production costs of one tonne of sugar depending on factory size conducted within the last couple of years in Poland may have various outcomes. The results of some of them may demonstrate that unit production costs at the largest factories are considerably higher that at small plants. This is caused by the fact that the most intensive phase of the restructuring process of the sugar industry in Poland, connected with large investment outlays and introduction of strategic restructuring activities, has been in progress for the last few years. Many sugar factories in the country, especially the large ones, are subject to a thorough modernization. Individual sugar corporations competing in the Polish market have been investing large sums in new machinery at selected plants. Furthermore, numerous large sugar factories are still overstaffed due to the slow rate of labor restructuring.

All this means that as long as certain issues are not 'put in order' at the largest sugar factories, e.g. use of energy and employment levels, unit production costs at these plants may, in fact, turn out to be higher than at small factories. This, in turn, means that the economies of scale effect in beet processing may for the next several years not be as evident in Poland as in the case of more advanced, West European countries.

5 Transformations in Structure and Ownership in the European Sugar Industry

The purpose of this chapter is to show to what extent some of the theoretical considerations from the previous section are confirmed in practice. First, it is portrayed how the number and average size of sugar factories has developed during the last five decades in the member states of the European Union. Subsequently, the process of ownership concentration in the European sugar industry is analyzed.

5.1 The Consolidation Process of Sugarbeet-processing Plants in Europe

The significance of an appropriate processing capacity and location of a sugar factory is reflected most clearly by structural changes that took place in the sugar industries of most European countries over the last few decades. One of the major strategies used by sugar corporations in Europe, aimed at the improvement in the productive and economic efficiency of their operations, has been the closure of small plants situated far from large beet-growing regions and the substantial expansion of the slicing capacities at factories selected for modernization.

In many cases, cessation of production at several obsolete and unfavorably located factories was followed by the construction of one large and modern manufacturing complex. Data presented in Table 7 shows how the amalgamation of sugar factories and refineries has developed in Europe since 1952. The trend towards the increasing consolidation of beet-processing facilities and the dynamics of this process are best portrayed by the example of countries in which the number of sugar factories was greatest fifty years ago. In France, Germany and Italy, the largest sugar manufacturers among states forming until recently the EU-15, the total number of sugar factories and refineries in 1952/53 was 264. In 2004/05 the corresponding number was 79, which means a reduction of 70%. Interestingly, the aggregate beet sugar production in all West European countries listed in Table 7 increased from about 5.3 million t in 1952/53 to 11.4 million t in 1972/73 and 18 million t in 1992/1993. During the campaign 2004/05 sugar factories in those countries produced 17.5 million t of beet sugar. At the same time, the sugarbeet-harvested area in the same group of countries increased from 1,463,000 ha in 1952/53 to 1,774,000 ha in 1972/72 and 2,093,000 ha in 1992/93. In the season 2004/05, it amounted to 1,655,000 ha (Zuckerwirtschaft; CEFS online database).

Table 7. Number of sugar factories and refineries, EU-25*, 1952/53-2004/05

		1952/53	1962/63	1972/73	1982/83	1990/91	1992/93	2001/02	2002/03	2003/04	2004/05
A	Austria	7	7	7	6	3	3	3	3	3	3
B	Belgium	39	25	19	16	12	10	9	9	9	6
DK	Denmark	10	7	6	6	5	4	3	3	3	3
E	Spain	62	62	47	37	27	26	14	14	12	11
EL	Greece	-	2	3	5	5	5	5	5	5	5
F	France (1)	123	115	78	62	54	50	36	36	34	34
FIN	Finland	6	7	7	6	5	4	3	3	3	2
GER	Germany (2)	74	66	56	48	79	52	30	28	27	27
I	Italy	67	80	59	39	31	25	20	20	19	18
IRL	Ireland	4	4	4	4	2	2	2	2	2	2
NL	Netherlands	13	13	12	10	7	6	5	5	5	5
P	Portugal	25	25	6	5	4	4	4	4	4	4
S	Sweden	19	10	8	8	7	6	3	3	3	2
UK	United Kingdom	27	24	23	17	14	12	8	7	7	7
	EU-15	**476**	**447**	**335**	**269**	**255**	**209**	**145**	**142**	**136**	**129**
CZ	Czech Republic	92	84	66	56	47	38	12	13	12	11
H	Hungary	12	11	11	12	12	12	7	7	6	5
LT	Lithuania	...	...	...	...	...	4	4	4	4	4
LV	Latvia	...	...	...	...	...	3	2	2	2	2
PL	Poland	76	76	76	79	78	78	76	65	54	43
SK	Slovakia	9	9	11	10	10	8	5	5	5	5
SL	Slovenia	...	...	...	...	...	1	1	1	1	1
	EU-25	**665**	**627**	**499**	**426**	**402**	**353**	**253**	**240**	**220**	**200**

* Luxemburg, Malta, Cyprus and Estonia are also member states of the European Union but since they do not produce sugar, they are not included in Table 7.
(1) Excluding factories in French Overseas Departments (2004/05: 5 sugar factories).
(2) Until 1989/90 Federal Republic only.

Source: Zuckerwirtschaft, F.O. Licht's International Economic Yearbook and Directory; IPC; Burak Cukrowy 2/2005, p. 32.

In conclusion, a more than threefold increase in sugar production in the former EU-15 between 1952/53 and 2004/05 was accompanied by an expansion of beet-harvested area of only 13%. In the same period, the number of sugar factories and refineries in the EU-15 member states was reduced by 73%. This betokens a significant improvement in the productive efficiency of sugarbeet cultivation and processing in Western Europe over the last few decades.

A particularly interesting case of consolidation in the sugar sector could be observed not long ago in Germany. After German reunification in 1989, the number of sugar factories on the enlarged territory of Germany rose to 79. This created the impression of a flashback since a similar number of plants existed in the

German Federal Republic in 1952. Nevertheless, the determination of the corporations which took over 43 plants in East Germany to implement a prompt, large-scale restructuring program had the effect that already during the 1994/95 campaign the total number of working sugar factories in the newly-formed German states amounted to only 9. Between the seasons 1990/91 and 2004/05 the number of sugar factories in the united Germany shrunk from 79 to 27.[36]

Apart from the aforementioned top three sugar producers in Western Europe, other countries of the region like Spain, Belgium and Great Britain conducted transformations of their sugar industries that were similar in scope. In other member states of the EU-15, the trend of changes was the same but due to a relatively small initial number of factories in those countries reorganization of their sugar industries was not as costly and challenging as in Germany or France. The consolidation process of sugarbeet-processing plants in Europe was influenced by the increasing competitiveness of cane-sugar producers and growing surpluses of sugar on the world market, leading to its decreasing price, as well as by technological progress.

In countries from the former Eastern bloc, structural changes in the sugar sector on a scale similar to Western Europe took place only in former Czechoslovakia. As shown in Table 7, the number of sugar factories on the present territory of the Czech Republic has fallen as drastically as in Western Europe. Many sugarbeet-processing plants in Czechoslovakia were closed down during socialist times in order to optimize the length of campaign in the remaining factories. In a few regions, several new plants were constructed, accompanied by the closure of a number of small and obsolete factories located in the vicinity of the new facilities.

The only country among large sugar producers in today's EU-25, where structural changes in the sugar industry were practically unheard of until the season 2002/2003, was Poland. Before 1990, this state of affairs was influenced to a great extent by the transfer of financial resources from profitable factories to plants which for various reasons found themselves in difficult economic situations. The latter received, in addition to this, generous government subsidies and low-interest loans what enabled them to proceed with sugar production despite a very poor performance. The abolition of central planning and the hardening of budget constraints for firms after Poland's change to a market economy in 1990 was not followed by the desirable structural changes in the sugar sector. Lack of consensus regarding a suitable restructuring strategy for the sugar industry during the first years of the transition period and uninterrupted, albeit limited, state protection of poorly performing plants did not favor structural reforms. While in most West European countries sugarbeet-processing plants were con-

[36] The restructuring process of the sugar industry in East Germany is analyzed in section 14 of this study.

tinually consolidated and modernized, in Poland the importance of such activities would seem to have been ignored. Even if local authorities were aware of the need for changes, they failed to take into account the significance of the time factor.

As portrayed in Table 8, a threefold and in some cases even an almost fourfold increase in the average daily slicing capacities of sugar factories could be observed throughout Western Europe between the campaigns 1967/68 and 2004/05.

Table 8. Average daily processing capacity of sugar factories (in 1000 t), EU-25, 1967/68-2004/05

		1967/68	1976/77	1986/87	1992/93	1999/00	2004/05	Change in % 1967/68: 2004/05
A	Austria	3.97	4.81	6.22	9.14	10.70	12.71	+220%
B	Belgium	2.66	4.13	6.37	7.91	10.02	12.92	+386%
DK	Denmark	4.54	5.88	6.78	9.37	10.05	10.09	+122%
E	Spain	1.68	2.47	4.00	4.72	7.35	8.91	+430%
EL	Greece	2.17	3.96	5.60	5.38	6.52	6.28	+189%
F	France	2.66	4.32	7.28	9.08	11.40	13.01	+389%
FIN	Finland	1.74	2.68	3.70	4.65	6.50	6.53	+275%
GER	Germany (1)	2.77	4.17	6.08	7.11	9.62	11.47	+314%
I	Italy	2.68	5.17	6.12	6.74	10.48	8.99	+235%
IRL	Ireland	3.20	2.88	4.25	7.66	8.00	8.53	+167%
NL	Netherlands	4.67	5.92	8.35	12.70	14.10	14.79	+217%
P	Portugal	...	1.10	1.25	1.25	3.13	4.57	-
S	Sweden	3.21	3.56	4.29	5.62	9.05	12.88	+301%
UK	United Kingdom	3.24	3.97	5.85	6.83	8.07	9.93	+206%
	EU-15	**3.01 (2)**	**3.93**	**5.44**	**7.01**	**8.93**	**10.11**	**+236%**
CZ	Czech Republic	...	...	...	...	3.16	3.86	-
H	Hungary	2.34	2.34	3.43	3.78	5.50	8.03	+243%
LT	Lithuania	...	...	...	...	2.90	2.97	-
LV	Latvia	...	...	...	...	1.96	2.20	-
PL	**Poland**	2.00	1.70	2.05	2.25	2.93	3.38	+69%
SK	Slovakia	...	...	...	...	3.20	3.14	-
SL	Slovenia	...	...	...	...	4.00	4.00	-
	EU-25					**7.08**	**8.06**	-

(1) Until 1989/90 Federal Republic only.
(2) Excluding Portugal.
Source: Zuckerwirtschaft; Krick 2000, p. 426; Sugar Economy Europe (Several Issues); IERiGŻ 2005.

With an average processing capacity exceeding 10,000 t of beet throughput per day and an average length of a campaign varying between 85 and 100 days, sugar factories in many West European countries produce today more than 100,000 t of sugar. There are also numerous plants where total sugar production during one campaign comes close to or exceeds 200,000 t. In France, the largest sugar manufacturer in Europe, the daily processing capacity of 5 out of 30 beet sugar factories equals or is greater than 20,000 t. The largest of the five plants, located in *Connantre*, is also the largest sugar factory in Europe. Its nominal daily pro-

cessing capacity amounts to 21,500 t per day. Only 6 factories in France have a processing capacity lower than 8,000 t of beet throughput per day.
As demonstrated in Table 9, sugarbeet-processing plants of that size are today something of a rarity in Western Europe. This situation prompted not long ago a number of organizations compiling various statistics regarding the European sugar industry to make some adjustments to the classification system of sugar factories according to their size. In the second half of the 1990s, one of the major providers of statistical data about sugar industries in Europe, the European Committee of Sugar Manufacturers (CEFS), based in Brussels, introduced into its classification system of sugar factories a new category comprising plants with a daily processing capacity larger than 15,000 t. Before this, all sites with a processing capacity exceeding 12,000 t of beet throughput per day were considered as very large by CEFS and constituted the largest size category.

All these developments mean that in the course of time, the meaning of the phrases "small factory", "medium-sized factory" and "large factory" has changed substantially with regard to sugarbeet-processing facilities in Europe (Krick 2000, p. 428).

Table 9. Classification of sugarbeet-processing plants according to their size, 10 largest sugar producers in the EU-25, campaigns 1993/94 and 2004/05

	France		Germany		Poland		United Kingdom		Italy		Spain		Netherlands		Belgium		Czech Republic		Denmark	
Processing capacity (in t per day)	1993/94	2004/05	1993/94	2004/05	1993/94	2004/05	1993/94	2004/05	1993/94	2004/05	1993/94	2004/05	1993/94	2004/05	1993/94	2004/05	1993/94	2004/05	1993/94	2004/05
<5000	11	2	10	1	75	34	2	1	3	-	10	2	-	-	1	-	39	9	-	-
5000-<8000	8	4	18	6	3	9	6	1	8	1	9	1	1	-	3	2	-	1	1	-
8000-<12000	15	7	11	9	-	-	2	2	10	7	2	8	1	1	2	3	-	1	3	2
12000-<15000	12	4	4	5	-	-	-	1	3	9	-	-	4	2	3	-	-	-	-	1
>15000	-	13	-	5	-	-	-	1	-	-	-	-	-	2	-	1	-	-	-	-
Total number	46	30	43	26	78	43	10	6	24	17	21	11	6	5	9	6	39	11	4	3

Source: CEFS online database; Cukier i Skrobia; F.O. Licht's International Economic Yearbook and Directory, IPC, Sugar Economy Europe.

The decreasing number of sugar factories in the EU-15 went hand in hand with a reduction in employment in the sugar industry. As portrayed in Table 10, the reduction in workforce employed during a campaign was more pronounced than the reduction in regular staff. This was due to the fact that even after a considerable expansion of the processing capacity of a sugar factory, the number of employees needed at individual stations during a campaign remains more or less unchanged. It tends rather to decline since the automation level of a sugar factory rises with its size. This, in turn, means that expansion of sugar production leads automatically to the improvement in labor productivity. As far as regular staff is concerned, a significant rise in sugar production usually leads to a slight increase since more people are needed to carry out various organizational, supervisory and administrative tasks (Render 1989, p. 47).

Table 10. Employment in the sugar industry, EU-15, 1993/94 and 2002/03

Processing season	Number of employees during the processing season	Number of employees between the processing seasons
1993/94	54,789	34,230
2002/03	35,362	24,934

Source: CEFS online database.

After the European Union's eastward enlargement in 2004, Poland became the third largest sugar manufacturer among the countries forming the EU-25. As can be seen in Tables 7 and 8, the total number and average size of sugar factories in this country differ substantially from what can be observed in highly developed member states of the EU. Although France and Germany produce every year twice as much sugar as Poland, the number of sugar factories in each of the two West European countries is only around half that of Poland. This is due to the fact that sugar factories in these countries are on average three times larger than that of sugar factories in Poland. This precludes sugar producers in Poland from benefiting from an economies-of-scale effect in beet processing and puts them at a significant disadvantage in their attempts to compete with producers from Western Europe. If fragmentation and underdevelopment of the beet-processing sector in Poland were eliminated, the country could very quickly become one of the most competitive beet sugar manufacturers in Europe. The availability of a relatively cheap labor force in Poland as well as favorable natural conditions for sugarbeet growing in many regions of the country constitute a priceless asset. Unfortunately, inefficiencies in sugarbeet processing and the unfavorable structure of beet plantations have the effect that Poland's comparative advantage in the production of sugarbeets is barely perceptible (Walkenhorst 1998, pp. 6-7; Miedziak 2003, p. 52).

5.2 Concentration of Ownership in the European Sugar Industry

The consolidation process of sugar factories in the EU-15 over the last three decades was accompanied by the gradual amalgamation of sugar companies. Their number shrank from 162 in 1972 to only 46 in 2004 (See Table 11). As was pointed out earlier, expansion of processing capacity in a sugar factory leads to a reduction in production costs per one tonne of sugar on condition that enough beets are available for full utilization of the enlarged capacity. Another necessary requirement for reaping the economies of scale in beet processing is a sufficiently large market share (production quota) of a particular sugar company.

Furthermore, reduction in production costs through consolidation and enlargement of sugar factories, their modernization and automation, is associated with substantial capital expenditure (Mahler op. cit, p. 105).

Table 11. Number of sugar and refinery companies by production year, EU-15

		1972/73	1982/83	1992/93	2002/03	2004/05
A	Austria	6	4	1	1	1
B	Belgium	14	11	7	6	2
DK	Denmark	2	2	1	1	1
E	Spain	16	13	8	3	3
EL	Greece	1	1	1	1	1
F	France	48	34	30	17	13
FIN	Finland	5	2	1	1	1
GER	Germany (1)	36	29	14	7	6
I	Italy	21	17	12	9	9
IRL	Ireland	1	1	1	1	1
NL	Netherlands	2	2	2	2	2
P	Portugal	6	5	3	4	3
S	Sweden	1	1	1	1	1
UK	United Kingdom	3	2	2	2	2
	EU-15	**162**	**124**	**84**	**56**	**46**

(1) Until 1989/90 Federal Republic only.
Source: Sugar Economy Europe 2004; CEFS online database.

The above limitations provide a strong stimulus for sugar producers in Europe to join forces. There are, however, also numerous other motives for mergers. Janz (2002, p. 24) suggests that a merger of two or more companies may lead, *inter alia*, to various rationalization effects and synergies not only in production but also in administration, marketing, research and development as well as in logistics. Furthermore, the same author points to the striving for market dominance and elimination of competitors as an important driving force of fusions.

Among the potential negative effects induced by decreasing number of competitors in a given industrial sector, Janz (ibid. p. 32) and Barney (2002, p. 339, 354-55) mention the possibility of secret cooperative agreements between individual producers aimed at the setting of higher prices for offered products. Such collusive behavior includes restriction of output and market sharing, both leading to an increase in price from which all companies involved benefit. In the recent past, sugar companies in the EU have been convicted several times by various competition authorities of operating in collusion.[37]

As the main motives for the mergers of a handful of sugar companies in Germany within the last few years, Janz (op. cit., p. 119) names the need to meet the increasing demands of customers and the mobilization of all possible cost-saving opportunities with the liberalization of world sugar trade.

---

[37] See Blume 2002, p. 75.

Until the beginning of the 1980s, the consolidation of sugar companies in Europe took place exclusively within the borders of individual countries. Since then, numerous sugar corporations have started to acquire sugar factories or entire sugar companies abroad (Kondrakiewicz op. cit., p. 101). The theoretical rationale behind this process is discussed separately in section 12 of this study. The focus of this chapter is to demonstrate solely the results of the internationalization of takeovers in the European sugar industry.

The amalgamation of sugar companies in individual countries and a series of trans-border mergers and acquisitions within the last two decades has led to a strong concentration of ownership in European Union's sugar sector. The ten largest sugar corporations currently control 75% of the entire EU-25 sugar production quota. As shown in Table 11, sugar industries in several member states of the former EU-15 are completely monopolized and some have an oligopolistic structure. The aforementioned consolidation processes contributed to the formation of industrial giants that are still strengthening their position. A prime example of such an organization is the multinational sugar corporation Südzucker, with its headquarters in *Mannheim/Ochsenfurt*, Germany. Its share of the EU-25 maximum sugar production quota exceeds by far that of other competitors (See Table 12).

Table 12. Maximum production quotas of 10 largest sugar companies in the EU-25*

Company	Maximum quota (in million tonnes)	in % of the EU-25 quota
1. Südzucker	3.8	21.8
2. Nordzucker	1.6	9.1
3. British Sugar	1.3	7.6
4. Tereos	1.2	6.7
5. Danisco	1.1	6.3
6. Pfeifer & Langen	0.9	5.0
7. Ebro Puelva	0.8	4.5
8. Polski Cukier	0.7	3.8
9. Copro B. & Italia Zuccheri	0.6	3.5
10. Suiker Unie	0.6	3.4
EU-25	**17.4**	**100**

* Before 2004/05 reclassification
Source: Südzucker (official web site).

Nonetheless, the amount of sugar produced by corporations placed behind Südzucker on the list of the largest sugar corporations in Europe is also tremendous. Their dynamic growth within the last two decades was the result of a wave of domestic and international mergers and acquisitions.

5.3 The Incorporation of Sugar Factories in Central and Eastern Europe into the Structures of West European Sugar Corporations

In the first half of the 1990s, West European sugar companies started to acquire sugarbeet-processing plants in Central and Eastern Europe. This was favored by the onset of privatization processes and the rapidly improving investment climate in the countries of this region after their transition to a market economy. Before 1990, sugar industries in individual central and east European states constituted state-owned monopolies. After the collapse of communism and the abolition of central planning in this group of countries, the state monopoly in sugar production was removed. In the following years, the bulk of sugar factories in these countries were gradually privatized, in most cases to strategic foreign investors. The form and pace of privatization differed between countries. In the Czech Republic, for example, the share capital of sugar factories was distributed initially free of charge to the public (voucher privatization). Until the end of 1993, 95% of state-owned enterprises from the food industry were privatized in this country with the help of the above method (Bavorova 2002, pp. 9-10). A few years later, foreign sugar companies took over several plants in the Czech Republic as a result of secondary ownership transfers. In Poland, negotiations started on the basis of a public invitation preceded by commercialization[38] constituted the dominant privatization method of sugar factories. In contrast to developments in the Czech Republic, the privatization of the Polish sugar industry moved forward very slowly. Up to 2005, 49 sugarbeet-processing plants in Poland were privatized, all to foreign investors. In September 2003, a national sugar corporation comprising all non-privatized sugar factories was established by decision of the Polish parliament.[39]

As in the case of Poland, privatization of sugar factories in Hungary began with the clarification of their legal status. This was followed by the sale of individual plants through public tender on a case-by-case basis. The Hungarian sugar industry quickly attracted strong interest from foreign investors. Already in the campaign 1993/94, 70% of the total volume of sugar produced in Hungary came from 6 sugar factories where West European sugar corporations had earlier acquired sizeable stakes.[40] In the second half of 1993, the privatization of sugar fac-

[38] Commercialization is a transformation of an enterprise into a joint-stock company or a limited-liability company by the Minister of the Treasury. The Treasury holds 100% of shares in such a company until its privatization (For details, see the web site of the Ministry of State Treasury of the Republic of Poland at www.mst.gov.pl).

[39] The privatization process of the sugar industry in Poland is discussed in detail in Section 13 of the present study.

[40] *Beghin-Say* held at that time a 40% stake in the sugar factories *Szerencs*, *Szolnok*, *Matracukor*; *AGRANA* possessed a 53% stake in two plants: *Petohaza* and *Kaposvar*, and

tories in Hungary was stopped and a national sugar corporation was created, composed of 5 plants (Schultes 1994, p. 689). Nevertheless, after the failure of this project (with the worsening economic condition of the plants included in the national corporation), these 5 factories were taken over by foreign investors (Solska 1999). Today, all working sugar factories in Hungary are controlled by foreign multinationals.

The very active involvement of West European sugar corporations in the privatization process of sugar industries in Central and Eastern Europe resulted in the complete domination of some sugar markets of this region. From the 10 largest sugar companies in Europe, 7 have sugarbeet-processing facilities in at least one of the countries that joined the EU in May 2004. All working sugar factories in Slovakia, Slovenia and Hungary are currently in the hands of several foreign sugar companies. 3 out of 4 beet-processing plants in Lithuania are majority-owned by the Danish company *Danisco*. The share of foreign-owned sugar companies in the total sugar production quota of Poland and the Czech Republic amounts to 60% and 80%, respectively. Among the sugar-producing countries that entered the EU in 2004, only Latvia has a sugar industry (two factories) that is still not connected with foreign capital. Apart from the acquisition of plants in the new member states of the EU, West European sugar corporations recently started to invest in countries that are currently preparing for accession. Following the takeover of 5 sugar factories in Moldova, Südzucker possesses 50% of the total sugar production quota in this country. *Südzucker* as well as *Pfeifer & Langen* also have controlling stakes in several sugarbeet-processing plants in Romania.

5.4 Outlook

It is very unlikely that in the foreseeable future the consolidation process of sugar factories in the European Union will come to a standstill. In states that joined the EU in 2004 there is still plenty of sugarbeet-processing plants whose capacity is too small to reap economies of scale. Therefore, it can be expected that the number of sugar factories in this group of countries will decline rapidly in the next few years. A further reduction in the number of sugarbeet-processing plants can also be expected in Western Europe. The pace of the amalgamation of sugar factories in the EU will depend on the outcome of talks between member states of the World Trade Organization (WTO) concerning the liberalization of the world sugar trade. In 2006, significant changes to the organization of the sugar

---

Tate & Lyle/Saint Louis Sucre had a 30% stake in the sugar factory *Kaba* through a joint sister company *Eastern Sugar* (Schultes 1994, p. 689).

market in the EU will be introduced.[41] It is quite certain that the implementation of the planned reform of the EU sugar regime will put enormous pressure on sugar companies to reduce the costs of sugar production. It will necessitate the closure of many sugarbeet-processing plants and the gradual concentration of the entire sugar production in factories with very large processing capacities, located in regions with a comparative advantage in sugarbeet production.

Apart from continuous amalgamation and increasing average processing capacity of sugar factories, further concentration of ownership may be expected in the European sugar industry within the next few years. It can be assumed, however, that the consolidation of sugar companies will proceed much more slowly and take place on a considerably smaller scale than the amalgamation of sugar factories. The concentration level of ownership in the European sugar industry is already at the present time very high and one should not expect too many mergers and acquisitions in this sector in the near future. There is no doubt that the European Commission's antitrust authorities will examine carefully each potential fusion in order to prevent large sugar companies from obtaining too large shares of the EU's sugar market. This should, *inter alia*, impede the establishment of cartels setting prices far above the marginal costs of production. Nonetheless, it can be expected that in the next few years the largest sugar corporations will continuously strengthen their position through takeovers of smaller sugar producers as well as through additional foreign direct investment in Central and Eastern Europe. Apart from setting their sights on further acquisitions in countries that joined the European Union in May 2004, several multinational sugar companies have designs on sugar industries in central and east European states outside of the EU.

6 Situation in the World Sugar Market, 1990-2004: International Analysis

The most significant feature of the developments in the world sugar market in the 1990-2004 time period was the systematic increase in the production of sugar and the continuous rise in the stocks of the commodity (an excess of production over consumption) from the marketing year 1994/95 onwards. Whereas in the marketing years 1990/91-1994/95, world production of centrifugal sugar amounted on average to 115 million t; in the 2000/01-2004/05 time period it totaled on average 142 million t. World ending stocks of sugar in the 1990/91-1994/95 time period amounted on average to 38 million t. The corresponding number for the years 2000/01-2004/05 is 64 million t. Consumption of

[41] Implications of the planned overhaul of the EU sugar regime are discussed in more detail in section 9.7 of the present study.

sugar increased continuously between the seasons 1990/91 and 2004/05. Nevertheless, apart from a few exceptions, it was always considerably lower than total sugar production (See Figure 9).

A progressive rise in the world stocks of sugar was accompanied by a gradual fall in its market price. The world market price of raw sugar plummeted from almost $ 300/mt in 1995 to less than $ 150/mt in 1999. The price of white sugar decreased in the same period of time from nearly $ 400/mt to $ 200/mt. After a short recovery in 2000 and 2001, resulting from an extraordinarily poor harvest in several major sugar-producing countries in 2000, world sugar prices in 2003 returned to a level similar to that recorded in 1999. One of the main reasons for these developments was the systematic increase in exportable surpluses of sugar in Brazil (See Figure 10). Another important factor that influenced a significant drop in world sugar prices in the second half of the 1990s were two economic and financial crises in Asia (lower demand) and Southern America (currency devaluation and liberalization of prices for ethanol led to a considerable increase in sugar production in Brazil) (European Commission 2003, p. 26). In the first half of 2004, the world market prices of sugar rose continuously and reached $ 202/mt (raw sugar) and $ 260/mt (white sugar) in July. This was due, among other things, to the fact that in the marketing year 2003/04 sugar production fell considerably in relation to the previous season (-4.7%). At the same time, the consumption of sugar increased slightly (+2.4%). This resulted in an appreciable reduction in world sugar stocks and, consequently, an increase in sugar prices.

Figure 9. World sugar balance, 1990/91-2004/05 (September/August), in million tonnes, raw sugar value*

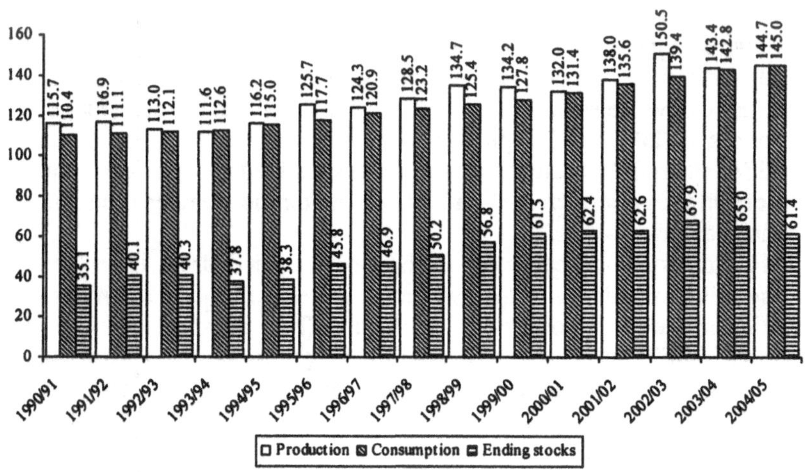

* Centrifugal sugar

Source: F.O. Licht's International Sugar and Sweetener Report (Several Issues); IERIGŻ (Several Issues).

Figure 10. World sugar prices and net exports, 1990-2004

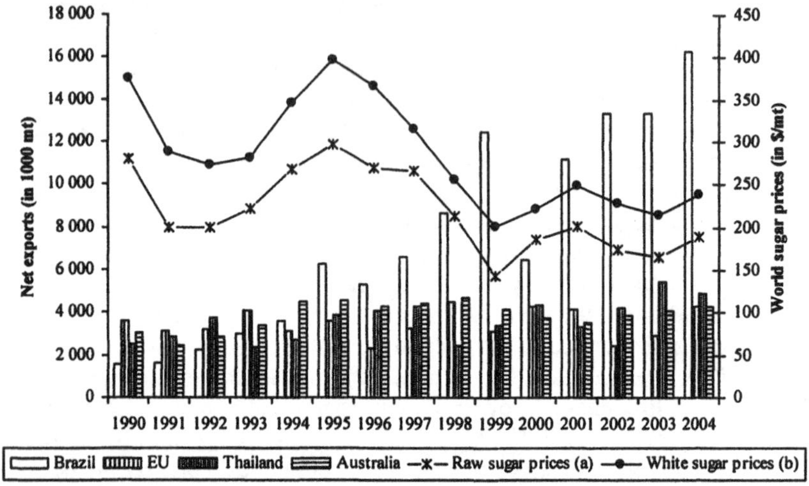

a) New York Contract No.11, f.o.b. & stowed, Caribbean ports (Annual averages)
b) London Contract No. 5, f.o.b. & stowed, European ports, in 50kg bags (Annual averages)
Source: F.O. Licht's International Sugar and Sweetener Report (Several Issues); Sugar Economy Europe (Several Issues).

The drop in sugar production in 2003/04 was caused mainly by unfavorable weather conditions in a number of countries. Insufficient rainfalls in Brazil had the effect that the cane harvest in the country in that season was lower than anticipated. Also in China, India and Thailand, production estimates had to be revised downwards (Sommer 2005, p. 34). In December 2004, the world market price of raw and white sugar amounted to $ 224/mt and $ 247/mt, respectively. The annual average world price of raw sugar in 2004 amounted to $190/mt and the annual average price of white sugar turned out to be $ 240/mt. The development of world sugar prices in 2005 will depend on the development of energy prices, the demand for ethanol, the extent of possible speculative buying of sugar in anticipation of further price increases and, of course, on the weather in major sugar-producing countries.

Another important development in the world sugar market in the period of time under investigation was the systematic increase in the share of cane sugar production in the total world sugar production. This share rose from 67.1% in the season 1990/91 to 76.9% in 2004/05 (See Figure 11). The gradual displacement from the world market of beet sugar by much cheaper cane sugar has been taking place for decades and the last 14 years constitute a continuation of this long-term trend.

One of the major factors that contributed within the last several years to the growing dominance of cane sugar over beet sugar was the increasingly strong pressure put on beet-sugar manufacturing countries by international organizations (e.g. WTO) and large exporters of cane sugar, especially Brazil and Thailand, to liberalize the world sugar trade.

Figure 11. World production of beet and cane sugar, 1990/91-2004/05, in million tonnes*

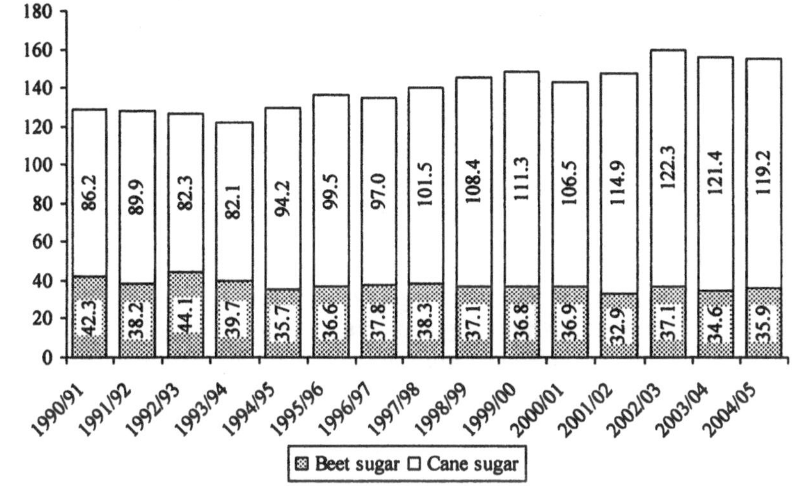

* Including non-centrifugal sugar in raw sugar value
Source: Sugar Economy Europe 2006, p. 16.

Figure 12. Sugarbeet and sugar cane harvested area (in 1000 ha); Sugarbeet and sugar yields per hectare, World, 1990-2004

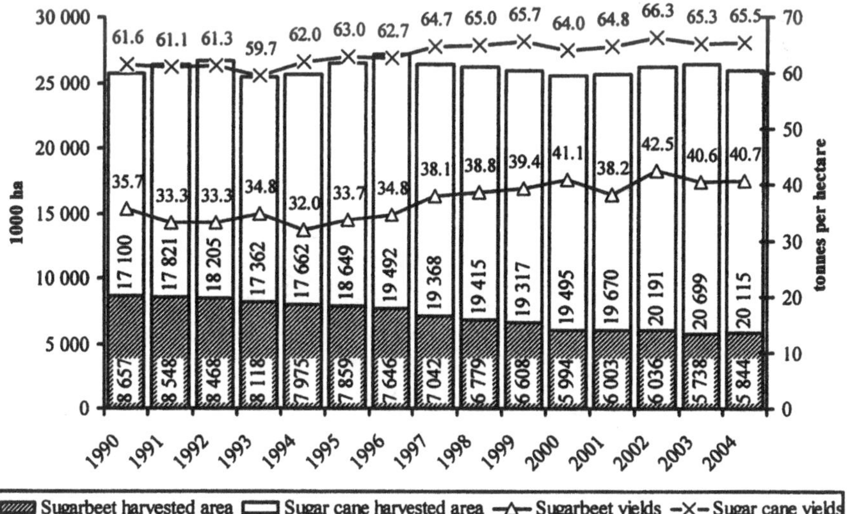

Source: FAOSTAT data (online database).

The considerable increase in the share of cane sugar production in world sugar production has been accompanied by a gradual fall in the sugarbeet harvested area and an expansion of the cane sugar harvested area. In the 1990-2004 time period, the former was reduced by 32% and the latter was enlarged by 18%. At the same time, the average sugarbeet yield per hectare increased from 35.7 t in 1990 to 40.7 t in 2004. Cane sugar yields rose in the same period of time from 61.6 t/ha to 65.5 t/ha (See Figure 12).

Brazil is currently the world's largest producer (28.3 million t in 2004/05) and exporter of sugar. Its share in world sugar production increased in the 1990/91-2004/05 time period from 8% to 20%. Brazil's share in world sugar exports rose in the same period of time from nearly 6% to 36% (Sugar Economy Europe 2006; Zuckerwirtschaft 1993/94). The country's imports of sugar are almost non-existent.

With total sugar production amounting to 21.4 million t, the EU-25 was placed second on the list of the largest sugar producers in the world in the marketing year 2004/05. The 21.4 million t constituted 15% of world sugar production. Exports and imports of sugar from/into the EU in 2004/05 amounted to 4.3 million t (9.4% of world sugar exports) and 2.5 million t (5.8 % of world sugar imports), respectively (Sugar Economy Europe 2006).

The third largest sugar producer in the world in the marketing year 2004/05 was India (14 million t). Its share in world sugar production amounted to 9.8% and was 2.1% lower than in the marketing year 1990/91. Sugar exports from India in 2004 constituted 0.3% of the world sugar exports. The corresponding number for 1990 is 0.2%. As in the case of Brazil, there were hardly any imports of sugar to India between 1990 and 2003. In 2004 the country imported 1.216 million t of sugar (Sugar Economy Europe 2006, p. 24).

Figure 13. Shares of selected countries in world sugar production in the marketing year 2004/05

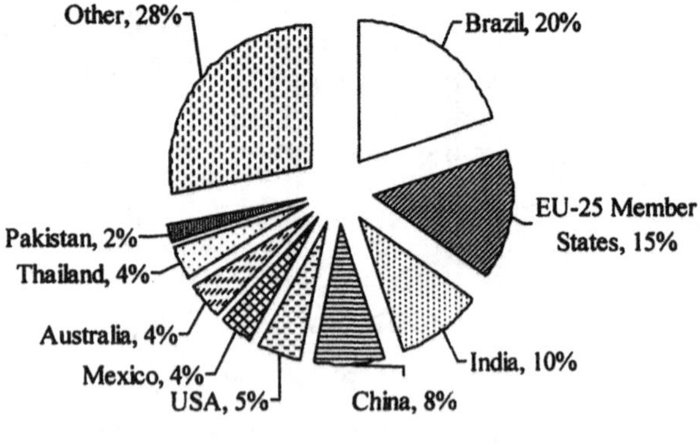

Source: Illustration by the author, based on Sugar Economy Europe 2006, pp. 11-15.

Figure 14. World's Top-10 exporters of sugar, in 1000 tonnes*

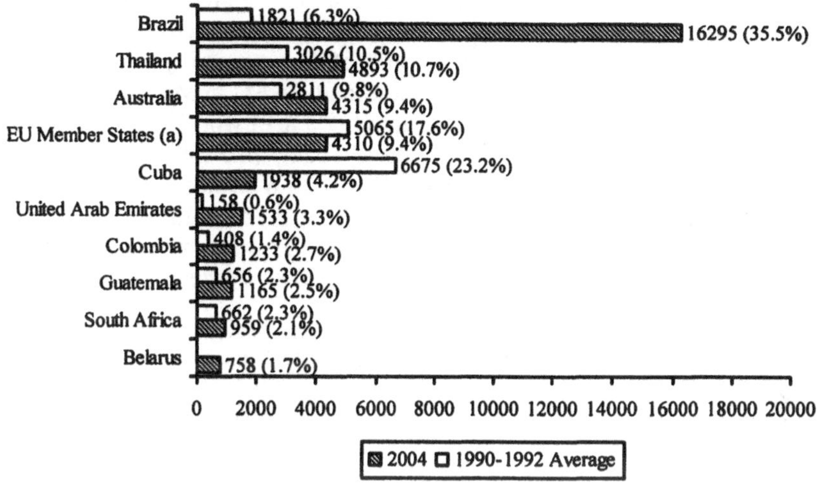

* Numbers in brackets stand for the countries' shares in world sugar exports.
a) For 1990-92: EU-12; For 2004: EU-25.
Source: Sugar Economy Europe 2006, pp. 22-25; Zuckerwirtschaft 1993/94, pp. 31-34.

Figure 15. World's Top-10 importers of sugar, in 1000 tonnes*

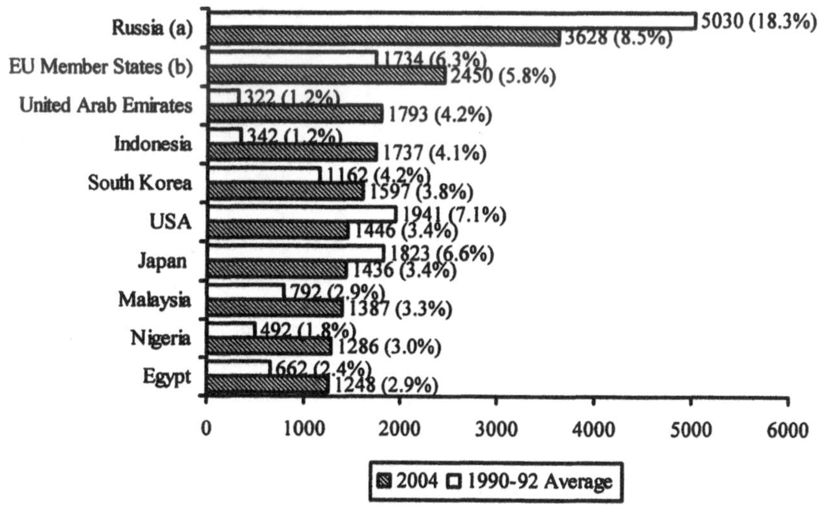

* Numbers in brackets stand for the countries' shares in world sugar imports.
a) For 1990-92 USSR; For 2004: Russia; b) For 1990-92: EU-12; For 2004: EU-25.
Source: Sugar Economy Europe 2006, pp. 22-25; Zuckerwirtschaft 1993/94, pp. 31-34.

In both Brazil and India, sugar is manufactured from cane.[42] The shares of selected countries in world sugar production in 2004/05 are presented in Figure 13.

Figures 14 and 15 portray the world's top-10 exporters and importers of sugar and their shares in world exports and imports of the commodity.

Production of sugar in the countries that joined the EU in May 2004 amounted in the marketing year 2004/05 to 3.8 million t (2.7% of world sugar production). The largest sugar producer in the EU-25 is Germany (4.7 million t in 2004/05). A similar amount of sugar is produced in France (4.6 million t in 2004/05). The third largest sugar producer in the EU-25 is Poland (2.2 million t in 2004/05). The shares of individual EU-25 member states in the aggregate sugar production of countries forming the enlarged EU are presented in Figure 16.

Figure 16. Shares of individual EU-25 member states in total sugar production of countries forming the enlarged EU, marketing year 2004/05

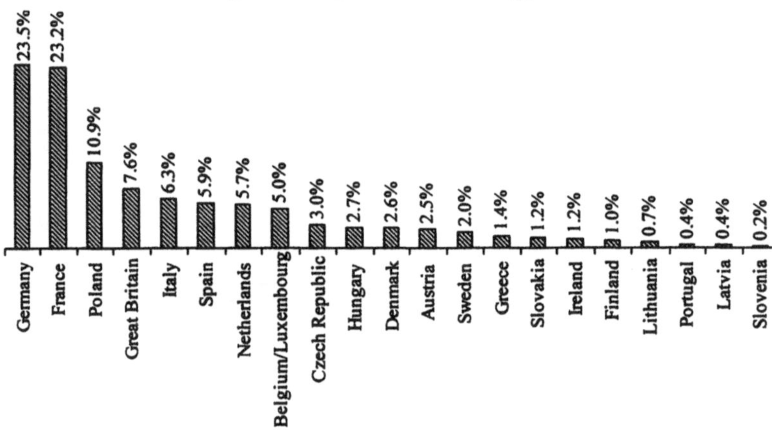

Source: Calculations by the author, based on Sugar Economy Europe 2006, p. 11.

The OECD forecasts in its Agricultural Outlook 2004-2013 that the world market price of sugar in the marketing year 2008/09 will amount to $ 150/mt for raw sugar and $ 179 for refined (white) sugar. The corresponding numbers for the season 2013/2014 are $ 176/mt and $ 204/mt (See Figure 17). According to OECD, the decreasing trend in the next few years will be brought about, *inter alia*, by systematically rising share of low-cost manufacturers in the world production and world exports of sugar. In the 2003/04-2013/14 time period, world production of sugar is expected to increase at an average annual rate of 1.7%. OECD projects that in the season 2013/14 sugar production worldwide will amount to 173.7 million t, i.e. 27.7 million t (19 %) more than in the marketing

[42] Small quantities of beet sugar are produced in India. In the marketing year 2004/05, beet sugar production in the country amounted to 30,000 t (Sugar Economy Europe 2006, p. 15).

year 2003/04. Consumption of sugar over the above projection period is expected to grow at an annual compound growth rate of 1.8% owing to "broad-based income growth and moderate increases in population" (OECD 2004, p. 9). Since production is going to exceed consumption in most years, there is little prospect for a sustainable rise in world sugar prices. In the marketing years 2010/11 and 2013/14, these prices are, in fact, expected to be considerably higher than in the season 2004/05 but only in nominal terms.[43] In real terms, i.e. when one takes into account inflation, the development of world sugar prices between 2003 and 2013 will have a downward trend (ibid., p. 15).

Figure 17. Projections of developments in the world sugar market, 2003/04-2013/14*

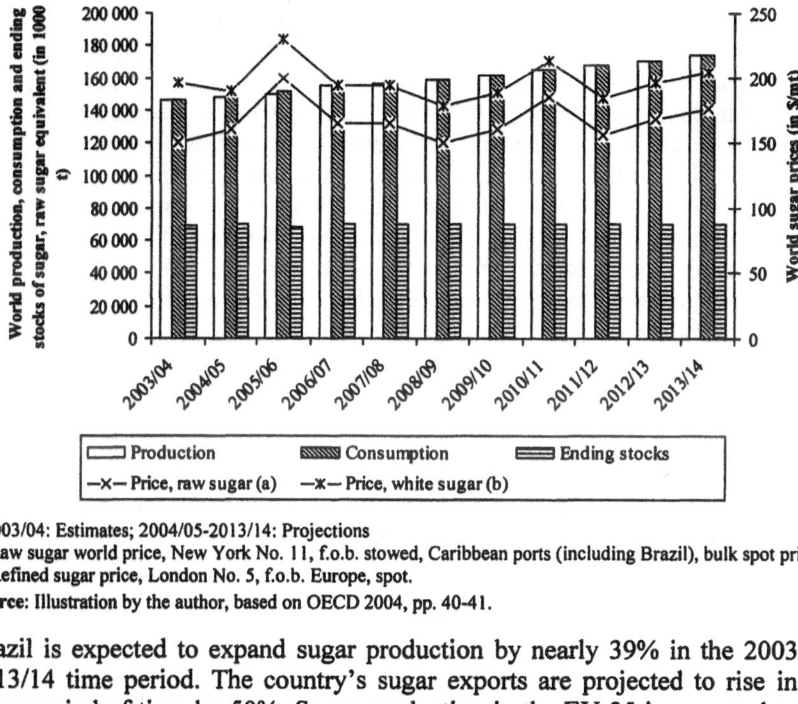

* 2003/04: Estimates; 2004/05-2013/14: Projections
a) Raw sugar world price, New York No. 11, f.o.b. stowed, Caribbean ports (including Brazil), bulk spot price.
b) Refined sugar price, London No. 5, f.o.b. Europe, spot.
Source: Illustration by the author, based on OECD 2004, pp. 40-41.

Brazil is expected to expand sugar production by nearly 39% in the 2003/04-2013/14 time period. The country's sugar exports are projected to rise in the same period of time by 50%. Sugar production in the EU-25 is expected to fall over the above projection period by about 2.2%. This drop will be entirely due to a reduction in the volume of sugar production in the countries forming until recently the EU-15. Whereas in old EU member states production of sugar is expected to decrease between 2003/04 and 2013/14 by 3.7%, in countries that

43 In nominal terms, the annual average raw sugar price in the marketing year 2013/14 is projected to exceed that recorded in the marketing year 2004/05 by about 10%. The corresponding number for white sugar is 7% (See OECD 2004, p. 41).

joined the EU in 2004 sugar production is expected to increase by 6.5%. Exports of white sugar from the EU-25 are expected to fall by 1.3%. At the same time, sugar imports into the EU-25 are projected to increase by almost 36%. Consumption of sugar in the EU-25 over the projection period is expected to fall by 3.7% (-2% in the former EU-15 and -11% in the new member states).
Ending stocks of sugar in the EU-25 are projected to fall slightly in the above period of time but the decrease will be insufficient to elevate considerably sugar prices within the Community. The same can be said about the expected development of global sugar stock-to-use ratio over the above projection period (ibid., p. 15).

Other major sugar producers, India, China and Thailand, are expected to expand sugar production in the 2003/04-2013/14 time period by 33%, 0.2% and 23%, respectively. China's annual sugar production will remain almost unchanged but the country's imports of sugar are expected to increase by 144% (from 800,000 t in 2003/04 to nearly 2 million t in 2013/2014). Consumption of sugar in China will rise at the same time by almost 15%. A considerable increase in sugar production in India will be driven by rapidly rising domestic demand for the commodity. Consumption of sugar in India over the projection period is expected to increase by nearly 4.5 million t (22%). Thailand, the second largest exporter of sugar is expected to increase sugar exports by 21%. Consumption of sugar in the country is projected to increase by 23%. Exports from another large sugar exporter, Australia, are expected to increase by 15%.
As far as the largest importers of sugar are concerned, it is projected that Russia's imports will increase between 2003/04 and 2013/14 by 21%. This development will be accompanied by a 17% rise in sugar consumption and by a 11.5% rise in sugar production in the country.

Figures 18-23. Production, consumption and sugar trade in selected countries, 2003/04, 2013/14, in 1000 tonnes, raw sugar value equivalent*

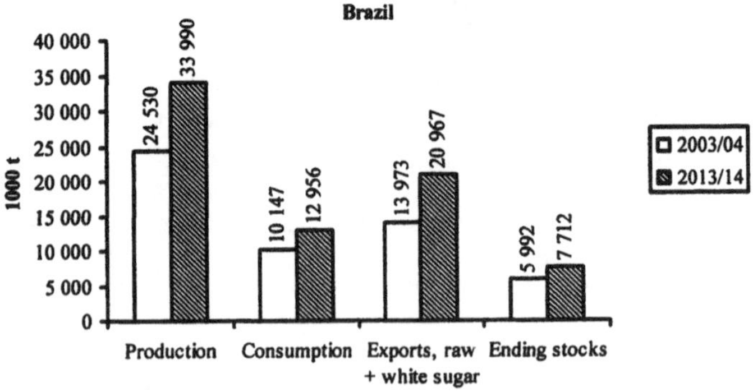

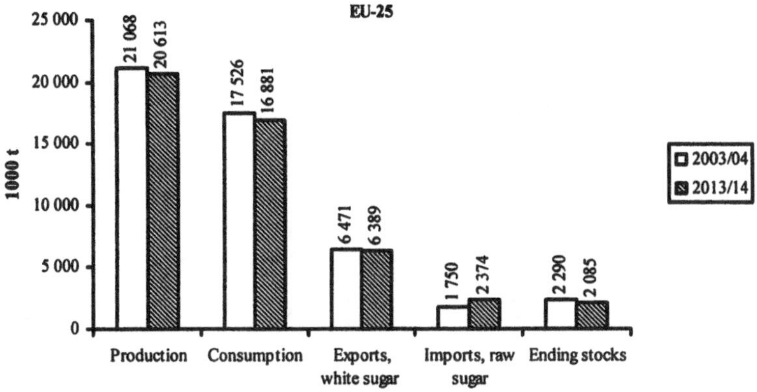
EU-25
25 000
20 000
15 000
10 000
5 000
0
1000 t
21 068
20 613
17 526
16 881
6 471
6 389
1 750
2 374
2 290
2 085
Production
Consumption
Exports, white sugar
Imports, raw sugar
Ending stocks
2003/04
2013/14

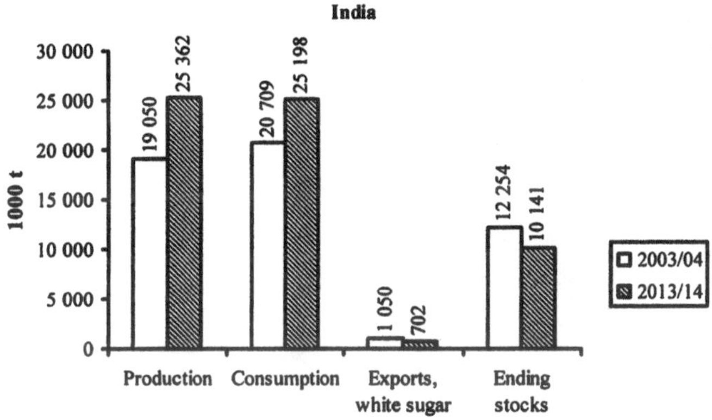
India
30 000
25 000
20 000
15 000
10 000
5 000
0
1000 t
19 050
25 362
20 709
25 198
1 050
702
12 254
10 141
Production
Consumption
Exports, white sugar
Ending stocks
2003/04
2013/14

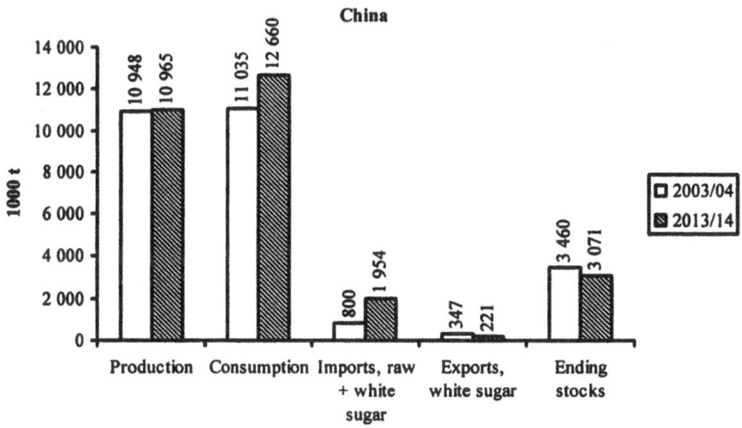
China
14 000
12 000
10 000
8 000
6 000
4 000
2 000
0
1000 t
10 948
10 965
11 035
12 660
800
1 954
347
221
3 460
3 071
Production
Consumption
Imports, raw + white sugar
Exports, white sugar
Ending stocks
2003/04
2013/14

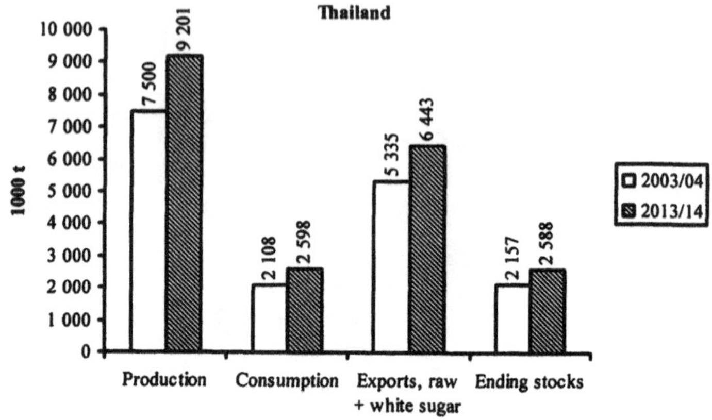

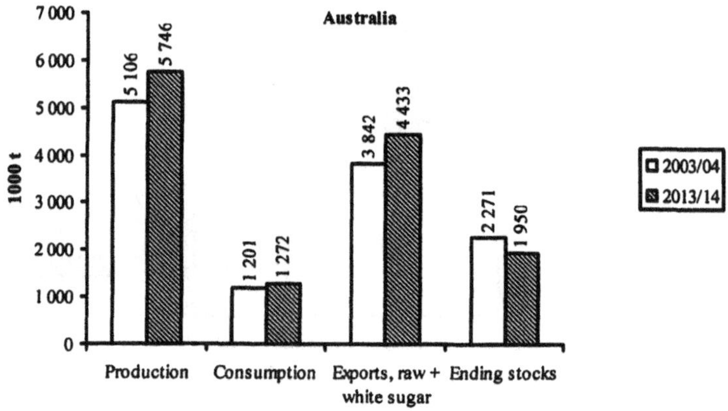

* 2003/04: Estimates; 2004/05-2013/14: Projections.
Source: 2004 OECD Agricultural Outlook Tables, 1970-2013 (OECD online database).

Indonesia's sugar imports are expected to increase by 17%. Sugar production in Indonesia is expected to increase by 27%. Projections regarding production, consumption and trade in sugar in selected countries in the marketing years 2003/04 and 20013/14 are presented in Figures 18-23.

It is important to mention here that the above projections take into account the accession of 10 new member states to the EU and are based on a number of assumptions relating to current and/or announced agricultural and trade policies in OECD member countries, on developments in non-OECD countries, on the current macroeconomic situation and its expected evolution as well as on concluded and ongoing trade negotiations in the WTO (OECD 2004, p. 3).

7 Developments in the Sugar Market in Poland and Changes of Productive Efficiency in the Domestic Sugar Industry: 1990-2004

In the first few years following Poland's transition to a market economy, the situation on the domestic sugar market was highly unstable owing to the lack of administrative arrangements regulating domestic sugar production and trade. Moreover, the liberalization of the sugar market in Poland after 1990 was accompanied by the dissolution of the state monopoly in sugar production. The 78 sugar factories existing at that time in the country became economically independent but almost all of them initially remained under state-ownership.[44] The production of sugar in Poland in the first half of the 1990s fluctuated between 2,037,000 t in 1990/91 and 1,373,000 t in 1994/95 (See Figure 24).

Figure 24. Sugar balance and retail price of sugar, Poland, 1990/91-2003/04

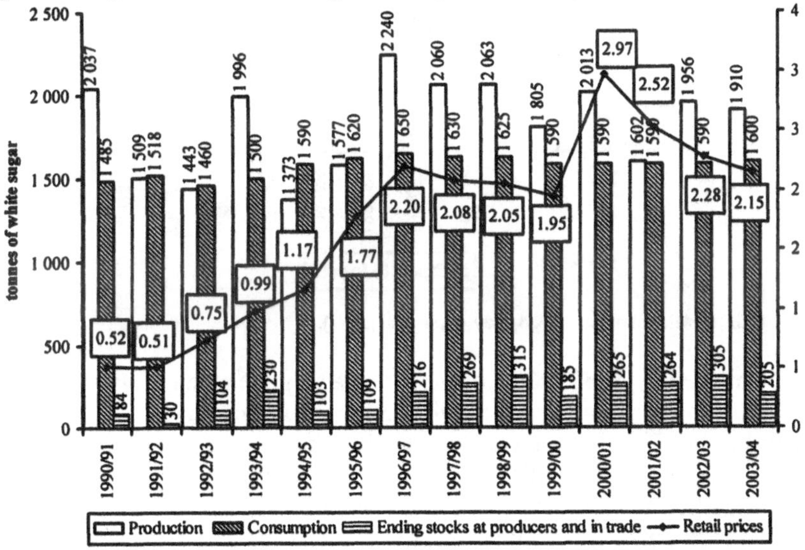

Source: IERiGŻ, Rynek Cukru: Stan i Perspektywy (Several Issues); GUS: Prices in the national economy.

With the exception of the season 1993/94, developments in the local sugar market did not result, however, in the build-up of sizeable sugar surpluses. In the event of considerable overproduction (1990/91 and 1993/94), excess sugar stocks were exported almost in full. Imports of sugar at the same time were negligible or

[44] Ownership transformations taking place in the Polish sugar industry in the 1989-2004 time period are described and discussed in section 13 of the present study.

non-existent (See Figure 25). Nevertheless, in most years in the 1990-1995 time period, consumption of sugar in Poland exceeded domestic production of the commodity. This had the effect that a continuous climb in the market price for sugar could be observed in the country between 1991 and 1996. In nominal terms, the average retail price of sugar in Poland in 1996 was 323% higher than in 1991. It must be pointed out, however, that prices of consumer goods and services increased in Poland in the 1991-96 time period by 292%. It means that in real terms the retail price of sugar in the country increased by 31%.

Figure 25. Export and import of sugar (in 1000 tonnes), Poland, 1990/91-2003/04

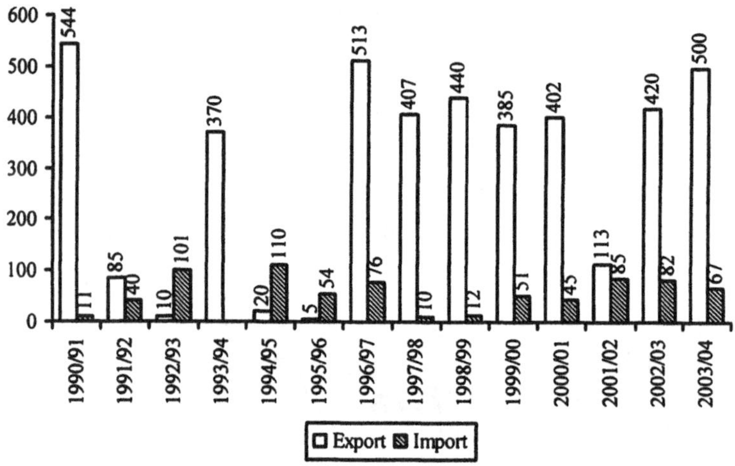

Source: IERiGŻ, Rynek Cukru: Stan i Perspektywy (Several Issues).

From the marketing year 1996/97 onward, the retail price of sugar started to gradually decline in Poland as a result of the presence of high sugar surpluses on the domestic market. This, in turn, was brought about by the fixing of excessive sugar-production quotas for domestic consumption, especially in the marketing years 1996/97-1998/99, and by a number of other shortcomings in the regulation of the sugar market in Poland, introduced in 1995.[45] As can be seen in Figure 24, sugar prices in the country recovered for a moment in the season 2000/01 after a three-year slump. This was mainly a result of an extraordinary intervention measure undertaken by the Polish government on the request of the sugar producers operating in Poland. This measure was a reduction in sugar production quota for domestic consumption (the A-quota) in the marketing year 1999/2000 from 1,650,000 t to 1,222,500 t.

[45] The main features of the regulation of the sugar market in Poland from 1995 onwards are presented in section 9 of the present study.

In the following years, the A-quota was again set at an unreasonably high level. Since most of the other flaws in the organization of the sugar market in Poland had not been eliminated, surpluses of sugar in the Polish market grew rapidly and the retail price of the commodity returned to a downward trend.[46] In 2003, this price fell in nominal terms to a level similar to that recorded in 1996 and was 21.5% higher than the retail price of sugar in 1995, i.e. the year when the regulation of the sugar market was introduced in Poland. In 2003, prices of consumer goods and services in the country had increased in relation to 1995 by 97.2%. This means that if we take into account inflation, it turns out that the retail price of sugar decreased in Poland in the 1995-2003 time period by 75.7%. The average producer price of sugar in the country in 2003 amounted to PLN 1.82/kg. In nominal terms, it was 29.1% higher than in 1995 (PLN 1.41/kg) but in real terms it had declined by 68.1%.

In 2004, both the average producer price and the average retail price of sugar in Poland skyrocketed in comparison with 2003 as a result of the country's EU accession and the accompanying adoption of a new regulatory framework for the domestic sugar sector.[47] The average retail price of sugar in Poland in 2004 amounted to PLN 3.14/kg and was, in nominal terms, 46% higher than in 2003. The average producer price amounted to PLN 2.63/kg, which in nominal terms means an increase by 44.5%. Prices of consumer goods and services in Poland rose in 2004 by 3.5% (www.stat.gov.pl).[48]

As far as trade in sugar is concerned, exports of the commodity from Poland in the first half of the 1990s were directed predominantly to countries of the former USSR (since 1992, mainly to Russia and to Belarus).[49] Only in 1990 did the vast majority of sugar exports from Poland go to France and the United Kingdom. These two countries and Germany were the main exporters of sugar to Poland in the 1990-1995 time period. Import of sugar to Poland became economically viable in 1992 and 1993 despite the introduction of a high import tariff (40%). This was due to a considerable decrease in world sugar prices at that time.

Not much had changed in the second half of the 1990s with regard to the destination of sugar exports from Poland. The major importers were still countries of

---

[46] Another factor that contributed to the formation of large sugar surpluses in Poland in the second half of the 1990s was the fact that the Agricultural Market Agency (*Agencja Rynku Rolnego*) was obliged by law at the end of 1996 to rebuild annually the reserves of C-quota sugar. This created additional sugar supply in the domestic market (IERiGŻ 4/1999, p. 3). Moreover, preferential imports of sugar from several central and east European countries (Czech Republic, Slovakia, Hungary, Romania) took place from 1996 onwards.

[47] The reasons for the significant increase in sugar prices in Poland in 2004 are explained in detail in section 9.5 of this study.

[48] Prices of consumer goods and services in the 1995-2004 time period increased in Poland by 104.1% (GUS).

[49] In the beginning of the 1990s, exports of sugar from Poland to countries of the former USSR often took the form of barter transactions.

the former USSR (Belarus, Uzbekistan, Russia and Ukraine). In 2002 and 2003, by far the largest part of total sugar exports from Poland was shipped to Ukraine.

Imports of sugar to Poland in the second half of the 1990s as well as in the 2000-2003 time period consisted mainly of preferential imports (reduced import tariff and/or special import quota) from a number of central and east European countries (Czech Republic, Slovakia, Romania and Hungary) as well as (non-preferential) imports from several EU member states (especially from Germany).

A significant change in the structure of sugar consumption took place in Poland in the 1990-2004 time period. The share of households in total sugar consumption in the country was decreasing systematically since 1990, accompanied by a gradual increase in the share of the food-processing industry. Sugar consumption in households rose between 1990 and 2004 by 11.2%. Consumption of sugar by the food-processing industry increased at the same time by 56% (See Figure 26).

Figure 26. Sugar consumption in Poland, 1990-2004

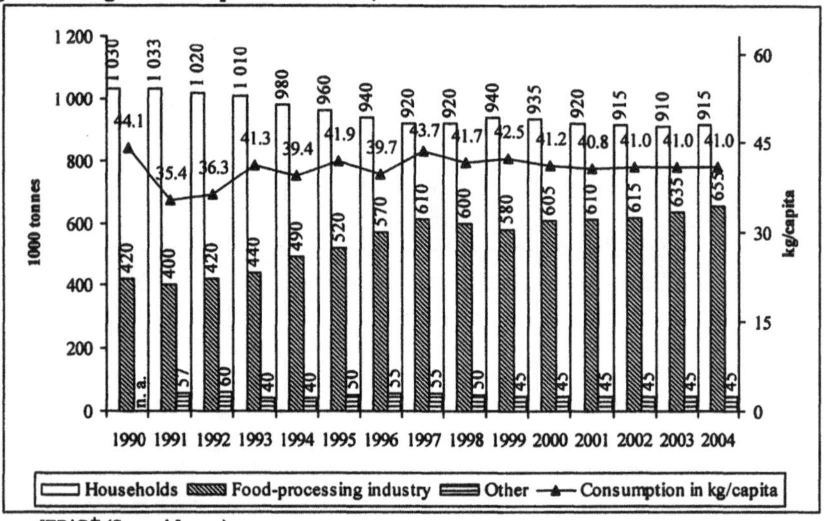

Source: IERiGŻ (Several Issues).

The average sugar consumption per capita in Poland fluctuated significantly in the first half of the 1990s (See Figure 26). A sharp drop in the value of this indicator in 1991 and 1992 was brought about *inter alia* by a significant fall in incomes and the decreasing consumption of high-calorie products. The most important factor, however, that contributed to the above development was the fact that Poland's transition to a market economy was followed by a considerable reduction in the domestic production of compotes, juices, beers, jams and confectionery products. This was the result of a significant increase in the import of such products to Poland in the first years of the 1990s. Export of these products from Poland decreased markedly at the same time (IERiGŻ 3/1993, pp. 16-17).

As was pointed out earlier in this study, the smaller the fragmentation level of sugarbeet plantations in a given country and the larger their size, the better is the cost efficiency of the sugarbeet harvest and the lower are the transportation costs of sugarbeets to sugar factories. Considering these facts, it must be said that several positive developments have been observed in Poland within the last 14 years with regard to the raw material base of the domestic sugar industry. The total number of sugarbeet growers in the country decreased in the 1990-2004 time period by 80%. At the same time, the average size of beet plantations increased by 226% (See Figure 27).

Figure 27. Number of sugarbeet growers (in 1000) and average size of sugarbeet plantations (in ha), Poland, 1990-2004

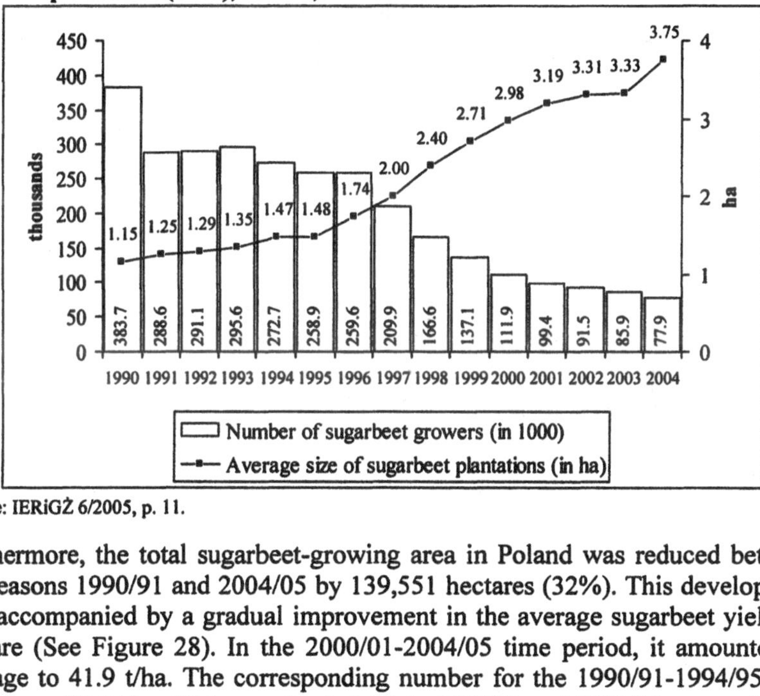

Source: IERiGŻ 6/2005, p. 11.

Furthermore, the total sugarbeet-growing area in Poland was reduced between the seasons 1990/91 and 2004/05 by 139,551 hectares (32%). This development was accompanied by a gradual improvement in the average sugarbeet yield per hectare (See Figure 28). In the 2000/01-2004/05 time period, it amounted on average to 41.9 t/ha. The corresponding number for the 1990/91-1994/95 time period was 33.7 t/ha. High sugarbeet yields in 1990/91 and 1993/94 were achieved mainly due to extraordinarily favorable weather conditions during the growing season.

The major reasons for a drastic decline in the number of sugarbeet growers and reduction in the sugarbeet-growing area between 1990/91 and 1991/92 included a slight fall in the profitability of sugarbeet production in relation to other crops (e.g. rape), the high labor input in sugarbeet production, the high sowing, nurturing and harvesting costs as well as the decreasing demand for sugarbeet leaves and beet pulp (IERiGŻ 3/1993, p. 8).

Figure 28. Sugarbeet-growing area and sugarbeet yields per hectare, Poland, 1990-2004

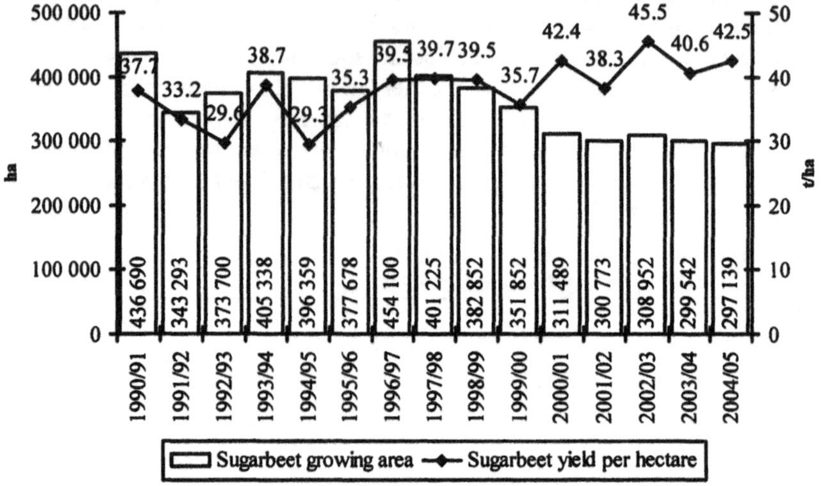

Source: IPC 2004; Malec 2005, p. 1.

A significant impact on the gradual decrease in the number of sugarbeet growers and the diminution of the beet-growing area in Poland in the following years was made by those sugar producers who employed various practices and policies in order to 'bring' beet plantations closer to processing plants and to improve the quality of procured sugarbeets. One of such practices included gradual withdrawal from cooperation with sugarbeet growers who were achieving poor sugarbeet and sugar yields and those situated far from sugar factories. Moreover, sugar producers have been working in close cooperation with beet growers on the continual improvement in sowing and growing techniques, the selection of appropriate types and quantities of seeds, fertilizers and plant protection products as well as the mechanization of the beet harvest. Advancements made in the above fields and the systematic increase in the productivity and quality of the beet harvest had the effect that the amount of sugarbeets needed for the production of a given volume of sugar was gradually decreasing. This was favored also by the increasing efficiency of sugar producers in the extraction of sugar from beets (See Figure 29).

Despite considerable progress in the restructuring of the raw material base in Poland between 1990 and 2004, a comparison of the current structure of sugarbeet plantations in the country with developments in Western Europe shows that there is still a lot of potential for further changes. Whereas in the season 2003/04 the average size of sugarbeet plantations in Poland amounted to 3.58 ha, in the EU-15 it amounted to 7.62 ha.

Figure 29. Development of selected indicators of productive efficiency in sugarbeet production and sugarbeet processing, Poland, 1990/91-2004/05

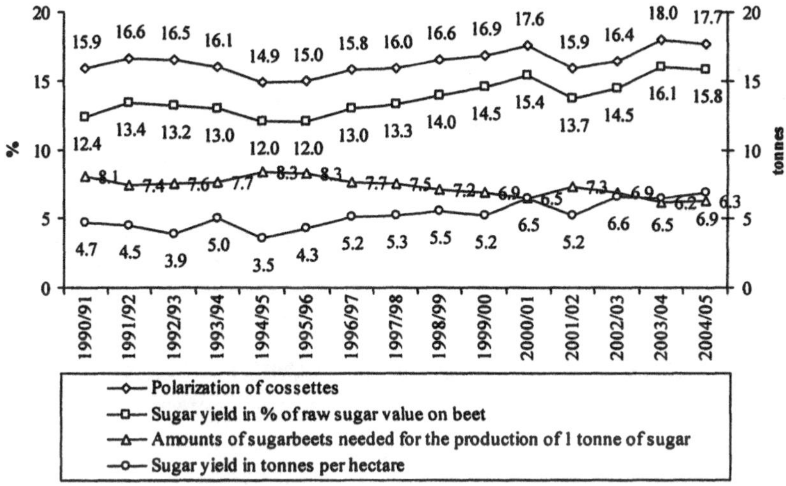

Source: IPC (Several Issues); IERiGŻ 2005, p. 18.

In France and Germany, the largest sugar producers in the EU-25, the average size of beet plantations amounted at the same time to 12.67 ha and 9.20 ha, respectively. A much better picture emerges from the comparison of the number of sugarbeet growers per one working sugar factory. In the season 2003/04 it amounted to 1,800 in the EU-15, 1,800 in Germany, 900 in France and 1,500 in Poland (IERiGŻ 12/2004, pp. 10-12; CEFS online database).

The average sugarbeet yield per hectare in countries forming the EU-15 amounted in the 2002/03-2004/05 time period to 59.3 t and was 38% higher than in Poland. In France it amounted to 74.6 t and in Germany to 58.2 t.

The average sugar yield per hectare between the seasons 2002/03 and 2004/05 amounted in the EU-15 to 8.8 t. The corresponding numbers for Poland, France and Germany are 6.7, 11.5, and 9.0, respectively (CEFS and IPC data).

The sugar yield in % of raw sugar value on beet in the former EU-15 in the 2002/03-2004/05 time period amounted on average to 16.3%. In Poland, the average value of this indicator in the same period of time amounted to 15.4%. In France and Germany it reached 16.1% and 16.9%, respectively (See Figures 30-32).

If we compare the above numbers with statistics presented in Figures 4-6 (subsection 3.4), it becomes clear that after 14 years of Poland's transition to a market economy there is still a considerable gap between productivity and quality of beet harvest (as well as extraction efficiency) in Poland and in leading sugar producing states in Western Europe. Agricultural yields achieved in west European countries are much higher than in Poland. And the fact that, e.g. in Germany, the average sugar yield in % of raw sugar value on beet currently amounts to on average 16.9% and in Poland to 15.4% means that about 0.6 tonne more of sugarbeets is needed for the production of one tonne of sugar in Poland than in Germany.

The number of working sugar factories in Poland decreased in the 1990/91-2004/05 time period from 78 to 43. In the season 2001/02, sugarbeets were still being processed at 76 plants (including 5 factories where one-day campaigns took place).

Figures 30-32. Average sugarbeet yield, sugar yield per hectare and sugar yield in % of raw sugar value on beet, 2002/03-2004/05, selected countries

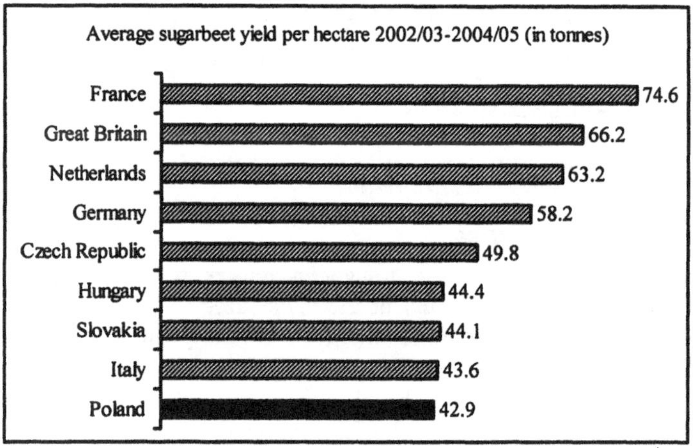

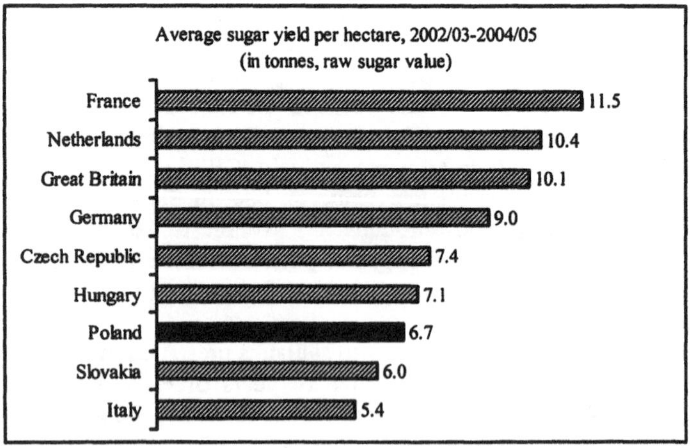

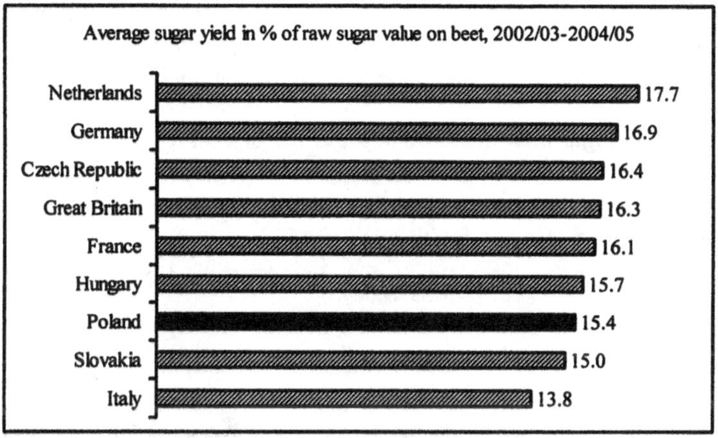

Source: CEFS; IPC; Sugar Economy Europe (Several Issues); F.O. Licht's World Sugar Statistics.

The consolidation of sugar factories in Poland actually began in the season 2002/03, when the Sugar Law of June 21, 2001, regulating the organization of the sugar market in the country, came into effect. In contrast to its previous version, provisions of the new law allowed for the cessation of sugar production at individual factories without the loss of sugar-production quota. In the season 2002/03, sugarbeet processing took place at 65 plants, one year later at 57. Sugar factories where beet processing was ceased belonged usually to the smallest in the domestic sugar sector. Their closure was in most cases accompanied by an increase in sugar production at other plants. This had the effect that the processing capacity per one working sugar factory in Poland increased from 2,064 t of beet throughput per day in 1990/91 to 3,380 in 2004/05 (IPC 2004, p. 7; Malec 2005). Total sugar production per one factory increased from 26,100 t in 1990/91 to 34,200 t in 2003/04 and 46,700 t in 2004/05. These developments led also to a gradual increase in the average length of a campaign in the last few years. Whereas in the campaign 2001/02 the duration of beet processing at sugar factories in Poland amounted on average to 49 days, the corresponding numbers for the campaigns 2003/04 and 2004/05 were 62 days and 87 days, respectively (STC 2004, p. 13; Malec 2005). Nevertheless, the length of a campaign at numerous factories in the country is still far from the theoretical optimum (85-90 days). This means that the domestic sugar industry as a whole is characterized by excess capacity. In other words, further amalgamation of sugar factories is necessary.

A considerable reduction in the use of resources could be observed in the sugar industry in Poland between the campaigns 1990/91 and 2003/04. The total use of energy in kWh/t of sugar decreased in this period of time on an industry-wide level by 51%. The average use of limestone decreased from 6.11% on beet in 1990/91 to 4.29% on beet in 2002/03, which constitutes a reduction of nearly 30%.

The use of coke declined at the same time by 41%, from 0.56% on beet to 0.33% on beet. Rationalization measures introduced at sugar factories in Poland have led also to an appreciable decline in the average use of coal and water (See Table 13).

The quality of sugar manufactured at sugar factories in Poland is similar to the quality of sugar produced in Western Europe. Virtually all sugarbeet-processing plants in the country manufacture "white sugar of standard quality" (EU-category II). Several factories produce additionally sugar fulfilling all necessary requirements to be classified as "extra white sugar" (EU-category I) (e.g. *Chybie*, *Krasnystaw*, *Nowy Staw*, *Ostrowite*, *Werbkowice*).[50]

A thorough analysis and discussion of possible future developments in the sugar market in Poland and in the domestic sugar industry is included in section 9.6 of the present study.

Table 13. Selected Information on the Sugar Industry in Poland, 1990/91-2004/05

	1990/91	1991/92	1992/93	1993/94	1994/95	1995/96	1996/97	1997/98	1998/99	1999/00	2000/01	2001/02	2002/03	2003/04	2004/05
Number of working sugar factories	78	78	78	78	78	76	76	76	76	76	76	76	65	57	43
Sugar production/factory (in 1000 t)	26.1	19.3	18.5	25.6	17.6	20.8	30.2	27.4	27.5	23.8	26.5	20.3	31.0	34.2	46.7
Average processing capacity (in 1000 t of beet throughput per day)	2.06	2.07	2.07	2.08	2.08	2.10	2.13	2.24	2.24	2.27	2.27	2.30	2.44	2.63	3.38
Average campaign length (a)	96	68	63	85	61	68	88	74	67	54	57	49	67	62	87
Recovery of sugar (in %)	78.1	80.8	80.1	81.1	80.4	80.4	82.4	83.1	84.4	86.0	87.4	85.6	87.9	89.4	89.7
Use of coke (in % on beet)	0.56	0.56	0.54	0.47	0.48	0.44	0.43	0.42	0.39	0.38	0.37	0.35	0.33	n.a.	n.a.
Use of coal (in % of c. fuel on beet)	6.37	6.80	6.42	5.91	5.71	5.21	4.98	4.67	4.57	4.20	4.11	4.74	4.62	n.a.	n.a.
Use of limestone (in % on beet)	6.11	6.19	6.12	5.49	5.46	5.13	5.07	5.06	4.80	4.76	4.55	4.43	4.29	n.a.	n.a.
Total use of energy (in kWh/t of sugar)	4414	4350	4178	3914	4097	3751	3339	3091	2880	2820	2702	2957	2857	2175	n.a.
Use of water (in % on beet)	224	188	146	112	95	81	66	60	50	43	41	37	31	n.a.	n.a.

a) Duration of sugarbeet processing (without interruptions) in days.

Source: IPC; STC (Several Issues); Malec 2005, p. 1; IERiGŻ 2005, p. 18.

8 Financial and Economic Condition of the Sugar Industry in Poland: 1990-2004

In 1990, the Polish sugar industry as a whole generated a net profit amounting to 12.7% of net income. This was mainly the result of a considerable increase in sugar prices following their deregulation in the second half of 1989. An increase

[50] See for example IPC 2004, pp. 28-30.

in sugar prices was accompanied by a gradual rise in sugarbeet prices but the latter was slower and less pronounced.[51] After the financially rewarding 1990, the economic situation of sugar factories in Poland disimproved with every following year. In 1992, 1993 and 1994, the net financial result of the sugar sector had a negative value (See Figure 33).

Figure 33. Financial results of the sugar industry in Poland, 1990-2004

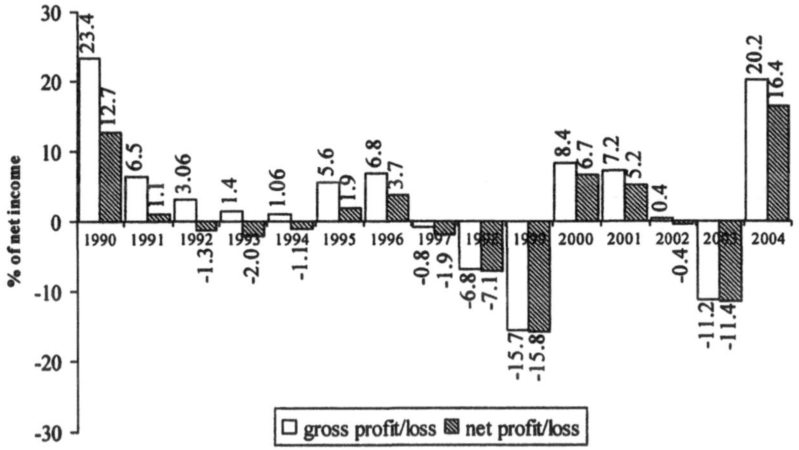

Source: IERiGŻ (Several Issues).

The major reasons for a substantial deterioration in the financial results achieved by the Polish sugar industry in the first few years following Poland's transition to a market economy included the imposition of heavy taxes on sugar factories and the introduction of an excessively high interest rate on bank loans as a means of fighting against hyperinflation. The total tax burden imposed on sugar factories in 1990 constituted 45.9% of their gross financial result. The corresponding numbers for the years 1991 and 1992 are 82.4% and 142.1%.[52] As far as the entire food industry is concerned, the tax burden in 1990, 1991 and 1992 amounted to 42.5%, 70.9% and 97.9% of the gross financial results achieved by the industry, respectively (IERiGŻ 3/1993, p. 13). Another significant reason for

---

[51] It is important to add here that sugar producers had at that time the possibility to freely negotiate the prices of sugarbeets with their suppliers. Most producers seem to have driven hard bargains since beet prices in Poland were low in the beginning of the 1990s. This enabled the producers to generate profits despite the fact that the market price of sugar was not high.

[52] The total tax burden consisted of income tax, and tax on the increase in salaries, as well as a dividend on the founding fund (*dywidenda od funduszu założycielskiego*) allotted to the national budget (IERiGŻ 3/1993, p. 13).

the worsening economic condition of the sugar industry in Poland in the early 1990s was the use of obsolete technology at many sugar factories and the accompanying excessive use of energy, water and other resources. A significant problem on a countrywide level was also the large share of fixed costs in the total costs of sugar production.

Moreover, the economic independence granted sugar factories after 1990 has turned out to be too challenging for many small plants since they were not able to compete successfully in a highly fragmented market with larger producers. Whereas in the first half of 1991, seven sugar factories operating in Poland (9%) had a negative net financial result, in the first half of 1993, the number of such plants came to 17 (22% of the total number of factories) (IERiGŻ 11/1993, p. 16). Total sugar production in Poland in the campaign 1993/94 considerably exceeded domestic demand for the commodity, owing to an extraordinarily large sugarbeet harvest. Since only a part of the resultant sugar surpluses were exported, the, up to then, significant rises in the domestic market price of sugar were suppressed. This meant that the sugar industry stayed on the defensive.

Considering the scope of the present study, it is important to mention at this point that the financial and economic condition of privatized sugar factories in Poland in the first three quarters of 1993 and in the first three quarters of 1994 was much better than the performance of state-owned plants. In contrast to the latter, privatized sugar factories generated a net profit (see Tables 14 and 15). It is also worth noting a considerably higher investment rate in the first three quarters of 1994 at privatized factories than at those owned by the state. Data presented in Tables 14 and 15 show furthermore that all sugar factories in Poland had to deal with high financial costs of their activity and that the liquidity ratio of most plants oscillated at around the lowest acceptable value (1).

Table 14. Indicators of the financial and economic condition of the sugar industry in Poland, 1993 (I half), 1994 (I half)

	I half of 1993				I half of 1994			
	Sugar factories				Sugar factories			
	Total (77)	S.-o. ent. (66)	Commer. (4)	Privat. (7)	Total (77)	S.-o. ent. (66)	Commer. (4)	Privat. (7)
Gross financial result (a)	1.1	0.6	3.3	3.6	-4.0	-4.9	-6.0	5.0
Net financial result (b)	-2.1	-2.5	-2.2	2.1	-6.1	-7.0	-9.0	3.3
Capital accumulation (c)	3.4	2.9	6.2	5.3	1.5	-2.3	-2.8	5.8
Financial costs (d)	14.6	15.0	10.8	14.7	12.8	12.8	11.3	14.2
Liquidity (e)	0.9	0.9	4.8	1.7	0.9	0.9	0.9	1.0
Investment rate (f)	0.7	0.7	0.6	0.7	0.7	0.6	0.3	3.4
Investment capability (g)	0.9	0.7	1.3	2.4	n.	n.	n.	0.7

S.-o. ent. = State-owned enterprises; Commer. = Commercialized; Privat. = privatized; n. = negative

a) Gross profit/loss in % of net income; b) Net profit/loss in % of net income; c) Sum of net profit/loss and amortization; d) Interest on bank loans in relation to net income; e) Ratio of working assets to current liabilities; f) Ratio of investment expenditure to amortization; g) Ratio of capital accumulation to investment expenditure

Source: IERiGŻ 10/1994 (No. 6), p. 17.

Table 15. Indicators of the financial and economic condition of the sugar industry in Poland, 1993 (I-III quarter), 1994 (I-III quarter)

	I-III quarter of 1993				I-III quarter of 1994			
	Sugar factories				Sugar factories			
	Total (77)	S.-o. ent. (66)	Commer. (4)	Privat. (7)	Total (77)	S.-o. ent. (66)	Commer. (4)	Privat. (7)
Gross financial result (a)	3.2	2.0	5.3	10.8	-0.1	-2.0	4.2	7.5
Net financial result (b)	-0.4	-1.2	-0.1	6.4	-2.7	-4.4	0.6	4.8
Capital accumulation (c)	4.3	...	...	...	1.3	-0.1	5.4	6.7
Financial costs (d)	11.9	...	...	...	10.8	11.6	6.9	8.9
Liquidity (e)	0.9	0.8	1.2	1	0.9	0.8	1.1	0.9
Investment rate (f)	0.9	...	...	...	1.3	0.9	0.8	7.0
Investment capability (g)	1.0	...	...	...	0.5	n.	1.3	0.5

S.-o. ent. = State-owned enterprises; Commer. = Commercialized; Privat. = privatized; n. = negative

a) Gross profit/loss in % of net income; b) Net profit/loss in % of net income; c) Sum of net profit/loss and amortization; d) Interest on bank loans in relation to net income; e) Ratio of working assets to current liabilities; f) Ratio of investment expenditure to amortization; g) Ratio of capital accumulation to investment expenditure

Source: IERiGŻ 4/1995 (No. 7), p. 20.

The methods of 'handling' financial difficulties among individual sugar factories in Poland in the beginning of the 1990s included postponement of payments for procured sugarbeets, payment for beets with sugar and sale of sugar at prices lower than the production costs (ibid., pp. 15-16).

In 1995 and 1996, the sugar sector in Poland looked as if it had pulled itself out of a long slump. The net financial result of the domestic sugar industry in 1995 was positive and amounted to 1.9% of net income. A year later, this indicator was almost twice as high (See Figure 33). Unfortunately, these developments had a temporary character and were the result of the following causes: a) consumption of sugar higher than production in the seasons 1994/95 and 1995/96, b) reduction in financial costs borne by sugar factories through a cut in the interest rate on bank loans, c) cancellation of debts of numerous sugar factories by banks and, d) favorable developments on the world sugar market (IERiGŻ 4/1997, p. 22; IERiGŻ 1999, p. 22).

In 1997, the financial and economic condition of the sugar industry in Poland again deteriorated substantially. The financial result of the whole sector was negative and, expressed in % of net income, had a similar value to that of the 1992-94 time period. This was the result of a very high sugar production in the season 1996/97, accompanied by sizeable sugar imports, followed by a gradual reduction in the market price of sugar. Nevertheless, the worst was yet to come. In 1999, the net financial result of the sugar industry amounted to -15.8% of net income. 94% of all sugar factories generated a net loss (IERiGŻ 6/2003, p. 24).[53] It turned out to be the deepest financial crisis the sugar sector had found itself in between the collapse of communism in Poland and the country's EU accession. The main reason for the crisis was the continuous drop in the market price of sugar after

[53] The corresponding numbers for 1997 and 1998 are 56% and 76%, respectively.

1996. This, in turn, was brought about by serious flaws in the regulation of the sugar market in Poland, which led to the appearance of several effects that have 'spoiled' the domestic sugar market.[54] Moreover, negative developments on the sugar market in Poland in the 1996-99 time period were accompanied by the formation of large surpluses of sugar on the world market and a gradual drop in world sugar prices. In the face of the above circumstances and deepening financial troubles, many sugar producers in Poland were selling sugar below the minimal selling price specified administratively and, in many cases, below the production costs. Techniques used by sugar producers to circumvent the law in order to protect their own situation, as well as the problems resulting from the employment of these practices, have been described in section 9 of the present study (subsection 9.5).

There is no doubt that crawling privatization of the sugar industry in Poland and the resultant lack of capital injection 'from outside' is another major factor that led the sector to near collapse in 1999. It was very difficult to react to the radical changes after 1990 in a situation when restructuring needs considerably exceeded the capital endowment of sugar factories.

As shown in Table 16, the financial results achieved by privatized sugar factories in 1995 and 1996 were much better than that of the sugar sector as a whole. In the following two years, the economic performance of both privatized plants and the sugar industry in Poland as a whole was miserable.

Table 16. Indicators of the financial and economic condition of the sugar industry in Poland, 1995-1998

	1995		1996		1997		1998	
	Sugar Industry	Privatized plants	Sugar Industry	Privatized plants	Sugar Industry	Privatized plants	Sugar Industry	Privatized plants
Gross financial result (a)	5.61	10.70	6.83	8.47	-0.79	0.33	-6.81	-9.59
Net financial result (b)	1.89	6.25	3.71	4.94	-1.93	-1.34	-7.09	-9.83
Capital accumulation (c)	5.71	8.32	7.06	6.98	2.14	1.65	-2.00	-4.90
Financial costs (d)	6.57	6.31	5.02	5.09	7.21	8.02	10.34	17.55
Liquidity (e)	1.10	1.30	1.16	1.16	1.06	0.98	1.05	1.19
Investment rate (f)	1.56	2.15	1.90	4.47	2.37	5.36	1.20	1.70
Investment capability (g)	0.96	1.87	0.9	1.37	0.22	0.1	-0.33	-0.58

a) Gross profit/loss in % of net income; b) Net profit/loss in % of net income; c) Sum of net profit/loss and amortization; d) Interest on bank loans in relation to net income; e) Ratio of working assets to current liabilities; f) Ratio of investment expenditure to amortization; g) Ratio of capital accumulation to investment expenditure

Source: IERiGŻ 4/1999, p. 23.

In 1998, both gross and net financial results of the whole industry were even slightly better than that of privatized plants. It must be pointed out, however, that sugar factories privatized in 1997 and 1998 were in a disastrous financial and economic situation at the time of their transfer into private hands (IERiGŻ

[54] These effects, as well as developments on the sugar market in Poland in the 1990-2004 time period, are described in detail in section 9 of the present study (subsection 9.5).

4/1999, p. 23). The average investment rate at privatized sugar factories in the years 1995-1998 was always higher than in the sugar sector as a whole.

A considerable reduction in the supply of sugar in Poland in 2000 (a cut in sugar production quota before the campaign 1999/2000 and an increase in the import tariff on sugar) boosted the price of the commodity on the domestic market and had the effect that the financial results of the sugar industry improved markedly in comparison with the previous year. After three consecutive seasons of being in the red, the sugar industry in Poland generated a net profit in 2000, amounting to 6.7% of net income. The effects of these interventions on the sugar market were still felt by local sugar producers in 2001. The market price of sugar in Poland in that year fell considerably, in fact, in relation to 2000, but it was still high enough to allow the domestic sugar industry to generate a net profit amounting to 5.2% of net income.

Apart from the 'disappearance' of a large part of the sugar surpluses from the market, a significant factor that contributed to the achievement of a fair profit by the sugar industry in Poland in 2000 and 2001 was the high sugar yield in % of raw sugar value on beet obtained on the country level in the campaigns 1999/2000 and 2000/2001. This was accompanied by cost reductions in other areas, e.g. in the use of energy and other supplementary materials utilized in sugar-beet processing. Nevertheless, getting rid of the large sugar stocks was crucial for the increase in the market price of sugar and for the improvement of the financial results achieved by sugar producers.

Since the aforementioned administrative cut in sugar production quota in Poland before the campaign 1999/2000 was followed by setting of an excessively high production quota in the following years, sugar surpluses on the domestic market again climbed to a high level in the second half of 2001 despite low sugar production in the campaign 2001/2002.[55] This development was also favored by a dynamic growth in isoglucose production in Poland from 1999 onwards. Production of the substance, a substitute for sugar, used for instance in soft drinks, increased in the country from 6,500 t in 1999 to 64,000 t in 2003, i.e. by 885%. Since the marketing year 2002/03, the supply of isoglucose has been constrained by the introduction of a production quota. Initially, the A-quota was set at 40,000 t and the B-quota at 2,200 t. In the marketing year 2003/04, the A-quota was increased to 60,000 t to the dissatisfaction, of course, of sugar producers (Gazeta Cukrownicza 2-3/2004, p. 39).

The above developments, as well as materialization of a number of additional effects resulting from the flawed organization of the sugar market in Poland (e.g. the sale of considerable amounts of C-sugar by the Agricultural Market Agency to bee-keepers in 2001; the sale of sugar by creditors of sugar factories; and pref-

---

[55] The low production was brought about by unfavorable weather conditions during the growing season of sugarbeets and by the resultant low agricultural yields.

erential imports of sugar from several CEECs), had the effect that after a sharp jump in 2000 the market price of sugar was to fall continuously in the following three years (See Figure 24 in section 7). This led inevitably to a drastic deterioration in the financial and economic situation of sugar producers in 2002 and 2003. In 2003, the sugar industry in Poland generated a net loss amounting to -11.4% of net income, which meant that the sector found itself in similar financial straits as in 1999. The share of sugar factories with a negative net financial result in the total number of sugar factories in Poland amounted in 2002 to 56%. In 2003 this share amounted to 86% (IERiGŻ 6/2004, p. 21).

In 2004, the net financial result of the sugar industry in Poland, measured in % of net income, reached its highest level since 1990. It amounted to 10.7%. 88.2% of all sugar factories generated a net profit in 2004 (IERiGŻ 2005, p. 21).

Table 17. Indicators of the financial and economic condition of the sugar industry in Poland, 1999-2004

	1999	2000	2001	2002	2003	2004
Gross financial result (a)	-15.7	8.4	7.2	0.4	-11.2	13.8
Net financial result (b)	-15.8	6.7	5.2	-0.4	-11.4	10.7
Capital accumulation (c)	-11.2	10.8	9.4	3.4	-7.1	13.8
Financial costs (d)	8.2	7.9	7.3	5.2	4.7	2.3
Liquidity (e)	0.88	1.06	1.12	1.14	1.07	1.40
Investment rate (f)	0.70	0.51	1.01	0.73	0.87	1.29

a) Gross profit/loss in % of net income; b) Net profit/loss in % of net income; c) Sum of net profit/loss and amortization; d) Interest on bank loans in relation to net income; e) Ratio of working assets to current liabilities; f) Ratio of investment expenditure to amortization
Source: IERiGŻ (Several Issues).

The radical improvement in the economic performance of sugar producers after a disastrous year 2003 was brought about a number of effects triggered off by Poland's EU accession in May 2004. Most importantly, the adoption of a new regulatory framework for the sugar sector in the country as well as mass sugar purchases by domestic consumers in March and April 2004 in anticipation of expected price increases in the future, resulted in a sharp jump in the market price of sugar, which remained at a high level until the end of 2004.
Developments in the sugar market in Poland shortly before and in the first months after the country's EU entry are described in detail in section 9.6 of the present study.

9 Regulation of the Sugar Market in the Enlarged European Union

Since 1968, the interests of sugarbeet growers and sugar producers in the EU have been safeguarded by the "common organization of the markets in the sugar sector" (CMO Sugar), a regulatory framework consisting of import tariffs against external competition, production quotas and levies, export refunds, guaranteed prices for certain amounts of sugar and sugarbeets, intervention purchases and other tools. The purpose of the present section is to present the basic instruments and the operating methods of the regulation of the sugar market in the EU, because a thorough acquaintance with the mechanisms behind the EU sugar industry is a necessary precondition for any serious discussion about restructuring processes in this industry. This section also discusses how the regulation of the sugar market has evolved in Poland since its introduction in 1995: in what ways the Polish system differed initially from the procedures adopted in the EU and how this influenced the competitiveness of domestic sugar producers. Finally, potential and actual effects of Poland's EU accession on the situation of domestic sugarbeet growers, sugar producers and consumers are discussed.

9.1 Objectives of the Common Agricultural Policy and the Common Organization of the Markets in the Sugar Sector

In the European Union, the quantity of sugar production, prices for sugarbeets and for certain amounts of manufactured sugar, as well as the sugar trade with third countries are regulated through the common organization of the markets in the sugar sector (CMO Sugar), one of the components of the Common Agricultural Policy (CAP), established in 1962. The main objectives of the CAP are defined as follows: to increase agricultural productivity; to ensure a fair standard of living for agricultural workers, especially through the increase in their incomes per capita; to stabilize agricultural markets; to guarantee regular supplies of agricultural products and to ensure reasonable prices for consumers (VSZ 2002, p. 6; USDA 1999). CMO Sugar, described often as the "EU sugar regime", was introduced in 1968 and has been functioning without any major changes up to time of writing (although some small modifications have been made to the scheme) .[56,57] It was excluded from the reforms of the CAP in 1992 and from the Agenda 2000 reform. The main purpose of the regulatory framework is to provide EU sugarbeet growers and sugar producers with fair and stable incomes, to stabilize prices and to guarantee self-supply of the EU market (European Commission 2004, p. 4).

---

[56] See Council Regulation No. 1009/67/EEC, Official Journal 308 of December 18, 1967 and Council Regulation (EC) No. 1260/2001 of June 19, 2001, Official Journal L 178 of June 30, 2001, with subsequent amendments.

[57] The last revision of the of the EU sugar regime took place in 2000, when the Council of Ministers decided that the regime would be extended until June 30, 2006.

9.2 The Cornerstones of CMO Sugar

Under the CMO Sugar, each member state of the EU is allocated for a given period of time two production quotas, "A" and "B", forming together the *maximum production quota.*[58] The Ministries of Agriculture of individual EU countries subsequently divide the national production quotas between the companies manufacturing sugar within their territories. The **A-quota**, or the *basic quota*, is the amount of sugar produced to meet domestic demand. For the marketing years 1995/96-2005/06, the total annual A-quota for the EU-15 was set at 11.9 million t of white sugar. **B-quota** sugar is intended to provide a surplus, so that demand can also be met in the event of a poor harvest or an extraordinary increase in the domestic demand. For the marketing years 1995/96-2005/06, the overall annual B-quota for the EU-15 has been set at 2.6 million t of white sugar. After the enlargement of the EU in May 2004, the maximum EU sugar production quota was increased by 2.96 million t of white sugar. The A-quota rose by 2.83 million and B-quota by 0.13 million t of white sugar (See Table 18).

The A- and B-quotas allocated to individual producers are covered by a full sales guarantee and a limited price guarantee. It means that sugar producers can sell quota sugar on the EU market or they can offer it to national intervention agencies, which are obliged to acquire this sugar and to pay the producers the so-called *intervention price.*[59] This price plays the role of a "safety net" which should ensure that the price of sugar on the EU market does not fall below a certain level.

---

[58] Sugar production quotas are currently allocated every five years. The present five-year period ends on June 30, 2006.

[59] Owing to a stable situation on the EU sugar market, and the fact that the market price of sugar has been considerably higher than the intervention price, only one intervention purchase took place until recently. In the marketing year 1986/87, the German Intervention Agency (*Bundesanstalt für Landwirtschaft und Ernährung*) bought 15,703 t of white sugar (Blume et al. 2002, p. 18). In the first quarter of 2005, intervention agencies in France, Belgium and Sweden received offers of white sugar totalling 320,000 t. 48,000 t were accepted by the intervention agency in France. Intervention purchases amounting to 32,000 t of white sugar took place in Belgium (Zuckerindustrie 4/2004, p. 254; Sugaronline Ebriefing of February 21, 2005). The above intervention offers were provoked, *inter alia*, by the formation of increasingly large sugar surpluses in the EU market, the lowering of mark-ups for EU sugar exporters and the more restrictive allocation of export licences by the European Commission from September 2004 onwards, and by the export of large quantities of sugar from the new into the old EU member states after the 2004 enlargement. In the end of May 2005, *Krajowa Spółka Cukrowa "Polski Cukier"* requested that the Agricultural Market Agency accept over 17,000 t of sugar, due to a significant decrease in the market price of the commodity. The intention to offer sugar for intervention was announced at the same time by other sugar producers operating in Poland (Nordzucker and Pfeifer & Langen) (Kozińska 2005). As of August 3, 2005, the total volume of sugar held in Poland's intervention stores stood at 80,833 t of white sugar (Zuckerindustrie 8/2005, p. 657).

Table 18. Sugar production quotas in the EU member states (in tonnes of white sugar)

		Maximum quota	A-quota	B-quota	B/A ratio (in %)
A	Austria	387,326.4	314,028.9	73,297.5	23.3
B	Belgium	819,811.6	674,905.5	144,906.1	21.5
DK	Denmark	420,745.5	325,000.0	95,745.5	29.5
E	Spain	996,960.9	957,082.4	39,878.5	4.2
EL	Greece	317,501.8	288,638.0	28,863.8	10.0
F	France (1)	3,768,991.4	2,970,359.4	798,632.0	26.9
FIN	Finland	146,086.7	132,806.3	13,280.4	10.0
GER	Germany	3,416,895.5	2,612,913.3	803,982.2	30.8
I	Italy	1,557,443.2	1,310,903.9	246,539.3	18.8
IRL	Ireland	199,259.7	181,145.2	18,114.5	10.0
NL	Netherlands	864,559.5	684,112.4	180,447.1	26.4
P	Portugal (2)	79,671.2	72,428.4	7,242.8	10.0
S	Sweden	368,262.2	334,784.2	33,478.0	10.0
UK	United Kingdom	1,138,626.9	1,035,115.4	103,511.5	10.0
	EU-15	14,482,142.5	11,894,223.3	2,587,919.2	21.8
CZ	Czech Republic	454,862.0	441209,0	13,653.0	3.1
H	Hungary	401,684.0	400454,0	1,230.0	0.3
LT	Lithuania	103,010.0	103010,0	0,0	0.0
LV	Latvia	66,505.0	66400,0	105.0	0.2
PL	Poland	1,671,926.0	1,580,000,0	91,926.0	5.8
SK	Slovakia	207,432.0	189760,0	17,672.0	9.3
SL	Slovenia	529,73.0	48157,0	4,816.0	10.0
	EU-25	17,440,534.5	14723213,3	2,717,321.2	18.5

(1) Including French overseas departments.
(2) Including the autonomous region of the Azores.
Source: EU basic sugar regulation, Chapter 2.

The combined application of other instruments of the common organization of the markets in the sugar sector, especially sugar import duties (€ 419/t of white sugar) and production quotas, keeps the market price of sugar in the EU higher than the intervention price (European Commission 2004, p. 5). Since the marketing year 1993/94, the intervention price has been fixed at € 631.9/t of white sugar.[60,61] The price relates to sugar fulfilling the requirements of the quality norms EU-category I and EU-category II.[62]

---

60 This price is calculated from the basic beet price by augmenting it by a sugar processing margin and the overall costs of beet transport to processors, and by subtracting the sugar producers' proceeds from sales of molasses (Blume et al. 2002, p. 20; VSZ 2002, p. 8). The intervention price of raw sugar is € 523.70/t (European Commission 2004, p. 5).

61 The intervention price of € 631.9/t of white sugar does not apply to all EU countries. For regions where the production of sugar is lower than its consumption, the so-called "deficit areas", and where production costs are high, the European Commission specifies each year a "derived" intervention price which exceeds slightly the basic intervention price. The derived intervention price is calculated by adding to the basic intervention price the estimated transport costs of sugar between surplus and deficit zones. In the marketing year 2004/05, derived intervention prices were determined for the following EU member states: Ireland,

It should be noted here that the price guarantee for B-quota sugar is much more limited than in the case of A-quota sugar. For the export of quota sugar, refunds are payable which make up the difference between the Community price and the much lower world market price. In the marketing years 2001/02 and 2002/03, the price obtained by EU sugar producers for sugar exported to third countries amounted on average to € 280/t and € 223/t of white sugar, respectively (European Commission 2004, p. 21).

Moreover, a quantity corresponding to the so-called "preferential imports" from ACP countries (African-Caribbean-Pacific) and India can be exported with refunds (See subsection 9.3). Export refunds are also paid to firms operating in the food-processing industry for sugar contained in various processed products, mainly foodstuffs and drinks, as a recompense for 'losses' connected with the use of (expensive) Community sugar in production. Apart from export refunds paid to sugar manufacturers for the export of quota sugar and to food processors, the EU also grants *production refunds* to the chemical and pharmaceutical industries for the sugar as well as the isoglucose and glucose used in the production of certain goods. The aim of the procedure is to make sure that companies operating in the above two industries are provided with Community sugar at a price similar to the world market price for sugar. This, in turn, should promote the use of sugar in chemicals and support the development of production of this type in the member states of the EU (European Commission 2004, p. 23; VSZ 2002, p. 11). The aforementioned production refunds apply to about 500,000 t in the EU-25 and their costs are covered by production levies (European Commission ibid., p. 23).

Sugar manufactured above the maximum quota, described as **C-sugar**, cannot be marketed within the EU and must be exported to third countries without any subsidies, at world market prices. Sugar producers who do not fulfill this condition incur very high financial penalties.[63] There is neither a sales volume guarantee nor a price guarantee for C-sugar. It is estimated that in the marketing year 2004/05, the quantity of sugar manufactured above the maximum production quota allocated to sugar producers in the EU-25 will amount to about 2 million t (European Commission 2004, p. 28).[64]

UK, Portugal, Finland (€ 646.50/t of white sugar), Spain (€ 648.8/t of white sugar) as well as Greece and Italy ((€ 655.3/t of white sugar) (See European Commission 2004, p. 6).

62 EU-category I and EU-category II quality specifications for sugar are presented in this study in section 10.1.

63 Detailed rules concerning the supervision of the intervention system and the monitoring of the implementation of other procedures included in the EU basic sugar regulation have been laid down in Commission Regulation (EC) No. 779/96 of April 29, 1996, Official Journal L 106 of April 30, 1996, pp. 009-019.

64 The highest amount of sugar manufactured above the EU maximum production quota was recorded in the marketing year 2000/2001. It totaled 3.8 million t of white sugar, which constituted 27% of the maximum quota (European Commission 2004, p. 28).

As is clear from Table 18, the ratios of B-quota to A-quota differ considerably between individual member states of the EU. Those countries that have the highest B/A ratios were assigned a high B-quota in the 1980s owing to a comparative advantage in sugar production. The purpose of such a decision was to encourage these countries to expand their volumes of sugar production (Blume et al., op. cit., p. 23).

Interestingly, the maximum sugar production quotas allocated to individual countries are not based on the actual consumption levels of the commodity but on the historical production levels (ibid., p. 22). This has been confirmed during EU enlargements up to now, since countries joining the Union have been allocated quotas corresponding more or less to the average volumes of production recorded during the five years preceding accession. Nevertheless, the A-quota assigned to individual countries has, since the establishment of the CMO Sugar, been set at a level corresponding to domestic consumption.

It is important to mention here that the allocated sugar production quotas are not transferable between member states of the EU. They can be transferred, however, between sugar companies operating in a given country. Such transfers can be conducted only on a limited scale since a given firm's quota can be reduced from year to year by no more than 10%. This restriction is not binding in a situation where the transfer is a result of a closure or a merger of sugar factories. Contrary to the production quotas, there are no restrictions on trade in sugarbeets and sugar between member states of the EU. Nevertheless, the volume of international trade in sugarbeets within the EU is very small. It takes place only in some frontier regions of EU countries (Blume et al. 2002, p. 22, 47).

In 1977, the production of *isoglucose*, a syrup with a high fructose content, obtained from starch, was included in the CMO Sugar. Isoglucose has a liquid form and is used by the soft drinks industry and some food processors as a substitute for sugar. Its EU market price is about 15% lower than the market price of sugar but its transport costs are higher and its storage quality is lower.[65] Production of isoglucose within the EU was, until enlargement in 2004, limited by the CMO Sugar to 300,000 t per year. After enlargement, this amount rose to 500,000 t since an isoglucose production quota of 200,000 t per year was allocated to Hungary, Poland and Slovakia. Like the sugar quota, the maximum production quota for isoglucose is divided into "A" and "B" quotas. Export refund arrangements specified for white sugar apply also to isoglucose (European Commission 2004, pp. 13-14).

---

[65] The production costs of isoglucose are lower than that of sugar and it is thus reasonable to assume that without the limitation of production of isoglucose in the EU, its consumption would be considerably higher than at the present time. Copper et al. (1995) have estimated that in the absence of any restriction regarding the production of isoglucose in the EU, the syrup could replace about 25% of the industrial use of sugar (Blume et al. 2002, p. 37).

Another natural sweetener whose production has been limited since 1994 by the CMO Sugar is *inulin syrup* (maximum production quota in the EU-25 totals 320,000 t). It is extracted from the chicory root and has a fructose content amounting to about 80-85%. Inulin syrup is sweeter than sugar and is used in the production of beverages, and ice cream, as well as in baking (Blume et al. 2002, p. 37). The EU market price of inulin syrup is about 30% higher than the price of sugar and the actual demand for this substance within the Community is much below the maximum production quota. For this reason, a large share of the quota (25-30%) is exported to third countries with refunds amounting to about € 30 million. Inulin syrup is produced in only three member states of the EU-25: France, the Netherlands and Belgium (European Commission 2004, p. 13). Isoglucose and inulin production quotas allocated to individual member states of the EU-25 are presented in Table 19.

Table 19. Isoglucose and inulin syrup production quotas in the EU member states (in tonnes of dry matter)

		Isoglucose			Inulin syrup		
		Max. quota	A-quota	B-quota	Max. quota	A-quota	B-quota
B	Belgium	71,591.6	56,150.6	15,441.0	215,246.8	174,218.6	41,028.2
E	Spain	82,579.0	74,619.6	7,959.4	-	-	-
EL	Greece	12,892.5	10,435.0	2,457.5	-	-	-
F	France (continental)	19,845.7	15,747.1	4,098.6	24,521.3	19,847.1	4,674.2
FIN	Finland	11,871.7	10,792.0	1,079.7	-	-	-
GER	Germany	35,388.8	28,643.3	6,745.5	-	-	-
I	Italy	20,301.9	16,432.1	3,869.8	-	-	-
H	Hungary	137,627.0	127,627.0	10,000.0	-	-	-
NL	Netherlands	9,099.1	7,364.6	1,734.5	80,949.9	65,519.4	15,430.5
PL	Poland	26,781.0	24,911.0	1,870.0	-	-	-
P	Portugal (mainland)	9,917.3	8,027.0	1,890.3	-	-	-
SK	Slovakia	42,547.0	37,522.0	5,025.0	-	-	-
UK	United Kingdom	27,237.3	21,502.0	5,735.3	-	-	-
	EU-25 TOTAL	507,679.9	439,773.3	67,906.6	320,718.0	259,585.1	61,132.9

Source: European Commission 2004, pp. 26-27.

Since sugar 'grows in the fields', as employees of the sugar industry often emphasize, sugar manufacturers in the EU pass on their sugar production quotas to sugarbeet growers in the form of *sugarbeet delivery rights*. Such rights are allocated normally to beet growers who have been supplying a given sugar factory with sugarbeets over a period of time. Sugarbeet processors do not have to acquire beets from farmers who do not possess valid delivery rights. The volume of delivery rights allocated to beet growers is determined on the basis of the expected sugar yield in % of raw sugar value on beet, and cannot be smaller than the amount needed to the production of the basic quota (VSZ 2002, p. 10).

Also like the sugar production quotas, the delivery rights are divided into "A" and "B" rights. Sugarbeet growers are paid different prices for A-, B- and C-beets, i.e. beets intended for the meeting of A- and B-quotas, and for C-sugar. For 1995/96 to 2005/06, the minimum price that sugar producers are required to pay for A-beets was € 46.72/t and the minimum price for B-beets was € 32.42/t.[66,67]

These prices are derived from the *basic price for beets* set administratively by the Council of Ministers in order to cover the costs borne by sugarbeet growers and provide them with a fair income. For the above period of time, the basic beet price was € 47.67/t.[68] A minimal price of beets used for the production of C-sugar is not specified in the EU basic sugar regulation. It is negotiated freely between sugarbeet growers and beet processors. The price that beet growers are paid for C-beets fluctuates between € 10/t and € 20/t, and is usually derived from the price obtained by processors for C-sugar on the world market (European Commission 2004, p. 11).

You will have noticed that the minimum price for A-beets constitutes 98% of the basic beet price and the minimum price for B-beets, 68% of the basic beet price. The difference between the basic beet price and the minimum beet prices constitutes the beet growers' contribution to the financing of *production levies* imposed on sugar producers in order to finance the refunds for the export of quota sugar to third countries.[69] Such levies are collected each year by authorized agencies located in individual member states of the EU. There is a basic levy amounting to 2% of the intervention price on A- and B-quota production, and a variable levy imposed on B-quota sugar. The latter is specified each year by the European Commission on the basis of the estimated costs of export refunds and may have the maximum level of 37.5% of the intervention price (European Commission 2002, p. 14). In the 1990-2002 time period, the production levy on A-quota sugar amounted on average to € 13/t and the levy on B-quota sugar averaged € 238/t. The weighted average levy on A- and B-quota production in the above period of time amounted to € 53/t of sugar (ibid., p. 15). If it turns out

---

[66] The above prices refer to sugarbeets of standard quality, i.e. beets "having a sound and fair merchantable quality and a sugar content of 16% at the reception point". If the delivered beets have a lower or higher sugar content from that specified in the EU basic sugar regulation, the beet growers are paid respectively lower or higher prices than the minimum prices specified in the regulation. The exact value of the discounts and extra payments are specified in cooperative agreements signed by sugarbeet processors and beet growers.

[67] In countries for which the European Commission sets a "derived" intervention price, the minimum beet price paid to beet growers is augmented by the so-called "regionalization premium" varying between € 2 and € 3 (European Commission 2004, p. 6).

[68] See Council Regulation (EC) No. 1260/2001 of June 19, 2001, Official Journal L 178 30.6.2001, with subsequent amendments.

[69] The production levy is funded in 58% by the beet growers and in 42% by the processors (European Commission 2004, p. 6).

that the levies collected in a given year are insufficient to cover the costs of export refunds, the European Commission lays down additional levies, the so-called supplement taxes. This mechanism guarantees that refunds for the export of quota sugar are fully funded by sugar producers and sugarbeet growers (VSZ, op. cit., p. 8).

It is important to add at this point that the export of refundable quota sugar to third countries is handled mostly by specialized traders for whom a number of *export tenders* are organized each year. The purpose of such tenders is to make sure that B-quota sugar is exported by firms requiring the minimum level of export refunds in order to compete successfully on the world market (European Commission 2004, p. 25). In the marketing years 2001/02, 2002/03 and 2003/04, the export refunds amounted on average to € 443, € 485 and € 512 per one tonne of white sugar, respectively (ibid., p. 22).

The key facts about the CMO sugar quota system and the guaranteed prices laid down in the regulatory framework are summarized in Figure 34 and Table 20.

Figure 34. The CMO Sugar quota system

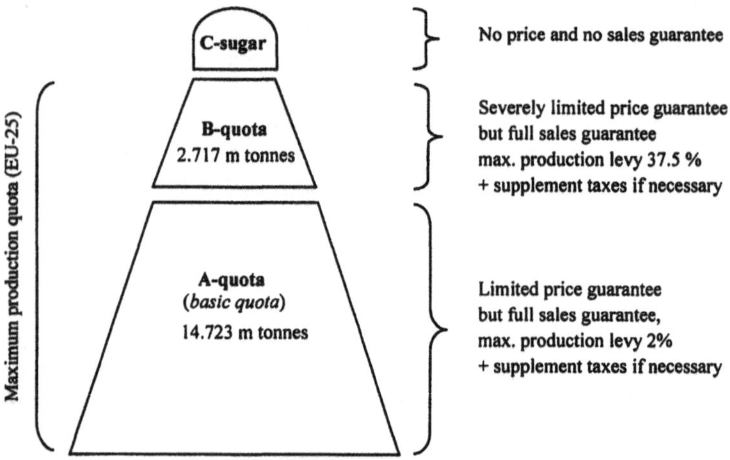

Source: Illustration by the author, based on EU basic sugar regulation.

Table 20. Prices under CMO Sugar (July 1, 1995 - June 30, 2006)

Intervention price for quota sugar = **€ 631.9/t** of white sugar
Basic price for beets = **€ 47.67/t** of beets of standard quality
Minimum price for A-beets = **€ 46.72/t** of beets of standard quality
Minimum price for B-beets = **€ 32.42/t** of beets of standard quality

Source: Illustration by the author, based on EU basic sugar regulation.

All sugar producers in the EU have the possibility to carry over a certain amount of sugar produced outside the maximum quota to the next year. In such a case, no production levy is imposed on the quantity that is carried over and there is no need to export the quantity to third countries. This amount must be stored for 12 months and in the following marketing year the A-quota allocated to a producer who decided for the above option is reduced by the quantity of sugar that was carried over. The amount of sugar that is carried over to the next year is, however, restricted. It cannot exceed 20% of the A-quota. Until the season 2000/01 inclusively, those sugar producers who took advantage of the possibility to carry over a particular quantity of sugar to the next year received reimbursements for the storage of sugar that they carried over. At the same time, storage levies were collected each year from beet processors. In the marketing year 2001/02, both storage reimbursements and storage levies were abolished, which had the effect that the aforementioned practice of carrying over certain amounts of sugar became unprofitable (Blume 2002, p. 23; VSZ 2002, pp. 10-11). Nevertheless, existing evidence shows that sugar producers who exceed the allocated maximum production quota in a given year tend to carry over one third of the overrun to the next year and to export two thirds of the quantity to third countries (European Commission 2004, p. 11).

9.3 Export and Import of Sugar

As was shown in section 6 of the present study, the enlarged EU, with exports amounting to about 4.3 million t, is the fourth largest sugar exporter in the world after Brazil, Thailand and Australia. In the last subsection, export refunds were presented among the basic components of the CMO Sugar. It must be pointed out, however, that during the Uruguay Round[70] of negotiations between member states of the WTO, concluded at the *Marrakesh* ministerial meeting in April 1994, the EU undertook to restrict the volume and value of export refunds for sugar. In accordance with the provisions of the Uruguay Round, export refunds paid to exporters of sugar, isoglucose and inulin syrup from the EU were limited to 1.273 million t or € 499 million.[71] Nevertheless, the limitation starts to apply over and above a quantity of preferential imports from ACP-countries and India,

---

[70] During the Uruguay Round of negotiations, the member states of the WTO undertook in a special agricultural agreement to introduce gradually the following liberalization measures in the 1995/96-2000/01 time period: (1) extension of market access with regard to agricultural products from third countries to 5% of domestic consumption, (2) reduction in import tariffs for sugar by 20%, (3) reduction in internal support by 20%, (4) reduction in the volume of refunded exports by 21% and (5) reduction in export subsidies by 36%. Liberalization measures of a similar extent are to be put into action also in the years to come. For the time period 2006/07 onwards, new conditions will be specified during negotiations launched at the Doha Ministerial Conference in November 2001 (VSZ 2002, p. 23).

[71] The above restrictions relate to sugar, isoglucose and inulin syrup in its natural state or added to processed fruit and vegetables (European Commission 2004, p. 22).

amounting to 1.6 million t. This means that, in practice, the limit consists of 1.6 million t of "ACP and India sugar" and an appropriation of €499 million which corresponds, at the current refund level, to one million t of sugar. In sum, the total amount of sugar that can be exported from the EU with a refund amounts to 2.6 million t (European Commission 2004, p 22).

In order to meet the provisions of the WTO agreements regarding the maximum volume of exports for which refunds can be paid, the European Commission each year adjusts the production quota allocated to individual member states of the EU. If it turns out that the quantity of refundable exports and the value of export refunds in a given marketing year are going to exceed the allowable levels, the A- and B-quotas allocated to sugar producers in the EU are reduced by a certain amount.[72] This procedure is called *reclassification* (ibid., p. 22, VSZ 2002, p. 9). In the marketing years 2000/01, 2002/03 and 2003/04 the EU maximum sugar production quota was reduced through reclassification by 0.5 million, 0.8 million and 0.2 million t, respectively (European Commission 2004, p. 23). No reclassification took place in the marketing year 2004/05.[73]

Sugar, milk, and milk products as well as eggs and cereals contained in processed products and exported with a refund, are also subject to a restriction resulting from the WTO agreements. The overall limit for all aforementioned products is € 415 million. 43% of this sum (€ 180 million) is allocated solely for sugar, which corresponds to about 450,000 t of the commodity. If this restriction is likely to be overrun in a given season, the EU food processors may be allowed to import a certain amount of sugar on the world market under the so-called inward processing arrangements (IPAs). In the marketing year 2002/03, the import of 90,000 t of sugar was made possible through IPAs.

Since the introduction of the CMO Sugar in 1968, the EU internal market has been protected against unbidden inflows of sugar from third countries, with the help of high import duties. Despite the obligation of the EU to gradually reduce import tariffs for sugar in accordance with the provisions of the Uruguay Round of WTO talks, the level of protection of the Community market remained practically unchanged up to the time of writing. There is a *fixed duty* on unprocessed sugar imported into the EU, amounting to € 419/t. In the case of raw sugar intended for refining, this duty amounts to € 339/t. Moreover, an additional *variable import duty* is applied when the so-called representative price falls below a certain level, specified during the aforementioned Uruguay Round of WTO negotiations, in a special safeguard clause for CMO Sugar. This 'trigger' price was set

[72] The European Commission estimates for this purpose every year (before October 1) the actual production surpluses within the EU and the total value of export refunds.

[73] The European Commission proposed to leave the EU sugar production quota for the marketing year 2004/05 unchanged since it had been estimated that the WTO export limits will not be exceeded, without the necessity of resorting to reclassification (*Zuckerindustrie* 8/2004, p. 554).

at € 531/t of white sugar, which corresponded at that time to the average price of imports to the EU. The representative price (€ 191/t in 2003) is the import price excluding the fixed import duty. Since it is similar to the world market price, which is considerably lower than the trigger price, the safeguard clause has been constantly in use since 1995. The function of the variable import duty (€ 115 in 2003) is to cover part of the difference between the representative price and the trigger price. In the last few marketing years, the protection of the Community market against imports, embracing the fixed import duty and the variable import duty, amounted on average to around € 500/t. If we add to this the shipping costs and the world price of sugar amounting to about € 200/t, it turns out that the overall protection offered to the Community sugar amounts to about € 700/t (European Commission 2004, pp. 15-16).

Despite a high level of protection of the internal market against imports from third countries, about 2.5 million t of sugar flow currently into the EU-25 in a year, which makes the Community the second largest sugar importer in the world after Russia (ibid., p. 15). This is due to the fact that over the last 30 years the EU has signed a number of bilateral and regional agreements with important trading partners. The major aim of such agreements has been the liberalization of trade between the signatory countries through the removal of existing trade barriers.

Since 1975, certain quantities of sugar from 19 ACP countries[74] and India enter the EU market each year, free of any import duties. Import of ACP sugar was included in the CMO Sugar after United Kingdom's EU accession, owing to earlier commitments made by this country to import raw cane-sugar for refining and for sale on the domestic market. In a special Protocol attached to the *Lomé* agreement, signed by the Community and 77 ACP States in 1975, the former party undertook to acquire certain amounts of sugar (cane, raw or white) from 19 ACP signatory states at guaranteed prices specified each year by the Council. At the same time, the ACP countries committed themselves to supplying that sugar (about 1.3 million t each year).[75] A similar agreement was reached at that time between the EU and India (European Commission 2004, p. 16). The ACP sugar can be marketed at any price within the EU but domestic intervention agencies

[74] These countries are: Barbados, Belize, Congo, Cote d'Ivoire, Fiji, Guyana, Jamaica, Kenya, Madagascar, Malawi, Mauritius, Uganda, St. Kitts and Nevis, Surinam, Swaziland, Tanzania, Trinidad & Tobago, Zambia and Zimbabwe (See European Commission 2004, p. 27).

[75] The 1975 *Lomé* agreement was replaced by an agreement signed in June 2000 in *Cotonou* (Belize). The *Cotonou* agreement took effect retroactively from March 2000 and remains in force for 20 years. It was ratified on April 1, 2003 and signed until October 2004 by two thirds of the countries concerned. Numbers regarding preferential imports of sugar included in the *Lomé* Protocol have not been changed. Unilateral trade preferences granted to ACP countries under the *Lomé* agreement will be switched from the beginning of 2008 onwards into economic partnership agreements since the former are at variance with WTO rules (For details see Nöhle 2004, pp. 704-705).

are obliged to purchase the quantities that cannot be sold at a price equal to or higher than the guaranteed (intervention) price.[76] This price amounts currently (marketing year 2004/05) to € 523.70/t of raw sugar and € 645.50/t of white sugar (derived intervention price specified for the UK) (ibid., p. 17). The export of sugar to the EU makes up about 70% of the total revenues of the sugar sectors in the ACP signatory states.[77] Access to the EU sugar market has had a significant impact on the socio-economic situation in most ACP countries (European Commission 2005, p. 1).

In the end of 2001, the EU abolished all import tariffs for sugar coming from the Western Balkans (Albania, Bosnia-Herzegovina, Croatia, Former Yugoslavian Republic of Macedonia (FYROM) as well as Serbia and Montenegro) as a part of a stabilization program developed for the region. In the marketing year 2002/03, imports of sugar from the aforementioned countries amounted to 300,000 t.[78] The average price paid for this sugar on the Community market was € 650/t. The large quantity of sugar imported from the Balkans was the main reason for reclassifications conducted in 2002/03 and 2003/04, in order to comply with the export refund restrictions resulting from the WTO agricultural agreements.[79] At the end of 2004, the European Commission presented a proposal to introduce tariff rate quotas for imports of sugar from the Western Balkans. In the first quarter of 2005, duty free imports of white sugar from Albania, where production of sugar does not take place, and from Bosnia and Herzegovina were officially restricted to 1,000 t and 12,000 t, respectively. Serbia and Montenegro was allowed duty free exports to the EU amounting to 180,000 t of white sugar. The quotas apply from July 1, 2005. Export limits for Croatia and FYROM are to be negotiated at a later date (Zuckerindustrie 11/2004, p. 775; Zuckerindustrie 3/2005, p. 166; Sugaronline Ebriefing: February 11, 2005).

In February 2001, the foreign ministers of the EU member states formed an agreement, described as the "Everything but the Arms" initiative, with 46 least developed countries (LDCs)[80], concerning the duty-free import of certain agricultural products, including sugar for which special arrangements were adopted. Under the agreement, the duty-free import of raw cane sugar from LDCs, intended for refining and set initially at 74,185 t, has been expanded by 15% with

---

[76] Intervention purchases of ACP sugar have not taken place up to the time of writing.

[77] See for example European Commission 2005, p. 3.

[78] Preferential imports from Serbia and Montenegro were suspended in 2003/04 (European Commission 2004, p. 18).

[79] It is important to add here that no export refunds are paid for exports of sugar from the EU to the Balkans. Only C-sugar produced in the EU can be marketed in that region. In 2003, nearly 365,000 t of Community sugar were exported to the Balkans in order to supply local demand, at an average price of € 218/t (European Commission 2004, p. 18).

[80] Including 6 signatories of the ACP Protocol: Belize, Madagascar, Malawi, Tanzania, Trinidad & Tobago, Zambia.

every successive year and can reach the maximum level of 129,751 t in 2005/06. In the years 2006, 2007 and 2008, import tariffs for sugar from LDCs will be reduced gradually by 20%, 50% and 80%, respectively. Quantity restrictions on these imports will be abolished in the marketing year 2009/10. From July 1, 2009, all kinds of sugar from LDCs will have duty-free access to the EU market (European Commission 2004, p. 19).

Under the Euro-Mediterranean Agreements, Turkey and Israel can export to the EU unrestricted amounts of *fructose*, a sugar contained naturally in a variety of fruits. These imports are exempted from any duties. A high sweetness of fructose means that one tonne of the substance used alone or in combination with glucose corresponds to two tonnes of sugar. Imports of fructose from Turkey and Israel into the EU have been rising systematically within the last years and amounted to 70,000 t in 2003. The average price paid for one tonne of these imports on the Community market amounted to € 800. Import of chemically pure fructose from other third countries is subject to a duty consisting of a 16% *ad valorem* duty and a fixed duty of € 507/t. A fructose import quota of 4,504 t is exempted from the fixed duty owing to the WTO agreements (ibid., p. 19).

For the marketing years 2001/02-2005/06, a "reduced rate of duty" is imposed on imports of raw cane sugar into the EU in order to provide domestic refineries (situated in the UK, France, Portugal, Finland and Slovenia) with "adequate supplies".[81] This preferential import quota amounts to nearly 1.8 million t expressed as white sugar.[82] It is covered partly by preferential imports from ACP countries and India (1.3 million t) as well as by imports under the "Everything but the Arms" initiative (0.1 million t). The remaining quantity is covered by Community production of raw cane sugar in French overseas departments (0.2 million t) and by preferential imports of the so-called CXL quota (0.08 million t). Preferential import of CXL quota is a result of GATT/WTO negotiations at the time of Finland's EU accession. This quota originating mainly from Cuba and Brazil is subject to a reduced import duty amounting to € 98/t. Its average import price lies between € 400 and € 420/t (European Commission 2004, p. 17).
Another 0.2 million t of raw cane sugar imported for refining, without duties, from the ACP states and India are intended for direct consumption (ibid., p. 20).[83]

Due to considerable surpluses of sugar on the Community market, the raw cane sugar imported to the EU each year at an average price of € 530/t, or an equivalent quantity of the Community beet sugar, must be re-exported at the much lower price of € 230/t. For the export of these quantities, export refunds are paid

[81] See EU basic sugar regulation (Article 39, point 1).

[82] The quota totals 1,796,351 t and is split as follows: UK (1,128,581 t), France (296,627 t), Portugal (291,633 t), Finland (59,925 t) and Slovenia (19,585 t) (EU basic sugar regulation, Article 39, point 2).

[83] For more details about the above trade agreements, see Nöhle 2004.

(€ 500/t). The annual cost of export refunds resulting from the re-export of the above quantities exceeds € 800 million (ibid., p. 21). Refiners of preferential raw cane sugar imported into the Community from ACP countries are provided with the so-called adjustment aid. This procedure was incorporated into CMO Sugar in 1986 in order to bring into line the conditions of competition between refineries processing solely cane sugar and plants processing sugarbeets. There is also an "additional aid" for sugar produced in French overseas departments. The above aids have been fixed by the Council at € 29.20/t since 1997. They are applicable to 1.2 million t of ACP sugar and 0.2 million t of sugar from the French overseas departments. The cost of these aids to the EU budget is € 41 million (ibid., p. 21).

9.4 Costs of CMO Sugar

The regulation of the sugar market in the EU is described often, especially by the representatives of the sugar industry, as "self-financing" or "budget neutral". This is, however, both figuratively and literally speaking, only half true. EU sugar producers and sugarbeet growers cover, in fact, through production levies, the costs of exports of quota sugar as well as isoglucose and inulin syrup, but the entire annual costs of the CMO Sugar are, on average, nearly twice that amount. In 1999, for instance, the actual gross budgetary expenditure on CMO Sugar amounted to € 2112.8 million. € 1203.6 million was financed through production and storage levies paid by sugarbeet processors and sugarbeet growers. The rest, i.e. € 909.2 million, constituted a net cost to the EU budget (See Table 21).

In the years 2000, 2001, 2002, 2003 and 2004 the actual gross budgetary expenditure on CMO Sugar was in a downward trend and amounted to € 2.10 billion, € 1.68 billion, € 1.59 billion, 1.44 billion and 1.42 billion, respectively.[84] The largest part of the expenditure was spent on export refunds (about 75% of the total expenditure in 2004). Production refunds provided to the chemical industry, refunds for the export of "non-Annex I" products, aid provided to the refiners of raw cane sugar, and aid for the disposal of raw sugar from the French overseas departments were other major elements of the gross budgetary expenditure on CMO Sugar in 2004 (European Commission 2004, pp. 23-24).

In the EU agricultural budget for 2005, accepted after a revision by the Council in December 2004, the planned budget spending on CMO Sugar is € 1.77 billion (USDA 2005, p. 3). The increase in 2005 in relation to the years 2000-2003 is connected with the 2004 EU enlargement and (the resultant) rise in export refunds.

[84] European Commission 2004, p. 24; European Commission 2004c, p. 7; European Commission 2005f, section 7, p. 3.

Table 21. CMO Sugar: Expenditure and Levies (Actuals 1995 to 1999 and Budget 2000, in € million)

	1995	1996	1997	1998	1999	2000
EXPENDITURE						
Measure						
Export refunds on sugar and isoglucose	1312.1	1230.0	1115.7	1265.5	1591.1	1493.0
Reimbursements of storage costs	398.8	361.1	362.4	349.5	342.8	316.0
Refunds on sugar used in the chemical industry	70.4	80.9	81.8	104.8	128.3	135.0
Measures to aid the disposal of raw sugar	15.0	15.4	14.2	12.8	11.2	12.0
Other interventions	34.7	23.9	33.8	44.1	39.4	40.0
Total expenditure	1831.0	1711.3	1607.9	1776.7	2112.8	1996.0
LEVIES (income)						
Sugar production levies	726.0	711.6	746.5	780.5	817.5	788.3
Isoglucose production levies	5.9	6.8	6.6	6.4	7.1	6.8
Inulin syrup production levies	1.1	1.6	2.2	2.8	2.0	3.0
Sugar storage levies	542.0	490.8	349.0	280.1	288.5	286.9
Levies on non-exported C sugar and C isoglucose production	0.3	0.8	9.9	0.3	0.4	p.m.
Charges levied on substituted C sugar and C isoglucose	0.8	0.0		0.0	0.0	p.m.
Additional levies	40.3	2.1	0.0	0.0	88.1	77.7
Total levies (income)	1316.4	1213.7	1114.2	1070.1	1203.6	1162.7
Net budgetary expenditure	514.6	497.6	493.7	706.6	909.2	833.3

Source: Court of Auditors 2001, p. 18.

The costs of all levies borne by EU sugar producers and beet growers are, in reality, passed on to the consumers by incorporating these costs in the price of sugar. In this way, sugar producers take advantage of the low price elasticity of demand for sugar (Court of Auditors 2001, p. 14). What is the overall price that EU consumers have to pay for the maintenance of the CMO Sugar? The most straightforward method of estimating these costs is to calculate the difference between the EU intervention price and the world market price for sugar. It must be pointed out, however, that the world market price cannot serve as a fully objective and authoritative indicator in such estimations (ibid., p. 14).

The costs of the regulation of the sugar market in the EU are reflected also in the *Producer Support Estimate* (PSE) and *Consumer Support Estimate* (CSE) for sugar, measured since 1986 by the Organization for Economic Cooperation and Development.[85]

OECD (2003, pp. 291-292) defines PSE as "*an indicator of the annual monetary value of gross transfers from consumers and taxpayers to support agricultural producers, measured at farm gate level, arising from policy measures which support agriculture, regardless of their nature, objectives or impacts on farm production or income. The PSE measures support arising from policies targeted*

[85] Until 1998, these measures were called "Producer Subsidy Equivalent" and "Consumer Support Equivalent". After redefining the measurement methods of the indicators, the OECD has substituted the terms with "Producer Support Estimate" and "Consumer Support Estimate", respectively.

to agriculture relative to a situation without such policies, i.e. when producers are subject only to general policies of (a given) country".
The monetary value of PSE for refined sugar in the EU in the years 1986-2004 is given in Figure 35, and the so-called percentage PSE for the same period of time is presented in Figure 36.

Figure 35. Producer Support Estimate for Refined Sugar, EU, 1986-2004 (in € million)

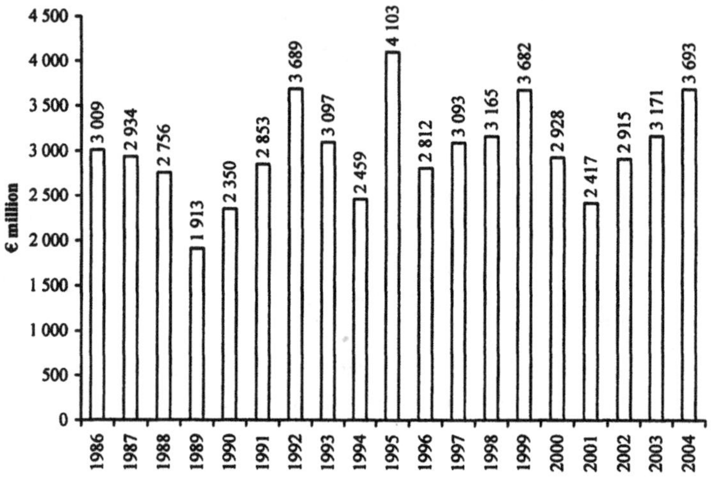

Source: OECD (PSE and CSE online database).

Figure 36. Producer Support Estimate for Refined Sugar, EU, 1986-2004 (in % of the value of total production)

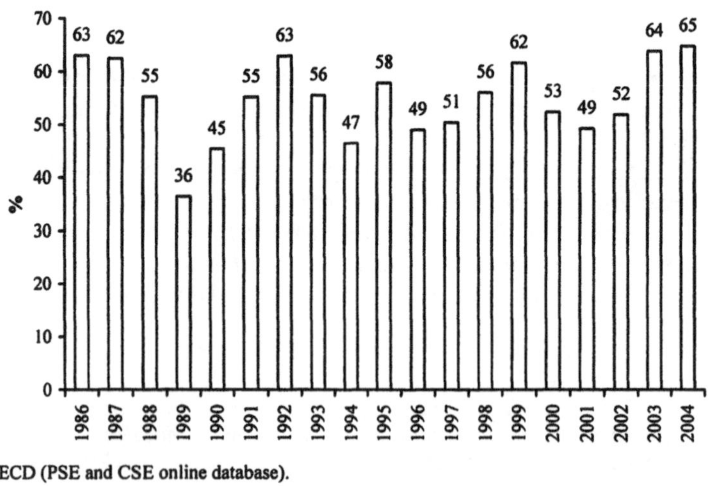

Source: OECD (PSE and CSE online database).

The percentage PSE is defined by the OECD as "*the ratio of the PSE to the value of total gross farm receipts, measured by the value of total production (at farm gate prices), plus budgetary support*" (ibid., p. 292).

CSE is defined by the OECD as "*an indicator of the annual monetary value of gross transfers to (from) consumers of agricultural commodities, measured at the farm gate (first consumer) level, arising from policy measures which support agriculture, regardless of their nature, objectives or impact on consumption of farm products. The CSE includes explicit and implicit transfers from consumers associated with: market price support on domestically produced consumption (transfers to producers from consumers); transfers to the budget and/or importers on the share of consumption that is imported (other transfers from consumers).* [...] *When negative, transfers from consumers measure the implicit tax on consumption associated with policies to the agricultural sector*" (OECD 2003, p. 285).

The "percentage CSE" is "*the ratio of the CSE to the total value of consumption expenditure on commodities domestically produced, measured by the value of total consumption (at farm gate prices), minus budgetary support to consumers (consumer subsidies)* (ibid., p. 285). The development of CSE and percentage CSE for refined sugar in the EU between 1986 and 2004 is portrayed in Figures 37 and 38, respectively.

Figure 37. Consumer Support Estimate for Refined Sugar, EU, 1986-2004 (in € million)

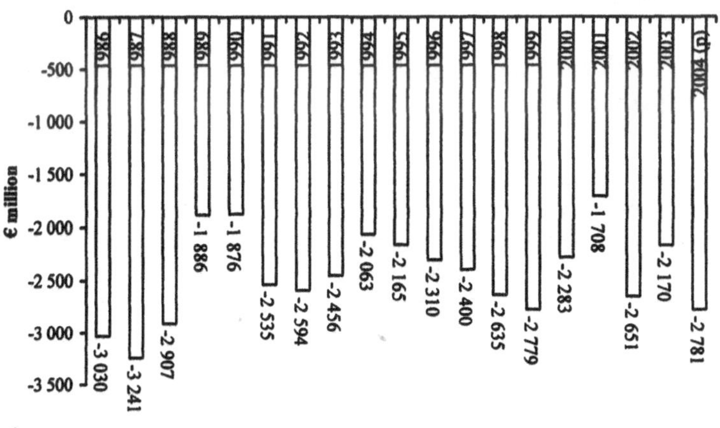

(p) = Preliminary
Source: OECD (PSE and CSE online database).

As can be seen in the graphics, the support to producers of sugar in the EU has remained high since 1986. After a number of temporary declines, it has always returned to the level recorded in the 1986-88 time period. Logically, the high support provided to producers of sugar has been accompanied by an incessantly high 'taxation' of the consumers of the commodity. The above facts have been used repeatedly in public debates by the advocates of the liberalization of the sugar market in the EU.

Figure 38. Consumer Support Estimate for Refined Sugar, EU, 1986-2004 (in % of the value of total consumption minus budgetary support to consumers)

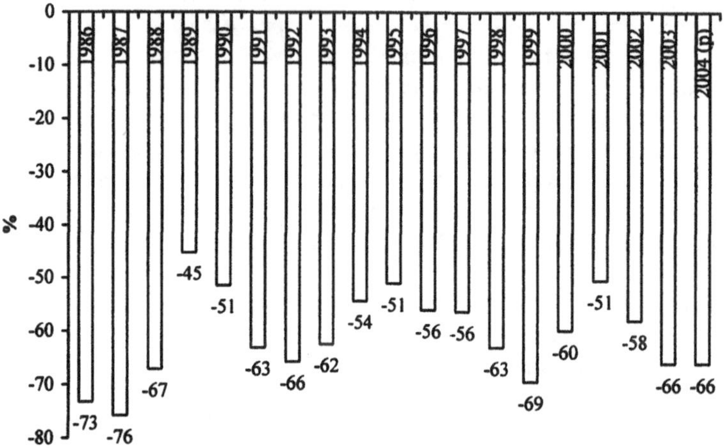

(p) = Preliminary
Source: OECD (PSE and CSE online database).

9.5 Organization of the Sugar Market in Poland before the Country's EU Accession

The first comprehensive regulatory framework for the sugar market in post-communist Poland was introduced when the Law on Regulation of the Sugar Market and Ownership Transformations in the Sugar Sector was passed in *Sejm*, the lower house of the Polish parliament, on August 26, 1994.[86] Regulations included in this legal act, called in short "the Sugar Law", created a new operational environment for the sugar sector, comprising sugar production quotas, export refunds, production levies, a minimal selling price for sugar on the domestic market, minimal price for sugarbeets as well as other instruments instituted in order to stabilize the situation on the domestic sugar market, to provide sugarbeet growers and sugar producers with fair and stable incomes and the consumers with a balanced and acceptable price of sugar (Świetlicki 2004, p. 39). The provisions of the Sugar Law started to apply from the beginning of the marketing year 1995/96, i.e., on October 1, 1995. Although the regulatory procedures introduced initially in Poland were similar to those adopted in the EU, they were in many

[86] Journal of Laws (1994) No. 98, item 473, with subsequent amendments.

ways different and, as it turned out later, included several serious shortcomings and loopholes.

On the basis of the aforementioned Sugar Law, sugar producers in Poland were allocated two production quotas "A" and "B". The **A-quota** was defined as the "*maximum amount of sugar that can be produced in a given year during the processing campaign and intended for sale on the domestic market between October 1 (of the current year) and September 30 of the following year*" (article 1a, point 1 of the Sugar Law). **B-quota** was defined as the "*maximum amount of sugar that can be produced in a given year during the processing campaign and intended for export, in natural form or in processed products with a sugar content exceeding 20%, between January 1 and December 31 of the following year, with the application of export refunds*" (article 1a, point 2 of the Sugar Law). At the same time, article 5 of the law obliged sugar producers to impose levies on all buyers of sugar intended for domestic sale in order to cover the costs of export refunds. These levies could not be higher than 7% of the value of sugar that was being sold, and were specified each year, as were the A- and B-quotas, by the Council of Ministers on the behalf of the Minister of Agriculture. Sugar producers were obliged also to transfer the above levies within 7 days of their collection to a special account at the Agricultural Restructuring and Modernization Agency (*Agencja Restrukturyzacji i Modernizacji Rolnictwa*). Sugar manufactured outside the A- and B-quota by individual producers was termed in the Sugar Law as **C-quota,** that must be exported without refunds. This referred also to processed products with a sugar content exceeding 20%.

As in the EU, sugar producers passed on their sugar production quotas to sugarbeet growers who were delivering beets to a given sugar factory for a period of time. Nevertheless, it was not before the season 2002/03 that beet growers in Poland were provided with the so-called beet growing and delivery rights obliging sugar factories to acquire beets from a particular grower. In other words, until 2001 producers of sugar operating in the Polish market had the possibility to decide each season freely with whom to sign a contract concerning the delivery of beets. In this way they were able to influence to a large extent the restructuring process of the raw material base in terms of 'bringing' it closer to a given factory and increasing the average size of beet plantations. Of course, virtually all sugar producers were using this opportunity although some of them do not want do admit it today.

Another difference between the organization of the sugar market in the EU and in Poland was that from 1995 to 2001, beet prices paid to farmers in Poland were specified each year by individual producers of sugar in cooperation with the representatives of beet growers delivering beets to a given factory. This had the effect that prices of beets differed between regions and between individual producers. After the introduction of the regulation of the sugar market in Poland, there were different prices for beets intended for the production of A-, B- and C-quota sugar.

Sale of sugar outside the A-quota in the domestic market was subject to a penalty payment amounting to 100% of the value of that sugar measured at the minimal selling price specified administratively each season by the Council of Ministers on the behalf of the Minister of Agriculture. For the marketing year 2001/02, for instance, the minimal selling price for sugar intended for sale on the domestic market was set at PLN 2/kg.[87] If, for example, a given sugar factory in this situation sold 100 t of its A-quota sugar domestically at PLN 1,50/kg (between October 1, 2001 and September 30, 2002) and the State Treasury controllers found out, the factory would have to pay a penalty fee totaling PLN 200,000 (PLN 2 x 100,000 kg). Nevertheless, as it will be shown later, many sugar producers in Poland were selling large amounts of A-quota sugar below the minimal selling price (especially in 1999) despite the risk of a severe punishment in form of the aforementioned penalties. This was provoked mainly by high surpluses of sugar on the Polish market (rising systematically since 1996), and by a very low market price of the commodity. This, in turn, was brought about predominantly by fundamental flaws in the regulation of the sugar market in Poland.

First of all, neither the Sugar Law of 1994 nor its new version passed on June 21, 2001[88] included information concerning the method on the basis of which the A- and B-quotas were specified by the Minister of Agriculture and suggested to the Council of Ministers. The A-quotas for the marketing years 1996/97-1998/99 were set at a level considerably exceeding domestic consumption, which was at that time at about 1,590,000 t (See Table 22).

It is important to mention here that in the EU, the A-quota allocated to individual member states has been always lower than or equal to domestic demand. Moreover, in contrast to the situation in Poland, it has been stable because it is specified for a period of five years. This policy and other instruments included in the CMO Sugar have for several decades effectively prevented the formation of large surpluses of sugar on the Community market. The establishment of excessive A-quotas by the Polish authorities in the aforementioned period of

---

[87] The minimal selling price of sugar intended for sale on the domestic market was specified by the Ministry of Agriculture on the basis of analyses conducted on the behalf of the Ministry by a group of experts from the Institute of Agricultural and Food Economics. The determination of the minimal selling price for a given marketing year in these analyses was guided by the following principles: 1) the minimal selling price must cover production costs of the most cost-efficient producers and be augmented by a margin (for the marketing year 1998/99, e.g., this margin was set at 6%), 2) increase in the minimal selling price must be in line with inflation, 3) estimations regarding the development of the market price of sugar on the domestic market should be taken into account (NIK 2000, pp. 41-42).

[88] See Journal of Laws (2001) No. 76, item 810, with subsequent amendments.

time constituted one of the major factors that triggered the formation of such surpluses in Poland and brought many sugar producers in the country to the brink of bankruptcy in the following years.

Table 22. Sugar production quotas in Poland, 1995/96-2004/05

Season	Sugar production quotas (in 1000 t of white sugar)			B/A ratio (in %)	Sugar price (in PLN/kg)	
	A	B	A+B		minimal	intervention
1995/96	1500	300.0	1800.0	20.0	1.16	-
1996/97	1630 (1)	122.9	1752.9	7.5	1.33	-
1997/98	1630	113.7	1743.7	7.0	1.50	-
1998/99	1650	109.1	1759.1	6.6	1.71	-
1999/00	1222.5	104.4	1326.9	8.5	1.71	-
2000/01	1520	104.4	1624.4	6.9	1.92	-
2001/02	1540	104.4	1644.4	6.8	2.00	-
2002/03	1540	104.4	1644.4	6.8	-	1.80
2003/04	1520	102.2	1622.2	6.7	-	1.85
2004/05	1580	91.9	1671.9	5.8	-	€ 0.6319

(1) The A-quota for the marketing year 1996/97 was set initially at 1,500,000 t but during the processing campaign 1996/97 it was increased to 1,630,000 t.
(2) Shortly before the campaign 1999/00 the A-quota was reduced by 25%, from 1,630,000 to 1,222,500 t.
Source: *Cukier i Skrobia* 2004, p. 36; Świetlicki 2004, p. 36.

It was no secret that the EU would allocate maximum sugar production quotas to aspirant countries from Central and Eastern Europe on the basis of historic production levels, just as it was done in the case of earlier enlargements of the Community. For countries that joined the EU in 2004, the reference period was 1995 to 1999. The willingness to get as high sugar production quota as possible after EU accession seems to the present author to be the only logical explanation for why in Poland the A-quota for the seasons 1996/97-1998/99 was set at such a high level. Another possible reason for such behavior could be the fact that the determination of a high sugar production quota was in the interest of sugarbeet growers. It relates especially to the A-quota since prices for sugarbeets intended for the production of this quota are much higher than for beets intended for the production of B- and C-quota sugar.

As was mentioned earlier, the Sugar Law of 1994 also introduced refunds for the export of B-quota sugar. This meant, in practice, that in a situation wherein sugar producers in Poland exported B-quota sugar below the minimal sugar price at which A-quota sugar could be sold domestically, the price difference was refunded to them in full. It is important to mention here that in contrast to the regulations adopted in the EU, according to which B-quota sugar can be sold domestically, is intended to provide a surplus and is subject to intervention purchases (intervention agencies are obliged to buy this sugar when offered), the Polish Sugar Law of 1994 stipulated that this quota was intended exclusively for export and that the Agricultural Market Agency (*Agencja Rynku Rolnego*) might purchase this sugar but it did not have to. Moreover, the aforementioned agency was not obliged to make intervention purchases of A-quota sugar. As far as intervention purchases are concerned, the Sugar Law of 1994 included only an ambiguous entry saying that the Agricultural Market Agency "may purchase sugar outside the A-quota, intended for the replenishment of national reserves".[89] In the same article of the 1994 Sugar Law, there was another entry allowing the Agricultural Market Agency to sell non-A-quota sugar acquired from domestic producers in the domestic market. At the same time, the Agency was exempt from financial penalties in the event of sale of that sugar below the minimal selling price.

Interestingly, in the marketing years 1995/96-2001/02, production levies for the coverage of costs connected with the export of B-quota sugar were imposed by sugar producers on the buyers of A-quota sugar, in accordance with the provisions of the 1994 Sugar Law. In other words, it was the domestic consumers who financed the reimbursements for the export of B-sugar. Maybe this was also the reason why the B-quota was, with exception of the marketing year 1995/96, continually set at a very low level by comparison with the A-quota.[90] In the 1996/97-2003/04 time period, it amounted on average to 108,000 t, which constituted about 7% of the A-quota. Of course, such a small B/A-quota ratio was not of benefit to the sugar producers since export of B-sugar with refunds constituted a lucrative business.

The passage of a new Sugar Law on June 21, 2001 did not bring any significant changes with regard to intervention purchases. Article 14, point 1 of the Law stipulated that the Agricultural Market Agency might purchase A- and B-quota sugar offered by domestic producers but it was not obliged to do so. In consequence, the Agency rejected many times the requests on the part of sugar manufacturers that it acquire quota sugar that could not be sold on the domestic market. It is important to remember here that intervention agencies in the EU member states have to make such purchases when the market price of sugar falls below the intervention price and sugar producers offer sugar for intervention. As was pointed out earlier, until recently this happened only once in the history of CMO Sugar. The regulation of the sugar market in the EU has effectively prevented the formation of large sugar surpluses without the necessity of resorting to intervention. The patchiness of the 1994 Sugar Law had the effect that intervention purchases did not take place in Poland even at a time when they were des-

[89] See Journal of Laws (1994) No. 98, item 473, Article 4a, point 1. Article 4a was added to the original version of the 1994 Sugar Law as a result of an amendment of the law accepted by the Polish Parliament on November 20, 1996 (Journal of Laws (1996) No. 152, item 724, article 1, point 5). The amended law came into effect on January 7, 1997.

[90] Naturally, this are only speculations since, as it was pointed out earlier, the Sugar Law did not include any information explaining how the A and B quotas were specified each year.

perately needed in order to eliminate gigantic surpluses of sugar in the domestic market and to 'save' the market price of this commodity. An extraordinary one-off intervention measure was undertaken in the country when the Ministry of Agriculture and Food Economy reduced the A-quota for the marketing year 1999/2000 from 1,650,000 t to 1,222,500 t on the joint request of all sugar producers. It goes without saying that the reduction was quite 'painful' for the manufacturers of sugar but given the failure of the regulation of the sugar market in force in Poland at that time and the lack of intervention by the Agricultural Market Agency, it was a necessary evil, allowing the curtailing of surpluses of sugar in the domestic market. It was expected that this would to be followed by an increase in the market price of sugar and, in consequence, by the improvement in the financial situation of sugar factories. And this was in fact the actual outcome of the radical reduction on the supply side. The average price of sugar on the Polish market rose from PLN 1.80/kg in September 1999 to PLN 2.30/kg in February 2000 (NIK 2000, p. 68). As it later turned out, the financial and economic situation of sugar factories in Poland in 2000 and 2001 improved considerably in relation to previous years.[91] Unfortunately, these positive developments were temporary. Since the beginning of 2003, everything has come back to 'normal'. Sugar producers operating in Poland have again started to generate sizeable losses owing to the reappearance of surpluses of sugar on the domestic market and, consequently, a plunge in the market price of the commodity. Although the A-quota for the marketing years 2001/02-2003/04 was scaled down markedly when compared with the 1996/97-1998/99 time period, it was still too high to reduce sugar surpluses and to limit their accumulation. The achievement of the above objectives was also impeded by the fact that in January 1999, isoglucose, a substitute for sugar used mainly in beverages, began to be produced in Poland. In 1999, 6,500 t of isoglucose was manufactured in the country. In following years, the volume of production of this substance rose rapidly and amounted to 16,800, 27,600, 43,500 and 64,000 t in the years 2000, 2001, 2002 and 2003, respectively (Świetlicki 2004, p. 38). In accordance with the provisions of the Sugar Law of 2001, a maximum production quota (A+B) of isoglucose was specified for the marketing year 2002/03 by the Council of Ministers on the behalf of the Minister of Agriculture.[92] The A-quota for the season 2002/03 was set at 40,000 t and the B-quota at 2,200 t. The A-quota for the marketing year 2003/04 was specified initially at 40,000 t but it was increased later to 60,000 t (ibid., p. 39).

The glut of sugar on the Polish market and the very low market price of the commodity were brought about not only by the specification of too large production quotas intended for domestic consumption, by the lack of intervention

[91] Detailed information on the development of the financial and economic situation of the sugar industry in Poland in the 1990-2004 time period is presented in section 8 of this study.

[92] See Journal of Laws (2001) No. 76, item 810, article 5.

and by the production of isoglucose. The regulation of the sugar market in Poland up to the marketing year 2001/02 inclusively, had also other flaws which gave rise to the emergence of a number of procedures that exacerbated the negative developments on the sugar market. One of such flaws was the fact that the Sugar Law of 1994 did not regulate issues connected with the monitoring of trade in quota sugar, including the C-quota. In other words, nobody was made responsible for the supervision of the sale of sugar in accordance with the provisions of the Sugar Law (NIK 2000, p. 46).[93] The effects could be observed especially in the second half of the 1990s. According to analyses conducted by the Supreme Chamber of Control, about 575,000 t of C-quota sugar was marketed in Poland in the 1997-99 time period. It was made possible, *inter alia*, by the dishonest behavior of a group of corrupt officials from several customs offices located on the Polish-German border. Out of 342 transports of sugar from Poland to Germany officially going through customs in *Kołbaskowo* between 1997 and 1998, 334 turned out to be fictional exports. In these 334 cases, customs officials provided false certificates confirming the export of a particular amount of C-sugar. In reality, this sugar did not leave Poland and was sold domestically. The orchestration of such swindles was driven by the willingness to take advantage of a significant price difference between sugar intended for domestic consumption and sugar intended for export (ibid., pp. 45-46).

Another procedure which resulted in the sale of considerable amounts of C-quota sugar on the domestic market was sugar factories' repayment of bank loans with sugar. The banks subsequently sold this sugar on the commodity market at a price far below the minimal selling price. This could take place because of the fact that the minimal selling price for sugar was binding only for the producers of the commodity. It means that after the acquisition of sugar from sugar factories, retailers could sell it at any price to the public. In this situation, A-quota sugar also was often marketed below the minimal selling price. This was orchestrated in three ways. Firstly, apart from C-sugar, sugar factories also used A-quota sugar for the aforementioned repayment of bank loans. Secondly, numerous sugar producers were circumventing the law by selling and buying their own A-quota sugar, which allowed them to subsequently sell that sugar on the market below the minimal selling price, as an 'acquired commodity'. Of course, A-sugar that was sold and bought by a given factory did not leave the plant. It turned into an acquired commodity solely as the result of a bogus transaction. In 1999, 137,300 t of sugar was sold in Poland as an 'acquired commodity' at prices that were on average PLN 0.39/kg lower than the minimal selling price (ibid., p. 10). Finally, sugar producers often concealed the price

[93] In November 1999, the Minister of State Treasury obliged the supervisory boards of state-owned sugar factories to submit detailed reports every month concerning the sale of sugar on the domestic market, including documents confirming the compliance of all practices with the regulation of the sale of sugar at or above the minimal selling price (NIK 2000, p. 48).

difference between the official selling price of A-quota sugar (equal to or higher than the minimal selling price), registered in the receipts, and the actual selling price (considerably lower than the minimal selling price) by burdening that sugar with various fictional selling costs, e.g. marketing costs, benefiting the purchasers of the sugar.[94] This method of getting round the regulations was widely used in Poland in 1999. The minimal selling price of sugar for the marketing year 1998/99 was set at PLN 1.71/kg. Nevertheless, the gigantic surpluses of sugar on the domestic market (about 300,000 t) and the poor economic situation of most sugar factories had the effect that sugar producers found themselves under strong pressure to look for ways of selling part of their A-quota sugar below that price. Therefore, a lot of sugar factories sold A-sugar at PLN 1.71/kg but at the same time paid money to the purchasers of that sugar, e.g. PLN 0.21/kg for marketing. In this way, the actual selling price amounted to PLN 1.50/kg. In 1999, over one million t of sugar marketed in Poland (half of the total production) was burdened with various selling costs amounting to PLN 353.6 million. The aforementioned marketing costs made up 68% of this sum. Due to the application of the above procedures, the actual selling price of sugar manufactured in the season 1998/99 was on average PLN 0.39/kg lower than the minimal selling price specified administratively (ibid., p. 10). Of course, this state of affairs had the effect that the sugar industry generated sizeable losses since the production costs of even the most cost-efficient producers exceeded the market price of sugar.

Investigations conducted by the Ministry of Finance revealed repeated use of the aforementioned fraudulent practices. In consequence, heavy financial sanctions in form of penalty fees, increase in the value added tax and/or corporate income tax were imposed on numerous sugar producers. Nevertheless, most of them avoided the payment of the penalties. The Ministry of Finance was not eager to enforce the payments since this would have been tantamount to forcing the bankruptcy of many factories. Individual producers filed appeals against the punitive actions and most legal proceedings concerning this issue were sooner or later concluded to the benefit of sugar producers. In most cases, the producers managed to convince those in authority that the sale of A-sugar below the minimal selling price through the application of practices described above was a result of an inadequate regulation of the sugar market, which led to the formation of large surpluses of sugar on the domestic market and compelled them to grasp at straws in order to survive.

---

94 Apart from marketing costs, A-quota sugar sold by sugar factories was burdened with transportation and transaction costs, costs connected with the unloading and reloading of sugar, costs of breaking lumps of sugar into smaller pieces as well as with distribution and counseling costs. Moreover, various commissions and discounts were granted to the buyers of sugar (NIK 2000, p. 43).

Apart from the factors named above, there was one more thing that contributed to the gradual accumulation of inordinate amounts of sugar on the Polish market from 1996. This was preferential imports of considerable quantities of sugar from the Czech Republic, Slovakia, Hungary and Romania, between 1997 and 1998. The import of sugar from these countries was subject in this period of time to a special, reduced tariff. In consequence, about 86,000 t of sugar was brought into Poland from abroad in the marketing years 1996/97 and 1997/98 (Stankiewicz 1999, p. 1). Nevertheless, the volume of imports was soon severely limited owing to a gradual introduction of higher tariffs on imports of sugar from the aforementioned countries. Whereas in 1997, imports of sugar to Poland from the Czech Republic amounted to 37,600 t, in 1998 it plummeted to 6,500 t after the increase in the import tariff. For the same reason, imports of sugar from Slovakia declined from about 11,000 t in 1998 to nothing in 1999. In September 1999, a general tariff on sugar imports, amounting to € 450/t, was imposed by the Council of Ministers in order to ensure effective protection of the domestic market (NIK 2000, p. 63).[95]

The aforementioned developments resulting from an inadequate regulation of the sugar market had an adverse effect not only on the situation of sugar producers operating in Poland but also on the situation of domestic sugarbeet growers. In the last few years preceding Poland's EU accession, many sugar factories in the country often fell into arrears in their payments for sugarbeets. Of course, this produced numerous conflicts and tensions between beet growers and processors, which is highly unfavorable given the strong bilateral interdependence of these two groups. In many cases, sugar producers paid the suppliers of sugarbeets with sugar manufactured during the processing campaign. It must be added here, however, that although delays in the payment for beet deliveries happened quite often, they did not take place amongst sugar factories privatized to foreign investors. This has been confirmed by the National Association of Sugarbeet Growers in Poland and is worth mention considering the scope of the present study.

At the end of 1996, the Sugar Law of 1994 was supplemented, *inter alia*, with an amendment stating that any sugar producer who does not start the processing campaign in a given season will loose their sugar production quota, which will be subsequently allocated by the Minister of Agriculture and Food Economy to

[95] The general sugar import tariff introduced in Poland in September 1999 was slightly higher than the tariff imposed on sugar imported to the EU. It remained at that level until Poland's EU accession and effectively prevented unbidden imports of sugar into the country. Nevertheless, until 2003, inclusively, preferential imports of small quantities of sugar from Hungary and Romania still took place. Moreover, a certain quota of imported sugar was subject to a reduced tariff (40% *ad valorem* but at least € 170/t), which resulted from the WTO-agreements. In 2003, this quota totaled 65,285 t. The overall quantity of sugar imported to Poland in 2003 amounted to 75,000 t (Chudoba 2004a; Chudoba 2004b, p. 5).

other producers who will "take over the raw material base of the producer".[96] It meant, in practice, that sugar companies operating in Poland at that point of time as well as those that were about to enter the Polish market, were deprived of the possibility to consolidate sugarbeet-processing plants and were compelled to keep even the smallest, ill-located and loss-making factories in operation. Due to the above regulation, processing campaigns at numerous sugar factories were launched and then ceased after only a few days, which was sufficient to fulfill the provisions of the Sugar Law and to keep the production quota. The campaigns 1997/98, 1998/1999, 1999/2000 and 2001/02 at the sugar factory in *Ciechanów* (British Sugar), for example, had a duration of 61 days, 7 days, 1 day and 1 day, respectively. At the sugar factory in *Michałów* (British Sugar), the campaign 1998/99 lasted 3.5 days and the campaigns 1999/2000 and 2001/02, only 1 day. The campaign 1999/2000 at the sugar factory in *Świecie* (British Sugar) had a duration of 3 days. At the factories in *Kętrzyn* and *Guzów* (both privatized earlier to British Sugar), the campaign 2001/02 lasted 1 day (STC 1998-2001). Sugar production quotas allocated to these factories for the aforementioned campaigns were manufactured at other plants controlled in Poland by British Sugar.

The necessity to conduct at least such short, 'fictional' campaigns in order not to lose production quota meant that sugar companies had to unnecessarily incur the very high costs connected with the maintenance of a number of obsolete and unprofitable plants. At the same time, the rule regarding the loss of production quota in the event of the definitive closure of a plant precluded the restructuring process of the sugar industry in Poland. In fact, it is important to remember that one of the greatest challenges of this process has been the consolidation of a large number of small facilities, dispersed throughout the country, into bigger and technologically advanced factories located in the regions with the most favorable conditions for sugarbeet growing. The aforementioned regulation, which made the implementation of this task impossible, remained in place until the beginning of the season 2002/03, i.e., until the moment when the Sugar Law of June 21, 2001 came into effect. Article 9, point 1 of the new Sugar Law stipulated that after a merger of one or more sugar producers, the production quotas of these producers are allocated by the Minister of Agriculture to the company established as a result of the merger. It meant, in practice, that a merger of, let's say, five sugar factories, forming five different companies, into one company, paved the way for the cessation of sugar production at certain plants which were subject to the merger, without the danger of losing the production quota allocated

[96] See Journal of Laws (1994) No. 98, item 473, Article 4, point 3a. Article 4, point 3a was added to the original version of the 1994 Sugar Law as a result of an amendment of the law accepted by the Polish Parliament on November 20, 1996 (Journal of Laws (1996) No. 152, item 724, article 1, point 4, letter d). The amended law came into effect on January 7, 1997.

to them. This was brought about by the fact that after the allocation of sugar production quota to a particular company consisting of several sugar factories, it is left to the decision of the management of the company as to where the entire quota will be produced and where sugarbeet processing will take place during every campaign thereafter.

The above regulation constituted one of the most significant changes introduced by the Sugar Law of 2001. This and a number of other new entries and corrections to the 1994 Sugar Law, included in the Sugar Law of June 2001, brought the regulation of the sugar market in Poland into a closer compatibility with the EU's CMO Sugar. Nevertheless, the architects of the new Sugar Law did not eliminate all the flaws contained in the old regulatory framework for the sugar sector. The minimal selling price of sugar, which turned out to be an inefficient instrument for stabilizing the market price of the commodity, was substituted with an intervention price. Sale of sugar below this price was forbidden not only for beet processors but also for retailers and for the Agricultural Market Agency. Unfortunately, the Agency was still not obliged to undertake intervention purchases of A- and B-quota sugar and such purchases did not take place because of lack of financial resources. This had the effect that except for the years 2000 and 2001, surpluses of sugar on the Polish market remained at a consistently high level until the end of 2003. Similarly, after a short recovery in 2000, the price of sugar on the domestic market was declining with every year and in 2003 it was back at the level recorded in 1996. It was only slightly higher than in 1995, the year when the regulation of the sugar market was first introduced in Poland (See Table 23).[97]

Apart from failing to intervene in the sugar market when necessary, the Agricultural Market Agency supported inefficient sugar factories since it acted often as a surety for state-owned plants that had lost their borrowing power.

Another important alteration included in the Sugar Law of 2001 concerned the setting of beet prices. Article 12, point 1 of the law obliged the Council of Ministers to determine each year (on the behalf of the Minister of Agriculture and Food Economy) the *basic beet price*, binding for all sugar producers. Moreover, the Minister of Agriculture and Food Economy was obliged to specify annually the *minimal prices* of beets intended for the production of A- and B-quota sugar.[98]

---

[97] It is important to mention here that in 2003, prices of consumer goods and services in Poland were higher than those recorded in 1995 by 97.2%. At the same time, the increase in the retail price of sugar on the Polish market amounted to only 21.5% (See Table 23). This means that if we take inflation into account, it turns out that the retail price of sugar in 2003 decreased in relation to 1995 by 75.7%. The producer price of sugar in 2003 increased in relation to 1995 by 29.1%. Nevertheless, if we add inflation to this, it comes out that in reality this price declined by 68.1%.

[98] See Journal of Laws (2001) No. 76, item 810, Article 13, point 5; Chudoba 2004d, p. 7.

Table 23. Prices of sugar in Poland, 1995-2003

Year	Prices of white sugar, in PLN/kg (including VAT)		Change indicator (Previous year = 100)	
	Producer price*	Retail price	Producer price	Retail price
1995	1.41	1.77	-	-
1996	1.78	2.20	126.2	124.3
1997	1.64	2.08	92.1	94.5
1998	1.72	2.05	104.9	98.6
1999	1.85	1.95	107.6	95.1
2000	2.36	2.97	127.6	152.3
2001	2.11	2.52	89.4	84.8
2002	2.10	2.28	99.5	90.5
2003	1.82	2.15	86.7	94.3

* These are official selling prices recorded in the accounts of sugar producers, and collected by the Central Statistical Office (GUS). The actual producer prices, especially in the years 1998-2001, were slightly lower due to the fact that A-quota sugar was often burdened with various fictional selling costs benefiting the purchasers of that sugar.

Source: Chudoba 2004c; Central Statistical Office (GUS), Online database (Prices in the national economy).

Provisions of the 2001 Sugar Law also changed the method of collecting levies for the coverage of export refunds resulting from the export of B-quota sugar. From the marketing year 2002/03, sugar producers were required to make money transfers amounting to 2% of the intervention price of sugar to the account of the Agricultural Market Agency. These payments related to A-quota sugar. Moreover, a production levy with a maximum level of 32% of the intervention price was imposed on B-quota sugar. If both levies turned out to be insufficient to cover the costs of export refunds, additional levies were to be imposed on the producers of sugar. Similar levies to those imposed on sugar producers were imposed on the producers of isoglucose and inulin syrup.[99]

All sugar producers operating in the Polish market were obliged also to submit to the Agricultural Market Agency detailed reports concerning the production and sale of sugar as well as customs documents confirming the export of C-quota sugar, within 30 days after the end of a marketing year.[100]

A very significant component of the 2001 Sugar Law was a section calling on the Minister of State Treasury for the establishment from all non-privatized sugar factories of a company named *Krajowa Spółka Cukrowa* (National Sugar Corporation).[101] This issue is described and discussed in detail in chapter 13 of the present study.

Last but not least, the Minister responsible for agricultural markets was obliged in the 2001 Sugar Law to determine the terms and conditions concerning the allocation of "beet growing and delivery rights" to individual sugarbeet growers.[102]

---

[99] See Journal of Laws (2001) No. 76, item 810, Article 16, points 1 to 6.

[100] See Journal of Laws (2001) No. 76, item 810, Article 6 point 3 and Article 7, point 2.

[101] See Journal of Laws (2001) No. 76, item 810, Article 18.

[102] See Journal of Laws (2001) No. 76, item 810, Article 3, point 9.

These conditions were formulated in an ordinance issued on March 15, 2002 by the Minister of Agriculture and Rural Development.[103] After the allocation of the "beet growing and delivery rights" by special commissions consisting of the representatives of beet growers and beet processors, it became a duty of the latter to purchase beets from growers possessing the rights.[104] At the same time, the restructuring process of the raw material base in terms of 'bringing' it closer to a given sugar factory and increasing the average size of beet plantations became fully dependent on the trade in the above rights between individual sugarbeet growers.

In conclusion, it can be said that despite numerous modifications, the regulatory framework for the sugar industry in Poland has not led to the achievement of goals specified at the time of its introduction and listed at the beginning of this section. Many of the aforementioned deficiencies in the organization of the sugar market in the country, included initially in the Sugar Law of 1994, were, in fact, eliminated after a thorough revision of the law in 1996 and after the introduction of a new Sugar Law in 2001. Nevertheless, all these changes did not result in a satisfactory stabilization of the incomes of beet processors and of the market price of sugar. Poland's accession to the EU in May 2004 and the accompanying full integration of domestic sugar producers and sugarbeet growers into the CAP was expected to plug all existing loopholes in the regulation of the sugar market and to bring about at least a short-term improvement in the situation of beet growers and sugar producers. The possible short- to medium-term implications of Poland's EU accession for domestic beet growers, beet processors and consumers of sugar are discussed in the next section of this study. Since the study was concluded in the end of 2005, some significant effects that could be observed shortly before and a few months after the country's EU entry are presented.

9.6 Implications of Poland's EU Accession for Local Sugar Producers, Consumers and Sugarbeet Growers

On July 1, 2004, i.e. from the beginning of the marketing year 2004/05, laws regulating the organization of the sugar market in Poland and other countries that joined the EU in May 2004 have been replaced by EU legislation. In other

[103] See Journal of Laws (2002) No. 26, item 260.

[104] In the allocation of the "beet growing and delivery rights", the aforementioned special commissions (named Mixed Commissions (*Komisje Mieszane*) considered beet growers who had signed beet delivery contracts with sugar producers for the campaign 2001/02. The volume of delivery rights allocated to individual growers was based on the quantity of beets delivered to a particular factory by a given sugarbeet grower within the previous five years (For details see Journal of Laws (2002) No. 26, item 260).

words, beet growers and beet processors from the new member states have started to operate according to new rules and regulations forming the EU's common organization of the markets in the sugar sector, a component of the Common Agricultural Policy.

As a result of EU-accession negotiations, finalized during the Copenhagen Summit in December 2002, Poland was allocated the following sugar production quotas for the marketing years 2004/05 and 2005/06: A-quota of 1,580,000 t and B-quota of 91,926 t. Moreover, the country was allocated an isoglucose production quota of 26.781 t (A-quota of 24,911 t and B-quota of 1,870 t).[105] The sugar production quota allocated to Poland was apportioned among individual sugar producers operating in the country on the basis of their shares in the maximum quota specified for the marketing year 2003/04. Poland's entire isoglucose production quota was allotted to one producer.

For the marketing years 2001/02 to 2005/06, the minimum price for sugarbeets used for the production of A-quota sugar was set in the EU basic sugar regulation at € 46.72/t and the minimum price for sugarbeets destined for the production of B-quota sugar at € 32.42/t.[106] Since the B-quota assigned to Poland constitutes 5.8% of the A-quota, it is not difficult to calculate that under the regulation of the sugar market in force in the EU at the time of writing, the minimal purchasing costs of sugarbeets intended for the production of quota sugar amount in Poland to € 45.9/t (46.72 x 0.942 + 32.42 x 0.058). In the marketing year 2003/04, the last season before Poland's EU accession, the minimal price that sugar producers in the country had to pay for A-beets amounted to PLN 122.84/t and for B-beets PLN 85.24/t. Since the B/A-quota ratio amounted in the marketing year 2003/04 to 6.7%, the minimal price paid by sugar producers in Poland for sugarbeets needed for the production of quota sugar totalled PLN 120.32/t.

In an ordinance issued on July 22, 2003, the Polish Council of Ministers has specified that in the first season following Poland's EU accession, prices paid by domestic sugar producers to domestic beet growers in PLN should be calculated on the basis of the average exchange rate PLN/€ in the time period July 1, 2004-June 30, 2005.[107] Such a "specific annual exchange rate" is applicable to the minimum sugarbeet prices for the currencies of those EU member states that have not adopted the euro. At the end of each marketing year, the European Commission

[105] Treaty of Accession of the Czech Republic, Estonia, Cyprus, Latvia, Lithuania, Hungary, Malta, Poland, Slovenia and Slovakia to the European Union, Annex II, pp. 142-145.

[106] Council Regulation (EC) No. 1260/2001 of June 19, 2001 on the common organisation of the markets in the sugar sector (Official Journal of the European Communities 30.06.2001 L 178, p.1).

[107] See Journal of Laws (2003) No. 141, item 1354.

issues a regulation containing the actual specific annual exchange rates for individual countries.[108]

Since contracts concerning the delivery of sugarbeets to be processed in the campaign 2004/05 were signed in the middle of 2004 and the purchase of these beets took place in late 2004, a commission composed of representatives of sugar producers and beet growers in Poland decided that the price of beets would be calculated on the basis of a working exchange rate of PLN 4.24 per 1 €. At the same time, it was specified that the sum of money paid to individual sugarbeet growers would be corrected after the end of the marketing year 2004/05 (after the announcement of the aforementioned specific annual euro exchange rate by the National Bank of Poland).

In the middle of 2005, it turned out that the actual average exchange rate PLN/€ in the time period July 1, 2004-June 30, 2005 amounted to PLN 4.20824 per 1€. On July 20, 2005, the European Commission issued a regulation including an entry stipulating that sugar producers in Poland should square accounts with the domestic beet growers for raw material delivered to sugar factories in the season 2004/05 using this exchange rate.[109] This means that, in theory, sugarbeet growers in Poland should give part of the payments received in 2004 back to the sugar producers (working exchange rate slightly higher than the actual exchange rate). In practice, the amount of money that beet growers 'owe' to the sugar producers for the season 2004/05 will be deducted from the payments provided to the beet growers in the season 2005/06.

9.6.1 Integration into the CAP: Effects for Sugarbeet Growers in Poland

Using the actual average exchange rate PLN/€ in the time period July 1, 2004-June 30, 2005, it turns out that after EU accession the price of sugarbeets used for the production of quota sugar increased in Poland by 61% in comparison with the marketing year 2003/04. Of course, Polish sugarbeet growers benefited greatly. Already before Poland's entry into the EU, sugarbeet growing in the country was more remunerative than the cultivation of other crops. According to analyses conducted by the Institute of Agricultural and Food Economics (*Instytut Ekonomiki Rolnictwa i Gospodarki Żywnościowej*), agricultural net income resulting from the production of sugarbeets in the period 1996-2001 was more than twice the net income resulting from the production of wheat. In the years 2002 and 2003, it was over 3.5 times higher (See Table 24).

A group of researchers from the aforementioned institute has demonstrated in a recent study that despite a slight increase in the costs of sugarbeet growing in

[108] See for example Commission Regulation (EC) No. 1291/2004 of July 14, 2004 (Official Journal of the European Union 15.7.2004 L243/21.

[109] See Commission Regulation (EC) No. 1180/2005 of July 20, 2005 (Official Journal of the European Union 21.7.2004 L189/32.

Poland, the net agricultural income resulting from this form of agricultural activity in the marketing year 2004/05 will amount to about PLN 4006/ha. This means that it will be almost three times greater than in the marketing year 2003/04 (PLN 1404/ha).[110]

Table 24. Costs and income resulting from the production of sugarbeets and wheat in Poland

Years	Value of production (a) (in PLN/ha)	Production costs (b) (in PLN/ha)	Net agricultural income (c) (in PLN/ha)	Work input (d) (in hours/ha)
		Sugarbeets		
1996-1998	4162	2360	1802	259.1
1999-2001	4813	3263	1550	203.1
2002-2003 (e)	5785	3870	1915	131.3
		Wheat		
1996-1998	1974	1083	891	63.4
1999-2001	2115	1442	673	46.9
2002-2003 (e)	2097	1570	527	33.4

a) The value of production was calculated by multiplying the yield of agricultural production (in quintals/ha) with the selling price of the production (in PLN/quintal) [1 quintal = 100kg], b) Direct and indirect production costs (without the estimation of costs connected with the input of work by farmers and their family members, c) Net agricultural income constitutes a difference between the value of agricultural production and costs of the production, d) Input of work by farmers and their family members, e) Estimates.
Source: Chudoba 2004d, p. 8.

Figure 39. Gross agricultural income resulting from the production of selected crops in Poland in 2004 (in PLN/ha)*

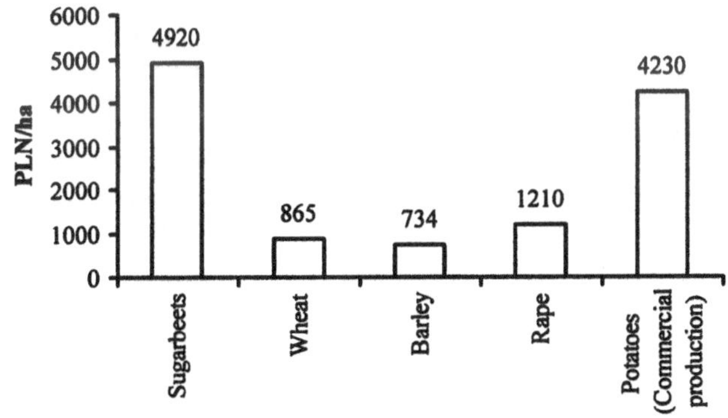

* Estimates; including direct payments
Source: Urban et al. 2005, p. 12.

Gross agricultural income resulting from the production of sugarbeets as well as selected other crops in Poland in 2004 is presented in Figure 39.[111]

---

[110] See Urban et al. 2005, p. 12.

[111] It is important to mention here that results of the study conducted by Urban et al. 2005 are not fully representative as far as the profitability of sugarbeet growing is concerned. Data about costs and profitability of sugarbeet growing was collected for the purpose of the above

Apart from profiting from a substantial increase in beet prices, beet growers in Poland have gained access already in the first year of the country's EU membership to EU funds in the form of simplified direct payments allocated on the basis of the area of the holding and covering all types of agricultural production.[112] In the countries that joined the EU in 2004, direct payments will be phased in over a period of ten years starting at a rate equivalent to 25% of the full EU-15 payment rate in 2004. In 2005, 2006 and 2007, this rate will rise to 30%, 35% and 40%, respectively.[113] Every following year the payment rate will be augmented by additional ten percentage points and will reach 100% of the EU normal level in 2013 (See Table 25).[114] It must be pointed out, however, that the simplified method of allocating direct payments to farmers (*Single Area Payment Scheme*), chosen by the Polish authorities during accession negotiations, has been introduced for a period of three years, i.e. until 2006. After this period, the simplified method may be extended for another two years. A quite different method of allocating direct payments to farmers is currently in use in the old member states. According to this scheme, direct payments do not apply to agricultural area and are allocated only to producers of selected crops. Production

---

study at farms using agricultural accounting. The average size of such farms amounts to 5.3 ha and is much larger than the average size of sugarbeet plantations in Poland (3.5 ha). This means that the profitability of sugarbeet growing as well as cultivation of other crops in Poland in 2004 was slightly lower than that presented in Figure 39. According to a study published in the beginning of 2005 in the quarterly *Burak Cukrowy*, gross agricultural income resulting from sugarbeet growing in the *Wielkopolska* region in the season 2004/05 amounted to PLN 4358/ha. Direct payments were excluded from the calculations conducted in the study. With direct payments, the income would rise to about PLN 4568/ha (See Paluch 2005, p. 9). Chudoba (2005, p. 12) has estimated that net agricultural income (including direct payments) resulting from the production of sugarbeets in Poland in the seasons 2004/05 and 2005/06 will amount to PLN 3710/ha. In the same study, the above author has shown that net agricultural income resulting from the production of sugarbeets in Poland in 2003/04 amounted to PLN 1740/ha.

112 The direct payments system applies only to farms larger than 1 ha, maintained in good condition and meeting certain environmental standards (exact requirements were specified in an ordinance issued by the Minister of Agriculture and Rural Development on April 7, 2004, published in Journal of Laws (2004) No. 65, item 600). In order to obtain direct payments, individual crop producers must each year submit a special application form to a regional office of the Agricultural Modernization and Restructuring Agency (*Agencja Restrukturyzacji i Modernizacji Rolnictwa*).

113 Direct payments and national contributions allocated to agricultural producers in Poland in 2004 amounted to PLN 210.53/ha and PLN 292.78/ha, respectively. In the case of hops, national contributions amounted to PLN 1013.81/ha (Journal of Laws (2004) No. 214, item 2168; www.doplaty.pl). In 2004, 1.385 million farmers in Poland were provided with direct payments having a total value of PLN 7.7 billion (Krupa 2005; PPR 2005).

114 Distribution of the payments is controlled and monitored under the Integrated Administration and Control System (IACS).

of sugarbeets, for example, is not covered by the scheme (Chudoba 2004d, p. 14; Nowak 2003, p. 1).

Table 25. EU direct payments and national supplementary contributions to be granted to farmers in new member states after the 2004 enlargement (in % of the full EU payment rate)

Years	EU contribution	National supplement	Overall maximum payment rate
2004	25	30	55
2005	30	30	60
2006	35	30	65
2007	40	30	70
2008	50	30	80
2009	60	30	90
2010	70	30	100
2011	80	20	100
2012	90	10	100
2013	100	0	100

Source: OECD 2003, p. 143.

During the phase-in period, the Polish government, and governments of other new member states, will have the possibility of supplementing direct payments, financed from the EU budget, with national contributions (*Complementary National Direct Payments*). Nevertheless, this possibility exists only with regard to certain crops, e.g. hops and tobacco, and the overall support level (direct payments + national contributions) provided to farmers in the 2004-2009 time period cannot exceed maximum allowable payment rates specified in the accession treaties (see last column in Table 2).[115] Until 2006, the national top-ups can be co-financed to a certain extent (40% of the total contribution) from rural development funds (OECD 2003, p. 141). Sugarbeet production is, however, excluded from the supplementary payments system. In the EU-15, sugarbeet growers receive neither direct payments nor national support.

As can be seen, sugarbeet growers as well as farmers engaged in other types of agricultural production in new member states experience a considerable rise in incomes in the first year following EU accession. It can be expected that the system of direct payments will lead to a gradual improvement in the standards of living in rural areas and will contribute positively to the lessening of income disparities and social distortions in these regions. Moreover, assuming that part of the increased incomes will be spent on investment projects, the inclusion of farmers from new member states of the EU into the CAP is likely to accelerate

[115] The full list of crops covered by the national contributions scheme is included in an ordinance issued by the Council of Ministers on April 6, 2004 (See Journal of Laws (2004) No. 65, item 596).

necessary restructuring and structural changes.[116] There is, however, a difference of opinion with regard to this issue. Some analysts in Poland forecast that in many cases direct payments provided to domestic farmers will be expended entirely on consumption and on maintenance of their own existence.[117] This refers especially to very small farms (1-2 ha), which are still common in Poland. In 2003, 17.5% of the total area under sugarbeet cultivation in Poland consisted of plantations that were smaller than or equal to 2 ha. The size of plantations covering another 31.4% of the overall sugarbeet-growing area in the country was between 2 and 5 ha (See Figure 40). A similar picture emerges when we look at all agricultural farms.[118]

This leads to the conclusion that the higher incomes of small-scale farmers resulting from access to CAP measures may in fact contribute to the ossification of current structures in agriculture in the first years following EU accession. From the opposite point of view, however, owners of middle-sized and large farms in Poland started to modernize production processes and to plough considerable sums of money into growth and development, already in the pre-accession period, by taking advantage of EU funds granted, *inter alia*, under the aegis of the SAPARD program.[119] Many large-scale farmers have indicated their intention to invest in the years following Poland's EU entry in the purchase of additional acreages of farmland and in the acquisition of modern machinery and equipment.[120] Considering the above facts, it is difficult to make long-term forecasts regarding the impact of EU accession on structural changes in the rural areas of the new member states. Experience from previous EU enlargements shows, how-

---

[116] What is meant here by necessary restructuring and structural changes is a consolidation of a large number of small farms into larger units, the relocation of production to regions with the most favorable natural conditions for a certain type of agricultural activity, and the specialization in production demanded by the market.

[117] See for example Zieliński 2004; Markiewicz 2004; Gazeta Wyborcza 2004, p. 2.

[118] According to the General Agricultural Census (*Powszechny Spis Rolny*) conducted in Poland in 2002, the total number of farms amounted in the country to 2.93 million. They covered an area of 16.9 million ha. The size of 51% of all farms did not exceed 2 ha. These covered, however, only 6.6% (1,121,500 ha) of the arable land. 50% (8,402,300 ha) of the arable land was covered by farms smaller than 15 ha. The average size of a farm in Poland amounted to 5.76 ha. From the total number of 2,172,200 farms that were engaged in some kind of agricultural activity, less than 950,000 produced predominantly for the market (FDPA 2004, pp. 68-69).

[119] Until October 12, 2004, EU funds totalling PLN 396.7 million were allocated to farmers in Poland under the SAPARD (Special Accession Program for Agriculture and Rural Development) for the co-financing of various investment projects. The vast majority of accepted projects (86%) were connected with the "increase in the diversity of farm production". SAPARD was initiated in Poland in July 2002. Applications for financial support under the aegis of the SAPARD program were accepted in Poland until the moment of the country's EU entry (FDPA 2004, pp. 19-20; 49-50).

[120] See for example Wesołowska et al. 2004; Szacki 2004.

ever, that EU accession is followed by an increase in the average size of farms and by a decline in the number of farmers in individual countries.

Figure 40. Structure of sugarbeet plantations in Poland, 1998-2003 (in % of total area under sugarbeet cultivation)

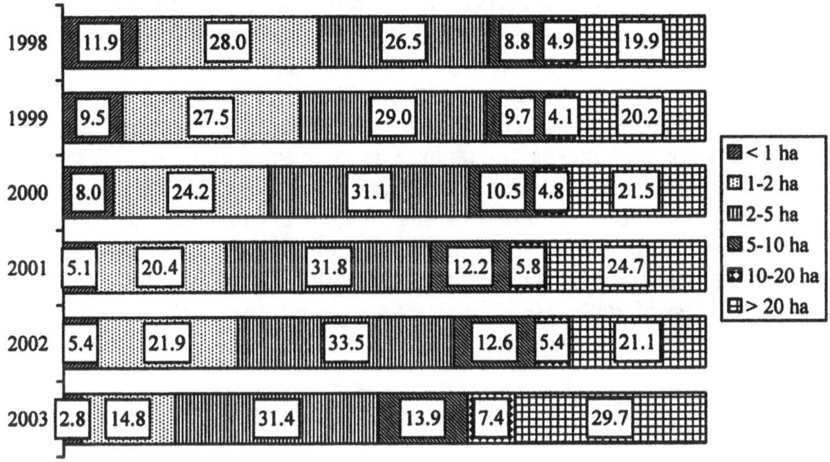

Source: IPC 2004, p. 37.

Apart from the obligation to obey regulations contained in the EU basic sugar regulation, beet processors and beet growers in the EU member states have the possibility of determining the exact terms of bilateral collaboration, in special agreements. Such an agreement was signed by the Association of Sugar Producers in Poland and the National Association of Sugarbeet Growers on May 13, 2004 in Warsaw. Regulations included in this document are in full conformity with the EU legislation and comprise such issues as allocation of "beet growing and delivery rights", payment conditions for sugarbeets delivered to sugar factories, quality requirements with regard to sugarbeets, terms of deliveries, etc.[121]

9.6.2 Consequences of Poland's EU Accession for Domestic Sugar Producers

As far as the impact of Poland's EU accession on the situation of sugar producers operating in the country is concerned, there are two important effects that could be observed already in the marketing year 2004/05. First of all, adoption of the CAP rules resulted in a significant increase in the costs of sugar production owing to the sharp rise in sugarbeet prices. In the seasons 1997/98-2002/03, the payment for sugarbeets delivered to sugar factories in Poland constituted on

[121] The full contents of the agreement were published, for example, in a special supplement to the quarterly *Burak Cukrowy* (4/2004). See also Kamieniarz 2004, p. 7.

average about 42 % of total production costs of sugar (excluding transportation costs). As was shown earlier, minimal prices of sugarbeets used for the production of quota sugar increased after Poland's EU accession by 61%. Assuming that other production costs rose by 10-15%, the 61% increase in sugarbeet prices has caused the share of sugarbeets in the overall production costs to rise to about 50-51%. Total production costs of sugar in Poland in the marketing year 2004/05 increased in relation to the previous year by 31-34%. At the same time, the intervention price for sugar was increased from PLN 1850/t in the marketing year 2003/04 to PLN 2659/t in the marketing year 2004/05 (at an exchange rate of PLN 4.20824 per 1 €). This means that as long as the current organization of the EU sugar market remains in force, the market price of sugar in Poland is likely to be high enough to compensate domestic sugar producers for the immense increase in sugarbeet prices. It can be expected that in the first two years following Poland's EU accession, sugar producers operating in the country are going to experience a considerable rise in incomes and an improvement in their financial and economic situation (See Table 26).

Table 26. Production costs of sugar and the financial result from the sale of sugar in Poland before and after the country's EU accession

	2002/03	2004/05-2005/06*
Sugar intervention price (in PLN/t, excl. VAT)	1800	2659 (a)
Market price of A-quota sugar (in PLN/t, excl. VAT)	1700	2792 (b)
Production costs of A-quota sugar (in PLN/t):	1940	2659 (c)
• raw material	900	1449 (d)
• other costs	1040	1210 (c)
Financial result from the sale of quota sugar:		
• at the intervention price (in PLN/t)	-140	0
• at market prices (in PLN/t)	-240	+133
	(-14% of net income (e))	(4.8% of net income)

* Projections

(a) The intervention price of € 631.9 was multiplied by 4.20824, i.e., the actual average exchange rate of PLN/€ in the time period July 1, 2004-June 30, 2005; (b) 105% of the intervention price; (c) Threshold values guaranteeing sale of sugar to the intervention agency without a loss; (d) The minimal price of sugarbeets intended for the production of quota sugar rose by 61%; (e) In the first half of 2003, the gross financial result of the sugar industry in Poland amounted to -14.6% of gross income.

Source: Chudoba 2004, p. 129; Analysis by the author.

Of course, this scenario can materialize only under the condition that the new regulatory framework for the sugar industry guarantee an effective protection against the formation of large surpluses of sugar in the domestic market and against other circumstances destabilizing the market price of sugar. Since differences between regulation of the sugar market in Poland and in the EU have been ironed out since the beginning of the marketing year 2004/05, the likelihood of fulfilling the above condition is good. The functioning of the sugar market in Poland after the country's EU accession will be supervised by the Minister of

Agriculture and Rural Development and by the President of the Agricultural Market Agency.[122]

The fact that sugar import duties between old and new member states of the EU were abolished on May 1, 2004 will certainly induce sugar producers in Poland to continue strategic restructuring processes in the face of more intense competition. It can be expected that due a significant rise in sugarbeet prices, sugar manufacturers and sugarbeet growers will continuously put a lot of effort into activities aimed at the increase in sugar content in procured sugarbeets, at the achievement of higher sugar yields per hectare and at the minimization of overall sugar losses. Moreover, it is quite certain that the trend towards the concentration of sugar production in regions with the best conditions for productive and cost-efficient sugarbeet growing will continue. Sugar producers will strive to reduce processing costs. This refers especially to the use of energy and other supplementary materials as well as to employment, since there is still a large potential for cost savings in these two areas at many Polish sugar factories. The pending reform of the EU sugar regime will have a strong influence on the type and pace of restructuring activities to be introduced in the coming years by sugar producers in Poland (See section 9.7).

Given the production quota allocated to Poland during accession negotiations, it can be expected that total sugar production in the country in the first two years of EU membership will remain at the pre-accession level. It may be even slightly higher than the average volume of production recorded in the last five years before Poland's EU entry. Chudoba (2004b, p. 11) estimates that production of C-sugar in the marketing years 2004/05 and 2005/06 will vary between 280,000 t and 380,000 t depending on sugarbeet and sugar yields. This author claims that maintenance of production of C-sugar on a high level will be favored by the considerable rise in prices of sugarbeets for the production of A- and B-quota sugar and by ongoing shortages of sugar in countries of the former USSR, a country to which a substantial part of sugar exports from Poland have been directed (ibid., p. 11). Results of the 2004/05 campaign show that the above forecasts are correct. Total sugar production in Poland amounted in the campaign to 2,008,384 t (Rybski 2005, p. 48). This means that production of C-sugar totalled 336,458 t. Due to the fact that production of sugar in Poland since EU accession considerably exceeds domestic consumption, it is important to export surpluses systematically to avoid fluctuations in the domestic market price. In the first three quarters of 2004, exports of sugar from Poland amounted to 322,200 t. The corresponding numbers for the first three quarters of 2002 and 2003 were 56,100 t and 270,600 t, respectively (Kozmana 2005). A considerable increase in the volume of exported sugar in 2004 in relation to previous years is attributed to a large extent to high exports to old EU member states after Poland's

[122] See Journal of Laws (2004) No. 42, item 386, section 6.

EU accession. Between May 2004 and September 2004, 118,000 t of sugar were exported from Poland to the EU-15 (ibid.).[123] On April 20, 2005, the European Commission extended the deadline for elimination of surplus sugar stocks in five countries which joined the EU in 2004. Poland is not on the list of theses five countries.[124]

9.6.3 Developments in the Sugar Market in Poland Before and After the Country's EU Accession

The possibility of a considerable increase in the market price of sugar in Poland after the country's EU accession, resulting from the adoption of a new regulatory framework for the domestic sugar sector, was discussed repeatedly in Polish newspapers and television shortly before the 2004 EU enlargement. This contributed to a large extent to the fact that such increases could be observed already several weeks before Poland's official EU entry in May 2004. In anticipation of future developments, thousands of consumers stormed supermarkets in April 2004 and emptied the shelves of sugar. Due to this situation, numerous vendors restricted for a period of time the maximum amount of sugar that could be acquired at one time by individual buyers. In consequence, the average retail price of sugar in Poland increased from PLN 2.18/kg in March 2004 to PLN 3.30/kg in April 2004, i.e. by 51%. The mass purchase of sugar for fear of high price increases constitutes an interesting phenomenon considering the fact that the price elasticity of demand for sugar is thought to be low. After the sudden hike in April 2004, the average retail market price of sugar in Poland rose systematically by a few percentage points until August 2004. In the following months it fell moderately (See Figure 41).

Similar to the retail prices, the average producer prices of sugar skyrocketed in Poland in April and May 2004 as a result of an extraordinary surge in demand. Nevertheless, a gradual decline in producer prices could be observed in the fol-

[123] Since the beginning of the marketing year 2004/05, companies from the new member states trading in sugar have to possess special licenses. Moreover, they have to bid for export refunds (quota sugar) in a series of tenders, against a large number of other trading companies.

[124] The new EU member states affected are Estonia, Cyprus, Latvia, Malta and Slovakia. Surplus stocks built up in these countries prior to their EU entry in May 2004 are to be eliminated by 30 November 2005. Authorities of the five countries will have until 31 March 2006 to provide proof of the elimination of the surpluses before the deadline. Any stocks remaining after 30 November 2005 will be subject to a charge, paid into the EU budget. After every enlargement of the EU, new member states are required to take measures to prevent local operators from building up speculative sugar stocks with the aim of benefiting from the high sugar price within the EU (European Commission 2005, p. 1).

lowing months. This was partly a consequence of the considerable curtailment of sugar purchases made by food processors, wholesalers and consumers, who stockpiled sizeable sugar reserves before May 2004 and used or sold them later over a longer period of time.[125] Another significant reason for the decrease was a gradual appreciation of the Polish zloty in relation the euro in the time period February 2004-February 2005. Whereas in May 2004 the average exchange rate of the euro amounted to PLN 4.73 per 1 €, in February 2005 it amounted to PLN 3.98 per 1 € (National Bank of Poland 2005). It had the effect that the intervention price for sugar, expressed in Polish zloty, fell systematically in the time period May 2004-February 2005. This was accompanied by a gradual fall in the average producer price and, to a lesser extent, the average retail price of sugar (See Figure 41).

Regardless of the above developments, at the end of 2004, sugar producers in Poland were much better off than a year earlier. It must be kept in mind that sugar sold in such large quantities shortly before and after Poland's EU accession was manufactured from sugarbeets purchased at 'old', non-EU, prices specified for the marketing year 2003/04. So, the year 2004 may long remain the most profitable year for sugar producers in Poland since the country's EU entry.

Figure 41. Development of sugar prices in Poland, January 2004-July 2005

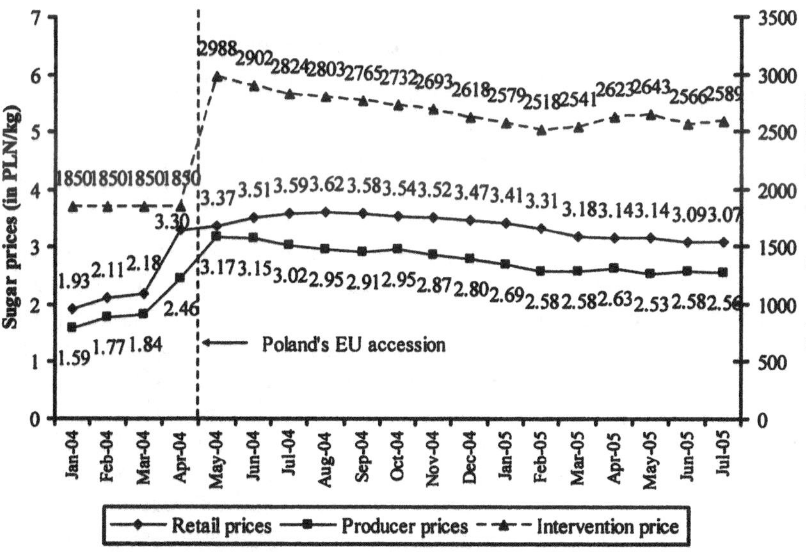

Source: Central Statistical Office (GUS), Online database (Prices in the national economy); NBP 2005.

[125] Sugar reserves made by food processors and wholesalers in Poland before the country's EU entry were not as large as was anticipated by sugar producers operating in the country.

In accordance with the principle that "there's no such thing as a free lunch", the sharp rise in the incomes of sugarbeet growers and the substantial increase in retail and producer prices of sugar in Poland after the country's EU accession were achieved at the cost to domestic consumers. It can be safely said that the considerable growth in sugar production costs in the marketing year 2004/05, resulting from the increase in raw material costs, was transferred by sugarbeet processors to a large extent to the consumers of sugar.[126] This becomes obvious not only after comparing manufacturing costs and market prices of sugar in Poland before and after the country's EU accession, but also after looking at the pre-accession value of the Consumer Support Estimate (CSE) for sugar in the country compared with the current EU level. In the period 2001-2003, the percentage CSE for sugar in Poland and in the EU amounted on average to -49% and -60%, respectively. As portrayed in Table 27, there was a large gap between the value of the percentage CSE for sugar in Poland and in the EU until 1995. As soon as the organization of the sugar market in Poland was regulated in a similar way as in the EU, this gap became considerably smaller. The more the regulatory framework for the sugar sector in Poland resembled the EU sugar regime and the closer came Poland's EU accession, the more the percentage CSE for sugar in the country was approaching that of the EU. In 2003, the value of this indicator was still considerably higher in Poland than in the EU, but already in the first year after the 2004 EU enlargement it will come down to the same level.

Table 27. Percentage CSE for Refined Sugar, Poland and EU, 1993-2003

	1993	1994	1995	1996	1997	1998	1999	2000	2001	2002	2003
Poland	-12	-23	-24	-43	-33	-43	-41	-66	-48	-50	-48
EU	-62	-54	-53	-56	-56	-63	-69	-60	-51	-62	-68

Source: OECD (PSE and CSE online database).

The sizeable increase in the market price of sugar in Poland after the country's EU accession has also had unpleasant consequences for industrial buyers of the commodity, e.g. manufacturers of confectionery products and the soft drinks industry. Domestic entrepreneurs involved in these business activities have been forced to look harder for cost reductions measures after the 2004 EU enlargement. Urban et al. (op. cit., p. 23) have demonstrated that production costs in the food-processing industry in Poland increased in 2004 by PLN 770 million owing to a substantial rise in sugar prices after the country's EU accession. Therefore, it can be expected that confectioners operating in Poland will pass on part of the increased production costs to domestic consumers by augmenting the selling prices of their products. The same can be said about manufacturers of most soft drinks and other products containing appreciable amounts of sugar.

[126] According to the study conducted by Urban et al. (2005), the sharp increase in the price of sugar in the middle of 2004 had the effect that consumers' expenditure in 2004 increased in Poland by about PLN 1.2 billion (Urban et al. 2005, p. 24).

According to estimates of the Association of Polish Manufacturers of Chocolate and Confectionery Products (*Stowarzyszenie Polskich Producentów Wyrobów Czekoladowych i Cukierniczych)*, in 2004, confectionery firms operating in Poland marketed products worth PLN 8.5-8.7 billion. This represents an increase by 6-7% in relation to 2003. Exports of the products had a value of PLN 1.2 billion, 10% more than a year earlier. About 30% of this sum was attributed to exports to non-EU countries (Prusek 2005). It is unlikely that the considerable rise in sugar prices in Poland in the middle of 2004 will bring about a substantial fall in the export of sweets to this group of countries in the coming years. EU producers of processed products containing Community sugar that are sold abroad are provided with export refunds compensating them for the difference between the (low) world market price of sugar and the (high) Community price. Preliminary results of analyses conducted by the Ministry of Agriculture and Rural Development in Poland show that the export of chocolate and confectionery products as well as soft drinks in the time period May 2004-December 2004 was considerably higher (in both value and volume) than in the time period May 2003 to December 2003.[127] Export of farm and food products in the time period May 2004 to December 2004 to former EU-15 countries increased in relation to the corresponding period of time in 2003 by 51.3%. Exports of such products to CIS countries rose at the same time by 20.5% (Ministry of Agriculture and Rural Development 2005).

Shortly before and after Poland's EU entry, there was widespread speculation in the domestic media about the danger that in the first weeks of the country's EU membership domestic producers of sugar and other commodities, as well as distributors and retailers, might breach the competition law and make unfair price-fixing arrangements. Nevertheless, such practices were not revealed on the sugar market and nobody was formally charged with employing such practices. As was pointed out earlier, the sudden rise in the market price of sugar in Poland in April and May 2004 was triggered off by the approaching introduction of a new regulatory framework for the domestic sugar sector, and by the resultant mass purchases of sugar by domestic consumers in anticipation of a high increase in the price of sugar after May 1, 2004.

Penalties for breaching competition law were toughened up in Poland directly before the country's EU entry, with the introduction of several amendments to the Law on the Protection of Competition and Consumers of December 15, 2000[128], as part of the adjustment of national legislation to EU norms. The new version of the law, which came into effect on May 1, 2004, allows the authorities to penalize a company that has seriously breached the competition law with a fine of up to 10% of its turnover, up to a limit of € 50 million.[129] Previously, the

[127] See for example Naszkowska 2005.
[128] See Journal of Laws (2000) No. 122, item 1319.
[129] See Journal of Laws (2004) No. 93, item 891, article 1, subsection 47, points 1 and 2.

penalty could not exceed € 5 million.[130] Moreover, companies involved in price-fixing cartels now have to be much more vigilant than before since whistle-blowers are treated leniently under the new regulations. If a firm involved in an illegal cartel provides on its own initiative concrete evidence for the existence of the cartel, it may be fully acquitted of all charges.[131] The Office for Competition and Consumer Protection (*Urząd Ochrony Konkurencji i Konsumentów*) is in charge of supervising and controlling the observance of the provisions of the competition law.[132]

9.6.4 Conclusions

Summarizing, it can be said without hesitation that the domestic sugarbeet growers benefited most in the first years of Poland's EU membership from the introduction of a new regulatory framework for the domestic sugar sector. They experienced a considerable improvement in their financial situation already in the first months of the marketing year 2004/05 owing to an appreciable increase in sugarbeet prices as well as their incorporation into the system of direct payments. Paradoxically, inhabitants of rural areas and farmers in Poland constituted the social group that was most afraid of the effects of EU accession on their situation. The attitude of this group to the idea of Poland's EU entry was, generally, negative, even a few weeks before and at the time of accession. Nevertheless, results of a study published at the end of 2004 by the Foundation for the Development of Polish Agriculture in a report entitled "Polish countryside after EU accession" show that this attitude changed dramatically within the first six months following the 2004 EU enlargement. Apart from expressing much more positive opinions about integration with the EU, country dwellers and especially farmers in Poland started to be increasingly optimistic about the economic situation in the country, about the direction of change and about their own employment prospects. Polish farmers turned from the greatest pessimists into the greatest optimists with regard to the above issues in the time period September 2003-September 2004.

The considerable rise in spirits in the countryside in the first months of Poland's EU membership was accompanied by a noticeable fall in the support among rural communities for populist parties which concentrated in the months preceding the EU accession on warning the public about disastrous implications of European integration. The metamorphosis in the mood in rural areas was brought about by the fact that none of the nightmare scenarios materialized which had been pres-

130 See Journal of Laws (2000) No. 122, item 1319, article 101, point 2.

131 See Journal of Laws (2004) No. 93, item 891, article 1, subsection 50.

132 It is worth mentioning here that in the beginning of May 2004, the National Bank of Poland set up a 24-hour confidential hotline where consumers could lodge reports about unjustified and extraordinarily high price increases observed in stores.

ented by the many opponents to EU accession in the lead-up to enlargement. Quite the contrary. Market prices and exports of agricultural products started to rise quickly and farmers were soon provided with direct payments for the first time. Moreover, they gained access to additional funds allocated under the aegis of several post-accession restructuring programs, financed from the EU budget.[133] According to provisional analyses conducted by Eurostat (the Statistical Office of the European Communities), published on December 17, 2004, real agricultural income per worker in Poland increased in 2004 by 73.5%. It was the second largest increase in the EU-25 after the Czech Republic, where agricultural income rose by 107.8%. The corresponding numbers for the EU-15 and EU-25 are 3.3% and 0.8%, respectively. In the countries that joined the EU in 2004, the rise in agricultural income amounted on average to 53.8%. This was brought about by integration into the CAP (subsidies), access to the Single Market (higher exports), increase of output in the agricultural sector due to a very successful harvest (good weather conditions) and higher producer prices (Eurostat 2004).
The Eurostat report shows clearly that the income gap between farmers in old and new member states of the EU is getting smaller and it seems very likely that such a trend will continue in the years to come. This does not change the fact, however, that the gap is still gigantic. Whereas in the Netherlands, for example, agricultural income per worker amounts on average to about € 32,000, in Poland the corresponding figure is € 1,900 (Sołtyk, op. cit.).

The above analysis concentrates predominantly on the short-term implications of Poland's EU entry for domestic sugar producers, consumers and sugarbeet growers. In view of recent developments, the formulation of forecasts for the time period 2006 onwards would be temerarious indeed. In July 2004, the European Commission tabled a plan for a comprehensive reform of the EU sugar regime. Implementation of the reform was due to begin in July 2005 but owing to uncertainties regarding the outcome of the Doha Round of WTO trade talks and the final decisions in the WTO panel ruling against the EU (subsidized re-exports of ACP-sugar and export of C-sugar), the starting date of the proposed reforms has been postponed until 2006. On June 22, 2005 the Commission presented a revised version of the reform plans. At the end of November 2005, the EU agriculture ministers reached agreement on the final parameters of the reform. Its implementation will have significant consequences for sugar producers, beet growers and consumers in Poland and other member states of the EU. Discussion of these consequences is included in the next subsection of the present study.

[133] See FDPA 2004, pp. 32-60.

9.7 Whither the European (and the Polish) Sugar Industry?

As was pointed out earlier in this study, the regulatory framework for the sugar sector in the EU has been functioning without any major changes since its introduction in 1968. Despite unremitting protests from cane-sugar manufacturing countries against export subsidies provided to EU sugar producers and against the protection of the Community market from the import of cheap cane sugar, the cornerstones of the EU sugar regime have not been changed for nearly four decades. Within the last few years, however, the EU policy regarding the organization of the internal sugar market has been subject to increasingly strong criticism expressed by numerous international institutions, e.g. Oxfam International, a consortium of organizations campaigning for policy changes aimed at reducing poverty and injustice. In a briefing paper issued in March 2004, Oxfam blames the EU for destroying opportunities for sugar exporters in developing countries and for hampering in this way the global efforts to alleviate human misery. At the same time, authors of the above publication call for a comprehensive reform of the EU sugar policy, including, *inter alia*, a cut of production quota and further expansion of market access for the least developed countries. This could, according to Oxfam, "benefit millions of people in poor countries" (Oxfam 2004, p. 1). More and more pressure has been put on the EU with regard to the organization of the sugar market by developing countries forming the G-20 group (including the world's largest exporters of cane sugar) and by the World Trade Organization.[134] The EU has committed itself during the Uruguay Round of WTO trade negotiations to gradually liberalize trade in sugar and to systematically reduce sugar export subsidies. In consequence, the volume of refundable EU sugar exports was reduced considerably in the 1995-2001 time period, through an adjustment of the production quotas allocated to individual EU member states (reclassification). It seems that the Doha Round of WTO trade talks launched in 2001 is likely to result in further agreements leading to the introduction of additional far-reaching liberalization measures in agriculture. A big step forward with regard to this issue was made on August 1, 2004 in Geneva, when trade negotiators from WTO member countries agreed on a negotiating framework "for estab-

[134] G-20 is an association of 20 member countries of the WTO, promoting and protecting the interests of the least developed and developing countries. The countries belonging to the association (Argentina, Bolivia, Brazil, Chile, China, Egypt, Ecuador, Philippines, India, Indonesia, Cuba, Mexico, Nigeria, Pakistan, Paraguay, RPA, Tanzania, Thailand, Venezuela and Zimbabwe) have half of the world's population and two thirds of the total number of farmers. The unofficial leader of G-20, Brazil, is probably the strongest supporter of the liberalization of world trade in agricultural products and of the abolition of subsidized export of sugar by the EU (Kuźmicz 2004).

lishing modalities in agriculture".[135] The deal signed in Geneva contained only a few dates and no precise information about the products to be involved and the structure of tariff and subsidies cuts. Highly developed countries have committed themselves in the Geneva deal to eliminate export subsidies and other forms of export support, and to cut imports tariffs for agricultural products after the conclusion of the Doha Round of trade negotiations. When this would happen remained largely uncertain until December 2005. During the Sixth WTO Ministerial Conference, held in Hong Kong, China (13-18 December 2005), trade ministers from the WTO member states accepted an agreement requiring the elimination of agricultural export subsides by 2013 (the EU accounts for about 90% of such spending) and committed themselves to providing duty-free and quota-free market access for most products from the 32 least developed countries "by 2008 or no later than the start of the implementation period" of any negotiated agreement.

In July 2003, Brazil, Australia and Thailand lodged a complaint with the WTO against subsidized re-exports of ACP-sugar and against (alleged) subsidization of exports of C-sugar by EU sugar producers. At the beginning of September 2004, the WTO made a ruling in this case saying that subsidized exports of C-sugar are illegal under WTO rules and that the EU is violating its commitments to the WTO by exporting much more subsidized sugar onto the world markets than it is permitted (*Zuckerindustrie* 8/2004, p. 552, 554; Knapp/Talk 2004, p. 7).[136] The European Commission filed an appeal against the ruling in January 2005.

On April 28, 2005 the WTO's Appellate Body made a final verdict in this case and upheld the major findings of the ruling.[137] This means that sooner or later the EU will have to take the consequences of the verdict into account and considerably reduce sugar exports, either through a cut in sugar production, the reorganization of its sugar policy, or a combination of both measures (Knapp/ Talks 2004, p. 2).

In the face of the above developments and future challenges, the EU authorities recently put the common organization of the markets in the sugar sector under close scrutiny and developed a plan of radical reforms, tabled by the European Commission on July 14, 2004. On June 22, 2005 the Commission presented a re-

135 For details see for example *The Economist*, August 7-13, 2004, pp. 59-60 or visit http:// www.wto.org/ english/tratop_e/agric_e/negs_bkgrnd23_julypack_e.htm.

136 As far as exports of C-sugar from the EU are concerned, the complainants have made the accusation that these exports benefit from subsidies by being "cross-subsidized effectively with revenues from production under A and B quotas" (European Commission 2004b, p. 1). In other words, the complainants claim that high profits resulting from sale of quota sugar on the Community market allow EU sugar producers to subsidize export of C-sugar. It is estimated that this hidden subsidy amounts to about € 1.49 billion (Knapp/Talks 2004, p. 7).

137 See European Commission 2005b; WTO 2005.

vised version of the reform plans.[138] The EU agriculture ministers agreed on the final parameters of the reform on November 24, 2005.
The reform shall be implemented over a period of four years, starting in the season 2006/07. The major changes to be introduced to the current regulatory framework for the EU sugar sector include:

- Reduction in the institutional support price for sugar by 36.0% (from € 631.9/t to € 404.4/t) over two years starting in the season 2008/09 (See Table 28).
- Reduction in the minimum price for sugarbeets by 39.7% (from € 43.63/t to € 26.29/t) over four years starting in the season 2006/07 (See Table 28).
- Abolition of the intervention system after a four-year phase-out period and the replacement of the intervention price by a reference price.
- Introduction of a private storage system as a safety net in case the market price falls below the reference price.
- Simplification of the quota system by merging the A- and B-quotas into one quota.
- Allocation of a decoupled payment to sugarbeet growers as a partial recompense (64.2% of the proposed price cut) for revenue losses resulting from the reform. The payment will be included in the Single Farm Payment. In countries giving up at least 50% of their quota, the possibility exists of an additional payment of 30% of the income loss for a maximum of five years, plus limited national aid.
- Voluntary restructuring scheme lasting 4 years (2006/07 to 2009/10) for EU sugar factories, and isoglucose and inulin syrup producers, consisting of a high, degressive payment to encourage factory closure and the renunciation of quota as well as in order to cope with the social and environmental impact of the restructuring process. This payment will be € 730 per tonne in years one and two, falling to € 625 in year three, and € 520 in the final year.
- A top-up payment (€ 4.68 per tonne of A- and B-sugarbeets) for sugarbeet producers affected by the closure of factories in the first year for which they have delivery rights.

---

[138] At the end of 2004, the Commission decided to postpone the starting date of reforms (season 2005/06) proposed in July 2004, due to serious reservations expressed by the parties concerned and due to uncertainty concerning the final verdict in the WTO panel ruling regarding EU sugar exports, as well as the outcome of the Doha round of trade negotiations. The revised plan of the overhaul of the EU sugar regime, proposed by the European Commission on June 22, 2005, takes into account, *inter alia*, the aforementioned WTO verdict.

- Increase in the isoglucose production quota by 300,000 t for the existing producer companies, phased in over a period of three years (100,000 t each year).
- Sugar for the chemical and pharmaceutical industries and for the production of bio-ethanol will be excluded from production quotas.

Table 28. Proposed institutional prices in the EU sugar sector

	Reference period	2006/07	2007/08	2008/09	2009/10
Institutional/Reference Sugar Price (€ /t)	631.9	631.9	631.9	541.5	404.4
Cumulative Reduction in the Institutional/ Reference Price	0.0%	0.0%	0.0%	-14.3%	-36.0%
Minimum Sugarbeet Price (€ /t)	43.63	32.86	29.78	27.83	26.29
Cumulative Reduction in Minimum Sugarbeet Price	0.0%	-24.7%	-31.7%	-36.2%	-39.7%

Source: Council Regulation (EC) No. 318/2006 of 20 February 2006 on the common organization of the markets in the sugar sector, Title II, Chapter I, Articles 3 and 5.

In order to give sugar producers "long term certainty about the rules they have to follow" in the future, the proposed new framework for the EU sugar sector is to remain valid until the season 2014/2015.[139]

The goal of the planned overhaul of the EU sugar regime is to bring sugar production within the Community in line with internal consumption, to expose the sugar sector to a greater extent to market forces and to achieve greater competitiveness of domestic sugar producers as well as a market balance guaranteeing the fulfilment of conditions specified in trade agreements concluded by the EU with various countries and those resulting from WTO negotiations. At the same time, the European Commission claims that it has taken into consideration the interests of sugarbeet growers, sugar producers and consumers in the EU in formulating the new strategy for the sugar sector. For this reason, the Commission proposed to stretch the introduction of the planned reforms over a period of years and to reach the target numbers gradually in order to enable all parties concerned to adjust to the new rules of the game as smoothly as possible. Regardless of this fact, there is no denying that the reforms will bring far-reaching changes for sugarbeet growers, beet processors and consumers in the enlarged EU.

First of all, the reform will result in a substantial reduction in the incomes of sugarbeet growers in all member states of the Community. In some regions, this form of agricultural activity will become economically non-viable. Many farmers are expected to withdraw from sugarbeet growing and to switch to the production of alternative crops. This refers especially to countries with unfavorable conditions for sugarbeet growing and to those where the cultivation of other crops may turn out more remunerative after the reform (e.g. Finland, Greece, Italy, Spain).

[139] For more details, see European Commission 2005c; European Commission 2005g.

Another significant effect of the reform will be a considerable fall in the processing margins of sugar producers in a number of countries, due to the expected drop in the EU market price of sugar to about € 404/t (assuming a 36% cut in the institutional support price for sugar—EU agriculture ministers agreement). The decrease in the market price of sugar to that level will make sugar production in many regions of the EU an unprofitable business.

Given the above facts and the strong interdependence between beet growers and beet processors, the impact of the reform on developments in the sugar industries of individual member states of the EU depends on the capacity of both domestic farmers and beet processors to adjust to the proposed price cuts (European Commission 2005d, p. 12).

According to analyses conducted by the European Commission, assuming an expected drop in the EU market price of sugar to about € 386/t (reform proposal of June 2005—cut in the institutional support price for sugar by 39%) and taking into account the projected *combined* profitability for sugarbeet growers and processors, sugar production is likely to be reduced drastically or even phased out after the introduction of the reform in Greece, Ireland, Italy and Portugal.[140] EU member states where sugar production is likely to be maintained but at a considerably lower level than in the season 2004/05 include: The Czech Republic, Spain, Denmark, Latvia, Lithuania, Hungary, Slovakia, Slovenia and Finland. In Austria, Belgium, France, Germany, the Netherlands, Poland, Sweden and the UK sugar production is likely to be affected but it is possible that in some of these countries the volume of sugar production will not decrease (ibid., pp. 13-14).

Preferential imports of sugar from ACP countries and India as well as from the least developed countries will be continued according to earlier arrangements. Access to the EU market for sugar imported from LDCs under the "Everything But the Arms" initiative will be extended gradually according to timetables specified earlier. Nevertheless, the guaranteed price paid for raw sugar imported under the preferential agreements will be reduced by about 40% from 2009/10 onwards. The price paid for preferential imports of white sugar, amounting in the marketing year 2004/05 to € 646.50/t (derived intervention price applicable to the United Kingdom), will also fall significantly.

Sugar producers from LDCs will gain unrestricted access to the EU market in 2009 but the cut in the institutional sugar price resulting from the reform will have the effect that for many of these producers as well as for producers from a number of ACP-countries the export of sugar to the EU will become unprofit-

[140] If sugar production in these four countries were phased out, the resultant drop in sugar production in the EU would amount to 9% of the EU-25 sugar production quota in the season 2003/04 (European Commission 2005d, p. 14).

able.[141] Moreover, the EU reserved the right to restrict sugar imports from LDCs (from 2008/09) if they increase by more than 25% each year (Oxfam 2005).
This means that the reform of the EU sugar regime is unlikely to contribute positively to the reduction of poverty in poor regions of the world from where sizeable amounts of sugar are imported currently at Community prices. Avoidance of the flooding of the Community market with sugar imports from the ACP states and LDCs from 2009 onwards was certainly one of the reasons why the European Commission opted to gradually reduce the current intervention price by more than one third until the marketing year 2009/10.[142]

The Commission estimates (on the basis of the June 2005 proposal) that after the introduction of the reform, annual preferential imports of sugar into the EU would increase between the seasons 2004/05 and 2012/13 by 1.6 million t (from 2.3 million t to 3.9 million t). The rise in imports would be almost fully attributed to an increased level of imports from the LDCs. Total exports of sugar from the EU are expected to fall by 2012/2013 from 3.1 million t to only 0.4 million t. EU subsidized sugar exports are projected to be zero (European Commission 2005d, p. 16). It must be pointed out here that reduction in EU sugar exports by about 2.7 million t does not have necessarily to be followed by a considerable increase in the world market price of sugar. The 'free space' made by the EU is likely to be filled by cane sugar from Brazil and Thailand. Therefore, it seems that a significant cut in EU sugar exports is not going to help the poorest countries exporting sugar onto the world market.[143]

Import tariffs on non-preferential sugar entering the EU will remain at a level guaranteeing an effective protection of the Community market against unbidden imports of the commodity.

Poland belongs to those member states of the EU where the reform of the EU sugar regime would not result in a considerable decline in the profitability of sugarbeet growing. Also the volume of sugar production is unlikely to decline substantially after the introduction of the reform. The costs of sugarbeet growing in Poland are at the moment much lower than in Western Europe.[144] Moreover, it must be kept in mind that already before the country's EU entry sugarbeet growing was more remunerative than the cultivation of other crops. Chudoba (2005, p. 12) and Urban et al. (2005, p. 12) have shown that in the first year of EU

---

141 For a more detailed analysis of possible effects of the proposed reform of the EU sugar regime for ACP states and for LDCs, see for example Knapp/Talks 2004, pp. 8-18.

142 In an official statement, the Commission states only that the proposed reduction in the institutional sugar price is provoked by the fact that it has been for a long time "out of touch with world trends and its current level is more than three times the prevailing world sugar price" (See European Commission 2004a, p. 5).

143 For a more detailed discussion of this issue, see for example Busse/Jerosch 2006, p. 104.

144 With similar sugarbeet yields per hectare, the variable costs of sugarbeet growing in Poland are about 40% lower than in Germany (Urban et al. 2005, pp. 9-10).

membership, net agricultural income resulting from sugarbeet growing increased in Poland by 113% (from PLN 1.740 to PLN 3.710 per hectare) and 197% (from PLN 1.404 to PLN 4.171 per hectare), respectively. Regardless of which of the two studies are closer to reality, it seems that even after a reduction in the minimum sugarbeet price by 39.7% by 2009/10, the net income resulting from sugarbeet growing in Poland will be, in nominal terms, much higher than in the season 2003/04, i.e. the last year before the country's EU entry.

The final version of the reform plan of the EU sugar regime envisages the introduction of a new, decoupled direct payment granted to sugarbeet growers to compensate them partially for income losses resulting from the reform (64.2% of the estimated revenue loss). Taking into account direct payments amounting to 60% of the estimated revenue loss (initial Commission proposal), *Urban* et al. (ibid., pp. 11–12) project that after the end of the phase-in period of the planned reform, the net agricultural income resulting from sugarbeet growing in Poland will be two and a half times higher than in the marketing year 2003/04. It is important to mention here, however, that calculations conducted by *Urban* et al. refer to farms using agricultural accounting (the average size of such farms amounts to 5.3 ha and is much larger than the average size of a sugarbeet plantations in Poland, of 3.5 ha). Moreover, *Urban* et al. in their calculations used price reductions proposed by the Commission in July 2004 (-37.0% for sugarbeets and -33.0% for the institutional sugar price). These differ slightly from the price reductions accepted by EU agriculture ministers on 24 November 2005 (-39.7% for sugarbeets and -36.0% for the institutional sugar price).

This leads to the conclusion that, at the national level, the income resulting from sugarbeet growing in Poland after the implementation of the reform of the EU sugar regime will be slightly lower than that projected by *Urban* et al. but this form of agricultural activity will still be attractive.

Commenting on the above calculations, Rybski (2005a, p. 154) claims that it is wrong to incorporate the aforementioned direct payments in estimations of future income resulting from sugarbeet growing, since "the payments will only be granted to farmers who produced sugarbeet under quota in the historical reference period (2000-2002) and will not be affected by any quota transfers, which may be made subsequently". In other words, farmers who were growing sugarbeets in the reference period will receive the direct payments regardless of whether they continue with sugarbeet growing or not. This argument is, however, insufficient to justify exclusion of the direct payment from the calculation of future income resulting from sugarbeet growing in Poland. It is obvious that the vast majority of farmers who will deliver sugarbeets to sugar factories in Poland in the years to come will consist of farmers who did this in the aforementioned historical reference period. Since they are eligible for the new direct payment, there is no reason to exclude it. The exclusion is justified only in the case of farmers who start to grow sugarbeets after the introduction of the reform (they will not fall under the historical reference period). Furthermore, if one decides to expand the sugarbeet-growing area in the future, the direct payment will not be paid for the additional acreages. Nonetheless, continual increases in the productivity and quality of the sugarbeet harvest in Poland have led to a gradual reduction in the sugarbeet-growing area in the country. This trend is very likely to continue in the future.

The above considerations demonstrate that after the implementation of the reform of the EU sugar regime, sugarbeet growing in Poland will still constitute a lucrative business (at least for those who have grown sugarbeets in the historical reference period). It is therefore unlikely that a large number of farmers in the country will withdraw from sugarbeet growing and switch to the production of other crops. Due to the considerable diversity of the soil and climatic conditions in Poland, it is indeed possible that a certain group of farmers will cease sugarbeet growing (on the grounds of low productivity and high growing costs) and start to grow maize, for example. It may turn out that for some sugarbeet growers the new direct payment plus income resulting from cultivation of some crop other than sugarbeet will bring higher profits than the continuation of sugarbeet growing. This refers, however, to a rather small group of farmers. In regions with unfavorable conditions for sugarbeet growing, the activity may still be more profitable than the cultivation of any other crop after the implementation of the reform of the EU sugar regime. A precondition for this is that sugarbeet growers in such regions increase the quality of the harvest and make efforts to reduce production costs. If this does not work, a part of sugarbeet production that was given up in one region can be 'moved' to more efficient growers situated elsewhere. From the point of view of sugar producers, this process is desirable as long as it does not take on very large proportions. And it is unlikely that it will happen in Poland.

The above analyses lead to the conclusion that the number of sugarbeet growers in Poland as well as the area under beet cultivation will continue to decrease. Nevertheless, it will be a slow-moving process. As shown in Figure 27, the allocation of the "beet growing and delivery rights" to sugarbeet growers in Poland has not brought to a halt structural changes at the raw material base of the domestic sugar industry. This will not change in the future. A gradual fall in the number of sugarbeet growers will be accompanied by a further increase in the average size of sugarbeet plantations. The achievement of a similar size of plantations to that currently found in countries forming the former EU-15 will, however, take some time.

The anticipated drop in the market price of sugar from € 631.9/t to € 404/t (-36.0%) and a simultaneous fall in the minimum price of sugarbeets from € 45.9/t to € 26.3/t (-39.7%) will cause the processing margins of sugar producers in

Poland to decrease but they will still be able to generate profits.[145] If we add to this the fact that the revised plan of the reform of the EU sugar regime does not envisage, at least initially, a compulsory reduction in the sugar production quota in the EU member states, it seems unlikely that the volume of sugar production in Poland would decline substantially after the implementation of the reform.[146]

The reform of the organization of the EU sugar market would force sugarbeet processors in Poland to continue activities aimed at increasing the cost efficiency of sugar production. This would include, *inter alia*, further consolidation of sugar factories and concentration of production in regions with the most favorable conditions for a productive sugarbeet harvest. It is, however, difficult to predict how fast these changes would materialize and what their extent would be. Given the course of sugar industry restructuring in Poland hitherto, the high costs of consolidation of sugar factories, and the current ownership structure in the Polish sugar sector (20 working sugar factories are in state hands), it can be expected that structural changes in the sugar industry will proceed slowly. The social aspect of restructuring makes the closure of 25 or 30 sugar factories within a short period of time highly unlikely. By the same token, the achievement of a daily processing capacity of 9,900 t (Walkenhorst model) in sugar factories in Poland, or even a doubling the current average capacity (3,400 t), is a distant prospect. Some sugar producers operating in Poland, e.g. Südzucker, claim that they do not intend to expand the processing capacity of sugar factories to more than 8,000 t of beet throughput per day, due to very high costs of such an undertaking.

It is known that before the beginning of the campaign 2005/06, sugarbeet processing will be ceased at the *Małoszyn* sugar factory (Südzucker Group). Furthermore, the management of *KSC "Polski Cukier"* has announced that by the campaign 2006/07, sugarbeet processing will have ceased at 7 factories controlled by the corporation (2 plants in 2005 and 5 plants in 2006). There are also rumors that two of the five factories currently owned by British Sugar in Poland (*Dobre* and *Unisław*) will be closed down in 2006.

If the above scenario comes to fruition, in the 2006/07 campaign, sugarbeet processing in Poland will take place at no more than 33 plants. It is important to point out, however, that in the case of *KSC "Polski Cukier"*, announcements about planned factory closures must be treated with caution since the restructuring process of this state-controlled company has been strongly politicized.

There is no doubt that information about the planned overhaul of the organization of the sugar market in the EU gladdened domestic consumers, especially industrial buyers of sugar. After the implementation of the reform, the market

---

[145] See for example Urban et al. 2005, p. 19.

[146] The European Commission hopes that voluntary restructuring in the least competitive regions of the EU, triggered by the proposed price cuts, will lead to a 'natural' quota reduction, guaranteeing a market balance and the meeting of commitments resulting from international trade agreements.

price of sugar in the EU will fall considerably. Consequently, production costs of processed goods containing large quantities of sugar will also decline. This in turn will lead to an improvement in the international competitiveness of soft drinks and confectionery products. Urban et al. (2005, pp. 23-24) project that the implementation of the proposed reform of the EU sugar regime would bring down production costs borne by food processors operating in Poland and using large quantities of sugar to a level similar to that recorded before the country's EU accession.

The reform is unlikely to have a significant effect on household consumption of sugar within the Community since the price elasticity of demand for this commodity is low.

Official announcement of the first version of the planned reform of the EU sugar regime by the European Commission in the middle of July 2004 provoked almost immediately an angry reaction from the representatives of sugar producers and sugarbeet growers, as well as from national governments in most member states of the enlarged EU. National and supranational associations of sugarbeet growers have criticized the proposed changes, especially with regard to the duration of the phase-in period (too short) and the extent of the planned reduction in sugarbeet prices. Beet processors and beet growers in many EU countries have worked out and presented a common stance on the Commission's proposals, saying that the reform plans in their original form are unacceptable and that the introduction of the reform would endanger thousands of jobs in rural areas and enforce the closure of numerous sugar factories. Furthermore, sugar producers and beet growers expressed opposition to the proposed starting date of the reforms, since in the marketing year 2000/01 it was decided that the current regulatory framework for the EU sugar sector would remain in force until the end of the marketing year 2005/06, i.e. until June 30, 2006. Beet processors and beet growers in many member states of the EU have stated that changes to the regulation of the sugar market before this deadline would be unfair since important investment decisions were made on the basis of previous arrangements. Sugar producers also protested against the level of proposed cutbacks in the institutional sugar price and suggested that it is too early to specify details of the reform before the finalization of the Doha Round of WTO trade negotiations.[147]

The National Association of Sugarbeet Growers and the Association of Sugar Producers in Poland took a decisive stand on the regulation of the sugar market in the EU and expressed a strong disapproval of the proposed reforms in an official statement signed jointly at the beginning of July 2004 in Warsaw. In short,

[147] For more information about the response of sugarbeet growers and sugar producers in the EU to the proposed reform of the EU sugar regime, see for example *F.A.Z.* 2004a; *F.A.Z.* 2004b; *Gazeta Cukrownicza* 7/2004, p. 180, 182-83; Hagelüken 2004; *Zuckerindustrie* 129 (2004) Nr. 7, pp. 486-487; *Zuckerindustrie* 129 (2004) Nr. 8, p. 601, 615-616; *Zuckerindustrie* 10/2004, p. 702.

in the document, the two associations rejected the vast majority of the changes proposed by the Commission and demanded prolongation of the current regulation of the sugar market in the EU without modification until the marketing year 2009/10.

These associations strongly condemned the planned merger of A- and B-quotas in individual EU member states. Such a move would, according the associations, be unjust for countries where the B-quota is at a very low level. Whereas in Poland the B/A-quota ratio amounts to 5.8%, the EU-25 average lies at 18.5%. In Germany and France this ratio amounts to 30.8% and 26.9 %, respectively.[148]

Contrary to the reaction of sugar producers and sugarbeet growers, the planned reform of the EU sugar regime was backed up by the Polish Federation of Foodstuffs Producers (*Polska Federacja Producentów Żywności*).[149]

Apart from organizations of sugar producers and sugarbeet growers and governments in most EU member states, the reform plans were criticized by countries benefiting from preferential imports of sugar to the Community market. LDC and ACP states announced that the proposed reduction of the institutional sugar price would be disastrous for many countries exporting sugar to the EU under the "Everything but the Arms" initiative, and demanded retention of the price at the current level. In March 2004, LDCs presented a proposal that stated that they would accept introduction of import quotas after 2008 under the condition that the prices paid to them for sugar exported to the EU would not be changed until 2019. The European Commission has refused the offer.

The sugar policy reform masterminded by the Commission did not meet the expectations of Oxfam International. The group argues that the reform will neither bring an end to overproduction and subsidized exports from the EU, nor will it lead to a considerable increase in imports from poor countries into the Community market. Oxfam points out that price reductions envisaged in the reform will impoverish many people in Africa since for many countries in the region the export of sugar to the EU will become unprofitable (Oxfam 2004a, p.3; Oxfam 2005).

In January 2005, the European Commission committed itself to providing support to ACP countries in order "to mitigate potential impacts of the EU sugar reform". The support would take the form of various trade and development measures, e.g. economic partnership agreements and activities aimed at the diversification of products and markets in sugar-dependent areas. The Commission has earmarked an initial assistance of € 40 million for ACP countries in 2006. Further financial support will be provided to the countries in the time period 2007-2013 (European Commission 2005, pp. 1-2; European Commission 2005e, p. 2).

---

[148] For a full version of the letter containing the joint position of the National Association of Sugarbeet Growers and Sugar Producers in Poland on reforms proposed by the European Commission in July 2004, see for example *Gazeta Cukrownicza* 7/2004, pp. 180-183.

[149] See for example *Gazeta Cukrownicza* 11/2004, p. 335.

According to analyses conducted by the European Commission, the annual budgetary costs of the organization of the sugar market during the phase-in period of the reform proposed in July 2004 (first version) would be similar to expenditures that would arise in the event of the maintenance of the status quo. The Commission claimed at that time that costs resulting from the introduction and implementation of new measures which are part of the reform, e.g. allocation of special direct payments to sugarbeet growers, would be counterbalanced by savings resulting from a substantial fall in expenditures for export refunds as well as from the cancellation of the refining aid and the abolition of production refunds for the chemical and pharmaceutical industries (European Commission 2004a, p. 11).

After the acceptance of the final version of the reform plans, it is estimated that payments provided to beet growers as a recompense for revenue losses resulting from the reform will total about € 1.7 billion. These payments will be financed entirely from the EU budget. At the same time, savings amounting to about € 800-900 million are expected to materialize as a result of a cut in export subsidies connected with the export of ACP sugar. It is not clear how export subsidies will be financed in the next few years since a production levy of € 12/t to be imposed on sugar producers is unlikely to suffice to cover these costs. Moreover, the EU budget will be burdened with the financial help to be provided to ACP countries (restructuring and diversification) (Sommer 2006, p. 51).

10 The Competitiveness of Sugar Producers: Analysis of Key Success Factors

In order to understand and assess the significance and the effects of various restructuring activities, we need to first examine the determinants and manifestations of competitiveness in a given industrial sector. The main purpose of this section is to define the term competitiveness with regard to the sugar industry. This section, together with the information provided hitherto, should allow an objective evaluation of the effectiveness of the restructuring activities implemented at sugarbeet-processing plants in Poland between 1990 and 2004.

10.1 Determinants of Competitiveness in the Sugar Industry

In the beginning of any discussion about the competitiveness of an economy (macro level), industry (meso level) or an economic unit (micro level), it needs to be pointed out that a universal definition of the term "competitiveness" does not exist in the economic literature. Hence, many authors discuss and analyze various aspects of competitiveness without explaining the meaning of the expression. There is, however, a general agreement among the theorists on this subject that competitiveness is derived from competition—the fundamental mechanism of the market economy—and that it is connected inseparably with this process.[150] For this reason, as indicated for example by Skawińska (2002, p. 73) and Wziątek-Kubiak (2003, p. 137), competitiveness is sometimes referred to as the ability of a given subject to compete successfully with other subjects. These authors emphasize at the same time that it relates to international markets, especially with regard to the member states of the EU. Similarly, Kokocińska (2002, p. 114) observes that ever increasing globalization is leading to a gradual displacement of the term "competitiveness" by the phrase "international competitiveness". Nonetheless, this interpretation of competitiveness is vague and ambiguous. Much more precise and meaningful is the definition proposed by Flejterski (1984, p. 391) who describes competitiveness as "*the ability to design, manufacture and market products whose prices, quality and other characteristics are more attractive to customers than those of equivalent products offered by the competitors*."

It is important to add at this point that according to Porter (1998, p. 33) competitiveness constitutes a microeconomic and not a macroeconomic measure since it is "firms, not nations, that compete on international markets". This is consistent with the well-known hypothesis formulated by Krugman (1994), according to which nations, in contrast to companies, cannot be eliminated from the market and the examination of their competitiveness is thus misguided.

As there are many definitions of competitiveness, there are also various approaches to the problem of measuring it. Many authors claim that the major indicator of competitiveness of firms is the profitability of their operations.[151] When an organization generates profits from its activities, this means that it is able to sustain its position in a competitive market and has a chance for further development through investment and innovation.

A change in the market share of a given firm is also considered as an indicator of the change in its competitiveness.[152] Nevertheless, the sole observation of changing market share of a company tells nothing about the actual reasons behind this. Therefore, additional factors need to be analyzed in order to identify these reasons and to get a comprehensive picture of a firm's situation (Wziątek-Kubiak op. cit., p. 117). The classification of market share as an indicator of the competitive position of firms is particularly problematic in the sugar industry. As we know from the previous chapters of the present study, the sugar market in the EU is strictly regulated from above and sugar production quotas are allocated to individual sugar producers by an authorized institution. Therefore, the possibilities for EU sugar producers to gain additional market shares are greatly limited. In practice, the

[150] See for example Skawińska 2002, p. 73; Stankiewicz 2002, pp. 17-45; Wziątek-Kubiak 2003, p. 37, 43.

[151] See for example Skawińska 2002, p. 74; Galli/Pelkmans 2000, p. 9; Wziątek-Kubiak 2003, p. 41.

[152] See Skawińska 2002, p. 209.

only path to growth is through mergers and acquisitions. Of course, one may claim that the expansion of a given sugar company as a result of takeovers of other sugar producers is a sign of its efficiency and financial strength. Nonetheless, it is misleading to consider it as a sign of increasing competitiveness, especially when a sugar corporation acquires from one of its competitors several inefficient and indebted plants (which constitutes in fact the acquisition their production quota).

The fundamental indicator by which the competitiveness of economic units should be judged is their productive efficiency. Wziątek-Kubiak (ibid., p. 21) claims that differences in the competitiveness of firms in an industry are a reflection of absolute differences in their productive efficiency. Competition prompts firms to constantly increase their productive efficiency in order to improve the cost efficiency of production. Efforts aimed at the increase in productive efficiency constitute according to Porter (1998, p. 21) the most significant method of competing. Porter is also the author of the generic competitive strategies model according to which there are two basic types of competitive advantage a firm can posses: *low cost* or *differentiation*. He calls these generic strategies because they can be applied to companies operating in any industry. A *cost leadership strategy* is one in which a firm strives to become the lowest-cost producer in a given industry and offer its usually standardized products or services to a broad market at the lowest prices. A firm that uses the *differentiation strategy* is one that tries to offer products or services with special features valued by a targeted group of customers. The extra value added provided thanks to the uniqueness of the offered products, which is accompanied by high production costs, allows the firm to charge a premium price. Porter advised companies to adopt one of the two aforementioned strategies and stay with it exclusively. He believed that a firm could lose its market identity and present a confusing image to its customers if it tried to execute more than one generic strategy at one time. This would lead a firm to having only a modest market share and the lowest return on investment in its industry. Porter called this dilemma being "stuck in the middle".[153] Nevertheless, it is today becoming more and more apparent that it is not enough to choose just one of the competitive strategies proposed by Porter in order to compete successfully in a given market. As observed for example by Zalewski (2002, p. 145), customers considering the purchase of a product or service look these days at the total yield coming from the purchase and usage of the product. This means that potential customers take into account in their decisions not only the price and/or quality of a product but also a number of other factors like the conditions of payment, method and timing of order and delivery, brand, assortment of products, the possibility of a trial period, customer service, etc. This development has been brought about by the fact that the number of firms offering products of high quality at low prices is constantly increasing as a result of fierce

[153] See Porter 1998, pp. 37-40.

uninterrupted low-cost competition. Price wars, the increasing incomes of customers and increasing market saturation have had the effect that the market power of customers in relation to the market power of producers is rising over time (ibid., p. 200). This in turn forces firms to improve continuously and simultaneously their cost efficiency, quality and flexibility. The importance of the last factor in gaining a competitive advantage in manufacturing was analyzed by Upton (1995), among others, who claims that flexibility manifests itself in quick response times to customers' orders, quick changeovers, and the ability to provide customers with a broad range and a large volume of products at any time. Moreover, this author suggests that the type of flexibility should always be tailored to the competitive environment of a given company. He emphasizes at the same time that operational flexibility is achieved by combining state-of-the-art technology and, which is even more important, efficient management of day-to-day activities (ibid., pp. 75-76). Finally, Upton (ibid., p. 80) points out that the training of human resources plays the key role in building flexibility since it is the only way to change the "this-is-the-way-we-have-always-done-it attitude" of employees. It seems to be of particular importance in transition economies.

All in all, it can be stated that focusing only on one of the two basic competitive strategies formulated by Porter at the moment creates rather the danger of lagging behind the competitors instead of being "stuck in the middle". For those firms which try to find the right balance between the cost efficiency and quality of production, and do not disregard the significance of flexibility aimed at the satisfaction of customer needs, the possibility of 'falling into a trap' is lesser than for those which stand stubbornly by one strategy adopted in the past. A prime example for a successful combination of the low-cost strategy with unceasing efforts at improvement in quality and satisfaction of customer needs is the activity and evolution of Toyota Motor Europe. For a long time Toyota played a marginal role in the European automobile market but owing to the design of several car models tailored to the tastes of European customers, continual improvement in productivity, reduction in costs and the ambition to be considered by European customers as the quality leader, the company's market share in Europe rose constantly between 1995 and 2004. In 2004, Toyota achieved an eighth consecutive record year of sales in Europe. With nearly 916,000 vehicles delivered, the company's sales rose by 10% over the previous year, up an estimated 2% in total market share. This resulted in a market share of 5%, the highest market share ever for Toyota in Europe (Toyota Europe 2005; Edmondson/Bonnet 2004, p. 26).

A very important remark by Porter (ibid., p. 34) is that determinants of competitiveness differ from industry to industry and that their definition depends on the focus of an investigation. Even if the factors which decided the competitiveness of firms operating in different sectors of the economy were the same, considerable differences in the relative importance of each of these factors may nevertheless exist. This means that apart from specifying the key success factors for a particular industry, it is also important to give them a weighting, as is also the case for the indicators of productive efficiency (Skawińska 2002, p. 77).

It needs to be pointed out at this point that changes in both productive efficiency and competitiveness should be measured over a longer period of time since efficiency and competitiveness cannot be turned on and off like a tap, but rather it usually takes several years before firms' efforts at improvement in these areas show any appreciable effects.

Another significant fact that needs to be considered in a discussion on competitiveness is that among all the factors that shape the competitive position of firms in a given industry there are some over which firms can exert influence and some which are beyond their control. With regard to this issue, Skawińska (2002, p. 59) distinguishes between "internal" and "external" factors, Kokocińska (2002, p. 114) between "efficiency-related" and "efficiency-unrelated" factors. In both cases, the former comprise the cost efficiency of production, quality and assortment of offered products and services, distribution, etc. In other words, all those areas which are dependent on the skills, capabilities and resources of firms. The determinants of competitiveness formed independently of the effectiveness of operations of economic units include the regulatory environment in a given industry, regional and/or national economic policy, social infrastructure, and environmental and demographic conditions.[154] Some of these factors may be influenced to some extent by firms, e.g. through lobbying politicians to introduce laws creating a more positive business environment, others are features that simply have to be accepted. Also, in this case it needs to be specified which external determinants of competitiveness are of special importance in a given industry (Skawińska 2002, p. 61).

It is worth adding here that some external factors, e.g. governmental support in the form of export subsidies or market protection, distort the actual competitiveness of firms and pose an impediment to its measurement. This is another reason why changing market share, shaped as it is by both internal and external factors, should not constitute the only indicator by which the change in competitiveness should be evaluated.[155]

The theoretical considerations of the present section, interviews conducted with representatives of sugar companies operating in Poland, and a thorough analysis of the situation on the European and world sugar markets, have formed the basis for a description of the main determinants of competitiveness in the sugar industry. They are presented in Figure 42.

---

[154] See for example Porter 1998a, p. 89; Galli/Pelkmans 2000, p. 9; Skawińska 2002, pp. 60-61; Kokocińska 2002, p. 114.

[155] See Wziątek-Kubiak 2003, pp. 50-51, 152-153.

Figure 42. Determinants of Competitiveness in the Sugar Industry

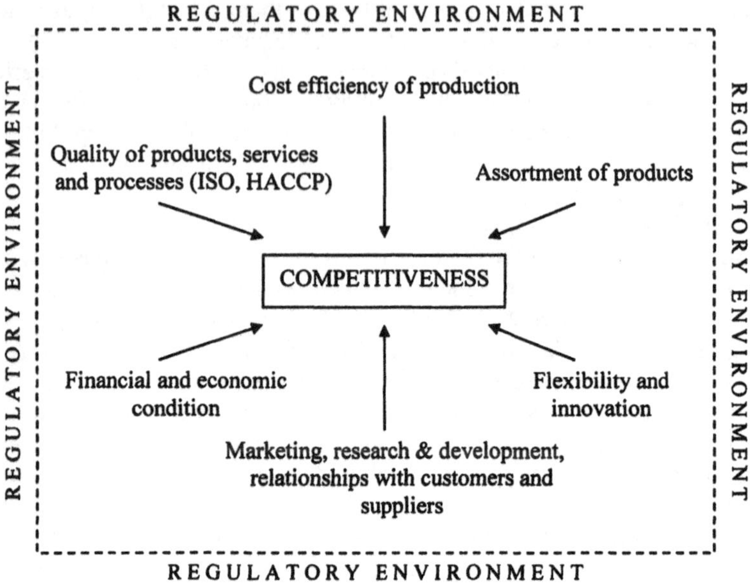

Source: Analysis by the author.

By far the most important source of competitive advantage in the sugar industry is the cost efficiency of production. A low market price of sugar and persistent surpluses in the commodity have the effect that only those sugar companies can survive in the medium to long term in the market, which are able to produce at a very low unit cost. For this reason, continual improvement in productive efficiency and reduction in costs should constitute the principal objective of restructuring activities for all European sugar manufacturers.

Another major determinant of competitiveness in the sugar industry and in the food-processing industry in general is the quality of products, services and processes.

Customers are placing more and more importance on the quality of products provided by the food business. This trend has been particularly clearly noticeable over the last decade throughout Central and Eastern Europe. As observed by Białasiewicz (2001, p. 36) in a report on various aspects of the quality of food on the eve of Poland's EU accession, "*The times when companies operating in the food-processing industry did not have to take special care about the quality of their products since everything disappeared immediately from the supermarket shelves are definitely over*". Increasing competition among suppliers, rising incomes and an increasing quality consciousness among consumers, as well as the introduction of rigorous sanitary and hygienic specifications, are the driving forces behind the continually rising quality requirements concerning foodstuffs, in the majority of central and east European counties. Nevertheless, in highly developed countries of the West also, the quality of products offered by the food-processing industry constitutes a crucial factor, which often plays a decisive role in shaping the competitive position of firms. Given the high surpluses of sugar on the European and world sugar market, manufacturers' quality assurance is a necessary requirement that needs to be met in order to be competitive, apart entirely from the cost efficiency of production.

The characteristics that "white sugar of standard quality" (EU-category II) manufactured in the member states of the European Union must possess are specified in Annex I to the EU basic sugar regulation.[156] In point 1 of the Annex it is stipulated that "white sugar of standard quality" shall be: a) of sound, genuine and merchantable quality; dry, in homogenous granulated crystals, free-flowing; b) have a minimum polarization of 99.7°, c) maximum moisture content of 0.06% and, d) maximum invert sugar content of 0.04%. Moreover, in order to be classified as "white sugar of standard quality" the number of points allocated to a given sugar and calculated on the basis of the value of three parameters (color type, ash content and color in solution) cannot exceed a total of 22, nor can it exceed 15 for the ash content, 9 for the color type and 6 for the coloring of the solution.

In order to be classified as "extra white sugar" (EU-category I), a sugar needs to satisfy the requirements a) - d) and the number of points obtained for ash content, color type and color in solution cannot exceed a total of 8, nor can it exceed 6 for the ash content, 4 for the color type and 3 for the coloring of the solution (Gruszecka 2000, p. 106). One point corresponds to: a) 0.0018% of ash content, determined using the ICUMSA method at 28° Brix; b) 0.5 units of color type using the Brunswick method; c) 7.5 units of coloring of the solution using the ICUMSA method (See Table 29).

In the campaign 2002/03, sugar manufactured, for example, in the *Opalenica* sugar factory had an ash content of 0.011%, a color type amounting to 1.40 units and a color in solution amounting to 33.00 ICUMSA units (IPC 2003, p. 52). This corresponds to 6.11 (0.011/0.0018), 2.8 (1.40/0.5) and 4.4 (33/7.5) points, respectively, which gives a total of 13.31 points. It means that sugar produced in *Opalenica* during the campaign 2002/03 fulfilled all necessary requirements to be classified as "white sugar of standard quality" (EU-category II).[157]

The ability to manufacture sugar fulfilling these requirements usually suffices to satisfy the demands of the vast majority of customers. Nonetheless, some clients require a product possessing quality parameters which allow its qualification as "extra white sugar" (EU-category I). In view of this fact, sugar manufacturers that are capable of providing customers with "extra white sugar", have a com-

[156] Council Regulation (EC) No 1260/2001 of June 19, 2001 on the common organization of the markets in the sugar sector (Official Journal of the European Communities 30.6.2001 L 178 with subsequent amendments, Annex I).

[157] Assuming that the requirements a)-d) were also satisfied.

petitive advantage over producers offering exclusively sugar of standard quality. It is worth mentioning here that sugar companies usually charge a higher price for sugar that meets quality requirements of EU-category I than for sugar classified as EU-category II. In order to make the transition from producing "white sugar of standard quality" to the production of "extra white sugar", a given sugar factory would have to introduce a number of changes in the technological process of sugarbeet processing, which would require, among other things, investment in new technology.

Table 29. Classification of sugar according to the number of points for ash content, color type and color in solution

	EU-category I (extra white sugar)	EU-category II (white sugar of standard quality)
Total number of points	**not more than 8 points**	**not more than 22 points**
Ash content	not more than 6 points	not more than 15 points
Color type	not more than 4 points	not more than 9 points
Color in solution	not more than 3 points	not more than 6 points

Ash content: 1 point = 0.0018% of ash
Color type: 1 point = 0.5 units
Color in solution: 1 point = 7.5 ICUMSA units

Source: Illustration by the author, based on information provided in Annex I of the Council Regulation (EC) No. 1260/2001 of June 19, 2001 on the common organization of the markets in the sugar sector, and in Gruszecka 2000, pp. 106-107.

Trading partners in Poland and other countries are currently interested not only in the quality specifications of a given final product but also in the quality of the entire process connected with its creation. Firms producing beverages, for example, usually use considerable quantities of sugar in various forms and of a particular quality and consistency. Since competition in the soft-drinks industry is intense and the power is with the buyers, no firm wants to risk its reputation and its customers' trust . For this reason, most of them want to be certain that the sugar they purchase and add to the soft drinks they produce has been manufactured in perfect sanitary conditions and according to procedures which have food safety as a priority.

Sugar producers, therefore, but not only they, introduce quality management systems at their productive facilities which ensure a hygienic manufacturing processes, improve the effectiveness of operations, and reinforce at the same time the esteem earned among customers and trading partners. The institution of a certain quality management system may be attested by a certificate issued by an accredited certification body after an official audit conducted at the request of a given company and aimed at the examination of the proper functioning of the system. The possession of certain types of certificates has a particularly high value for potential trading partners, and often constitutes a prerequisite for the beginning of cooperation between firms (ibid., p. 36). In the food-processing industry, the most popular and recognized quality management systems include the Hazard Analysis and Critical Control Point (HACCP) and a series of management system standards developed by the International Organization for Standardization (ISO).[158]

HACCP constitutes "a systematic approach to the identification, evaluation, and control of food safety hazards" from the moment of production and procurement of the raw material, throughout manufacturing and distribution, to the consumption of a finished product (USDA 1997). The word "hazards" stands here for "biological, chemical, or physical agents that are reasonably likely to cause illness or injury in the absence of its control" (ibid.). Any HACCP system has a precautionary character and its main goal is to prevent food safety risks at every stage of creation and distribution of foodstuffs. The application of programs such as Good Hygienic Practice (GHP) and Good Manufacturing Practice (GMP) is considered a necessary precondition to the development and implementation of a HACCP system at an enterprise (Białasiewicz op. cit., p. 39; USDA 1997). GHP and GMP embrace a number of basic sanitary, hygienic and environmental standards and practices that must be employed in each segment of the food-processing industry. Many of them are specified in governmental regulations and guidelines. The development of a well-functioning HACCP system is based on the following principles: hazard analysis (collection and evaluation of information on hazards associated with a particular food), identification of critical control points, determination of critical limits, establishment of monitoring procedures, corrective actions as well as verification, record-keeping and documentation procedures.[159] The maintenance of an effective HACCP system requires regular verification of all procedures and the introduction of updates and revisions whenever needed (USDA, ibid.). It necessitates also the thorough education and training of all individuals involved so that they are aware of the significance of food safety, understand their role in ensuring it and fulfill their responsibilities correctly and efficiently.

On the basis of the European Council Directive 93/43/EEC of June 14, 1993 on the hygiene of foodstuffs, which came into effect in December 1995, food business operators in all member states of the European Union are obliged to ensure that food safety procedures are "identified, implemented, maintained and reviewed on the basis of principles used to develop the HACCP system" (Article 3, point 2 of the directive).[160] The directive therefore can be considered as a call to all firms operating in the food-processing industry on the territory of the EU

---

[158] ISO is an international abbreviation of International Organization for Standardization derived from the Greek word *isos* meaning "equal" (ISO 2002, p. 2).

[159] For a precise delineation of each of the seven principles, see USDA 1997.

[160] See Official Journal of the European Communities L 175, 19/07/1993 pp. 1–11.

to institute the HACCP system. After coming into force, the above directive was incorporated gradually in the national laws of individual member states of the EU. In Germany, for instance, this happened in August 1997, in Austria in February 1998. In Poland, the requirement to institute a HACCP system was made legally binding for food-business operators on January 1, 2004, when the Law on the Health Condition of Nourishment and Nutrition of May 11, 2001 came into force.[161] The above regulation, however, excludes manufacturers of primary products (raw materials), e.g. sugarbeets from the requirement to introduce the HACCP system but obliges them to adopt and adhere to the principles of GMP and GHP.[162]

Management system standards developed by ISO since 1947 are, in most cases, adopted by firms voluntarily, but they constitute the best-known standards worldwide and within the last few decades have become an international emblem of first-rate quality and environmental management. The most popular and widespread ISO standards belong to the ISO 9000 and ISO 14000 families. Standards from the ISO 9000 family (revised and consolidated in 2000) are generic quality management requirements regarding the manufacturing, distribution and servicing of products. The phrase "quality management" stands here for the organization and implementation of processes or activities aimed at the satisfaction of customer needs and the fulfillment of regulatory requirements applicable to a particular product or service. ISO quality management standards are general rules, guidelines and/or procedures developed to help organizations to systematize the management of various operations and to make it more efficient. The ISO 14000 series of standards refers to environmental management, i.e. the minimization of harmful effects of organizations' activities on the natural environment. Apart from helping firms to organize and coordinate quality and environmental management, the ISO standards require them to strive continually to improve performance in these fields. The satisfaction of customer needs and regulatory requirements, as well as an efficient use of time, money and other resources, underlie the development of individual ISO standards and constitute the main rationale behind their employment (www.iso.org; Zalewski 2002, p. 155).

As in the case of HACCP, a company that adopts a system of procedures in conformity with a given ISO norm, and provides its employees with appropriate training, can apply for an ISO-certification, which is granted for a period of 3 years by a competent auditing body. If a given ISO standard has been adopted by an organization as part of the regulatory-framework in a particular country, a conformity assessment is usually conducted on the behalf of a regulatory author-

[161] See Journal of Laws (2001) No. 63, item 634, article 30, point 2; amended by a regulation passed on July 24, 2002 and published in Journal of Laws (2002) No. 135, item 1145, article 1, point 14, letter a, as well as by a regulation passed on October 30, 2003 and published in Journal of Laws (2003) No. 208, item 2020, article 1, subsection 24.

[162] See Journal of Laws (2003) No. 208, item 2020, article 1, subsection 24.

ity. In a situation where a firm implements an ISO standard voluntarily, a conformity assessment is carried out by an auditing body at the request of the firm in order to increase its trustworthiness among trading partners and customers (ISO 2002, pp. 2-12). A certified quality or environmental management system is monitored every six months. After the expiration of the aforementioned three years, another comprehensive audit is carried out in order to test whether the system is still functioning well. In Poland, HACCP and ISO certificates are issued by the Polish Center of Testing and Certification (*Polskie Centrum Badań i Certyfikacji S.A.*), a member of IQNet (The International Certification Network), as well as by several foreign accredited certification bodies operating internationally.[163]

As far as the ISO 9000 family is concerned, the most difficult aspect for companies was until recently the fulfillment of quality management requirements specified in the ISO 9001 norm, since it embraced all processes connected with the design, manufacturing, distribution and servicing of a product. ISO 9002 comprised the manufacturing and distribution processes and the ISO 9003 norm concerned only individual stages of manufacturing (Białasiewicz, op. cit., p. 37). After a thorough revision of standards for quality management conducted by ISO technical committee in 2000, the ISO 9000 series (developed in 1987 and revised only once, in 1994) was replaced by the ISO 9000:2000 series. The 2000 revision brought *inter alia* a reduction in the number of standards and the introduction of explicit requirements for achieving customer satisfaction and continual improvement, specified on the basis of previous findings and taking into account the changing demands of the market. Organizations that were certified to the 1994 versions of ISO 9001, ISO 9002 or ISO 9003 before the release of the revised standards on December 15, 2000, were given a three-year deadline by ISO and IAF (International Accreditation Forum) to migrate to one consolidated standard named ISO 9001:2000. It means that ISO certificates in the 1994 versions lost their accredited status with the IAF and its national accreditation body members on December 15, 2003 (www.iso.org).

There is no doubt that the successful institution and maintenance of a well-functioning HACCP system, as well as the fulfillment of quality management requirements specified in the ISO 9001:2000 norm, increases considerably the competitive position of firms operating in the food-processing industry, including sugar producers. HACCP and ISO 9001:2000 certificates constitute at the present time fundamental credentials that any food processor in the European Union needs to possess in order to compete successfully in the domestic and/or foreign market. Nevertheless, as indicated for example by Białasiewicz (op. cit., p. 11),

---

[163] These certification bodies include the British Standards Institution (BSI), Bureau Veritas Quality International (BVQI), DQS Deutsche Gesellschaft zur Zertifizierung, Germanischer Lloyd Certification GmbH (GLC), KEMA, Lloyd's Register Quality Assurance Ltd, SGS International Certification Services Ltd and TÜV Cert (www.iso.org).

it is not enough to satisfy basic quality standards required by customers and trading partners if one is to be victorious in competition with one's main rivals. This author suggests that companies operating in the food-processing industry should look beyond the established norms and strive to design and manufacture products of higher quality than those offered by the competitors.

The next significant source of competitive advantage in the sugar industry is the assortment of offered products. Until not long ago, most sugar manufacturers in Europe produced only one type of sugar, which was packed and sold in 50 kg and 1 kg bags. Nevertheless, owing to competition between individual sugar companies, technological progress and the increasing demands of the market, a lot has changed with regard to this issue over the last 15-20 years. Apart from refined sugar of various crystal sizes (fine and extra fine sugar), households are today also offered different types of gelling and preserving sugars, used in the preparation of jams and jellies. There are also white and brown sugar cubes as well as candy sugars intended especially for tea and coffee; sanding and powdered sugar for the decoration of desserts, cakes, etc. Firms that use sugar as a raw material for the production of other products can also choose between different types of the commodity (granulated sugar of various crystal sizes, various sugar syrups, fondants, glutens, etc.). Moreover, it has become common practice to store manufactured sugar in silos instead of bags, which enables sugar companies to provide customers with a flexible packaging service. It should be pointed out, however, that the above developments are, at the time of writing, still at a much more advanced stage in West European countries than in Central and Eastern Europe. Whereas in Germany, France and/or the United Kingdom, for example, all sugar factories have been storing their sugar in silos for many years, in Poland such facilities have only recently been constructed in a limited number of factories. For many, the expenditure connected with the erection of a modern and sufficiently large silo is simply too great. Similarly, the assortment of products offered by the sugar industry in Poland and other former Soviet-type economies of the region is not as wide as in Western Europe, despite the progress in this area that has taken place here since 1990. Nonetheless, regardless of the main location of operations and the current product range, all sugar manufacturers in Europe are continually making concerted efforts to widen the assortment of products offered and to come up with innovative ideas allowing to gain a competitive advantage over major rivals. While the cost efficiency of production remains the *sine qua non* of competitiveness in the sugar industry, providing customers with a diversified range of prime quality products and ensuring a flexible service (packaging, conditions of payment, timing of deliveries, etc.) is very important if one is to compete successfully in the European sugar market.

Another significant factor influencing the competitiveness of economic units operating in the sugar industry is the management of marketing activities. Marketing is often mistakenly connected only with the advertising and selling of products. In reality, however, it covers a much broader spectrum of tasks undertaken in order to recognize and satisfy customer needs while meeting the goals and supporting the mission of a given company (Kotler/Armstrong 2001, p. 36). The role of marketing managers is to analyze and assess the market potential for a given product, mastermind and implement the optimal combination of the marketing-mix instruments (product attributes, pricing strategy, promotional activities, distribution strategy), and to build and cement profitable relationships with customers, based on superior customer value and satisfaction.[164]

Some may claim that as far as the sugar industry is concerned, marketing, especially the analysis of customer needs and promotion, are not as important as in the case of many other business organizations since sugar constitutes an undifferentiated commodity for which there is a universal and inelastic demand. By the same token, the idea may seems plausible at first that sugar companies should concentrate principally on continual improvement in the cost efficiency of production and quality of offered products with little emphasis placed on marketing. Nonetheless, such an approach is wrong for the reason that efficient marketing management can positively influence sales results even at companies manufacturing basic commodities, such as sugar, flour or rice (Daniels/Radebaugh 2001, p. 560).

It was pointed out earlier in this section that flexibility and innovation increase the competitiveness of sugar producers. We should add at this point that development of innovative products by research and development (R&D) personnel must be always preceded by the identification of latent customer needs and undiscovered gaps in the market. And this is obviously the task of the marketing department. Innovations are born in the R&D laboratories of business organizations, usually as a consequence of signals sent by the marketing people (Hill 2002, p. 532).

In view of persistent surpluses of sugar in a highly competitive sugar market, it is particularly important for sugar companies to make every effort to retain and build long-term relationships with current customers. Of course, attracting new customers is also significant, but keeping the existing ones and cultivating lasting partnerships with them is vital for the success of economic units operating in the sugar industry. The achievement of this objective depends to a great extent on the efficiency of the activities undertaken by marketing managers. Therefore, their role in the creation of the competitive advantage of one sugar company over another should not be underestimated.

Apart from building and maintaining lasting relationships with customers, it is of crucial importance for the competitiveness of beet sugar producers that they establish such relationships with suppliers and other partners forming the sugar supply chain. This chain consists of sugarbeet growers, providers of supplemen-

[164] See for example Kotler/Bliemel 2001, pp. xxxiii-xxxiv, 1-52; Kotler/Armstrong op. cit., p. 14.

tary materials used in sugarbeet processing, sugar manufacturers, distributors, and retailers. As rightly observed by Kotler and Armstrong (op. cit., p. 29), "[many companies] *know that their fortunes rest not only on how well they perform but also on how well their entire supply chain performs against competitors' supply chains.*" For all sugarbeet processors, particularly significant along the supply chain is the relationship they set up with sugarbeet growers. This is due to the fact that the productivity and quality of beet harvest have a decisive impact on the cost efficiency of sugar production. For this reason, sugar producers work in close cooperation with sugarbeet growers during the entire year and support them in their efforts aimed at superior performance, through training, exchange of ideas, professional advice on the techniques of sugarbeet cultivation, etc. The joint commitment of sugar producers and sugarbeet growers to continually increase the productivity and quality of the beet harvest is beneficial for both parties, since the scale of payment for delivered sugarbeets now depends on their sugar content.

Last but not least, it is important to add to the list of major "internal" determinants of competitiveness in the sugar industry the financial and economic situation of sugar companies. The introduction of restructuring activities at sugar factories, especially those of a strategic type, and the financing of core operations both require investment of considerable amounts of financial resources. Apart from expending their own capital, sugar producers usually rely on bank loans in the preparation and implementation of processing campaigns. Wide-ranging and costly restructuring projects are also to a large extent financed with the help of bank borrowings. In this situation, it is vital for sugar companies to maintain a level of liquidity that satisfies the requirements of lenders and facilitates access to external funds. The long-term profitability of operations constitutes a necessary precondition for the achievement of sufficient liquidity to meet the demands of creditors and also allows producers to engage in strategic restructuring as well as in R&D activities.

It was mentioned earlier in this subsection that the competitiveness of firms in any industry depends not only on their productive and economic efficiency and on the capabilities they possess, but also on external factors such as the regulatory framework concerning a given branch of the economy, macro-policies, environmental and demographic conditions, social infrastructure etc. Of all these factors, the regulation of the sugar market in individual European countries, both EU and non-EU members, has had the greatest influence on the competitiveness of local sugar producers.

Since 1968, the European Union's common organization of the markets in the sugar sector has been enabling beet sugar manufacturers and sugarbeet growers operating in the EU to generate stable profits from their operations despite the considerably higher production costs of beet sugar compared to the production costs of cane sugar, and despite persistent surpluses of sugar on the world market.

Shortly after the transition to a market economy in the beginning of the 1990s, central and east European countries started to gradually introduce policy measures aimed at the regulation of their domestic sugar markets in a much the same way as happened in the EU. As we learned in section 9, a comprehensive regulation of the sugar market in Poland was instituted in 1995 when the Sugar Law of August 26, 1994 came into effect. Unfortunately, a number of significant shortcomings in the regulatory framework had the effect that surpluses of sugar on the domestic market rose in the following years and the market price of sugar was only slightly higher (and sometimes even lower) that the costs of its production. Due to this state of affairs, virtually every sugar producer in Poland found itself in serious financial and economic straits throughout the 1996-2003 time period. The regulation of the sugar market in the EU and the evolution of such regulation in Poland provide a prime illustration of the impact that intervention by national and/or supranational governments can have on the competitive position of economic units.

10.2 Crucial Indicators of Productive Efficiency in the Production of Beet Sugar

It has been specified above that one the fundamental determinants of the competitiveness of economic units is their productive efficiency. Some indicators of productive efficiency in the beet sugar industry were presented already in sections 3 and 4 of this study. It was shown, among other things, that at the end of the 1980s, productivity in the Polish sugar industry, as well as agricultural yields, were much lower than in west European countries. The purpose of this subsection is to determine which changes in which indicators of productive efficiency have the greatest impact on the cost efficiency and competitiveness of sugar producers, and to determine the relative importance of these indicators.

It was shown earlier that the cost efficiency of beet sugar production depends not only on the efficiency of sugarbeet processing at factories but also on the productivity and quality of the sugarbeet harvest. Therefore, in the case of the beet sugar industry, it seems reasonable to divide indicators of productivity and cost efficiency into those connected exclusively with sugarbeet production and those reflecting the efficiency of sugarbeet processing. It is important to mention here that, in general, sugar producers have considerably lesser control over the quality of procured sugarbeets and the productivity of the harvest than over the effectiveness of sugarbeet processing at a plant. Of course, sugar companies provide sugarbeet growers with various advisory services and assistance regarding the appropriate cultivation of sugarbeets, but the extent to which such activities attain the desired results is always uncertain. Their outcome depends on the skills and capabilities of individual farmers and, which cannot be forgotten, on the weather conditions in a given growing season.

The key indicators of the productivity and quality of the beet harvest, and the measures reflecting productivity and cost efficiency of sugarbeet processing, are presented separately in Table 30.

Table 30. Indicators of productivity and cost efficiency in sugarbeet production and processing

Key indicators of productivity in sugarbeet production	Key indicators of productivity and cost efficiency in sugarbeet processing	Mixed indicators
• Polarization of cossettes*** • Sugarbeet yield per hectare**	• Total sugar production during a campaign*** • Duration of a campaign** • Overall sugar losses (in % on beet)** • Recovery of sugar (in %)** • Labor productivity (in tonnes of white sugar per employee)** **Use of supplementary materials**: • Total use of energy (in kWh/t of beet/sugar)*** • Use of coal (in % on beet/sugar)** • Use of el. energy (in kWh/t of beet/sugar)* • Use of coke (in % on beet)* • Use of limestone (in % on beet)* • Use of water (in % on beet)*	• Sugar yield (in % of raw sugar value on beet)*** • Sugar yield per hectare**

*** highly important, ** important, * less important

Source: Analysis by the author.

The third column of Table 30 contains two indices of productivity described as "mixed indicators". These measures reflect the efficiency of both sugarbeet production and sugarbeet processing. A high sugar yield in % of raw sugar value on beet implies a high polarization of cossettes (sugar content in sliced beet roots) and low sugar losses during the technological process of sugarbeet processing in a given campaign. Nonetheless, in order to assess to what extent a high sugar yield in % of raw sugar value on beet was the result of good work by the sugarbeet growers (and Mother Nature) and to what extent was it an effect of efficient sugar extraction, a comparison of polarization of cossettes and overall sugar losses is necessary.[165]

[165] If, for instance, the average polarization of cossettes in a given campaign amounted to 15% on beet and the sugar yield in % of raw sugar value on beet amounted to 13%, it means that overall sugar losses during sugarbeet processing totaled 2%. Overall sugar losses can be also assessed by looking at the value of the indicator referred to as the "recovery of sugar". This is calculated by dividing the sugar yield in % of raw sugar value on beet by the polarization of cossettes. In the above example, the recovery of sugar amounts to 86.7%.

As with the sugar yield in % of raw sugar value on beet, the sugar yield per hectare reflects productive efficiency in sugarbeet production and, to a lesser extent, sugarbeet processing. As was mentioned already in section 3, it is calculated as a quotient of total sugar production and sugarbeet-harvested area. A high sugar yield per hectare indicates a high sugarbeet yield per hectare, high polarization and efficient processing.

Apart from the indicators of productivity and cost efficiency listed in Table 30, measures such as the average distance between a sugar factory and its beet-procurement area, total beet-procurement area, and total number of sugarbeet growers also constitute significant points of reference in the evaluation of the cost efficiency of sugar production at a given location. The first of these three measures is taken particularly often into account in such an analysis. This is because the transport and storage of sugarbeets are quite costly and the reduction to a minimum of the average distance between a sugar factory and the raw material base is of particular interest for any sugar producer.

The number of stars placed next to each indicator included in Table 30 signifies the relative importance of the value of the indicator for the cost efficiency of beet sugar production. Individual indices were weighted in this way on the basis of analyses conducted in section 4 of the present study, with special consideration given to the structure of costs in the production of one tonne of beet sugar in Poland in the marketing years 1997/98-2003/04. Furthermore, the theoretical discussion in section 4.3 was taken into account, concerning the relationship between the size of a sugar factory and the economic efficiency of beet sugar production.

In order to evaluate the efficiency of sugarbeet production and processing at a given sugar factory (and its raw material base), one could look solely at the most significant indicators of productivity: polarization of cossettes; total sugar production during a campaign; use of energy (per one tonne of manufactured sugar); sugar yield in % of raw sugar value on beet. This also allows one to easily calculate the overall sugar losses and the recovery of sugar. Nevertheless, such an analysis would provide an oversimplified and inexact picture of the actual efficiency of production at a particular plant. Much more informative would be a study comprising, apart from the above key measures, the length of a campaign, labor productivity, and the sugar yield per hectare. The inclusion of the remaining indicators of productive efficiency in the analysis (sugarbeet yield per hectare and use of other supplementary materials) would allow a more precise identification of the sources of efficiency and inefficiency. For, clearly, in any investigation aiming to assess the efficiency of a particular sugar producer, the more indicators of productivity taken into account which have a considerable impact on the cost efficiency of sugar production, the more instructive will be the findings of the investigation.

11 Privatization and the Determinants of Enterprise Restructuring

The major challenges facing the sugar industry in Poland after the country's transition to a market economy in 1990 can be inferred to a large extent from the contents of the first few sections of the present study. It is clear that what was sorely needed was improvement in the overall competitiveness of the local sugar sector, through comprehensive restructuring. In the previous section, the major determinants of competitiveness and productive efficiency in the sugar industry were identified. This, together with the description of characteristics of the sugar industry in Poland at the time of the country's jump to a market economy (chapter 3) reveals in how many areas the economic transition enforced far-reaching changes. A significant improvement in competitiveness of the local sugar industry required, above all, the consolidation of a large number of small sugar factories dispersed throughout the country and the concentration of sugar production in areas where the conditions for sugarbeet growing and processing are, from the point of view of economics, most favorable. Another urgent need was that action be taken to improve the productivity and quality of the sugarbeet harvest and to increase the average size of sugarbeet plantations. Other significant tasks included the thorough modernization of selected factories, an increase in productivity and the improvement of environmental safeguards. In short, the Polish sugar sector needed a comprehensive restructuring. The measure supposed to ensure a swift and effective implementation of this process was the privatization of sugar factories.

The aim of this section is to precisely define the terms "privatization" and "enterprise restructuring" with reference to economic literature, and to pinpoint the actual goals of these undertakings. Another issue analyzed here are the various types and methods of measurement of microeconomic restructuring.

11.1 Privatization of State-owned Enterprises in Poland: Objectives and Methods

EBRD (1999, p. 92) defines privatization as a transfer of economic assets and activity from the state into private ownership. In the economic literature, privatization of state-owned enterprises is often called "privatization from above" since it requires state activism. The contribution to the development of the private sector through the emergence of *de novo* firms is referred to as "privatization from below".[166] Ownership transformations in the sugar industry in Poland fall into

[166] See, for example, PWE 1998, p. 164; Winiecki 2001, p. 8, Wagener 1997, p. 1; Wagener et al. 2000, pp. 3-4, Bałtowski 2002a, p. 17.

the first category, and virtually all issues discussed here relate to the privatization and restructuring of already existing companies.

11.1.1 The Goals of Privatization from Above

Generally, the goals of privatization can be divided into macroeconomic and microeconomic ones. The main macroeconomic objective of privatization includes change of ownership structure in the economy from a monopolistic market structure into a highly competitive one. The major microeconomic goal of privatization is the improvement in the productive efficiency and competitiveness of enterprises through their thorough-going restructuring.[167]

Considering privatization in its broader sense, Surdykowska (1997, pp. 14-17), Bałtowski (1998, p. 33), Savas (2000, p. 119) and Olesiński (2000, p. 46) point out that it should additionally:

- Reduce the role of government in the economy
- Reduce the cost of government
- Generate revenues, both by selling assets and then by collecting taxes from them
- Reinforce competition
- Promote the development of capital markets in transition economies
- Accelerate economic development
- Attract new domestic and foreign investors (capital inflow)
- Improve the quality of goods and services
- Increase customer orientation

Although all the objectives listed above are significant, the microeconomic goal of privatization is of primary importance given the purpose of this study and the methodology used in its empirical section.

The goals of privatization and the rationale behind this process are dealt with also in theories concerning ownership structure and private property rights. Two economic doctrines that emerged in the second half of the twentieth century play dominant roles at the present time in relation to these issues. The first, an intellectual formation called *property rights school*, established in the 1970s, proclaims a firm advocacy of individual ownership and entrepreneurship. According to this theory, among the various forms of ownership creating different economic incentives and motives, private property brings about the most effective behavior of firms (Bałtowski 1998, p. 17). The second important contribution to the economic theory regarding ownership structure is the *public choice theory*. It says that "*Privatization, which liberates an enterprise from the burden of political involve-*

[167] See for example Wagener 1994, pp. 13-16; Marinov et al. 1998, p. 29; Bałtowski 1998, pp. 33-38; Olesiński 2000, p. 46; Bałtowski 2002a, p. 27.

ment and economic guidelines that are not in compliance with market principles, reduces the capacity of politicians to influence the activity of enterprises in a way that would serve their own purposes or reflect the demands of pressure groups at the cost of economic efficiency, streamlines the economic purposes of enterprises and improves their operational effectiveness" (Tittenbrun 1995, p.84).[168]

According to Bałtowski and Mickiewicz (2000, p. 434), the liberation of state enterprises from political influence constitutes a prerequisite for all other potential benefits of privatization, such as better management, innovation and increased productivity. Analyzing the property rights structure in post-communist countries, Welfens and Jasiński (1994, p. 109) conclude after reviewing several works of Staniszkis, Hayek and Mises that fragmented private property is of crucial importance since it constitutes "an institution that makes the market work". They describe real socialism as a situation where "economics is abolished, and everything becomes politics" (ibid., p. 102), which is an accurate recapitulation of the facts and developments presented in section 3 of the present study. Moreover, these authors indicate that private property guarantees the most efficient allocation of resources, and describe a system that is not based on private ownership as destitute of initiative and responsibility (ibid., p. 109).[169] While underlining the superiority of private ownership and the necessity of privatization in transition economies, virtually all pro-market economists point at the same time to competition as another vital factor leading to innovation and to the improvement in economic efficiency.[170] Lavigne (1999, p. 163), for example, claims that privatization will yield the expected results, in terms of allocative efficiency, only if it is complemented by the existence of a market environment characterized by the interaction of many buyers and sellers.

11.1.2 Delineation of Selected Privatization Paths

The Privatization Law passed on July 13, 1990 constituted the main legal basis for the transfer of enterprises from state to private ownership in Poland.[171] In the following years, a multi-track approach was taken to privatization in this country, including *indirect privatization* (capital privatization, mass privatization program, bank-led restructuring, increase of capital) and *direct privatization* (leasing of a company's assets to a new company set up by its employees; sale of company's assets to a domestic or foreign investor, following the formal announcement of

[168] The above quotation comes from Bałtowski and Mickiewicz 2000, pp. 433-434, where its original version (in Polish) has been translated into English.

[169] The same view is presented *inter alia* by Moore 1992, p. 118; Sachs 1993, p. 29 and Machan 2002, pp. 4-5.

[170] See for example Welfens and Jasiński 1994, p. 66; Wagener 1997, pp. 2-3; Lavigne 1999, p. 163.

[171] See Journal of Laws (1990) No. 51, item 298, with subsequent amendments.

bankruptcy; use of a company's assets as a contribution in kind to the initial capital of a joint venture company set up by the Treasury and a private investor; genuine liquidation).[172]

In the following part of the present subsection, the capital privatization of a company and the leasing of a company's assets to a new company set up by its employees are described in detail, since these two privatization methods played the key role in the privatization process of the sugar industry in Poland.

11.1.2.1 Indirect Privatization (Capital Method)

Indirect privatization (capital method) in Poland has its origin in the Act of Commercialization and Privatization of State Enterprises of August 30, 1996. It can be considered a new version and extension of the Privatization Law of July 13, 1990.[173] In the first phase of privatization of a state-owned enterprise with the capital method, the enterprise is transformed by the Minister of State Treasury into a joint-stock company or a limited-liability company. This process, called "commercialization" or "corporatization", is initiated at the request of the enterprise itself, its founding organ or on the initiative of the Minister of State Treasury. 100% of shares in the 'new' company are held initially by the State Treasury, which is represented at the General Assembly of Shareholders by the Minister of State Treasury. The operations of the company are administered by a management board consisting either of executives 'inherited' from the transformed state-owned enterprise or of new natural persons appointed as a result of a competition organized by the Ministry of State Treasury. According to the provisions of the Act of Commercialization and Privatization of State-Owned Enterprises of August 1996, the director of a commercialized state-owned enterprise shall be appointed as the president of the first management board of the company established as a result of commercialization, unless he does not agree to hold such an office.[174] In such a situation, a natural person may be commissioned by the company to perform managerial duties on a one-man board of management.[175] The activities of a joint-stock company and the decisions of its management are inspected and appraised by a supervisory board consisting of five

[172] For a short description of each type of all aforementioned privatization methods, see Bałtowski/Mickiewicz 2000, pp. 436-441.

[173] Journal of Laws (1996) No. 118, item 561, with subsequent amendments. The Act of Commercialization and Privatization of State Enterprises came into effect on April 8, 1997 and replaced at the same time the Privatization Law of July 13, 1990.

[174] See Journal of Laws (2002) No. 171, item 1397, article 6, point 2.

[175] According to article 17, point 2 of the Act on Commercialization and Privatization of State-Owned Enterprises, this person shall be selected in a competition carried out by the supervisory board. The General Assembly of Shareholders decides as to the conduct of the competition.

persons including two employees' representatives. In the case of commercialization of an enterprise in the agricultural or food industry, farmers (or fisherman) shall have one representative on the supervisory board. It is not necessary to appoint a supervisory board at a limited liability company established as a result of commercialization of a state-owned enterprise. The Minister of State Treasury or a person appointed by him performs the supervision of the company's activities.[176]

The shares of companies transformed in accordance with procedures described above may be sold to potential investors by the Minister of State Treasury. The sale may take the following forms:

- Public offering
- Public tender
- Negotiations started on the basis of a public invitation
- Acceptance of the offer by the entity issuing the announcement

In the following part of this subsection, the sale of a company's shares through negotiations based on public invitation is briefly delineated, since this procedure was applied widely in the privatization process of the sugar industry in Poland. In general, the method was used in the privatization of medium and large companies whose controlling stakes were to be sold to qualified domestic or foreign investors.

The privatization of a commercialized state-owned enterprise according to the formula under consideration begins with the invitation of potential investors to enter negotiations, through an advertisement published in the national press. The announcement is made by the Minister of State Treasury. Before this takes place, the Minister orders a comprehensive analysis of the enterprise's situation and often of the entire sector in which the company operates.

In addition, a contract is signed between the Ministry of State Treasury and an advisor required to help in negotiations with potential buyers.[177] The number of shares to be sold, their price, and the terms of payment, constitute the principal subject of such negotiations. An important part of negotiations and a significant factor by the final choice of investor are the so-called *privatization packages*. An *investment package*, for instance, comprises investment commitments that a strategic investor is required to satisfy over a specified period of time following privatization. In many cases, it is not only determined how much money the investor is supposed to invest, but also quite often on exactly what kind of investment projects the investor should concentrate in the future, e.g. replacement or modernization of a particular piece of equipment. Apart from the investment package, a *social package* is also negotiated. It includes an obligation on the part

[176] Journal of Laws (2002) No. 171, item 1397, article 11, points 1 and 2.

[177] Domestic and foreign advisory companies, as well as law firms, have been usually appointed for this purpose (See http://www.mst.gov.pl).

of the investor to keep the employment level at a privatized company unchanged for a period of years (in the case of the sugar industry, usually between 24 and 36 months). Moreover, investors often commit themselves to providing the employees of privatized enterprises with various benefits and services (e.g. a one-off salary bonus for all workers, training, etc.). Sometimes an *environmental package* is negotiated separately or as part of the investment package. It covers investment commitments connected with environmental improvements (Bałtowski 2002a, p. 137). Depending on the industry in which a company operates, other packages are negotiated with potential investors. During the indirect privatization of sugar factories in Poland (capital method) a *sugarbeet-growers package* constituted an inherent and crucial component of any privatization deal. The agreements included guarantees concerning the maintenance of the existing beet-growing area, as well as an obligation on the part of the investors to give preference, in contracting of sugarbeet deliveries, to farmers who had delivered beets to the plant over a period of some years before privatization.

If a large number of prospective investors respond to an invitation of the Minister of State Treasury to enter negotiations regarding privatization of a commercialized state-owned enterprise (or group of enterprises), their number is limited to two or three after examination of submitted offers and preliminary talks. Eventually, one investor is selected with whom the detailed terms and conditions of the privatization deal are settled (including the aforementioned packages).[178]

11.1.2.2 Direct Privatization (Leasing of a Company's Assets to a New Company set up by Its Employees)

This method of privatizing state-owned enterprises, called also *employee leasing* or *leverage employee buy-out*, was most commonly used in Poland since the beginning of the privatization process in the country (Bałtowski 2002a, p. 140). In the first half of the 1990s, several Polish sugar factories were transferred into private hands using this privatization method.[179]

The basic feature of employee leasing is that a state-owned enterprise is given for use against lease payments, mainly to insiders. The ownership of the enterprise is transferred to leaseholders gradually over a period of years. It needs to be emphasized, however, that the privatization method under discussion has been applied primarily to companies in a strong economic situation and having a strong potential for further development and growth. These requirements constitute a kind of safeguard increasing the probability that leaseholders will be able to run

[178] The above depiction of the operation of indirect privatization (capital method) has been put together predominantly on the basis of information provided on the official website of the Polish Ministry of State Treasury (URL: http://www.mst.gov.pl).

[179] For details, see section 13 of the present study.

the privatized enterprise efficiently in the future and meet the terms and conditions of the lease. Other requirements that must be met in order to lease a company from the State Treasury are specified in the Act of Commercialization and Privatization of State-Owned Enterprises of August 30, 1996. Article 51, point 1 of this act stipulates that the leasing of a company to its employees may take place where all of the following conditions are satisfied:

1) more than half of the total number of employees of the state enterprise, or employees and farmers or fishermen respectively, have joined the company
2) the shareholders of the company are only natural persons, unless the Minister competent for the State Treasury permits legal persons to participate in the company
3) the paid up initial capital of the company is no lower than 20% of the amount of the founder's fund and the fund of the enterprise on the day on which the balance sheet for the financial year preceding the issue of the order of direct privatization is drawn up
4) at least 20% of shares have been taken up by persons not employed by the privatized enterprise

The last requirement was not included in the Privatization Law of July 13, 1990. It was introduced in the Act of Commercialization and Privatization of State-Owned Enterprises of August 30, 1996. The reason why legislators decided on such an amendment was that, in most cases, privatization through employee leasing, comprising exclusively insiders, does not guarantee a sufficient influx of capital for investment and innovations at the privatized company. The phrase "persons not employed by the privatized enterprise" in point 4 refers to passive and active outside investors (the latter willing to participate in the management of the enterprise) whose involvement in employee leasing should eliminate the aforementioned weakness of this privatization method.[180]

An agreement about the lease of a state-owned enterprise to its employees (and partly to outside investors) may not exceed 15 years.[181] Nonetheless, the leaseholder and the State Treasury may decide on the transfer of the ownership of the enterprise before the end of the period for which the lease agreement has been concluded. In such a case, the remaining part of the payment due shall be paid in installments. It needs to be mentioned, however, that this is possible only after the leaseholder has made a payment of at least one third of the due amount specified in the lease contract and after the balance sheet and the profit and loss account for the second financial year from the date of conclusion of the contract

[180] See www.mst.gov.pl (Direct privatization paths).

[181] Article 52, point 1 of the Act of Commercialization and Privatization of State-Owned Enterprises of August 30, 1996.

have been approved.[182] According to article 54, point 1 of the Act of Commercialization and Privatization of State-Owned Enterprises of August 30, 1996, the detailed principles regarding the determination of leasing repayments, release from the repayments, as well as the method of securing the unpaid part of the dues (if the ownership of the enterprise was transferred to the leaseholder before the full repayment of the amount specified in the lease contract) shall be determined through a formal ordinance issued by the Council of Ministers.

As was mentioned earlier, the two methods outlined above served as the main formulas in the privatization process of the sugar industry in Poland. Nevertheless, it has to be emphasized that a few sugar factories in the country were privatized through the *increase of capital* and contribution of a factory to a *joint venture* established in cooperation with a foreign investor.[183] These privatization methods were used for sugar factories in a poor financial situation and in urgent need of capital.

11.2 Definitions, Types and Measurement Methods of Enterprise Restructuring

The transition from a planned to a market economy enforced an absolute reorganization in the way enterprises functioned. This might be also the simplest definition of enterprise restructuring but economic literature provides a much more detailed explanation of this complex process and specifies the various elements of which it has been composed, particularly in former Soviet-type economies. Carlin et al. (1995, pp. 427-428) describe restructuring as a process of transforming state-owned firms into "value-maximizing" units. This can be achieved by changing the structure of an enterprise along four axes: "internal organization, employment, output and investment." Further, the authors indicate that restructuring is the opposite of passivity, whereby enterprises do not make any effort to meet the challenges of a changing environment. Since continual changes in the economic environment of firms enforce various adaptive measures, they are considered to be the fundamental motive for enterprise restructuring.[184] A thorough acquaintance with the external factors influencing the competitive position of firms in a particular industry is therefore a prerequisite for the effectiveness and soundness of any decision regarding restructuring activities. It is thus decisive as regards the efficiency of management and, consequently, the success or failure of firms. Restructuring is aimed at ensuring the survival of an

182 See Article 52, points 3 and 4 of the Act of Commercialization and Privatization of State-Owned Enterprises of August 30, 1996.
183 For details, see section 13 of the present study.
184 See for example Suszyński 2003, p. 20.

enterprise in a competitive market and at providing solid foundations for long-term development and growth (Suszyński 2003, p. 62).

In the economic literature, a division into two basic types of microeconomic restructuring has been established: *reactive* and *strategic* restructuring.[185] *Reactive restructuring* involves short-term improvement in cost competitiveness without major investments in plant and equipment.[186] This might include minor adjustments to the production process, e.g. closing particular product lines, changing the product mix, downsizing, selling dilapidated machines or even entire plants, usage of cheaper or higher quality inputs, disposal of non-productive assets, better organization of work, reorganization of management, search for new markets for existing products etc.[187] Reactive restructuring is usually a response to an enterprise's long-standing economic troubles. It is supposed to bring about a recovery from a crisis and, in many cases, prevent the bankruptcy of an enterprise.

Strategic restructuring, often also described in the literature as "deep" or "growth-driven", involves a forward-looking strategic orientation. It is considered to be fundamental to the growth of firms and requires considerable financial resources. Investments in new technologies, development of new products, upgrading of the existing ones and introduction of structural and organizational changes are characteristic of this type of restructuring.[188] Other deep restructuring activities include developments in the areas of financial control, marketing and sales, quality control and information systems (Estrin et al., op. cit, p. xx). It is generally accepted that strategic restructuring plays a key role in a firm's adaptation to the market economy and in the gaining of a strong competitive position on the market.[189]

In contrast to reactive restructuring, the introduction and implementation of strategic restructuring requires specialist know-how and a deliberate business strategy. Obviously, this type of restructuring is more difficult than reactive restructuring and takes much longer. At the same time, it needs to be emphasized that reactive restructuring does not have to be considered as a prerequisite to more complicated strategic restructuring. Each of these restructuring types has a different function and they can be carried out simultaneously (Grosfeld/Roland 1995, p. 8).

---

185 See Grosfeld/Roland 1995, pp. 6-7; Roland 2000, p. 234; Bornstein 2001, p. 189.

186 Reactive restructuring is also often referred to as "defensive", "shallow" or "survival-driven" (See for example Ernst et al. p. 294; Carlin/Landesmann 1997, p. 78; Commander et al. 1999, p. 6; Lipowski 2001, pp. 54-55; Domadenik et al. 2002, pp. 4-5).

187 See Estrin et al. 1995, p. xx; Grosfeld/Roland 1995, pp. 6-7; Commander et al. 1999, p. 6; Lipowski 2001, p. 55, Meyer 2002, p. 11

188 See EBRD 1999, p.141, Suszyński 2003, p. 126.

189 See for example Meyer 1998a, pp.12-13; Suszyński 2003, pp. 125-127; Lipowski 2001, p. 55.

Another important division of restructuring activities, widespread in the economic literature and differing from that described above, is the distinction between *operational*, *organizational* and *financial* restructuring.[190] This division is based on the main three areas of change linked with the thorough restructuring of enterprises in transition economies. *Operational restructuring* includes a wide area of rearrangements in the core activity of a company. It is characterized by the adjustment of virtually all the resources of an enterprise to changes in the environment and to the requirements of the market. Reduction in costs and improvement in the quality of offered products constitute the principal purpose of this type of restructuring. Examples of operational restructuring include the new definition of the scale and scope of operations, improvements in labor productivity as well as the enhancement of the quality and variety of products, which is usually accompanied by changes in the technological base and the introduction of innovations in the production process. Such alterations necessitate the institution of a wide range of supplementary activities, connected particularly with the training of employees. The cessation of production of non-profitable commodities, the reduction of vertical integration through outsourcing and changes in the areas of marketing and distribution are also typical for operational restructuring, which covers the greatest span of activities from all thee types of restructuring described here (Suszyński 2003, p. 126). The aim of *organizational restructuring* is to adapt the organizational structures and procedures within an enterprise to the strategy specified by the enterprise (ibid., p. 152).[191] It includes changes concerning the number of departments, forms of organization, ways of communicating, allocation of responsibilities, etc. Referring to the strict hierarchy at state-owned enterprises under socialism, Meyer (1998a, pp. 12-13) points out to the necessity to redefine relations and interactions between individuals within an enterprise in the direction of a flatter organizational structure. Another crucial part of organizational restructuring emphasized *inter alia* by this author is the introduction of new managerial techniques, together with the selection of managers who can utilize them and run a firm efficiently. An important task of organizational restructuring, especially in transition economies, is the development of state-of-the-art information systems allowing for the convenient storage, processing and transmission of data relevant to strategic decision-making (Suszyński op. cit., p. 157). *Financial restructuring* is concentrated on the improvement in the financial and economic condition as well as long-term viability of an enterprise. The major tasks of this type of restructuring in transition economies include reduction in the level of indebtedness, maintenance of liquidity and constant

---

190 See for example Suszyński 2003, p. 126; Marinov et al. 1998, p. 33. Suszyński (ibid., p.126) uses a division into *operational* and *financial* restructuring and classifies *organizational* restructuring as an element of the former.

191 The above definition refers to a classic theory formulated by Chandler (1962), according to which the structure of an enterprise follows its strategy.

enhancement of shareholder value (ibid., p. 160). Strategies used to meet the above objectives encompass increase of capital, reduction in costs, introduction of a strict budgetary control and discipline, and reorientation of financial management towards cost and profit analysis. Other examples of financial restructuring include rationalization in the use of company's assets (asset engineering) and in the sourcing of finance.

Given the above division of enterprise restructuring into reactive and strategic restructuring, as well as into operational, organizational and financial restructuring, it is noteworthy that activities connected with, for example, organizational restructuring can also be classified as reactive or strategic restructuring (ibid., p. 191). It should also be mentioned that many authors underline the timelessness of the restructuring process. Pohl et al. (1997, p.1), for instance, claim that "*Firms in all countries must continuously restructure to maintain profitability in the face of a changing economic environment, technological progress, and competition from other firms*".[192] Moreover, both theorists and practitioners dealing with enterprise restructuring suggest that it is today becoming increasingly important that firms do not restrict their restructuring activities merely to responses to changes in their environment. It is equally important that managers of enterprises in all industries identify future trends beforehand so that a company's ability to adapt is greater than the speed of changes (Roland Berger Strategy Consultants 2002).[193]

An interesting and important issue discussed in numerous studies is the problem of which should come first: privatization or restructuring. It is generally accepted that some pre-privatization restructuring is advisable and can produce positive results in terms of economic transformation. Pełka (1994, p.34), for example, rightly claims that restructuring before privatization increases the attractiveness of an enterprise for potential investors. Nevertheless, there are numerous studies which demonstrate that due to the lack of sufficient capital and managerial expertise in former Soviet-type economies, the scope of restructuring activities prior to privatization is mostly limited to reactive restructuring. Megyery and Sader (1996, p. 30) postulate that before privatization, governments should focus on activities like labor force reduction and the shedding of liabilities, but investments in the modernization or expansion of existing facilities should be left to the new owners of privatized enterprises. Nevertheless, in this case also it depends greatly on the managerial know-how of private investors and their access to financial resources if privatization is to be followed by the introduction of much-needed strategic restructuring.

Many authors claim that privatization constitutes a particular form of restructuring, with the fundamental aim of finding an owner who will take the responsi-

---

192 See also OECD 2002, p. 9

193 See also Skawińska 2002, p. 7, pp. 66-67; Suszyński 2003, pp. 23-24.

bility for activities leading to the proper development of an enterprise. Meyer (1998b, p. 17) says directly that "*The major, if not the main task of microeconomic restructuring is the transfer of enterprises from state ownership to private ownership*". It should create a stimulus for managers of privatized companies to undertake strategic restructuring followed by the increase in productive efficiency and competitiveness. Suszyński (op. cit., p. 127) and Lipowski (op. cit., p. 54) consider privatization as the main form of "ownership restructuring", connected with fundamental changes in the ownership structure and control at a given enterprise. Both authors place ownership restructuring on the same level as operational, organizational and financial restructuring.

The measurement of enterprise restructuring takes various forms in empirical studies. Djankov and Murrell (2000, p.4) distinguish between *quantitative* and *qualitative* indicators of microeconomic restructuring. The former are based on accounting information and measure actual enterprise performance with respect to productivity and profitability. A typical feature of quantitative research is that it tests cause-and-effect relationships and expresses these relationships with numbers (White 2000, p. 46; Rudestam and Newton 2001, p. 27). Qualitative indicators, on the other hand, show, for example, whether a given firm has introduced organizational changes, new products, new marketing expertise, etc. Such descriptive information is mostly obtained from surveys or questionnaires completed with the help of the managerial staff of firms. Its meaningfulness with regard to the investigation of restructuring efficiency is thus rather low. Djankov and Murrell (op. cit., p. 4) point to quantitative indices (numerical data) as being prevalent in economic research and that "measure directly the prime objective of enterprise restructuring—the improvement in economic performance". Whereas qualitative studies concentrate on the description and discovery of a phenomenon, quantitative research focuses on hypothesis testing and verification (Rudestam and Newton, op. cit., p. 36). Quite often, qualitative and quantitative research techniques are combined. The use of a variety of research methods in scientific research is termed *method triangulation*. As indicated by White (2000, op. cit., pp. 66-67), such an approach allows one to look at a given problem from a number of perspectives and facilitates the understanding and accurate interpretation of obtained results. It needs to be mentioned at this point, however, that both quantitative and qualitative studies examining the effectiveness of restructuring must be preceded by a scrupulous analysis of the factors which have a decisive impact on the competitiveness of organizations operating in a particular industry. If, for example, the costs of production constitute one of the key success factors in a given industry, a common practice in a mixed research is the collection of qualitative information about what has been done over a specified period of time in order to reduce these costs at a given enterprise. At the same time, the most important statistically recordable measures of productivity are identified and weighted according to their relative importance for production costs. Finally, it is analyzed how they have changing during the same time period. This relates also to all other measurable variables which influence to a large extent the competitiveness of an organization. As far as variables reflecting the economic performance of firms are concerned, more or less standardized scales are used regardless of the type of industry under investigation. Many authors emphasize that examination and assessment of restructuring efficiency through the comparison of selected quantitative variables at a given enterprise (or group of enterprises) should comprise a period of several years.[194] An investigation of post-privatization restructuring effectiveness should indicate the value of selected variables, reflecting productivity and economic efficiency, shortly before the privatization of an enterprise, at the time of its privatization, and at least three years after the ownership transformation (Bałtowski 2002b, p. 52). The number of analyzed variables may vary depending on the scope of the research and the availability of data.

Apart from restructuring, there are also several other approaches to the introduction of changes within an enterprise. One of these alternative ways of reorganizing the operations of a firm is called *reengineering* or *business process reengineering*.[195] Like restructuring, the goal of reengineering is substantial improvement in productivity, quality of products, competitiveness and shareholder value. Nevertheless, firms using reengineering as a method of solving problems start with a blank sheet of paper, rethink existing business processes, and transform them radically in order to ensure the achievement of these objectives (Hammer 1990, pp. 104-105, Chen 1999, pp. 187-188, Smart et al. 1999, p. 288). The aim of restructuring is, in contrast, a gradual repair of individual operational areas and not the starting of everything from scratch. Reengineering begins with the formulation of the mission of an enterprise. Subsequently, the key problems in existing processes are identified and then innovative solutions and breakthrough concepts are introduced, completely changing the way things were done before (Malhotra 1998; Chen, op. cit., pp. 188-189). Hence, reengineering is often referred to as a radical redesign and reinventing of an enterprise as a whole with the purpose of a significant improvement in performance measures such as productivity, cycle times, and quality.[196] The reengineering process embraces organizational structure and operations, as well as the value system of an organization. All these aspects are thoroughly rearranged, with great emphasis being placed on customer needs.

There are a large number of management tools that can be used as part of or in combination with restructuring. As indicated by Suszyński (op. cit., p. 63), re-

---

194 See for example Bałtowski 2002b, p. 52.

195 The concept of *reengineering* was first introduced by Hammer (1990), and by Davenport and Short (1990), and used also by Hammer and Champy (1993).

196 See for example Hammer and Champy 1993; Johansson et al. 1993, p. 15; Schnetzer 1999, p. 18.

structuring is a flexible process, open to modern concepts and methods of managing change within an enterprise. The author claims that, in many cases, such methods have been developed as an alternative to restructuring, but emphasizes at the same time that they can be used constructively as a complement to this process, making it much more efficient.[197] Bain & Company's Management Tool Survey 2003, carried out among senior executives of 708 companies in Europe, Asia, Africa, and North and South America, revealed that there has been a considerable increase in the use of various management tools. According to the report, the average amount of management tools used by companies around the world rose from 10 in the year 2000 to 16 in 2002. The most popular tools, used in 2002 by more than 80% of surveyed firms, included *strategic planning*, *benchmarking* and *mission and vision statements* (Bain & Company 2003, p. 2). Nonetheless, the authors of the above survey underline that the choice of individual management tools should always be adjusted to a given industry and the type of operations in which a company in engaged. As suggested by an executive of one of the organizations surveyed by Bain & Company: "Just because something worked for the next guy doesn't mean it's going to fit right into your business system and culture" (ibid., p. 8). A common approach to management used, for example, by many food and beverage companies is called *total quality management* (TQM).[198] Its main feature is that all units of an enterprise focus on maximum satisfaction of the needs of customers by providing them with products and services of the highest quality. Such continual improvement in the quality of offered products, as well as an unceasing nurturing of customer relationships, combined also with a great importance placed on the reduction in production costs, lie at the heart of TQM. The achievement of certain quality standards and norms by a particular organization is often confirmed by certificates (for example ISO 9000 series, HACCP) issued by authorized institutions. It does not mean, however, that once they possess such certificates firms are entitled to rest on their laurels. TQM represents the eternal search for quality improvements, the elimination and prevention of deficiencies, and the reduction of costs.[199]

---

[197] See also Schnetzer 1999, p. 37.

[198] 57% of companies participating in the aforementioned survey pointed to TQM as one of the management tools they used in 2002.

[199] A comprehensive overview of various management tools and their features can be found on the web site of Bain & Company (URL: http://www.bain.com/management_tools/ home.asp). For a more detailed delineation of TQM, see for example Hradesky 1995, Zink 1997 or Suszyński 2003, pp. 54-57.

11.3 Social Aspects of Industrial Restructuring in Transition Economies

As in all post-communist countries, the restructuring process of state-owned companies in Poland after the country's transition to a market economy has constituted a knotty and sensitive socio-political problem. The abolition of central planning, the introduction of market principles, and the hardening of budget constraints enforced a gradual rise in labor productivity, achieved mainly by means of bringing employment levels at overstaffed industrial enterprises to realistic dimensions. The exposure of economic activity to market forces and the implementation of strict budgetary discipline resulted in the liquidation of many enterprises. Economic and political transformation also initiated a slow-moving process of shifting production and employment from heavy industry and agriculture to light industry and the services sector. This was brought about by substantial changes on both the demand and the supply side. The end of artificial 'labor hoarding', known since the socialist times, the continuous increase in productivity, and structural changes leading to a substantial reallocation of labor had the effect that a large number of people became unemployed. In a lot of cases, this was particularly prevalent in areas where the conditions for finding alternative employment were highly unfavorable. All these developments were accompanied by the ever-increasing privatization of state-owned enterprises. Therefore, many started to express the view that privatization constitutes the main source of the social costs of economic transformation, since it leads inevitably to redundancies and, consequently, to unemployment. One of the most expressive responses to this assertion has been formulated by Balcerowicz (1998, p. 185), who points out that while it is always possible to find several cases where privatization led to a considerable reduction in the workforce, the statement that privatization leads to unemployment is an extreme generalization. The author recommends that one see the whole picture and, instead of comparing current employment with its earlier levels, advises the comparison with the employment levels that would exist if privatization had not occurred after Poland's changeover to a market economy. Using the same line of argument, the authors of the World Investment Report 2000 indicate that a reduction in employment following the privatization of an enterprise does not constitute a loss for the economy if the enterprise was in difficulties and would have gone bankrupt in the absence of privatization (UNCTAD 2000, p.183). It is thus unfounded to claim that the social costs of restructuring in former socialist countries are a consequence of privatization. The problem of rising unemployment should be considered rather as a price that has had to be paid for many years of inefficient 'housekeeping', and of serious distortions and misallocation of resources under central planning. As indicated by Bałtowski (1998, p. 38), the social costs of transformation should be seen primarily as the costs of learning to operate in an economic system based on private property, economic freedom and competition.

Regardless of the above considerations, it is evident that undesirable social effects of transition to market economy do exist and pose one the greatest problems connected with this process. The elimination of excess employment levels at industrial enterprises constitutes a major challenge in any restructuring program in the former Soviet-type economies. Unfortunately, this also means that enterprise restructuring is often regarded by employees as something that seriously endangers their jobs and not as a chance for a rapid increase in competitiveness, allowing for survival in the short run and giving hope for prosperity and growth in the long run (Suszyński op. cit., p. 150). Since the goals of restructuring match more or less those of privatization, an ownership change equally evokes in employees a sense of menace and uncertainty. At the same time, those who firmly oppose the introduction of necessary reforms are often unaware that they do it at their own expense. Due to this fact, it has been of crucial importance to explain carefully, to everyone who is directly concerned, the aims of restructuring, in order to obtain social agreement for changes (ibid., p. 151). Another vital task has been to open employment prospects for those for whom restructuring means a loss one's job (mainly blue-collar workers and people employed in agriculture). As far as the last problem is concerned, one solution is the creation of favorable conditions for the establishment of new places of work in a given country or region, through the reduction in corporate taxes and the introduction of other incentives luring investment and arousing entrepreneurship. Another option is the support of worker mobility from depressed regions to areas where jobs are available. A common practice at enterprises undergoing a thorough restructuring in transition economies has been the allocation of redundancy payments to laid-off workers, allowing for professional requalification, and facilitating the search for a new occupation. It needs to be added at this point, however, that the possibility of making such payments has been strongly limited, due to the fact many companies simply could not or cannot afford it. For obvious reasons, employees of enterprises taken over by foreign investors are in a relatively good position with regard to this issue. A similar role is played by unemployment benefits paid by the government to displaced workers for a fixed period of time. Nevertheless, even if such compensations are spent entirely on retraining and re-education, the likelihood for redundant workers of finding new jobs, especially if they are middle-aged, is still low. As indicated by Hare (2003, p. 13): "*A 45-year old steelworker, for example, will often find the process of adapting to new types of employment practically impossible, and many simply never make it. Thus the retraining of such workers is not only costly, but quite often inefficient*".

Undoubtedly, all the aforementioned policy interventions and initiatives combined together contribute greatly to the reduction in social costs of economic transformation and industrial restructuring. Nevertheless, the case of Polish transition demonstrates that they are insufficient in the arduous combat against rising unemployment in former socialist countries. Apart from using the instruments described above, it is becoming increasingly important, in regions facing massive unemployment, to support various forms of entrepreneurship by non-governmental organizations. As indicated by Hausner (2004, pp. 13-14), what is presently much needed in areas heavily affected by unemployment are not large-scale governmental programs but small social projects aimed at gradually changing the direct environment of those "socially excluded" and awakening in them the spirit of initiative that has been, in many cases, dulled by long-term inactivity.

The most alarming situation exists in regions which were the hubs of the declining industries, and in towns with one large company giving employment to a significant part of the local population. A prime example of enterprises that played such a role in Poland are sugar factories. Most of them are situated in the suburbs of small cities or in country areas. In such cases it is extraordinarily difficult to carry out painful restructuring programs and the process becomes strongly politicized. As was mentioned already in previous sections of the present study, one of the greatest challenges in the restructuring of the sugar industry in Poland has been the consolidation of existing sugar factories through the closure of small, inefficient and/or ill-located plants. Nevertheless, the social aspect of restructuring is one the main reasons why privatization and restructuring of the sugar sector in the country was delayed for a long time. Polish authorities bowed many times to the pressure of various lobbies and hesitated to make economically rational but unpopular decisions. Therefore, the privatization process of the Polish sugar industry has not been completed and the restructuring of this industry branch proceeds sluggishly. Nonetheless, sugarbeet processing at many plants was ceased within the last few years. Some of the remaining ones are gradually being modernized and their processing capacities are expanded slowly but surely.

The hitherto theoretical considerations show clearly that the adaptation of the sugar industry in Poland to the demands of the market economy have posed a considerable restructuring challenge in a number of areas. It is obvious that apart from substantial financial resources (not available domestically), it required a certain know-how. In this situation, the strategy that seemed to ensure swift and effective restructuring of the Polish sugar sector was the privatization of sugar factories to foreign investors.

One of the main goals of the next section is to discuss the potential microeconomic benefits and costs of the privatization of state-owned enterprises to foreigners.

12 Foreign Direct Investment

Before embarking on a thorough analysis of the privatization process of the sugar industry in Poland and an examination and evaluation of the restructuring effectiveness of foreign investors who participated in this undertaking, it is important to clarify the meaning of the term foreign direct investment (FDI) and to show how the possibilities for such an activity have developed in the country under discussion within the last few decades. Moreover, it needs to be explained what prompts firms to move their operations abroad and why do they choose a particular region or country for this purpose. Finally, we will look at the potential microeconomic benefits and costs of privatization-related FDI inflow for the host country.

12.1 What is FDI?

In the World Investment Report 2001, UNCTAD defines FDI as "*an investment involving a long-term relationship and reflecting a lasting interest and control of a resident entity in one economy in an enterprise resident in an economy other than that of the foreign direct investor*" (UNCTAD 2001, p. 275). Furthermore, it is assumed that the foreign investor "*exerts a significant degree of influence on the management of the enterprise resident in the other economy*", and that the investment "*involves both the initial transaction between the two entities and all subsequent transactions between them and among foreign affiliates*". Finally, UNCTAD points out that FDI "*may be undertaken by individuals as well as business entities*" (ibid., p. 275).

The International Monetary Fund provides a similar definition in its Balance of Payments Manual, saying that "*FDI is an investment made with the objective of obtaining a lasting interest in an enterprise operating in an economy other than that of the investor, the investor's purpose being to have a significant degree of influence on the management of the enterprise*" (IMF 1993, p. 86).

The expressions "long-term relationship" and "lasting interest" help to distinguish FDI from foreign portfolio investment (FPI). FPI is an investment made by individuals, firms or public bodies in foreign financial instruments, e.g. government bonds or foreign stocks (Hill 2002, p. 182).

A firm undertaking FDI becomes a *multinational corporation* (MNC), often also called a *transnational corporation* (TNC). An equity participation of 10% is regarded by both IMF and UNCTAD as a threshold to qualify an investment as FDI and to distinguish it from portfolio investment. Similarly, according to the U.S. Department of Commerce, FDI occurs "*when a US citizen, organization or affiliated group takes an interest of 10% or more in a foreign business entity*" (ibid., p. 182).

Among various classifications of FDI, the most significant one is the division into *horizontal* and *vertical* FDI. Horizontal FDI is undertaken to produce (and sell) the same or similar kinds of goods abroad (in the host country) as in the home country. Vertical FDI can take two forms. A *backward vertical* FDI is an investment in an industry that provides low-cost inputs for a firm's domestic production processes. *Forward vertical* FDI, on the other hand, is undertaken in an industry abroad that sells the outputs of a firm's domestic production (ibid., p. 197; Moosa 2002, p. 4; Navaretti et al., 2002, p. 14).

There are three types of FDI: *greenfield investment, cross-border mergers and acquisitions (M&As)*, and *joint ventures*. Greenfield investment takes place when a company establishes a completely new production, distribution or other form of activity in a foreign country, using primarily its own resources. FDI may occur also through the acquisition of, or merger with, an existing firm in the host country. Meyer and Estrin (1998c, p. 3) isolate a special form of acquisition which they call *brownfield investment*. The authors use this term with reference to an acquisition that is followed by reconstruction and/or extensive renovation of a plant, the replacement of most pieces of machinery, rebuilding of infrastructure, far-reaching changes in the organizational structure, reorganization of work, etc. The vast majority of cross-border M&As are acquisitions, with mergers contributing to only a few percent of all M&As worldwide.[200]

FDI can also take the form of a joint venture with an existing firm in the host country or with another company that is foreign to the host country (Moosa op. cit., p. 16).

12.2 Development of Possibilities for FDI in Poland

After the end of World War II, FDI in Poland was practically impossible. The communist regime allowed only exceptionally for joint investment projects with enterprises from the COMECON countries.[201] A hugely unfavorable environment regarding FDI inflows and the autarkical policy adopted by the communist leaders accounted for the lack of interest among foreigners in doing business in Poland and other states from the central and east European region. Nonetheless, increasing foreign debt and the deepening economic crisis in Poland in the middle of the 1970s prompted the local authorities of the time to introduce regulations encouraging FDI inflow to the country. Two ordinances issued by the Council of Ministers on February 6[202] and May 14[203], 1976 initiated the regulation of foreign

[200] See for example UNCTAD 2000, p. 99.

[201] Council for Mutual Economic Assistance (COMECON or CMEA) constituted a trading system established in 1950 between countries of the Eastern bloc to intensify activities aimed at the development of a Soviet military-industrial complex.

[202] Journal of Laws (1976) No. 11, item 63, with subsequent amendments.

[203] Journal of Laws (1976) No. 19, item 123, with subsequent amendments.

business activity in Poland. Although the new legislation made possible selected types of direct investment, it did not guarantee sufficient property rights protection for foreign investors and required them to go through a number of cumbersome and costly procedures in order to even set foot on Polish ground. Consequently, the reluctance of potential investors to enter the Polish market remained unchanged over the following years (Szymaniak 2001, p. 11; Karaszewski 2001, pp. 156-157).

The next significant acts regarding FDI in Poland were passed on July 6, 1982[204] and April 23, 1986[205]. The former invited Polish emigrants to invest in the territory of their homeland but allowed only for business projects on a limited scale. Nawrocki (1989, pp. 10-11) reports that by the end of 1983, nearly 500 such firms had started operations in Poland. The law of April 23, 1986 enabled foreign investors to establish joint ventures in Poland, with local partners. A new version of this act, which came into effect on December 23, 1988[206], allowed also for the formation of purely foreign joint ventures. Both laws included highly favorable conditions regarding the taxation of the business activities to which they referred, as an additional incentive to invest in Poland. In 1989, 247 joint ventures with foreign participation were established in Poland. One year later, 734 such companies began activities in the country (Karaszewski op. cit., p. 158). Nevertheless, at the end of the 1980s, many potential foreign investors were still deterred from entering the Polish market by the grave and uncertain political and economic situation in the region. Moreover, they still had to satisfy many conditions and obtain numerous official permissions in order to start business activity on Polish territory. Many of them doubted the reliability of the guarantees given by local institutions and lacked confidence in the effectiveness of contract enforcement (Szymaniak op. cit., p. 13).

The radical reforms of the Balcerowicz Plan and the beginning of the privatization process of the Polish economy were accompanied by the passage of the law of June 14, 1991[207], broadly regulating the legal position of foreign investors in Poland. Among the main rationale behind the enactment of the law, Szymaniak (ibid., p. 14) mentions "*the creation of an investment environment similar to that of highly industrialized countries and an aspiration to standardize the rights and conditions to undertake business activity by domestic and foreign entities.*" In the following years, several amendments to the above law were put into force. The most important changes have been included in a law passed on March 29, 1996[208] in connection with Poland's prospect of joining the OECD and the long-term goal of EU accession. It introduced, among other things, the

---

[204] Journal of Laws (1982) No. 19, item 146, with subsequent amendments.
[205] Journal of Laws (1986) No. 17, item 88, with subsequent amendments.
[206] Journal of Laws (1988) No. 41, item 325, with subsequent amendments.
[207] Journal of Laws (1991) No. 60, item 253, with subsequent amendments.
[208] Journal of Laws (1996) No. 45, item 199.

principle of "national treatment" of foreign-owned economic units and reduced considerably the number of permissions that foreigners needed to acquire in order to start operations in Poland.[209]

Finally, the Business Activity Law of November 19, 1999[210] can be considered as a crowning achievement of legislative processes leading to the liberalization of FDI activities in Poland. According to the law: "*Foreign persons may undertake and conduct business activity in the Republic of Poland according to the principle of reciprocity insofar as the international agreements ratified by Poland do not stipulate otherwise, just like an entrepreneur who maintains his/her permanent residence or seat in Poland. Faced with a lack of reciprocity, foreign persons may establish only limited partnerships, limited liability companies and joint stock companies in order to undertake and conduct business activity in the Republic of Poland and they may join such companies and purchase interest and shares of stock therein.*"[211]

Although there are still some minor barriers to the business activities of non-residents in Poland, foreign investors today enjoy national treatment in the country. They operate on the basis of general business legislation and under the same tax and labor codes as domestic firms. The law currently in force guarantees a high level of protection for private property. Poland is already strongly integrated into international structures as a member of WTO (1995), OECD (1996), NATO (1999) and the European Union (2004). This fact contributes greatly to the attractiveness of this country as a location for FDI (EBRD 2001, p. 10).

In the 1992-2002 time period, a significant role in promoting Poland as a destination country of FDI was played by the Polish Agency for Foreign Investment (PAIZ). Established in 1992 as a non-profit organization and a joint-stock company wholly-owned by the State Treasury, PAIZ assisted foreign businesses in establishing a presence in Poland. In 2003, PAIZ merged with the Polish Information Agency (PAI) to form a new body, the Polish Information and Foreign Investment Agency (PAIiIZ). As in the case of PAIZ, the Agency serves potential foreign investors by: providing reliable and customized information on the economic and legal environment in Poland; facilitating the initial stages of their investment process; helping to identify the most appropriate location for their business activities; and overall guidance through all the formal procedures in dealing with central and local authorities.[212]

As shown in Figures 43 and 44, Poland's transition to a market economy in 1990 was followed by a considerable influx of FDI into the country, especially in the second half of the 1990s. The adoption of legislation which was increasingly friendly towards foreign business activity, the gradual stabilization of the

---

[209] For details, see Szymaniak op. cit., p. 15; Karaszewski op. cit., p. 160.
[210] Journal of Laws (1999) No. 101, item 1178.
[211] Journal of Laws (1999) No. 101, item 1178, article 6, points 2 and 3.
[212] See http://www.paiz.gov.pl.

economic and political situation, as well as the process of integration into the EU, were continually improving the investment climate in Poland and had the effect that annual FDI flows to the country showed an upward trend with every year.

Figure 43. FDI inflow into Poland, 1990-2004 (in $ million)

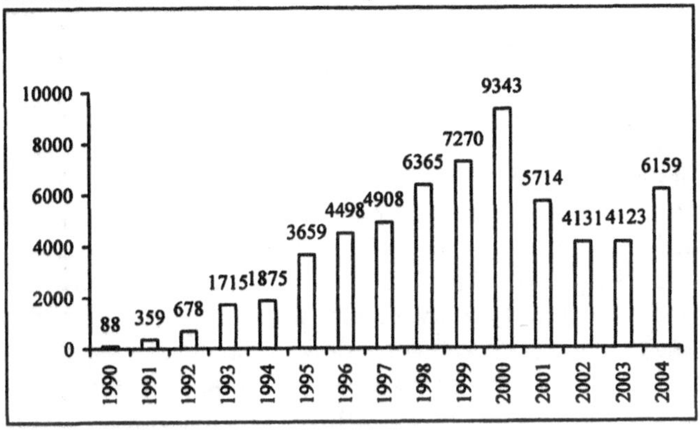

Source: NBP (balance of payments based on transactions).

Figure 44. FDI stock in Poland, 1990-2004 (in $ million)

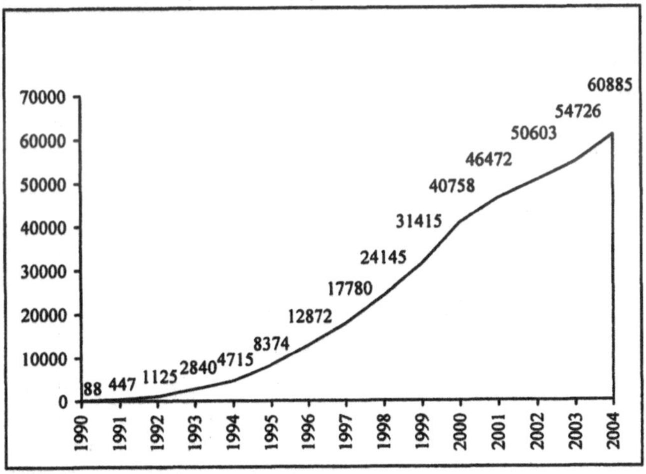

Source: NBP (balance of payments based on transactions).

After reaching its peak in 2000, however, a substantial decline in FDI inflow to Poland could be observed in the following years. This was due mainly to a noticeable slowdown in the privatization process of state-owned enterprises and to the fact that in the 2001-2005 time period Poland lost the race for numerous big investment projects, undertaken by west European corporations in other central and east European countries instead (Slovakia, Czech Republic, Hungary).[213]

12.3 Selected Theories explaining the Determinants of FDI

A matter of considerable importance regarding FDI is the question of why companies undertake direct investment abroad instead of, for example, exporting or licensing their products, and what factors are decisive in the choice of a particular location for such an activity. The present subsection contains an overview of selected theories related to these issues. Its main purpose is to facilitate the identification and understanding of the reasons for which west European sugar corporations decided to participate in the privatization process of the sugar industry in Poland. It should help also to identify potential economic effects of privatization-related FDI inflow to a host county. Finally, it should reveal what actions governments can take to affect positively the inflow of foreign investment and how they can influence the benefits expected from FDI inflow. In the opinion of John Dunning, author of one of the most significant theories explaining FDI (see subsection 12.3.7), "*Any assessment of the impact of the activities of multinationals on the welfare of host countries requires some understanding of the reasons why transnational corporations undertake FDI.* [...] *This is because the consequences of FDI on a particular host country are a function of the interaction between the competitiveness of its location-bound resources and the competitive advantages of the investing firms*" (Dunning 2001, p. 34).

12.3.1 Internalization Theory (Market Imperfections)

The basic assumption of the internalization theory is that whenever companies recognize that the net benefits of moving operations abroad outweigh those offered by an external trading relationship due to the existence of *market imperfections*, they will choose the former type of international activity (Du Pont 2002, p. 12; Rymarczyk 2004, pp. 36-37).[214] Moreover, according to this theory, the possession of some significant, firm-specific advantage allowing a given firm to compete successfully in a foreign market is considered as a *sine qua non* for FDI.

As far as horizontal FDI is concerned, of relevance are market imperfections that arise when there are either obstacles to the free flow of products between countries or when there are barriers to the sale of know-how (Hill op. cit., p. 191). Obstacles to free trade of products are mainly a result of protectionist policies of governments in the form of tariffs, quotas and other instruments which make

[213] See for example Kublik 2004; Kublik/Kostrzewski 2005; Gazeta Wyborcza 2005.

[214] See also Hymer 1976; Buckley/Casson 1976; Rugman 1981; Rugman 1985, pp. 570-575; Williamson 1985.

exporting too expensive. Barriers to the sale of know-how appear when the transfer of unique technological, marketing or managerial knowledge possessed by companies is fraught with risk. There are three circumstances under which such situation may occur: (1) when a firm has valuable know-how that cannot be protected effectively by a licensing contract and may therefore be easily assimilated and used by existing or potential competitors; (2) when a firm needs strict control over the operations of a foreign subsidiary in order to maximize its market share and earnings abroad, and (3) when the transfer of a firm's skills and know-how through a license or through franchising is very difficult (e.g. a specific organizational culture or management know-how) (ibid., pp. 192-193; Navaretti et al., op. cit., pp. 16-17, Buckley 2002, pp. 106-107).

Backward vertical FDI is undertaken, according to the internalization theory, to reduce transaction costs and to eliminate risks concerning the supply of inputs procured in a foreign country and used in the domestic production processes. It can be achieved, for example, through the acquisition of a foreign oil refinery. FDI of this type should also reduce uncertainty with regard to the prices and delivery of imported raw materials (Moosa op. cit., pp. 32-33). Furthermore, a firm may decide on backward vertical FDI if it does not want to give away to other firms its technological expertise concerning the process of finding and/or extracting a particular raw material (Hill, op. cit., p. 198).

A significant shortcoming of the internalization theory is that is does not explain why companies choose a particular country as a location of FDI.

12.3.2 Product Life-Cycle Theory

The product life-cycle theory proposed by Raymond Vernon in the 1960s assumes that companies from highly developed countries undertake FDI at a particular stage in the life cycle of an innovative product they pioneer in their home market (Hill op. cit., p.195; Rymarczyk 2004, pp. 43-45). Vernon argued that in a situation when such a product becomes standardized in the home market but the demand for the product in other advanced countries is large enough to support local production, companies will move production to these countries. This is caused by the appearance of competition in the home market, which is accompanied by increasing cost pressures. As market saturation proceeds also in the new locations but the demand for the same product rises high enough in developing countries, companies will take advantage of the lower labor costs in these regions to shift their production there. In this way, over time, a particular country can switch from being an exporter of a product to an importer. Although Vernon's theory clearly reflects the patterns showing how production of products developed initially in the U.S. migrated around the world between 1945 and 1975, it has several weaknesses. As Hill (ibid., p.195) and Giddy (1978) rightly point out, it does not explicitly explain why a company (even when the conditions mentioned above are met) should choose FDI over licensing or exporting. The aforementioned authors claim that sufficient demand for a particular product abroad does not automatically justify its local production. Exporting may still be profitable because of scale economies arising from serving the global market from one location. Similarly, licensing a product in order to manufacture it in countries with large demand may be more profitable than FDI. Hill (ibid., p. 195) claims that due to the fact that it ignores these assumptions, the product life-cycle theory possesses only a limited usefulness to explain FDI.

Another limitation of Vernon's theory lies in the difficulty of applying it to current trends in the world economy. While Vernon assumed that most new products are first introduced in the U.S., today's globalization and integration of world economies accounts for simultaneous introduction of such products in the U.S., Japan and Western Europe. Moreover, the rapid progress in communication and transportation contributes to an unprecedented dispersion of production around the world. Components of new products are produced in accordance to the theory of comparative advantage in those locations "*where the mix of factor costs and skills is most favorable*" (ibid., p. 137).

12.3.3 Developmental Theories by Porter and Ozawa

By the end of the twentieth century, several theories had been developed which together with Vernon's earlier "product life cycle" form a group described by Meyer (1998b) as *developmental theories*. The theories presented in this sub-section differ considerably, however, from Vernon's hypothesis and are thus discussed separately. Moreover, they seem to be of particular relevance with regard to FDI in Central and Eastern Europe, which justifies their detailed exploration, considering the scope of the present study. The common premise of the theories outlined here is that the comparative advantages of individual countries change with their economic development, that FDI influences structural change in an economy and, conversely, the structure of an economy determines the type of FDI it attracts and/or undertakes.[215]

Porter (1998, pp. 545-560) defined four basic stages of economic development: *factor-driven, investment-driven, innovation-driven* and *wealth-driven.* The above author indicates that each country's progress on the ladder of development begins with the utilization of unskilled labor and natural resources in the production of labor-intensive goods (*factor-driven stage*). Subsequently, individual countries direct their efforts towards a production that requires skilled human capital and advanced technology (*investment-driven stage*). The third stage, *innovation-driven,* takes place when a given country accumulates abundant highly skilled human capital and promotes R&D activities. A typical feature of

[215] See Meyer 1998b, p.80.

this stage of development is that innovative and modern products start to play a dominant role in exports, shaping in this way the comparative advantage of a given country. An economy in the *wealth-driven* stage of development strives to sustain and preserve the wealth level that has been already achieved.

Ozawa (1992) combined Porter's theory with inward and outward FDI flows to explain the phenomenon of changing comparative advantages. He suggests that economies in the *factor-driven* stage of development are the destination of FDI from more advanced countries looking for cheap natural resources and low-cost labor. As soon as the less developed country enters the *investment-driven* stage, its indigenous firms will also undertake FDI seeking for low-cost labor, and the country simultaneously starts to attract more capital-intensive FDI, e. g. in the building or construction industry. In the *innovation-driven* stage, both inward and outward FDI flows will embrace sectors characterized by highly skilled human capital and advanced technology. In this way, Ozawa's theory suggests that the interaction of comparative advantages and FDI accounts for dynamic changes in their structure. Ozawa emphasizes additionally that the economic openness of countries and a favorable investment environment constitute necessary conditions for economic growth. Because of a considerable gap in the economic development between west European and central and east European countries, the above theory can be applied to explain certain FDI flows from the former to the latter (Meyer 1998b, p. 81-86; Wysokińska 1998, pp. 113-118).

Referring to Kojima and Ozawa (1984), Meyer (ibid., pp. 83-85) presents the view that in the face of changing comparative advantages, firms domestically engaged in the production of labor-intensive goods and operating successfully in a particular industry for many years, gaining at the same time valuable know-how and experience, and which are not able to sustain profitability because of competition from imports, rising labor costs and/or appreciation of currency in the domestic market (*push factor*), have two alternatives: they can either shift with their workforce to another sector or move their entire production (or the labor-intensive, unprofitable activities) abroad, benefiting from location-specific advantages of the host country (*pull factor*). The author points out that this mechanism accounts for the existence of large, established multinational corporations, and medium-sized enterprises which move abroad for the first time. The latter prefer a foreign location in proximity to their home market, where gaining initial experience is easier.

12.3.4 Portfolio Theory

The internalization of business activity takes place, according to the *portfolio theory,* because of the willingness of investors to reduce the risk of locating capital in only one country. This risk is connected with the development of the economic and political situation in a given region, the development of demand for a particular product in the local market, appreciation and depreciation of local currency, etc. It is assumed that diversification of an investment portfolio by investing in several countries increases individual investors' or organizations' chances of achieving stable profits.[216] Rymarczyk (op. cit., p. 50) indicates that FDI allows firms the possibility of reducing uncertainty, not only with regard to sales results and economic performance, as is also the case of exporting, but also with regard to the availability of and access to factors of production (natural resources and workforce). At the same time, the author points out that, in general, firms undertaking FDI are burdened with a considerably higher investment risk than companies operating only in the domestic market. For this reason, reduction of uncertainty (with regard to return of invested capital) through dispersion of business activity over several countries cannot be the only reason why companies decide for FDI (ibid., p. 51).

12.3.5 Strategic Behavior (Oligopolistic Reactions)

Knickerbocker (1973) and Graham (1978, 1985) are cited in economic literature dealing with international business as the fathers of a theory according to which FDI may be a result of a strategic rivalry between firms competing in oligopolistic industries.[217] On the basis of research comprising 187 large U.S. corporations operating internationally, the former author observed that in a situation where an industry is dominated by a limited number of firms, any significant move of one of them results in imitative behavior by the others. Knickerbocker argues that such behavior relates also to FDI activities and claims that when one member of an oligopoly establishes operations abroad, other members will follow to prevent the initiator of the process from gaining a "first-mover advantage".[218] Extending Knickerbocker's hypothesis to a situation where "two or more MNCs encounter each other in different regional markets", Hill (op. cit., p. 195) provides an imaginative description of their rivalry by using the following metaphor: "*Rather like chess players jockeying for advantage, firms will try to match each other's moves in different markets to try to hold each other in check. The idea is to ensure that a rival does not gain a commanding position in one market and then use the profits generated there to subsidize competitive attacks in other markets.*"

Referring to Knickerbocker's "follow-the-leader" hypothesis with regard to FDI, Meyer (1998b, p.73) presents an alternative explanation of the phenomenon. He argues that such imitative practices can be a result of one of the following: (a) followers may presume that the leaders have undertaken extensive market research before making the final decision about entering a particular market, and their investment therefore signifies an investment opportunity; (b) the leaders

[216] See for example Buckley 2002, p. 105; Rymarczyk op. cit., p. 50; Umiński 2002, pp. 37-38.
[217] See for example Hill op. cit., p.193; Rymarczyk op. cit., pp. 37-39.
[218] See Hill op. cit., p.193; Meyer 1998b, p.72; Rymarczyk 2004, p. 38.

contribute through their investment to the development of infrastructure in the host country, which makes the location more attractive for suppliers, customers and, subsequently, competitors; (c) both competitors simply react to a common external stimulus such as market liberalization.

Another example of the strategic behavior of firms is a backward vertical FDI undertaken with the purpose of gaining control over appreciable deposits of a particular raw material, which should hinder the entry of new competitors to a given industry. Conversely, a firm may establish an independent distribution network for its products in a foreign country (forward vertical FDI) in order to simplify access to a highly competitive market dominated by a small number of local companies (Hill, op. cit., pp. 197-198).

In contrast to the aforementioned ideas formulated by Knickerbocker, Edward M. Graham (op. cit.) claims that FDI may be the effect of retaliatory policies of international competitors with a monopolistic position in their home markets. More precisely, the above author argues that such a firm 'invaded' by a foreign competitor in the domestic market will respond in the same way by investing in the home market of the 'invader' (Meyer 1998b, p. 72; Meyer/Estrin 1998, p. 7).

12.3.6 Location Hypothesis

According to the location hypothesis, FDI takes place because of the existence of differences between countries with regard to the availability of factors of production (labor and natural resources), the costs and quality of these factors, overall investment climate, size and structure of a given market, etc.[219] The immobility and attractiveness of some of the elements may give many firms a strong stimulus to move their operations to a particular country in order to take advantage of the positive local conditions. A company may, for instance, build a plant in a foreign country where it has access to a cheap source of a raw material used in large quantities in the domestic production process and procured predominantly from abroad. In this way, the company can reduce costs of production thanks to a significant reduction in transportation and transaction costs. Such an investment would additionally eliminate uncertainty concerning the supply of the raw material (Moosa 2002, p. 36).

Similarly, a firm engaged in the production of labor-intensive goods may be attracted to a foreign location by the availability of a considerably cheaper workforce than in the home country. It must be mentioned here, however, that the decision of a multinational corporation to undertake FDI in a particular region depends not on the wage differential between the home and host country of the investment but on relative, productivity-adjusted labor costs in the latter. This is

---

219 See for example Hymer op. cit., pp. 114-15; Moosa op. cit., pp. 33-36; Rymarczyk op. cit., p. 41.

due to the fact that low wages may often mean low labor productivity (Carstensen/Toubal 2003, p. 8). In the case of industries where high employee qualifications are required, a company will be attracted to a foreign country with abundant skilled, low-cost human resources. A firm operating in a capital-intensive industry may decide for direct investment abroad because of the lower costs of capital in the host country than in the home country (ibid., p. 37).

In contrast to the internalization theory, which explains the reasons of FDI activity without providing an answer to the question as to why firms decide to establish operations in a particular country, the location hypothesis makes it clear why companies choose a given location but it fails to demonstrate why they internationalize in the first place.

12.3.7 Eclectic Paradigm of International Production

The eclectic paradigm (OLI-paradigm) developed by John Dunning (1977, 1980, 1988) constitutes the most comprehensive theory explaining FDI. It integrates several existing theories related to this issue and suggests that a company will undertake FDI in a particular country when the following three conditions are met:

(a) The company must possess some kind of *ownership-specific* (O) advantage over firms operating in the same industry abroad and serving or intending to service the same market. Such an advantage may take the form of a specific technological or/and managerial know-how, a patent, brand name, trademark, etc. It may also result from the company's exclusive or privileged access to certain tangible assets or markets. The (O) advantage(s) must be powerful enough to compensate the investor for the disadvantages of operating in a foreign country.[220]

(b) The exploitation of the firm's ownership-specific advantages can be best achieved from a foreign country offering valuable *location-bound* (L) resources and/or capabilities (e.g. oil deposits, sugarbeet plantations or cheap and skilled labor).

(c) The company perceives that it is in its interest to internalize (I) the use of its ownership advantages (through FDI) rather than to externalize it (through exporting or licensing) (Dunning 1988b, pp. 10-12; Dunning 2001, p. 36; Rymarczyk op. cit., pp. 47-49).

Summarizing the main assumptions of the OLI-paradigm, Rymarczyk (ibid., p. 49) indicates that the theory is based on the premise that the greater are the ownership advantages of an enterprise over firms in foreign countries and the more profitable is the exploitation of these advantages in the countries due to

---

[220] Such 'costs of foreignness' in the host country of FDI arise when local firms have easier access to information, labor and/or capital markets, or when they enjoy preferential treatment by local authorities (Blattner 2002, p. 6; Hollensen 2001, p. 46; Buckley 2002, p. 100).

their location-specific characteristics, the stronger is the stimulus for the enterprise to internalize the use of the advantages.

Apart from all the determinants of FDI that have been presented up to now in this section, Dunning (op. cit., pp. 64-66) and Moosa (op. cit., pp. 50-58) emphasize the importance of a number of additional factors that firms take into account when considering direct investment in a particular country. These include corporate tax rates, political stability, competition policy, general macroeconomic stabilization as well, as the availability and quality of transport and communications infrastructures. According to the former author, national governments aiming to attract FDI should concentrate primarily on the creation of an investment environment where organizational and transaction costs of economic activity are minimal, and leave the decision on what is produced and how it is produced to *"the collective will of thousands of firms and hundreds of thousands, or millions, of consumers."* (Dunning, ibid., p. 66). Nonetheless, the afore-cited author claims that governments should at the same time provide support for the appropriate functioning of the market by promoting *"an up-to-date legal, financial and commercial infrastructure, an educated labor force, an adequate transportation and telecommunications network, a strong anti-monopoly policy, a sound macroeconomic policy, and a wealth-creating culture, without which the market cannot do the job expected of it"*. Concluding his considerations regarding the role of national governments in the establishment of a favorable investment climate, Dunning observes that administrations which apart from their social and strategic responsibilities are constantly reducing transaction and coordination costs of economic activity *"are likely to be the most successful, not only in attracting the right kind of FDI, but [in doing] so at the least real costs."* (ibid., p. 66). It is important to add here that multinational corporations are deeply hesitant about investing in any highly politicized environment, characterized by an excessive bureaucratic red tape and unpredictable decision-making. Megyery and Sader (1996, pp. 7-9) claim that in order to be successful, privatization programs in transition countries targeting foreign investors should be guided by three fundamental principles: political commitment, business orientation and fairness.

12.3.8 Industrial Networks and Alliance Capitalism

The network approach is based on the assumption that in order to be successful in the global marketplace, each company depends to a smaller or larger extent on assets and resources controlled by other firms, and that companies gain access to these resources by entering into cooperative relationships with other organizations.[221] By the same token, authors of the *network model* suggest that business

[221] See for example Rymarczyk op. cit., pp. 51-52; Hollensen, op. cit., p. 47.

corporations cannot be viewed as isolated market players but as actors interacting bilaterally with, and linked to, other actors, through exchange relationships (Hollensen, op. cit., p. 60; Buckley 2002, p. 122). Entry into a network by an outsider is possible only if existing members of the network have some significant motives for starting cooperation with the new entity. In the early stage of their evolution and functioning, industrial networks have, by definition, a domestic character (Hollensen, op. cit., p. 61). Internalization of business activity through FDI is driven, according to the network approach, by the willingness of firms to strengthen their competitive position in a globalized economy. This, in turn, can be best achieved through the extension of cooperative relationships beyond national borders (Rymarczyk 2004, p. 52). Such relationships allow a company to avoid very high expenditures connected with production and allow the coordination of multiple activities within a single ownership (Dunning 2001, p. 42). A cross-border network system may be established, often on the initiative of a firm located in the host country of a direct investment and offering access to a network that is, for various reasons, valuable for the foreign investor. For example, the takeover of a company in Central and Eastern Europe by a west European multinational corporation gives the former the opportunity to integrate domestic production processes into the global production, marketing and distribution network of the multinational. In exchange, the investing firm gains access to the local market and to the network system of the acquired firm. Existing cooperative relationships of a given company in the domestic market are likely to be continued abroad when a firm undertaking FDI requires one of its suppliers to follow it into the foreign country. If the supplier fails to do that, it may not be able to keep its ties with the firm in the home market.

The phenomenon of migrating business networks can be represented by the example of a sugar producer and a beverages manufacturer. Let us assume that in country A, sugar producer X is the major supplier of Coca-Cola (See Figure 45). Let us imagine further that at a certain point of time Coca-Cola acquires a number of productive facilities in country B to serve the local market and to export to countries E, F and C. At the same time the company also wants sugar producer X to provide it with sugar of the same type and quality in country B as in country A. Unfortunately, it is impossible for X to export to country B as much sugar as Coca-Cola asks for. Nonetheless, in order to satisfy the needs of its main customer, X takes over several sugar factories in country B. X is aware of the fact that its major competitors operating in country A already possess sugarbeet-processing plants in country B. X knows also that if it did not invest in country B, Coca-Cola would probably soon switch to a new supplier operating in both country A and country B. It is very likely that this would lead to the cessation of cooperation between X and Coca-Cola in country A.

Apart from demonstrating how international networks work and how they may be formed, the above example shows that such cooperative relationships are dynamic, i.e. their structure is often modified or readjusted as a reaction to changes within a network or in its environment. An organization will stay inside a business network as long as it contributes to proper functioning of the network and as long as other members of the network perceive that a cooperative relationship with the organization brings advantages.

Figure 45. Example of an international business network

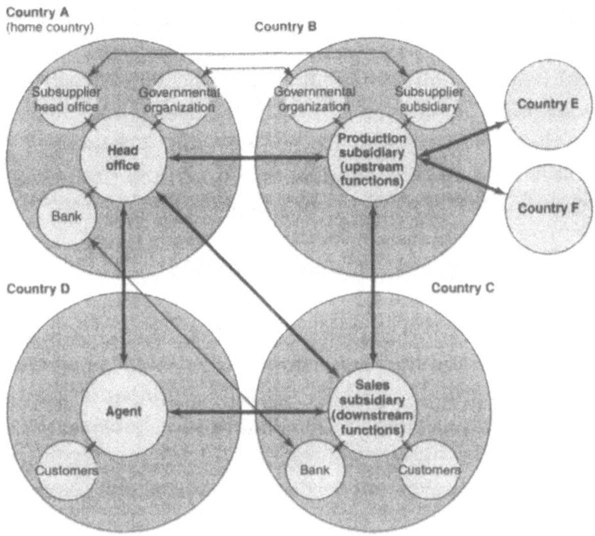

Source: Hollensen 2001, p. 62.

Similarly, any firm that is not fully satisfied with the system of business connections it has established may break the ties with existing partners and engage in new relationships (Buckley 2002, p. 122; Hollensen 2001, p. 61; Rymarczyk op. cit., p. 52). It is worth adding here that the existence of individual business networks is in most cases very difficult for third parties to observe (including potential entrants), since members of such structures are linked to each other by a number of ties (economic, technical, legal, social, administrative, etc.) (Hollensen, ibid., p. 61). Quite often it is not in the interest of individual actors in a network to make all their cooperative relationships widely known.

Referring to the increasingly widespread formation of clusters of affiliated companies interacting in a number of markets, Dunning (2001, pp. 37-43) describes the phenomenon as a movement from hierarchical to *alliance capitalism*. The author observes at the same time that more and more organizations consider the fact of belonging to a business network as a form of competitive or ownership-specific advantage. Inspired by the considerable changes in the "extent, form and depth of economic relations between individuals and organizations" over the last three decades, Dunning recently extended his eclectic paradigm of international production presented earlier in this section. The author claims that among a wide range of wealth-creating and firm-specific intangible assets that are today decisive as regards the success or failure of companies operating internationally, a crucial role is played by *relational assets* or, in short, *R-assets,* which can be deployed productively only in combination with the R-assets of other economic actors (Dunning 2003, p. 4). Such assets are defined by Dunning as "*The stock of a firm's willingness and capability to access, shape and engage in economically beneficial relationships; and to sustain and upgrade these relationships*". R-assets consist of a variety of ingredients including trust, dependability, spirit of community, work ethic, avoidance of instability, etc. The content and optimum configuration of these ingredients is context-specific and depends on the objectives of the partners in a cooperative relationship, on their reasons for entry into the relationship and on the type of the relationship (ibid., p. 3).

12.3.9 Regional Economic Integration and FDI

The experience of the last few decades, connected for example with succeeding enlargements of the EU and the establishment of NAFTA, has made it clear that regional economic integration (REI) has had a significant impact on FDI flows within the integrating area. Hence, the relationship between REI and inward/ outward FDI flows in the integrating region has been analyzed in an increasing number of studies dealing with international business and examining the determinants of FDI.[222]

As was pointed out earlier in this study, gradual integration into international organizational structures and, most of all, the commencement of accession negotiations with the EU, which enforced introduction of far-reaching legislative changes, contributed greatly to a sizeable inflow of FDI into Poland between 1995 and 2004. The same can be said about the majority of other former Soviet-type economies that joined the EU in May 2004.[223]

Barry (2002, p.7) argues that EU accession is likely to "change substantially the nature, origin and sectoral destination" of FDI flows to central and east European countries. The author claims that EU membership eliminates most of the uncertainty about future policy and about EU accession itself, i.e. factors

[222] See for example Blomström/Kokko 1997; Buckley 2004.

[223] It was shown in the empirical part of the present study that the prospect of EU accession by a number of countries from Central and Eastern Europe constituted one the most significant factors that prompted several west European sugar corporations to establish operations in these countries long before they became full members of the EU. The main rationale behind such early engagement of west European sugar companies in Central and Eastern Europe was the desire to control sugar production quota that is allocated administratively within the EU and is currently not transferable between countries.

which previously deterred foreign investors from establishing operations in capital- and training-intensive sectors in Central and Eastern Europe. Referring to *The Irish Times* of May 25, 2001, Barry (ibid., p. 7) quotes executives in the U.S. technology and pharmaceutical sectors who predict that corporate America will direct its focus away from Western Europe to countries like Poland, Hungary, the Czech Republic and Estonia as soon as they join the EU. In the opinion of foreign investors, EU accession guarantees the creation of a transparent business environment and institutional stability in the new member states, which will release many of the blockages that have discouraged some multinational corporations from investing in the aforementioned locations (Barry ibid., p. 15; Bevan/ Estrin 2000, p. 6; Grabbe 2001, p. 30).

At the time of their EU entry, Portugal, Spain and Greece were, with regard to GDP per capita and economic structure, in a similar situation to Poland on the brink of EU accession. The first two of the Mediterranean countries enjoyed a sharp upturn of inward FDI during the first six years of their membership in the EU, owing to the adoption of *acquis communautaire* and improved credibility in the eyes of foreign investors (See Figure 46).

Figure 46. FDI flows to new EU member states prior to and after accession (in $ million)

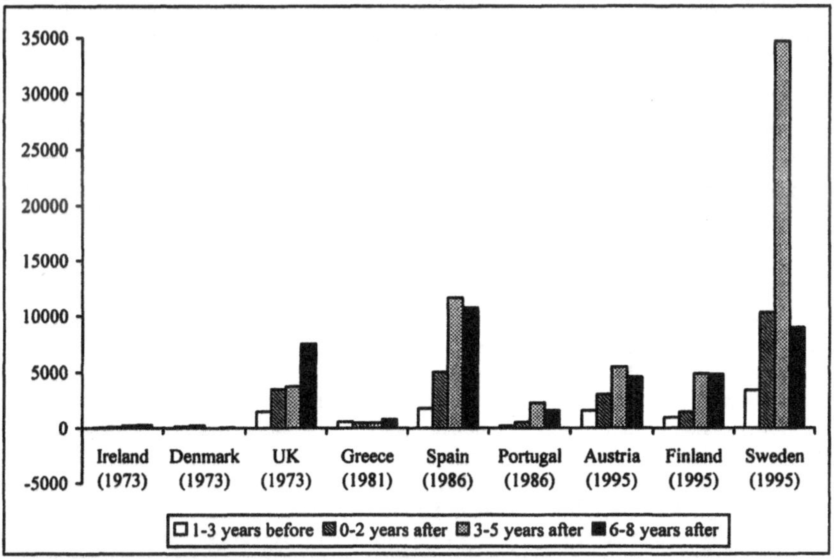

Source: Calculations by the author, based on data collected by UNCTAD (FDI online database).

Greece's EU accession was, in contrast to the developments in Spain and Portugal, not followed by a considerable rise in FDI inflow to the country. It was brought about mainly by the fact that the attitude of the Greek government (led by Prime Minister Papandreou) towards foreign investors was at that time strong-

ly antagonistic (Winiecki 2002, p. 126). Nonetheless, a substantial growth in FDI inflows to the United Kingdom, Austria, Finland and Sweden during the first years of their EU membership shows clearly that in countries with a favorable investment climate and a stable economic and political situation, EU accession constituted a turning point that initiated a period of outstanding success in attracting inward FDI. Denmark and Ireland did not experience a dramatic growth in inward FDI in the first eight years after EU entry but at the time when the two countries joined, FDI in Europe and elsewhere was on a relatively small scale. The popularity of this form of international business activity and the rapid growth in its world stock began for real in the middle of the 1980s. Moreover, EU enlargement in 1973 coincided with the beginning of a recession and with the end of Europe's Golden Age. The crisis was influenced to a large extent by two oil shocks, in 1973 and 1979, and by a considerable slowdown of world productivity growth (Barry 2003, pp. 4-5).
Under such circumstances, the accumulated annual increase in FDI stock in Europe remained at a moderate level until the middle of the 1980s. As shown in Figure 46, among the three countries that joined the EU in 1973, only the United Kingdom enjoyed an appreciable rise in inward FDI in the first eight years following accession.[224] Between 1991 and 1994, a considerable decrease in FDI inflows could be observed in many European countries. This was due mainly to the west European recession and the crisis of the European Monetary System (Winiecki 2002, p. 126).

The above developments and earlier theoretical considerations allow one to expect that FDI influx to Poland and other new member states of the EU will intensify after May 1, 2004. Nevertheless, economic theory suggests that apart from factors connected with REI and having a positive impact on FDI flows within the integrating region (e.g. improved transparency of the legal environment and predictability of future policies in countries joining the EU), there are

[224] It needs to be emphasized, however, that absolute FDI inflows to the UK after the country's EU accession exceeded those recorded in Ireland since the UK is a much larger economy. For this reason, it is highly advisable to measure proportionate rather than absolute increases in FDI inflows in order to get an accurate picture of the actual developments. Prof. Frank Barry from the University College Dublin points out to the fact that FDI inflows to Ireland averaged about $ 35 million between 1971 and 1973, and were at around $ 250 million in the late 1970s. This constitutes a huge increase, especially when reflected in the change of employment numbers at domestic and foreign-owned firms. Numbers of those employed in foreign-owned industry in Ireland rose by almost 25% between 1973 and 1980. By 1980 Ireland had a far higher share of its manufacturing employment in foreign-owned firms than most EU economies have even today. FDI inflows to Ireland skyrocketed in the second half of the 1990s, contributing greatly to a rapid development of the local economy. Denmark experienced the sharpest increase in inward FDI in its history in the years 1998-2001, with average annual inflows amounting to $ 17 billion (See UNCTAD: FDI online database).

also factors that may have an adverse effect on FDI activity and FDI stock in individual countries participating in the integration process. If, for instance, a large number of FDI projects in country A were conducted by firms headquartered in a neighboring country (B) in order to substitute exports because of high trade barriers, then a regional economic integration of the two economies (reduction or complete abolishment of trade and investment barriers) may lead to the withdrawal of many foreign investors from country A, if they recognize that exporting from the home country (B) will be more profitable (Blattner 2002, p. 11; Blomström/Kokko 1997, p. 5). In a situation when most FDI flows from country B to country A have been motivated by the willingness of foreign investors to exploit locally their unique expertise in a given field, REI between the two countries does not provide the investors with a reason to pull out of the existing engagement in country A (Blomström/Kokko, ibid., p. 8). These two examples demonstrate that the effect of REI on FDI depends to some extent on the reason of entry of foreign investors to a particular market before the integration has occurred. By the same token, it can be concluded that REI has different implications for investors from the participating countries and for external investors (ibid., p. 5). Furthermore, the consequences of REI for the direction and type of FDI flows depend on the characteristics of the integrating economies (e.g. location-specific advantages, stage of economic development, initial level of market protection, competitiveness of local firms, existing economic relationships, etc.).[225] In other words, REI is not likely to affect all participants of the process in the same manner with regard to inward FDI flows. This implies also that drawing any general conclusions about the interdependence between REI and FDI flows within the integrating area would be hazardous. It can be stated, however, that REI is likely to result in a considerable inflow of FDI to those participating countries which possess strong location-specific advantages (e.g. natural resources or low-cost labor) and where integration is accompanied by positive changes in the institutional environment (ibid., pp. 14-17).

12.4 Potential Benefits and Costs of Privatization-related FDI Inflow: Micro-level Approach

This chapter seeks to identify potential microeconomic effects of FDI inflow to a host country as a result of privatization from above. It analyses FDI as a source of capital and technological knowledge. In the last part of the subsection, we will look at possible effects on employment of the privatization of enterprises to foreign investors.

[225] For a detailed discussion of this issue, see Blomström/Kokko 1997, pp. 6-17.

12.4.1 FDI as Source of Capital

One of the major problems inhibiting the introduction and implementation of restructuring activities (especially that of strategic type) at state-owned enterprises in former Soviet-type economies after their 'leap' to a market economy has been the lack of the financial resources needed for this purpose. With scant savings, domestic governments have been ill-equipped to cope with the difficult task of restructuring thousands of distressed industrial enterprises. The inflow of capital provided by private investors to cash-starved enterprises is vital in such a situation. A politically attractive option would be privatization of state-owned enterprises to domestic entrepreneurs, but in transition economies not many possess enough money and know-how to finance and carry out successful restructuring. These obstacles may be overcome with the help of foreign investors who usually have access to funds not available to host-country firms. Apart from the possibility of investing their own capital, foreign companies are more likely than the domestic ones to obtain credit from local banks and on the international capital markets since they provide reliable guarantees to lenders.

Numerous studies focusing on FDI in developing countries in Latin America and Central and Eastern Europe show that in the case of entry of a foreign investor to the local markets through acquisition of an enterprise, be it state-owned or private, the initial expense for the purchase of shares of the enterprise turns out to be only a small part of the total capital invested.[226] In the early phase of Polish transition, investment expenditures at firms privatized to foreign investors were in the first years following privatization much higher than at companies privatized domestically (especially to insiders). Between 1996 and 1999, the investment gap between these two groups of enterprises shrunk considerably but total investment expenditures and their share in total revenues were still higher at the former (Bałtowski 2002b, p. 79; UNCTAD 2000, p. 170). Foreign firms' share in total investment outlays in Poland increased from 20% in 1994 to 33% in 1996 and 40% in 1997. In manufacturing, this share amounted to 56% (Kamiński/Smarzyńska 2001, p. 8). Negotiations between host-country governments and a foreign investor acquiring a particular state-owned enterprise, often result, apart from the determination of an adequate price for the shares of the enterprise, in the investor's commitment to invest a certain amount of capital in the acquired firm in the years to come. Such commitments often constitute a very significant part of privatization deals in transition economies. Empirical studies show that, on the macro-level, foreign investors with stakes in privatized state-owned enterprises in Poland do fulfill investment obligations specified in privatization contracts.[227]

[226] See for example UNCTAD 2000, pp. 168-170; Bałtowski 2002b, pp. 77-79.

[227] See for example Ministry of State Treasury 2002b, p. 23; Jarosz 1997, p. 158; Bałtowski 2002b, pp. 83-87.

In the long term, however, the contribution of inward FDI to the generation of capital and income at host country firms, and in the host country in general, is not obvious. The assessment of this contribution is complicated due to the fact that not only the initial inflow of capital to the host country but also its outflow (in the form of transfer of profits) to the home country of the foreign investor must be taken into account. The possibility of the repatriation of profits from enterprises in Poland privatized to foreigners has often been loudly proclaimed by opponents of the participation of foreign capital in the privatization process of the Polish economy. Groups hostile to the privatization of state-owned enterprises to foreign investors have repeatedly used the argument that in a situation where the accumulated value of remittances of profits to the home country of a privatization-related FDI equals the total capital invested in the acquisition and restructuring of a given enterprise, any additional transfer of money to the home country of the foreign investor is tantamount to 'draining' the host economy of its wealth. It must be said, however, that the evaluation of inward FDI on the basis of such straightforward calculations is wrong, since apart from the measurable effects of inward FDI on the host country (investment of a certain amount of capital), there are also many direct and indirect spillover benefits of such investment (e.g. transfer of technological, marketing and/or managerial know-how) which have a significant impact on the possibility for profit and capital accumulation by local firms (Karaszewski 2001, p. 56). Moreover, as it was suggested earlier in this study with regard to changes in employment at privatized enterprises, it is always good to consider what would have happened in developing countries with state-owned enterprises taken over by foreign investors if their privatization had not occurred. As far as companies requiring substantial financial restructuring and investment in technological upgrading are concerned, had they not been privatized to multinationals, it would have lead in many, if not in most cases, to bankruptcy and liquidation.

For all these reasons, any judgment on the contribution of inward FDI on capital formation in the host country should be preceded by a thorough analysis of a number of factors and concentrate on individual investment projects.

12.4.2 Transfer of Technology

Investment in cutting-edge technology constitutes an inextricable and crucial part of continuous enterprise restructuring in developing, middle-developed and industrialized countries. The need for such investment in post-communist economies in Central and Eastern Europe, trying to close the developmental gap between themselves and the wealthy Western neighbors, has been enormous. Unfortunately, in most countries of the region, the possibilities for the modernization of production processes at industrial enterprises through the development and incorporation of modern technologies have been limited, partly because of insufficient funds and partly because of a lack of expertise. This means that developing and middle-developed countries have to rely to a large extent on more advanced economies for the technology needed to increase productivity and the competitiveness of domestic firms, and to stimulate industrial growth. One way of gaining access to modern technology in post-communist countries is the privatization of state-owned enterprises to foreign investors, preferably to established multinationals. It seems reasonable to assume that after the entry into a foreign market through FDI, multinational corporations are determined that operations in the new location be highly efficient, and that they will thus put in a lot of effort, in technological terms, in order to ensure this (UNCTAD 2000, p.174). If an FDI project is connected with the acquisition of an enterprise using outdated methods of production and antiquated machinery, the foreign investor is very likely to furnish the acquired plant with new technologies in order to improve productivity and overall cost efficiency. Obviously, this does not have always to be valid since it is not unusual that FDI is not accompanied by the institution of state-of-the-art technologies in the host country. Foreign investors prefer often to derive rents from existing technologies in host country operations (Karaszewski 2001, p. 57; UNCTAD 1999, p. 36).

It has to be pointed out that the term technology comprises much more than simply machinery and equipment, with which it is usually associated. Żukowska-Gagelmann (2001, p. 36) defines technology as "*a form of industrial knowledge, possessed by an individual firm, industry or country, which refers to the method of production of goods and services from inputs*". The author distinguishes between two major types of technological knowledge, and terms them *codifiable* and *non-codifiable*.[228] Nevertheless, since in the economic literature the use of the expressions *tangible* and *intangible* technology is more widespread, they are also used by the present author throughout this study. A typical feature of *tangible technology* is that it can be passed from one user to another in the form of manuals (e. g. blueprints for products, scientific formulas, specifications for manufacturing processes, etc.) or in form of physical assets such as machines and apparatuses used for a particular purpose. *Intangible technological knowledge* embraces tacit skills acquired in the course of many years of experience in a given field, or owing to the engagement in R&D activities. Examples of intangible technological expertise include marketing and management techniques, specific corporate culture as well as other forms of know-how embodied in the employees, products and processes of a given organization (Chen 1996, p. 4).[229]

Schnepp et al. (1990, p. 3) define transfer of technology as "*a process by which expertise or knowledge related to some aspect of technology is passed*

[228] Umiński (2002, p. 25) distinguishes between *hardware* and *software* technology.

[229] The role of managers seems to be of particular importance in the implementation of restructuring processes at enterprises in post-communist economies. This issue is therefore discussed separately in the next subsection.

from one user to another for the purpose of economic gain." Many authors proposing their own definition of technology transfer emphasize additionally that such a transfer is not achieved until the transferee absorbs, understands and can utilize the technology that has been transferred.[230] Intangible technological knowledge is usually highly personal, difficult to formalize, rooted in the routines and personnel of innovative organizations and not easy to replicate in a new environment. Therefore, its transfer is much more difficult than in the case of tangible technology. Firm-specific intangible knowledge can be assimilated through a gradual learning process and often requires the mobility of employees and/or considerable investment in upgrading of skills of the transferees (Radosevic 1999, pp. 14-15; UNCTAD 1999, p. 34; Żukowska-Gagelmann, op. cit., p. 38). It can be transmitted, e.g., through licensing or franchising, when the licensor/franchiser helps to train personnel of the licensee/franchisee and to incorporate the modern technology in the production processes. Nonetheless, international technology trade is dominated today by flows of industrial knowledge between parent companies and affiliates of multinational corporations. Subsidiaries of MNCs located in developing and middle-developed countries acquire technology from their parents in the form of patents as well as through the import of machinery, equipment, inputs and services (Chen 1994, p. 1; Chen 1996, p. 5; Rugman 1983; Żukowska-Gagelmann, ibid., p. 40).

Apart from direct transfers of technology from MNCs to their foreign affiliates, a lot of attention is devoted in economic literature to the positive spillover effects of such transfers on indigenous firms.[231] A positive spillover effect may occur, for instance, when a foreign subsidiary of a particular MNC relies increasingly on local suppliers for inputs, at the same time setting high requirements with regard to the quality, packaging and conditions of delivery (Winiecki 2002, p. 123; UNCTAD 1999, p. 40). Spillovers of this type are more likely to materialize when FDI is a result of acquisition of an existing firm than in the case of a greenfield investment since the local firm may already have strong links with domestic suppliers before privatization. If such links turn out to be useful and efficient, the foreign investor will retain and strengthen them. In the case of greenfield investment, the development of contacts with local suppliers usually takes more time and effort (UNCTAD 2000, p. 176).

Technological spillovers to local firms can also take place through *demonstration effect*, *competition effect* and *labor mobility* (Żukowska-Gagelmann op. cit., p. 53-55). Demonstration effect is a result of imitative behavior of local firms through observation of practices utilized by multinationals. Competition effect comprises a number of measures undertaken by local firms as a response to the entry of a foreign competitor to the domestic market. Among such activ-

---

[230] See for example Chen 1994, p. 2; Chen 1996, p. 4.

[231] See for example Winiecki 2002, p.123-124; Żukowska-Gagelmann 2001, pp. 51-58.

ities, Żukowska-Gagelmann (ibid., p. 53) cites reduction in costs, increase in productivity, improved motivation of employees as well as acquisition of modern technology and enhancement of the quality of products and services.

Mobility of labor also constitutes a significant channel for the transfer of technological knowledge, especially of that described earlier as intangible. It takes place when, for example, a local firm hires former employees of a multinational corporation who had been trained by their previous employer.

The extent of the aforementioned positive linkages depends, however, on the absorptive abilities of local firms in a particular country. There is a general agreement in the economic literature that the likelihood of positive spillovers for local firms, resulting from the presence of MNCs in the domestic market, increases as the developmental gap between host economies and that of foreign investors becomes smaller.[232] The existence of a large gap means that the technological capability of firms in a host country is too weak for the incorporation of modern foreign technologies and innovative organizational practices (Żukowska-Gagelmann op. cit., p. 56-57).

Apart from the potential positive spillover effects described above, the entry of an MNC into a developing county, with all its organizational strengths and modern technology, may put strong pressure on domestic firms operating in the same industry. MNCs may eventually crowd them out. Unlike indigenous enterprises, local consumers obviously benefit from such a scenario since it leads usually to the availability of cheaper and better products. Many authors and politicians citing Joseph Schumpeter refer to the process of disappearance of uncompetitive firms and the emergence of new, efficient ones as "creative destruction".[233]

Analyzing the effects of FDI in Poland over the period 1993-97, and concentrating on technology transfer, Żukowska-Gagelmann (op. cit., p. 183) found out that foreign-owned firms make a positive contribution to productivity growth and modernization in domestic industry as a whole. Nevertheless, the author did not observe positive spillovers from foreign-owned to domestic firms. The same result was obtained by Konings (2000). One of the reasons for this state of affairs is the fact that because of poor quality standards of local suppliers, many foreign firms import inputs from abroad. Another obstacle to the emergence of positive spillovers is caused by low mobility of the labor force from multinationals to domestic firms. Payment of much higher wages and attractive social packages guaranteed by the former make the move of an employee from a foreign-owned company to an indigenous firm a rare phenomenon. The third major reason for scant positive spillover effects of inward FDI in Poland is the

---

[232] See for example Winiecki 2002, p.123; Żukowska-Gagelmann ibid., p. 57.

[233] See for example Kornai 2000, p.14 or Greenspan 2001, p. 1.

inability of local firms to imitate many of the practices used by foreign firms because of the lack of capital (Żukowska-Gagelmann op. cit., p. 183).

12.4.3 FDI as a Conduit for Foreign Managerial Expertise

The demand for managers who understand the requirements of the market economy was in the early phase of transition in former Soviet-type economies of Central and Eastern Europe no weaker than the demand for capital. Most managers of state-owned enterprises in the region were engineers who had never been trained in the skills needed in a capitalist system.[234] This is no surprise for anybody who remembers the environment of the communist regime. Paternalistic protection of industrial enterprises by the state, in the form of soft budget constraints as well as limitation of managerial responsibilities in the fulfillment of administrative plans did not call for creative leaders. Analyzing the behavior of enterprises in Central and Eastern Europe in the early stages of transition, Estrin et al. (1995) and Meyer (1997) observed that when exposed to the realities of the market economy, the qualifications of local managers were good enough to make short-term adjustments to the production process in the form of defensive restructuring activities but were not adequate to cope with the more difficult strategic restructuring tasks. According to McDonald (1993), the best solution to this problem is privatization of state-owned enterprises to foreign corporations which tend to bring to former Soviet-type economies efficient managerial practices developed over several decades of operations in the market economy. This author used several examples of early privatizations in Poland to demonstrate that business practices introduced by Western investors rapidly transformed ailing state-owned companies into highly market-oriented and internationally competitive firms. McDonald (ibid.) also provides examples of domestic privatizations with dispersed ownership, which reveal that local managers often simply lack the skills necessary to run a large industrial enterprise in a capitalist system. In the words of the author: "*These managerial shortcomings are not the product of intellectual limitations. Rather, they are the legacy of a communist system that forced enterprises to think only in terms of production and directed managers to maximize output with a shortage of inputs. Polish and other Eastern managers were highly skilled at this task but almost entirely unprepared for the demands of a market economy*" (McDonald ibid., p. 5). The same can be said about marketing skills since in planned economies enterprises did not have marketing departments. Again, foreign managerial expertise and experience can serve to remedy this.

Dobrinsky (1996) presents a similar point of view to that of McDonald. Dobrinsky claims that privatization alone does not necessarily solve the problem

[234] See Meyer 1997, p. 12.

of proper corporate governance and managerial motivation. Especially in the case of dispersed ownership, perverse managerial behavior may be persistent. Privatization in the form of sale to strategic foreign investors leads, in contrast, almost invariably to effective restructuring (Dobrinsky 1996, p. 402). Also Krkoska (2001, p.8) claims that the experience of ten years of transition in Central and Eastern Europe has shown that strategic foreign investors have usually been better able to implement difficult restructuring processes than managers at state-owned firms and at those privatized domestically. Nevertheless, it must be emphasized that as far as the impact on the quality of management is concerned, it would be foolish to generalize about the superiority of privatization to foreigners over other forms of privatizations. There are certainly a lot of cases throughout Central and Eastern Europe where the transfer of a state enterprise into the hands of an indigenous investor led to phenomenal results and where privatization of a firm to a foreign company was not followed by the institution of modern and efficient management techniques. Moreover, some may claim that the above theoretical considerations can be applied primarily to the first phase of transition in Central and Eastern Europe since at the present time there are a lot of natives of the countries concerned working in the domestic market who have gained a solid education and practical experience within the last 14 years, and are thus well prepared to perform managerial functions at any business organization. Additionally, they are normally better acquainted than foreigners with the situation in the local markets and with the habits and tastes of domestic customers (UNCTAD 1999, p. 41). If all this is true, one may suggest that both multinational corporations launching operations in Central and Eastern Europe and indigenous firms (private and state-owned) can rely nowadays exclusively on local human resources when recruiting management personnel responsible for the planning and coordination of day-to-day activities. This would indicate further that the importance of inward FDI as a conduit for innovative management and marketing skills is gradually lessening in middle-developed post-communist European countries. Unfortunately, a large survey conducted by the European Bank for Reconstruction and Development in Central and Eastern Europe in May 2000 reveals that while foreign investors have no difficulty in finding a skilled workforce in the region, two thirds of the surveyed reported that they cannot find managers locally with the requisite skills and experience and are using expatriates instead (EBRD 2000, p. 9). This implies that the shortage of Western-type managerial knowledge in Central and Eastern Europe is still considerable and that even now privatization of state-owned enterprises to foreigners constitutes a great opportunity to bring in modern business practices to the region. Last but not least, one cannot forget to take into account the positive spillover effects of inward FDI regarding the transfer of managerial and organizational know-how to domestic firms (See previous subsection).

In conclusion, the utilization of host and home country management personnel at affiliates located in Central and Eastern Europe seems to be the most beneficial option for MNCs.

12.4.4 Employment Effects

Whereas it is axiomatic that greenfield-type FDI inflows create new jobs in the host country, acquisition of a local company by a foreign investor can often lead to a reduction in employment at the company as a result of post-privatization restructuring activities and rationalization measures. Nevertheless, the opposite may also occur since a takeover of an enterprise by a multinational corporation can be followed by an increase in employment, especially in a longer term (UNCTAD 2000, p. 180). The actual employment impact of privatization-related FDI depends to a large extent on the type of industry in which the investment takes place, on the short-term and long-term objectives of the investor, and on the condition of a given enterprise at the time of its privatization (UNCTAD 1994, p. 166). If, for instance, an MNC operating in a labor-intensive industry, e. g. machine engineering or the food-processing industry, acquires an overstaffed plant in a developing country, a more 'painful' streamlining of employment is likely to occur than in the case of a FDI project in a highly capital-intensive sector where production processes are almost fully automated. It needs to be pointed out, however, that from the point of view of economics, rationalization of employment resulting in a noticeable increase in productivity and cost efficiency constitutes a positive development despite the fact that it is usually accompanied by some social costs, especially in developing countries.

The social aspects of industrial restructuring were discussed in some depth in section 11.3 of the present study. It remains only to be added here that privatization of a state-owned firm to a foreign investor is likely to have positive qualitative effects on employment. Multinational corporations operating in developing and middle-developed countries usually invest considerably more in training than local firms and use more innovative training and development methods. Moreover, they tend to pay superior salaries to those directly employed and provide them with more attractive fringe benefits than those offered by domestic firms (ibid., pp. 187-198). Employees occupying managerial positions as well as blue-collar workers at Polish enterprises privatized to foreigners confirm this, on the national level, by reporting higher wages, better training opportunities and better conditions of work in the post-privatization period (Jarosz 1998, pp. 152-158).

Apart from direct employment effects of privatization-related FDI inflow to a host country, there are a number of indirect consequences of such investment. Some of them, e.g. the emulation of foreign managerial techniques by local firms through various channels, were described already in preceding subsections.

Foreign investors may contribute to the generation of employment in the host country through the purchase of raw materials, components and services from local suppliers and/or subcontractors (*backward linkages*). Similarly, they can positively influence generation of jobs in the host country by cooperating with local distributors of their products (*forward linkages*) (UNCTAD 1994, p. 192). Advisory services and other forms of assistance provided by foreign investors to local suppliers of raw materials are likely to improve the quality of the workforce and contribute positively to skill formation in the host country (ibid., p. 204; UNCTAD 1999, pp. 39-40). Close cooperation between sugar factories privatized to foreign investors in Poland and local sugarbeet growers is a perfect example of such a process.

According to UNCTAD's World Investment Report 1994, indirect employment effects of FDI in the host countries are, in principle, positive and quite often generate the same or a greater number of jobs than the direct investment itself (ibid., p. 1994). Nonetheless, the extent of these externalities depends, as in the case of direct employment effects themselves, on the industry in which a privatization-related FDI project takes place, on the goals and sourcing strategy of the foreign investor (procurement of inputs locally or abroad) and the initial situation of the acquired enterprise.

12.4.5 Conclusions

It can be stated on the basis of the above theoretical considerations that given the restructuring challenges facing the sugar industry in Poland in the beginning of the 1990s, the privatization of sugar factories in the country to foreign investors seems to have been the right policy to follow at that time, in order to ensure effective restructuring. In theory, foreign investors were equipped with everything what was domestically scarce or simply unavailable and which was necessary to restructure the Polish sugar industry and make it internationally competitive. Apart from much needed financial resources, foreign investors possessed experience as well as valuable technical and managerial know-how, gained during many years of operations under market economy conditions. By the same token, they were expected to succeed in implementing the necessary strategic restructuring processes (such as the consolidation of sugar factories and the thorough modernization of selected plants) and increasing the overall productivity efficiency in the Polish sugar sector.

The above considerations on potential benefits and costs of the privatization of state-owned enterprises to foreign investors serve as the basis for the formulation of hypotheses tested in the empirical part of this study.

13 The Privatization Process and the Current Framework of the Sugar Industry in Poland

After Poland's "leap to a market economy" in 1990, the state monopoly in sugar production was removed and the 78 sugar factories existing at that time in the country became individual economic units. They remained, however, under state-ownership. In the following few years, the financial situation of most plants was systematically worsening. This was a result of uncontrolled, survival-driven competition between individual sugar manufacturers in a new, market-oriented environment. The disappearance of governmental subsidies, a substantial increase in the interest rates on bank loans as well as overproduction and inefficiencies in beet processing and structural distortions were other important factors putting many sugar producers in Poland in a difficult situation. In the early years of the transition period, Polish authorities did not introduce any strategic plan of action aimed at the restructuring of the indigenous sugar industry. At the same time, structural changes as well as the modernization of small, undercapitalized and technologically obsolete sugar factories needed to be dealt with immediately. This, however, required a fair amount of financial resources, which were not available domestically.

In the years 1992-1993, various institutions and groups of experts drafted several restructuring programs for the Polish sugar sector. One such scheme was prepared by Rolimpex Ltd (UK) at the request of the Ministry of Agriculture in December 1992. In the first months of 1993, the Inter-ministerial Team for Restructuring and Privatization of the Agricultural Environment (*Międzyresortowy Zespół ds. Restrukturyzacji i Prywatyzacji Otoczenia Rolnictwa*), led by Prof. Roman Urban, and the Antimonopoly Office, developed two further projects (Ministry of State Treasury 2001, p. 65). Nevertheless, it was not before the middle of 1994 that the Polish government decided on a definite course of action. The end product of all the debates regarding the restructuring of the sugar industry in Poland was the Law on Regulation of the Sugar Market and Ownership Transformations in the Sugar Sector, passed on August 26, 1994.[235] One of the main provisions of the law was the establishment of four sugar holdings (*Pomorsko-Poznańska Spółka Cukrowa*, *Mazowiecko-Kujawska Spółka Cukrowa*, *Śląska Spółka Cukrowa* and *Lubelsko-Małopolska Spółka Cukrowa*) charged with the privatization of all state-owned sugar factories.[236] The allocation of regions to individual holdings as

---

[235] Journal of Laws (1994) No. 98, item 473; Journal of Laws (1996) No. 152, item 724.

[236] Apart from calling for the establishment of four sugar holdings and the specification of their tasks, the Sugar Law of August 26, 1994 also included a set of market regulations for the sugar sector in Poland. Individual elements of the sugar regime introduced in Poland on the basis of the Sugar Law of August 1994, its functioning, shortcomings and modifications are discussed in detail in section 9.5 of this study.

well as the location of sugar factories that found themselves on their territories are portrayed in Figure 47.

The aforementioned regulation imposed the transfer to the sugar holdings of 51% of the share capital of all state-owned sugar factories (which were transformed first into State Treasury Corporations). After the completion of this process, individual holdings were to be privatized to strategic investors.

Two sites, *Klecina* and *Chełmica*, were closed down in 1995 due to a disastrous financial situation. 13 other sugar factories in Poland were privatized individually and/or created alliances with foreign investors.

As a result of a joint venture of *British Sugar*, *Rolimpex* and "*Cukrownie Toruńskie*", a new company called *SugarPol* was established in 1989, with *British Sugar* holding a 51% majority shareholding. The company comprised two factories, *Unisław* and *Ostrowite*. In 1994, *SugarPol* acquired a third factory, in *Świecie*.

In 1991, assets of the sugar factory in *Gostyń* were leased to a new company set up by its employees. Shortly afterwards, four other plants located in the vicinity of *Gostyń* were privatized in the same way (*Góra Śląska*, *Kościan*, *Miejska Górka*, *Wschowa*). In the years 1996-97, the plants in *Kościan*, *Miejska Górka* and *Gostyń* were taken over by *Pfeifer & Langen* (Germany) through a secondary ownership transfer. In 1999, the same company took over the sugar factory in *Góra Śląska*.

Sugarbeet-processing plants located in *Środa Wielkopolska*, *Garbów, Guzów, Dobre and Kętrzyn* were privatized individually and were not incorporated into holdings. The first two of the five plants were taken over by *Pfeifer & Langen* and *Tate & Lyle*, respectively. *Tate & Lyle* sold later its stake in *Garbów* to *Südzucker*. The sugar factories in *Guzów, Dobre* and *Kętrzyn* were acquired by *Rolimpex*. In 2000, *British Sugar* took over all three plants through a secondary ownership transfer.

Due to a very poor economic situation, the sugar factories in *Głogów*, *Ropczyce*, *Włostów*, *Strzyżów*, *Glinojeck*, *Michałów*, *Ciechanów* and *Pelplin* were privatized to strategic foreign investors individually (through the increase of capital) before the end of the establishment of holdings (Ministry of State Treasury 2002, p.12). Nevertheless, their transfer into private hands was carried out by sugar holdings.

In 1999, the German company *Nordzucker* became a majority owner of the sugar factory in *Opalenica* after the acquisition of a controlling stake from the creditor of the plant, *Bank Gospodarki Żywnościowej* and from *Rolimpex S.A*. In 2000, *Nordzucker* purchased an additional package of shares of *Opalenica* from *Pomorsko-Poznańska Spółka Cukrowa*. Also, the already privatized sugar factory in *Wschowa* was taken over by *Nordzucker* in 2000 (acquisition of majority stake from an individual investor).

The share capital of 61 plants was incorporated systematically into the four holdings. This took much more time, however, than had been anticipated. The regis-

tration of individual holdings in the appropriate courts (granting of a legal status) took place in the first half of 1996 (NIK 2000, p. 48).[237] It was preceded by the choice of head offices and the appointment of members of the management and supervisory boards of each holding by the Ministry for Ownership Transformations.[238] Commercialization and incorporation into individual holdings of all non-privatized sugar factories (except for two cases) ended in June 1998.[239]
The slow pace of this process was brought about partly by the fact that for a certain period of time many plants did not fulfill all the necessary requirements (specified in the Sugar Law of 1994) for the transformation into a joint-stock company, due to their poor economic situation. Moreover, managers of many factories were not very enthusiastic about entering into the sugar holdings, since it was tantamount to the loss of autonomy. Some feared that after such a reform, sugar factories in good economic condition would have to support loss-generating plants. Furthermore, employees of sugar factories that attracted strong interest of foreign investors were afraid that formation of holdings would lead to a slow-down of privatization and an increase in political influence on the activity of their enterprises (Kondrakiewicz 2000, p. 127; Langowski/Sopińska-Węglowska 2002).

An ordinance issued on June 20, 1995 by the Council of Ministers, stipulated that the privatization of sugar holdings (not individual plants) could take place through the increase of share capital of individual holdings (issue of new shares and takeover of these shares by qualified outsiders).[240] 49%-stakes in each sugar factory incorporated into holdings remained initially in the hands of the State

[237] The registration of the first holding (*Mazowiecko-Kujawska Spółka Cukrowa*) took place on April 1, 1996. The last of the four holdings (*Pomorsko-Poznańska Spółka Cukrowa*) was registered on June 20, 1996 (NIK 2000, p. 48).

[238] In the second half of 1996, the Ministry for Ownership Transformations was dissolved. Its duties and tasks were taken over by a new department of governmental administration, the Ministry of State Treasury (See Journal of Laws (1997) No. 141, item 943, article 25, with subsequent amendments).

[239] The incorporation of sugar factories into *Lubelsko-Małopolska Spółka Cukrowa* ended on December 31, 1996. At *Mazowiecko-Kujawska Spółka Cukrowa,* this process was finalized on April 2, 1997. At *Śląska Spółka Cukrowa,* 51% of the share capital of the last sugar factory (*Ziębice*) was incorporated on May 26, 1998. Contribution of shares of the last sugar factory (*Pelplin*) to *Pomorsko-Poznańska Spółka Cukrowa* took place on June 24, 1998 (NIK 2000, p. 49; Kondrakiewicz 2000, p. 128). The sugar factory in *Szczecin* remained, until 2003,the only sugarbeet-processing plant in Poland which was still a state-owned enterprise. For a long period of time, the plant was under the so-called curative proceedings, due to its poor economic situation. At the end of 2003, the factory in *Szczecin* was commercialized, and was incorporated into *KSC* in 2005. The sugar factory in *Wieluń* (number 44 in Figure 47) was incorporated into *Śląska Spółka Cukrowa* with a delay, since restitution claims had been lodged earlier concerning its assets. In the end, the factory was taken over together with other plants forming *Śląska Spółka Cukrowa* by *Südzucker*.

[240] Journal of Laws (1995) No. 75, item 375.

Treasury. A large part of these stakes was to be allocated at a later time, free of charge, to farmers (15%) and employees of privatized sugar factories (15%).[241]

It is important to mention here that a reserve amounting to 5 % of the share capital of each State Treasury Corporation was created in Poland for restitution purposes. In the case of enterprises whose share capital was to be contributed to sugar holdings, this reserve was increased by another 4% (Ministry of State Treasury 2001, p. 66).

The Minister of State Treasury signed a contract with an advisor who was to help in implementing the privatization process of factories incorporated into the four sugar holdings on October 15, 1997. According to a privatization timetable included in an annex to the ordination issued on June 20, 1995 by the Council of Ministers, such contract should have been signed within 6 months after the registration of the last sugar holding. In reality, it took nearly 16 months (NIK 2000, p. 54). This delay had the effect that the preparation of pre-privatization analyses by the appointed advisor and the beginning of the privatization process also took place behind time.[242]

On November 3, 1999, the Council of Ministers issued an ordinance changing the rules and timetable of the privatization of sugar holdings.[243] It included an entry saying that "Privatization of sugar holdings may be preceded by sale of packages of shares (being in possession of holdings) of individual sugar factories or their groups, according to principles and procedures specified by General Assembly of Shareholders of a given sugar holding in accordance with article 18 of the Act on Commercialization and Privatization of August 30, 1996." In other words, the new ordinance paved the way for privatization of individual sugar factories and groups of plants. Previously, the ordinance of June 20, 1995 prescribed privatization of entire holdings.[244]

The ordinance of November 3, 1999 provided a legal basis for a change to the privatization strategy concerning *Pomorsko-Poznańska Spółka Cukrowa*, *Mazowiecko-Kujawska Spółka Cukrowa* and *Lubelsko-Małopolska Spółka Cukrowa*, specified by the Minister of State Treasury at the end of 1998 (NIK 2000, p. 59). According to the new privatization scheme, clusters of sugar factories concentrated in the

---

241 Journal of Laws (1996) No. 152, item 724, article 1, point 8.

242 In the years 1997-1999, the Ministry of State Treasury allocated for the preparation of pre-privatization analyzes of the four sugar holdings financial resources from the PHARE program totaling ECU 484.651 (NIK 2000, p. 54).

243 Journal of Laws (1999) No. 93, item 1069.

244 In an audit examining the implementation of the provisions of the Sugar Law of August 26, 1994 (carried out between December 1999 and April 2000), the Supreme Chamber of Control questioned the legality of the ordinance of November 3, 1999. It expressed doubts about whether it was constitutional that an ordinance prescribing privatization of entire holdings be complemented by a new one, making possible the sale of assets of holdings before their privatization in due course. After a thorough investigation of this issue by lawyers, it turned out that introduction of such an amendment was permissible.

above three holdings were to be privatized regionally to strategic investors. It was expected that the sale of sugar factories in this way would make the privatization process easier and lead to a swift transfer of state property into private hands. Another rationale behind the choice of this privatization method was that a take-over of several plants located in a given region by one strategic investor would facilitate their consolidation at a later time.

In compliance with the new governmental strategy, individual holdings divided factories within their territorial reach into groups. *Lubelsko-Małopolska Spółka Cukrowa* and *Mazowiecko-Kujawska Spółka Cukrowa* created three such groups each; *Pomorsko-Poznańska Spółka Cukrowa* established five groups of plants.[245] At *Śląska Spółka Cukrowa,* such division did not take place. The existence of "natural hubs of sugarbeet plantations" and the location of sugar factories on their territories constituted an important factor taken into account in the establishment of individual holdings and groups of factories designed for privatization (Ministry of State Treasury 2002, p.13).[246]

As soon as the Minister of State Treasury published advertisements in the national press inviting investors to enter negotiations concerning the regional privatization of commercialized sugar factories, potential bidders could start applying for the acquisition of all factories concentrated in *Śląska Spółka Cukrowa* and particular groups of plants formed in the remaining three sugar holdings.[247] The first winner of preliminary negotiations was selected on March 31, 2000, when the French company *Saint Louis Sucre* was granted the exclusive

---

245 *Lubelsko-Małopolska Spółka Cukrowa* established the following three groups of plants: Krasnystaw Group (comprising the sugar factories in *Krasnystaw, Klemensów, Rejowiec, Strzyżów, Werbkowice, Wożuczyn*), Lublin Group (sugar factories in *Częstocice, Lublin, Łapy, Opole* and *Sokołów*) and Ropczyce Group (sugar factories in *Ropczyce, Łubna, Przeworsk* and *Włostów*). *Mazowiecko-Kujawska Spółka Cukrowa* established the following three groups of plants: Mazowiecka Group (*Borowiczki, Brześć Kujawski, Dobrzelin, Leśmierz, Mała Wieś* and *Ostrowy*), Chełmża Group (*Chełmża, Krasiniec* and *Mełno*) and Gdańsk Group (*Malbork, Nowy Staw*). *Cukrownie Toruńskie*, a company providing various services for the sugar industry, also went into the composition of *Mazowiecko-Kujawska Spółka Cukrowa. Pomorsko-Poznańska Spółka Cukrowa* established the following five groups of plants: Szczecin Group (*Gryfice, Kluczewo, Szczecin*), Gdańsk Group (*Pelplin, Pruszcz Gdański* (the Gdańsk Group, comprising in total four plants (*Malbork, Nowy Staw, Pelplin, Pruszcz Gdański*), was created jointly by *Pomorsko-Poznańska Spółka Cukrowa* and *Mazowiecko-Kujawska Spółka Cukrowa*), Bydgoszcz Group (*Janikowo, Kruszwica, Nakło, Tuczno, Żnin*), Poznań Group (*Opalenica* and *Szamotuły*) and Kalisko-Konińska Group (*Gosławice, Gniezno, Witaszyce, Zbiersk, Zduny*).

246 Up to April 2000, sugar holdings invested PLN 1,742,000 in the preparation of restructuring programs and pre-privatization analyses (NIK 2000, p. 56).

247 The sugar factory in *Głogów* was excluded from the privatization of the entire Silesian holding (*Śląska Spółka Cukrowa*). Due to the fact that the plant found itself on the brink of bankruptcy, the authorities of *ŚSC* decided to privatize it individually. On November 17, 1999, a majority stake in *Głogów* was acquired by *Pfeifer & Langen* (NIK 2000, p. 55).

right to enter into the final phase of negotiations regarding the purchase of 16 factories clustered in *Śląska Spółka Cukrowa* (NIK 2000, p. 54).
By the end of March 2003, 49 sugarbeet-processing plants in Poland had been privatized (including all aforementioned individual privatizations). All of them were taken over through a primary and/or secondary ownership transfer by foreign sugar corporations. German sugar companies were particularly actively involved in the privatization process of the sugar industry in Poland. *Südzucker* (the largest sugar manufacturer in the EU), *Nordzucker* (the second largest) and *Pfeifer & Langen* acquired together 38 sugar factories in the country. *British Sugar*, *Rolimpex*, *Tate & Lyle* (all three from the UK) and *Danisco* (from Denmark) took over 11 plants.[248] Many Polish sugar factories were in very poor economic condition at the moment of their transfer into private hands. Nonetheless, strategic investors had to pay a fair price in order to come into the possession of controlling stakes in privatized sugar factories. In privatization deals carried out by the State Treasury, the average selling price of a sugar factory, expressed in PLN per one tonne of total sugar production quota allocated to the plant, amounted to about PLN 2,000 (Pro-Invest International 2001, p. I-4).
In many cases, the increase in the capital of an ailing sugar factory, conducted by a strategic investor immediately after privatization, was connected with financial expenditures similar to those incurred by the purchase of shares of the factory (ibid. p. I-4).

The number of factories sold to foreign investors was very likely to expand since West European sugar corporations were eager to make further purchases. Moreover, the Sugar Law of August 26, 1994 stipulated that all sugar factories were to be privatized. A surprising decision of the Polish government on the withdrawal from this process and the establishment of a national sugar corporation named *Krajowa Spółka Cukrowa "Polski Cukier"* (National Sugar Corporation "Polish Sugar") (*KSC*) created a decisive obstacle on the way to the completion of privatization through the sale of commercialized sugar factories to strategic investors. The new Sugar Law, passed on June 21, 2001 provided the legal basis for this turnaround.[249] According to the law, *KSC* was to comprise all sugar factories that had not yet been privatized. This sudden change of governmental policy was imposed by the increasing opposition of various groups hostile to privatization with foreign involvement, including some sugarbeet growers, employees of some sugar factories and several members of the Polish parliament. The Polish government thus abandoned its strong commitment to privatization of the sugar sector. As a result, crucial decisions in the process were overturned at the last minute. The formal signature of an authenticated deed on the establishment of *KSC* took place in Warsaw on August 26, 2002.

248 Sugar factories acquired by *Rolimpex*, *Tate & Lyle* and *Danisco* were taken over at a later point in time by *British Sugar* and *Südzucker* through a secondary ownership transfer.
249 Journal of Laws (2001) No. 76, item 810, article 20.

Figure 47. Sugar industry in Poland

POLSKI CUKIER	SÜDZUCKER	NORDZUCKER	PFEIFER & LANGEN	BRITISH SUGAR
1 GRYFICE	12 JAWOR*	45 OPALENICA	51 GŁOGÓW*	62 PELPLIN*
2 SZCZECIN*	13 MAŁOSZYN	46 SZAMOTUŁY*	52 GOSTYŃ	63 CIECHANÓW*
3 KLUCZEWO	14 PASTUCHÓW*	47 WSCHOWA*	53 GÓRA ŚLĄSKA	64 MICHAŁÓW*
4 JANIKOWO	15 PUSTKÓW*	48 CHEŁMŻA	54 KOŚCIAN*	65 GLINOJECK
5 KRUSZWICA	16 STRZELIN	49 KRASINIEC*	55 MIEJSKA GÓRKA	66 OSTROWITE
6 NAKŁO	17 ŚWIDNICA	50 MEŁNO*	56 ŚRODA	67 ŚWIECIE*
7 TUCZNO	18 WROCŁAW		57 GOSŁAWICE	68 UNISŁAW
8 ŻNIN*	19 BABORÓW*		58 GNIEZNO*	69 DOBRE
9 MALBORK	20 CEREKIEW		59 WITASZYCE*	70 GUZÓW*
10 NOWY STAW	21 CHYBIE		60 ZBIERSK*	71 KĘTRZYN*
11 PRUSZCZ GD.*	22 RACIBÓRZ		61 ZDUNY*	
27 BOROWICZKI*	23 WRÓBLIN			
28 BRZEŚĆ KUJAW.	24 ŁAGIEWNIKI*			
29 DOBRZELIN	25 OTMUCHÓW			
30 LEŚMIERZ	26 ZIĘBICE*			
31 MAŁA WIEŚ	44 WIELUŃ*			
32 OSTROWY	72 ŁUBNA			
33 KLEMENSÓW*	73 ROPCZYCE			
34 KRASNYSTAW	74 WŁOSTÓW*			
35 REJOWIEC*	75 GARBÓW*			
36 WERBKOWICE	76 STRZYŻÓW			
37 WOŻUCZYN	43 PRZEWORSK*			
38 CZĘSTOCICE				
39 LUBLIN				
40 ŁAPY				
41 OPOLE				
42 SOKOŁÓW*				

* Locations where sugarbeet processing was ceased until the beginning of the campaign 2004/05.

Source: *Zuckerindustrie* 126 (2001) Nr. 9; *Rynek Cukru* Nr. 23/*Czerwiec* 2003, Cukier i Skrobia 2005.

In October 2003, *KSC* officially became a capital group comprising 22 sugarbeet-processing plants spread over seven provinces of Poland. A part of the share capital of *KSC* was to be allocated free of charge to sugarbeet growers (15%) and to employees (15%) of individual plants incorporated into the company. The rest of the share capital was to be transferred into their hands for a payment.

Before the 2001 Sugar Law came into effect, Germany's *Nordzucker* fulfilled virtually all the necessary requirements connected with the acquisition of six sugar factories in the vicinity of *Szczecin* and *Gdańsk*.[250] On November 15, 2000, *Saint Louis Sucre* (part of the *Südzucker Group* since 2002) signed a preliminary contract with the Polish Ministry of State Treasury concerning the aforementioned takeover of 16 plants in Silesia.[251] After the passage of the 2001 Sugar Law, the above two transactions were blocked by the Ministry of Internal Affairs. Both *Nordzucker* and *Saint Louis Sucre* filed complaints with the courts.

On March 26, 2003, after more than two years of legal confrontations, the Ministry of State Treasury gave final approval to the sale of the Silesian holding to *Saint Louis Sucre*.[252] Conversely, the Court of Appeal in *Gdańsk* rejected on May 14, 2003 a formal complaint lodged by *Nordzucker* and decided that two of the six factories that the company wanted to acquire (*Malbork* and *Nowy Staw*) were to be incorporated into *KSC*. A similar verdict was later reached with regard to the remaining four plants (*Pruszcz Gdański, Gryfice, Szczecin* and *Kluczewo*). The sugar factories *Malbork, Nowy Staw, Pruszcz Gdański, Gryfice,* and *Kluczewo* were later incorporated into *KSC* (the last three in January 2005). *Szczecin* was administered until recently by *KSC* on behalf of the Polish State Treasury. It was incorporated into the corporation in May 2005.

At the time of writing, it is still not clear what is going to happen with the factory in *Leśmierz*. 30% of share capital of this plant was distributed to its employees and sugarbeet growers prior to the decision on the establishment of *KSC*. Since the State Treasury holds a majority stake in *Leśmierz*, it may seem logical that the factory should be incorporated into the national sugar corporation. This is also the outcome that the State Treasury and the management of *KSC* would like to see reached. Nevertheless, employees and sugarbeet growers of *Leśmierz* are unwilling to join *KSC* and prefer to remain 'independent'. The State Treasury, on the other hand, does not have a sufficient amount of votes in the

---

[250] In Figure 47, these factories are marked with the numbers 1-3 and 9-11. *Mazowiecko-Kujawska Spółka Cukrowa* and *Pomorsko-Poznańska Spółka Cukrowa* jointly chose *Nordzucker* as a potential strategic investor for the sugar factories in *Pruszcz Gdański, Malbork* and *Nowy Staw*.

[251] Factories 12-26 and 44 in Figure 47.

[252] The sugar factory in *Ziębice* was incorporated into *Śląska Spółka Cukrowa* but it went bankrupt after a preliminary privatization contract regarding the purchase of *ŚSC* by *Saint Louis Sucre* was signed by the representatives of the company and by the Polish Ministry of State Treasury. Therefore, the factory 'fell out' from the transaction.

General Assembly of Shareholders in order to make a ruling sealing the incorporation of *Leśmierz* into *KSC*.

After 14 years of ownership transformations in the Polish sugar industry, five large capital groups have crystallized in the sector. The current make-up of the sugar market in Poland is presented in Figure 48.

Figure 48. Market shares of sugar companies in Poland, 2004

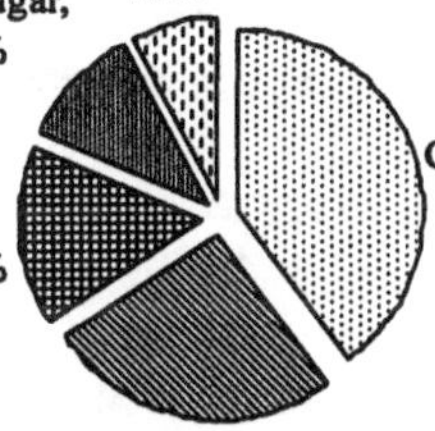

Source: IERiGŻ 6/2005, p. 19.

Many experts share the opinion that the most opportune moment to commence a large-scale consolidation and restructuring process of the sugar industry in Poland appeared immediately after the collapse of communism and central planning in the country.[253] The organizational structure of the sugar sector in 1989 provided a good basis for the privatization and amalgamation of sugar factories concentrated in 13 grouped enterprises.[254] Instead of initiating such a reform, grouped enterprises were liquidated and 78 plants began a solitary struggle for survival. In this way, the early opportunity to launch necessary restructuring processes in the Polish sugar industry was lost. Developments of the following years validated the theory that in the case of slow privatization and restructuring, many impediments to the processes are likely to emerge on the way.[255] This refers mainly to the eventuality of fading social agreement with reforms, especially among those who have an interest in maintaining the status quo.

It is recognized by many authors that the transfer of enterprises from state to private ownership constitutes the major task of microeconomic restructuring.[256] Nevertheless, if the fulfillment of this task is tantamount to the loss of the remnants of political influence on the economy, it is unlikely that those in power will make special efforts to speed up privatization. Of course, this does not have always

253 See for example Malec 2002, p.230; Rygielski 2003, p. 50.
254 See Appendix 1.
255 See for example Lipton/Sachs 1990; Balcerowicz 1997, pp. 208-234; Bałtowski/Mickiewicz 2000, p. 434; Bałtowski 2002a, p. 28 and 228.
256 See for example Meyer 1998b, p.17.

to be true, but it turned out to be valid in the case of Polish transition. As the number of state-owned enterprises gradually decreased after the country's 'leap' to a market economy, the political character of entities still in the hands of the state was getting stronger year by year. By the same token, the pressure of political lobbyists to keep such entities out of the clutches of private (especially foreign) investors was also growing. By the end of the 1990s, the share of the state sector in Poland's GDP had shrunk to 35% (EBRD 1999, p. 24). In this situation, the value of sugar holdings as objects of political ascendancy was gaining increasing importance, since the four holdings and nearly 60 sugar factories under their authority offered about 200 posts in supervisory boards (Bałtowski 2002a, p. 228).

The plausibility of the above considerations was confirmed after the parliamentary elections in Poland in 1997 and 2001, when serious reshuffles were made in the supervisory boards of individual holdings and most commercialized sugar factories. Obviously, such a 'carousel of posts' also took place at other entities controlled by the state. It goes without saying that the motivation of civil servants supervising State Treasury Corporations on the behalf of the government to accelerate privatization is very weak, if not null. Members of supervisory boards are interested rather in preventing ownership changes in order to keep their jobs for as long as possible and to allow things to muddle along.

Audits conducted by the Polish Supreme Chamber of Control in the years 1995-2000 revealed that sugar holdings delayed the privatization and restructuring of sugar factories incorporated into their structures and burdened them at the same time with the costs of their own functioning.

The reluctance of succeeding governments to privatize and to initiate radical restructuring programs was growing stronger with every year. This was brought about not only by the increasingly political character of state-owned enterprises. The more advanced was the transformation process of the Polish economy, the worse was the public attitude towards privatization. Surveys conducted regularly by the Public Opinion Research Center (CBOS) demonstrated that social support for ownership changes and other reforms deteriorated considerably in the years 1998-2003 compared with the early years of transition. There were several reasons for this development: rising unemployment; a lagging economy; disappointment of a large group of people who felt that they had lost out on the transition to capitalism; as well as the disclosure of several swindles and shabby affairs connected with privatization from above. All this had the effect that in the 1999-2003 time period the number of Poles who believed in benefits arising from privatization was constantly shrinking. In late 2003, it was considerably smaller than the number of those who thought that privatization has an adverse effect on the Polish economy. The most recent survey examining the public attitude towards privatization was carried out by CBOS in January 2005. Although results of the survey show a slight improvement in the opinions about privatization in comparison with

2003, the attitude of 40% of Poles towards this process remains still negative (CBOS 2005, p. 2).[257]

Given the above developments, it should not come as a surprise that the privatization process of the Polish economy slowed down considerably at the end of the 1990s. The governments elected in 1997 and 2001 shied away from making bold decisions in this field, since such a move could have exposed them to the displeasure of a large group of voters. At the same time, billions of PLN of public money were spent on propping up moribund state-owned enterprises. Moreover, as time went by, various activists were showing more and more zeal in stirring up a revolt against the "sale of national jewels to foreigners at rock-bottom prices". This relates in great measure to the privatization process of the sugar industry in Poland. Apart from shelving the privatization of sugar factories, the Polish government effectively prevented their closure and amalgamation through the enactment of appropriate legislation.

As a result of all these developments, employment in the sugar industry in Poland was slowly decreasing in the years following the country's transition to a market economy. By the same token, labor productivity in the local sugar sector was improving at snail's pace and was barely perceptible over a long period of time. It started to rise considerably from the season 1998/99 onwards (See Figures 49 and 50, and Tables 31 and 32).

Summarizing the issues discussed in this section, it has to be pointed out once again that the unending postponement of privatization of the sugar industry in Poland systematically increased the extent of political involvement in this sector. It had the effect that, from a certain moment on, all significant decisions concern-

---

257 In October 2003, only 19% of Poles surveyed by CBOS agreed that privatization is beneficial to the Polish economy while 43% claimed that it does not bring any good. In the years 1990-1999 (with the exception of 1992), the number of those who claimed that privatization brings benefits for the Polish economy was considerably higher than the number of those who think that it does not bring any benefits. Unfortunately, in the years 2000-2003, the results of the opinion polls examining public attitude towards privatization, conducted by CBOS, turned upside down. Among the main beneficiaries of privatization, people surveyed by CBOS in October 2003 named swindlers and crooks (48%), civil servants involved in ownership transformations (39%), and foreigners (34%). At the same time, the surveyed persons claimed that the majority of Poles (63%), Polish economy in general (51%) and employees of privatized enterprises (48%), lost most on privatization (CBOS 2005, pp. 2-8). A similar survey conducted by CBOS in January 2005 demonstrated that 25% of Poles argue that privatization is beneficial to the Polish economy while 40% expressed an opposite point of view. Among the main beneficiaries of privatization, people surveyed by CBOS in January 2005 named again swindlers and crooks (44%), civil servants involved in ownership transformations (42%), and foreigners (40%). At the same time, the surveyed persons claimed that the majority of Poles (71%), Polish economy in general (45%) and employees of privatized enterprises (44%), lost most on privatization (CBOS 2005, pp. 2-8).

ing the sugar industry were dominated by politics, while economics became a matter of secondary importance. The culmination of this process was marked by the governmental resolution calling for the establishment of the national sugar corporation *Krajowa Spółka Cukrowa "Polski Cukier"*.

Figure 49. Average employment level in the sugar industry in Poland (in thousands), 1994-2004*

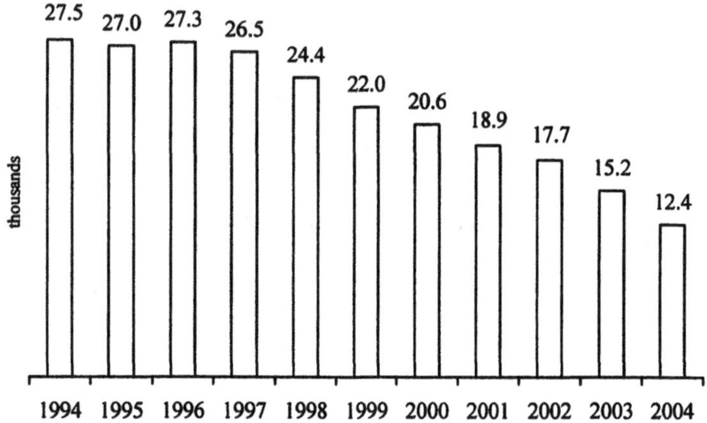

* Average employment level during the year.
Source: GUS 2005.

Figure 50. Average labor productivity in the sugar industry in Poland (in tonnes of white sugar per one employee*), 1994-2004

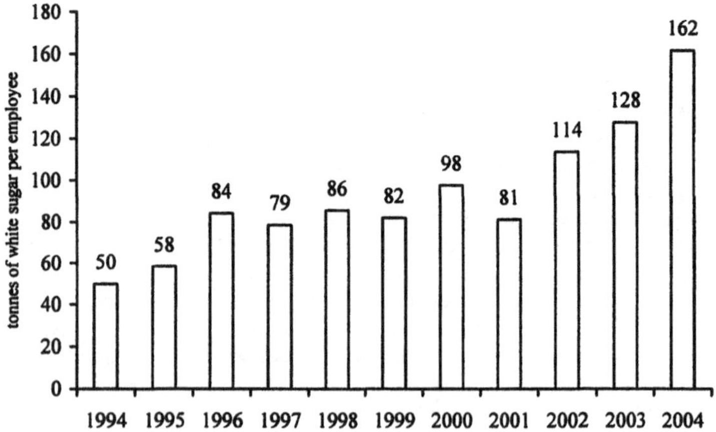

* Average employment level during the year.
Source: Calculations by the author, based on GUS (employment) and IPC (sugar production) data.

Table 31. Employment in the sugar industry in Poland, 2002/03-2004/05

	2002/03	2003/04	2004/05
Campaign employment*	24,679	21,288	15,174
Inter-campaign employment**	13,618	10,235	8,646
Campaign employment per 1 working sugar factory	392	387	441
Inter-campaign employment per 1 working sugar factory	216	186	212

* Regular staff + Campaign workforce; ** Regular staff

Source: Rybski 2005, p. 49.

Table 32. Productivity of sugar production in Poland, 2002/03-2004/05

	2002/03	2003/04	2004/05
Total sugar production (in t) per 1 employee. Campaign employment	80.2	91.4	132.4
Production of quota sugar (in t) per 1 employee. Campaign employment	64.4	78.5	110.2
Total sugar production (in t) per 1 employee. Inter-campaign employment	145.3	190	232.3
Production of quota sugar (in t) per 1 employee. Inter-campaign employment	116.8	163.4	193.4
Total sugar production (in t) per 1 working sugar factory	31.413	35.372	46.707
Production of quota sugar (in t) per 1 working sugar factory	25.238	30.399	38.882

Source: Rybski 2005, p. 49.

14 Theorizing on the Optimal Structure of the Sugar Industry in Poland: Analysis and Discussion of Walkenhorst's Model

Despite the fact that a micro-level approach was taken in this study in order to evaluate the impact of privatization of the sugar industry in Poland on the restructuring process of this sector, it is necessary to conduct certain macro-level analyses if one is to be able to attempt an answer to the main research question. As was pointed out repeatedly in previous chapters, one of the greatest challenges facing the restructuring process of the Polish sugar industry has been the consolidation of a large number of small sugar factories dispersed over the whole country and the concentration of sugar production in areas where the conditions for sugarbeet growing and processing are, from the point of view of economics, most favorable. For this reason, it is essential to find out in which regions of Poland the soil and climatic conditions are best for sugarbeet growing, where the costs of this form of agricultural activity are lowest, how many beet-processing plants are needed in the country, how much sugar they should produce and, finally, where they should be located. The purpose of this section is to answer these questions and to arrive at a picture of the optimum structure of the sugar industry in Poland. In the first part of the section, the natural conditions for sugarbeet growing and the distribution of the major sugarbeet-growing regions in the country are examined. Subsequently, a mathematical programming model, aimed at the specification of the economically optimum structure of the sugar industry in Poland, is detailed and analyzed.

In section 4 of this study, it was indicated that sugarbeets are very demanding crops with regard to the quality of soil and climatic conditions such as rainfall and temperature. A highly fertile soil supplemented with minerals and other nutrients is a sine qua non for a good sugarbeet harvest and for the achievement of high yields. It is therefore self-evident why sugarbeets in Poland (and other European countries) are grown most abundantly in regions where the suitability to agriculture of the soils and other natural conditions is greatest. As shown in Figure 51, sugarbeets cover the greatest part of the total area under cultivation in the following former Polish provinces: Leszno (*leszczyńskie*), Legnica (*legnickie*), Wrocław (*wrocławskie*), Zamość (*zamojskie*), as well as Włocławek (*włocławskie*) and Płock (*płockie*).[258]

Figure 51. Share of beet-growing area in total area under cultivation (in %), old administrative division of Poland (1975-1999)

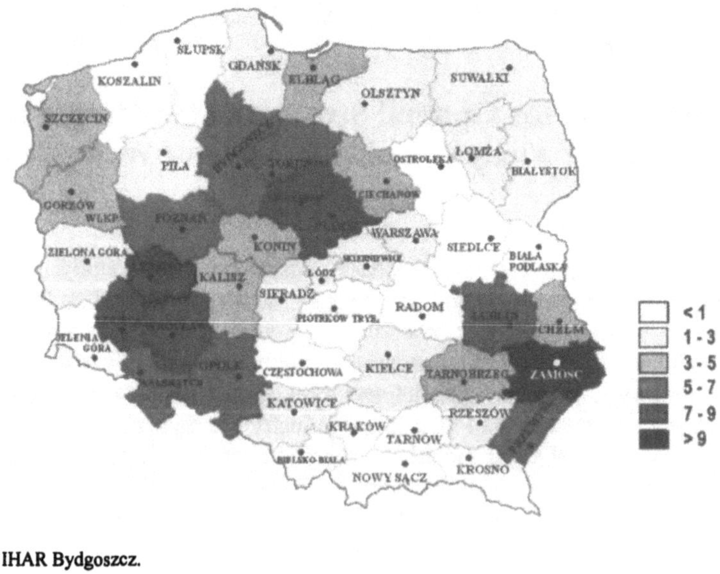

Source: IHAR Bydgoszcz.

---

258 In the 1975-1998 time period, Poland was divided into 49 provinces (voivodships). Their territories and capital cities are portrayed in Figure 51. On January 1, 1999, the 49 provinces were replaced by only 16 (Figure 52) as a result of a reorganization of the old administrative division of the country (For more details see for example http://www.staff.amu.edu.pl/~zbzw/ ph/pro/plpro.html).

If we take the new administrative division of Poland (16 provinces), introduced in 1999, it turns out that the share of sugarbeet-growing area in the total area under cultivation is highest in the Opole (*opolskie*) and the Kuyavian-Pomeranian (*kujawsko-pomorskie*) voivodships (See Figure 52).

Figure 52. Share of beet-growing area in total area under cultivation (in %), new administrative division of Poland (from 1999 onwards)

Source: GUS 2003, p. 42.

A comparison of the above two maps with information provided in Figures 53 and 54 leaves no doubt that there is a direct correlation between the quality of soils and the overall natural conditions for agriculture and the distribution of sugarbeet-growing regions in Poland. It is important to mention here that on the national level, the quality of Polish soils with regard to their agricultural suitability is considerably lower than in many West European countries, e.g. France, the Netherlands and the western part of Germany.[259] Less than one fourth of ploughland soils in Poland can be classified as good or very good (classes I-IIIb). Soils of the poorest quality (classes V-VI) cover more than 30% of ploughland in the country (Andrzejewski/Baranowski 1993).

---

[259] Owing to their location in the Atlantic climate zone (favorable conditions for agriculture), the quality of soils in the above countries is about 25% higher than in Poland which lies in a temperate climate zone (less favorable conditions for agriculture). Moreover, Poland has a poorly developed water network (water deficits) in relation to most other European countries, due to a large-scale deforestation carried out in the past and due to mistakes made in the management of water resources. This refers especially to the central belt of the Polish lowland (Andrzejewski/Baranowski 1993).

Figure 53. Evaluation of the soils of Polish farmland (in points) according to communes

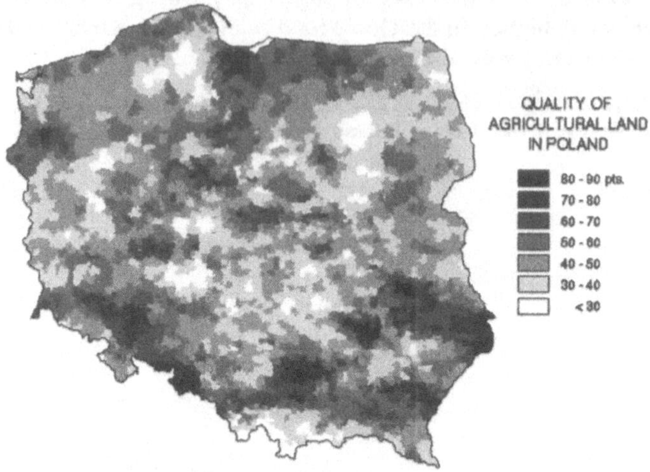

Source: Andrzejewski/Baranowski (1993).

Figure 54. Evaluation of the natural conditions* for agriculture in Poland (in points) according to communes

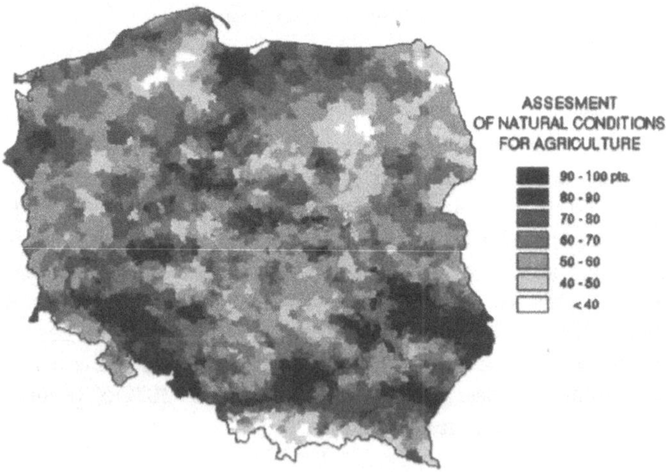

* Including soil conditions, agroclimate, surface and water features of the terrain.
Source: Andrzejewski/Baranowski (1993).

The most soil (in ha) suitable for sugarbeet growing is located within the borders of the following old Polish provinces: Opole (*opolskie*) [63,000 ha], Zamość (*zamojskie*) [58,000 ha], Bydgoszcz (*bydgoskie*) [52,000 ha], Olsztyn (*olsztyńskie*) [51,000 ha], Elbląg (*elbląskie*) [48,000 ha], Poznań (*poznańskie*) [44,000 ha], Szczecin (*szczecińskie*) and Kielce (*kieleckie*) [42,000 ha each] (Brzeziński 2002, p. 6).

If we take another look at the map with the new administrative division of Poland, we will see that these regions went into the composition of eight new Polish provinces which abound with sugarbeet plantations—the two mentioned earlier (Opole and Kuyavian-Pomeranian voivodships) as well as the Lower Silesian (*dolnośląskie*), Greater Poland (*wielkopolskie*), Pomerania (*pomorskie*), West Pomerania (*zachodniopomorskie*), Lublin (*lubelskie*) and Świętokrzyskie (*swiętokrzyskie*) voivodships. Since not only the quality of soils but also other natural conditions within these provinces are favorable for sugarbeet growing, it can be said, in short, that large basins of sugarbeet plantations in Poland are situated in the right places.

The theoretical considerations included in section 4 of the present study, especially those concerning the transport costs of sugarbeets to factories, lead to the conclusion that from the point of view of economic efficiency the entire sugar production should be located on the territory of these eight provinces. The bulkiness and heaviness of sugarbeets, as well as their sensitivity to long storage periods, have meant that in an effort to keep the costs of beet transport and sugar losses at a minimum, virtually all sugar factories in highly developed west European countries are today located in close proximity to major sugarbeet-growing regions.[260]

As we have learned in previous chapters, before 1990, many sugar factories in Poland were built for political reasons in regions where beet plantations are scarce and fragmented, and where the conditions for sugarbeet growing are highly unfavorable. A prime example of such a plant is the sugar factory *Łapy* (no. 40 in Figure 47). Moreover, several beet-processing plants (e.g. *Lublin* and *Szczecin*) found themselves in the immediate vicinity of large city centers. This has caused a number of difficulties for those who run such factories (such as higher costs of meeting environmental standards and of carrying out a campaign than in rural areas, antagonisms with the representatives of the local community, etc.).

For the above reasons, a major challenge of the restructuring process of the sugar industry in Poland, next to the consolidation of a large number of small factories, has been the relocation of a part of production to regions offering better conditions for the achievement of good agricultural yields and high cost efficiency of beet processing.

It is important to add at this point that the main potential advantage of the consolidation of sugar factories in Poland has been not only the increase in the processing capacity of selected sugar factories in order to reap economies of

[260] See the example of Germany at http://www.zuckerwirtschaft.de/2_1_1.html.

scale. In a short run, this restructuring measure was much needed to increase the utilization level of the processing capacity at individual plants. The existence of a large number of sugar factories located often side by side had the effect that the length of a campaign at many of them was for a long time far from the theoretical optimum. This was brought about partly by an insufficient availability of sugarbeets in many regions to serve fully the needs of local factories and partly by the fact that the demand for sugar in Poland and the production quota allocated administratively to individual plants from 1995 onwards were considerably smaller than the cumulative processing capacity of the sugar industry. As time went by, the adverse effects of structural distortions in the Polish sugar industry became increasingly visible. A considerable increase in the average daily beet throughput could be observed at many factories in the second half of the 1990s owing to the gradual introduction of technological enhancements in beet processing. This had the effect that the time needed to produce a certain amount of sugar at such plants was getting shorter with every campaign. Consequently, an increasing number of sugar factories needed only a few weeks to manufacture the amount of sugar allocated them in their production quota. Therefore, they 'strayed' ever further from the optimum duration of a campaign (85-90 days).

Of course, not in all of the aforementioned eight new Polish provinces where sugarbeets are grown in large quantities are the soil and climatic conditions identical. The costs of sugarbeet production and conditions for the achievement of high sugar yields differ between these regions. Therefore, the determination of the optimal location of sugar factories and the economically optimal volume of production in individual locations requires a more sophisticated analysis. Such an investigation was conducted in the middle of the 1990s by Peter Walkenhorst who published the results in 1998 in a book entitled *Restructuring the Sugar Industry in Poland: Transition from State Socialism to the Common Agricultural Policy*. In order to specify location and size of sugar factories allowing for the maximization of profits in the Polish sugar sector, the author designed a non-linear optimization model. Three major determinants of the optimal location and size of beet-processing plants were incorporated into the model: (a) regional differences in the costs of sugarbeet production, (b) sugarbeet transport costs, and (c) the economies of scale in beet processing.[261] Sugar factories that were in operation in Poland at the time of the model's construction were taken as potential future locations of beet-processing plants.[262] It must be emphasized, following Walkenhorst, that the results of the modeling constitute an idealistic scenario since they presents "the outcomes of market allocation under perfect competition" or "actions that an enlightened social planner would take to maximize social

[261] For a more detailed description of the model, see Walkenhorst 1998, pp. 52-62.

[262] Walkenhorst observed that all new plants constructed in East Germany after 1990 as a result of privatization and a comprehensive restructuring of the local sugar industry had been located in regions where sugar production took place previously.

welfare" (Walkenhorst 1998, p. 10). This means that the model portrays an industry structure that is likely to emerge after a full privatization and liberalization of the sugar sector. Nevertheless, it shows "the desired direction of change" on the way to maximum efficiency and can be therefore helpful for policy makers in the development of restructuring strategies (ibid., p. 10).

The model was validated through a comparison of the model's predictions with the actual outcome of the restructuring process of the sugar industry in East Germany in the time period 1989/90-1994/95. Already in the middle of the 1990s, the validation proved highly successful since the structure of the sugar industry in the former territory of the GDR resembled closely that obtained as a result of the modeling. A comparison of the current structure of the sugar industry in East Germany with that envisaged by Walkenhorst shows that they are identical in several aspects. The model correctly predicted the total number of sugar factories and their average daily processing capacity (See Table 33).

Table 33. Sugar industry in East Germany, 1989/90, 2004/05 and Walkenhorst's model predictions

	GDR 1989/90	East Germany 2004/05	Model prediction
Total Sugar Production (in tonnes)	624,000	1,100,000	788,400
Number of Sugar Factories	43	6	6
Average Daily Processing Capacity of Sugar Factories (in tonnes)	1,550	10,950	10,950
Total Employment	14,478	845* (993)**	2,605

* Regular staff (excluding apprentices), ** Regular staff + Campaign workforce

Source: Walkenhorst 1998, p. 64; information provided by the management of individual sugar factories; analysis by the author.

Moreover, the distribution of individual sugar factories predicted by the model is very close to the actual outcome of sugar industry restructuring in the new German federal states. As shown in Figure 55, the location of three out of six plants has been foreseen perfectly (*Anklam*, *Güstrow* and *Könnern*). The location of another two factories does not differ greatly from the model's predictions. Increase in labor productivity at sugarbeet-processing plants in East Germany in the 1989/90-2004/05 time period was, however, higher than that envisaged by the model.

The above facts indicate that although Walkenhorst's model takes into account only three factors with a significant impact on the direction of structural changes and restructuring processes in the sugar sector, the accuracy of its predictions means that it can indeed serve as a very useful tool in the formulation and verification of reform policies.

The simulation of the economically optimal structure of the sugar industry in Poland by Walkenhorst in the middle of the 1990s demonstrated that privatization and liberalization of the sector would result in a consolidation of 78 sugar factories existing at that time in the country into only 13 scale-efficient plants with an average capacity of 10,500 t of beet throughput per day (See Table 34).

Figure 55. Location and size of sugar factories in East Germany, 1989/90, 2004/05 and Walkenhorst's model prediction

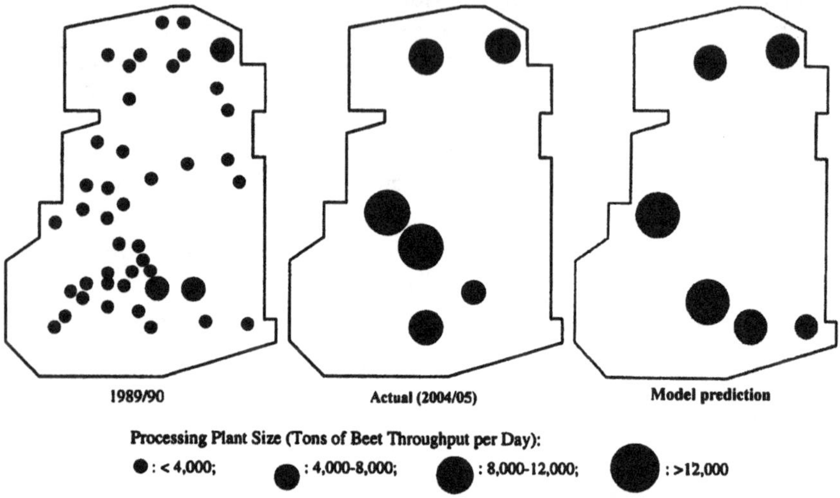

Source: Walkenhorst 1998, p. 65; www.zuckerwirtschaft.de; analysis by the author.

Table 34. Sugar industry in Poland, 1994/95, 2004/05 and Walkenhorst's model predictions

	1994/95	2004/05	Model Prediction 1995 (privatization, liberalization)	Model Prediction 2000/01 (EU accession, historical beet delivery rights)
Total Sugar Production (in million t)	1.490	2.008	1.631	1.548
Number of Sugar Factories	78	43	13	13
Average Daily Processing Capacity of Sugar Factories (in t)	2,069	3,760	10,458	9,929
Total Employment	28,700	8,646* (15,174)**	5,363	5,142

* Regular staff; ** Regular staff + Campaign workforce.

Source: Walkenhorst 1998, p. 67, 71; Walkenhorst 2001, p. 89; Rybski 2005, p. 49; Świetlicki 2005, p. 36; analysis by the author.

The location and size of individual sugar factories, predicted by the model, as well as the actual outcome of sugar industry restructuring in Poland up to 2004/05, inclusively, are shown in Figure 56. As can be seen, the model predicted that in the economically optimal situation the entire sugar production would be situated in the vicinity of major sugarbeet-growing centers, i.e., regions with a comparative advantage in sugarbeet growing (See Fig. 51 and 52).

Figure 56. Location and size of sugar factories in Poland, 1994/95, 2004/05 and Walkenhorst's model prediction

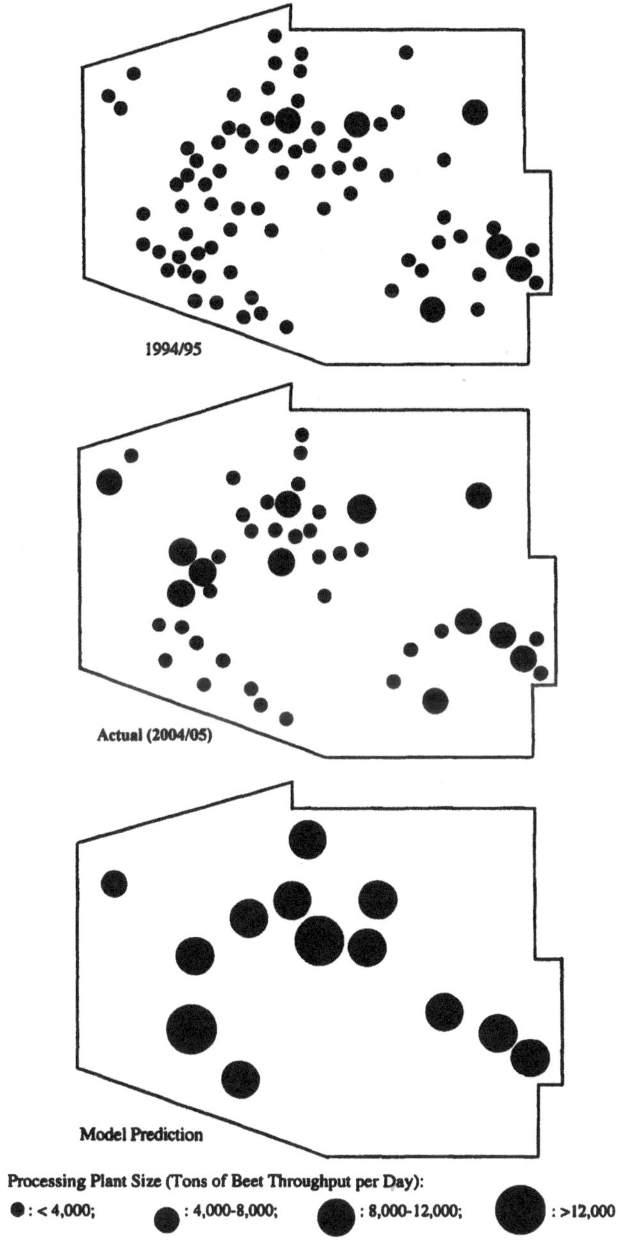

Source: Walkenhorst 1998, p. 72; analysis by the author.

The processing capacity of two sugar factories would exceed 12,000 t of beet throughput per day. 10 plants would have a daily processing capacity lying between 8,000 and 12,000 t, and only one factory would process 4,000 to 8,000 t of beets per day. At the time when Walkenhorst was modeling the optimal structure of the sugar industry in Poland, the daily processing capacity of only 6 out of 78 sugar factories operating in the country exceeded 4,000 t. This makes clear once again how great was the fragmentation of the local sugar industry in the beginning of the 1990s and how great was the need for consolidation of existing factories in order to reap economies of scale in beet processing and to improve in this way the economic efficiency of sugar production. Similarly, reduction in total employment in the sector from 28,700 to 5,363, predicted by the model, indicates a high level of overmanning in the Polish sugar industry and an enormous potential for improvement in labor productivity.

At the end of 2000, Walkenhorst complemented his earlier analyses in an article published in 2001 in the *European Review of Agricultural Economics*.[263] In the face of Poland's endeavors to join the EU, the determination of the optimal structure of the sugar sector in the country was extended by Walkenhorst in the above study by a simulation of several pre-accession and accession scenarios. One of the scenarios ("scenario V") assumed full integration of Poland into the CAP and the allocation to the country of a sugar production quota "equal to its rated production capacity" in the 1994-95 time period. Another significant assumption of the scenario was that sugarbeet growers in Poland would be granted non-tradable sugarbeet delivery rights based on historical production levels (Walkenhorst 2001, p. 67). Since at the time of writing Poland has joined already the EU, we know that the provisions of this scenario are the closest to reality. Therefore, presented in the last column of Table 34 are the results of calculations aimed at the specification of the optimal structure of the sugar industry in Poland which take into account these provisions. As can be seen, the total number of sugar factories remained unchanged in comparison with model predictions assuming full privatization and liberalization of the sugar sector in Poland (model predictions in 1995). Total sugar production, average processing capacity of sugar factories and the total employment level in the Polish sugar industry, envisaged by Walkenhorst in the above EU accession scenario, are only slightly lower than in the case of earlier analyses. The optimal location of individual plants remains the same.

Since sugarbeet delivery rights allocated to beet growers in Poland after the country's EU entry are tradable between individual growers, transfer of these rights to farmers located in the vicinity of sugar factories and to regions with the best conditions for sugarbeet growing is, contrary to Walkenhorst's assumption, possible. Nevertheless, sugar producers' capacity to influence the materialization

---

263 See Walkenhorst 2001.

of such processes is greatly limited. In theory, they have to rely completely on the beet growers and hope that the 'inconvenient' ones will sell their delivery rights to those that better suit producers' priorities.

It is important to emphasize that the structure of the sugar industry in Poland envisaged by Walkenhorst's model is not suited to the drawing of conclusions and the making of recommendations about the future of individual plants. This is due to the fact that a number of factors that may have a strong influence on decisions concerning the location of sugar factories had not been incorporated into the model, e.g. the state of repair and technological advancement of existing plants, the distance of individual factories from transportation networks and from major population centers, and regional changes in sugarbeet production costs.[264] The model predicts, for instance, the maintenance and expansion of sugar production at the location of the sugar factory *Lublin,* which is situated inside a city inhabited by more than 350,000 people. Furthermore, the model envisages abandonment of sugar production at the sugar factories *Łapy* and *Ropczyce* due to high beet-procurement costs in regions where they are located. Nevertheless, as was rightly observed by Walkenhorst, the two plants have certain qualities which allow one to state that they "can continue to function for a period of years at low operating expenses" and bring profits (Walkenhorst 1998, p. 132). These qualities include the relatively good condition of machinery and equipment at the time of modeling, a large initial processing capacity and, from the point of view of the owners of the plants, geographical proximity to the market.

For the above reasons, predictions of Walkenhorst's model may be very helpful in the estimation of the developmental potential of existing factories but such an investigation would have to be supplemented by additional analyses. The model is designed predominantly for the determination of the optimal structure of the sugar industry as a whole and for the specification of the optimal spatial distribution of sugar factories at a national level (ibid., p. 132).

It can be clearly seen in Figure 56 that contrary to the developments in East Germany, the actual structure of the sugar industry in Poland differs considerably from that predicted by Walkenhorst's model. Despite the abandonment of sugar production in many locations within the last decade, the number of sugar factories in the country and their average processing capacity are still far from the theoretical optimum. The explanation of this state of affairs is quite simple. Whereas the model shows an industry structure that would have emerged as a result of privatization and liberalization of the sugar sector, these conditions had been fulfilled in Poland only partially, and certainly to a much lesser extent than in the former GDR. The transfer of individual factories into private hands after 1990 progressed at a very slow pace. Most plants were privatized in the years

---

[264] See Walkenhorst 1998, pp. 64-66.

1997-2003. As we learned in section 13, the privatization process of the Polish sugar industry was not completed, and 26 plants went into the composition of the national sugar corporation between 2002 and 2005. The liberalization of the sugar sector in Poland took place from 1991 to 1994. Nevertheless, it was not accompanied by large-scale privatization of sugar factories. Regulations included in the 1994 Sugar Law prevented structural changes in the Polish sugar sector, since the closure of a beet-processing plant by its owner resulted in the loss of the sugar production quota allocated to the plant. It was not before the 2001 Sugar Law came into effect that sugar companies operating in Poland could set about consolidating individual factories without the risk of losing part of their production quota.

A completely different approach was taken by the privatization and restructuring process of the sugar industry in the former GDR after the German reunification. In 1990, the 43 sugar factories existing in East Germany were sold by the *Treuhandanstalt*, the agency responsible for the privatization of state-owned enterprises, to several West German sugar corporations (*Pfeifer & Langen*, *Südzucker*, *AG Uelzen-Braunschweig* and *Zucker Verbund Nord*) and to the Danish company *Danisco* for a symbolic price of 1 German Mark (Walkenhorst 1998, pp. 45-46). The new owners of the 43 plants were given a free hand in designing the restructuring process and decided almost immediately on a restructuring strategy which can be described as a shock therapy. Within five years, the 43 factories were consolidated into only 9 highly productive, scale-efficient and profitable facilities.[265]

34 factories situated in regions with unfavorable conditions for sugarbeet growing were closed down, four plants were modernized, three were expanded, and two completely new ones were built (*Könnern* in 1993 and *Klein Wanzleben* from 1992 to 1994). Post-privatization investment in East German sugar factories amounted to ECU 1.2 billion. The results of post-privatization restructuring activities were phenomenal. In only five years, the average daily beet throughput of East German sugar factories increased from 1,550 to 7,700 tonnes, which allowed them to benefit from the economies-of-scale effect in beet processing. Energy efficiency and labor productivity improved greatly. Employment in the industry fell from about 14,500 in 1989/90 to 1,500 in 1994/95. Total sugar production in East Germany increased in the same period of time by 50%, from 624,000 to 932,000 tonnes (Walkenhorst 1998, p. 64). The use of better seed and better machinery as well as the introduction of modern farm management practices had the effect that sugarbeet yields and quality standards very quickly approached the levels of West German plants. Sugar factories in former GDR are today in a good economic condition and meet the highest technical standards in Europe.

---

[265] Between 1995 and 2004, another 3 plants were closed down.

Two key factors that contributed to the rapid pace and overall success of sugar industry restructuring in East Germany were the ample capital endowments and know-how on the part of the investors, and an absence of administrative and political obstacles to the closure of inefficient and unfavorably located factories. Even if such obstacles appeared at a certain point of time, they were easily overcome. The capital strength of the companies which took over beet-processing plants in East Germany allowed them not only to cover the costs of all necessary investment but facilitated also the cumbersome process of labor restructuring. Owing to generous redundancy payments and other forms of compensation and support provided to laid-off workers, the inevitable reduction in employment level took place without any major conflicts or frictions. Of course, it would be false to say that social costs of sugar industry restructuring in East Germany were inexistent but they were certainly much lower than the costs that would materialize if privatization of sugar factories to West European sugar corporations did not take place.

As was pointed out earlier, the major administrative obstacle to the closure of inefficient and ill-located sugar factories was eliminated in Poland in 2002. The consolidation process of sugarbeet-processing plants in the country has gathered pace since then despite the fact that many factories are still in the hands of the state. This, in turn, means that the restructuring process of the sugar industry in Poland remains a highly politicized issue. It is, nonetheless, very likely that EU membership and the pending reform of the EU sugar regime will enforce further concentration of sugar production in the country. It is therefore highly probable that in a few years the structure of the sugar industry in Poland will resemble much more that envisaged by Walkenhorst's model than is the case at the time of writing. There is even still a chance that it will be almost identical to the model prediction, as in the case of the sugar industry in East Germany. This is, however, to say the least, improbable.[266]

---

[266] For a detailed analysis of the potential effects of Poland's EU entry and the pending reform of the EU sugar regime on structural changes in the local sugar industry, see for example Iwan 2005.

15 Types and Effectiveness of Restructuring Activities implemented by Individual Sugar Producers in Poland up to the Campaign 2004/05

This section forms the empirical part of the present study. Its main purpose is to analyze and evaluate the effectiveness of restructuring activities implemented up to the season 2004/05 at Polish sugar factories taken over by foreign investors, as well as at plants incorporated into *KSC "Polski Cukier"*. Case studies included in this section contain, among other things, the results of analyses carried out according to the methodology described in section 1.3. The obtained results are used to test hypotheses formulated at the beginning of the study (section 1.1).

15.1 British Sugar

British Sugar, headquartered in Peterborough/UK, is the third largest sugar producer in the EU-25. In the marketing year 2004/05, a maximum sugar production quota of 1.3 million t gave this internationally active company a market share of 7.6% in the EU sugar market.

British Sugar is the leading supplier of sugar to the UK market. It provides more than half of the country's annual requirements of the commodity. The remainder is met mostly by cane sugar imports from the African, Caribbean and Pacific sugar producing states. British Sugar sells its products on the UK's retail market under the brand name *Silver Spoon*.

In the season 2004/05, British Sugar operated six sugarbeet-processing plants in the UK located in East Anglia, the North-East, and the East and West Midlands. The factories produce each year 1.3 million t of sugar from around 9 million t of sugarbeets (the UK's entire crop). The raw material processed at British Sugar's plants in the UK is grown on 135,000 hectares and supplied by 7,000 beet growers. With around 550,000 t of sugarbeet feed as well as over 50,000 t of pressed pulp and molasses produced each year, British Sugar is amongst the largest manufacturers of high energy animal feed in the UK. It is distributed to more than 20,000 livestock farmers across the UK under the brand name *Trident* (within the framework of a sister company ABNA (Associated British Nutrition & Agriproducts).

According to research conducted by Reading University, the British beet sugar industry supports around 20,000 jobs in the farming, processing and transport industries. Since 1991 British Sugar, has been owned by Associated British Foods plc (ABF), one of Europe's largest food and ingredients companies with annual sales of £ 5.2 billion and over 35,000 employees in Europe, Australasia, the United States and Latin America.[267]

British Sugar's overseas operations have been steered since 1994 by British Sugar Overseas Ltd (BSO). This investment organization was established by ABF with the aim of developing businesses in South East Asia and Eastern Europe for the manufacture of sugar and related products. BSO currently controls a number of sugar factories in China and Poland. At the time of the establishment of BSO, British Sugar was already present in the latter country. In 1989, the company formed there a joint-venture company with *Rolimpex S.A.* and *Cukrownie Toruńskie,* called *SugarPol (Toruń) Sp. z o. o.*. It initially comprised two sugar factories, *Unisław* and *Ostrowite.*[268] In 1994 *SugarPol* acquired a third plant in Poland, in *Świecie*. After the establishment of BSO, *SugarPol* became the nucleus of that organization. In the following years, BSO took over further 7 sugar factories in Poland (details in the next subsection). All factories were then gradually consolidated, so that in the season 2004/05, BSO operated 4 sugarbeet-processing plants in the country. They produce around 200,000 t of sugar every year.

In 1995, BSO commenced its business activity in China as a result of a joint-venture with a local sugar company. This initial investment concerned one cane-sugar factory at *Shibie* in Guangxi Province, South East China. In the following years, BSO gradually expanded its engagement in the Chinese market. At the time of writing (August 2005), the company has majority control in four cane-sugar factories in the region, producing in total around 450,000 t of sugar. BSO intends to increase sugar production in China to about 500,000 t in the near future. The company is actively seeking opportunities to acquire additional cane sugar factories in the country.

Apart from the above business activity in China, BSO holds a majority stake in *Lianhua-BSO,* a company producing 20,000 t of crystalline dextrose every year, using glucose syrup made from maize starch. Production of the substance takes place at a plant located 600 km north-west of Shanghai. *Lianhua-BSO* dextrose products have a wide range of applications in the manufacture of food, confectionery and pharmaceutical items such as intra-venous drips, oral rehydration products, tablets and powdered medicines.

15.1.1 British Sugar in Poland

British Sugar's investment in Poland (*SugarPol*) initiated ownership transformations in the domestic sugar industry and the involvement of foreign capital in this

---

[267] British Sugar was acquired by ABF from *Berisford International.*

[268] *British Sugar* had a 51% majority shareholding in the joint-venture company. The British party declared an investment of $ 10 million and *Cukrownie Toruńskie* brought to the Company, as a contribution in kind, the two sugar factories *Unisław* and *Ostrowite*. *Rolimpex S.A.* received a 4% stake in *SugarPol* for its capital contribution.

process. Interestingly, the fact that this investment project came off was to a large extent a matter of serendipity. At the time when the joint-venture was formed, British Sugar was owned by *Berisford International*. Since the then owners of the company had roots in Poland and had already established trade links with the country, they decided to invest there as soon as it became possible. The management of the *Ostrowite* and *Unisław* plants was at the same time actively looking for an investor. In this way, the first joint-venture company in the Polish sugar sector was formed in October 1989. Berisford's/British Sugar's attitude to the investment was described by Dr. Stansiław Dziedzic, Business Development Director at BSO in Poland, as follows: "We have an opportunity to invest, we buy the two factories and let's wait to see how it will develop".

After the takeover of *Berisford International* by ABF in 1991, the new parent company of British Sugar had to decide whether to expand business activity in Poland or not. Since British Sugar's early engagement in the joint-venture concerning *Ostrowite* and *Unisław* had shown that direct investment in Poland could be successful, it decided to expand. In 1994, *SugarPol* acquired a third sugar factory in Poland, a bankrupt plant in *Świecie*.

In October 1997, *BSO Polska* acquired a majority stake in *Cukrownia Glinojeck* S.A., the largest sugarbeet-processing plant in Poland.[269] One year later *BSO Polska* underwrote Glinojeck's share acquisition of two neighboring factories *Michałów* (80.6 %) and *Ciechanów* (81.8 %). In 1999, *BSO Polska* acquired a minority stake in *SugarPol* from *Rolimpex S.A.*, increasing its own shareholding in the company to 72 %.

Finally, in 2000, *BSO Polska* acquired four additional sugar factories in Poland (*Guzów, Dobre, Kętrzyn* and *Pelplin*) from *Rolimpex S.A.* and *Danisco*.[270] A company called *SugarTor Sp. z o. o.* was formed from three of the plants (*Guzów, Dobre* and *Kętrzyn*).[271]

In the second half of 2004, *BSO Polska* acquired 33.4% and 1% of the share capital of the *Glinojeck* and *Pelplin* sugar factories, respectively, from *KSC "Polski Cukier"*. In this way, *BSO Polska* increased its stake in the *Glinojeck* sugar factory to 92% and in the *Pelplin* plant to 99%.

In the campaign 2004/05, sugarbeet processing took place at four sugar factories taken over by British Sugar in Poland: *Dobre*, *Glinojeck*, *Ostrowite*, and *Unisław*.

---

269 *BSO Polska* took over *Glinojeck* through a capital increase and the acquisition of all 25,000,000 new shares of the plant issued as a result of a capital increase. This gave BSO a 51% stake in the *Glinojeck* sugar factory.

270 Before the takeover by *BSO*, the *Guzów* plant was owned by *Rolimpex S.A.* The *Pelplin* sugar factory had been owned since 1998 by *Danisco*. *Dobre* and *Kętrzyn* were in the hands of a joint-venture company (*RolDan*) formed by *Danisco* and *Rolimpex*.

271 The location of individual sugar factories taken over by British Sugar in Poland is shown in Figure 47 (page 233).

BSO Polska group's combined A/B quota of 183,000 t represents 11% share of the domestic sugar industry's total production quota.

Table 35. Sugar factories taken over by British Sugar in Poland

Date	Factory location	Processing capacity*	Privatization method
1989	*Ostrowite*	1,300	Joint-venture
1989	*Unisław*	1,300	Joint-venture
1994	*Świecie*	1,600	Acquisition
1997	*Glinojeck*	6,400	Indirect privatization
1998	*Ciechanów*	2,000	Indirect privatization
1998	*Michałów*	1,400	Indirect privatization
2000	*Guzów*	1,600	Secondary ownership transfer
2000	*Dobre*	2,700	Secondary ownership transfer
2000	*Kętrzyn*	2,200	Secondary ownership transfer
2000	*Pelplin*	1,700	Secondary ownership transfer

* Average beet throughput per day (in tonnes) at the time of the takeover by British Sugar/BSO.
Source: IPC (Several Issues).

15.1.1.1 Operational Restructuring

One of the major components of operational restructuring implemented within the BSO group in Poland up to the season 2004/05 was the cessation of sugarbeet processing at six sugar factories and the concentration of sugar production in only four locations: *Glinojeck*, *Dobre*, *Ostrowite* and *Unisław*. The main goal of this undertaking was to optimize the utilization level of the processing capacity at the strategic sites and to maximize the economic efficiency of operations. In 2002, sugarbeet processing was ceased at the *Ciechanów*, *Guzów*, *Kętrzyn*, *Michałów* and *Świecie* plants. Beet processing at the *Pelplin* sugar factory was ceased in 2004.

A number of factors were taken into account in the choice of factories destined for closure: state of repair of individual plants; location; economic performance; processing capacity. Decisions on the closure of a given factory were based on comprehensive economic analyses. To give an example, the decision on the cessation of sugarbeet processing at the *Kętrzyn* sugar factory came to many as a surprise. The location of the factory in the vicinity of the border between Poland and Russia as well as the existence of large sugarbeet plantations in the region weighed in favor of continuing sugar production at the *Kętrzyn* plant. Nonetheless, analyses carried out by BSO showed that it would be more economically viable to close down this small sugar factory and to process the raw material delivered to the plant in *Glinojeck* despite the considerable distance between the two locations. It is important to mention here that, until recently, one of the major problems of *Glinojeck* was that the factory suffered from shortages of the raw material supplies needed for full utilization of its processing capacity.

Modernization activities implemented by BSO at sugar factories taken over in Poland up to the season 2004/05 were focused on the increase in the cost efficiency of operations, the improvement in the quality of manufactured sugar, and environmental protection. By far the largest amount of capital was invested by BSO in the modernization of the *Glinojeck* sugar factory. According to information provided by Andrzej Zarzycki, Managing Director of the Glinojeck plant until 2005, BSO invested around PLN 110 million in the technological modernization of *Glinojeck* in the 1998-2003 time period (major investment projects are listed in Table 36). The value of investments at the remaining sugar factories taken over by BSO in Poland was considerably lower. Up to the season 2004/05, it did not exceed PLN 100,000 at any of the plants acquired in the second half of the 1990s.[272]

Table 36. Major investment projects at the Glinojeck sugar factory, 1998-2004

- automation and computerization of production processes
- sugar silo (capacity: 30,000 t)
- modernization of the sugarbeet storage yard (incl. new machinery for unloading of sugarbeets from trucks)
- modernization of the packing department (incl. new palletizer)
- modernization of the sugar house (among other things new crystallizers (mixers) for magma 3, modernization of the condenser's station, new control room)
- modernization of the reception facilities (new falling film evaporator, new predefecation (preliming) station, modernization of carbonation tanks (carbonation I and II), thin juice heater (heating preceding carbonation II)
- modernization of barometric water coolers
- new scale for coke and limestone
- change of electronic appliances at the unloading of lime kiln
- closed water circuit

Source: BSO Polska; Klimaszewski/Branicki 2004, pp. 90-91; Branicki/Dziadowiec 2005, p. 68.

BSO Polska emphasizes, however, that improvements in productivity, cost efficiency of operations, and quality of manufactured sugar achieved by the company in Poland up to the season 2004/05 are attributable mainly to the transfer of know-how, i.e. streamlining of production, employment of Western manufacturing and management practices, training and motivation of local employees, etc. In the first years of British Sugar's presence in Poland, the use of the company's agricultural expertise contributed greatly to a considerable increase in the productivity and quality of the sugarbeet harvest (details in subsection 15.1.1.3).

It can be said that as far as restructuring activities implemented by British Sugar/ BSO in Poland until the season 2004/05 are concerned, the transfer of managerial and technical know-how, the institution of new control and reporting systems,

[272] The major investment projects implemented by BSO in Poland in the first half of the 1990s were the construction of a new sugar house, equipped with a modern distributed control system, at the *Ostrowite* plant in 1994, as well as installation of tanker loading for bulk sugar in *Unisław* and *Ostrowite*.

and the systematic streamlining of operations played, generally, a more important role than filling individual factories with state-of-the-art machinery and equipment.[273]

From the beginning of British Sugar's/BSO's presence in Poland, the company's investment in development in the country has been dependent on the financial results achieved by local sugar factories. For this reason, in 2002 and 2003, when the sugar industry in Poland generated losses owing to unsound regulation of the local sugar market, investments within the *BSO Polska* group took place on a very limited scale. They were made up of activities that were essential for the maintenance of individual plants. At the same time, *BSO Polska* points out that profits made by its units have been always reinvested in Poland and not transferred elsewhere.

In May 2005, *BSO Polska* announced on its official website that the company intends to invest PLN 170 million in further modernization of the *Glinojeck* sugar factory by the campaign 2006/07, in order to make it "one of the most efficient and modern plants in Europe". Initially, *BSO Polska* did not provide any details on what the PLN 170 million would be spent but in the last quarter of 2005, most of the investment plans were disclosed.

At the end of August 2005, the *Glinojeck* sugar factory signed a contract worth PLN 16.3 million with *Mostostal Płock S.A.* The contract concerns the construction of three tanks for condensed juice, each with a capacity of 35,000 t. Storage of juice in the tankers will allow sugar crystallization to be carried out for quite a long period after the end of the beet-processing season. The processing capacity of the *Glinojeck* plant is to be expanded to 11,500 t of beet throughput per day by the beginning of the campaign 2006/07. It is expected that beet processing at the factory in the campaign 2006/07 will have a duration of 100 days. After that, a juice-crystallization campaign lasting about 50 days will take place. Other investment projects to be implemented at the Glinojeck sugar factory by the campaign 2006/07 include:

- new sugarbeet pump
- new extraction tower
- new raw material laboratory (to be completed in the last quarter of 2005)
- modernization of the juice purification station (installation of additional clarifiers, saturation and main liming tanks, GP filters for juice straining).
- new falling film evaporators (more efficient use of energy)
- expansion of sugarbeet reception facilities (to be completed before the campaign 2005/06)
- modernization and enlargement of the sugarbeet storage yard
- sugar segregation station (nearing completion in the second half of 2005)
- enlargement of the sugar storehouse (in progress in the second half of 2005)

[273] See for example Farrow et al. 1993; Gąsowski 1998.

It is very likely that Poland's EU accession as well as a high profit generated by *BSO Polska* in 2004 had a strong influence on the above investment decisions. It seems also quite certain that the plans will have significant implications for the future of the remaining working sugar factories controlled by *BSO Polska*. There have been suggestions that the *Unisław* and *Dobre* plants are to be closed down in 2006.

Setting these speculations aside, let us take a look at the effects of operational restructuring within the *BSO Polka* group up to the season 2004/05, inclusively.

In the season 1995/96, i.e. when a comprehensive regulatory framework for the sugar sector in Poland was introduced for the first time, the total volume of sugar production at the ten sugar factories taken over in the country by BSO amounted to 144,112 t (14,411 t per factory). In the campaign 2004/05, the four *BSO Polska* plants where beet processing still took place produced 206,872 t (51,718 per one factory). As a result of cessation of beet processing at six locations, sugar production at the *Ostrowite*, *Unisław*, *Glinojeck*, and *Dobre* plants increased between the time of their takeover by BSO and the season 2004/05 by 134%, 158%, 117% and 42%, respectively (See Figure 57).

In the campaign 2002/03, total sugar production at the *Glinojeck* sugar factory exceeded 100,000 t for the first time. *Glinojeck* was the first, and so far the only, sugar factory in Poland to cross this threshold .

Figure 57. White sugar production (in tonnes of white sugar), BSO Polska

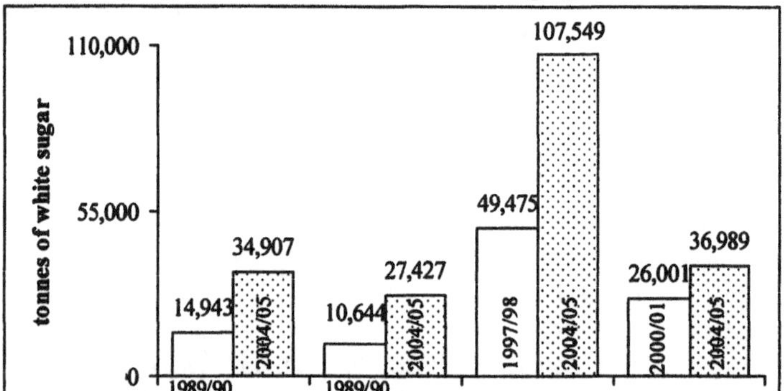

Source: IPC (Several Issues).

The daily beet throughput at the *Ostrowite*, *Unisław*, *Glinojeck* and *Dobre* sugar factories averaged at the time of their takeover by BSO 2,901 t. In the campaign 2004/05, it amounted on average to 3,704 t, an increase of 28%. The greatest increase in the average daily beet throughput took place at the *Glinojeck* sugar factory. It amounted to 119% (See Figure 58).

Figure 58. Average beet throughput per day (in tonnes), BSO Polska plants

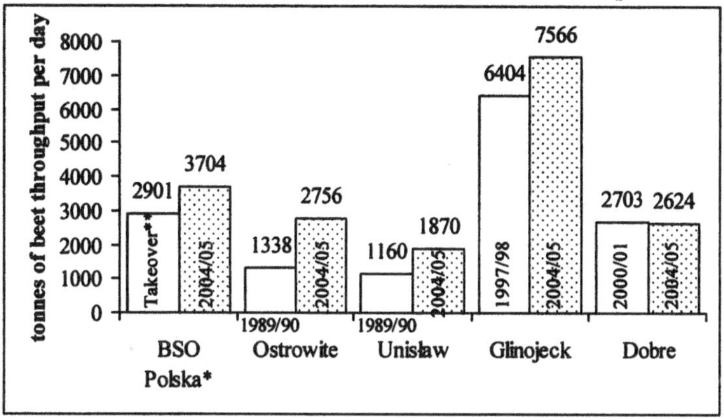

* Unisław, Ostrowite, Glinojeck, Dobre.

** Takeover = Ostrowite and Unisław (campaign 1989/90), Glinojeck (campaign 1997/98), Dobre (campaign 2000/01).

Source: STC (Several Issues); BSO Polska.

The consolidation of ten sugar factories into four had the effect that the average length of a campaign within the *BSO Polska* group had been optimized by the season 2002/03. At the time of the takeover of the *Glinojeck* sugar factory by BSO, sugarbeet slicing at the plant during the processing season lasted only 59 days (campaign 1997/98). Beet slicing at the *Dobre* sugar factory at the time of its takeover by BSO had a duration of 61 days (campaign 2000/01).[274]

Between 1998 and 2001, sugarbeet slicing at the *Ciechanów*, *Guzów*, *Kętrzyn*, *Michałów* and *Świecie* plants was launched during the processing season and then ceased within a few days. The purpose of this procedure was to keep the production quota allocated to the above factories.[275] Sugar production quotas allocated to these factories were manufactured during the aforementioned seasons at other plants controlled in Poland by BSO, where 'normal' campaigns took place.

In the season 2001/02, i.e. the last season when sugarbeet processing took place at all ten sugar factories taken over by BSO in Poland, the average duration

[274] Campaign length at the *Ostrowite* and *Unisław* plants at the time of their takeover by British Sugar (1989) is not taken into account due to the fact that the regulatory framework for the sugar sector in place in Poland in the beginning of the 1990s differed considerably from that introduced in the season 1995/96 (production quotas, etc.).

[275] As we learned in section 9.5 of this study, the law which regulated the functioning of the sugar industry in Poland until the season 2002/03 stipulated that sugar producers would lose the production quota allocated to a given sugar factory if beet slicing were not started at the factory during the processing season.

of beet slicing within the *BSO Polska* group came to 52 days (excluding the five plants where the so-called fictional, one-day campaigns took place).[276]

After a definite cessation of beet processing at the *Ciechanów*, *Guzów*, *Kętrzyn*, *Michałów* and *Świecie* plants in 2002, the average duration of beet slicing at the remaining five factories forming the *BSO Polska* group increased in the season 2002/03 to 89 days. In 2004, beet processing was ceased for good at another sugar factory controlled by *BSO Polska*, the *Pelplin* plant. The length of beet slicing at the *Glinojeck*, *Dobre*, *Ostrowite* and *Unisław* factories in the campaign 2004/05 averaged 90 days (See Figure 59).

Figure 59. Days of beet slicing, BSO Polska, 2001/02-2004/05

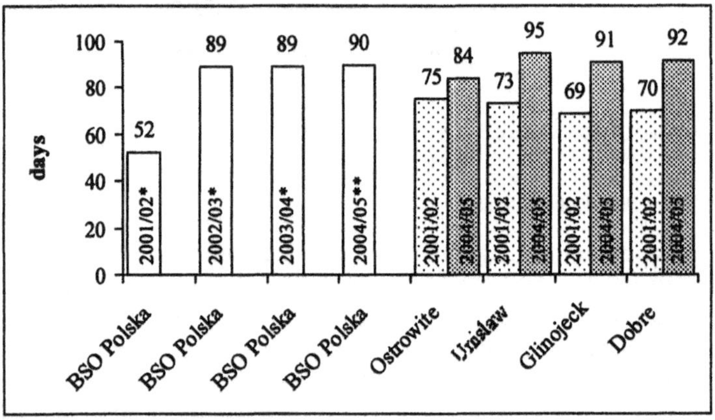

* Ostrowite, Unisław, Glinojeck, Dobre, Pelplin.
** Ostrowite, Unisław, Glinojeck, Dobre.
Source: IPC (Several Issues); BSO Polska.

Cessation of sugarbeet processing at six locations and gradual labor restructuring at the remaining four factories led to a significant reduction in employment within the *BSO Polska* group by the season 2004/05. At the time of their takeover by BSO, regular staff at the *Ciechanów*, *Guzów*, *Kętrzyn*, *Michałów* and *Pelplin* factories amounted on average to 190-200 workers.

In the campaign 1989/90, the *Ostrowite* sugar factory employed in total 401 workers (209 regular workers and 192 campaign workers). Total sugar production at the factory amounted to 14,943 t. Taking into account the overall employment level, labor productivity at the *Ostrowite* plant amounted to a mere 37 t per worker. Labor productivity counting only regular staff amounted to 71 t per worker (See Figures 60 and 61).

---

[276] If one takes into account also factories where 'fictional' campaigns took place, it turns out that beet slicing during the campaign 2001/02 at plants forming the *BSO Polska* group lasted on average 27 days!

Figure 60. Employment level, *Ostrowite* sugar factory, 1989/90 and 2004/05

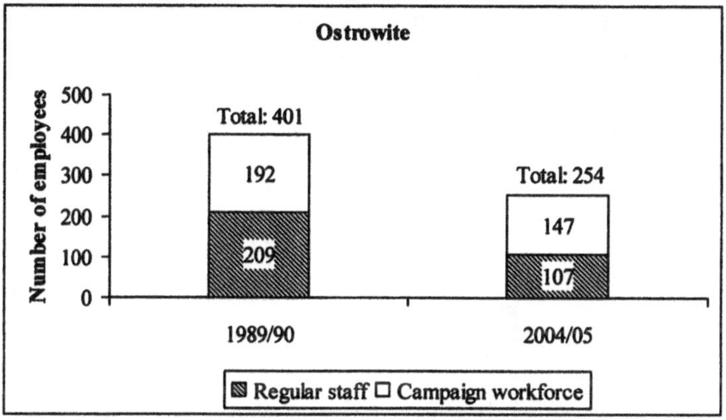

Source: BSO Polska.

Figure 61. Sugar production and labor productivity, *Ostrowite* sugar factory, 1989/90 and 2004/05

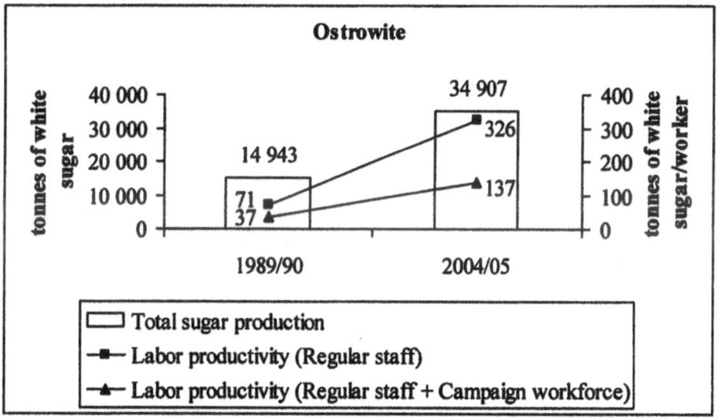

Source: Gąsowski 2004, p. 18; BSO Polska; calculations by the author.

In the campaign 2004/05, 254 workers (107 regular workers and 147 campaign workers) manufactured 34,907 t of white sugar at the *Ostrowite* sugar factory. Labor productivity counting regular staff and campaign workforce amounted at the factory to 137 t per one worker. This means an increase of 270% in relation to 1989/90. If we take into account only regular staff, it turns out that labor productivity at the *Ostrowite* plant in the season 2004/05 (326 t/worker) was 359% higher than in the campaign 1989/90 (71 t/worker) (See Figures 60 and 61).

359 workers (253 regular workers and 106 campaign workers) were employed at the *Unisław* sugar factory at the time of its takeover by British Sugar (campaign 1989/90). Sugar production at the *Unisław* plant in the campaign 1989/90

totaled 10,644 t. This means that labor productivity at the factory, counting the overall employment level, amounted at that time to only 30 t per worker. Labor productivity counting only regular staff was not much higher: it came to 42 t per worker.

Figure 62. Employment level, *Unisław* sugar factory, 1989/90 and 2004/05

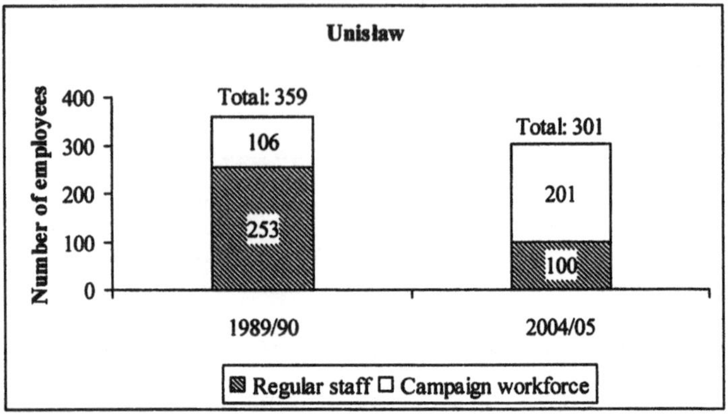

Source: BSO Polska.

Figure 63. Sugar production and labor productivity, *Unisław* sugar factory, 1989/90 and 2004/05

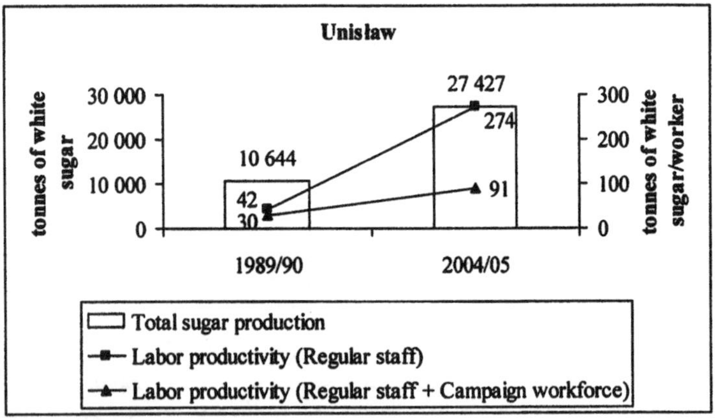

Source: Gąsowski 2004, p. 18; BSO Polska; calculations by the author.

In the campaign 2004/05, the *Unisław* sugar factory employed in total 301 workers (100 regular workers and 201 campaign workers). They manufactured 27,427 t of white sugar. Labor productivity counting the overall employment level at the *Unisław* plant in the campaign 2004/05 amounted to 91 t per worker. It was 203% higher than in the season 1989/90. If we take into account only regular staff, labor productivity at *Unisław* in the campaign 2004/05 amounted to 274 t per worker, an increase of 552% in relation to the season 1989/90 (See Figures 62 and 63).

As far as employment levels at *Glinojeck*, the largest sugar factory in the *BSO Polska* group, is concerned, shortly after the takeover of the plant by BSO it amounted to 886 workers (432 regular workers and 454 campaign workers) (campaign 1998/99). Sugar production in the campaign 1998/99 totaled 74,181 t.

Figure 64. Employment level, *Glinojeck* sugar factory, 1998/99 and 2004/05

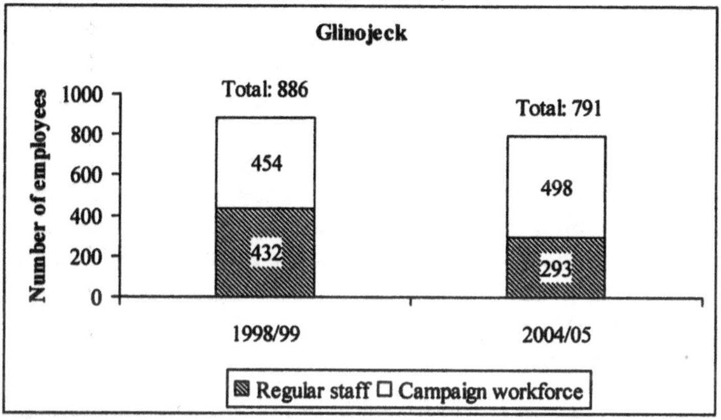

Source: BSO Polska.

Figure 65. Sugar production and labor productivity, *Glinojeck* sugar factory, 1998/99 and 2004/05

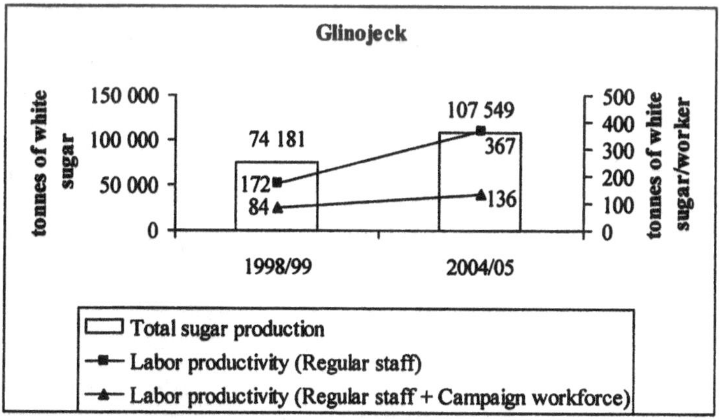

Source: IPC 1999, p. 22; BSO Polska; calculations by the author.

Consequently, labor productivity at the plant, in relation to overall employment, amounted in the season 1998/99 to 84 t per worker. Labor productivity calculated on the basis of regular staff amounted to 172 t per worker (See Figures 64 and 65).

In the campaign 2004/05, labor productivity counting regular staff and campaign workforce amounted at the *Glinojeck* sugar factory to 136 t per worker. This constitutes an increase of 62% in relation to the season 1998/99. Labor productivity referring to regular staff amounted to 367 t per worker, 113% higher than in the campaign 1998/99 (See Figure 65).

The total number of workers at the *Dobre* sugar factory at the time of its takeover by BSO was 341 (139 regular workers and 202 campaign workers) (campaign 2000/01). Sugar production at the *Dobre* plant in the campaign 2000/01 totaled 26,001 t. Labor productivity at the factory, counting regular staff and campaign workforce, amounted to 76 t per worker. Taking into account only the regular staff, labor productivity at *Dobre* in the season 2000/01 amounted to 187 t per worker (See Figures 66 and 67).

In the campaign 2004/05, the *Dobre* sugar factory employed in total 304 workers (107 regular workers and 197 campaign workers). Labor productivity in the season 2004/05, counting regular staff and campaign workforce, amounted at *Dobre* to 122 t per worker, 60% higher than in the campaign 2000/01. Labor productivity in the campaign 2004/05 at the *Dobre* sugar factory, counting only regular staff, amounted to 346 t per worker, which constitutes an increase of 85% in relation to 2000/01 (See Figures 66 and 67).

The above analyses clearly show that labor productivity increased considerably within the *BSO Polska* group between the takeover of individual sugar factories in Poland and the campaign 2004/05. As far as the four sugar factories where beet processing still took place in the season 2004/05 are concerned, labor productivity improved significantly at two of them (*Ostrowite* and *Unisław*).

Figure 66. Employment level, *Dobre* sugar factory, 2000/01 and 2004/05

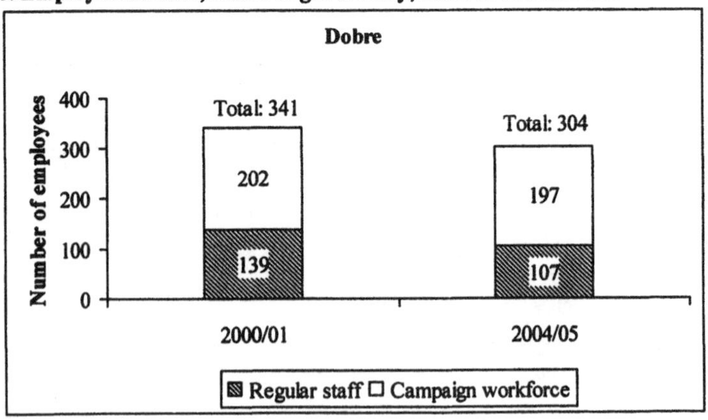

Source: BSO Polska.

Figure 67. Sugar production and labor productivity, *Dobre* sugar factory, 2000/01 and 2004/05

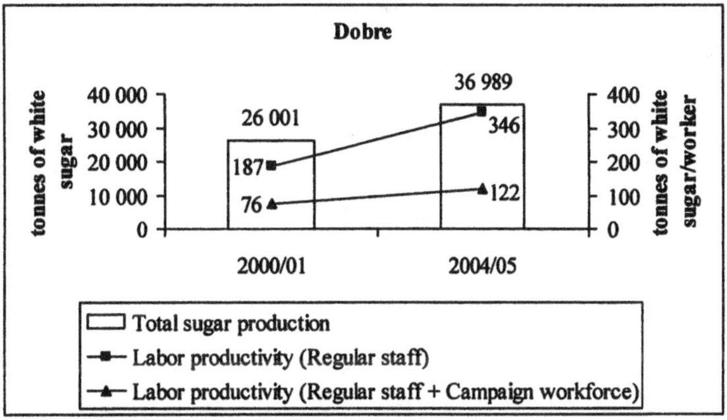

Source: IPC 2001, p. 22; BSO Polska; calculations by the author.

Despite a noticeable progress in this area at the *Glinojeck* and *Dobre* plants, there is certainly still potential for further efficiency increases at the two locations. The overall employment level at the *Glinojeck* sugar factory in the campaign 2004/05 was two to three times higher than at factories of similar size in Western Europe. In particular, the number of campaign workers at the *Glinojeck* plant was still enormous in the season 2004/05 (nearly 500 people). The management of the factory points out, however, that this is attributable largely to the fact that a considerable number of workers were employed in the campaign 2004/05 at several sugarbeet-purchasing centers belonging to the *Glinojeck* plant. These centers are to be closed in 2005, so campaign employment at the *Glinojeck* sugar factory in the campaign 2005/06 is likely to be much lower than in the season 2004/05.

Labor restructuring within the *BSO Polska* group up to the season 2004/05 was carried out predominantly through the use of standard methods used in this process, i.e. a guaranteed employment period granted to workers at the time of a takeover of a given factory and a program of voluntary redundancies. In the case of factories destined for closure, *BSO Polska* took additional measures aimed at the minimization of the social costs of restructuring. Generally, the strategy of the company was to seek investors willing to take over the infrastructure of a closed factory, to launch there some form of business activity, hiring at least part of the factory staff. The extent of the social problems resulting from factory closure differed from case to case. Its dimension depended to a great measure on the location of a factory and the possibilities of an alternative employment in the region. Sometimes, it depended also on the willingness of laid-off factory workers to take on alternative jobs. How labor restructuring was implemented by *BSO*

Polska at individual factories taken over by the company in Poland and what are the results of these activities up to the season 2004/05 is described below.

Unisław and Ostrowite

For nearly ten years after the formation of *SugarPol*, *BSO Polska* did not make any efforts to reduce the employment level at the *Unisław* and *Ostrowite* plants. "As long as we could afford it, any drop in employment occurred naturally"; so describes the situation Dr. Stanisław Dziedzic from *BSO Polska*. Nevertheless, when dark clouds began to gather over the sugar industry in Poland in 1997, due to developments in the domestic sugar market (inadequate regulation, low market price of sugar), *BSO Polska* has started to reduce employment at individual plants, including *Unisław* and *Ostrowite*, as one of the methods of cutting production costs. Downsizing at the two locations did not, however, take the form of group lay-offs but mainly voluntary redundancies and individual dismissals.

Świecie

At the time of the takeover of the *Świecie* sugar factory by *SugarPol*, the employment level at the plant was already very low. Shortly before the factory was acquired by *SugarPol*, it went bankrupt and its staff found itself out of work. After the takeover of *Świecie* by *SugarPol*, BSO hired back the workers of the plant (about 30 people) and beet processing was continued at the factory for a number of years. When the decision on the closure of *Świecie* was made by BSO, the workers of the plant were provided with redundancy payments and left their jobs. According to *BSO Polska*, the social problem of labor restructuring in *Świecie* was small. The employment level at the local sugar factory was very low and the factory staff consisted mainly of qualified workers.

The infrastructure of the *Świecie* plant was sold by BSO to a developer who dismantled the factory and is currently waiting for the prices of land and property to go up before selling what is left.

Glinojeck

BSO Polska agreed on a social package with the employees of the *Glinojeck* sugar factory after the takeover of the plant, despite the fact that the company was not obliged to do so by the privatization contract. The staff of *Glinojeck* demanded a social package from the new owner of the plant, arguing that workers of other factories taken over by foreign investors had obtained certain guarantees and privatization bonuses. BSO met these demands by providing the workers of the *Glinojeck* plant with a guaranteed employment period and with a salary increase. Up to 2004, labor restructuring at the *Glinojeck* sugar factory was implemented exclusively through voluntary redundancies. At the time of writing (second half of 2005) there have also been individual lay-offs at *Glinojeck*.

Ciechanów

At the time of the takeover by BSO/*Glinojeck*, 168 regular workers were employed at the *Ciechanów* sugar factory. 93 workers accepted voluntary redundancies proposed by the board of directors of the *Glinojeck* plant and left their jobs within the first year after the takeover of *Ciechanów* by BSO/*Glinojeck*.[277] Another 15 workers accepted redundancy payments in the second year. 16 workers from *Ciechanów* were employed at the *Glinojeck* sugar factory. After the rejection of several job offers, 12 employees of the transport department at the *Ciechanów* plant were laid off. They received redundancy payments that were considerably higher than those required by law.

After cessation of beet processing at *Ciechanów,* the remaining workers were employed by companies that took over the infrastructure of the factory and started a business activity in the plant. In 2004, six companies employing in total 60 people were engaged in various forms of business activities on the territory of the *Ciechanów* sugar factory. A building materials sales outlet and a petrol station were built in the former sugarbeet storage yard of the plant. The former sugar storehouse currently serves as a wholesale outlet for office equipment and wood products. In another building, plastic containers are produced. The number of people employed at the former factory in *Ciechanów* is, according to *BSO Polska*, very likely to rise in the near future since there are new investment projects under way (*Tygodnik Ciechanowski* 2004).

Dr. Dziedzic from *BSO Polska* claims that of all the factories taken over by the company in Poland, the social problems of restructuring were most serious at the *Ciechanów* plant. For this reason, *BSO Polska* is satisfied with the fact that labor restructuring at the location has turned out well and that the company managed to find investors willing to take over the infrastructure of the local factory. It is, however, worth mentioning that apart from the aforementioned employees of the transport department at the *Ciechanów* sugar factory, it was difficult to persuade many other workers into leaving their posts at the factory and accepting an alternative job. In certain cases, even an employment guarantee of 12 months in a new workplace was not enough.

Michałów

Labor restructuring at the *Michałów* sugar factory was carried out by BSO predominantly by means of voluntary redundancies. As in the case of *Ciechanów*,

---

[277] At the time of the takeover of *Ciechanów*, BSO/*Glinojeck* gave the staff of the factory a guarantee of employment over a certain period of time.

people employed at the *Michałów* plant were initially given a guarantee by BSO/ *Glinojeck* of employment over a certain period of time.

Despite the favorable location of *Michałów* (30km to Warsaw), BSO has encountered serious difficulties in finding investors willing to acquire the infrastructure of the factory after cessation of beet processing at the plant. Up to 2004, two small companies had started business activity on the grounds of the *Michałów* sugar factory. One of them manufactures refrigerators for cars and employs about 5-10 people. The other one provides freight transportation services. According to *BSO Polska*, the social problem of restructuring at *Michałów* is much smaller than elsewhere since the laid-off workers of the plant are very likely to find new jobs in Warsaw and/or the surroundings.

As far as the infrastructure of *Michałów* is concerned, *BSO Polska* adopted a similar strategy as in *Ciechanów*, i.e. division of land and property into a number of pieces and sale to investors. *BSO Polska* has transferred part of the machinery from *Ciechanów* and *Michałów* to factories where beet processing still takes place. The rest was either sold or scrapped.

Dobre

As portrayed in Figure 66, the employment level at *Dobre* did not change much from the time of the takeover of the factory by BSO to the campaign 2004/05. A slight reduction in the number of regular workers occurred naturally and was not the result of deliberate labor restructuring.

Guzów

After the takeover of *Guzów*, BSO offered people employed at the factory voluntary redundancies. The redundancy payments were equal to 12 months of salary. Nearly the entire staff of *Guzów* wanted to accept the payments and leave their jobs at the factory. Nevertheless, BSO did not let everybody go since a certain number of workers were needed at the plant until its closure. *Guzów* is located about 45-50km far from Warsaw, close to the neighboring city of *Żyrardów*. Finding employment in this region is much easier than in most other parts of Poland. This, as well as the fact that the workforce taken over by BSO with the *Guzów* factory consisted of qualified workers, made labor restructuring at the factory quite easy. It is important to add that the employment level at *Guzów* had been reduced considerably by the previous owner of the plant, *Rolimpex S.A.*, before the takeover of the factory by BSO.

After the cessation of beet processing in *Guzów*, the local factory was dismantled and most of the buildings were pulled down in order to minimize tax payments. At the time of writing (September 2005) *BSO Polska* has not yet decided whether it will launch some alternative production in *Guzów*.

Kętrzyn

The majority of workers employed at the *Kętrzyn* plant accepted voluntary redundancies offered by BSO and left their jobs before the season 2004/05. Part of the infrastructure of *Kętrzyn* was taken over by an investor, after cessation of sugar production at the factory. Nevertheless, no business activity had been launched at the plant by the end of 2004. The investor scrapped many of the objects left in the factory. BSO is seeking for other firms willing to invest on the territory of *Kętrzyn*.

Pelplin

In the end of 2004, labor restructuring and asset engineering at the *Pelplin* sugar factory was at an early stage. Beet processing at the plant was ceased after the end of the season 2003/04. The staff of *Pelplin* was offered generous redundancy payments by BSO. Many workers have accepted them and have already left their jobs.

Apart from the above activities aimed at the reduction in costs and improvement in productivity, *BSO Polska* has been continually training its staff and personnel, in order to maintain a consistent level of quality of products and services. Immediately after the formation of *SugarPol*, British Sugar delegated a group of experts to Poland with the task of helping to increase the efficiency of operations in the country. One of the first measures was to make workers and beet growers aware of the need for a more efficient use of resources. Employees of various factory departments were sent to the UK and other West European countries to receive training. An ongoing educational program for beet growers delivering raw material to factories forming *SugarPol* was started shortly after the establishment of the joint-venture company (See also section 15.1.1.3).

Staff and personnel training still plays a vital role within the *BSO Polska* group at all levels. One of the company's strategic goals is to continually train its employees to become "multi-skilled". At the same time, *BSO Polska* strives to gradually increase productivity and workers' salaries. For the above reasons, the company organizes management courses, financial courses, etc. Furthermore, *BSO Polska* provides support for employees wanting to get certain qualifications on their own initiative (e.g. MBA studies or CIMA certificates in business accounting).

One of the key areas of underperformance identified by BSO at individual sugar factories in Poland at the time of their takeover by the company was poor extraction efficiency. Recovery of sugar at the *Ostrowite*, *Unisław*, *Glinojeck* and *Dobre* plants at the time of their takeover by BSO amounted on average to 81.8%. In the campaign 2004/05, recovery of sugar at the four factories averaged 90.4 % (+ 10.5%). The value of this indicator of efficiency at the *Ostrowite*,

Unisław, *Glinojeck* and *Dobre* plants in the campaign 2004/05 was, respectively, 23%, 8%, 11% and 2% higher than at the time of their takeover by BSO (See Figure 68).

Figure 68. Recovery of sugar, BSO Polska

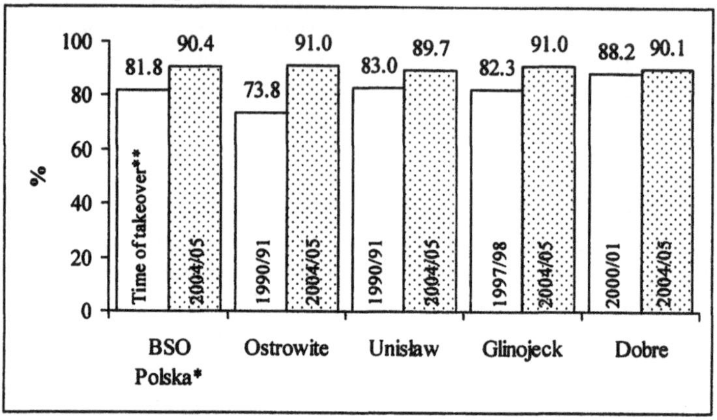

* Ostrowite, Unisław, Glinojeck, Dobre.
** Time of takeover = Ostrowite and Unisław (campaign 1990/91), Glinojeck (campaign 1997/98), Dobre (campaign 2000/01).
Source: STC (Several Issues); Gazeta Cukrownicza 1/2005, p. 31; calculations by the author.

Figure 69. Sugar yield in % of raw sugar value on beet, BSO Polska

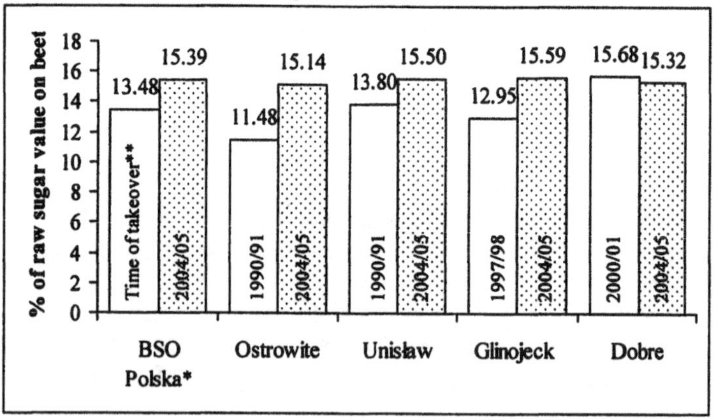

* Ostrowite, Unisław, Glinojeck, Dobre.
** Time of takeover = Ostrowite and Unisław (campaign 1990/91), Glinojeck (campaign 1996/97), Dobre (campaign 2000/01).
Source: STC (Several Issues); Gazeta Cukrownicza 1/2005, p. 31.

The average sugar yield in % of raw sugar value on beet at the *Ostrowite*, *Unisław*, *Glinojeck* and *Dobre* plants amounted at the time of their takeover by BSO to 13.48%. In the campaign 2004/05, it averaged at the four factories 15.39%

(+14%). Sugar yield in % of raw sugar value on beet at the *Ostrowite* plant in the campaign 2004/05 was 32% higher than in the season 1990/91. At the *Glinojeck* and *Unisław* sugar factories, it was, respectively, 20% and 12% higher than at the time of the takeover of the plants by BSO. At *Dobre*, the sugar yield in % of raw sugar value on beet at the time of the takeover of the factory by BSO was almost equal to the one recorded in the season 2004/05 (See Figure 69).

Modernization activities and rationalization measures implemented by BSO at sugar factories taken over in Poland led to a considerable reduction in the consumption of resources used in the production of sugar by the season 2004/05.

A significant decrease in energy consumption took place at the *Ostrowite*, *Unisław*, *Glinojeck* and *Dobre* plants between the time of their takeover by BSO and the season 2004/05. Initially, the total use of energy (heat and electrical energy) for sugar production at the plants averaged 4095 kWh/t of sugar. The corresponding figure for the campaign 2004/05 is 2285 kWh/t of sugar, which constitutes a decrease of 44%. At the *Ostrowite* and *Glinojeck* plants, total energy consumption in the season 2004/05 was 55% lower than at the time of the takeover of the factories by BSO (campaign 1990/91 for *Ostrowite*, and 1996/97 for *Glinojeck*[278]).

Figure 70. Total energy consumption (in kWh/t of sugar), BSO Polska

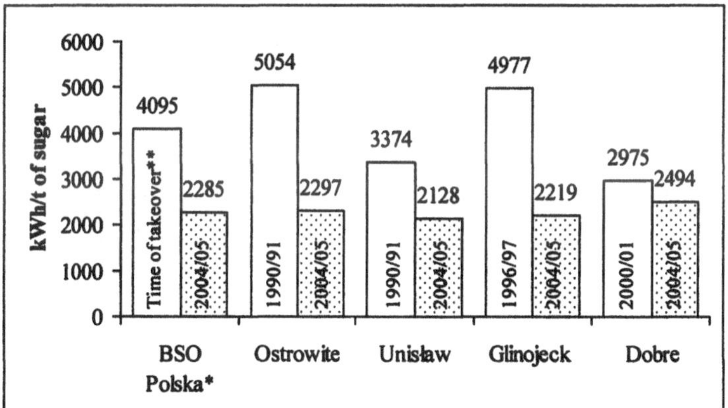

* Ostrowite, Unisław, Glinojeck, Dobre.
** Time of takeover = Ostrowite and Unisław (campaign 1990/91), Glinojeck (campaign 1996/97), Dobre (campaign 2000/01).
Source: STC (Several Issues); BSO Polska, calculations by the author.

Total use of energy in the campaign 2004/05 at the *Unisław* sugar factory was 37% lower than in the season 1990/91 (time of takeover by BSO). At *Dobre*, total energy consumption in the campaign 2004/05 was 16% lower than at the time of the takeover of the factory by BSO (See Figure 70).

278 Data on energy consumption at the *Glinojeck* sugar factory in the season 1997/98 is not available.

Despite a significant reduction in the use of energy at the *Ostrowite*, *Unisław*, *Glinojeck*, and *Dobre* plants from the time of their takeover by BSO to the season 2004/05, it seems that there is still room for further improvement in this field. The average energy consumption at factories forming the *BSO Polska* group was in the campaign 2004/05 slightly higher than at plants controlled by other foreign sugar companies operating in Poland.

At the time of the takeover of *Ostrowite*, *Unisław*, *Glinojeck*, and *Dobre* by BSO, the use of coal at the four plants averaged 6.03% on beet. Unfortunately, current information about the use of coal at the factories is not available. It is only known that in the campaign 2002/03, coal consumption at the *Glinojeck* sugar factory was 44% lower than in the season 1996/97, i.e. shortly before the takeover of the plant by BSO. The use of coal at the *Ostrowite* plant in the season 2002/03 decreased by 33% in relation to the campaign 1990/91. At *Unisław* and *Dobre*, coal consumption in the campaign 2001/02 was, respectively, 25% and 8% lower than at the time of the takeover of the factories by BSO (See Figure 71).

Figure 71. Use of coal (in % on beet), BSO Polska

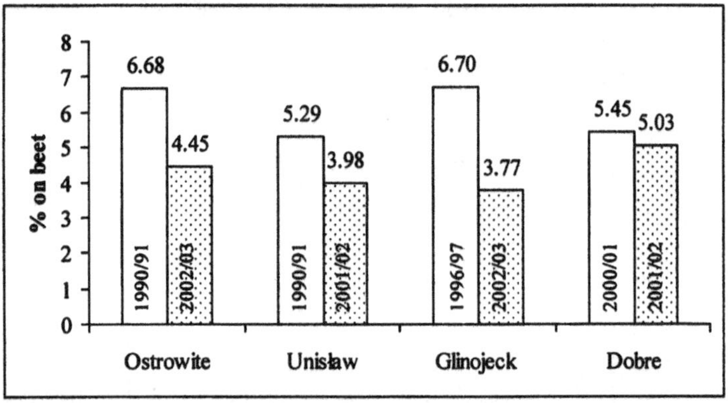

Source: IPC (Several Issues).

At the time of their takeover by BSO, the average use of coke at the *Ostrowite*, *Unisław*, *Glinojeck*, and *Dobre* plants amounted to 0.45% on beet. The corresponding figure for the season 2004/05 is 0.24% on beet, which means a decrease by 46%. At both the *Unisław* and *Glinojeck* plants, the use of coke in the campaign 2004/05 was 54% lower than at the time of the takeover of the factories by BSO. The use of coke at *Ostrowite* and *Dobre* in the campaign 2004/05 was 36% lower than at the time of the takeover of the factories by BSO (See Figure 72).

In the campaign 2004/05, limestone consumption (in % on beet) at *Ostrowite*, *Unisław*, *Glinojeck* and *Dobre* was, on average, 38% lower than at the time of the takeover of the plants by BSO. The greatest reduction in the use of limestone up to the season 2004/05 took place at the *Glinojeck* sugar factory (-53%). Limestone consumption at the *Unisław* plant in the campaign 2004/05 was 45% lower than in the season 1990/91. At *Ostrowite* and *Dobre*, the use of limestone decreased between the time of the takeover of the factories by BSO and the campaign 2004/05 by 13% and 27%, respectively (See Figure 73).

Figure 72. Use of coke (in % on beet), BSO Polska

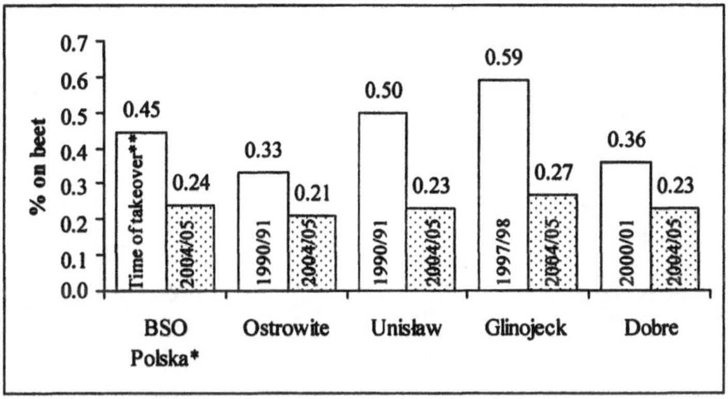

* Ostrowite, Unisław, Glinojeck, Dobre.
** Time of takeover = Ostrowite and Unisław (campaign 1990/91), Glinojeck (campaign 1997/98), Dobre (campaign 2000/01).
Source: IPC (Several Issues); BSO Polska.

Figure 73. Use of limestone (in % on beet), BSO Polska

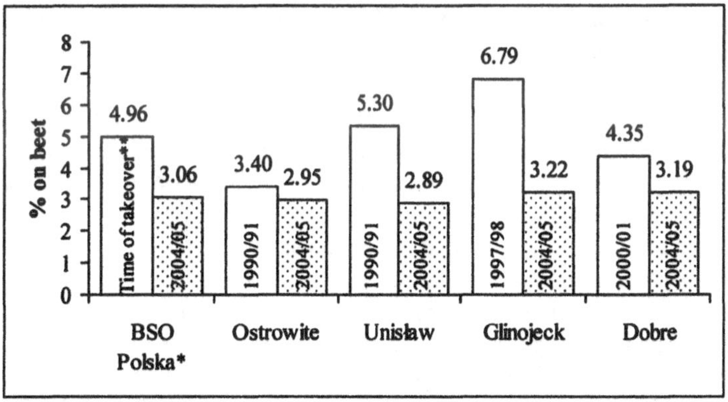

* Ostrowite, Unisław, Glinojeck, Dobre.
** Time of takeover = Ostrowite and Unisław (campaign 1990/91), Glinojeck (campaign 1997/98), Dobre (campaign 2000/01).
Source: IPC (Several Issues); BSO Polska.

A substantial reduction in the use of fresh water (in % on beet) took place at the *Ostrowite*, *Unisław*, *Glinojeck*, and *Dobre* sugar factories between the time of their takeover by British Sugar/BSO and the campaign 2002/03.[279]

[279] Information on the use of fresh water at *BSO Polska* plants in the seasons 2003/04 and 2004/05 is not available.

The average use of fresh water at the four factories decreased by 93%. As shown in Figure 74, the *Glinojeck* sugar factory did not use fresh water at all in the campaign 2002/03.

Figure 74. Use of fresh water (in % on beet), BSO Polska

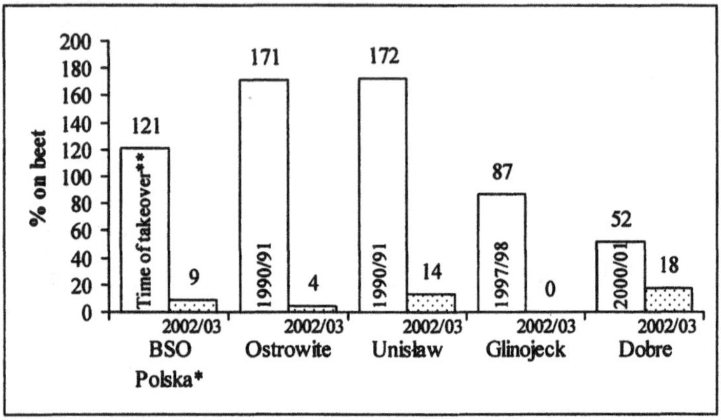

* Ostrowite, Unisław, Glinojeck, Dobre.
** Time of takeover = Ostrowite and Unisław (campaign 1990/91), Glinojeck (campaign 1997/98), Dobre (campaign 2000/01).
Source: IPC (Several Issues); Branicki 2003, p. 81.

In the campaign 2002/03, a system of identifying and analyzing "lost opportunities" was introduced at factories forming the *BSO Polska* group. Every deviation from the theoretically optimum performance specified before each campaign for individual factory departments (e.g. beet throughput per day, energy consumption, etc.) is documented and thoroughly analyzed. This measure is meant to help to avoid certain problems in the future as well as to facilitate investment decisions (Branicki 2003, p. 82, 86).

Apart from activities aimed at a general increase in the productivity and cost efficiency of operations, BSO focused on the improvement in the quality of sugar manufactured at individual plants. This refers particularly to *Ostrowite* and *Unisław* where the quality of sugar at the time of the takeover of the factories by British Sugar fell far short of West European standards and did not fulfill the requirements of existing and potential customers of the company. One of the factors that induced British Sugar to take actions aimed at the improvement in quality of sugar produced in *Ostrowite* and *Unisław*, was an arrangement made by the company with Coca-Cola. At the time when British Sugar established operations in Poland, Coca-Cola was looking for a local provider of sugar fulfilling certain quality requirements. British Sugar committed itself to making the necessary investment in *Ostrowite* and *Unisław* in order to be able to supply Coca-Cola with sugar matching the strict quality specifications required by the company.

Coca-Cola undertook, in return, to buy, over a number of years, sugar manufactured at Polish factories controlled by the British company.

Within a short period of time, *SugarPol* has established itself as the number one producer of high quality sugar in Poland. *Unisław* was the first Polish sugar plant/producer to replace Western sugar companies as the supplier of Coca-Cola Poland. By the campaign 1995/96, the quality of sugar manufactured at the *Unisław* and *Ostrowite* plants was of the same quality as sugar produced by BSO in the UK.

For the purpose of quality control, British Sugar upgraded and refurbished the laboratories of the *Ostrowite* and *Unisław* plants, introducing the most modern test equipment and the newest analytical methods. A microbiological lab was established at the laboratory of the *Unisław* factory. It also services other sugar factories in the *BSO Polska* group. One of the measures that contributed greatly to a significant improvement in the quality of sugar manufactured in *Ostrowite* and *Unisław* (as well as other sites taken over by BSO in Poland at a later period of time) was the automation of magma boiling.

In 1995, the *Ostrowite* and *Unisław* plants were the first sugar factories in Central and Eastern Europe to be granted ISO 9002 quality certificates (Spetch at al. 1996, p. 34).[280] After the takeover of *Glinojeck* and *Dobre* by BSO, quality management systems based on the ISO 9001:2000 standard were also instituted at these two sites. All working sugar factories forming the *BSO Polska* group are currently certified to the above standard. Furthermore, at all four sugar factories currently forming the *BSO Polska* group, the HACCP system had been instituted by the campaign 2004/05. An accreditation certifying the institution and proper functioning of HACCP was granted to *SugarPol* in 1999, in 2001 to the *Glinojeck* sugar factory and in January 2004 to the *Dobre* plant. All management systems implemented at *BSO Polska* units are approved and monitored by Lloyd's Register Quality Assurance.

In the season 2004/05, all working sugar factories controlled in Poland by BSO manufactured "white sugar of standard quality" (EU-category II). The total number of points for physico-chemical parameters of sugar produced at the *Unisław* and *Ostrowite* plants has for years been very close to the threshold allowing to classify that sugar as "extra white sugar" (EU-category I). This threshold has often been crossed at the two factories within the last few years. Throughout the entire processing season 2002/03, for example, the *Ostrowite* plant manufactured "extra white sugar". The values of selected physico-chemical parameters of sugar manufactured at BSO plants in the campaign 2004/05 are presented in Table 37.

BSO Polska claims that it is currently able to produce "extra white sugar" at all four factories run in Poland. Nevertheless, the company does not do this since the demand for the product is modest and its production costs much higher than those

[280] The certificates were granted by Lloyd's Register Quality Assurance.

of the production of "white sugar of standard quality". For this reason, certain quantities of "extra white sugar" are manufactured at *BSO Polska* units every year and provided to customers who need it.

Table 37. Selected physico-chemical parameters of sugar manufactured at BSO Polska plants, campaign 2004/05

	Color in solution [ICUMSA units]	SO2 [mg/kg]	Ash content [mg/kg]	Non-soluble substances [mg/kg]	Turbidity [ICUMSA units]
Dobre	20.8	2.9	0.010	2.7	22.8
Unisław	20.2	2.6	0.011	2.4	20.2
Ostrowite	17.7	2.6	0.009	2.3	10.2
Glinojeck	22.4	3.4	0.010	2.6	18.8
Average	**20.3**	**2.9**	**0.010**	**2.5**	**18.0**

Source: Branicki/Dziadowiec 2005, p. 67.

Since the beginning of its presence in Poland, British Sugar/BSO has been gradually expanding the assortment of products offered by the domestic units of the company. After the installation of necessary equipment at *Ostrowite* and *Unisław*, in the mid 1990s, the two factories were the first in Poland to sell sugar bulk-loaded onto tankers. Up to then, sugar delivered to the food and beverages industry in Poland was packed and conveyed exclusively in 50kg bags. Within the *BSO Polska* group, bulk sugar is currently offered by the *Ostrowite, Unisław, and Glinojeck* plants. In *Glinojeck* and *Unisław* sugar is also packed in the so-called big bags (1000kg).

As far as products destined for the retail market are concerned, *BSO Polska* has been continually widening their range. *BSO Polska* currently offers white sugar in bags of various size, baking sugar, coarse sugar, white and brown sugar cubes, brown sugar, icing sugar as well as sachettes and sticks.[281] Since 1999, the above products have been sold in the Polish retail market under the brand name "*Srebrna Łyżeczka*". "*Srebrna Łyżeczka*" is the Polish equivalent of the brand name under which British Sugar's products are sold in UK—"Silver Spoon". The packaging plant for the "*Srebrna Łyżeczka*" retail brand is located in *Glinojeck.*

Sugar acquired in large quantities by food and beverages producers is marketed by *BSO Polska* under the industrial brand "*SugarPol*" in 25kg bags, 1000kg big bags and in bulk. Tankers painted blue, and bearing the *SugarPol* logo, can be seen quite often on the main roads leading to Warsaw, Łódź and Toruń (Budny 2004).

The systematic improvement in quality of sugar manufactured at *BSO Polska* units and the expansion of the product range offered by the company was accompanied by a new, individual approach towards clients' requirements. A number of services were introduced for this purpose. One such service is the so-called

[281] For more details, see http://www.srebrnalyzeczka.pl.

vendor management, a system of monitoring the sugar stocks kept by customers and delivering new supplies whenever needed. Telemetric systems, stock controls and electronic data interchange (EDI) are currently in constant use in the everyday activities performed by *SugarPol*. The above tools enable swift and efficient management of orders and deliveries.

About 50% of the sugar manufactured every year by *BSO Polska* units is sold in the retail market. The other half is acquired by industrial buyers. A certain portion of the customers of *BSO Polska* are the clients of British Sugar in the UK market.

Interestingly, the assortment of products offered is, according to the management of *BSO Polska*, of secondary importance for the competitiveness of a sugar producer in Poland, since white sugar makes up for about 95% of total sales. Moreover, Dr. Dziedzic from *BSO Polska* claims that the quality of sugar is slowly ceasing to be an asset, due to the fact that, in contrast to a few years ago, nearly all sugar producers in Poland are able to provide it.

Shortly after the formation of *SugarPol*, British Sugar/BSO started to carry out activities aimed at the minimization of any negative environmental impact of operations. The first stage in the improvement of environmental care in *Unisław* and *Ostrowite* was to tackle the waste water/fresh water usage problem. Water circuits at the two factories were closed and, as portrayed in Figure 74, the use of fresh water was reduced to a great extent. Waste water production was also reduced considerably. Neither *Ostrowite* nor *Unisław* had any form of water treatment at the time of the formation of *SugarPol*. After being used in the production process, waste water at the former plant was simply returned to an adjacent lake. Within a short period of time, the problem of sewage treatment at *Ostrowite* and *Unisław* was solved by British Sugar by building their own treatment plants and/or sending sewage to municipal treatment plants. In consequence, biological life in the aforementioned lake in *Ostrowite* was soon restored after the lake had been dead for many years. As was shown earlier, technological modernization and rationalization measures implemented at the *Ostrowite* and *Unisław* plants in the post-privatization period led to a significant reduction in the use of energy, coal and coke. This was accompanied by the lowering of the emission of pollutants into the atmosphere. Moreover, activities aimed primarily at the improvement of the quality of manufactured sugar (physico-chemical parameters) contributed greatly to the reduction of the detrimental environmental impact of operations in *Ostrowite* and *Unisław* (Farrow et al. 1993, p. 258, 291; Gąsowski 1998, p. 486). In the beginning of 2005, the *Ostrowite* plant was granted ISO 14001 certificate by Lloyd's Register Quality Assurance. *Ostrowite* is the second sugar factory in Poland, after *Chybie,* to receive this certification.

A similar approach to environmental care as in *Ostrowite* and *Unisław* was taken by BSO at the *Glinojeck* sugar factory after the takeover of the plant by the company (closure of the water circuit, etc.).

Since 2003, *BSO Polska* has started to place great emphasis on activities aimed at minimizing the risk of accidents. An internal safety management system consistent with specifications of the OHSAS 18001 standard was instituted at all working sugar factories controlled by the company.[282] Information campaigns, factory audits, emergency drills, as well as the obligation on factory staff to follow certain procedures (clothing, etc.), are the main preventive measures introduced within the *BSO Polska* group in order to avoid accidents and to improve health protection.[283] In 2004, the *Unisław* sugar factory was granted a certificate confirming the institution of a safety management system fulfilling the requirements of the OHSAS 18001 norm.

14 accidents took place in total at the *Ostrowite* (1), *Unisław* (6), *Glinojeck* (4) and *Dobre* (3) plants in the time period January 2004-October 2004. All such occurrences are documented and analyzed in detail. Subsequently, appropriate action is taken to minimize the risk of similar accidents in the future. Also, every single case of first aid being given to workers at the factories' clinics is reported (Powaga 2004, p. 14).

15.1.1.2 Organizational Restructuring

One of the major elements of organizational restructuring implemented within the *BSO Polska* group up to 2005 was the gradual incorporation of individual sugar factories/companies into *SugarPol (Toruń) Sp. z o. o.* and *Cukrownia Glinojeck S.A.* in order to facilitate decision-making processes and to minimize administrative costs. The current organizational structure of *BSO Polska* is presented in Figure 75.

The make-up of *SugarPol (Toruń) Sp. z o. o.* did not change for many years after the *Świecie* sugar factory was taken over by the company in 1994. Since the cessation of beet processing at the *Świecie* plant (2002), *SugarPol* currently consists of the two factories from which the company was formed in 1989, *Unisław* and *Ostrowite.*

Cukrownia Glinojeck S.A. initially included only the beet-processing plant in *Glinojeck*. In 1998, the *Ciechanów* and *Michałów* sugar factories were taken over by the company. After the takeover of *Dobre, Kętrzyn, Guzów* and *Pelplin* by *BSO Polska* in 2000, a company named *SugarTor Sp. z o. o.* was formed from the first three plants. The *Pelplin* sugar factory formed until recently a separate

---

[282] OHSAS 18001 (Occupational Health and Safety Assessment Series) is an international occupational health and safety management system specification, intended to help organizations to control occupational health and safety risks. It was developed in response to widespread demand for a recognized standard against which to be certified and assessed. For more details see http://www.ohsas-18001-occupational-health-and-safety.com.

[283] See Gruszczyńska 2004.

company (*Cukrownia Pelplin S.A.*) controlled by *BSO Polska* (99.8% of the share capital).

In the second half of 2005, *Cukrownia Glinojeck S.A.* took over both *SugarTor Sp. z o. o.* and *Pelplin S.A.* This became possible only after the acquisition by *BSO Polska* of a minority stake in the *Glinojeck* sugar factory from the sugar corporation *KSC "Polski Cukier"* in the second half of 2004.

According to information provided by *BSO Polska*, the last stage of adjusting the organizational structure of the company to the adopted strategy will be the merger of *SugarPol (Toruń) Sp. z o. o.* and *Cukrownia Glinojeck S.A.* Nevertheless, the acquisition of a minority stake (28% of the share capital) in *SugarPol* by BSO from *KSC "Polski Cukier"* is a necessary precondition for this undertaking.

Figure 75. Organizational structure of BSO Polska (as of September 2005)

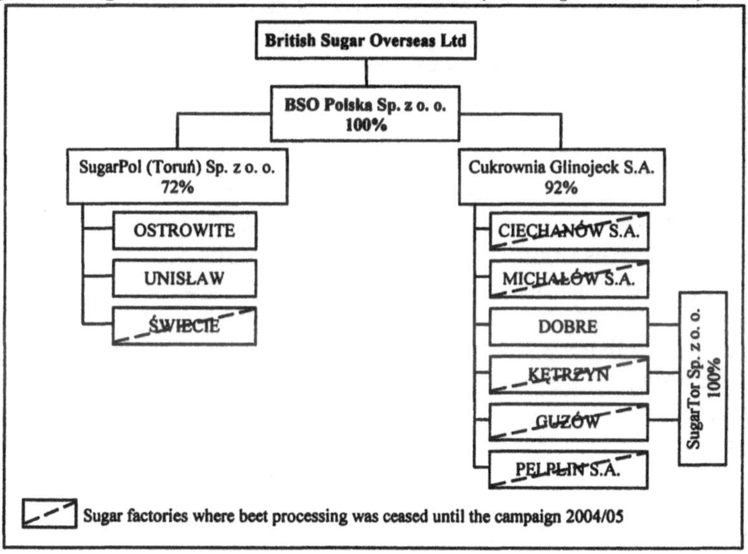

Source: Illustration by the author, based on information provided by BSO Polska.

Since their takeover by BSO, all the sugar factories in Poland have been administered by Polish managers. Nevertheless, from the beginning of British Sugar's presence in Poland, they have been supported by technicians from the UK who have been visiting the Polish sugar factories and taking an active part in the implementation of restructuring processes. Apart from being trained in Poland, Polish managers have also been sent for training to the UK.

Strategic decisions concerning BSO's operations in Poland are taken by the board of directors of *BSO Polska Sp. z o. o.* This board is made up of four persons and was chaired until recently by Mr. Andrew Armstrong, who took up a new post at an ABF company in the USA in 2005. At that time, Mr. David R. Langlands was appointed the new chair of the board of *BSO Polska*.

Apart from the gradual adjustment of the organizational structure to the adopted strategy, British Sugar/BSO introduced profound changes to the management and to the operational methods of the enterprises taken over in Poland. This refers especially to *SugarPol*, whose formation coincided with Poland's transition from a centrally-planned to a market economy. Immediately after the establishment of the joint-venture company, British Sugar began to transform the *Ostrowite* and *Unisław* plants from passive enterprises, whose activity was limited for many years to the meeting of certain production targets, into fully market- and customer-oriented businesses. This included, *inter alia*, the establishment of a marketing and sales department and initiation of a number of marketing activities such as visiting current and potential customers and the commissioning of market research by professional consultants. A database was created on developments in the Polish sugar market and on customers' details, to be used for analyses and future reference. A computer-based reporting system for sales and revenues from sales was instituted to help the management of *SugarPol* to monitor current developments in this field and to react quickly to changes. At the same time, a detailed monitoring of costs was instituted which allowed managers to carry out profitability analyses and to calculate product prices in relation to production costs. Moreover, a system was established to monitor the inter-campaign factory maintenance and full-year overhead costs (Farrow et al. 1993, pp. 257-258).

Another organizational change introduced by British Sugar at the *Unisław* and *Ostrowite* plants shortly after the formation of *SugarPol* was the abolition of a hierarchical system that severely limited the independence and responsibility of functional managers, who were now empowered to manage their own areas (Gąsowski 1998, p. 486).

At the present time, all activities such as sales-order processing, distribution, logistics, and procurement are coordinated by *BSO Polska Sp. z o. o.* on behalf of its subsidiary companies. The business unit of *BSO Polska Sp. z o. o.* that manages the development of the company's retail business is the *Srebrna Łyżeczka Business Unit*. The management of relationships with industrial customers, raw material supplies, financial management, supply chain management, and human resource management are coordinated by the *SugarPol Business Unit*.

In July 2002, *BSO Polska* formed *Co-Products Polska*, a separate business unit focusing on the production and distribution of fodder made from beet pulp and molasses. *Co-Products Polska* manufactures, *inter alia*, one of the most nutritious and increasingly popular farm animal feeds, named *Tofi*. In 2004, the *Co-Products Polska Business Unit* was incorporated into the Raw Material Department of *BSO Polska* in order to facilitate cooperation of the unit with farmers delivering sugarbeets to BSO plants in Poland.

Virtually all processes, from resource planning, customer relationship management, and service management to financial management and supply chain management within the *BSO Polska* group are currently handled using a software solution provided and installed by *Epicor/Scala Polska* (formerly *Scala Business Solutions Sp. z o. o.*).[284]

15.1.1.3 Raw Material/Agricultural Management

After the establishment of *SugarPol (Toruń) Sp. z o. o.*, one of the first restructuring measures introduced at the company was the formation of the Agricultural Development Department. This was accompanied by the launch of an agricultural development program aimed at the improvement in the productivity and quality of the sugarbeet harvest as well as at the reduction of growing costs. Under the aegis of this program, a team of Polish and UK agriculturalists, led by Mr. Brian Farrow[285], assisted farmers in adopting more advanced cultivation techniques, through training programs and advice. Some beet growers were offered the opportunity to visit British Sugar plants in the UK and took responsibility for grower-instruction programs after coming back to Poland. A number of experimental plots were sown each year in the beet-procurement areas of the *Unisław* and *Ostrowite* plants to demonstrate improved cultivation methods. Equipment was brought in from the UK to support the above processes. Moreover, local production was begun of cultivation equipment such as subsoilers and modern leveling harrows, to make them available to growers at as low a price as possible. One of the major reasons for poor sugarbeet yields achieved at the raw material base of *Unisław* and *Ostrowite* until 1989 was the damaged soil structure resulting from traditional cultivation practices (Farrow et al. 1993, pp. 256-257).[286]

On the basis of soil analyses carried out in a new laboratory (*Unisław*), beet growers were given detailed recommendations on the appropriate application of fertilizers and plant protection products. A computer program developed in the UK was installed for this purpose. Previously, the amount of pesticides and fertilizers used by farmers delivering raw material to *Ostrowite* and *Unisław* was often excessive. Quite often it was applied at the wrong time. Therefore, there was a lot of room for productivity increase and for the achievement of considerable cost savings. *SugarPol's* agricultural team made its beet growers aware of the need for costs control and more efficient crop nutrition (ibid. pp. 256-257; Hollowell 1995, pp. 39-40).

Since sugarbeets were very often drilled into excessively acidic soil, a large-scale campaign of supplying farmers with lime was initiated. Furthermore, the

---

[284] See www.epicor.pl and/or www.epicor.com.

[285] Mr. Farrow was responsible for the coordination of raw material/agricultural management at *BSO Polska* until 2002.

[286] See also Spetch et al. 1996.

highest class sugarbeet seeds chosen on the basis of *SugarPol's* own trials were distributed to farmers on advantageous financial terms. Other activities undertaken systematically in order to maximize crop yields and to minimize growing costs included: the transfer from a traditional pre-drill weed control to post-drill systems of weed control; providing beet growers with financial aid in the purchase of new machinery and equipment (precise drills, subsoilers, sprayers, plows, sowers, combine harvesters, etc.) as well as herbicides and fertilizers; the establishment in 1994 of a number of centers where overhauls and repairs of sprayers and drills were carried out; the organization (since 1994) of an annual event called "Field Days" (demonstration of beet growing techniques at experimental plots, providing growers with expert advice on all aspects of beet growing, presentation of modern machinery, equipment, seeds, plant production products, etc.) (Antkowiak 1995, pp. 18-19; Gąsowski 1998, p. 485).[287]

These activities led quickly to the realization of the desired results. The pH of soil improved to the optimum level for sugarbeets. Also, the sugar content in beets procured by *Ostrowite* and *Unisław* was increasing gradually.

After laying the foundations for the achievement of high agricultural yields, the mechanization of farm work was systematically introduced at plantations forming the raw material base of *SugarPol*. At the time of the formation of the joint-venture company, the raw material base of *SugarPol* consisted of a large number of small plantations where the use of horses and human power in the cultivation and harvest of sugarbeets was in common use. In order to change this state of affairs, British Sugar provided beet growers, *inter alia*, with credits for the purchase of modern agricultural machinery as well as with instructions on the proper use of the new equipment.

Another significant restructuring measure introduced at *SugarPol* with regard to the company's raw material base was a change of the time of the year when sugarbeet sowing is started. While some allowance was made if weather conditions were unfavorable, the beginning of this process was, as a rule, rescheduled from the second half of April to the end of March At the same time, action was taken to delay harvesting as much as possible. This was made possible by the systematic increase in the share of beets collected with the use of self-propelled combine harvesters as well as modern cleaner-loader machinery. The purpose of the above changes was to improve the quality of the harvest (longer growing season and longer exposure to sun = higher sugar content in beets) and to stretch the harvesting season over as long a period of time as possible so that raw material can be processed systematically and almost immediately after the harvest (without laying on the field for a long time, and losing quality).

---

[287] At the present time, "Field Days" are organized by *BSO Polska* once a year for all units of the group. In 2005, the event took place in *Długołęka*.

An Agricultural Development Department was also formed at the *Glinojeck* sugar factory after the takeover of the plant by BSO. In the following years, similar measures to those introduced at *SugarPol* were brought into practice at the raw material base of *Glinojeck* and other factories taken over by BSO in Poland.

In the season 2004/05, polarization of cossettes at *Ostrowite*, *Unisław*, *Glinojeck*, and *Dobre* was, on average, by nearly 0.6 percentage points higher than at the time of the takeover of the plants by British Sugar/BSO. The greatest increase in the quality of the beet harvest took place in *Ostrowite* and *Glinojeck* (See Figure 76).

Figure 76. Polarization of cossettes (in %), BSO Polska

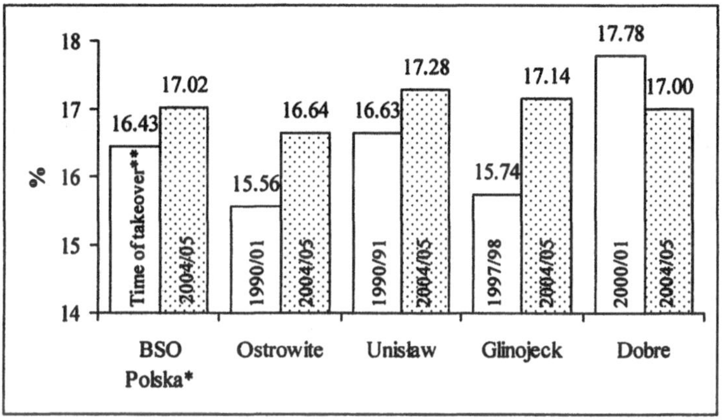

* Ostrowite, Unisław, Glinojeck, Dobre.
** Time of takeover = Ostrowite and Unisław (campaign 1990/91), Glinojeck (campaign 1997/98), Dobre (campaign 2000/01).
Source: IPC (Several Issues); Gazeta Cukrownicza 1/2005, p. 31.

Due to the fact that cessation of beet processing at six sugar factories was accompanied by the takeover of their raw material base by the remaining four plants, polarization of cossettes at all sugar factories acquired in Poland by British Sugar/BSO at the time of their takeover by the company is presented in Figure 77.

The average sugarbeet yield per hectare within the *BSO Polska* group in the season 2004/05 amounted to 41.1 t. At the time of the takeover of individual factories in Poland by British Sugar/BSO, the average sugarbeet yield per hectare at the plants amounted to 33.4 t (See Figure 78).

The average sugar yield per hectare at the ten factories taken over by British Sugar/BSO in Poland amounted at the time of their takeover by the company to 5.26 t. In the campaign 2004/05, the average sugar yield per hectare within the *BSO Polska* group amounted to 6.33 t, which means an increase of 20% (See Figure 79). Data on sugar yields recorded in the season 2004/05 at individual factories forming the *BSO Polska* group is not available.

Figure 77. Polarization of cossettes (in %), BSO plants at the time of their takeover by BSO and BSO Polska average in the season 2004/05

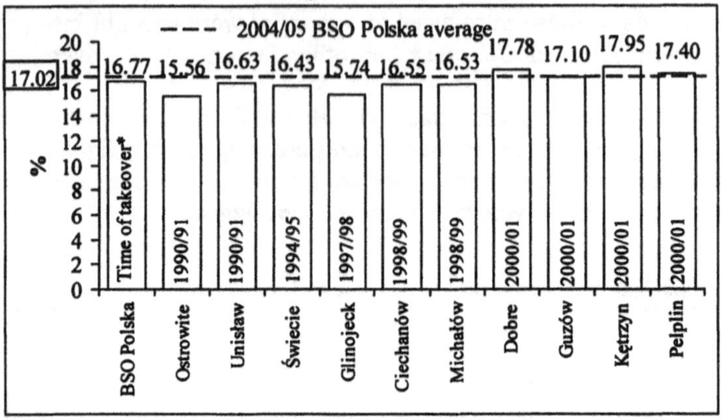

* Time of takeover = [Ostrowite and Unisław (campaign 1990/91) + Świecie (campaign 1994/95) + Glinojeck (campaign 1997/98) + Michałów and Ciechanów (campaign 1998/99) + Dobre, Guzów, Kętrzyn and Pelplin (campaign 2000/01)]/10.

Source: IPC (Several Issues); Gazeta Cukrownicza 1/2005, p. 31.

Figure 78. Sugarbeet yield (in tonnes per hectare), BSO plants at the time of their takeover by BSO and BSO Polska average in the season 2004/05

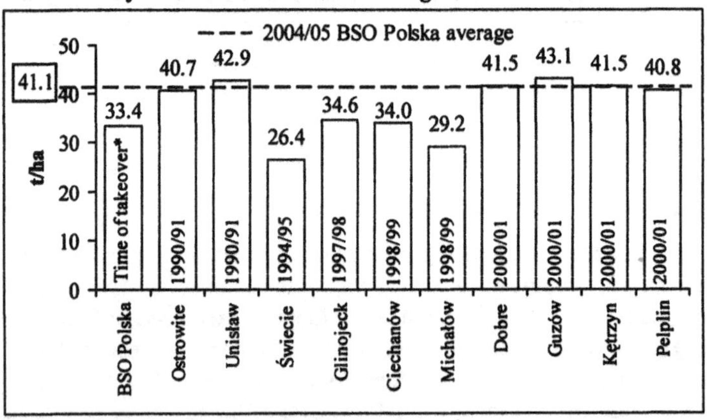

* Time of takeover = [Ostrowite and Unisław (campaign 1990/91) + Świecie (campaign 1994/95) + Glinojeck (campaign 1997/98) + Michałów and Ciechanów (campaign 1998/99) + Dobre, Guzów, Kętrzyn and Pelplin (campaign 2000/01)]/10.

Source: IPC (Several Issues); BSO Polska.

The beet-procurement area of all factories taken over by British Sugar/BSO in Poland totaled 38,373 ha at the time of their takeover by the company. In the season 2004/05, the beet-procurement area of the *BSO Polska* group amounted to 32,668 ha (-15%).

Figure 79. Sugar yield (in tonnes per hectare), BSO plants at the time of their takeover by BSO and BSO Polska average in the season 2004/05

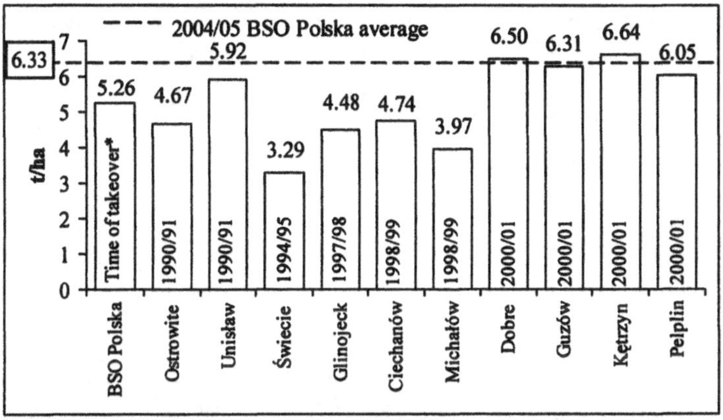

* Time of takeover = [Ostrowite and Unisław (campaign 1990/91) + Świecie (campaign 1994/95) + Glinojeck (campaign 1997/98) + Michałów and Ciechanów (campaign 1998/99) + Dobre, Guzów, Kętrzyn and Pelplin (campaign 2000/01)]/10.

Source: IPC (Several Issues); BSO Polska.

The raw material base of factories where beet processing had ceased by the campaign 2004/05 was taken over by those plants which were still operational. The total beet-procurement area of *Ostrowite*, *Unisław*, *Glinojeck*, and *Dobre* amounted at the time of the takeover of the factories by British Sugar/BSO to 23,068 ha. Information about the size of the beet-procurement area of individual plants in the season 2004/05 is not available.

An enormous drop in the number of beet growers delivering raw material to factories forming the *BSO Polska* group took place up to the season 2004/05. At the time when British Sugar/BSO was taking over individual factories in Poland, 20,746 farmers were delivering sugarbeets to the (ten) plants. In the seasons 2003/04 and 2004/05, *BSO Polska* contracted beet supplies with 8,449 and 8,152 farmers, respectively. Farmers delivering sugarbeets to factories where beet processing had ceased by the campaign 2004/05 were 'taken over' by the plants which were still working. The change in the number of beet growers delivering raw material to the *Ostrowite*, *Unisław*, *Glinojeck*, and *Dobre* plants from the time of their takeover to the campaign 2003/04 is presented in Figure 80. Information on the number of farmers delivering sugarbeets to individual plants in the season 2004/05 is not available.

Since the decrease in the beet-procurement area of *BSO Polska* up to the season 2004/05 was much less pronounced than the drop in the number of beet growers delivering raw material to factories forming the group, it is clear that a considerable increase in the average size of beet plantations forming the raw material base of *BSO Polska* has taken place. As shown in Figure 81, the average size of beet plantations forming the raw material base of all ten sugar factories taken over by British Sugar/BSO in Poland amounted at the time of their takeover by the company to 2.63 ha. In the season 2004/05, the size of beet plantations forming the raw material base of the BSO Polska group averaged 4.0 ha.

Figure 80. Number of beet growers, BSO Polska

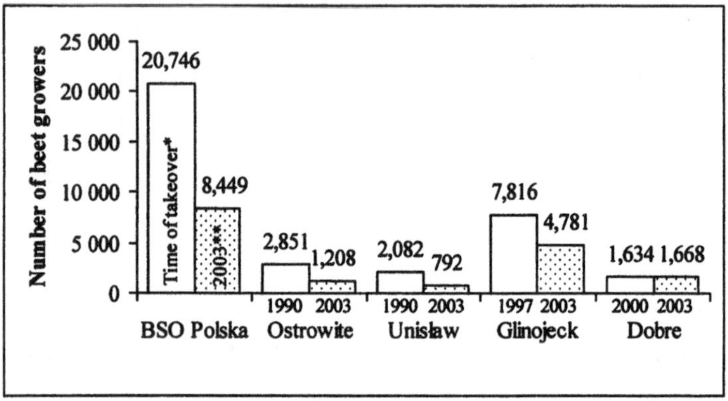

* Time of takeover = [Ostrowite and Unisław (campaign 1990/91) + Świecie (campaign 1994/95) + Glinojeck (campaign 1997/98) + Michałów and Ciechanów (campaign 1998/99) + Dobre, Guzów, Kętrzyn and Pelplin (campaign 2000/01)]

** Ostrowite + Unisław + Glinojeck + Dobre.

Source: IPC (Several Issues); BSO Polska.

Figure 81. Average size of sugarbeet plantations (in ha), BSO Polska

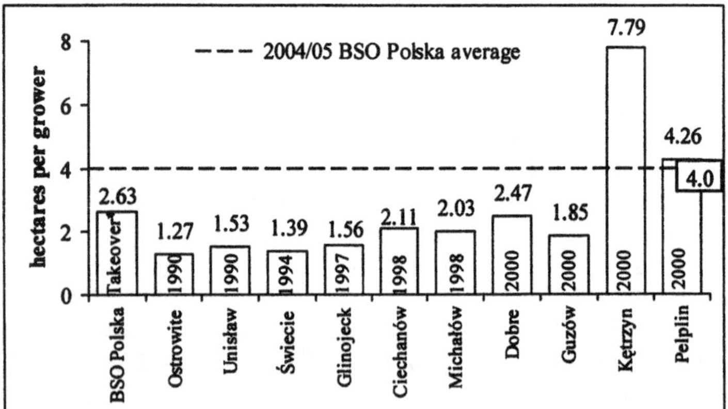

* Time of takeover = [Ostrowite and Unisław (campaign 1990/91) + Świecie (campaign 1994/95) + Glinojeck (campaign 1997/98) + Michałów and Ciechanów (campaign 1998/99) + Dobre, Guzów, Kętrzyn and Pelplin (campaign 2000/01)]/10

Source: IPC (Several Issues); BSO Polska.

A number of factors influenced the substantial fall in the number of beet growers and considerable rise in the average size of beet plantations within the *BSO Polska* group up to the season 2004/05. It was partly a result of the gradual increase in the productivity and quality of the beet harvest (less and less sugarbeets needed for the production of a certain amount of sugar), and partly a consequence of deliberate actions taken by British Sugar/BSO to 'bring' beet plantations closer to individual factories and to increase their average size. Up to 2002, this was achieved to a certain extent by getting rid of 'inconvenient' farmers, i.e. those situated far away from the beet-processing plants and those with very small beet plantations. Cessation of cooperation with such farmers was carried out lawful, but in the opinion of the disadvantaged, not completely fair, methods. They included contracting beet deliveries only with farmers growing beets on an area exceeding a certain threshold specified by a sugar factory and/or burdening beet growers with the costs of transporting raw material to factories. It is important to mention that as long as the employment of such practices was legal, virtually all sugar producers in Poland made use of them. Nevertheless, since the allocation of the "beet growing and delivery rights" to beet growers in Poland in 2002, sugar producers operating in the country cannot use these procedures anymore. Structural changes at the raw material base of the sugar industry have been since then almost fully dependent on the will and activity of the growers (trade with the delivery rights, or withdrawal from sugarbeet growing on their own initiative).

Coming back to restructuring activities in the field of raw material/agricultural management within the *BSO Polska* group, a number of significant changes were introduced up to the season 2004/05 with regard to the collection and storage of sugarbeets, as well as in the logistics of their deliveries to sugar factories. These changes include the coverage of sugarbeet piles with lignin (helping to minimize sugar losses) and the preliminary cleaning of a gradually increasing share of procured sugarbeets on the fields (to minimize the amount of soil transported unnecessarily to sugar factories). The popularization of the latter required investing considerable sums of money in modern cleaner-loader machinery.

The share of raw material delivered to sugar factories directly from the fields by professional freight companies has been systematically increased within the *BSO Polska* group. This has been accompanied by the gradual liquidation of regional sugarbeet-purchasing centers. At the time of the takeover of individual sugar factories in Poland by British Sugar/BSO, 53 such centers were run by the ten plants. The *Glinojeck* sugar factory had 25 regional beet-purchasing centers at the time of the takeover of the plant by BSO. By the season 2003/04, the number of beet-purchasing centers within the *BSO Polska* group had been reduced to five (*Ciechanów*-1, *Glinojeck*-2, *Guzów*-1, *Kętrzyn*-1).

In addition to the introduction of the above changes, a detailed schedule for the collection, preliminary cleaning and delivery of sugarbeets to individual factories is specified every season within the *BSO Polska* group. Due to the gradual increase in the share of the raw material pre-cleaned on the fields and delivered to factories by freight companies, a certain method of piling sugarbeets into heaps was made obligatory. Moreover, the monitoring of the state of these sugarbeet piles was introduced.

A scheme for paying farmers on the basis of the average polarization of cossettes at individual factories was initiated within the *BSO Polska* group in the season 2001/02. Previously, beet growers were paid according to the weight of their beet supplies. In the campaign 2004/05, beet growers delivering raw material to factories forming the *BSO Polska* group were paid on the basis of the average polarization of cossettes recorded at individual plants during the processing season. In the coming season, *BSO Polska* plans to introduce a scheme for paying farmers individually on the basis of the sugar content in the delivered sugarbeets from that farmer. Samples of each beet delivery will be taken for this purpose. The adoption of such a system is in the interest of the most efficient beet growers since it increases their financial returns. Moreover, it motivates farmers to make efforts to maximize the quality of their beet harvest. This, in turn, is in the interest of sugar producers.

It is worth mentioning at this point that farmers supplying *BSO Polska* plants with raw material have always been paid for beet deliveries on time, regardless of the developments in the sugar market.

At the present time, the Agricultural Development Department of *BSO Polska* continues its close cooperation with beet growers and provides them with training as well as advisory services on all aspects of beet growing. On the basis of tests carried out at experimental plots, the optimal varieties and types of sugarbeet seeds, fertilizers and plant protection products are selected and distributed to beet growers. At the same time, beet growers are instructed on how and when to use them. Moreover, the automation of field work is ongoing.

In June 2004 *BSO Polska* launched a website (www.plantator-bso.pl) directed primarily at beet growers and compiled by employees of the raw material departments of factories forming the *BSO Polska* group. The website gives beet growers, among other things, the opportunity to contact and consult agricultural inspectors by e-mail. Furthermore, growers can acquaint themselves on the website with the current offers of *Co-Products Polska* and download publications with advice concerning all the phases of sugarbeet growing. The website serves also as one of the tools of informing beet growers about current events or meetings, as well as informing them of changes to the legislation regulating the sugar market in Poland (Konarska-Gębala 2004).

Last but not least, it is important to mention that *BSO Polska* supports the realization of the desired structural changes at the raw material base of factories forming the group. The company encourages small-scale farmers and those growing sugarbeets far away from sugar factories to sell their growing and delivery rights. *BSO Polska* makes this group of growers aware of the existing opportunities connected with the withdrawal from sugarbeet growing and acts as a middle man between those who want to sell and those who want to buy beet-growing and delivery rights.

15.1.1.4 Financial Restructuring

At the time of the takeover of individual sugar factories in Poland by British Sugar/BSO, the financial and economic condition of most of them was very poor. The poor financial situation of the *Unisław* and *Ostrowite* plants in the end of the 1980s, and the pressing need for an injection of capital, were the main reasons why the management of the factories was urgently seeking an investor.

The *Świecie* sugar factory was acquired by *SugarPol*/BSO from the liquidator of the plant. The entire staff of *Świecie* had at that time already been laid off and the factory had filed for bankruptcy. After the takeover of *Świecie* by *SugarPol*/BSO, the case was withdrawn from the bankruptcy court at the last minute.

The financial situation of the *Glinojeck* sugar factory at the time of its takeover by BSO was disastrous. In 1997, the plant was heavily indebted and filed for bankruptcy. Due to this state of affairs, *Glinojeck* was privatized individually before the completion of the incorporation of all state-owned sugar factories into holdings, charged with their transfer into private hands. The *Michałów* and *Ciechanów* plants were also in dire financial and economic straits at the time of their takeover by *Glinojeck*/BSO. For this reason, they were also privatized individually.

The financial situation of the four sugar factories acquired by BSO from *Rolimpex* and *Danisco* in 2000 was considerably better than that of plants taken over earlier by the company. The most urgently needed financial restructuring at *Guzów, Dobre, Kętrzyn* and *Pelplin* had been carried out by their previous owners.

The main component of the financial restructuring implemented by BSO at factories taken over in Poland and in a difficult financial situation was the improvement of their liquidity through a capital increase, the reduction in debts and the introduction of strict financial control. Increase of capital was carried out by BSO at the *Glinojeck*, *Michałów* and *Ciechanów* plants. In *Unisław* and *Ostrowite*, British Sugar concentrated initially on the improvement of poor financial control. The company instituted at the two factories a modern budgeting system as well as efficient, computer-based monitoring and reporting systems. Through operational restructuring (introduction of technological enhancements, rationalization measures, etc.) British Sugar/BSO gradually created the conditions for the generation of profits at the sugar factories taken over in Poland.

As far as asset engineering is concerned, British Sugar/BSO systematically unloaded non-productive assets. A number of processes were outsourced. In the case of cessation of beet processing at a given factory, part of the fixed assets was transferred from the location to other plants; the rest was either sold or scrapped. The details on decisions taken concerning the infrastructure of factories where beet processing had ceased by the season 2004/05 were given earlier, in the analysis of labor restructuring within the *BSO Polska* group (section 15.1.1.1).

Information on the financial results achieved by *SugarPol* up to 1994 is not available. Since the financial results achieved by sugar factories in Poland in the 1995-2004 time period depended strongly on developments in the domestic sugar market, the analysis of these results for any sugar company operating in the country would not hold a lot of interest, and is therefore not included in this section. Generally, the *BSO Polska* group, like the other sugar producers operating in Poland, generated fair profits in 1995, 1996, 2000, 2001 and 2004.

15.1.1.5 Conclusions

Analyses carried out in this case study have shown that restructuring activities implemented by British Sugar/BSO in Poland up to the season 2004/05 had a number of highly desirable results.

First of all, the takeover of ten sugar factories in Poland by British Sugar/BSO has brought at least half of them back from the brink of closure. Financial restructuring conducted at individual plants in the post-privatization period warded off the threat of bankruptcy and created good prospects for their long-term functioning.

One of the most significant achievements of the operational restructuring implemented within the *BSO Polska* group up to the season 2004/05 is the consolidation of ten factories into four more scale-efficient and more cost-efficient plants. The consolidation led to the optimization of the campaign length at the strategic locations. It meant also, among other things, an end to *Glinojeck's* eternal struggle with raw material shortages.

The considerable reduction in employment within the *BSO Polska* group, resulting from cessation of beet processing at six locations and labor restructuring at the remaining plants, was carried out without major social disturbances. This was accompanied by a considerable increase in labor productivity within the group.

After establishing operations in Poland, the British company set standards in several fields, for example in the quality of manufactured sugar and in quality management in general (*Unisław* and *Ostrowite* were the first sugar factories in Poland at which ISO and HACCP systems were instituted). As regards the assortment of products, British Sugar/BSO quickly mounted a challenge to competitors in the Polish market by offering industrial buyers sugar in bulk and in big bags.

There is no doubt that British Sugar/BSO's direct investment in Poland resulted in a significant transfer of know-how, with regard to all aspects of sugarbeet growing, as well as operations management.

Despite many positive developments and the high efficiency of restructuring activities implemented by British Sugar/BSO in Poland up to the season 2004/05, not everything is perfectly in place as of yet. There is, for instance, still a lot of room for further reduction in energy consumption at factories forming the *BSO Polska* group. Moreover, the employment level at individual plants, especially the *Glinojeck* sugar factory, is relatively high. This means that labor productivity can still be improved. The same can be said also about the productivity and quality of the beet harvest at the raw material base of *BSO Polska*, in spite of significant achievements made in this field. Further structural changes at the raw material base of *BSO Polska* (in the average size of beet plantations and their average distance from individual sugar factories) would also be very positive developments in the years to come. Nevertheless, the materialization of such changes has depended since 2002 almost exclusively on the activity of the beet growers.

The length of BSO's involvement in Poland, the hitherto restructuring effectiveness, and investment plans announced recently, are evidence of the company's long-term commitment to invest and develop business activity in the country. This, in turn, means that, in all probability, the competitiveness of sugar factories forming the *BSO Polska* group will increase systematically in the future.

15.2 Nordzucker

With a maximum sugar production quota of 1.6 million t, Nordzucker AG, headquartered in *Braunschweig*, Germany, is the second largest sugar producer in the EU-25. The 1.6 million t constituted 9.3% of the production quota of all 25 EU member states in 2004.

Nordzucker AG was established as a result of several mergers of sugar companies based in the northern and central part of Germany.[288] The main shareholders of Nordzucker AG are sugarbeet growers, who hold 96.6% of the company's share capital via *Nordzucker Holding AG, Union-Zucker Südhannover GmbH* and *Nordharzer Zucker AG*. The remaining part of the share capital of Nordzucker AG is held by direct shareholders who have stakes in all three holding companies forming the Nordzucker AG. In contrast to its main competitor, the Südzucker AG, Nordzucker AG is not listed on the stock-exchange. The current capital structure of Nordzucker AG is presented in Figure 82.

Figure 82. Capital structure of Nordzucker AG

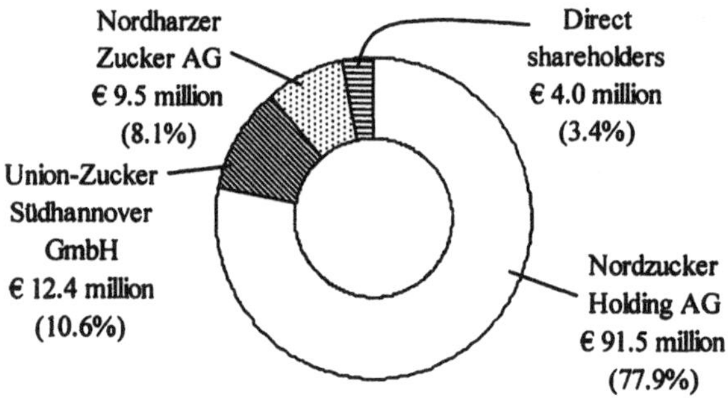

Source: Nordzucker AG, Annual Report 2004/05, p. 15.

In the campaign 2004/05, Nordzucker AG operated eight white sugar factories in its domestic market. Together, they processed on average 90,000 t of sugarbeets per day. The plants are located in the federal states of Lower Saxony, Sachsen-Anhalt and Mecklenburg-Western Pomerania. Nordzucker's market share in Germany in 2004 amounted to 30%. As well as its domestic operations, Nordzucker also manufactures sugar at five factories it owns abroad - two in Poland (*Opalenica, Chełmża*), two in Hungary (*Szerencs, Szolnok*) and one in Slovakia

[288] In 1997 *Zuckerverbund Nord AG* (ZVN), based in *Braunschweig*, merged with *Zucker-Aktiengesellschaft Uelzen-Braunschweig* (ZAG), based in Uelzen, to form *Nordzucker AG*. In 2003, *Union-Zucker-AG Südhannover*, based in *Nordstemmen*, was integrated into the company as a result of a fusion.

(*Trencianska Tepla*).[289] Moreover, Nordzucker holds a minority stake (33.5%) in two sugar factories in the Czech Republic (*Dobrovice, Ceske Mezina*). Nordzucker's activities abroad are coordinated by the company's *Sugar International* division.

In the season 2004/05, sugar factories belonging to the Nordzucker Group manufactured 1.86 million t of sugar. The company's sales and net consolidated income in 2004/05 amounted to € 1,235 million and € 65 million, respectively. 65% of Nordzucker Group's total sales were generated by activities in Germany, 16% were generated in Poland, 7% in Slovakia and 2% in Hungary. 64% of the net consolidated income of the Nordzucker Group in the season 2004/05 was generated in Germany. Investment in property, plants and equipment within the Nordzucker Group totaled € 59 million. The average number of employees working at the Nordzucker Group in the season 2004/05 amounted to 3,334. 43% of this sum (1,437) was employed in Germany. As of November 1, 2004, 1,909 people were employed by Nordzucker in Hungary (709), Poland (578) and Slovakia (622).

16,417 farmers cultivated sugarbeets for the Nordzucker Group in 2004 on an area of 209,873 ha. 10,300 farmers (63%) delivered raw material to Nordzucker's plants located in Germany. The beet-procurement area of Nordzucker AG totaled 150,000 ha (71%). Since autumn 2004 Nordzucker sells household sugar products in all European countries under the brand name *SweetFamily*.

Apart from sugar production, Nordzucker has been continually expanding activities in the non-sugar segment through its *Business Development* division.[290] The company recently entered the sweetener market. In November 2004 Nordzucker AG established *InnoSweet GmbH*, headquartered in *Braunschweig*, as a 100% subsidiary. *InnoSweet* concentrates on global trading in special sweeteners such as polyols, artificial sweeteners and special sugars for the food, healthcare and pharmaceutical industries. Another focus of the company is a customized development of innovative sweetener systems.

Nordzucker also has a 50% stake in *SweetGredients GmbH & Co. KG*, a joint venture with the Danish food producer *Arla Foods Ingredients amba*. *SweetGredients* is the only worldwide producer of *tagatose*, a diabetic-safe, dentally-sound sweetener produced from lactose.

In 2000, Nordzucker acquired a 50% stake in *Syral S.A.* This company, based in *Marckolsheim*, France, manufactures and sells sweetening ingredients derived from wheat and maize. The sweetening ingredients are used by the food and beverage industries as well as the pharmaceutical industry. In the financial year 2003/04 (1 October 2003 - 30 September 2004), *Syral's* sales had a value of € 176.7

---

[289] In the season 2004/05, Nordzucker's market shares in Hungary, Poland and Slovakia amounted to 36%, 9% and 39%, respectively.

[290] With the exception of *Hübner-Medopharm Group* which is fully consolidated because of Nordzucker's 98% stake in the company.

million and the company's net income amounted to € 0.6 million. The average number of employees working at *Syral* in 2003/04 amounted to 270.

Another company owned by the Nordzucker Group is *Hübner-Medopharm Group.*[291] Its main business is the production and sale of natural food supplements, pharmaceuticals and cosmetics. *Hübner* products are sold in more than 30 countries. They are distributed predominantly through health food stores and pharmacies. In 2004, *Hübner* recorded a turnover of € 32.6 million and a net income of € 1.3 million. The company employed 232 people.

Nordzucker holds a 50% stake in the *Amino Group*, including *Amino GmbH, esparma GmbH* (*Osterweddingen*, Germany) and *SA Bioproducts Pty Ltd* (Durban/South Africa). The entire Group employed about 290 people in 2004.

Amino GmbH manufactures raw sugar juice, amino acids and other ingredients from molasses. It also adds dietary value to nutritional products, dietary supplements, indication-driven supplements and pharmaceutical applications which are marketed worldwide.

Esparma GmbH is a pharmaceutical company with about 70 employees. It produces medical products and cosmetics as well as pharmaceuticals used in neurology, urology, pediatrics and the treatment of diabetes. In June 2004, Nordzucker sold its interest in esparma to *Salutas Pharma GmbH*, a *Hexal Group* company. Distribution activities including approvals and brands were sold to *Wockhard Ltd*, an Indian pharmaceutical group.

SA Bioproducts Pty Ltd, in which *Amino GmbH* has a 40% stake, develops and sells amino acids. The company employs over 100 people.

In addition to the above activities Nordzucker holds a 50% stake in *Norddeutsche Zucker-Raffinerie GmbH* in *Frellstedt*, Germany. The company purifies the raw sugar juice from *Amino* to produce liquid sugar and a number of specialized products.

In 2004, the sales of the *Amino Group* totaled € 29.4 million. The Group generated a net loss of € 3.4 million.[292]

15.2.1 Nordzucker in Poland

Nordzucker's investment in Poland began with the acquisition of a majority stake (51.16% of the share capital) in the sugar factory in *Opalenica* from the creditor of the plant, *Bank Gospodarki Żywnościowej* (46.94%) and from *Rolimpex S.A.* (4.22%). In 2000 *Nordzucker* purchased an additional package of shares (28.59% of the share capital) of *Opalenica* from the sugar holding *Pomorsko-Poznańska Spółka Cukrowa*. Also in 2000 Nordzucker took over another five sugar factories

[291] Nordzucker has a 98% stake in the company.

[292] The above overview is based on information contained in the Annual Report 2004/05 of the Nordzucker AG as well as information provided on the web sites of individual companies belonging to the Nordzucker Group.

in Poland. A majority stake in *Wschowa* sugar factory was acquired by the company from an individual investor and the employees of the plant in spring 2000. At around the same time the *Szamotuły* sugar factory was privatized to Nordzucker. In autumn 2000, the company took over the sugar factories *Chełmża, Mełno* and *Krasiniec*.[293]

Table 38. Sugar factories taken over by Nordzucker in Poland

Date	Factory location	Processing capacity*	Privatization method
1999/2000	*Opalenica*	4,500	Indirect privatization/Sec. ownership transfer
2000	*Wschowa*	2,600	Secondary ownership transfer
2000	*Szamotuły*	2,100	Indirect privatization (Holding privatization)
2000	*Chełmża*	5,100	Indirect privatization (Holding privatization)
2000	*Mełno*	2,300	Indirect privatization (Holding privatization)
2000	*Krasiniec*	2,300	Indirect privatization (Holding privatization)

* Average sugarbeet throughput per day (in tonnes) at the time of takeover by Nordzucker.
Source: Nordzucker Polska; IPC 2000, pp. 19-21 (processing capacity).

The number of sugar factories taken over by Nordzucker in Poland was very likely to expand, since the company was in advanced talks with the Polish government on the acquisition of six additional plants (*Gryfice, Kluczewo, Szczecin, Malbork, Nowy Staw* and *Pruszcz Gdański*) in the north-western part of the country.[294] Negotiations concerning the takeover took place shortly before the decision was made to establish the national sugar corporation *KSC "Polski Cukier"*, incorporating all state-owned sugar factories. When the Sugar Law of 2001 came into effect, the privatization deal was blocked by the Ministry of Internal Affairs. Since at that time Nordzucker fulfilled most of the requirements connected with the acquisition of the six factories, it filed a complaint to the court. On May 14, 2003, the Court of Appeal in *Gdańsk* ruled that two of the six factories that Nordzucker wanted to acquire (*Malbork* and *Nowy Staw*) should be incorporated into *KSC "Polski Cukier"*. A similar verdict was made later with regard to the remaining four plants (*Pruszcz Gdański, Gryfice, Szczecin* and *Kluczewo*). As we learned already in section 13 of the present study, all six sugar factories had been gradually incorporated into the *KSC* by May 2005.

The main reason for Nordzucker's participation in the privatization process of the sugar industry in Poland was a "geographical expansion of the company's core activities in the sugar sector". The company has followed its customers in this way in order to serve their needs in the domestic markets. A continued expansion

293 The locations of individual sugar factories in Poland that have been taken over by Nordzucker are presented in Figure 47 (page 233).

294 In Figure 47, these factories are marked with the numbers 1-3 and 9-11. *Mazowiecko-Kujawska Spółka Cukrowa* and *Pomorsko-Poznańska Spółka Cukrowa* have jointly chosen *Nordzucker* as a potential strategic investor for the sugar factories in *Pruszcz Gdański, Malbork* and *Nowy Staw*.

and stabilization of the sugar segment constitutes one of the strategic goals of Nordzucker. For this reason, in the last few years the company has also invested in Hungary, Slovakia and the Czech Republic.

When Nordzucker was beginning its investments in Poland, the goal of the company was to achieve a market share of 20% in the country. Since Nordzucker did not acquire as many sugar factories in Poland as it wanted, this goal has not been achieved so far. Nevertheless, the management of the Nordzucker Group points out that the company is still interested in increasing its market share in Poland.

After the carrying-out of necessary financial restructuring at sugar factories taken over in Poland, Nordzucker's focus in the country turned to restructuring activities aimed at improving the cost efficiency of sugar production. This was to be achieved by reducing the use of resources and introducing other rationalization measures as well as increasing the productivity of both sugarbeet processing and sugarbeet production. The restructuring activities also had the aim of increasing the quality of manufactured sugar and improving environmental care.

From the total number of six sugar factories taken over by Nordzucker in Poland, sugarbeet processing for the campaign 2004/05 took place at two plants - *Chełmża* and *Opalenica*.

15.2.1.1 Operational Restructuring

One of the most significant operational restructuring measures implemented by Nordzucker in Poland by the season 2004/05 was the consolidation of six sugar factories taken over in the country into two plants and the concentration of the entire sugar production in the two locations. After thorough economic analyses, the sugar factories in *Chełmża* and *Opalenica* were chosen by Nordzucker for comprehensive modernization. The following factors were taken into account in the choosing of the two strategic locations: a) the location of individual sugar factories in relation to major beet-growing regions, b) the size and state of repair of the factories, and c) the geographical location of individual plants (distance to the market, distance from city centers). The principal purpose of the cessation of sugarbeet processing at four locations was to increase the utilization level of the processing capacity at the *Chełmża* and *Opalenica* plants to the optimum and to prolong the length of a campaign at the two factories to about 95 days.

In the campaign 2000/01, total sugar production at all six sugar factories taken over by Nordzucker in Poland amounted to 173,040 t (28,840 t per sugar factory). The campaign length at the plants in the season 2000/01 averaged 61 days. In the seasons 2001/02 and 2002/03, the campaign lengths were 55 days and 60 days, respectively. After the end of the campaign 2002/03, sugarbeet processing was ceased in *Mełno*, *Szamotuły* and *Wschowa*. This led to an increase in the average campaign length in *Chełmża*, *Krasiniec* and *Opalenica* to 73 days in the

season 2003/04. In consequence of the cessation of sugar production in *Krasiniec* after the campaign 2003/04, the campaign lengths of 2004/05 in *Chełmża* and *Opalenica* were 97 days and 90 days, respectively (See Figure 83).
The campaign 2000/01 at the *Chełmża* sugar factory lasted 71 days. At the *Opalenica* plant it had a length of 66 days (57 days in 1999/2000).

Figure 83. Campaign lengths (in days), Nordzucker group in Poland, 2000/01-2004/05

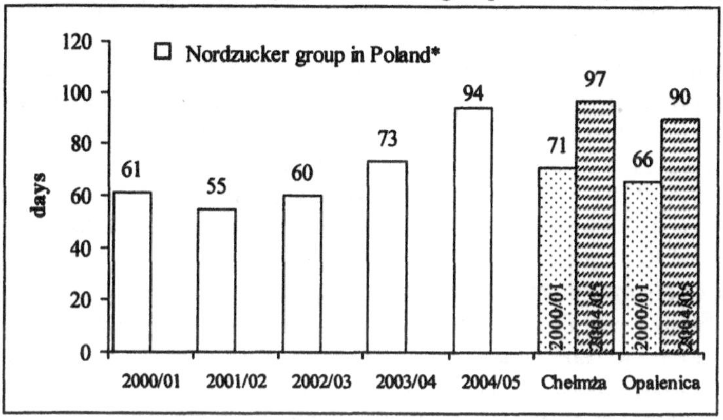

* 2000/01-2002/03 = Chełmża, Krasiniec, Mełno, Opalenica, Szamotuły, Wschowa; 2003/04 = Chełmża, Krasiniec and Opalenica; 2004/05 = Chełmża and Opalenica.
Source: Wawro 2005, p. 100, IPC 2001, pp. 19-20.

Figure 84. Sugar production, Nordzucker group in Poland (in tonnes of white sugar), 2000/01 and 2004/05

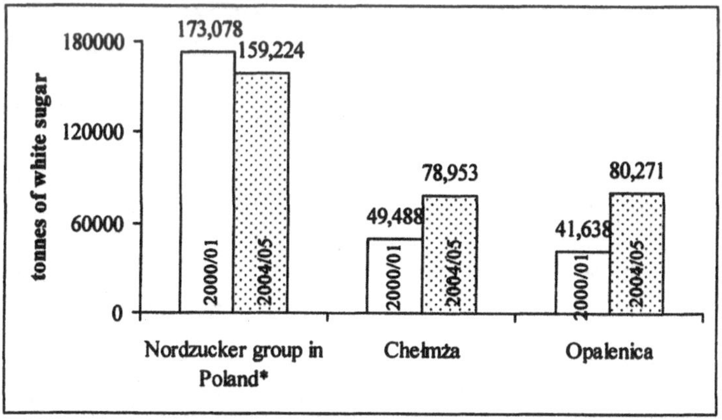

* 2000/01 = Chełmża, Krasiniec, Mełno, Opalenica, Szamotuły, Wschowa; 2004/05 = Chełmża and Opalenica
Source: IPC 2001, pp. 22-24; Nordzucker AG.

At the time of their takeover by Nordzucker, the *Chełmża* sugar factory produced 49,488 t of sugar and the *Opalenica* plant 41,638 t (campaign 2000/01). As a result of cessation of sugarbeet processing in *Mełno*, *Krasiniec, Szamotuły* and *Wschowa*, sugar production in *Chełmża* and *Opalenica* in the campaign 2004/05 rose to 78,953 t (+60%) and 80,271 t (+93%), respectively (See Figure 84).

Concentration of sugar production in *Chełmża* and *Opalenica* was accompanied by a thorough modernization of the two factories.

In the 2000-2004 time period, Nordzucker invested over € 45 million in tangible assets in Poland.[295] Most of this sum was invested in the modernization of the *Chełmża* and *Opalenica* plants. In *Krasiniec*, *Mełno*, *Szamotuły* and *Wschowa*, modernization activities were conducted on a much smaller scale. Their main goal was to improve the quality of sugar and to keep production costs to a minimum. The major investment projects at the *Opalenica* plant were implemented between 1999 and 2002. A comprehensive modernization of the *Chełmża* sugar factory took place in 2003 and 2004. The major investment projects implemented by Nordzucker at the above two locations by the campaign 2004/05 are listed in Table 39.

Not all of the machinery and equipment installed in the post-privatization period at the *Chełmża* and *Opalenica* sugar factories was brand new. A considerable amount of the machinery had been used before, either at German or Polish plants where sugarbeet processing had been ceased. The installation of such machinery in *Chełmża* or *Opalenica* was preceded by a general inspection.

It is important to mention that the type of modernizing activities to be implemented at sugar factories taken over by Nordzucker in Poland was dictated to a great extent by the provisions of privatization contracts. Investment obligations were specified in the so-called "investment packages". At the time of the takeover of the *Opalenica* sugar factory, for example, Nordzucker had been obliged in the privatization contract to invest PLN 27 million in the modernization of the plant in the 1999-2002 time period. The privatization contract also included a detailed list of investment projects to be implemented at the factory. Apart from the investment commitments, Nordzucker was obligated by the privatization contract to invest PLN 11 million in the clearance of the *Opalenica* plant's debts. Since Nordzucker took over the *Opalenica* sugar factory at the same time as the *Szamotuły* plant (one privatization deal), the privatization contract also included investment obligations for the latter. Nordzucker was obliged to invest PLN 2.5 million in the modernization of *Szamotuły* and PLN 8 million in the clearance of the factory's debts.

All investment obligations included in privatization contracts were fulfilled by Nordzucker by the season 2004/05 and the total value of investment projects implemented by the company at sugar factories taken over in Poland exceeds considerably the contractual commitments.

---

[295] According to information provided in Annual Reports (2001/02-2004/05) of Nordzucker AG.

Table 39. Major investment projects, *Opalenica* and *Chełmża* sugar factories, 1999-2004

Opalenica
Major investment projects: **Extraction**: extraction tower (BMA, 6000 t/d), countercurrent cossette mixer, 8 beet-pulp presses (Stord), **Evaporation station**: falling film evaporation apparatus (5000 square meters heating surface), Booster (640 square meters), new condensate flasher **Reception facilities**: Press chamber filter- Putsch 100 A3 **Sugar house/Crystallization**: automation of sugar boiling, pan seeding system, pan seeding apparatuses for white sugar, pan seeding apparatuses for raw sugar, central control station (Siemens PCS7), installation of new heating chambers and mixers for boiling apparatuses, thick juice collecting tank from high-grade steel, new sugar transport (from the sugar house to the silos) elements, cooling crystallization for magma 3 (2x300 t) **Drying/Packaging/Storage**: 2 drying- and cooling plants, sugar segregation unit, packing machinery (Hesser: 35t/8h), palletizer; big-bag (22t/h), three sugar silos (two with a capacity of 10,000 t of sugar each and one with a capacity of 40,000 t), loading station for bulk sugar **Sugarbeet unloading**: modernization of sugarbeet-storage yard, introduction of dry unloading, *Bütfering* system (equipment for tipping out sugarbeets from vehicles)
Chełmża
Major investment projects: **Extraction**: scalder (BMA), extraction tower (BMA), countercurrent cossette mixer, automation of sugar boiling, **Reception facilities**: beet pulp presses plant with 10 beet pulp presses (HP 1800, SMAG), renovation of high-voltage and low-voltage switchgears, new power transformer, modern evaporation station (5000 square meters heating surface) enabling a low use of steam, change of main liming, construction of barometric water cooler, defecation mud presses **Sugar house/Crystallization**: thorough modernization of the sugar house, central control station (Siemens PCS7), pan seeding system, pan seeding apparatuses for white sugar, pan seeding apparatuses for raw sugar, installation of new heating chambers and mixers for boiling apparatuses, thick juice collecting tank from high-grade steel, new sugar transport (from the sugar house to silos) elements, **Drying/Packaging/Storage**: sugar silo (capacity: 60,000 t of sugar), modern drying station and sugar packaging room, new sugar storehouse, sugar segregation (sieving) and dispatching station (segregation capacity: 80t/h, tank trucks loading capacity: 120t/ha), *Bütfering* system (equipment for tipping out sugarbeets from vehicles) **Sugarbeet unloading**: modernization of sugarbeet-storage yard

Source: Wawro 2005; Rząpała 2005; Wawro/Küster 2004, p. 495.

Apart from an "investment package", privatization contracts signed by Nordzucker in Poland also included a "social package" and a "sugarbeet growers' package". They contained a number of guarantees and commitments concerning the employees of sugar factories taken over by Nordzucker and farmers delivering raw material to individual factories. More details are presented in a later part of this chapter.

One of the main objectives of the modernizing activities implemented by Nordzucker in Poland by the season 2004/05 was a reduction in energy consumption at factories taken over in the country. As shown in Figure 85, the use of energy in the boiler house within the Nordzucker group in Poland was reduced between the seasons 2000/01 and 2004/05 from 423 to 273 kWh per one tonne of processed sugarbeets, a decrease of 35%.

At the time of their takeover by Nordzucker, the use of energy in the boiler houses at the *Chełmża* and *Opalenica* sugar factories amounted to 446 and 456 kWh/t of beet, respectively (campaign 2000/01). The corresponding numbers for the season 2004/05 are 285 kWh/t of beet for *Chełmża* (-36%) and 261 kWh/t of beet for *Opalenica* (-43%) (See Figure 85).

Figure 85. Energy consumption (boiler house, in kWh/t of beet), Nordzucker group in Poland, 2000/01-2004/05

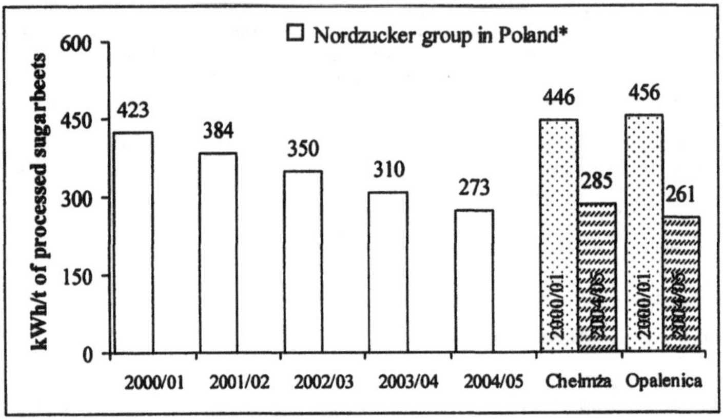

* 2000/01-2002/03 = Chełmża, Krasiniec, Mełno, Opalenica, Szamotuły, Wschowa; 2003/04 = Chełmża, Krasiniec and Opalenica; 2004/05 = Chełmża and Opalenica.
Source: Wawro 2005, p. 101, Nordzucker AG.

Figure 86. Electric energy consumption (in kWh/t of beet), Nordzucker group in Poland, 2000/01-2004/05

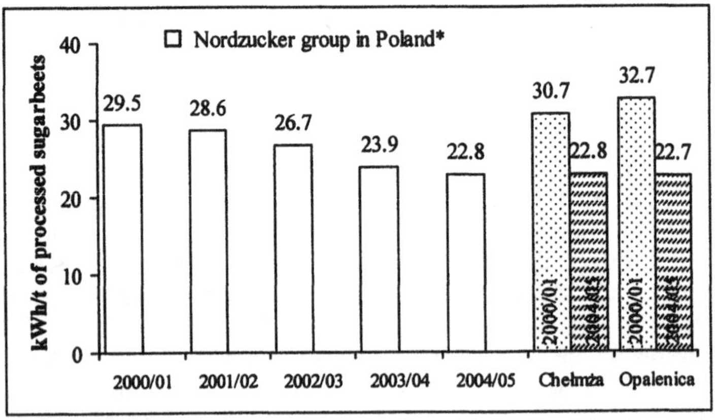

* 2000/01-2002/03 = Chełmża, Krasiniec, Mełno, Opalenica, Szamotuły, Wschowa; 2003/04 = Chełmża, Krasiniec and Opalenica; 2004/05 = Chełmża and Opalenica.
Source: STC 2001 (part I), p. 30; Wawro 2005, p. 101.

Electric energy consumption at Nordzucker plants in Poland decreased between 2000 and 2004 from 29.5 to 22.8 kWh/t of processed sugarbeets, i.e. by 23%. In the campaign 2000/01, the use of electric energy at the *Chełmża* and *Opalenica* sugar factories amounted to 30.7 and 32.7 kWh/t of beet, respectively. In the season 2004/05, electrical energy usage amounted to 22.8 KWh/t of beet in *Chełmża* (-26%) and 22.7 kWh/t of beet in *Opalenica* (-31%) (See Figure 86).

Total use of energy, measured in kWh per one tonne of manufactured sugar, at the *Chełmża* and *Opalenica* plants in the campaign 2000/01 amounted to 3476 kWh/t and 3024 kWh/t, respectively. In the campaign 2004/05, it amounted to 2058 kWh/t at the *Chełmża* sugar factory (-41%) and 1812 kWh/t at the *Opalenica* plant (-40%).

The replacement of coal boilers by two gas boilers as warm water boilers (heating) at the *Opalenica* sugar factory led to a significant reduction in costs resulting from energy consumption during the refurbishment (inter-campaign) period and to an improvement in environmental care. As shown in Figure 87, dust and sulfur dioxide emissions were reduced drastically at the *Opalenica* plant after the installation of the two gas boilers.

Figure 87. Dust and sulfur dioxide emissions at the *Opalenica* sugar factory, before and after installation of two gas boilers

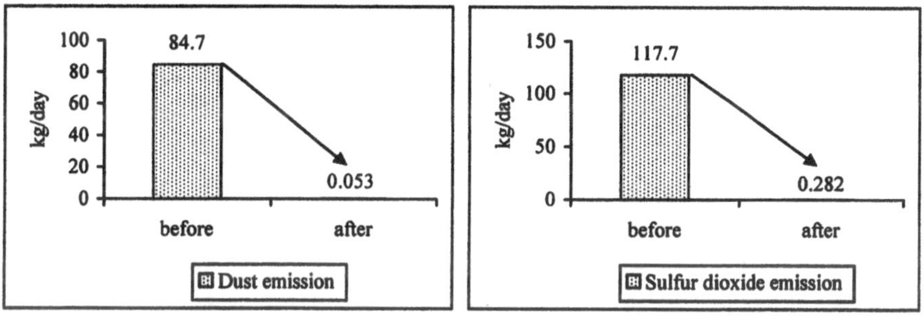

Source: Küster/Wawro 2004, p. 495.

As well as resulting in a considerable decrease in energy consumption, modernization activities and rationalization measures introduced by Nordzucker at sugar factories taken over in Poland led to a significant drop in the use of other resources.

The use of limestone at factories forming the Nordzucker group in Poland was reduced by 32% between the seasons 2000/01 and 2004/05. At the *Chełmża* and *Opalenica* plants it was reduced at the same time period by 37% and 30%, respectively (See Figure 88).

The use of coke within the Nordzucker group in Poland decreased by 19% between the campaigns 2000/01 and 2004/05. In *Chełmża* and *Opalenica* it dropped by 33% and 6%, respectively (See Figure 89).

Coal consumption at Nordzucker plants in Poland decreased by 23% between the seasons 2000/01 and 2004/05. At the *Chełmża* sugar factory it dropped by 20% and at the *Opalenica* plant it fell by 29% (See Figure 90).

According to information provided by *Nordzucker Polska*, the usage of fresh water at the *Chełmża* and *Opalenica* plants in the campaign 2001/02 amounted to 28.45% and 57.50% on beet, respectively.

Figure 88. Limestone consumption (in % on beet), Nordzucker group in Poland, 2000/01-2004/05

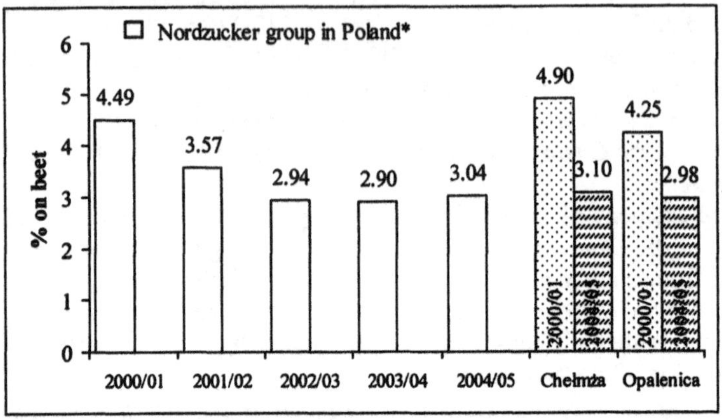

* 2000/01-2002/03= Chełmża, Krasiniec, Mełno, Opalenica, Szamotuły, Wschowa; 2003/04= Chełmża, Krasiniec and Opalenica; 2004/05= Chełmża and Opalenica.
Source: STC 2001 (part II), p. 22; Wawro 2005, p. 101.

Figure 89. Use of coke (in % on beet), Nordzucker group in Poland, 2000/01-2004/05

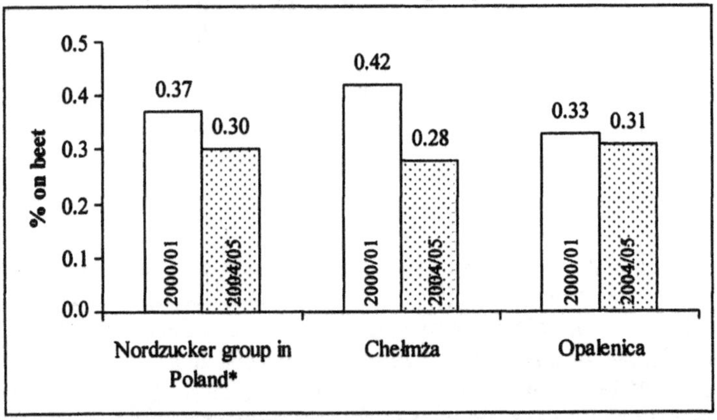

* 2000/01= Chełmża, Krasiniec, Mełno, Opalenica, Szamotuły, Wschowa; 2004/05= Chełmża and Opalenica.
Source: IPC 2001, pp. 43-45; Nordzucker AG.

In the campaign 2004/05, the usage of fresh water at the *Chełmża* sugar factory amounted to 16.57% on beet (-42% in relation to 2001). In *Opalenica* it amounted to 12.67% on beet (-78 % in relation to 2001).[296]

[296] According do IPC data, the usage of fresh water at the *Chełmża* and *Opalenica* plants in the campaign 2001/02 amounted to 17% and 77% on beet, respectively (See IPC 2002, pp. 28-29).

Figure 90. Use of coal (in % on beet), Nordzucker group in Poland, 2000/01 and 2004/05

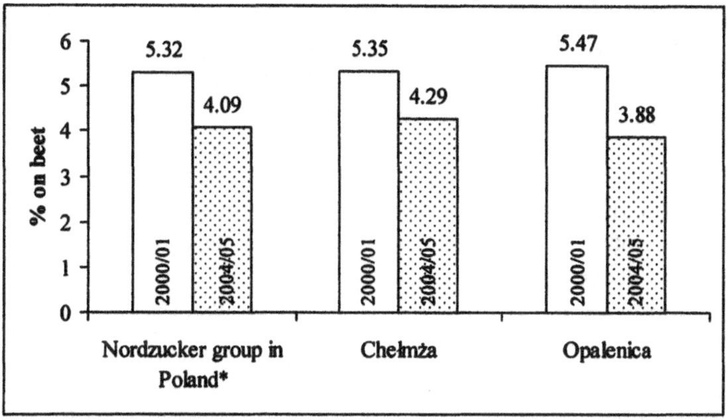

* 2000/01= Chełmża, Krasiniec, Mełno, Opalenica, Szamotuły, Wschowa; 2004/05= Chełmża and Opalenica.
Source: IPC 2001, pp. 43-45; Nordzucker AG.

The consolidation of six sugar factories into two plants and a large-scale labor restructuring led to a significant increase in labor productivity within the Nordzucker group in Poland by the season 2004/05. In 2000, the company employed 2,837 workers in the country (as of November 1, 2000). The corresponding number for 2004 is 578, which is a decrease of 80% (See Figure 91). As was shown earlier, total sugar production within the group was reduced by only 8% (from 173,078 t to 159,224 t) in the same period of time. This resulted in an overall increase in labor productivity, measured in tonnes of sugar per employee, by 350%.

Figure 91. Staff development, Nordzucker group in Poland, 2000-2004

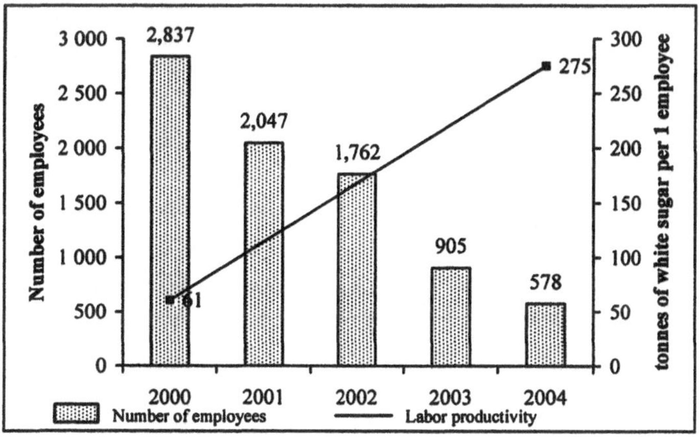

Source: Annual Reports (2001/02-2004/05) of the Nordzucker AG.

Between the seasons 1999/2000 and 2004/05, employment (regular staff plus campaign workforce) at the *Opalenica* sugar factory was reduced by 48% (from 491 to 254 workers). Since total sugar production at *Opalenica* increased by 122% at the same time (from 36,079 t in 1999/00 to 80,271 t in 2004/05), the accompanying increase in labor productivity amounts to 330% (from 73 t to 316 t per employee). If we only take regular staff into account, the increase in labor productivity at the *Opalenica* sugar factory is 277% (from 127 t to 478 t per employee). Regular staff at the *Opalenica* sugar factory was reduced by 41% between the campaigns 1999/2000 and 2004/05. The campaign workforce was reduced by 58% (See Figures 92 and 93).

Figure 92. Employment level at the sugar factory in *Opalenica*, 1999/2000 and 2004/05

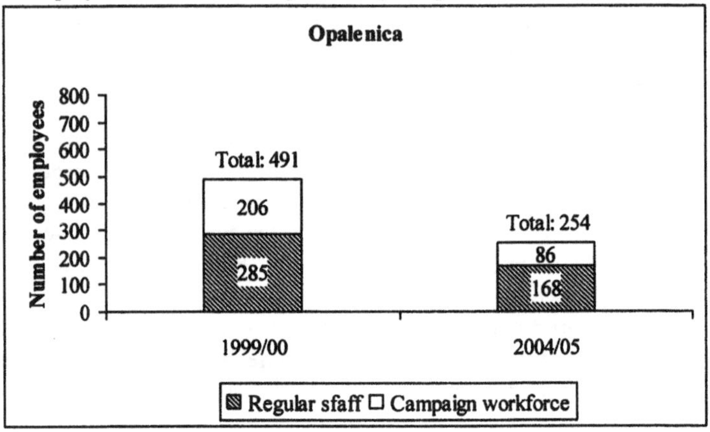

Source: Nordzucker AG.

Figure 93. Sugar production and labor productivity at the sugar factory in *Opalenica*, 1999/2000 and 2004/05

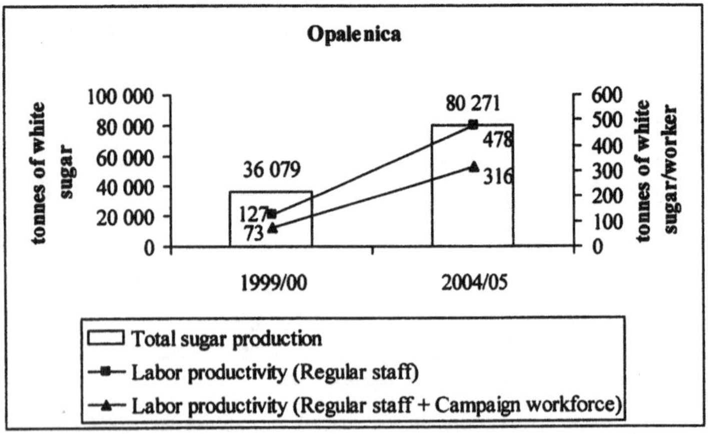

Source: Nordzucker AG, IPC 2000, p. 23.

Total employment at the *Chełmża* sugar factory was reduced by 63% between the campaigns 1999/2000 and 2004/05 by (from 690 to 255 workers). The volume of sugar produced at the plant in the season 2004/05 was 89% greater than in the campaign 1999/2000. The resultant rise in labor productivity was 412% (from 61 t to 310 t per employee).

Figure 94. Employment level at the sugar factory in *Chełmża*, 1999/2000 and 2004/05

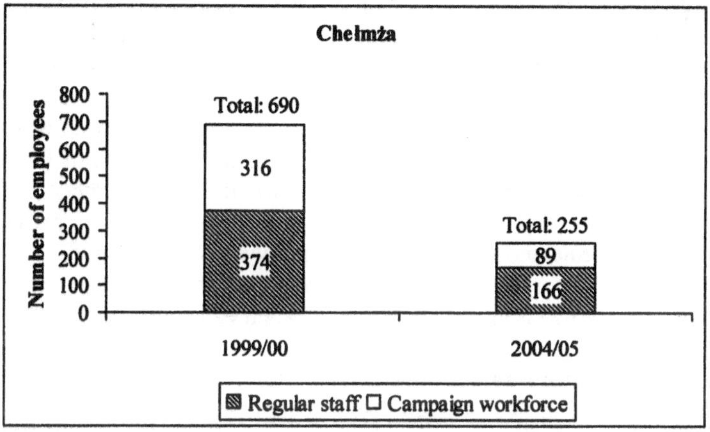

Source: Nordzucker AG.

Figure 95. Sugar production and labor productivity at the sugar factory in *Chełmża*, 1999/2000 and 2004/05

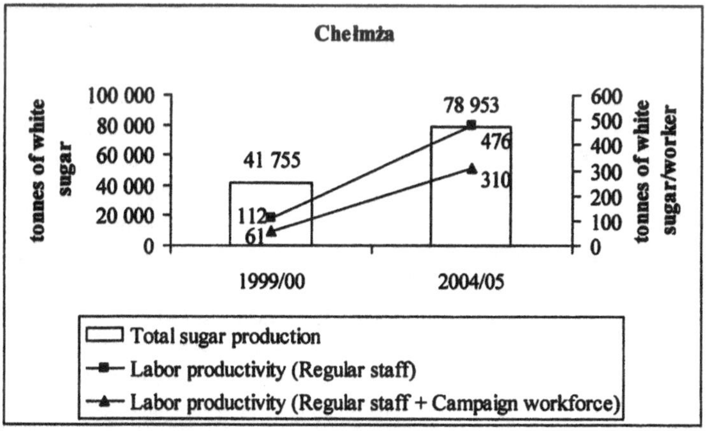

Source: Nordzucker AG; IPC 2000, p. 22.

Labor productivity counting only regular staff increased by 326% (from 112 t to 476 t per employee) (See Figure 95). Regular staff at the *Chełmża* sugar factory was reduced by 56% between the seasons 1999/2000 and 2004/05. The campaign workforce was cut by 72% in the same time period (See Figure 94). Such a significant reduction in the campaign workforce indicates far-reaching automation and computerization of production processes.

One of the key measures introduced by Nordzucker in Poland in order to reduce the numbers employed at their sugar factories in the country was a voluntary staff reduction program initiated in 2001.

During privatization negotiations with the labor unions of sugar factories that were taken over in Poland, Nordzucker offered the employees of individual plants a social package consisting of a guaranteed period of employment of 36 months and the aforementioned voluntary redundancies. Employees who wanted to leave their jobs before the end of the guaranteed employment period received payments equivalent to a monthly salary multiplied by the number of months left until the end of the guaranteed employment period. Furthermore, Nordzucker undertook to cover the costs of staff training in the post-privatization period, provided that the training was connected with the work done by a given employee.

In *Opalenica*, *Szamotuły* and *Wschowa*, the social package had an additional component - a one-off privatization bonus for each employee. It took the form of a salary increase of PLN 200.

The Nordzucker group throughout Poland supplemented the voluntary redundancies program with an outplacement and redeployment program.

After the closure of the *Szamotuły* sugar factory, a certain number of employees of the plant were hired by an investor who had acquired it from Nordzucker and launched an alternative business activity there. At the end of 2004, Nordzucker was in advanced talks with an investor interested in taking over the *Mełno* sugar factory.

As shown in Figure 96, the average sugar yield in % of raw sugar value on beet within the Nordzucker group in Poland in the campaigns 2000/01 and 2004/05 was more or less at the same level.

The extraction efficiency at the *Chełmża* and *Opalenica* sugar factories increased slightly between the seasons 2000/01 and 2004/05 (See Figure 97).

As far as the quality and assortment of products is concerned, highly positive developments could be observed at the Nordzucker group in Poland between 2000 and 2004. In consequence of post-privatization modernizing activities and technological enhancements as well as the institution of quality management systems, the quality of sugar offered by sugar factories acquired by Nordzucker in Poland improved considerably. Both the *Chełmża* and *Opalenica* plants currently manufacture "white sugar of standard quality" (EU-categrory II).

At the time of their takeover by Nordzucker, the product range of the *Chełmża* and *Opalenica* sugar factories was limited to 50kg and 1kg bags. By the season 2004/05 this product range had been widened by bulk sugar loaded onto tank tracks (industrial buyers), big bags (1000 kg), sugar sticks, lump sugar, powdered sugar and extra fine sugar.

Figure 96. Sugar yield in % of raw sugar value on beet, Nordzucker group in Poland, 2000/01 and 2004/05

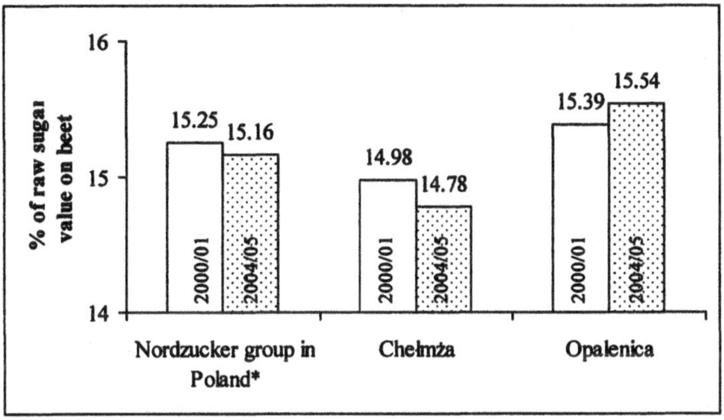

* 2000/01= Chełmża, Krasiniec, Mełno, Opalenica, Szamotuły, Wschowa; 2004/05= Chełmża and Opalenica.
Source: STC 2001, p. 18, Nordzucker AG.

Figure 97. Recovery of sugar, Nordzucker group in Poland, 2000/01 and 2004/05

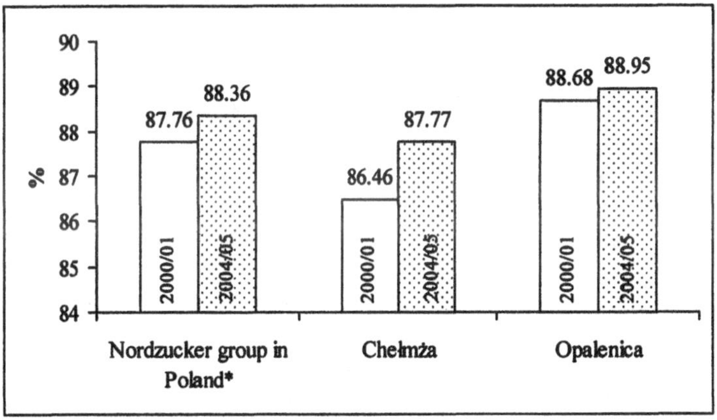

* 2000/01= Chełmża, Krasiniec, Mełno, Opalenica, Szamotuły, Wschowa; 2004/05= Chełmża and Opalenica.
Source: STC 2001, p. 11, Nordzucker AG.

The packaging of products manufactured at Nordzucker plants in Poland also changed after their takeover by the company. Initially, household sugar products were marketed by Nordzucker in Poland in blue bags under the brand name *Promyk* (sunbeam). Since autumn 2004 Nordzucker sells household sugar products in all European countries (in blue bags) under the brand name *SweetFamily*. Nordzucker decided that after the introduction of this new brand name in Poland, the old brand name (*Promyk*) would remain on new sugar packages for a certain period of time, bearing the *SweetFamily* inscription and logo; this was a customer-orientated decision.

About 60-70% of sugar manufactured at Nordzucker plants in Poland is sold either in bulk or in large bags to industrial buyers. According to the management of *Nordzucker Polska*, the main competitive advantages of the company are the high quality of their sugar and their ability to provide customers with sugar in bulk and in bags of various sizes at any time. As expressed at the end of 2004 by Dr. Adam Koziołek, Nordzucker's representative in Poland: "We are currently able to indulge every whim of our customers".

Chełmża and Opalenica are the first two factories in Poland to be certified on the basis of PN-EN (*Polska Norma*) ISO 9001:2000. The system was instituted at both plants in 2002. It is designed to improve customer satisfaction and quality assurance. In 2003, the HACCP system was instituted in *Chełmża* and *Opalenica*. Certification confirming the institution and proper functioning of the above quality management systems is renewed annually after audits have been carried out by authorized bodies. According to information provided by Nordzucker, possession of such certificates is a necessary requirement for the company's major customers.

In all its countries of operation, Nordzucker attaches a lot of weight to a continual increase in job safety and health protection. The company rigorously pursues a target of "zero accidents" and a minimal level of sick leaves. In order to avoid accidents, Nordzucker introduced a number of preventive measures and a risk management program at their Polish sugar factories. The preventive measures include accident benchmarking[297], internal audits[298], the organization of emergency drills and the introduction of certain requirements and rules with regard to clothing and behavior at a sugar factory (e.g. the requirement to wear a helmet (for everybody entering the sugar factory), the requirement to wear special clothing, shoes, glasses, masks and earplugs (for workers in individual factory departments)). Furthermore, information campaigns aimed at the avoidance of unnecessary accidents are organized regularly at Nordzucker plants in Poland. Factory workers also have the possibility of contributing to the improvement in job safety by putting forward their own proposals through the *Nordzucker Brain Pool*. A large number of suggestions submitted by factory workers are put into practice. The employees of Nordzucker plants in Poland where no accidents occur for a given period of time are provided with salary bonuses. The value of

[297] Any accident that takes place in a Nordzucker group factory is thoroughly analyzed and discussed with factory workers. Subsequently, appropriate preventive measures are taken in order to avoid similar accidents in the future. Each accident is documented, classified and recorded in a statistical benchmarking database. The compiled statistics are communicated to all employees.

[298] Internal audits are in the form of monthly walking rounds of the entire sugar factory. The purpose of the audits, which are carried out each month by a special commission, is to identify places where health and safety hazards exist and to eliminate the likelihood of accidents at such places through appropriate preventive measures.

the bonuses rises in direct proportion to the length of time without accidents. The Nordzucker group uses vaccination campaigns as one of its methods of minimizing sick leaves (lost workdays) at their Polish plants.

In 2004 Nordzucker instituted a work safety and health management system consistent with OHSAS 18001 specifications at the *Chełmża* and *Opalenica* sugar factories.

The above activities resulted in a significant decrease in the number of accidents within the Nordzucker group in Poland. 25 accidents took place at Nordzucker plants in Poland in 2001. The corresponding numbers for 2002, 2003 and 2004 are 3, 13 and 0, respectively (Wawro 2004a, p. 93; Gazeta Cukrownicza 7/2005, p. 210). An increase in the number of accidents in 2003 is attributed to the fact that numerous modernizing activities were implemented in that year at individual sugar factories.

At the end of September 2004, 1300 days had passed since the last accident at the *Opalenica* sugar factory. This fact, as well as the employment of the best practices in job safety, had been noticed by the National Labor Inspectorate (*Państwowa Inspekcja Pracy*). In November 2004, *Wielkopolski Cukier S.A.* (*Opalenica* sugar factory), was awarded the prize "Employer-Organizer of Safe Work" with a congratulatory letter from the President of Poland for remarkable achievements in the area of workforce protection (Gazeta Cukrownicza 12/2004, p. 338).

Other awards obtained by the *Opalenica* sugar factory/*Wielkopolski Cukier S.A.* in the 2001-2004 time period include: "Business Fair Play Certificate" ("*Przedsiębiorsto Fair Play*") [2001], "Polish Prestige" ("*Polski Prestiż*") [2001], the honorary title of the "Approved Partner Program" ("*Solidny Partner*") for reliability and responsibility in business [2002], "Market Leader" ("*Lider Rynku*") (in sugar production and distribution) [2002], AGRO POLAND-EURO QUALITY emblem (for white sugar PN-A-74850) [2002], "*Wielkopolska Jakość*" trademark [2002] and "Euro Leader" (in sugar production and distribution) [2003].

Quality management, health and safety management and environmental management systems instituted at Nordzucker plants in Poland are integrated into a single, company-wide business management system. As well as the institution of the aforementioned management systems in Poland, Nordzucker also established a system of managing and responding to customers' complaints.

In 2003, Nordzucker instituted computer software in its laboratories at sugarbeet-processing plants in all its countries of operation. Installation of the software at all Nordzucker plants standardized control processes as well as the types and frequency of analyses carried out at laboratories within the entire Nordzucker group. Data from individual laboratories is transmitted, with the use of the software, to a central database. On the basis of information collected in the database, reports containing various statistics are compiled and made available to all users (Wawro 2004a, p. 94).

Since the establishment of operations in Poland, Nordzucker has continually organized a large number of vocational training courses for employees. The main goal of the courses is to provide employees with the new skills needed to adapt to technological and organizational changes introduced as a result of restructuring. As well as being trained in Poland, employees from various departments (and of various ranks) have been sent to Germany for training.

Nordzucker's operations in Poland are administered by Polish managers. German managers sit on the boards of directors of individual factories/companies. Technicians and engineers from Germany visit Nordzucker plants in Poland and act as consultants on the implementation of major investment projects.

15.2.1.2 Organizational Restructuring

One of the most significant changes introduced as part of organizational restructuring in the Nordzucker group in Poland by the season 2004/05 was the merger of all six sugar factories/companies taken over by Nordzucker in the country into two companies: *Wielkopolski Cukier S.A.* and *Pomorski Cukier S.A.* The establishment of the two companies formed the basis for the consolidation of individual sugar factories/companies (the cessation of sugarbeet processing at selected locations).

Wielkopolski Cukier S.A., headquartered in *Opalenica*, was established on February 20, 2002. The fixed assets necessary for sugar production were incorporated into the new company on December 20, 2002, predominantly from the *Opalenica* and *Szamotuły* plants. Since the campaign 2003/04, the *Opalenica* sugar factory is the only working sugarbeet-processing plant in *Wielkopolski Cukier S.A.* After the closure of the *Szamotuły* and *Wschowa* factories in 2003, *Opalenica* took over the raw material base of the two plants.

Pomorski Cukier S.A., with a registered office in *Chełmża*, was established on March 4, 2003. The fixed assets necessary for sugar production were incorporated into *Pomorski Cukier S.A.* from the *Chełmża* sugar factory. Since the campaign 2004/05, it is the only working sugar factory in *Pomorski Cukier S.A.* Cessation of sugarbeet processing in *Mełno* and *Krasiniec* (in 2003 and 2004, respectively) was accompanied by the takeover of the raw material base of the two plants by *Chełmża*.

As well as allowing the consolidation of individual factories without the loss of production quota, the establishment of *Wielkopolski Cukier S.A.* and *Pomorski Cukier S.A.* streamlined management processes and led to a considerable reduction in administrative costs within the Nordzucker group in Poland.

The organizational structure of *Wielkopolski Cukier S.A.* and *Pomorski Cukier S.A.* was adjusted to the structure of Nordzucker units in Germany. At the head of each of the two companies in Poland there is a board of directors consisting of two people at *Pomorski Cukier S.A.* and three people at *Wielkopolski Cukier S.A.*

(as of August 2005). Moreover, each company has managing directors responsible for the fields of technology, raw material and finances. There are also a number of process managers in each department.

Figure 98. Evolution of the organizational structure of the Nordzucker group in Poland

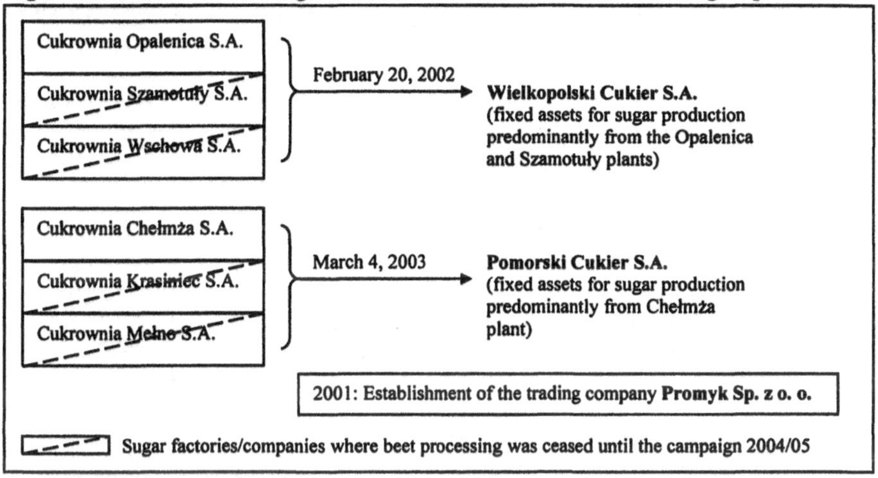

Source: Original diagram by the author.

The last step on the way to adjusting the organizational structure of the Nordzucker group in Poland to the adopted strategy will be a merger of *Wielkopolski Cukier S.A.* and *Pomorski Cukier S.A.* into one company named *Nordzucker Polska S.A.* The merger is due to be finalized by September 2005. The main goal of this move is to reduce administrative costs to the minimum.

Distribution of sugar manufactured at Nordzucker plants in Poland as well as all marketing activities are handled by *Promyk Sp. z o. o.*, a trading company established in 2001 and headquartered in *Przeźmierowo.*

In the time period between March 2002 and September 2003, the management information system SAP was instituted at individual units of the Nordzucker group in Poland. This system has been used at Nordzucker units in Germany for many years.

The institution of SAP at Nordzucker units in Poland took place in two stages and was carried out by the *Business Consulting Center Sp. z o. o.* (BCC). During the first stage (March 2002-January 2003), several modules of SAP were instituted at the *Poznań* group of Nordzucker units in Poland (*Wielkopolski Cukier S.A.*, *Nordzucker Polska Sp. z o. o.*, *Nordzucker Polska Spółka Komandytowa* and *Cukrownia Opalenica S.A.*). The SAP modules instituted at the *Poznań* group comprise the following functional areas of management: Financial Accounting (FI), Fixed Assets Accounting (FI-AA), Controlling (CO), Materials Management (MM), Sales and Distribution (SD), Human Resources (HR). The SAP implementation in human resources management covered the following functionalities: personnel administration, work time management, payroll settlement and organizational structure management.

Additionally, an interface between SAP and a system that handles accounts with sugarbeet growers ("*Plantator*") was developed and implemented by BCC consultants.

In the second stage of SAP implementation within the Nordzucker group in Poland (April 2003-September 2003), the above modules of SAP were instituted at *Pomorski Cukier S.A.* and *Cukrownia Chełmża S.A.* This project was also carried out by BCC (See Figure 99).

Figure 99. SAP implementation at Nordzucker units in Poland

First stage (March 2002-January 2003):

Wielkopolski Cukier S.A. *Nordzucker Polska Sp. z o. o.* *Nordzucker Polska Spółka Komandytowa* *Cukrownia Opalenica S.A.*	FI, FI-AA, CO, MM, SD, HR, interface between SAP and the "Plantator" system

Second stage (April 2003-September 2003):

Pomorski Cukier S.A. *Cukrownia Opalenica S.A.*	FI, FI-AA, CO, MM, SD, HR, interface between SAP and the "Plantator" system

Source: BCC 2004.

The institution of SAP within the Nordzucker group in Poland greatly facilitated the collection of and access to information, reduced the time needed to communicate this information, and minimized errors. Furthermore, it enabled early risk identification and constant risk monitoring. In short, SAP implementation led to a significant increase in the time and cost efficiency of a large number of processes. As expressed by Mr. Andrzej Nowak, a member of the board of directors of *Wielkopolski Cukier S.A.*: "*Thanks to an efficient execution of SAP implementation in consecutive units of our group, we make a significant step in the reorganization of the Nordzucker group in Poland towards an integrated, economically sound organism, fully oriented to customers' needs*" (BCC 2004, p. 3).

15.2.1.3 Raw Material/Agricultural Management

Restructuring activities in this field within the Nordzucker group in Poland were concentrated in the 2000-2004 time period on the increase in the productivity and quality of the sugarbeet harvest and on the improvement in the cost efficiency of the collection, storage and delivery of sugarbeets to sugar factories.

The provision of sugarbeet growers with advisory services and instructions on appropriate sowing and growing techniques as well as on the choice and proper use of seeds, fertilizers and plant protection products played a major role in activities aimed at the increase in agricultural yields. The advisory services had been provided mainly in the form of training courses as well as through close cooperation between employees of the raw material departments at individual factories and the sugarbeet growers. Furthermore, before each campaign farmers delivering sugarbeets to Nordzucker plants in Poland receive guides containing various instructions and advice. A special edition of the quarterly "*Burak Cukrowy*", including, among other things, practical advice on all phases of sugarbeet growing and harvesting methods, is supplied throughout the year free of charge to beet growers delivering sugarbeets to Nordzucker plants in Poland.

One of the methods of popularizing the use of modern sowing, growing and harvesting techniques within the Nordzucker group in Poland is the organization of an event called "*Dni Buraka*" (Sugarbeet Days). The event takes place every year (usually in June) at two locations: in *Trzcianka*, near *Opalenica* (since 1996) and in *Kowroz*, near *Chełmża* (since 2000). The Sugarbeet Days include practical demonstrations at a number of experimental plots (these relate to all phases of sugarbeet growing) as well as presentations prepared by companies producing sugarbeet seeds, fertilizers and plant protection products. Moreover, modern sowing, harvesting, cleaning and loading machinery are presented (Leśniak 2004).

Between 2000 and 2004, the Nordzucker group in Poland introduced a number of new methods of harvesting and preserving sugarbeets in the fields in order to minimize sugar loss in the procured raw material. One such measure is the coverage of sugarbeet piles with lignin at a late stage of the campaign (lignin protects sugarbeets from going rotten due to the cold). At the time of Nordzucker's takeover of individual sugar factories in Poland, the use of this practice on sugarbeets delivered to the plants was scant. As portrayed in Figure 100, more and more sugarbeets procured by Nordzucker plants were covered with lignin in the following years. In the campaign 2004/05, 86% of the total number of sugarbeets delivered to Polish Nordzucker plants (after November 11) had been covered with lignin.

The aforementioned activities secured high quality levels in the raw material procured by Nordzucker plants in Poland and led to a considerable increase in the sugar yield per hectare in the 2000-2004 time period.

The average polarization of cossettes within the Nordzucker group in Poland in the campaign 2000/01 was 17.38%. In the season 2004/05, average polarization in sugarbeets within the group amounted to 17.16% (See Figure 101).

Since the campaign 2004/05, the amount of money paid to beet growers for raw material delivered to Nordzucker plants in Poland is dependent on sugar content. Each delivery is evaluated individually (For details see Opielewicz 2005 for example). Previously, the payments provided to beet growers were calculated on the basis of the average polarization of cossettes in a given campaign (taking all deliveries into account).[299]

Figure 100. Coverage of sugarbeet piles with lignin, Nordzucker group in Poland, 2000-2004*

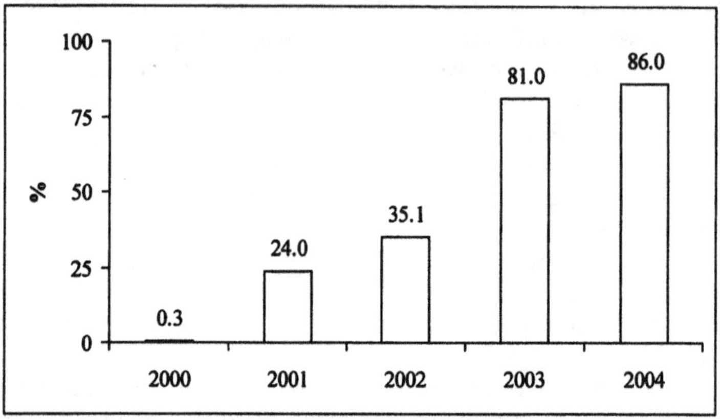

* In % of sugarbeets delivered to Nordzucker plants in Poland after November 11.
Source: Wawro 2005, p. 100.

Figure 101. Polarization, Nordzucker group in Poland, 2000/01-2004/05*

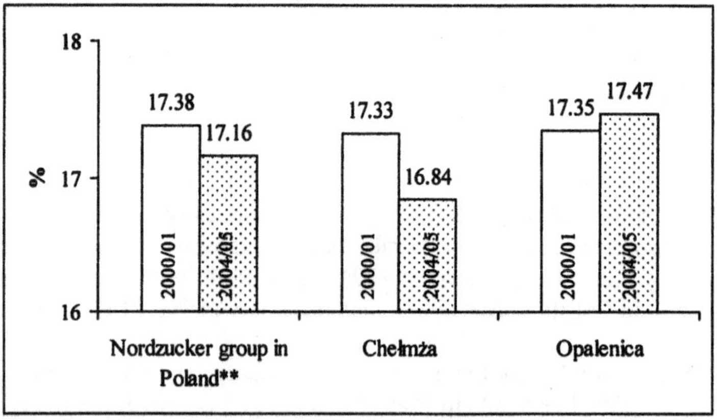

* For 2000/01: polarization of cossettes; for 2004/05: Polarization in sugarbeets.
** 2000/01= Chełmża, Krasiniec, Mełno, Opalenica, Szamotuły, Wschowa; 2004/05= Chełmża and Opalenica.
Source: IPC 2001, pp. 25-27; Nordzucker AG.

299 Such a system disadvantaged the most efficient farmers and did not give any incentive to make efforts to improve the quality of the harvest. The ability to calculate payments individually on the basis of sugar content in delivered sugarbeets requires investing considerable sums of money in the necessary equipment.

The average sugar yield per hectare of the Nordzucker group in Poland in the campaign 2004/05 amounted to 7.5 t and was 14% higher than in the season 2000/01 (6.6 t/ha) (See Figure 102).

Figure 102. Sugar yield (in tonnes per hectare), Nordzucker group in Poland, 2000/01-2004/05

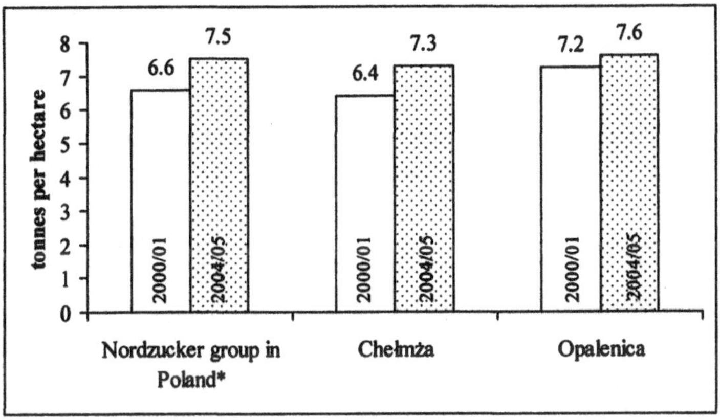

* 2000/01= Chełmża, Krasiniec, Mełno, Opalenica, Szamotuły, Wschowa; 2004/05= Chełmża and Opalenica.
Source: IPC 2001, pp. 16-18; Nordzucker AG.

The average sugarbeet yield of the Nordzucker group in Poland in 2000 and 2004 was equal. It amounted to 43.5 t/ha.

At the time of the takeover of individual sugar factories in Poland, Nordzucker was obliged by privatization contracts to maintain the size of the beet-procurement area and to give priority to existing beet growers in the allocation of beet delivery contracts. Furthermore, the company committed itself to the procurement of sugarbeets from existing sugarbeet-growing regions, forming the raw material base of the Nordzucker plants in Poland even in the case of cessation of beet processing at a given location. This fact as well as the granting of beet growing and delivery rights to beet growers in Poland in 2002 have strongly constrained Nordzucker's abilities to influence structural changes at the raw material base of their factories in Poland. For this reason, up to the campaign 2004/05, such changes within the Nordzucker group in Poland took place on a very limited scale and materialized naturally (withdrawal from sugarbeet growing, trade between farmers in beet delivery rights).

According to Mr. Stanislaw Barnaś, Chairman of the National Association of Sugarbeet Growers in Poland, the Nordzucker group did not employ any prohibited and/or unfair practices in the 2000-2004 time period aimed at bringing sugarbeet plantations closer to sugar factories or at increasing their average size. As expressed by Mr. Barnaś during an interview in February 2004: "They [the Nordzucker group in Poland] do not wriggle out of anything [responsibilities and commitments concerning the beet-procurement area and the beet growers]." It is worth mentioning here that farmers supplying the Nordzucker group in Poland with raw material have always been paid on time for their deliveries, regardless of the situation in the domestic sugar market.

Between the campaigns 2000/01 and 2004/05, the beet-procurement area of the Nordzucker group in Poland decreased by only 8.4 % (from 26,249 ha to 24,057 ha). Cessation of sugarbeet processing at 4 locations was accompanied by a 'takeover' of their raw material base and farmers by the *Chełmża* and *Opalenica* factories. In consequence, the beet-procurement area of the *Chełmża* plant rose by 60% between the seasons 2000/01 and 2004/05 (from 7,768 ha to 12,434 ha). The beet-procurement area of the *Opalenica* sugar factory increased by 87% during the same time period (from 6,226 ha to 11,623 ha) (See Figure 103).

Figure 103. Beet-procurement area of the Nordzucker group in Poland, 2000/01-2004/05

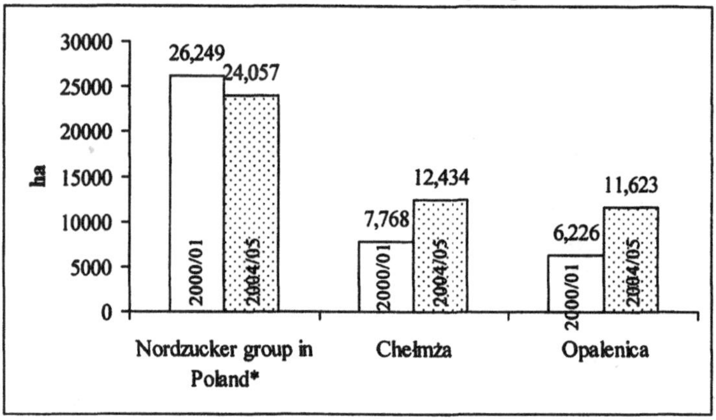

* 2000/01= Chełmża, Krasiniec, Mełno, Opalenica, Szamotuły, Wschowa; 2004/05= Chełmża and Opalenica.
Source: IPC 2001, pp. 13-15; Nordzucker AG.

The number of sugarbeet growers delivering raw material to Nordzucker plants in Poland dropped in the 2000-2004 time period from 7,561 to 5,718 (-24.4%). The number of farmers delivering sugarbeets to the *Chełmża* and *Opalenica* plants increased between the seasons 2000/01 and 2004/05 by 40.4% (from 2,619 to 3,676) and 59.5% (from 1,280 to 2,042), respectively (See Figure 104).

The average size of the sugarbeet plantations forming the raw material base of the Nordzucker group in Poland increased by 17.9% between 2000 and 2004 (from 3.85 ha to 4.54 ha). During the same time period, the average size of the beet plantations forming the raw material bases of the *Chełmża* and *Opalenica* plants increased by 13.8% (from 2.97 ha to 3.38 ha) and 17.1% (from 4.86 ha to 5.69 ha), respectively (See Figure 105).

By the season 2004/05 a number of steps had been taken by the Nordzucker group in Poland to increase the cost efficiency of the collection, storage and delivery of sugarbeets to sugar factories. One such activity was the introduction of six-row combine harvesters for use in the sugarbeet harvest. But due to the large number of small sugarbeet plantations remaining in the beet-procurement area of the Nordzucker group in Poland, the use of the harvesters is not total.

Figure 104. Number of sugarbeet growers, Nordzucker group in Poland, 2000/01 and 2004/05

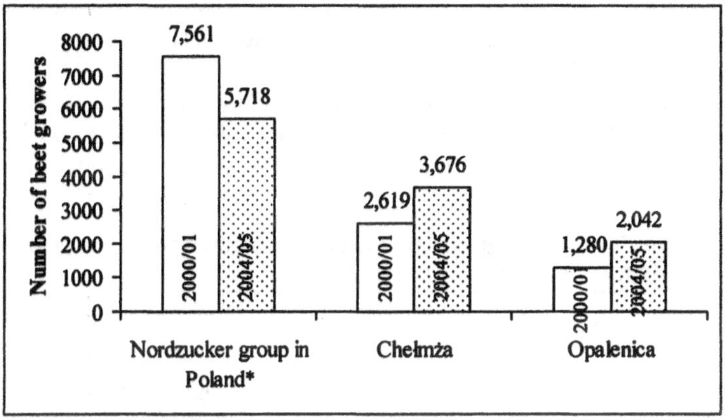

* 2000/01= Chełmża, Krasiniec, Mełno, Opalenica, Szamotuły, Wschowa; 2004/05= Chełmża and Opalenica.
Source: IPC 2001, pp. 13-15; Nordzucker AG.

Figure 105. Average size of sugarbeet plantations, Nordzucker group in Poland, 2000/01 and 2004/05

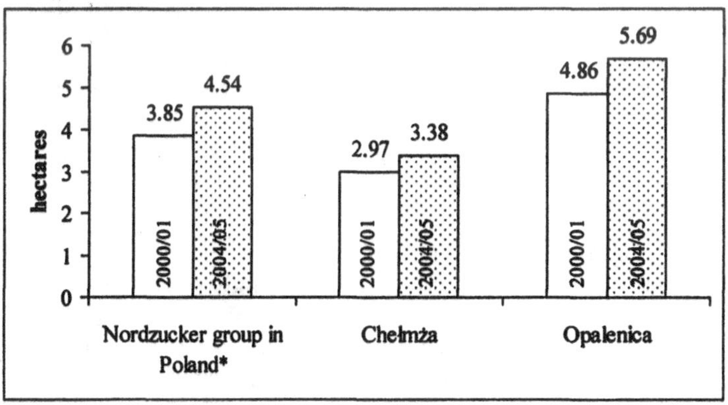

* 2000/01= Chełmża, Krasiniec, Mełno, Opalenica, Szamotuły, Wschowa; 2004/05= Chełmża and Opalenica.
Source: IPC 2001, pp. 13-15; Nordzucker AG.

Another restructuring measure was the liquidation of regional sugarbeet-purchasing centers and the introduction of sugarbeet transport directly from the fields to sugar factories by professional freight companies.[300] This change was accompanied by a thorough modernization of sugarbeet storage yards at the *Chełmża* and *Opalenica* sugar factories.[301] In the campaign 2004/05, 100% of sugarbeets procured by the Nordzucker group in Poland were delivered to *Chełmża* and *Opalenica* by professional haulage companies. A special method of piling sugarbeets on the edges of fields was made obligatory in order to optimize the time and cost efficiency of loading sugarbeets onto trucks. Furthermore, the share of sugarbeets that went through the process of preliminary cleaning on the fields was increased systematically in the 2000-2004 time period.

Less than one quarter of sugarbeets delivered to Nordzucker plants in Poland in the campaign 2000/01 were pre-cleaned on the fields. In the season 2004/05, 100% of sugarbeets delivered to Nordzucker plants in Poland went through preliminary cleaning (See Figure 106).[302]

Figure 106. Preliminary cleaning of sugarbeets on the fields, Nordzucker group in Poland, 2000-2004*

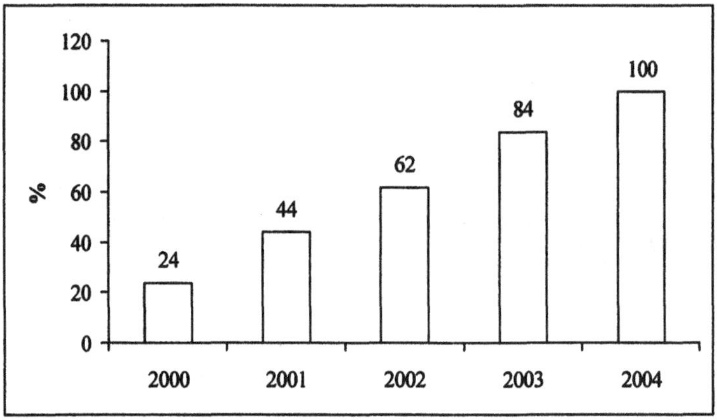

*** In % of the total amount of sugarbeets delivered to Nordzucker plants in Poland.**
Source: Wawro 2005, p. 100.

The above changes in sugarbeet harvesting and in the way of transporting sugarbeets to factories were accompanied by an increasingly widespread use of modern loading and cleaning machinery at the sugarbeet plantations that form the raw material base of the Nordzucker group in Poland.

Raw material is delivered to Nordzucker plants in Poland in a "just-in-time" system. It means that a detailed schedule of beet deliveries is specified before each

[300] The six sugar factories taken over by Nordzucker in Poland had 18 sugarbeet-purchasing centers at the time of the takeover. All of them had been liquidated by the campaign 2004/05.

[301] See ZPBC 2005.

[302] The main purpose of pre-cleaning sugarbeets on the fields is to minimize the volume of soil attached to sugarbeets and transported unnecessarily to sugar factories.

campaign. During the processing season, there are no long lines of trucks waiting to enter the *Opalenica* and *Chełmża* factories, as there used to be in the past, and sugarbeets delivered to the two plants are processed within a short period of time. A detailed schedule of beet deliveries also ensures that the harvested raw material is not stored for many days on the fields, losing quality at the same time. Owing to the installation of beet-pulp and defecation-mud presses at the sugar factories in *Opalenica* and *Chełmża*, the streets of the cities remain dry and clean during the time of campaign.

In 2002, the Nordzucker group carried out a survey among farmers delivering sugarbeets to the *Chełmża* sugar factory. More than 99% of the surveyed farmers evaluated cooperation between the sugar factory and themselves as either good (42.4%) or satisfactory (56.7%). According to 90.5% of the surveyed persons, the subject matter of the training courses organized by the raw material department of the *Chełmża* sugar factory met their expectations. 92.41% expressed satisfaction with the trend towards the collection of harvested sugarbeets directly from the fields by professional haulage companies.[303]

15.2.1.4 Financial Restructuring

The sugar factories taken over by Nordzucker in Poland were heavily indebted at the time of the takeover. The liabilities of the *Opalenica* and *Chełmża* plants amounted to several dozen million of Polish zloty. Nordzucker spent about PLN 200 million in the clearance of debts and on increasing the capital of the sugar factories acquired in Poland. Other measures introduced by the company in order to ensure sufficient liquidity of individual plants and to create conditions for the generation of profit included the minimization of costs and the introduction of strict financial discipline.

As far as asset engineering is concerned, non-productive fixed assets were either sold to private investors or given away to the local communities. The sale of certain fixed assets took place with the condition of the 'takeover' of a number of factory workers by the buyer. The price of such assets was often dependent on the number of factory staff taken over by the investor. As was mentioned earlier, after the closure of the *Szamotuły* sugar factory a number of its employees were hired by an investor who had acquired the plant from Nordzucker and launched an alternative business activity there.

Many of the activities previously conducted by factory staff, e.g. sugarbeet clearing, transport, canteens, cleaning, security, were outsourced in the post-privatization period. In a number of cases, companies consisting of former factory workers were commissioned to provide the outsourced services (e.g. security

[303] For more details see Żurawska 2003.

services by security staff previously employed at the sugar factory, cleaning by former factory cleaning crews, etc.).

The implementation of wide-ranging restructuring activities in the 2000-2004 time period and, most importantly, the instability of the Polish sugar market until 2004, meant that the Nordzucker group generated a profit in Poland for the first time in 2004 (See Table 40).

Table 40. Business development, Nordzucker group in Poland, 2000-2004*

	2000	2001	2002	2003	2004
Turnover	45	92	77	72.4	94
EBIT	6	10	-8	-5.7	27.8
Annual surplus	0	0	-15	-11.1	24.6
Tangible asset investment	5	10	4	9.8	16.4
Equity capital	6	8	4	15.3	45.8

* All values in € million.
Source: Nordzucker AG (Annual Reports 2001/02-2004/05).

A net profit of € 24.6 million was achieved in 2004 as a consequence of developments in the sugar market in Poland after the country's EU accession (the adoption of a new regulatory framework for the domestic sugar sector and the resultant increase in the market price of sugar) and a largely completed restructuring program within the Nordzucker group in Poland (cost savings).

15.2.1.5 Conclusions

The above analyses show that restructuring activities implemented by the Nordzucker group in Poland in the 2000-2004 time period resulted in a considerable improvement in the productivity and cost efficiency of sugar production.

Operational and organizational restructuring processes within the group had been largely completed by the season 2004/05. The consolidation of the six Polish sugar factories taken over by Nordzucker into two more scale-efficient plants led to the prolonging of the campaign to the optimum at the strategic locations.

A thorough technological modernization of the *Chełmża* and *Opalenica* plants made production processes more environmentally friendly and was followed by a noticeable reduction in the consumption of major resources (cost savings). Since the consolidation of sugar factories was accompanied by increasing automation of production at the strategic sites and by large-scale labor restructuring, a significant rise in labor productivity had taken place within the Nordzucker group in Poland by the season 2004/05. The number of employees working at the group was cut by 80% between 2000 and 2004, however the downsizing was carried out in a way that avoided conflicts and social disturbances.

The organizational changes implemented by Nordzucker in Poland by the season 2004/05 as well as the restructuring activities in the field of "raw material/agricultural management" (sugarbeet growing, harvesting, logistics) are evidence of the transfer of know-how. They contributed to an increase in the productivity and quality of the sugarbeet harvest as well as an improvement in the overall efficiency of operations.

The introduction of new work safety standards at Nordzucker's Polish sugar factories resulted in a significant increase in labor safety as well as a reduction in the number of accidents at the plants.

The financial result achieved by the Nordzucker group in Poland in 2004 shows that after the introduction of EU sugar market regulations in the country (May 2004), the units of the group were able to generate profits allowing for further development and the continuation of restructuring processes.

Although in most areas things had already been 'put in order' at the Nordzucker group in Poland by the season 2004/05, there are still a number of restructuring challenges for the years to come. The structure of the raw material base of the group, for example, is far from optimal. An increase in the average size of the sugarbeet plantations that form the raw material base would pave the way for improvements in agro-technology. This in turn would lead to a productivity increase and additional cost savings. However, as was already pointed out several times in this study, structural changes in the raw material base of the sugar industry in Poland are dependent almost exclusively on the will and activity of the sugarbeet growers.

Finally, it must be mentioned once again that Nordzucker still hopes to increase its market share in Poland in the future through the acquisition of additional sugar factories in the country.

15.3 Pfeifer & Langen

Among the sugar corporations that participated in the privatization process of the sugar industry in Poland, Pfeifer & Langen (P&L), headquartered in *Köln* (Cologne), Germany, is at least in one sense exceptional. The company is a family enterprise with the legal form of a limited partnership—a rarity in today's European sugar business.

P&L was founded by three Cologne industrialists, Emil Pfeifer, Valentin Pfeifer and Eugen Langen, in 1870. Shortly afterwards, the region where the activities of P&L were initially concentrated, the Rhineland area, developed into a major center of a modern sugarbeet economy. Today, P&L is the third largest sugar producer in Germany and the sixth largest in the EU-25, with a maximum sugar production quota slightly over one million tonnes (about 5% of the total sugar production quota of the EU-25).

In 2004, the company employed 915 people in its domestic market (excluding campaign workforce) and had a turnover of € 656 million (*Zuckerindustie*/Sugar Industry 7/2005, p. 574).

Within the last 30 years, P&L has systematically strengthened its competitive position in the home market, with the takeover of a number of sugar companies in Rhineland and Westphalia, the construction of new sugarbeet-processing plants, and the application of modern production techniques. In 1991, after the reunification of Germany, P&L acquired stakes in several sugar companies located on the territory of the former German Democratic Republic, through its subsidiary *Diamant-Zucker KG*. Two years later, P&L began processing sugarbeets at an enormous new technologically advanced plant built in *Könnern*, in the newly formed German state of *Sachsen-Anhalt* (Saxony-Anhalt).[304] In the old, West German states, P&L manufactures sugar at four locations: in *Appeldorn*, where it runs a factory with a daily beet-processing capacity of 7,500 t; *Elsdorf* (9,500 t/d); *Euskirchen* (10,000 t/d); and *Lage* (7,500 t/d).

As well as its domestic operations, P&L also owns a factory in *Bazancourt* near Reims (France) producing glucose syrups, native and modified wheat gluten, soluble wheat proteins and native starch.

Between 1995 and 2001, P&L took over 11 sugar factories in Poland. At the end of 1998, the company came also into the possession of controlling stakes in two sugar factories in Romania. Since 2001, P&L owns shares in one sugar factory in Hungary, in *Kapsvár*. Moreover, P&L has distribution and sales offices in Barcelona, Milan and in the aforementioned *Kapsvár*.

A wide variety of products offered by P&L to households and to industrial buyers is marketed in Germany under the brand names "*Kölner Zucker*" and

---

304 The daily beet processing capacity of the sugar factory in *Könnern* currently amounts to 16,500 t.

"*Diamant Zucker*".[305] In other countries, they are sold under the brand name "*Diamant*".

Apart from being one of largest sugar producers in Europe, P&L is also engaged in a number of other business activities. In 1967, the firm began production of potato crisps at a plant in *Wevelinghoven* (Germany) and established an affiliate company named *Intersnack*. Today, *Intersnack* is Europe's leading provider of crisps, manufactured at 13 factories situated in nine countries. The company employs 3,700 people world-wide. In Germany, *Intersnack*'s products are marketed under the brand names *funny, frisch, chio* and *Wolf Bergstraße*. In other countries, the company sells its products under the brand names *Vico, Chipi, Slovakia* and *Bohemia*.

In 1971, P&L and Willibert Krüger established jointly a company named *Krüger GmbH & Co. KG*, focusing initially on the production of instant teas. The firm grew rapidly and gradually expanded its product range. It is currently a key market player in Europe among the producers of instant tea, coffee and cocoa drinks. Moreover, the *Krüger* group, today employing more than 4,000 people, is a major producer of chocolate and hazelnut chocolate spread as well as soluble, effervescent vitamin tablets. The group also supplies many food processors with a variety of half-finished products. Articles of the *Krüger* group are manufactured at 19 plants located in 14 countries. About 120,000 t of sugar are used annually by companies belonging to the *Krüger* group in the production of its products.

It is worth mentioning that the sugar segment contributes about one third of P&L's total revenues. This makes the firm one of the most strongly diversified companies among major European sugar producers (Kohnke 2005, pp. 43-44).

15.3.1 Pfeifer & Langen in Poland

The activity of P&L in the Polish market began in 1995, when the corporation acquired a 47% stake in a sugar factory located in *Środa Wielkopolska*, as a result of the establishment by the Polish State Treasury and P&L of a limited liability company "*Cukrownia Środa Sp. z o. o.*".[306]

In 1996 and 1997, P&L took over another three plants in Poland: *Miejska Górka* (1996), *Kościan* (1996) and *Gostyń* (1997). These factories were privatized to insiders in the years 1991-92 (employee leasing) and P&L acquired them through a secondary ownership transfer.[307]

---

305. For detailed information about the product range of P&L, see the official website of the company (www.pfeifer-langen.de).

306 6% of the share capital of *Środa* was taken over by its employees and sugarbeet growers, and the rest remained under the control of the State Treasury.

307 As a result of the primary ownership transfer, the share capital of the sugar factories in *Miejska Górka* and *Kościan* was taken over by the employees of the plants, by sugarbeet growers and by third parties. The entire share capital of the sugar factory in *Gostyń* was, in

In 1999 P&L took over the sugar factory in *Głogów*, which had earlier been incorporated into *Śląska Spółka Cukrowa* but due to a disastrous economic situation and owing to the fact that it was situated quite far away from other plants concentrated in the holding, was privatized individually.[308]

Apart from the plant in *Głogów*, P&L acquired yet another Polish sugar factory in 1999 that had been privatized to its employees and sugarbeet growers in the years 1991-92, namely, the plant in *Góra Śląska*. Finally, in July 2001, P&L took over the sugar factories in *Gniezno, Gosławice*, *Witaszyce*, *Zbiersk* and *Zduny*, which together formed a subgroup (*Kalisko-Konińska* Group) of *Poznańsko-Pomorska Spółka Cukrowa*, one of the four sugar holdings established in the second half of the 1990s.[309]

The maximum sugar production quota allocated to the above 11 sugar factories totals 260,000 t and gives P&L in Poland a market share of 16.6%. According to the executives of P&L, it was market share that the company was seeking when it entered the Polish market.

Table 41. Sugar factories taken over by P&L in Poland

Date	Factory location	Processing capacity*	Privatization method
1995	*Środa Wielkopolska*	2,300	Direct privatization
1996	*Kościan*	3,200	Secondary ownership transfer
1996	*Miejska Górka*	2,600	Secondary ownership transfer
1997	*Gostyń*	3,800	Secondary ownership transfer
1999	*Głogów*	3,000	Indirect privatization (Holding privatization)
1999	*Góra Śląska*	4,000	Secondary ownership transfer
2001	*Gniezno*	2,800	Indirect privatization (Holding privatization)
2001	*Gosławice*	3,900	Indirect privatization (Holding privatization)
2001	*Witaszyce*	3,000	Indirect privatization (Holding privatization)
2001	*Zbiersk*	2,500	Indirect privatization (Holding privatization)
2001	*Zduny*	2,600	Indirect privatization (Holding privatization)

* Average beet throughput per day at the time of takeover by P&L.
Source: IPC (Several Issues).

contrast, taken over exclusively by the employees of the factory. It needs to be added here that investments and modernization activities conducted by P&L at the factory in *Gostyń* had already begun in 1996, i.e., one year before the company took over a large shareholding in the plant through the increase of capital. This was due to the fact that the employees of *Gostyń* demanded during initial negotiations that P&L provide the factory with financial resources for modernization activities as a precondition for "more advanced talks" on the takeover of the plant.

308 On November 17, 1999, P&L acquired 51% of the share capital of the factory in *Głogów* for nearly PLN 29 million (NIK 2000, p. 55).

309 P&L paid PLN 97.2 million for 51% of the share capital of factories forming the *Kalisko-Konińska* Group. The sugar production quota allocated to the plants in the campaign 2000/01 amounted in total to 101,282 t. This means that P&L had to pay PLN 960 for each tonne of production quota allocated to factories from the KK-Group.

Among the most significant determinants of its investment in Poland, P&L cites in the first place the company's "awareness about Poland's prospect of EU accession and about the existence of national sugar production quotas that are not transferable between countries". Through its involvement in the privatization process of the Polish sugar industry, P&L wanted to gain access to a large market and to reap economies of scale.

The initial restructuring strategy of P&L in Poland after the establishment of operations in the country was consistent with the major microeconomic goals of privatization formulated in the theoretical part of the present study. As its general objective, P&L set itself the improvement in the competitiveness of acquired sugar factories, through the introduction of a number of restructuring activities. In the 1995-2004 time period, these activities were concentrated mainly on the improvement in the productivity and quality of the sugarbeet harvest, the modernization of technological processes at selected factories through investment in new machinery and equipment, labor restructuring, the improvement of environmental standards and the installation of modern information systems. Out of the total number of 11 plants taken over by P&L in the Poland, sugarbeet processing during the campaign 2004/05 took place at five locations: *Gosławice, Gostyń, Góra Śląska, Miejska Górka* and *Środa Wielkopolska*.

15.3.1.1 Operational Restructuring

Up to the beginning of the campaign 2004/05, P&L invested nearly PLN 250 million in the technological modernization of the sugar factories taken over in Poland. The principal purposes of investment activities in this field were the reduction in the use of energy and other resources during the processing campaign, the improvement in the quality of manufactured sugar (color in solution, ash content and granularity), the creation of optimal conditions for the storage of sugar (prolongation of the maximum storage period, assurance of appropriate temperature and humidity in storage silos), the introduction of new packaging methods, and the improvement of environmental standards (construction and/or modernization of water purification plants).

The implementation of the above policies required the acquisition of new machinery and apparatuses and/or modernization of existing equipment. The technological modernization conducted by P&L in Poland had been concentrated predominantly on five sugar factories that were selected as "strategic locations": *Gosławice, Gostyń, Góra Śląska, Miejska Górka* and *Środa Wielkopolska*.

On the basis of comprehensive economic analyses, P&L decided to relocate the entire production to the above factories and to gradually cease sugarbeet processing at the remaining six plants taken over in Poland. The fundamental criterion taken into account by the choice of factories for modernization was the location of individual plants in relation to certain beet-growing regions. P&L committed itself to the concentration of sugar production in areas with the lowest costs of sugarbeet growing and with the highest crop quality and productivity. This, along with the distance of individual factories from major beet-growing regions was key in the choice of strategic sites. Other factors that played a role in the selection of factories destined for a thorough modernization included the state of repair of individual plants (sugar house, turbine room), the ease of transport of product to customers (road infrastructure), environmental issues, and the distance of the factories from city centers. The decision to cease beet processing at the sugar factory in *Kościan*, for instance, was dictated, among other things, by the fact that the plant was located within the borders of quite a large city. Nonetheless, the factories in *Kościan* and in *Głogów* were modernized to some extent before their closure. Up to the moment of cessation of sugar production at a given plant, P&L introduced modernization activities that were necessary in order to make the quality of sugar produced in that plant as high as possible and to minimize production costs. The major investment projects implemented by P&L at individual sugar factories in Poland up to the beginning of the campaign 2004/05 are listed in Table 42.

As can be seen, the takeover of sugar factories listed in Table 42 by P&L was followed by a considerable infusion of capital into the plants, in the form of various modernization activities. The activities included the introduction of technological enhancements, rationalization measures, and the acquisition of new machinery and equipment. As well as acquiring new machinery, machines were also transferred from sugar factories controlled by P&L in Germany. Most capital was invested in technological modernization of the factories in *Gostyń*, *Miejska Górka*, *Środa Wielkopolska* and *Gosławice*. Two common modernization measures introduced at all plants where sugarbeet processing still took place in the campaign 2004/05 were the computerization and automation of the production process, and the rationalization of energy usage. The greatest number of technological innovations was introduced at the factory in *Gosławice*. According to Mr. Janusz Pierun, the representative of P&L in Poland, by the beginning of the season 2004/05, the company had fulfilled all its investment obligations with regard to sugar factories taken over in Poland. Such obligations constituted, in some cases, a part of the privatization deals. At the time of the takeover of the *Kalisko-Konińska* group, for example, P&L was obliged by the privatization contract to invest at least € 6 million in the group, in fixed assets, by December 31, 2002. It was specified in the contract that the investment should be made in "new, modern machinery or used equipment being in a good state of repair and meeting European standards". Furthermore, it was determined that the equipment should be purchased at prices that would be no higher than the market prices established in trade exchange. Today, it is known that the value of investment in modernization of the *Kalisko-Konińska* group, conducted by P&L up to the campaign 2004/05, considerably exceeded the level specified in the privatization contract. As shown in Table 42,

PLN 38 million was spent by P&L on technological restructuring of the sugar factory in *Gosławice.*

Table 42. Major investment projects, Pfeifer & Langen plants in Poland

Głogów	Gosławice	Gostyń	Góra Śląska
Total investment: PLN 10 million	Total investment: PLN 38 million	Total investment: PLN 70 million	Total investment: PLN 12 million
- construction of a new packing department - sugar packaging line (1 kg bags; capacity: 110 bags/minute) - modernization of sugar silo (storage capacity: 20,000 t)	- modernization of the packing department - modern packer (Hesser, 1kg bags, capacity: 118 t/24h) - thorough modernization of the sugar house (installation of 4 new strike pans and modernization of the existing ones; introduction of a fully computerized system of continuous, cascading high raw boiling and raw boiling; installation of new centrifuges) - thorough modernization of reception facilities (new defecation mud press, new carbonation tanks, crystallizer, evaporator, pumps, filters) - installation of minglers - reconstruction of sugarbeet storage yard - installation of 7 modern beet pulp presses - automation and computerization of the production process - rationalization of energy and heat economy	- thorough modernization of the sugar house - thorough modernization of reception facilities - automation and computerization of the production process - reconstruction of sugarbeet storage yard - construction of a water purification plant - raw material laboratory - rationalization of energy and heat economy	- modernization of sugar silo - rationalization of energy and heat economy - automation and computerization of the production process
Kościan	**Miejska Górka**	**Środa Wielkopolska**	
Total investment: PLN 12 million	Total investment: PLN 60 million	Total investment: PLN 50 million	
- modernization of water purification plant - partial modernization of the sugar house (e.g. evaporator)	- modernization of the packing department - thorough modernization of the sugar house - modernization of sugar silo - thorough modernization of reception facilities - automation and computerization of the production process - reconstruction of the sugarbeet-storage yard - modernization of raw material laboratory - rationalization of energy and heat economy - construction of a water purification plant	- construction of a new packing department - thorough modernization of the sugar house - thorough modernization of reception facilities - construction of a sugar silo (storage capacity 65,000 t) - automation and computerization of the production process - rationalization of energy and heat economy - construction of a water purification plant	

Source: Gazeta Cukrownicza 4/2003, pp. 112-114; Burak Cukrowy 1/2004, p. 4; Gazeta Cukrownicza 4/2004, pp. 86-88; Information provided by Pfeifer & Langen Polska; Nowe Cukrownictwo 3/2003, pp. 5-8.

Apart from the *Kalisko-Konińska* group, there were also certain contractual investment obligations with regard to the *Miejska Górka* and *Kościan* factories. According to Mr. Pierun, all of these obligations were met.

Technological modernization and rationalization activities implemented by P&L in Poland led to an appreciable reduction in the total use of energy and other resources at all sugar factories which were in operation during the processing campaign 2004/05. At the time of the takeover of the factories, the overall use of energy (boiler house) for sugar production at the plants amounted on average to 2831 kWh/t of sugar. In the campaign 2003/04 it amounted on average to 1626 kWh/t of sugar, a decrease of 43%.

Figure 107. Total use of energy (boiler house, in kWh/t of sugar), P&L plants in Poland

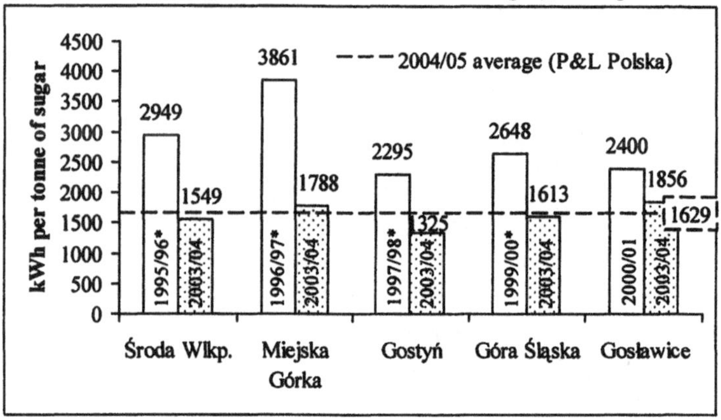

* Calculations by the author based on IPC data.
Source: IPC (Several Issues); Jórdeczka/Małkowski 2004, p. 87.

In the whole sugar industry in Poland, total energy consumption in the campaign 2003/04 averaged 2175 kWh/t of sugar (see IPC 2004, pp. 31-32).

Unfortunately, data on energy consumption at individual P&L plants in the campaign 2004/05 is not available. It is known that of all P&L plants in Poland, the total use of energy in the campaign was lowest at the factory in *Gostyń,* where it amounted to 1374 kWh/t of sugar. At the entire P&L group in Poland, it amounted on average to 1629 kWh/t of sugar and was only slightly higher than a year earlier.[310]

Limestone consumption at the five P&L plants that were in operation in the 2004/05 campaign averaged 4.22% on beet at the time of their takeover by P&L. In the campaign 2004/05, the use of limestone at the five plants averaged 3.16% on beet. This means a reduction of 25% (See Figure 108). The lowest limestone consumption among all working P&L plants in Poland in the campaign 2004/05 was recorded at the factory in *Gostyń* (2.69% on beet).

---

[310] See Jórdeczka 2005.

The average use of limestone in the sugar industry in Poland in the campaigns 2001/02 and 2002/03 amounted on average to 4.44% and 4.29% on beet, respectively. Data for the campaigns 2003/04 and 2004/04 is not available.

Figure 108. Use of limestone (in % on beet) at P&L plants in Poland

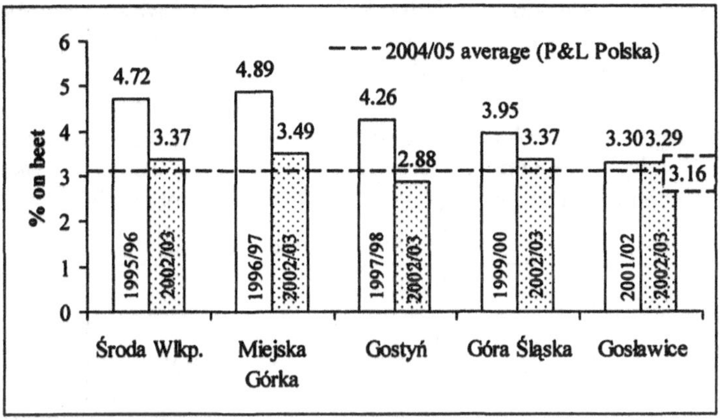

Source: IPC, STC (Several Issues); Jórdeczka 2005.

A considerable reduction in the use of fresh water took place at the five plants under analysis after their takeover by P&L. At the time of the takeover, it amounted on average to 43% on beet.

Figure 109. Use of fresh water (in % on beet) at P&L plants in Poland

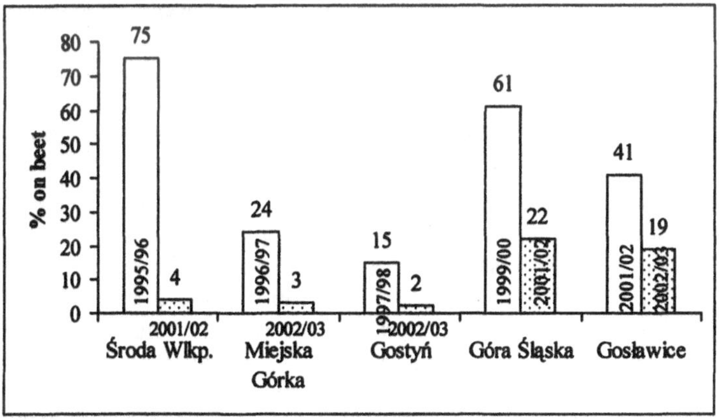

Source: IPC (Several Issues).

In the campaign 2001/02, the last campaign for which data for all five plants is available, fresh water use at the plants averaged 15.2% on beet (a reduction of 65%). If we remove from the calculation of the 2001/02 average the factory in *Gosławice* (which was taken over by P&L in 2001), the average fresh water use at the remaining four plants amounted to merely 8.8% on beet. As shown in Figure 109, the use of fresh water at the *Gosławice* plant was reduced by 54% in the campaign 2002/03.

The use of coke at P&L factories that were processing beets in the campaign 2004/05 amounted at the time of their takeover by P&L to 0.32% on beet. In the campaign 2001/02 - again, this is the last campaign for which data for all five plants is available - the use of coke averaged 0.27% on beet (a drop of 15.6%). At the sugar factory in *Gosławice*, the use of coke was reduced by 10.7% between the campaigns 2001/02 and 2002/03 (See Figure 110). In the campaign 2002/03, coke consumption in *Miejska Górka* and *Gostyń* amounted on average to 0.27% and 0.22% on beet, respectively. Information concerning the use of coke at P&L plants in Poland in the seasons 2003/04 and 2004/05 is not available.

Figure 110. Use of coke (in % on beet) at P&L plants in Poland

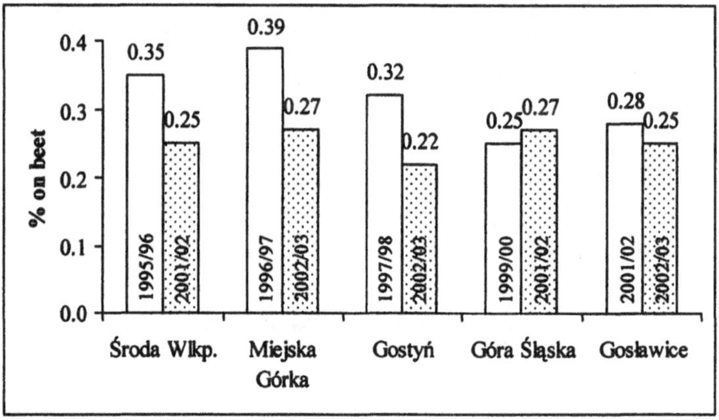

Source: IPC (Several Issues).

Average coal consumption at P&L plants where beet processing took place in the season 2004/05 amounted at the time of the takeover of the factories by P&L to 4.18% on beet. The corresponding figure for the campaign 2002/03, the last campaign for which data is available, is 3.49% on beet (a drop of 17%).

The 11 sugar factories taken over in Poland by P&L produced at the time of their takeover 291,600 t of sugar (26,500 per one factory). Consolidation of the 11 plants into five units by the campaign 2004/05 led to a considerable increase in total sugar production at individual factories. Aggregate sugar production at the five sites that were in operation in the campaign 2004/05 amounted at the time of their takeover by P&L to 153,000 t (30,596 per factory). In the campaign 2003/04, the five plants manufactured in total 229,000 t of sugar (45,960 per factory).[311] After the cessation of beet processing in *Zbiersk* and *Zduny* in 2004, total sugar production at the five plants where beet processing took place in the campaign

[311] In the meantime, sugarbeet processing was terminated at the factories in *Głogów*, *Gniezno*, *Kościan* and *Witaszyce*.

2004/05 rose to 319,600 t (63,920 per one factory) (See Figure 112). This means that sugar production at P&L plants in Poland that were in operation during the 2004/05 campaign has increased by 109% since their takeover by P&L.

Figure 111. Use of coal (in % on beet) at P&L plants in Poland

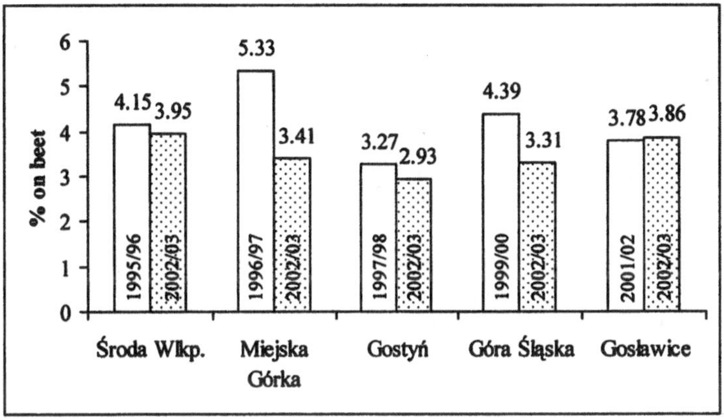

Source: IPC (Several Issues).

Figure 112. Sugar production (in 1000 tonnes of white sugar) at P&L plants in Poland

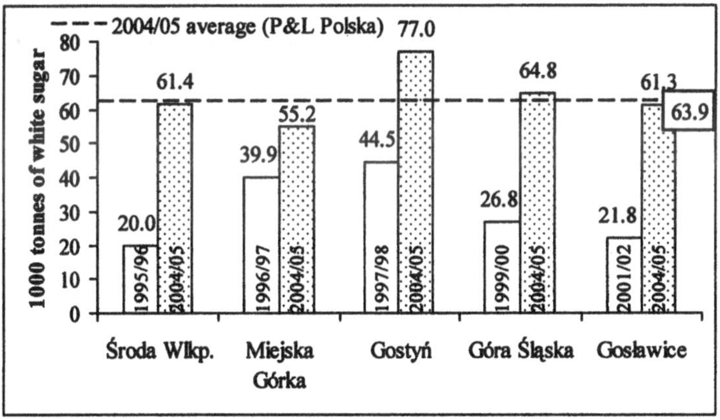

Source: IPC (Several Issues); Pfeifer & Langen Polska.

Sugar production in the campaign 2004/05 was lowest at the plant in *Miejska Górka*, where it amounted to 55,154 t. It was highest at the sugar factory in *Gostyń* (76,955 t) (Jórdeczka 2005). The greatest increases in total sugar production from the time of the takeover by P&L to the campaign 2004/05 took place at the factories in *Środa Wlkp.* (+207%), *Gosławice* (+181%) and *Góra Śląska* (+141%).

The average beet throughput per day at the five factories that were in operation in the campaign 2004/05 amounted at the time of their takeover by P&L to 3,334 t/d. In the campaigns 2003/04 and 2004/05, it amounted to 3,864 t/d and 4,067 t/d, respectively.

The consolidation of sugar factories by P&L in Poland was accompanied by a gradual increase in the campaign length at individual plants. Whereas the campaign 2001/02 at P&L factories that were in operation in the season 2004/05 lasted on average 53 days, the campaign 2003/04 had an average duration of 71 days. As was already mentioned earlier, in the season 2003/04, beet processing took place for the last time at the factories in *Zbiersk* and *Zduny*. The length of the 2003/04 campaign at these plants amounted to 18 days and 12 days, respectively. After cessation of beet processing at these two factories in 2004, an increase in sugar production and prolongation of the length of a campaign took place in the season 2004/05 at the remaining five P&L plants. The campaign 2004/05 at these plants lasted on average 100 days (from 96 to 105 days at individual plants).

Modernization activities and rationalization measures implemented by P&L at sugar factories taken over in Poland led to an appreciable improvement in the key indicators of productivity in beet processing up to the campaign 2004/05. Sugar yield in % of raw sugar value on beet, at factories that were in operation in the campaign 2004/05, amounted on average at the time of their takeover by P&L to 13.25%. The corresponding number for the campaign 2003/04 was 16.57%, which constitutes an increase of 25%.

Figure 113. Sugar yield in % of raw sugar value on beet at P&L plants in Poland

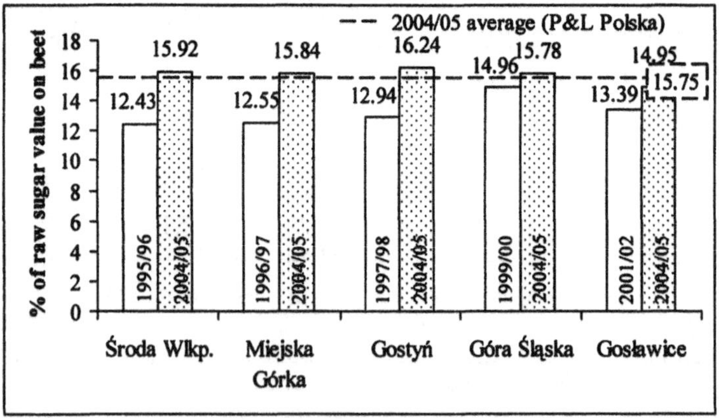

Source: IPC (Several Issues); Jórdeczka 2005; Pfeifer & Langen Polska.

In the campaign 2004/05, the average sugar yield in % of raw sugar value on beet at factories controlled by *P&L Polska* fell moderately in relation to the previous season. It amounted to 15.75% (See Figure 113).

A significant improvement in extraction efficiency took place at the five P&L sugar factories in Poland that were in operation in 2004/05. At the time of their takeover by P&L, recovery of sugar at the plants averaged 84.38%. In the campaigns 2003/04 and 2004/05, it amounted on average to 88.42% and 88.05%, respectively (See Figure 114). This change indicates a considerable reduction in sugar losses during sugarbeet processing.

Figure 114. Recovery of sugar at P&L plants in Poland

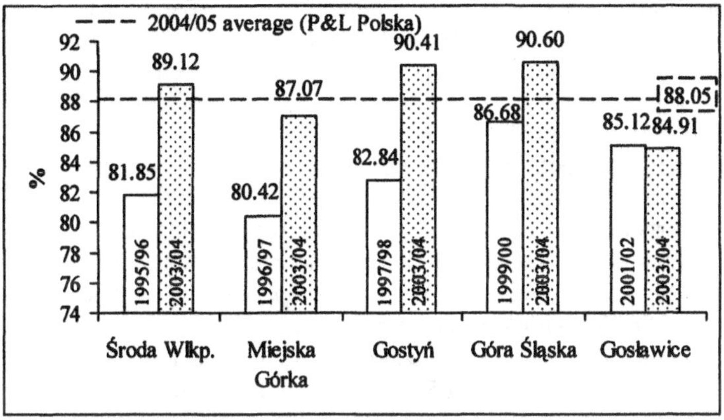

Source: IPC (Several Issues); Gazeta Cukrownicza 1/2005, p. 31.

Of course, the amalgamation of the 11 sugar factories taken over in Poland by P&L into five plants, as well as the automation and computerization of production processes at the strategic locations, was accompanied by a significant reduction in employment and by an increase in labor productivity within the *P&L Polska* group. In 2004 alone, 700 people employed at factories controlled by *P&L Polska* were laid off. Overmanning was most pronounced at factories in the *Kalisko-Konińska* group. Information about the employment level at individual plants at the time of their takeover by P&L is not available, but it is known that in 2001 regular staff at factories controlled by *P&L Polska* totaled about 2,500 employees. In the campaign 2004/05, it amounted to 845. The campaign workforce in the season 2004/05 totaled 715 employees. This means that average labor productivity, measured in tonnes of sugar per employee, amounted to 378 (regular staff) and 205 (regular staff + campaign workforce).

Apart from making use of the standard methods of labor restructuring, such as a program of voluntary redundancies[312], *P&L Polska* introduced in February 2004

[312] As the first step in its labor restructuring, *P&L Polska* introduced a program of voluntary redundancies. In the first phase of the program, in 2001, the company offered its employees redundancy payments amounting to their monthly salary multiplied by the number of months left to the expiration of the guaranteed employment period specified in the privatization contracts. About 500-600 employees accepted the offer and left their jobs. After a period of time, *P&L Polska* again offered its employees voluntary redundancies but this time the redundancy payments were equal to 15 months of salary. The second phase of the program of voluntary redundancies was expanded by an additional element. As a result of

a special activization program for laid-off workers. The company charged a professional outplacement firm (*IMC Kariera*) with the task of finding new jobs for laid-off workers and providing them with vocational training aimed at the improvement of their chances in the job market. The activization program included: a) analysis of the skills of individual workers; b) support and advice by job search as well as the preparation of job applications, covering letters, resumes; c) consultations with counselling psychologists; d) search of job offers; e) the organization of courses (free of charge) aimed at the improvement of the professional qualifications of individual workers.

Participation in the activization program was voluntary. Nine professional activization centers (with 30 career advisors, 13 entrepreneurship trainers and 14 economists) were established under the aegis of the program. Some of the laid-off workers started their own businesses. The outplacement company engaged by *P&L Polska* provided them with support in the preparation of business plans and in the assessment of individual business projects.

Of the 352 people that joined the activization program, 190 had found a new job by the beginning of February 2005. About 40 of those 190 people were employed by *Volskwagen* in Poznań and by *Mahle* in Krotoszyn (engine blocks foundry). The program is to be wound up at the end of April 2005 (Bogdziewicz 2005; Information provided by *P&L Polska*).

A number of laid-off workers who participated in the program of voluntary redundancies introduced by *P&L Polska* in the time period 2001-2003 established various repair shops and small companies. *P&L Polska* provided these companies with the opportunity to acquire machinery and equipment from the firm (e. g. part of the P&L's fleet, lathes, grinders, milling machines, etc.) on favorable purchase terms. Furthermore, *P&L Polska* has commissioned companies established by its former employees to provide certain services (e. g. carpentry services, painting, etc.).

On the grounds of two sugar factories where sugarbeet processing was ceased, companies were established which had been created by former employees of *P&L Polska*. The boiler house at the sugar factory in *Kościan*, for example, was taken over by an employee partnership, and provides heat to two housing estates. About

---

the so-called holding privatization (*Kalisko-Konińska* group), 15% of the share capital of privatized sugar factories was granted free of charge to sugarbeet growers and another 15% to employees of the plants. Many employees of *P&L Polska* declared that they would take the voluntary redundancies under the condition that the company acquire from them the obtained shares. In such cases, *P&L Polska* in fact purchased the shares. The amount of money paid to individual employees for their shares was, on average, equal to eight months of salary. If we add to this sum redundancy payments amounting to 15 months of salary, it turns out that employees who participated in the second phase of the program of voluntary redundancies introduced by *P&L Polska* were provided with financial resources equal to 22 months of salary.

20 people are employed at the company. *P&L Polska* found an investor who took out a lease on the grounds of the *Zbiersk* plant and adapted it for the manufacture of cardboard boxes, employing between 40 and 50 people at the location.

As far as the product range of sugar factories taken over by P&L in Poland is concerned, at the time of the takeover of the plants, it consisted of white sugar in 1 kg bags, 50 kg bags and partly also in big bags (1000 kg). In the post-privatization period P&L widened the product range and diversified sugar packaging. At the present time, sugar manufactured at beet-processing plants controlled by *P&L Polska* is packaged in small bags of various size (from 250g to 5kg), 25 kg bags, 50 kg bags and big bags. Moreover, bulk dispatch is possible. P&L in Poland also manufactures cube sugar and powdered sugar (three different types of packages). The company also offers household clients in Poland extra fine sugar, jam sugar, various types of rock candy sugar, sticks, cinnamon sugar and even cane sugar ("Dry Demerara", "Dark Muscovado"). Not all of the above specialties are manufactured in Poland. Some are produced at P&L's sites located in other counties (predominantly in Germany), and imported when needed. Such a solution is, according to P&L, much more economically viable than the establishment of a new production line for each product. The demand for certain products in Poland is simply too low. *P&L Polska* also offers a number of products for industrial buyers, e. g. fondant used predominantly in the confectionery and bakery industry as a filling or coating glaze. It is offered by *P&L Polska* in 15 kg cartons.[313]

About 50% of sugar manufactured by *P&L Polska* is purchased by industrial buyers and the other 50% by retailers.

All working sugar factories controlled by *P&L Polska* manufacture "white sugar of standard quality" (EU-category II). Since the demand for "extra white sugar" (EU-category I) in Poland is, according to P&L, low and the costs of its manufacture are high, the company imports such sugar from its German plants whenever needed.

At all working P&L plants in Poland, the HACCP system has been instituted within the last few years. ISO management systems have also been instituted at most factories.[314] Although P&L sites in Poland have certificates confirming the institution of the aforementioned systems, the management of the company claims that possession of such certificates has only a "symbolic character". P&L's representative, Mr. Janusz Pierun, points to the fact that before signing a contract with

[313] For details, see www.pfeifer-langen.pl.

[314] *Góra Śląska* (ISO 9002: 1994- first certification in 1999 (Sale and production of molasses, pellets, fondant glaze)), *Miejska Górka* (ISO 9001: 2000- first certification in 2001 (Sugar and molasses production)), *Środa Wlkp.* (ISO 9002: 1994- first certification in 2001 (Production of white sugar (KN + KD) powdered sugar, powdered sugar with additives, refined sugar, liquid and invert sugar)); *Pfeifer & Langen Polska S.A.* in Gostyń (ISO 9001: 2000- first certification in 2002 (Sugar production) (Białasiewicz 2001, pp. 100-101; P&L Polska).

a given sugar producer, potential customers send often their own inspectors to sugar factories to verify the hygienic conditions and quality standards.

Asked what were the main competitive advantages of *P&L Polska*, Mr. Pierun cited the popularity of the brand name "*Diamant*" in the domestic market, the cost efficiency of production, and the possession of a wider assortment of products and patents than the major competitors. P&L holds, for example, a patent for rock candy. Other sugar companies have rock candy in their product range, commissioned from P&L.

15.3.1.2 Organizational Restructuring

In order to adjust the organizational structure in Poland to their strategy, P&L gradually merged the sugar factories/enterprises taken over in the country into two companies. The sugar factories in *Gostyń*, *Miejska Górka*, *Góra Śląska*, *Środa Wlkp.*, and *Kościan* were merged in 2001, to form *Pfeifer & Langen Polska S.A.*, headquartered in *Gostyń*. In fact, it was *Gostyń* that took over the other four factories.

The other six factories acquired by P&L in Poland were merged in two phases into *Cukrownia Gniezno S.A.*, with its headquarters in *Konin*. In autumn 2003, the sugar factory in *Gniezno* took over the *Gosławice* plant (phase I). The company established as a result of this merger took over the factories in *Głogów*, *Witaszyce*, *Zbiersk*, and *Zduny* in February 2004 (phase II).

It must be pointed out at this point that the merger of companies in the *Kalisko-Konińska* group was imposed by the provisions of the privatization contract signed by P&L and the sugar holding *Poznańsko-Pomorska Spółka Cukrowa*.[315] On December 22, 2004, *Pfeifer & Langen Polska S.A.* in *Gostyń* and *Cukrownia Gniezno S.A.* in *Konin* were merged to form *Pfeifer & Langen Polska S.A.*, headquartered in *Poznań* (See Figure 115).[316]

The major stimulus for the merger of individual sugar factories into two and, eventually, one company was the fact that it enabled P&L to consolidate the factories without the danger of losing the sugar production quota allocated to the plants. Another significant rationale behind the mergers was the willingness to streamline management within the P&L group in Poland. After the merger of the plants into one company, a two-person board of directors of the company was established. This considerably facilitated the decision-making processes. Previous to this, the number of managerial posts had been reduced at individual sugar factories in order to increase the self-reliance of those holding operational positions.

---

[315] As well as stipulating the merger of the factories in the *Kalisko-Konińska* group into one company, the privatization contract also contained an *investment package*, a *social package* and a *beet-growers' package*. Some of the obligations included in the individual packages were described earlier in this case study.

[316] *Cukrownia Gniezno S.A.* in Konin took over *Pfeifer & Langen Polska S.A.* in Gostyń.

Figure 115. Evolution of the organizational structure of P&L Polska

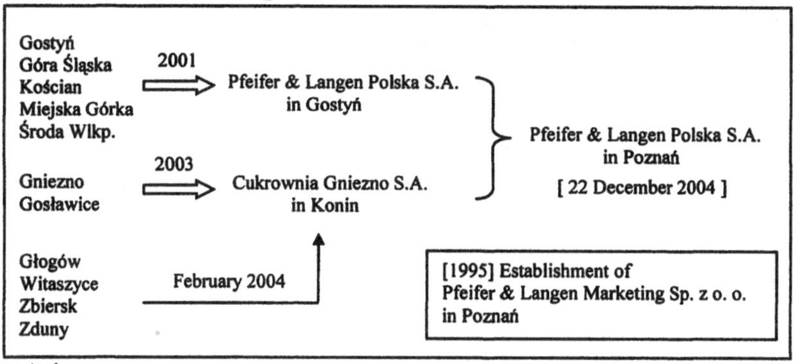

Source: Author.

From the beginning of P&L's presence in Poland, managerial positions at the company have been held by Polish managers. Nevertheless, members of the board of directors of P&L in Germany have visited Poland regularly and provided advice on various issues. Key decisions concerning restructuring activities within the *P&L Polska* group are made jointly by executives from *P&L Polska* and from the German headquarters of P&L. As pointed out by Mr. Pierun: "*If there is a problem to solve or if an important decision is to be made, we arrange a meeting, be it in Poznań, Cologne or Brussels; we share our opinions and adopt eventually a certain strategy, a certain course of action*".

The above mergers and subsequent factory closures were accompanied by the 'absorption' of the raw material bases of individual factories. In the campaign 2004/05, the beet-procurement area of *P&L Polska* was divided into nine beet-growing regions. Due to the consolidation of the 11 sugar factories into five plants where beet processing still took place in the season 2004/05, the nine regions were merged in December 2004 into five beet-growing regions concentrated around the five factories.

As well as the organizational changes described above, P&L created in Poland a body with a strictly market-oriented character. In 1995, *Pfeifer & Langen Marketing Sp. z o. o.*, was established, with its headquarters in Poznań. The company is responsible for the marketing and distribution of sugar and other products manufactured at plants controlled by *P&L Polska*. Moreover, *Pfeifer & Langen Marketing* carries out continuously market analyses aimed at "better acquaintance with customer's needs and preferences". The firm also provides existing and potential customers with advisory services and undertakes activities aimed at strengthening the brand name "*Diamant*" under which P&L products are marketed in Poland.

During the 2001-2004 time period, *P&L Polska* installed several modules of the well-known enterprise information software system SAP R/3 (now mySAP

Enterprise Resource Planning) facilitating the storage, processing and transmission of data, as well as management of specific business tasks. The modules installed by *P&L Polska* include the following functional areas: Financial Accounting (FI), Fixed Assets Accounting (FI-AA), Controlling (CO), Materials Management (MM) and Sales and Distribution (SD), Human Resources (HR), basis module (technical-basis). The SAP R/3 system was installed at *P&L Polska* by *Business Consulting Center Sp. z o. o.*, a consulting company specializing in implementing, developing and outsourcing SAP systems. The stages of the installation of SAP R/3 at *P&L Polska* are presented in Figure 116.

Figure 116. Stages of instituting SAP R/3 at P&L Polska units

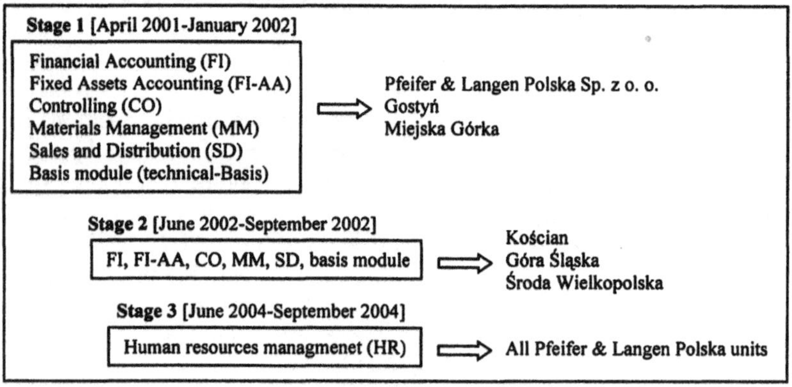

Source: www.bcc.com.pl; Pfeifer & Langen Polska.

15.3.1.3 Raw Material/Agricultural Management

The raw material base of sugar factories taken over by P&L in Poland was the object of the first major restructuring activities implemented by the company in the country. From the beginning of its presence in Poland, P&L systematically incorporated local sugar factories and beet growers into a system of advisory services for sugarbeet growers, provided by an inter-company organization called LIZ for short (*Landwirtschaftlicher Informationsdienst Zuckerrübe*). The main goal of LIZ, which came into operation in Germany in 1991, is to provide farmers with professional advice on all aspects of sugarbeet growing. A large body of advisors employed at the raw material departments of individual sugar factories provides the above services 'in the field' year round. Moreover, a web site is available where sugarbeet growers can find detailed information about how to prepare the fields for sowing and what methods to use in a given season. LIZ constitutes also a communication and cooperation platform between the raw material departments of sugar factories controlled by P&L in Poland and other countries.[317]

[317] For details, see www.liz.pl.

Up to the campaign 2004/05, P&L had invested about PLN 80 million in agriculture in Poland. The major investments in this field included the acquisition by individual sugar factories of modern sowers, combine harvesters, spraying machines and sugarbeet cleaners. Initially, the machinery was only made available to sugarbeet growers during the campaigns. Later, most of the equipment was acquired from factories by individual beet growers.

Investment in agriculture within the *P&L Polska* group also included the organization of dozens of meetings with sugarbeet growers, the establishment of experimental plots, and beet-growing demonstrations. An event called "Field Days", organized by P&L, is attended by about 3000-5000 people every year.

In order to minimize sugar losses in the procured sugarbeets and to reduce the amount of beet tare (soil adhering to procured sugarbeets) brought into factories, P&L introduced the practice of preliminary sugarbeet cleaning on the fields. In the campaign 2004/05, more than 96% of sugarbeets delivered to sugar factories controlled by *P&L Polska* underwent preliminary cleaning. The corresponding figures for the campaigns 2003/04 and 2002/03 were 88% and 62.6%, respectively (Jórdeczka/Małkowski 2004, pp. 86-87; www.liz.pl). Other practices introduced by P&L include the coverage of sugarbeet piles with lignin and the systematic insertion of probes into the piles in order to control and prevent the materialization of undesired effects such as rotting.

The investments in agricultural equipment at *P&L Polska* had had the effect that the sugarbeet harvest at the company's raw material base has changed dramatically within the last few years. At the present time, wide-tired combine harvesters (for example, made by *Kleine*) are used. After digging up the sugarbeets, the harvester cuts off the leaves from the beets and puts them into a bunker which is built in to the harvester. Subsequently, the harvester deposits the beets at the edge of the field where they are cleaned by a sugarbeet cleaner, loaded onto large trucks and transported directly to sugar factories. At the time of the takeover of individual sugar factories in Poland by P&L, a large part of sugarbeets processed at the plants was delivered first to regional purchasing centers. Beets were often stored in the centers for a longer period of time before being transported to sugar factories. Each of the factories taken over by P&L had between six and ten such centers at the time of the takeover. They had all been closed by the campaign 2004/05 and all sugarbeets processed at factories controlled by *P&L Polska* are presently delivered by professional transportation companies, directly from the fields to the individual sugar factories. *P&L Polska* hires firms to dig up the sugarbeets, collect them and carry out the preliminary cleaning. Mr. Pierun points out that "The task of the beet growers is to sow sugarbeets and to take care of proper tillage. The rest is done by others".

As a result of the above activities conducted by *P&L Polska* in cooperation with suagrbeet growers, a considerable improvement in the productivity and quality of beet harvest has taken place at the raw material base of the group. The average sugar content in beets procured by factories that were in operation in the campaign 2004/05 amounted at the time of their takeover by P&L to 15.82%.[318] In the campaign 2003/04, it averaged 18.73%, which means an increase of 18.4%. The average sugar content in sugarbeets processed at factories controlled by *P&L Polska* in the campaign 2004/05 amounted to 17.89% (see Figure 117).[319]

Figure 117. Polarization of sugarbeets, P&L Polska

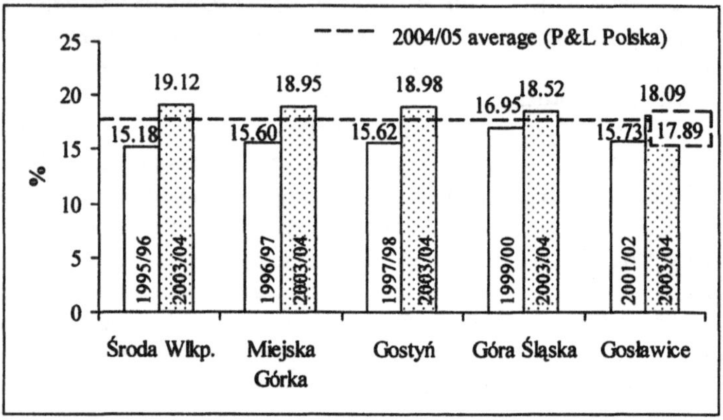

Source: IPC (Several Issues); www.liz.pl.

The average sugar yield per hectare at the beet-growing regions of factories that were in operation in the campaign 2004/05 amounted at the time of their takeover by P&L to 5.38 t/ha. In the campaign 2003/04, it averaged 6.28 t/ha (+ 16.7%). In the campaign 2004/05, the average sugar yield per hectare at *P&L Polska* totaled 7.80 t/ha. If we take into account only beet-growing regions of factories where sugar production took place in the campaign 2004/05, the average sugar yield per hectare amounted to 7.92 t/ha (See Figure 118).

The average sugarbeet yield per hectare in the beet-procurement area of the 11 sugar factories taken over in Poland by P&L amounted at the time of the takeover to 39.6 t/ha. In the campaign 2004/05, the average sugarbeet yield per hectare within the *P&L Polska* group amounted to 43.5 t/ha.

As regards structural changes at the raw material base of sugar factories, such as the increase in the average size of beet plantations and 'bringing' the beet-procurement area closer to individual plants, Mr. Pierun from *P&L Polska* claims that the processes have materialized "naturally".

[318] Since *P&L Polska* measures sugar content in procured beets at the factory gates, the above indicator refers to polarization of sugarbeets and not polarization of cossettes.

[319] The 17.89% average includes all nine beet-growing regions in which the beet-procurement area of *P&L Polska* was divided until December 2004. The sugar content in beets procured from beet-growing regions of factories that were in operation in the campaign 2004/05 amounted to 17.80%.

Figure 118. Sugar yield per hectare (in tonnes), P&L Polska

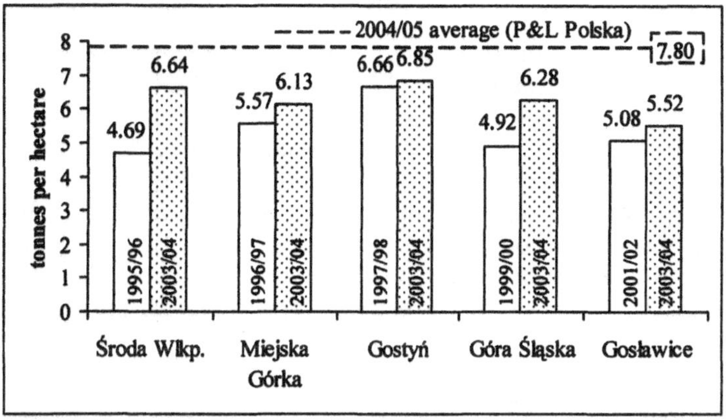

Source: IPC (Several Issues); www.liz.pl.

Mr. Pierun emphasizes that *P&L Polska* has never pressurized beet growers situated far away from the nearest sugar factory or those achieving poor agricultural yields to withdraw from sugarbeet growing. The major factor that has contributed to a gradual reduction in the number of beet growers delivering sugarbeets to factories controlled by *P&L Polska* is the fact that since 1995 the company has been paying beet growers for the sugar content in the delivered raw material and not for its weight. Due to this payment scheme, the least productive beet growers withdraw sooner or later from beet growing and switch to other crops.

Before the 2001 Sugar Law came into effect, and before beet growers in Poland were allocated the "beet growing and delivery rights", the costs of transporting sugarbeets to factories controlled by *P&L Polska* were borne by beet growers. This had the effect that many of those who had to drive very long distances retired from beet growing. In this way, the beet-procurement area of *P&L Polska* 'moved' gradually closer to the factory chimneys. Furthermore, a gradual increase in the quality and productivity of the sugarbeet harvest, achieved thanks to agro-technological progress, has brought about a systematic reduction in the amount of sugarbeets needed for the production of a given volume of sugar.

At the present time, beet transportation costs are split between sugar producers and beet growers. The exact terms and conditions concerning this issue are specified in the so-called "branch agreement" (*porozumienie branżowe*) signed in Warsaw on May 13, 2004 by the Association of Sugar Producers in Poland and the National Association of Sugarbeet Growers.

As has been repeatedly pointed out in this study, regulations contained in this agreement (and earlier in the 2001 Sugar Law) restricted sugar producers' influence on structural changes. Mr. Pierun says that the only thing that sugar producers can do now is "To make beet growers aware of the economic implications of their activities but at the end of the day it is up to them what decisions they make".

The beet-growing area of sugar factories taken over in Poland by P&L amounted at the time of their takeover to 51,234 ha. In the season 2004/05, the beet-growing area of *P&L Polska* totaled 46,550 ha (-9.1%). The total number of beet growers delivering raw material to the 11 factories taken over by P&L amounted at the time of their takeover to 16,716. In the campaign 2004/05, 10,532 beet growers delivered sugarbeets to factories controlled by *P&L Polska* (-37%). The average size of beet plantations forming the beet-procurement area of *P&L Polska* increased from 3.21 ha (at the time of the takeover of individual plants) to 4.65 ha in the season 2003/04 (+45%). The corresponding figure for the season 2004/05 is 4.44 ha (IERiGŻ 6/2005, p. 12).

15.3.1.4 Financial Restructuring

According to information provided by *P&L Polska*, the financial and economic condition of the sugar factories in *Środa Wielkopolska*, *Gostyń*, *Góra Śląska*, *Kościan,* and *Miejska Górka* was satisfactory at the time of their takeover by P&L. What was needed at the plants was investment in their modernization.

As shown in Table 43, the financial and economic situation of the sugar factory in *Głogów* at the time of its takeover by P&L was quite bad. In the financial years 1997 (1 October 1996-30 September 1997) and 1998 (1 October 1997-30 September 1998), the plant generated a net loss of PLN 5.9 million and PLN 6.7 million, respectively.

The financial and economic condition of the factories in the *Kalisko-Konińska* group was also difficult at the time of their takeover by P&L. In August 1999, the net working capital of the group had the value of PLN -110.4 million [320]. One year later, the value of this indicator was even worse, at PLN -152.6 million (See Table 44).

In August 2000, the long-term financial obligations of the factories forming the *Kalisko-Konińska* group totaled PLN 41.1 million. It must be pointed out, however, that the long-term liabilities of the sugar factory in *Gniezno* constituted 64% of this sum (see Table 44). The net financial result of the *Kalisko-Konińska* group in August 1999 and August 2000 amounted to PLN -44.3 million and PLN -19.7 million, respectively. This state of affairs made it impossible to finance investment expenditures with the help of bank loans, since factories from the *Kalisko-Konińska* group did not satisfy the standards required by the banking law. As can been seen in Table 44, the situation of the factories in *Gniezno*, *Witaszyce*, *Zbiersk* and *Zduny* was the major cause for the poor financial and

---

[320] Net working capital = current assets – short-term liabilities – prepayments and accrued income.

economic condition of the *Kalisko-Konińska* group as a whole. The economic situation of *Gosławice* was not that dramatic. It does not change the fact, however, that the credit rating and overall financial health of the factory were poor.

Table 43. Financial situation and economic performance of the *Głogów* sugar factory (financial years 1997 and 1998)*

	1.10.1996-30.09.1997	1.10.1997-30.09.1998
Sales income	46,746,293.67	44,511,001.06
Equity capital	17,211,957.43	10,507,933.06
Sales profit/loss	- 2,741,694.13	- 439,315.42
Operating profit/loss	- 2,997,497.04	- 1,236,052.29
Short-term liabilities	16,474,165.25	26,717,302.54
Long-term liabilities	7,584,537.16	-
Net financial result	- 5,945,439.71	- 6,704,024.37
Total value of assets	43,050,067.84	38,501,081.13
Fixed assets	31,559,076.11	29,230,941.38
Current assets	10,635,151.73	8,523,719.75

* All values in PLN
Source: Monitor Polski No. B-78, pp. 20-22.

Table 44. Long-term liabilities, net financial result and net working capital of factories forming the Kalisko-Konińska group, August 1999 and August 2000*

Sugar factories	Long-term financial obligations		Net financial result		Net working capital	
	August 1999	August 2000	August 1999	August 2000	August 1999	August 2000
Gniezno	26,616.50	26,331.90	- 4,987.50	- 17,520.20	- 31,669.60	- 70,461.50
Gosławice	5,214.40	4,111.40	- 10,333.20	3,145.80	- 12,347.50	- 5,888.80
Witaszyce	5,273.90	3,845.60	- 12,067.90	- 5,470.70	- 30,143.00	- 35,629.60
Zbiersk	3,214.50	2,342.90	- 7,167.40	1,098.80	- 18,850.10	- 19,704.70
Zduny	8,594.90	4,518.00	- 9,704.10	- 923.20	- 17,378.30	- 20,921.70
Total	48,914.20	41,149.80	- 44,260.10	-19,669.50	- 110,388.50	- 152,606.30

* All values in PLN thousands.
Source: Dolata 2000, pp. 5-6.

In order to ensure sufficient liquidity of factories taken over in Poland, P&L increased the capital of plants in financial difficulties and repaid their debts. As for the *Kalisko-Konińska* group, P&L was obliged by the privatization contract to carry out a "guaranteed increase of capital" of the plants in the group, amounting to "at least PLN 50 million". P&L was required to acquire shares resulting from the capital increase using its own financial resources and to spend that sum on the clearance of liabilities of individual plants. The capital increase conducted by P&L at the *Kalisko-Konińska* group totaled PLN 53 million. It did not include the plants in *Zduny* and *Witaszyce*. P&L also increased the capital of *Gostyń, Miejska Górka,* and *Głogów* after their takeover (by about PLN 12 million in total). P&L also carried out a capital increase in *Góra Śląska* and *Kościan*.

Later, P&L concentrated on activities aimed at the creation of the conditions for generation of profits at individual plants. These activities included asset engineering and the introduction of strict financial discipline.

At factories taken over by P&L in the 1995-1999 time period, the company first off-loaded non-productive assets such as kindergartens, hotels, holiday resorts, etc. In plants taken over through a secondary ownership transfer, most of such activities had already been sold off by their previous owners. Part of machinery and equipment from factories where beet processing had ceased by the campaign 2004/05 was transferred to the remaining plants. Machinery that was no longer needed was either sold (e.g. electric turbines) or scrapped.

Up to the season 2004/05, the implementation of certain activities at factories forming the *Kalisko-Konińska* group, such as the sale of machinery and infrastructure of closed plants, was restricted by privatization contracts. P&L was allowed to start these processes after paying off the creditors of individual factories and after conducting the guaranteed investments specified in the privatization contract. Therefore, at the time of writing *P&L Polska* was at a preparatory stage of selling/leasing the infrastructure of closed sugar factories.

A significant part of asset engineering within of P&L *Polska* consisted of labor restructuring described in subsection 15.3.1.1.

The financial results achieved by sugar factories taken over by P&L in Poland depended strongly in the 1995-2004 time period on developments in the domestic sugar market. *P&L Polska* units generated fair profits in 1995, 1996, 2000, 2001 and 2004. As was shown in section 8 of this study, the other seasons were lean years for the sugar industry in Poland, primarily due to loopholes in the organization of the sugar market and the resultant high sugar surpluses and low market price of the commodity. Therefore, a thorough examination of the development of the financial situation of individual sugar producers would tell us little and would serve little purpose.

In 2004, the turnover of the P&L group in Poland amounted to € 196.6 million and was 36% higher than in 2003 (€ 144.4 million) (Zuckerindustrie 7/2005, p. 575).

15.3.1.5 Conclusions

The above analyses show clearly that restructuring activities implemented by Pfeifer & Langen in Poland up to the campaign 2004/05 resulted in the materialization of a number of desirable effects. Most importantly, technological modernization conducted at strategic sites, as well as activities at P&L's raw material base, led to an appreciable improvement in the productivity and cost efficiency of sugar production, as well as in the quality and productivity of the beet harvest.

Owing to a swift and efficiently carried out consolidation of 11 sugar factories into five, the average sugar production at the five selected strategic locations increased from 30,596 t at the time of their takeover by P&L to 63,920 t in the campaign 2004/05. Considering the pronounced economies-of-scale effect in beet processing, this development can be considered as one of the major achievements of the restructuring processes implemented hitherto by P&L in Poland.

It has been demonstrated that sugar factories chosen by P&L for thorough modernization benefited from a considerable infusion of capital and modern technology up to the campaign 2004/05. Rationalization measures and innovations introduced by *P&L Polska* at individual sugar factories and their activities in the area of raw material/agricultural management are an indication of the transfer of valuable know-how.

As well as introducing strategic restructuring activities leading to the improvement in the cost efficiency of sugarbeet processing, P&L substantially widened the product range of its units in Poland and considerably improved the quality of manufactured sugar.

The construction of new water-purification plants, the modernization of the existing ones, the reduction in the use of major resources (energy, coal, coke), and the application of other activities, have had the effect that production processes at *P&L Polska* units have become much more environment-friendly within the last few years.

Finally, the way in which labor restructuring was conducted within the *P&L Polska* group should serve as a model and is proof of the company's strong sense of social responsibility. The provision of generous voluntary redundancies for laid-off workers and the implementation of a professional activization program on a large scale allowed the minimization of the social costs of necessary restructuring processes.

15.4 Südzucker

The Südzucker Group, headquartered in *Mannheim/Ochsenfurt* (Germany) is currently by far the largest sugar producer in Europe. Its share in the maximum sugar production quota of the EU-25 in the marketing year 2004/05 amounted to 21.8% (3.8 million t).

The first significant step on the way to the establishment of this gigantic sugar corporation was the merger of five south German sugar companies into *Süddeutsche Zucker-AG* in 1926. After merging with *Zuckerfabrik Franken GmbH* in 1988, the company changed its name to *Südzucker AG*. The main shareholders of *Südzucker AG* are sugarbeet growers who hold 56% of the company's share capital via the *Süddeutsche Zuckerrübenverwertungs-Genossenschaft eG* (SZVG). Other major owners are Austrian shareholders, via ZSG, with some 10% of the share capital, and the remaining 34% of Südzucker shares are widely held (free float).[321]

In the following years, Südzucker grew rapidly through its foreign investments in *AGRANA* (Vienna, Austria), *Raffinerie Tirlemontoise* (Brussels, Belgium) and *Saint Louis Sucre* (Paris, France). The company has thus developed from a regional sugar producer into an international group with nearly 17,500 employees worldwide[322] and an annual turnover of € 4.8 billion. Apart from possessing 11 sugarbeet-processing plants in Germany and having a large market share in the local market (40%), Südzucker today, through its affiliate companies, manages the activity of numerous sugar factories in Belgium (3), Austria (3), France (5 sugar factories and 1 refinery), Poland (12), Slovakia (2), Hungary (2), the Czech Republic (2) as well as in Romania (1 factory and 1 refinery) and Moldova (3) (See Figure 119).

Südzucker's sugar segment produces a wide variety of products for both households and the food-processing industry. In the 2004/05 campaign, Südzucker's sugar segment produced 5.1 million t of sugar from 31 million t of sugarbeets. The group's turnover and operating profit in the sugar segment in the season 2004/05 amounted to € 3.5 billion and € 360 million, respectively. Capital expenditures in tangible assets in this segment amounted to € 144 million.

In addition to the sugar segment, Südzucker has built up a fast-growing segment of highly refined specialties. This segment includes *Palatinit*, *ORAFTI* (both companies producing food ingredients, such as sugar substitutes and intense sweeteners, for functional food products), *AGRANA* (starch production for both the food and non-food sectors at three locations in Austria, one site in Hungary and one site in Romania), *PortionPack Europe* (production and marketing of portion-

---

[321] 50% of the free float is held by institutional investors (including commercial businesses) and the other half is divided among private investors (about 31,100 private shareholders).

[322] Average employment level during the year.

packed articles (sugar, sauces, non-food items)), *Surafti* (production of bakery preparations with a sugar base), and the *Freiberger Group* (deep frozen Italian specialties, e.g. pizzas, pastas, baguette-based meals).

Südzucker also has a number of more recent interests: Bioethanol (production by *Saint Louis Sucre* in Eppeville (France); a new site under construction in Zeitz, Sachsony-Anhalt, (Germany); fruit additives and fruit juice concentrates with *Vallø-Saft A/S* (Denmark); a 45% stake in *Steirerobst AG*, with production sites in Austria, Hungary, Poland, Romania and Ukraine; and *Atys S.A.* (France).[323]

Südzucker Group's revenues in the special products segment in the marketing year 2004/05 amounted to € 1.3 billion. Operating profit in this segment in the same year totaled € 163 million and capital expenditures amounted to € 356 million.

Südzucker Group's earnings after income taxes in the marketing year 2004/05 amounted to € 358 million. Restructuring activities and special items resulted in total expenses amounting to € 46 million.[324]

Figure 119. Location of sugar factories belonging to the Südzucker Group

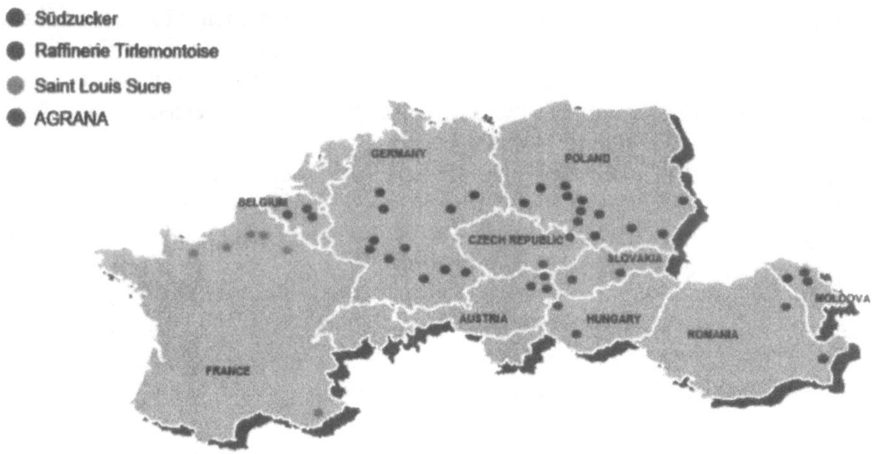

Source: Südzucker 2004, p. 20.

[323] From the total number of 17,500 employees of the Südzucker Group, 12,000 are employed in the sugar segment and the remaining 5,500 in the special products segment.

[324] The above company profile is based on information provided on the official web site of the Südzucker Group (www.suedzucker.de).

15.4.1 Südzucker in Poland

Südzucker's investment in Poland began with the acquisition of stakes in several sugar factories in the south-eastern region of the country in the second half of the 1990s. The plants, which were privatized individually, were in poor financial condition, and desperately needed an injection of capital. In 1997, Südzucker took over the sugar factories *Łubna* and *Ropczyce* through an increase of capital. A year later, Südzucker took over the sugar factory in *Włostów* as a result of the acquisition of a majority stake in the plant by the sugar factory in *Ropczyce* (after an increase of the share capital at the former). In 2000, Südzucker acquired two more sugarbeet-processing plants in Poland, *Garbów* and *Strzyżów*. The sugar factory in *Garbów* had been privatized earlier to another foreign investor (Tate & Lyle) and the takeover of the plant by Südzucker constituted a secondary ownership transfer.[325] The site in *Strzyżów* was taken over by Südzucker through an increase of the share capital of the plant.[326] In 2002, Südzucker acquired the sugar factory in *Przeworsk* (as a bankrupt's estate).

On November 15, 2000, *Saint Louis Sucre* (belonging since 2002 to the *Südzucker Group*) signed a preliminary contract with the Polish Ministry of State Treasury concerning the takeover of 16 plants in Silesia, forming the *Śląska Spółka Cukrowa* sugar holding (See Table 45).[327] After the passage of the 2001 Sugar Law, this transaction was blocked by the Ministry of Internal Affairs. *Saint Louis Sucre* filed a complaint with the courts.

On March 26, 2003, after more than two years of legal confrontations, the Ministry of State Treasury gave final approval to the sale of the Silesian holding to *Saint Louis Sucre*. The transfer of 95% of the share capital of the holding to *Saint Louis Sucre* took place on April 8, 2003.[328]

In the meantime, one of the 16 factories forming the holding, *Ziębice*, went bankrupt and 'fell out' from the transaction. Nonetheless, the sugar production quota of the factory was allocated to other plants of *Śląska Spółka Cukrowa*. They also absorbed the raw material base of *Ziębice*.

---

[325] Prior to the takeover of *Garbów* by Tate & Lyle, the sugar factory was transferred from the state into private hands as a result of restitution of property seized under Communist rule.

[326] Südzucker paid PLN 35.6 million for the acquired part of the increased share capital of the *Strzyżów* sugar factory.

[327] In Figure 47, these factories are marked with the numbers 12-21 and 44.

[328] *Saint Louis Sucre* paid about PLN 250 million for the acquired share capital of *Śląska Spółka Cukrowa*. The company was additionally obliged by the privatization contract to carry out a capital increase totaling another PLN 250 million. It also undertook to invest PLN 100 million in the modernization of sugar factories forming *Śląska Spółka Cukrowa* within 3 years after the finalization of the privatization deal. Furthermore, *Saint Louis Sucre* was obliged to spend PLN 55 million within 6 years of the takeover of the factories forming *Śląska Spółka Cukrowa* on "developmental investments" (Naszkowska 2003; Bałtowski 2002, p. 228; Information provided by *Südzucker Polska*).

In the season 2004/05, a maximum sugar production quota of 422,000 t gave the Südzucker group in Poland a market share of 25.3%. According to Dr. Thomas Kirchberg, chairmen of the board of directors of *Südzucker Polska*, a market share of at least 25% is what Südzucker strove to achieve when the company entered the Polish market. At the same time, Dr. Kirchberg admits that Südzucker wanted to acquire more sugar factories in the south-eastern region of Poland than it actually did. From the beginning, the company targeted the south-western and the south-eastern part of Poland as potential investment locations, since soil quality and other natural conditions in these regions are favorable for cost-efficient and productive sugarbeet production.

Table 45. Sugar factories taken over by Südzucker in Poland

Date	Factory location	Processing capacity*	Privatization method
1997	Łubna	2,300	Indirect privatization
1997	Ropczyce	7,400	Indirect privatization
1998	Włostów**	1,900	Indirect privatization
2000	Garbów**	1,800	Secondary ownership transfer
2000	Strzyżów	2,800	Indirect privatization
2002	Przeworsk**	3,100	Takeover of bankrupt's estate
2003	**Śląska Spółka Cukrowa**:		Indirect privatization (Holding privatization)
	▪ Baborów**	1,300	
	▪ Cerekiew	3,500	
	▪ Chybie	2,100	
	▪ Jawor**	2,200	
	▪ Łagiewniki**	2,100	
	▪ Małoszyn	3,900	
	▪ Otmuchów	3,400	
	▪ Pastuchów**	1,400	
	▪ Pustków**	2,000	
	▪ Racibórz	2,300	
	▪ Strzelin	3,000	
	▪ Świdnica	3,100	
	▪ Wieluń**	1,200	
	▪ Wrocław	3,000	
	▪ Wróblin	2,700	

* Daily processing capacity (in tonnes of beet throughput per day) at the time of the takeover by Südzucker.
** Sugar factories where sugarbeet processing had ceased by the campaign 2004/05
Source: Südzucker Polska.

The large size of the Polish market, the competitiveness and developmental potential of the local sugar industry, the relatively high sugar consumption per capita in Poland, and the prospect of EU accession, were the major reasons for Südzucker's participation in the privatization process of the Polish sugar industry. Südzucker was aware of the fact that due to the local character of sugarbeet growing and sugar production as well as the system of allocating non-transferable sugar production quotas to individual member states of the EU, its presence in

Poland and the achievement of "an acceptable market share" was possible only through the establishment of operations in the country.

An analysis and assessment of the restructuring activities implemented by Südzucker in Poland requires that one make a clear distinction between sugar factories located in the south-eastern part of the country and plants taken over by the company in Silesia in 2003. There are two major reasons why such a separation is necessary. Firstly, 5 out of the 6 sugar factories situated in south-eastern Poland and owned by Südzucker were taken over by the company in the 1997-2000 time period. This implies that the restructuring processes conducted by Südzucker in the region are at a much more advanced stage than in Silesia. Moreover, enough time has passed to see and to evaluate the effects of restructuring activities implemented by Südzucker in south-eastern Poland.

The situation with the plants in Silesia is different. A number of significant post-privatization restructuring measures have been introduced at the group since the takeover of the factories in March 2003. Nonetheless, a preliminary assessment of the effectiveness of the restructuring program embracing the plants will not be possible before the end of the season 2007/08. At the time of writing it is, for instance, still not decided by Südzucker which of the Silesian factories are to become the strategic locations of the future, i.e. plants which will be thoroughly modernized and where production will be concentrated in the following years. Südzucker is waiting for definite conclusions in discussions on the parameters of the reform of EU sugar regime to be introduced in 2006 before making such key decisions. Moreover, the cessation of sugar production at plants forming *Śląska Spółka Cukrowa* is restricted by the privatization contract. *Saint Louis Sucre* was obliged by the contract, *inter alia*, to maintain beet processing at 8 plants of the Silesian holding until the campaign 2007/08, inclusively. Finally, a precondition for consolidation of sugar factories in Silesia (and elsewhere in Poland) without the loss of production quota is the merger of two or more plants into one unit. This is usually a lengthy process. It requires to obtain a number of permissions and must go through a great many bureaucratic stages before it can be finalized. At the time of writing, Südzucker is in the process of merging all the sugar factories forming *Śląska Spółka Cukrowa* into one economic unit—*Cukier Śląski* (See Nowe Cukrownictwo 3/2004, p. 6).

The only Silesian plant selected for a comprehensive modernization and expansion by Südzucker so far is the *Cerekiew* factory. It is important to mention at this point that Südzucker has ruled out the construction of new sugar factories in Poland and the expansion of the processing capacities of existing plants beyond 5,000-8,000 t of beet throughput per day. This would be, according to Dr. Kirchberg, too costly and economically unviable.

The second argument for distinguishing between sugar factories situated in south-eastern Poland and the Silesian plants is that the restructuring criteria and priorities specified initially by Südzucker were quite different for the two regions.

Dr. Kirchberg points out that in south-eastern Poland, Südzucker was compelled to restructure "what the company managed to acquire". In other words, from the small number of plants taken over in the region by Südzucker, two or three were viewed as suitable sites for modernization (judged on size, state of repair, location, etc.). The large number of sugar factories taken over by Südzucker in Silesia gives the company many more possibilities and more room for maneuver in the years to come.

Even given all this, a common goal of restructuring activities implemented by Südzucker throughout Poland has been the continual improvement of the competitiveness of individual plants through the increase in the quality and productivity of the sugarbeet harvest, the reduction in the costs of beet processing through the technological modernization of sugar factories and the introduction of rationalization measures, as well as the improvement in the quality of manufactured sugar.

From the total number of 21 sugar factories taken over by Südzucker in Poland, sugarbeet processing in the campaign 2004/05 took place at 12 plants: *Łubna*, *Ropczyce* and *Strzyżów* in south-eastern Poland as well as *Cerekiew*, *Chybie*, *Małoszyn*, *Otmuchów*, *Racibórz*, *Strzelin*, *Świdnica*, *Wrocław* and *Wróblin* in Silesia.

15.4.1.1 Operational Restructuring

As far as the south-eastern region of Poland is concerned, Südzucker's modernization activities have been concentrated in *Ropczyce*, *Łubna* and *Strzyżów*. The cessation of sugarbeet processing at the three other locations in the region was driven predominantly by Südzucker's desire to optimize (increase) the utilization level of the processing capacity of the first three factories and to prolong in this way the campaign length at the plants.

Several factors were taken into account in the choice of factories destined for modernization: processing capacity, location, state of repair, etc. The main advantage of the sugar factory in *Ropczyce* was its large nominal processing capacity. The location of *Strzyżów* in the vicinity of a major beet-growing region was decisive in the continuation of sugar production at the plant. In the case of the sugar factory in *Łubna*, the close proximity of the plant to the market (Kraków and surroundings) played a decisive role in its choice as a strategic location.

The main objective of modernization activities implemented by Südzucker up to the season 2004/05 in *Ropczyce*, *Łubna* and *Strzyżów* was a reduction in the use of energy and other resources as well as improvement in the quality of manufactured sugar. Moreover, the company introduced rationalization measures in the following fields: logistics, storage, collection of sugarbeets, and employment level. Up to the campaign 2004/05, Südzucker invested € 20 million in the modernization of sugar factories in south-eastern Poland. Major investment projects are listed in Table 46.

Table 46. Major investment projects, Südzucker plants in south-eastern Poland

Łubna	juice purification, defecation mud press, beet pulp press, evaporation station, boiling station A, centrifugal station B
Ropczyce	evaporation station, filter station, boiling station A, centrifugal station A, B, C, new white sugar whirling machines, sugar silo (capacity: 40,000 t of sugar), packing department, sugar packing line (1kg bags, capacity: 240,000 of 1 kg bags/day), new sugar segregation station , modern palette machines in the packing department, sugar storehouse and distribution station, sugarbeet storage yard, low-voltage switchboard,
Strzyżów	evaporation station, filter station, centrifugal station B, C, beet pulp press, defecation mud press, boiling station, sugarbeet storage yard, modernization of the sugar house, sugar dedusting, scales, water purification plant

Source: Südzucker Polska; Bücherl 2005, pp. 311-313; Information provided on the web sites of individual sugar factories.

It is important to mention here that in contrast to *Śląska Spółka Cukrowa*, the takeover of sugar factories in south-eastern Poland by Südzucker was not accompanied by an obligation on the part of the company to implement certain investments in the post-privatization period or to provide employees of individual sugar factories as well as sugarbeet growers with certain guarantees and benefits. In a privatization through an increase of capital or a takeover of a bankrupt's estate (as in the case of *Przeworsk* sugar factory) such *packages* are usually not included in the privatization deal.

In the present study, we will examine, according to the adopted methodology, the changes in productive efficiency at plants that were privatized to individual foreign investors up to the beginning of the campaign 2001/02 and where sugarbeet processing still took place in the season 2004/05. From the total number of 21 sugar factories taken over by Südzucker in Poland, there are three plants that fulfill the above conditions: *Łubna*, *Ropczyce* and *Strzyżów*.

The consolidation of six sugar factories taken over by Südzucker in south-eastern Poland into three plants led to a sizeable increase in the total volume of sugar production at the three strategic locations. At the time of their takeover by Südzucker, the six sugar factories in south-eastern Poland produced in total 155,473 t of sugar (25,912 t per factory). Sugar production at the *Łubna*, *Ropczyce* and *Strzyżów* plants totaled at that time 100,817 t (33,606 per factory). After the cessation of sugarbeet processing at three locations (*Garbów*, *Przeworsk*, *Włostów*), total sugar production in *Łubna*, *Ropczyce* and *Strzyżów* in the campaign 2004/05 rose to 168,950 t (56,317 t per one factory). This means an increase by 68%, which constitutes a very positive development, considering the economies-of-scale effect in beet processing (See Figure 120).

The concentration of sugar production in *Łubna*, *Ropczyce* and *Strzyżów* led to a better utilization of the processing capacities of the three plants and to an appreciable increase in the length of a campaign at the factories. The campaign 2000/01 at the six sugar factories taken over by Südzucker in south-eastern Poland had an average length of 54 days. In *Łubna*, *Ropczyce* and *Strzyżów*, it averaged 51 days.

In consequence of the cessation of sugarbeet processing at the *Garbów*, *Przeworsk* and *Włostów* plants, the campaign 2004/05 in *Łubna*, *Ropczyce* and *Strzyżów* had an average length of 86 days (See Figure 121). As was shown in the theoretical part of the present study, a campaign length of 85-90 days is considered, from the point of view of economic efficiency, as the optimum length of a campaign in Poland.

Figure 120. Sugar production at Südzucker plants in south-eastern Poland (in 1000 t of white sugar)

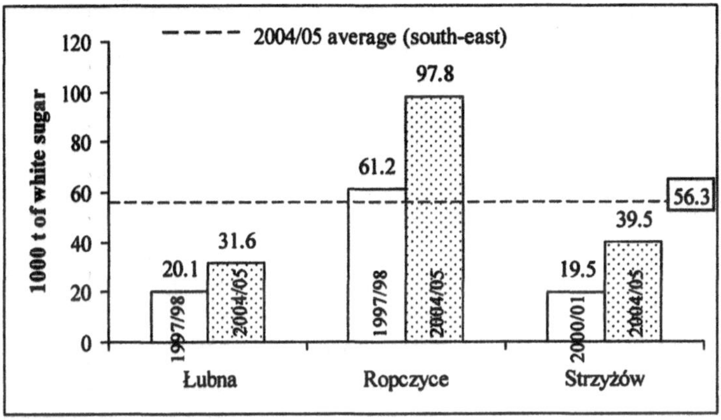

Source: IPC (Several Issues), Südzucker Polska.

Figure 121. Campaign lengths at Südzucker plants in south-eastern Poland (in days)

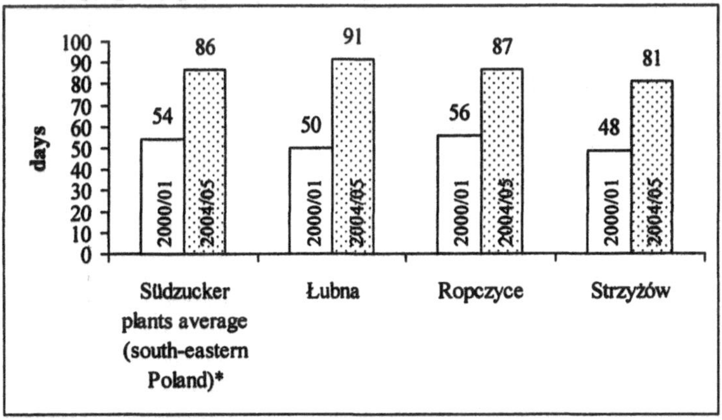

* The 2000/01 average comprises all sugar factories taken over by Südzucker in south-eastern Poland (*Garbów*, *Łubna*, *Przeworsk*, *Ropczyce*, *Strzyżów*, *Włostów*). The 2004/05 average is taken from the factories that were in operation in the campaign 2004/05 (*Łubna*, *Ropczyce* and *Strzyżów*).

Source: STC (Several Issues); Südzucker Polska.

Data on total energy consumption at the *Łubna*, *Ropczyce* and *Strzyżów* plants at the time of their takeover by Südzucker and during the campaign 2004/05 show that rationalization activities conducted by the company in this field led to good results. At the time of the takeover of the three factories by Südzucker, total energy consumption at the plants amounted on average to 3,558 kWh/t of sugar. In the campaign 2004/05, it averaged 1,860 kWh/t of sugar, which constitutes a reduction of 48% (See Figure 122).

Figure 122. Total energy consumption (in kWh/t of sugar, boiler house), *Łubna*, *Ropczyce* and *Strzyżów*

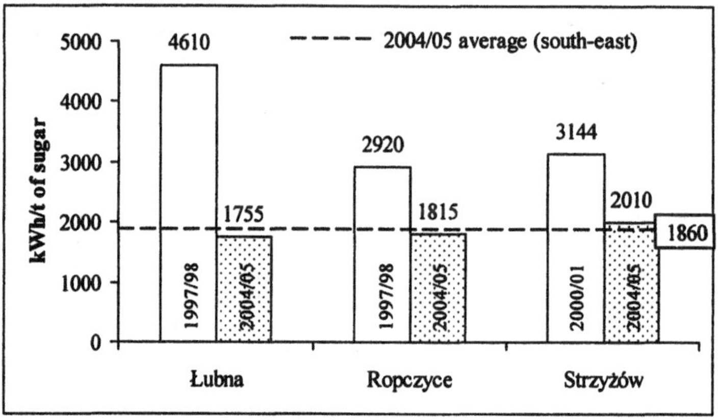

Source: STC 2001, p. 26; Südzucker Polska.

Figure 123. Limestone consumption (in % on beet), *Łubna*, *Ropczyce* and *Strzyżów*

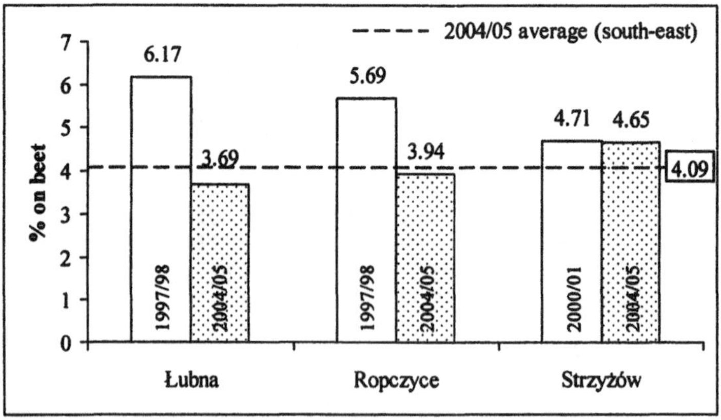

Source: IPC (Several Issues), Südzucker Polska.

The use of other resources at the above factories has also reduced considerably since their takeover by Südzucker. The average use of limestone at the *Łubna*, *Ropczyce* and *Strzyżów* plants amounted at the time of their takeover to 5.52% on beet. In the campaign 2004/05, it averaged 4.09% on beet (- 26%). As shown in Figure 123, a significant cut in the consumption of limestone took place in the post-privatization period at the *Łubna* and *Ropczyce* plants.

The average use of coal at the *Łubna*, *Ropczyce* and *Strzyżów* plants amounted at the time of their takeover to 5.19% on beet. In the campaign 2004/05, it averaged 4.57% on beet, which constitutes a reduction of 12%.

The average use of coke at the *Łubna*, *Ropczyce* and *Strzyżów* plants amounted at the time of their takeover to 0.48% on beet. In the campaign 2004/05, it averaged 0.31% on beet, which constitutes a reduction of 37% (See Figure 124).

Figure 124. Use of coke (in % on beet), *Łubna*, *Ropczyce* and *Strzyżów*

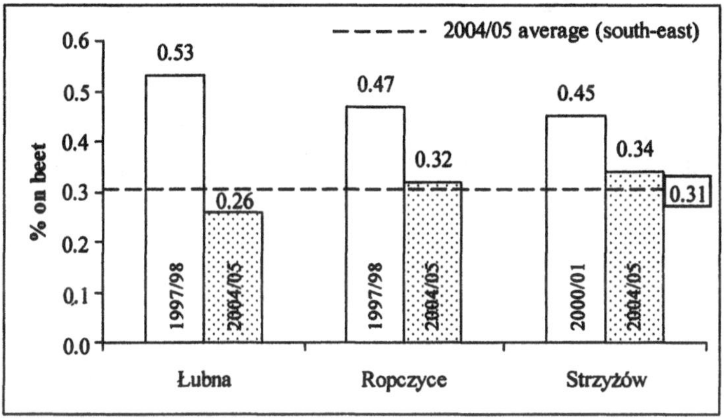

Source: IPC (Several Issues), Südzucker Polska.

Figure 125. Use of fresh water (in % on beet), *Łubna*, *Ropczyce* and *Strzyżów*

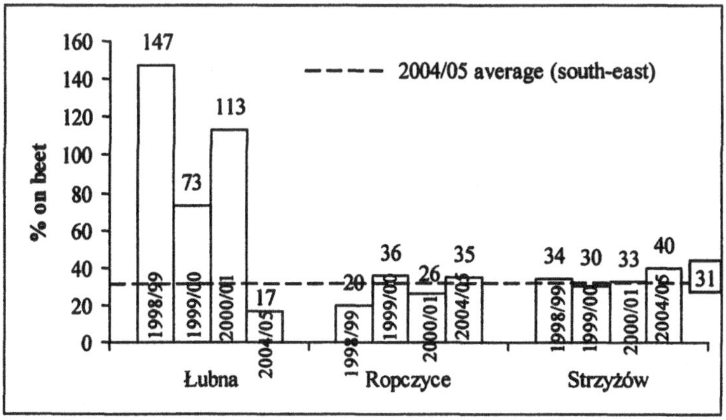

Source: IPC (Several Issues); Südzucker Polska.

The use of fresh water at the above three plants in the campaign 1998/99 amounted on average to 67% on beet. It was highest at the *Łubna* sugar factory

(147% on beet). In the campaign 2004/05, the average use of fresh water at the *Łubna*, *Ropczyce* and *Strzyżów* plants amounted to 31% on beet. Whereas fresh water use decreased considerably at the *Łubna* plant after its takeover by Südzucker, it increased slightly at the Ropczyce sugar factory. It remained more or less unchanged at the *Strzyżów* plant (See Figure 125).

Modernization activities and rationalization measures implemented by Südzucker at the *Łubna*, *Ropczyce* and *Strzyżów* plants led to an appreciable improvement in the key indicators of productivity by the campaign 2004/05. The average sugar yield in % of raw sugar value on beet at the three factories amounted at the time of their takeover by Südzucker to 13.24%. The corresponding number for the campaign 2004/05 is 16.09%, which constitutes an increase of 21% (see Figure 126).

Figure 126. Sugar yield in % of raw sugar value on beet, *Łubna*, *Ropczyce*, *Strzyżów*

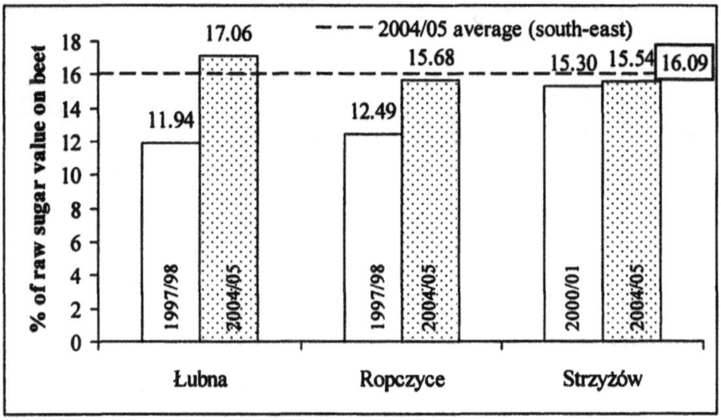

Source: IPC (Several Issues); Südzucker Polska.

A significant improvement in extraction efficiency took place at the *Łubna*, *Ropczyce* and *Strzyżów* factories since their takeover by Südzucker. At the time of the takeover, recovery of sugar at the three plants averaged 83.72%. In the campaign 2004/05 it amounted on average to 89.93%. The greatest increase took place at the *Łubna* sugar factory (see Figure 127). An increase by 7.4% at all three plants indicates a considerable reduction in sugar losses during sugarbeet processing. It must be added here, however, that recovery of sugar for *Łubna*, *Ropczyce* and *Strzyżów* in 2004/05 was calculated on the basis of polarization of cossettes including the raw material base of factories that were merged with the above plants/companies in the post-privatization period and closed subsequently (*Przeworsk*, *Garbów and Włostów*). When taking into account only the 'original' raw material base of *Łubna*, *Ropczyce* and *Strzyżów*, recovery of sugar at the plants in the campaign 2004/05 averaged 88.7%.[329]

[329] *Ropczyce* (88.7%), *Strzyżów* (88.1%), *Łubna* (89.3%).

Figure 127. Recovery of sugar, *Łubna*, *Ropczyce* and *Strzyżów*

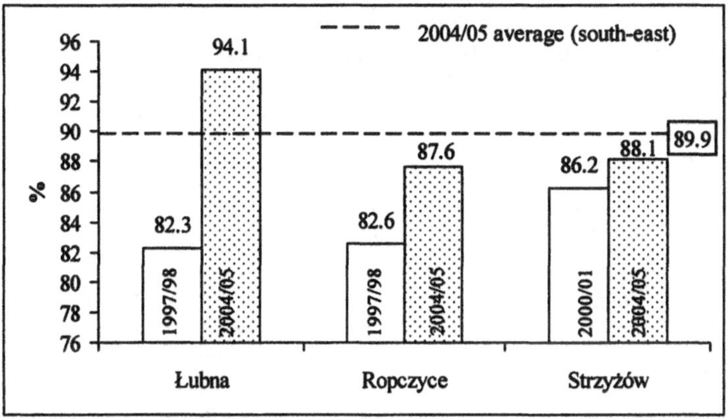

Source: IPC (Several Issues); Südzucker Polska.

An appreciable improvement in labor productivity could be observed at the *Łubna*, *Ropczyce* and *Strzyżów* plants in the period from their takeover by Südzucker up to the campaign 2004/05. It was achieved with gradual staff reduction and automation of production processes, as well as a significant increase in total sugar production at the three plants after cessation of sugarbeet processing in *Garbów*, *Przeworsk* and *Włostów*.

As shown in Figure 128, regular staff at the *Łubna* sugar factory has been reduced since the takeover of the plant by Südzucker almost by a half.

Figure 128. Employment level, *Łubna* sugar factory, 1997/98 and 2004/05

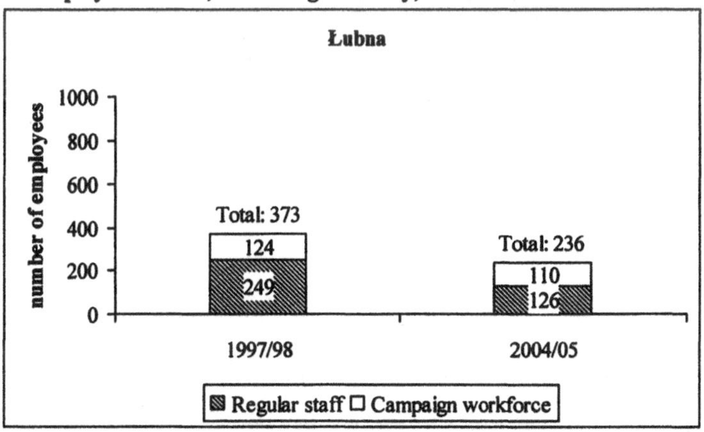

Source: Südzucker Polska.

Also the number of workers employed during a campaign declined slightly (-11%). This development was accompanied by a significant increase in total sugar production at *Łubna* and, consequently, an appreciable growth in labor productivity, expressed in tonnes of sugar per one employee. If we take into account only regular staff, labor productivity at the *Łubna* factory increased in the 1997/98-2004/05 time period by 210%. Labor productivity comprising regular staff and campaign workforce increased at the same time by 148% (See Figure 129).

Figure 129. Sugar production and labor productivity, *Łubna* sugar factory, 1997/98 and 2004/05

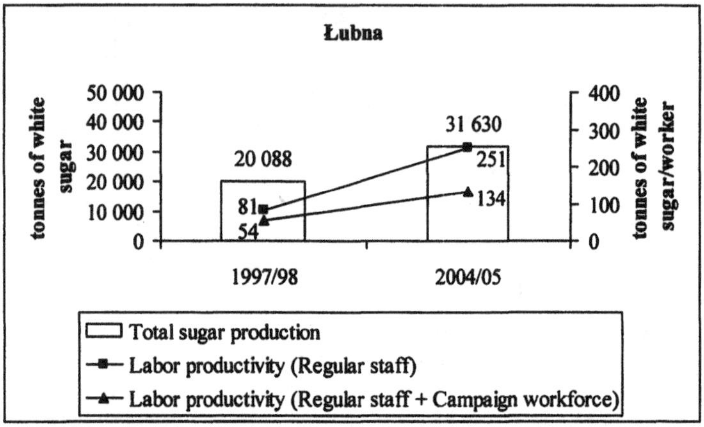

Source: Südzucker Polska; IPC.

The total number of employees (regular staff + campaign workforce) at the *Ropczyce* sugar factory decreased by 26% between the takeover of the plant by Südzucker and the campaign 2004/05.

Figure 130. Employment level, *Ropczyce* sugar factory, 1997/98 and 2004/05

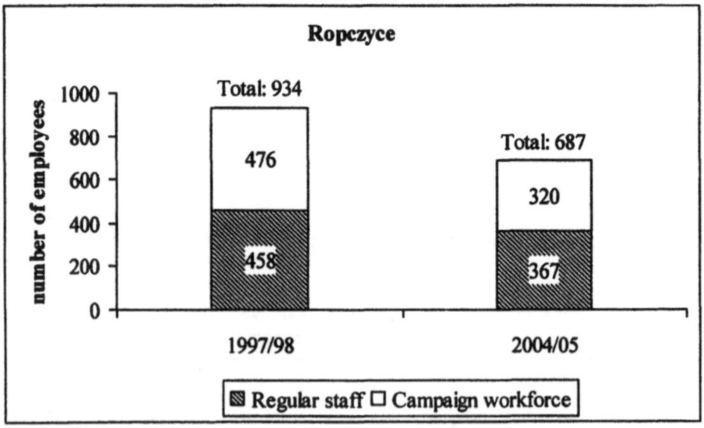

Source: Südzucker Polska.

Regular staff was reduced by 20% and campaign workforce by 33%. The accompanying increase in total sugar production at *Ropczyce* from 61,234 t in 1997/98 to 97,780 t in 2004/05 has caused labor productivity to rise by 98% (regular staff). Labor productivity at the factory, counting regular staff and campaign workforce, rose by 115% during the same period (See Figures 130 and 131).

Figure 131. Sugar production and labor productivity, *Ropczyce* sugar factory, 1997/98 and 2004/05

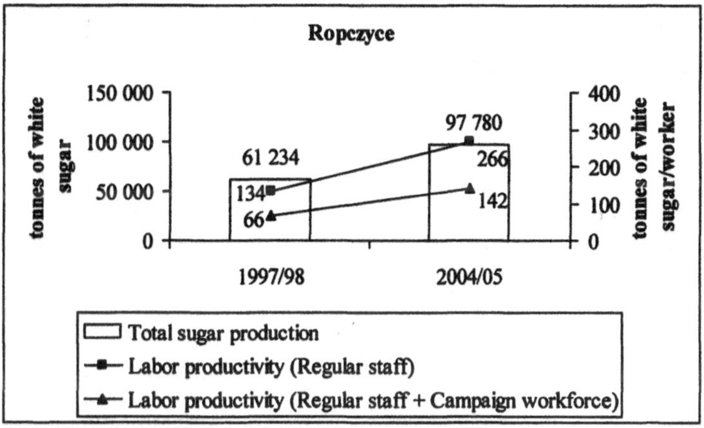

Source: Südzucker Polska; IPC.

The overall employment level at the *Strzyżów* sugar factory has been reduced by 56% since the takeover of the plant by Südzucker. Regular staff at *Strzyżów* decreased by 50% in the 2001/02-2004/05 time period.

Figure 132. Employment level, *Strzyżów* sugar factory, 2000/01 and 2004/05

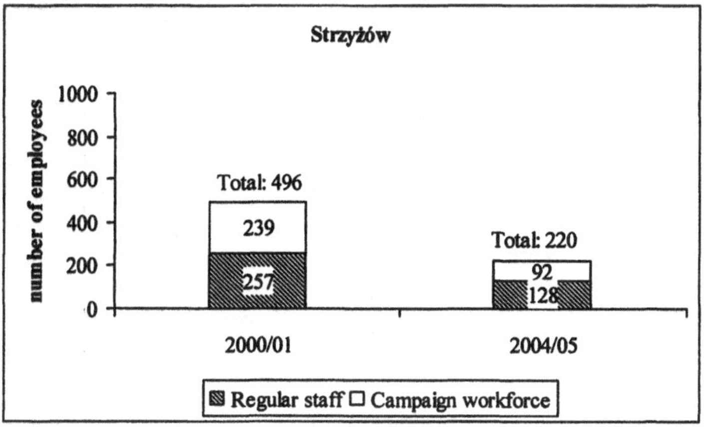

Source: Südzucker Polska.

The number of workers employed at the factory during the campaign dropped by 61% in the same time period (See Figure 132). Such a significant reduction in campaign workforce indicates that automation and computerization of production processes was introduced in the post-privatization period. As shown in Figure 133, labor productivity at the *Strzyżów* plant increased by 307% (regular staff) between 1997/98 and 2004/05. Labor productivity comprising regular staff and campaign workforce increased at the same time by 361%.

Figure 133. Sugar production and labor productivity, *Strzyżów* sugar factory, 2000/01 and 2004/05

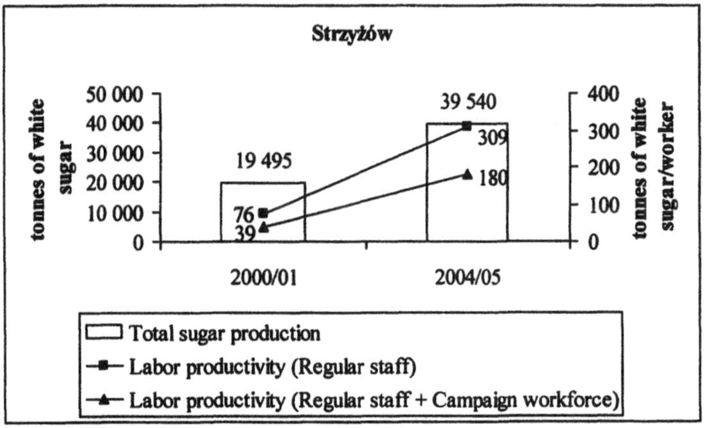

Source: Südzucker Polska.

The number of regular workers at all three sugar factories (*Łubna*, *Ropczyce* and *Strzyżów*) amounted at the time of their takeover by Südzucker to 964. Campaign workforce totaled 839 people. The corresponding numbers for the campaign 2004/05 are 621 and 522, respectively.

Total sugar production at the three sugar factories increased from 100,817 t at the time of their takeover by Südzucker to 168,950 t in the campaign 2004/05. This means that aggregate increase in labor productivity at *Łubna*, *Ropczyce* and *Strzyżów* since their takeover by Südzucker till the campaign 2004/05 amounts to 160% (regular staff). Aggregate increase in labor productivity comprising regular staff and campaign workforce at all three plants amounts to 164%.

It is important to mention at this point that the sugar factories *Garbów*, *Przeworsk* and *Włostów* (plants where sugarbeet processing had ceased by the campaign 2004/05) employed at the time of their takeover by Südzucker, on average, more than 200 regular workers.[330]

[330] *Garbów*: 167 workers (1999/00), *Strzyżów*: 293 workers (2000/01), *Włostów*: 165 workers (1998/99).

In the campaign 2003/04, the Südzucker group in Poland employed 3,128 regular workers plus 3,262 seasonal workers at 17 working sugar factories. With a total sugar production amounting to 487,793 t, average labor productivity within the group amounted to 156 t per one employee (regular staff) and 76 t per one employee (regular staff + campaign workforce).

During the campaign 2004/05, sugarbeet processing within the Südzucker group in Poland took place at 12 sugar factories. They manufactured 517,891 t of sugar. Regular staff at the plants amounted in total to 1,819 people and campaign workforce totaled 1,489. The average labor productivity within the entire group amounted to 285 t per employee (regular staff). Labor productivity comprising regular staff and campaign workforce amounted to 157 t per employee. This means that labor productivity at Südzucker group in Poland increased in the campaign 2004/05 by 83% (regular staff) and 107% (regular staff + campaign workforce) in relation to the previous season.

As it is easy to see, this remarkable increase is attributable to the fact that regular staff of the Südzucker group in Poland was reduced between the seasons 2003/04 and 2004/05 by 42% and campaign workforce was cut at the same time by 54% (See Figure 134). The drastic downsizing affected predominantly the Silesian factories.

Figure 134. Employment level and labor productivity (in t per one employee) at sugar factories of the Südzucker group in Poland, 2003/04 and 2004/05

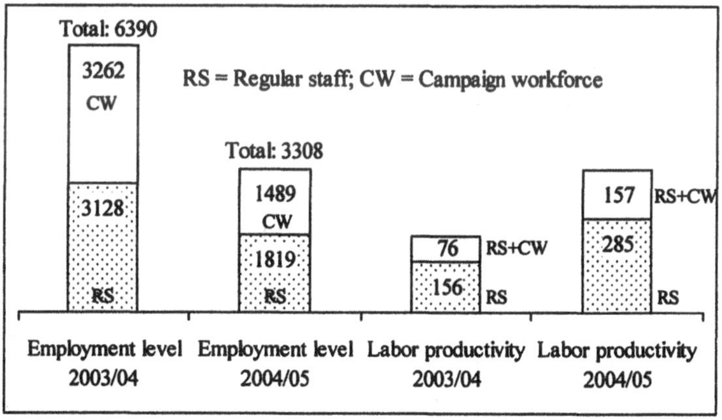

Source: Südzucker Polska.

At all sugar factories destined for closure, Südzucker agreed on a certain social package with employees. The company provided workers of individual plants either with a guaranteed period of employment and, simultaneously, a program of voluntary redundancies, or, in the case of the closure of a factory, with redundancy payments. Laid-off workers of closed factories were provided with redundancy payments varying between 18 and 24 months of salary. In both Silesia and south-eastern Poland, Südzucker offered its employees a combination of a guaranteed employment period and voluntary redundancies. The guaranteed period of employment amounted to 40 months. Those who left their job before the end of this period (either on their own initiative or as a result of being laid off) received payments equivalent to a monthly salary multiplied by the number of months left until the end of the guaranteed period of employment.

Apart from providing laid-off workers with some form of redundancy payments, at most locations, Südzucker offered them training and retraining opportunities aimed at the improvement of their chances on the job market. Such opportunities existed, for example, at the *Przeworsk* sugar factory. Nonetheless, the offer met with little interest on the part of the employees of the plant. More enthusiasm for training was shown by employees of the *Garbów* sugar factory and the Silesian plants. Südzucker hired a professional vocational training provider and charged it with the task of preparing employees of the *Garbów* sugar factory, as well as factories in Silesia, for the job market. Those who participated actively in the program obtained certificates proving the completion of a given course.

No alternative production was started by Südzucker at factories where beet processing was ceased. At the time of writing the company was looking for investors willing to take over the infrastructure of individual plants.

As far as restructuring activities at *Śląska Spółka Cukrowa* are concerned, two major rationalization measures were implemented between the takeover of the holding by *Saint Louis Sucre* in 2003 and the campaign 2004/05. The first of these measures is the cessation of sugarbeet processing at 6 plants (*Baborów*, *Jawor*, *Łagiewniki*, *Pastuchów*, *Pustków* and *Wieluń*) in order to increase the utilization level of the processing capacities of the remaining Silesian sugar factories and to prolong the campaign length at the locations. The closure of the above six plants and labor restructuring at the remaining sites in Silesia led to a significant reduction in the overall employment level within the Südzucker group in Poland. As was shown earlier, more than 1,300 regular workers of the group were laid off in 2004, predominantly in Silesia. According to information provided by Südzucker, the vast majority of the laid-off workers took voluntary redundancies and left the company on their own initiative.

The cessation of sugar production at six Silesian sugar factories resulted in a considerable increase in the average length of a campaign at the remaining plants located in the region. Nonetheless, in the campaign 2004/05, the processing capacity of some of them was still not being fully utilized and the length of a campaign at the factories was not yet optimal. The campaign 2004/05 at Südzucker plants in Silesia lasted on average 83 days, which is very close to the theoretical optimum (85-90 days). Nevertheless, at the *Chybie* sugar factory, for example, the campaign 2004/05 had a length of merely 60 days. In order to optimize campaign length at all Silesian sugar factories, *Südzucker Polska* decided in the beginning of

2005 on the cessation of sugarbeet processing at the *Małoszyn* sugar factory before the beginning of the campaign 2005/06.

Apart from the aforementioned consolidation of sugar factories in Silesia and the accompanying labor restructuring, Südzucker implemented a number of modernization activities in the region, aimed at the reduction in energy consumption and other resources, overall increase in productive efficiency, and improvement in the quality of manufactured sugar.

Up to the campaign 2004/05, investment expenditures of Südzucker at *Śląska Spółka Cukrowa* totaled € 14 million. The major investment projects are listed in Table 47.

Südzucker Polska emphasizes that during the five years preceding the takeover of *Śląska Spółka Cukrowa* by *Saint Louis Sucre*, investment in modernization of factories forming the holding was almost non-existent.

Another significant restructuring measure implemented by Südzucker in Silesia by the season 2004/05 was optimization of freight charges for the transportation of sugarbeets to local sugar factories. Moreover, a number of innovations in the collection, transport and reception of beet supplies were introduced. All these activities and their results are described thoroughly in subsection 15.4.1.3.

As concerns the quality of sugar produced at factories controlled by the Südzucker group in Poland, all plants where beet processing took place in the campaign 2004/05 manufactured "white sugar of standard quality" (EU-categrory II).

The total number of points for color type, ash content and color in solution, on the basis of which sugar is classified into categories, in the campaign 2004/05 at Südzucker plants in Poland was between 10 and 20 points.[331]

Up to the season 2003/04, there was a wide diversity among sugar factories forming the Südzucker group in Poland with regard to the quality of manufactured sugar. Sugar produced at some of them did not satisfy the requirements of the EU-category II norm. This had the effect that not all customers of the Südzucker group Poland were provided with sugar of the same quality. According to Dr. Kirchberg, significant progress had taken place with regard to this issue by the season 2004/05. Differences in the quality of sugar manufactured at individual factories forming the Südzucker group in Poland were reduced considerably.

At the *Chybie* sugar factory, Südzucker manufactures, apart from "white sugar of standard quality" (EU-category II), also "extra white sugar" (EU-category I). Nonetheless, Dr. Kirchberg claims that due to a low demand for "extra white sugar" in the Polish market, local production of large qualities of sugar fulfilling quality requirements of this category is, at the moment, unnecessary and economically non-viable.

---

[331] As was shown in section 10.1 of this study, in order to be classified as "white sugar of standard quality", the number of points allocated to sugar and calculated on the basis of the value of three parameters (color type, ash content and color in solution) cannot exceed a total of 22, or 15 for the ash content, 9 for the color type and 6 for the coloring of the solution.

Table 47. Major investment projects at Südzucker plants in Silesia

Cerekiew	sugarbeet storage yard, juice purification, evaporation station, thick juice, extraction, silo (capacity: 40,000 t of sugar (under construction in the end of 2004)), sugar segregation
Chybie	emission control
Jawor	sugarbeet loading device
Łagiewniki	sugarbeet loading device
Małoszyn	beet pulp press, defecation mud press, sugarbeet loading device
Otmuchów	beet pulp press, defecation mud press, evaporator
Pustków	sugarbeet loading device
Racibórz	barometric water circulation, boiler house, sugarbeet loading devices, evaporation station
Strzelin	juice purification, beet pulp press, sugarbeet loading device, evaporation station, sugarbeet storage yard (sugar beet reception station)
Świdnica	beet pulp press, utilization of steam from the evaporating crystallizer (strike pan), sugar cooling, evaporation station
Wrocław	big bag, beet pulp press, sugarbeet loading device
Wróblin	scale (factory yard), beet pulp press, boiling station, water purification plant

Source: Südzucker Polska.

By the season 2004/05, *Südzucker Polska* had instituted the HACCP system at all working sugar factories. The *Ropczyce* and *Chybie* plants also possess certificates confirming the institution of ISO 9001:2000 (sugar production). The latter factory also obtained ISO 14001 and ISO 18001 certificates.

In order to increase job safety and to minimize the risk of accidents, Südzucker provided workers of its sugar factories in Poland with appropriate training and protective clothing/equipment. It is the responsibility of the boards of directors of individual plants/companies to ensure the safety of all employees.

The types of products manufactured at sugar factories taken over by Südzucker in Poland has not changed much since the time of the takeover. Household sugar, powdered sugar and sugar cubes as well as liquid sugar, invert sugar and refined sugar were already being manufactured at individual plants at the time of their acquisition by Südzucker. Production of these products continues. New products that Südzucker started to manufacture in Poland after the establishment of operations in the country are jam sugar, brown sugar and sugar sticks. The company emphasizes that it is able to provide customers in Poland with all the products offered by the Südzucker group in Germany and other countries.[332] Import of certain products to Poland, for instance rock candy sugar or nibs sugar, is, according to Dr. Kirchberg, more economically viable than the launch of local production. This is due to the very low demand for some products in the Polish market.

About 60% of sugar manufactured by the Südzucker group in Poland is purchased by retailers and the remaining 40% by industrial buyers. Sugar packed in 1 kg bags is by far the most popular item among products offered by Südzucker in Poland.

[332] For an overview of the product range of the Südzucker Group, see www.suedzucker.de.

15.4.1.2 Organizational Restructuring

The long-term goal of Südzucker with regard to the organizational structure in Poland has been a merger of all sugar factories/companies controlled in the country into one company, *Südzucker Polska Sp. z o. o.*, established in March 2004. The facilitation of management and decision-making processes, as well as cost savings, are the main rationale behind this undertaking. The evolution of the organizational structure of Südzucker in Poland since 2003 indicates clearly that the company is really striving to achieve the aforementioned goal.

In 2003, the *Garbów* and *Łubna* sugar factories (forming separate companies) were merged into one company—*Cukier Małopolski S.A.* One year later, a merger of *Cukier Małopolski S.A.* and the *Przeworsk* sugar factory took place. The two mergers allowed for cessation of beet processing at two out of three plants forming *Cukier Małopolski S.A.* without the loss of sugar production quota allocated to individual factories. In the campaign 2004/05, *Cukier Małopolski S.A.* consisted of only one working sugar factory: *Łubna* (See Figure 135).

At the end of 2004, the *Ropczyce* sugar factory merged with the *Włostów* plant to form *Cukrownia Ropczyce S.A.* Since sugarbeet processing in *Włostów* was ceased, *Cukrownia Ropczyce S.A.* consists currently of one factory: *Ropczyce*. Südzucker would like to incorporate *Cukrownia Ropczyce S.A.* as soon as possible into *Südzucker Polska Sp. z o. o.* but at the time of writing it was impossible due to the possession of the so-called "golden share" of the *Ropczyce* plant by the Polish State Treasury. Südzucker faces the same problem with the *Strzyżów* plant (*Cukrownia Strzyżów S.A.*).

Südzucker Polska Sp. z o. o. is the leading company of the entire Südzucker group in Poland. It coordinates all the activities of Südzucker in Poland and provides the remaining companies with a number of services (e.g. electronic data processing, legal services, acquisition of various machinery and resources, e. g. coal, coke, limestone, automobiles, apparatus, etc.). Nevertheless, as long as the subordinate companies form separate enterprises, each of them has its own board of directors, board of trustees, accounts department, etc. Of course, this state of affairs makes decision-making processes within the group complicated and costly. As was mentioned earlier, Südzucker is striving to merge all companies into one unit but this means overcoming cumbersome legal procedures and is dependent to a large extent on the will of the Polish State Treasury.

A plan of merger of the 15 sugar factories/companies in Silesia into one company (*Cukier Śląski*) was signed on October 25, 2004. The *Świdnica* sugar factory/company is due to take over the remaining 14 plants. At the time of writing (May 2005) *Südzucker Polska* is holding advanced talks with the Polish State Treasury concerning the merger. The process is expected to be finalized in the second half of 2005 at the latest. Südzucker also plans in the near future to merge the three companies situated in south-eastern Poland (*Cukrownia Strzyżów S.A.*, *Cukrownia*

Ropczyce S.A. and *Cukier Małopolski S.A.*). The final step would be the incorporation of *Cukier Śląski* as well as the company established as a result of the merger of the three companies in south-eastern Poland into *Südzucker Polska Sp. z o. o.*

Figure 135. Organizational structure of Südzucker Polska (as of May 2005)

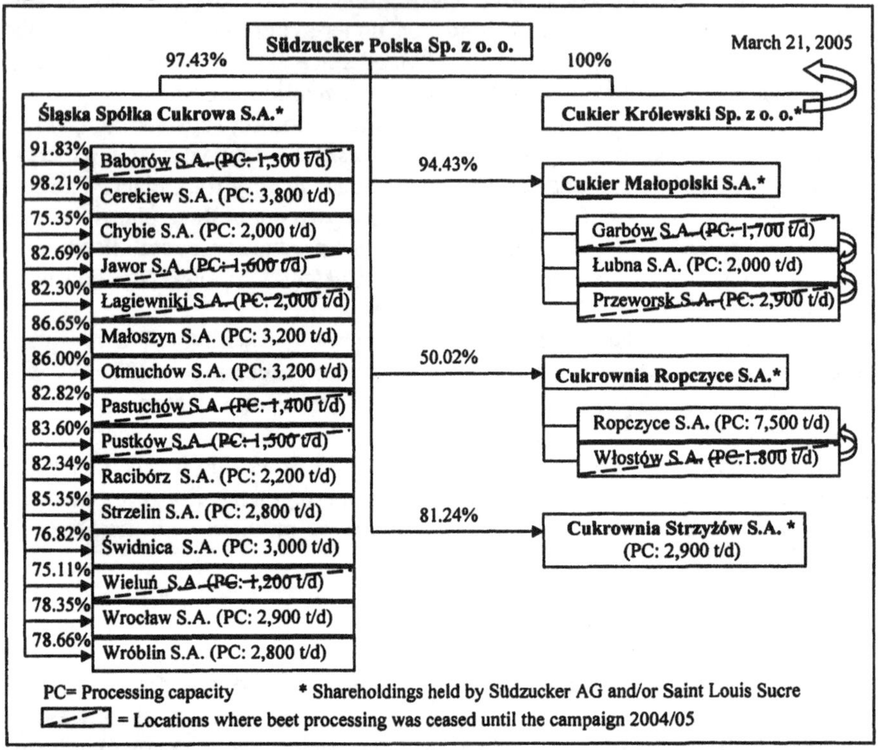

Source: Südzucker Polska.

In 1999, Südzucker established in Poland a trading company named *Cukier Królewski Sp. z o. o.*[333] Initially, the company was responsible for the marketing and distribution of sugar and other products (e.g. molasses) manufactured at Südzucker plants located in south-eastern Poland. Since 2003, *Cukier Królewski* provides the above services for all units controlled by *Südzucker Polska*. "Cukier Królewski" is also the brand name under which products of the Südzucker group are marketed in Poland. Due to the fact that the Südzucker group in Poland operates over quite a large area, *Cukier Królewski* has two regional offices situated in Ropczyce and Cerekiew. Apart from selling products of the Südzucker group,

[333] See www.cukier-krolewski.pl.

the company promotes the brand name "Cukier Królewski" in the Polish and European markets through various marketing activities. Moreover, *Cukier Królewski* provides existing and potential customers with advisory services and conducts extensive research aimed at the identification of customers' needs and preferences. On March 21, 2005, *Cukier Królewski* was incorporated into *Südzucker Polska Sp. z o. o.* and became a trading department of the company (See Figure 135).

The board of directors of *Südzucker Polska Sp. z o. o.* consists of five persons. Four of the board members are German managers. All of them are long-serving employees of Südzucker. Moreover, two managerial posts at the functional departments into which *Südzucker Polska Sp. z o. o.* is divided, e.g. controlling, are occupied also by specialists from Germany. Such a make-up of the board of directors and composition of staff at individual departments of *Südzucker Polska Sp. z o. o.* creates favorable conditions for the transfer of Western managerial practices and know-how—one of the expected benefits of the inflow of privatization-related FDI to Poland and other central and eastern European countries. As far as the remaining companies of the Südzucker group in Poland are concerned (as well as individual sugar factories), they are administered by Polish managers.

In March 2004, the installation of a business management software system called Microsoft Business Solutions–Axapta was completed at three companies of the Südzucker group in Poland: *Cukier Królewski*, *Cukrownia Ropczyce S.A.* and *Cukier Małopolski S.A.* Axapta is a multiple language, multiple currency enterprise resource planning (ERP) solution that helps small and mid-size organizations to automate processes, accelerate operations, reduce errors, increase cost efficiency. Microsoft Axapta includes applications for financial management, customer relationship management, supply-chain management, human resource management, project management, and analytics. Fully customizable, this all-in-one solution helps businesses to collaborate more effectively with customers, partners, employees, and suppliers.[334] Axapta was instituted at the Südzucker group in Poland by *CSF Polska Sp. z o. o.*, a certified partner of Microsoft Business Solutions.[335]

15.4.1.3 Raw Material/Agricultural Management

Up to the season 2004/05, Südzucker has taken a number of actions with regard to the raw material base of sugar factories acquired in Poland in order to increase the quality and productivity of the beet harvest. The company established a number of experimental plots with the aim of identifying the optimal type of sugar-

[334] See http://www.microsoft.com/businesssolutions/default.aspx.

[335] For more information about institution of Axapta at the Südzucker group in Poland see CSF 2004 and/or Microsoft 2004.

beet seeds as well as the optimal growing and plant protection methods. Such plots were established by Südzucker initially in south-eastern Poland and after the takeover of *Śląska Spółka Cukrowa*, also in Silesia.[336] On the basis of the experiments, as well as own know-how and experience, Südzucker has provided sugarbeet growers in Poland with appropriate training and advice.[337] Furthermore, the company has gradually introduced the automation of the beet harvest, since at the time of the takeover of individual plants in south-eastern Poland many activities were carried out manually. Südzucker propagated the use of modern machinery on farms and acted as a middleman between beet growers and firms selling modern beet harvesters. In the season 2004/05, about 60% of sugarbeets procured by the Südzucker group in Poland were harvested with the help of six-row combine harvesters. More than 20 specialized loader machines, so-called "mice", were in use at the raw material base of the Südzucker group in Poland in the campaign 2004/05.

Südzucker also introduced into Poland a number of changes with regard to the method and timing of the harvest as well as the storage of sugarbeets. A common problem at the raw material base of individual plants at the time of their takeover by Südzucker was that during the harvesting season, sugarbeets were left for many days in the soil after the top of the plants had been cut off. This had the effect that sugarbeets were losing a lot of sugar before they were collected and delivered to sugar factories. Introduction of several innovations in the harvesting and storage of sugarbeets led to a considerable reduction in sugar losses resulting from the aforementioned inefficiencies.

As concerns the storage of sugarbeets on the fields, *Südzucker Polska* popularized at its raw material base a particular method of collecting sugarbeets into piles and covering them with lignin.[338] The latter measure was used for about 40% of sugarbeets procured by the Südzucker group in Poland in the season 2004/05. At the time of the takeover of individual sugar factories by Südzucker in the country, the coverage of sugarbeet piles with lignin at the raw material base of the plants was not used at all.

As shown in Figures 136 and 137, the above activities led to a significant increase in the sugar content in sugarbeets procured by Südzucker factories located in south-eastern Poland as well as a considerable growth in the productivity of

336 For details, see for example Skwierz 2005.

337 Apart from close cooperation of inspectors employed at the raw material departments of individual sugar factories with sugarbeet growers, the Südzucker group in Poland organizes annually an event called "Sugarbeet Days" during which modern agricultural machinery and sugarbeet-growing techniques are presented and popularized. Moreover, the Südzucker group in Poland provides its sugarbeet growers with a special edition of the quarterly "*Burak Cukrowy*" containing various advice, reports, studies and information about current affairs within the Südzucker group and in the sugar industry.

338 See for example Kuczyński 2005.

the beet harvest in the region. The average polarization of cossettes at the *Łubna*, *Ropczyce* and *Strzyżów* plants amounted at the time of their takeover by Südzucker to 15.8%. In the campaign 2004/05 it averaged 17.9%, which constitutes an increase of 13.3%. This growth is wholly attributable to a considerable improvement in the polarization of cossettes at *Łubna* and *Ropczyce* since at the *Strzyżów* sugar factory it remained more or less unchanged since the takeover of the plant by Südzucker. It is important to add here that polarization of cossettes for *Łubna*, *Ropczyce* and *Strzyżów* in the season 2004/05 was calculated taking into account the raw material base 'taken over' by the three plants from *Przeworsk*, *Włostów* and *Garbów*. Polarization of cossettes at the 'original' raw material base of *Łubna*, *Ropczyce* and *Strzyżów* in the season 2004/05 amounted on average to 18.14%.[339]

Figure 136. Polarization of cossettes, *Łubna*, *Ropczyce* and *Strzyżów**

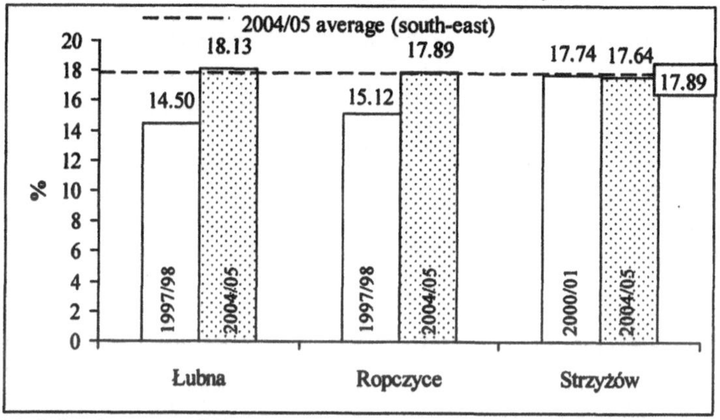

For 2004/05 including the raw material base of Przeworsk, Garbów and Włostów.
Source: IPC (Several Issues); Südzucker Polska.

The average sugarbeet yield per hectare at the raw material base of *Łubna*, *Ropczyce* and *Strzyżów* amounted at the time of the takeover of the factories by Südzucker to 37.7 t. The corresponding number for the campaign 2004/05 is 44.7 t (+ 19%).

The average sugar yield per hectare achieved by the six sugar factories taken over by Südzucker in south-eastern Poland amounted at the time of the takeover to 5.23 t. The value of this indicator for *Łubna* and *Ropczyce* was at that time well below 5 t (See Figure 138). In the campaign 2004/05, the average sugar yield per hectare with regard to Südzucker factories located in south-eastern Poland amounted to 7.09 t/ha. The sugar yield per hectare at *Łubna* and *Ropczyce* increased since the time of the takeover of the plants by Südzucker till the campaign 2004/05 by 73% and 51%, respectively.

---

[339] Ropczyce: 17.67; Łubna: 19.10; Strzyżów: 17.64.

Figure 137. Sugarbeet yield per hectare (in tonnes), *Łubna*, *Ropczyce* and *Strzyżów**

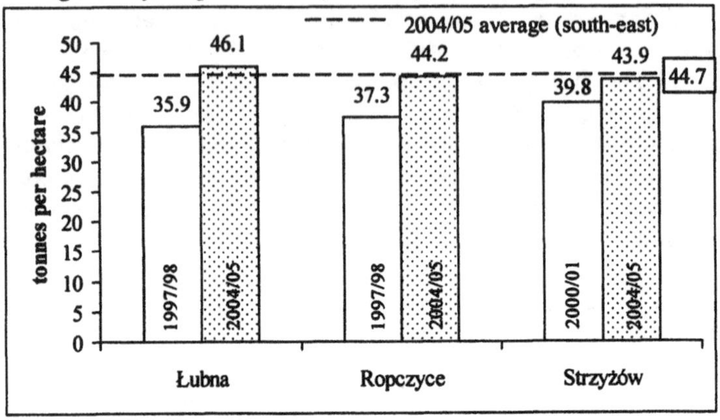

* For 2004/05 including the raw material base of Przeworsk, Garbów and Włostów.
Source: STC (Several Issues); Südzucker Polska.

Figure 138. Sugar yield per hectare (in tonnes), Südzucker plants in south-eastern Poland

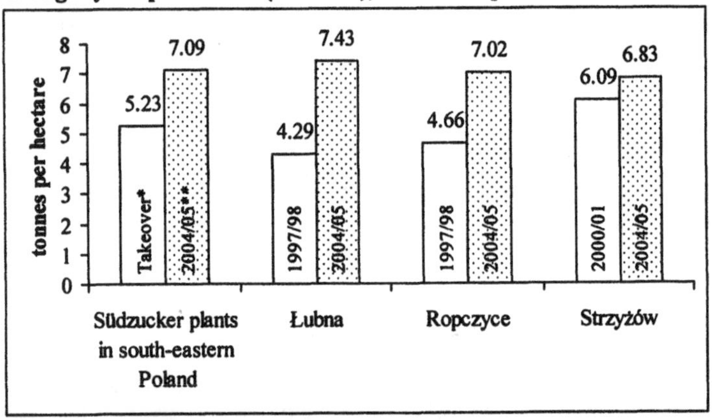

* Takeover = [Garbów (2000/01) + Łubna (1997/98) + Przeworsk (2002/03) + Ropczyce (1997/98) + Strzyżów (2000/01) + Włostów (1998/99)]/6
** 2004/05 = [Łubna + Ropczyce + Strzyżów]/3.
Source: IPC (Several Issues); Südzucker Polska.

The sugar yield per hectare recorded in *Strzyżów* at the time of the takeover of the factory by Südzucker was at a relatively high level (6.09 t/ha). One of the reasons for this is certainly the fact that natural conditions for sugarbeet growing are highly favorable in the region of the raw material base of the *Strzyżów* factory. From the takeover of *Strzyżów* by Südzucker until the season 2004/05, sugar yield per hectare achieved at the location rose by 12% (See Figure 138).

Apart from the aforementioned activities aimed at increasing the quality and productivity of the beet harvest, significant changes in the logistics of sugarbeet deliveries to sugar factories had been introduced within the Südzucker group in Poland by the campaign 2004/05. At the time of the takeover of individual factories by Südzucker, delivery of sugarbeets to beet-processing plants was predominantly by beet growers using their own means of transport. A large portion of the harvest was not delivered directly to sugar factories but rather to regional sugarbeet-purchasing centers. Sugarbeets were stored at the centers for a period of time and subsequently transported to sugar factories with their own fleet of vehicles. There were about 220 regional beet-purchasing centers within today's Südzucker group in Poland in 1997. The majority of them were situated in south- eastern Poland. The *Ropczyce* sugar factory alone had at that time about 60-70 such centers. By the campaign 2004/05, the number of regional beet-purchasing centers within the Südzucker group in Poland had been reduced to 19. The *Ropczyce* plant still has the most regional beet-purchasing centers of any of the sugar factories owned by the Südzucker group in Poland.

In the campaign 2004/05, 95% of sugarbeets procured by the Südzucker group in Poland were brought directly from the fields to individual sugar factories. Most transports were organized and carried out by specialized shipping companies. In this campaign, the share of beet deliveries using beet growers' own means of transport in the total deliveries was greatest at the Silesian sugar factory *Wróblin*, where it amounted to about 25% (Kuczyński 2005).

Before sugarbeets are transported to sugar factories, they go through the process of preliminary cleaning on the fields. This is to reduce the volume of soil attached to sugarbeets and transported unnecessarily to sugar factories, thereby increasing transport costs. In the campaign 2004/05, 93% of sugarbeets procured by the Südzucker group in Poland were pre-cleaned on the fields. At the time of the takeover of individual sugar factories in Poland by Südzucker, only about 5% of sugarbeets procured by the plants went through preliminary cleaning.

Prior to the allocation of "beet growing and delivery rights" to beet growers in Poland, *Südzucker Polska* favored contracting beet deliveries to farmers situated in the vicinity of individual sugar factories, those achieving good agricultural yields and/or having large sugarbeet plantations. This fact, as well as a gradual increase in the productivity and quality of beet harvest at the raw material base of the Südzucker group in Poland, had the effect that the number of beet growers delivering sugarbeets to factories belonging to the group was falling systematically. At the same time, the average size of beet plantations forming the raw material base of the Südzucker group in Poland was rising. The total number of beet growers delivering sugarbeets to the six factories taken over by Südzucker in south-eastern Poland amounted at the time of their takeover by the company to 22,027, of which 72% (15,944) were delivering to the *Łubna*, *Ropczyce* and *Strzyżów* plants. In the campaign 2004/05, the number of beet growers delivering sugarbeets to these three factories, even with the closure of the other three, amounted in total to 8,631. The greatest reduction in the number of beet growers took place in *Ropczyce*. At the time of the takeover of *Ropczyce* by Südzucker, 8,917 beet growers were delivering to the factory. The corresponding number for the campaign 2004/05 is 3,674, which means a decrease of 59% (See Figure 139).

Figure 139. Number of sugarbeet growers, Südzucker plants in south-eastern Poland

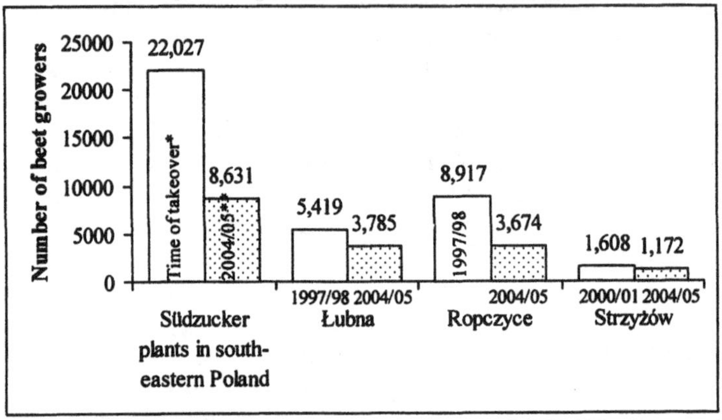

* Time of takeover = Garbów (2000/01) + Łubna (1997/98) + Przeworsk (2002/03) + Ropczyce (1997/98) + Strzyżów (2000/01) + Włostów (1998/99)
** 2004/05 = Łubna + Ropczyce + Strzyżów (including beet growers 'taken over' from Włostów, Przeworsk and Garbów).
Source: IPC (Several Issues); Südzucker Polska.

The total beet-procurement area of the six plants taken over by Südzucker in south-eastern Poland amounted at the time of their takeover to 30,918 hectares. 68% (20,760 ha) of this area formed the beet-procurement area of *Łubna*, *Ropczyce* and *Strzyżów*. In the campaign 2004/05, the beet-procurement area of the three plants covered 24,947 ha. This increase of 20% in relation to the time of the takeover of the factories by Südzucker is due to two factors: a) 'absorption' by *Łubna*, *Ropczyce* and *Strzyżów* of the beet-procurement area of factories where beet processing had ceased by the campaign 2004/05 (*Garbów*, *Włostów* and *Przeworsk*); b) increase in sugar production at *Łubna*, *Ropczyce* and *Strzyżów* after cessation of beet processing at *Garbów*, *Włostów* and *Przeworsk*.

As shown in Figure 140, the greatest increase in the beet-procurement area took place at the *Łubna* plant. The beet-procurement area of *Ropczyce* decreased slightly in the 1997/98-2004/05 time period.

The above developments were, as we have said, accompanied by a gradual increase in the average size of beet plantations forming the raw material base of the Südzucker group in south-eastern Poland. At the time of the takeover of the six plants located in the region, the average size of beet plantations forming the raw material base of the factories was 1.54 ha. As concerns the then raw material base of *Łubna, Ropczyce* and *Strzyżów*, the size of beet plantations averaged

1.44 ha. In the season 2004/05, the average size of beet plantations forming the raw material base of the three factories was 2.92 ha, an increase of 103% (See Figure 141).

Figure 140. Beet-procurement area of Südzucker plants in south-eastern Poland (in ha)

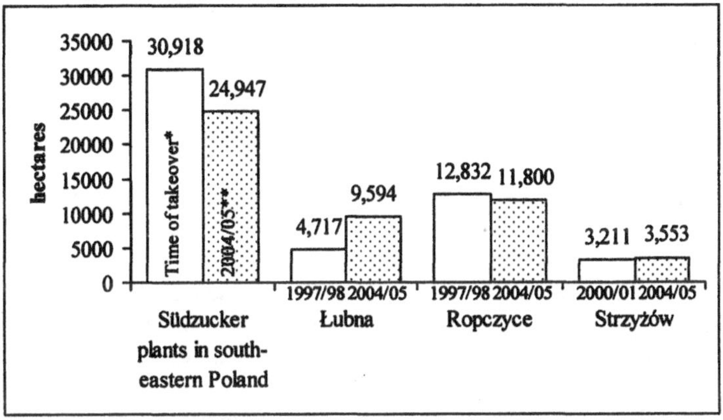

* Time of takeover = Garbów (2000/01) + Łubna (1997/98) + Przeworsk (2002/03) + Ropczyce (1997/98) + Strzyżów (2000/01) + Włostów (1998/99)
** 2004/05 = Łubna + Ropczyce + Strzyżów (including the raw material base of Garbów, Przeworsk and Włostów).
Source: IPC (Several Issues); Südzucker Polska.

Figure 141. Average size of sugarbeet plantations (in ha), Raw material base of Südzucker plants in south-eastern Poland

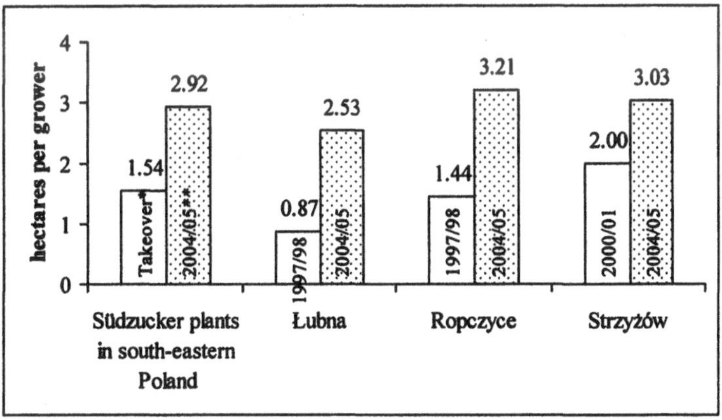

* Takeover = Average size of beet plantations at the raw material base of Garbów (2000/01), Łubna (1997/98), Przeworsk (2002/03), Ropczyce (1997/98), Strzyżów (2000/01) and Włostów (1998/99)
** 2004/05 = Average size of beet plantations at the raw material base of Łubna, Ropczyce and Strzyżów.
Source: IPC (Several Issues); Südzucker Polska.

As was pointed out earlier in this study, structural changes with regard to the raw material base of the sugar industry in Poland have depended, since the season

2002/03, almost exclusively on the will and activity of sugarbeet growers (trade with "beet growing and delivery rights", or withdrawal from sugarbeet growing).

The number of sugarbeet growers delivering raw material to all factories of the Südzucker group in Poland in the season 2004/05 amounted to 16,412 (Dobrowolski 2005, p. 3). 7,781 (47%) growers delivered sugarbeets to the Silesian plants of the group. The beet-procurement area of the Südzucker group in Poland in the season 2004/05 covered 70,572 ha. This means that the average size of beet plantations forming the raw material base of the group amounted to 4.3 ha. This indicates that sugarbeet plantations in Silesia were slightly larger than plantations in south-eastern Poland.

The beet-procurement area of Südzucker's Silesian factories covers an area of about 30,000 square kilometers. One of the major rationalization measures implemented by Südzucker at *Śląska Spółka Cukrowa* up to the campaign 2004/05 was the optimization of freight costs of transport of sugarbeets to individual factories. On the basis of complex, computer-based analyses taking into account several parameters (e.g. distance of individual beet plantations to sugar factories, processing costs at individual plants, quality of sugar), beet deliveries from individual plantations were directed to a given sugar factory. Such a reorganization of beet deliveries was introduced at *Śląska Spółka Cukrowa* for the first time in the campaign 2004/05. The introduced changes led to a reduction in the average distance of beet transports at *Śląska Spółka Cukrowa* from 33 km to 29 km (even though several factories forming *Śląska Spółka Cukrowa* were closed at the same time). Considering the fact that 2.14 million t of sugarbeets were procured by the Silesian plants of the Südzucker group in the season 2004/05, shortening the distance of individual beet transports by an average of 4 km makes a huge difference and leads to considerable cost savings. As a result of the above adjustments, nearly 726,000 t of sugarbeets were 'exchanged' between individual factories. Apart from resulting in a considerable reduction in beet transport costs, optimization of beet deliveries at *Śląska Spółka Cukrowa* contributed to an increase in the average length of a campaign at the various factories. In order to see how the reorganization of beet deliveries at *Śląska Spółka Cukrowa* worked in practice, we will look at the example of the *Świdnica* sugar factory.

In 2004, the *Świdnica* sugar factory signed contracts with 935 farmers for beet deliveries totaling 200,000 t. The average distance between individual beet plantations and the *Świdnica* plant amounted to 25.43 km. As a consequence of the optimization of freight costs introduced at *Śląska Spółka Cukrowa* in the season 2004/05, *Świdnica* 'handed over' 68,580 t of sugarbeets (contracted with 325 farmers) to other factories and 'took over' 47,787 t of sugarbeets (contracted with 179 farmers) from other plants (See Figure 142). The amount of sugarbeets processed at the *Świdnica* sugar factory in the campaign 2004/05 decreased in this way to 179,000 t. Most importantly, the average distance of individual beet transports decreased from 25.43 km to 20.03 km.

It must be added here that the way in which beet deliveries within *Śląska Spółka Cukrowa* are reorganized may change in the future depending on decisions concerning factory closures and on structural changes at the raw material base of the Silesian factories of the Südzucker group.

Figure 142. Optimization of sugarbeet deliveries at *Śląska Spółka Cukrowa* by the example of *Świdnica* sugar factory

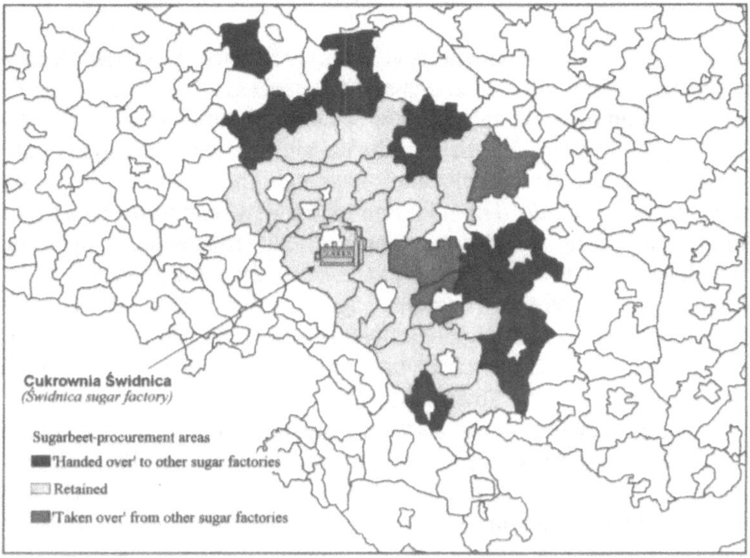

Source: Südzucker Polska.

The optimization of freight costs within the Südzucker group before the campaign 2004/05 concerned not only the raw material base of sugar factories forming *Śląska Spółka Cukrowa* but also the beet-procurement area of the *Ropczyce* and *Przeworsk* plants. A part of the beet-procurement area of these two factories is located in Silesia. Until recently, sizeable amounts of sugarbeets (about 28,000 t) processed in *Ropczyce* and *Przeworsk* were transported to the factories from Silesian sugarbeet plantations, over a very long distance and at a high cost. This was due to chronic shortages of sugarbeets in the vicinity of the above two plants. After cessation of beet processing at three out of six sugar factories in south-eastern Poland, the problem of insufficient sugarbeet supplies in the region disappeared. In the campaign 2004/05, the beet-procurement area of the *Ropczyce* and *Przeworsk* plants in Silesia was 'taken over' by sugar factories forming *Śląska Spółka Cukrowa* as part of the optimization of freight costs.

Another significant rationalization measure implemented by Südzucker at *Śląska Spółka Cukrowa* in the season 2004/05 was the introduction of several innov-

ations with regard to the logistics of beet deliveries to individual sugar factories and their reception at the plants.
All formalities connected with the purchase and delivery of sugarbeets to factories forming *Śląska Spółka Cukrowa* have been handled since the season 2004/05 with the help of bar codes and smart cards provided to beet growers and persons transporting sugarbeets to individual plants. The above tools replaced the so-called "beet delivery booklets" possessed by farmers and "beet transport letters" provided to haulers.
The reception of sugarbeet deliveries at factories forming *Śląska Spółka Cukrowa* as well as the settlement of accounts and the process of giving out beet pulp to growers are carried out with the support of a computer software named "*Plantator*" (*Beet Grower*). The weighing of sugarbeets, and the identification of individual beet growers and beet plantations takes place with the use of the aforementioned bar codes and smart cards. The adoption of the new, computer-based system of coordinating, weighing and documenting beet deliveries helps to avoid mistakes (due to manual data entry, for example) and saves time and money.[340]
As a result of closing down all regional sugarbeet-purchasing centers of the Südzucker group in Silesia in 2004, sugarbeets procured by factories forming *Śląska Spółka Cukrowa* were delivered in the campaign 2004/05 to individual plants directly from the fields (Pawłowska 2004).

Restructuring activities at the raw material base of the Südzucker group in Poland will be concentrated in the coming years on the continual improvement of productivity and quality of the beet harvest. At the end of 2004, Dr. Kirchberg said that the principal medium-term goal of the Südzucker group in Poland with regard to its raw material base is the achievement of an average sugar yield per hectare of 10 t. "Maybe we will get there in five years"- so the words of the chief executive of *Südzucker Polska*. Another desire of the Südzucker group in Poland is to move its raw material base gradually to the largest and most efficient farms.

15.4.1.4 Financial Restructuring

The financial and economic condition of sugar factories taken over by Südzucker in south-eastern Poland was disastrous at the time of the takeover. At some of them, bankruptcy proceedings had been already begun; at the others, it was about to begin. They were thus in desperate need of an injection of capital. As was mentioned earlier, this was the reason why the factories were privatized individually. In the case of the privatization of the *Przeworsk* sugar factory, Südzucker took over a bankrupt's estate.

---

[340] For more details, see Kuczyński 2005; Pawłowska 2004.

Most sugarbeet-processing plants acquired by Südzucker in Silesia were heavily indebted and their overall financial situation was poor.

After the takeover of individual sugar factories in Poland, Südzucker took several steps to improve their liquidity and to reduce debts. Almost immediately after the acquisition of the Silesian factories, Südzucker conducted a capital increase at the plants, amounting to about PLN 240 million. The financial situation of sugar factories in south-eastern Poland was improved through a capital increase and/or debt restructuring.

At times when banks were unwilling to give sugar factories credits (due to their poor financial situation and the developments in the sugar market) some plants acquired by Südzucker in Poland were offered credit by *Südzucker AG* in order to improve their liquidity.

Financial restructuring at sugar factories taken over by Südzucker in Poland also included the introduction of a number of changes to the financial management. All major transactions became subject to approval by the supervisory board. In order to prevent competition between individual sugar factories controlled by Südzucker, *Cukier Królewski* was made responsible for the marketing and distribution of sugar manufactured within the entire group.

As far as asset engineering is concerned, this was conducted by Südzucker until the campaign 2004/05 on a limited scale. Some activities that did not belong to the core activity of individual sugar factories were sold off. This refers, for example, to a construction company which was part of the *Ropczyce* sugar factory at the time of its takeover by Südzucker.

As regards factories that were closed down by Südzucker in the post-privatization period, the company has been trying to find investors to take over their infrastructure and use it for some form of business activity. Nonetheless, at the end of 2004, these processes were at an early stage and there were as yet no investment projects worth mentioning. Dr. Kirchberg emphasizes that the consolidation of sugar factories taken over by Südzucker in Poland was initiated not long ago, since until recently (2002) it was tantamount to the loss of production quota. As long as individual plants remained in operation, 'juggling' with their assets was impossible. By the same token, more advanced asset engineering is to be conducted within the Südzucker group in Poland from 2005 onwards.

Due to the fact that in the 1995-2004 time period, the financial results achieved by the sugar industry in Poland depended strongly on developments in the domestic sugar market, changes to the financial situation of sugar factories taken over by Südzucker in the country are not analyzed in this subsection. Generally, the Südzucker group as well as other sugar companies generated profits in Poland in 1995, 1996, 2000, 2001 and 2004. As shown in section 8 of this study, the other seasons constituted lean years for the domestic sugar industry due to loopholes in the organization of the sugar market, high sugar surpluses and a low market price of the commodity.

15.4.1.5 Conclusions

The above analyses show clearly that restructuring activities implemented in Poland up to the campaign 2004/05 by the largest European sugar producer resulted in a number of desirable effects. As far as sugar factories taken over by Südzucker in south-eastern Poland are concerned, the length of time since the takeover allows for a preliminary assessment of the efficiency of post-privatization restructuring. Above all, Südzucker saved the factories from almost certain bankruptcy through comprehensive financial restructuring. Operational restructuring and agricultural management led to a considerable increase in productivity. This refers to both the factories that were chosen for a thorough modernization and their raw material base. Productivity growth was accompanied by an appreciable reduction in the use of resources as well as computerization and automation of production processes. Consolidation of six sugar factories into three more scale-efficient plants led to a prolongation of the campaign length to the optimum. All this contributed to an improvement in the cost efficiency of production and, consequently, the competitiveness of individual factories. The increase in the quality of manufactured sugar as well as the broadening of the product range are other factors that influenced the growth in competitiveness.

As concerns sugar factories taken over by Südzucker in Silesia, it is too early to evaluate the effectiveness of post-privatization restructuring. Nevertheless, a number of significant restructuring activities have been implemented at the Silesian plants. Most importantly, Südzucker managed to get factories forming *Śląska Spółka Cukrowa* out of the serious financial difficulties in which they found themselves before privatization. Moreover, during the first year of its presence in Silesia, numerous rationalization measures were introduced by Südzucker in the collection and storage of sugarbeets as well as their delivery to sugar factories (optimization of freight costs and innovations in logistics).

Another fact worthy of note is the considerable increase in labor productivity within the Südzucker group in Poland, achieved through large-scale labor restructuring, and, most importantly, labor restructuring which was not accompanied by any serious social disturbances.

The realization of all above activities and the materialization of their results would be impossible without considerable capital investment. Moreover, organizational changes implemented by Südzucker in Poland, and the innovations introduced in the collection, storage and delivery of sugarbeets in Silesia are proof of the transfer of know-how.

15.5 State-owned Sugar Factories/Krajowa Spółka Cukrowa S.A.

The principal aim of this research is to analyze and evaluate the effectiveness of restructuring undertaken by foreign investors participating in the privatization of the sugar industry in Poland. However, in a situation where 40% of the sugar produced in the country is manufactured by factories that remain in state hands, such an analysis would be incomplete without taking a look at the course and effectiveness of restructuring processes taking place at this group of plants. Above all, it can facilitate the assessment of the contribution of foreign investors to the restructuring process of the sugar industry in Poland.

The structure of this subsection is almost the same as that of the remaining ones that form the empirical part of the present study. However, its scope differs slightly from the rest. The main purpose of this subsection is to identify differences and similarities with regard to the types and effects of restructuring processes that were implemented at privatized and state-owned sugar factories by the season 2004/05, inclusively.

In 1995, two state-owned sugar factories, *Klecina* and *Chełmica*, went bankrupt and were closed down. Between 2001 and 2003, the same happened to the factory in *Ziębice*. At the end of August 2002, the national sugar holding *Krajowa Spółka Cukrowa S.A.* (*KSC*) was formed on the basis of provisions made in the Sugar Law of 2001.[341] It incorporated most of the non-privatized sugar factories in Poland. In October 2003, the holding officially became a sugar corporation, comprising 22 sugarbeet-processing plants spread over seven provinces of Poland.[342] In the first half of 2005, another four state-owned factories functioning as independent economic units, *Pruszcz Gdański*, *Gryfice*, *Kluczewo* and *Szczecin*, were incorporated into *KSC* (details in section 13 of this study). As the last of the four, the sugar factory in *Szczecin* entered into the *KSC* in May 2005.[343] As a result of the above developments, *KSC* became the largest sugar producer in Poland, with a market share of nearly 40%.[344] There remains one state-owned sugar factory in Poland, *Leśmierz*, which has not become part of *KSC*, although the national sugar corporation holds a majority stake in the plant. 30% of the

---

[341] *Cukrownie Toruńskie*, a trading company providing services for the sugar industry, was also incorporated into *KSC*.

[342] As well as the official name, *KSC* also uses the abbreviation *KSC "Polski Cukier" S.A.* (KSC "Polish Sugar" S.A.), reflecting the reason for and goal of its establishment – the formation of an indigenous sugar corporation with the ability to compete successfully with foreign-owned sugar companies).

[343] After the incorporation of the *Szczecin* sugar factory into *KSC*, the seed capital of the company amounted to PLN 976,880,501.

[344] In the 2004/05 campaign, the maximum sugar production quota of *KSC* (excluding the *Leśmierz* sugar factory) amounted to 636,970 t (A-quota of 601,949 and B-quota of 35,021 t).

share capital of *Leśmierz* was distributed to its employees and sugarbeet growers prior to the establishment of *KSC*. The employees and sugarbeet growers of *Leśmierz* are unwilling to join *KSC* and prefer to remain 'independent'. The State Treasury does not have a sufficient amount of votes in the General Assembly of Shareholders to make a ruling sealing the incorporation of *Leśmierz* into the national sugar corporation.

The locations of the sugar factories that form *KSC* are presented in Figure 143. The factory in *Leśmierz* is controlled by the corporation, so it has also been included in the chart.

Figure 143. Locations of factories owned and/or controlled by Krajowa Spółka Cukrowa "Polski Cukier"

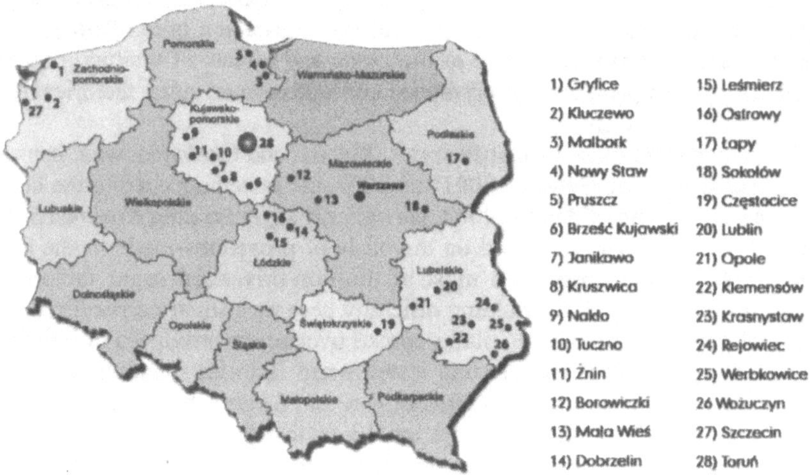

Source: KSC 2005, p. 7.

As of September 30, 2005, 83.4% of the seed capital of *KSC* was owned by the Polish State Treasury and 16.6% was in the hands of the employees (8.8%) and the beet growers (7.8%) of the corporation (KSC 2006, p. 7). At the time of writing (January 2006), the procedure of distributing part of the seed capital of *KSC* free of charge to employees and beet growers from factories forming the company was in progress. After the finalization of this process (July 2008), the capital structure of *KSC* will have the following make-up: State Treasury (77.85%), beet growers (10.8%), and employees (11.35%) (KSC 2005, p. 6). The target capital structure of *KSC* has been specified in the Sugar Law of June 21, 2001. Article 20, point 3 of the law stipulates that the Council of Ministers is to determine, in an ordinance, a program of privatizing *KSC* and a way of selling company shares exclusively to beet growers who deliver raw material to *KSC* plants and to employees of the factories that form the national sugar corporation.

As a result of the privatization, the entire share capital of *KSC* is to be gradually transferred into the hands of the beet growers and employees of the company. Individual shareholders will be able to sell their shares only to other employees of *KSC* and/or to beet growers who have contracts for raw material delivery with factories in the national sugar corporation. This means that the attainment of a majority stake in *KSC* by a foreign investor will be impossible.

According to the methodology adopted in this study, it is too early to evaluate the effectiveness of restructuring activities carried out at *KSC* in the season 2004/05. It is for this reason that analyses included in this subsection focus on the description of major restructuring activities that were implemented between 1990 and 2004 at the factories that form the company today. Nevertheless, a clear distinction between restructuring processes implemented prior to and after the incorporation of individual plants into *KSC* has been made. How major indicators of productivity and cost efficiency changed in the 1990-2004 time period at the factories that currently form *KSC* is examined, and we will look also at the development of the indicators at individual plants up to and after their incorporation into *KSC*.

15.5.1 Operational Restructuring

Until the formation of four sugar holdings in Poland in 1999, operational restructuring implemented since 1990 at state-owned sugar factories that currently form *KSC* was not guided by any governmental strategy. Restructuring activities in this field were introduced, in general, at the discretion of the management of individual plants in order to increase overall efficiency of operations. In fact, all of the factories were in the hands of a single owner, the state, but they operated as independent economic units. Each of them was competing for survival with other state-owned and private sugar producers in Poland. At the same time, the state provided support to factories which found themselves in a difficult financial situation. It often acted as guarantor for bank loans. Such paternalistic protection by the state was much less pronounced than under communist rule, but it was still there. Consolidation of the group of factories owned by the state and the materialization of highly desired structural changes was out of the question under the above circumstances.

The management of individual plants systematically introduced various rationalization measures to reduce the usage of energy, coal, coke and other resources. As will be shown later, the effectiveness of such activities differed from factory to factory. Due to the fact that between 1990 and 2004 there were only a few seasons when sugar producers in Poland generated fair profits (due to flawed regulation of the sugar market and low prices of sugar), state-owned plants lacked the capital for the implementation of large investment projects. Therefore, operational restructuring carried out at this group of factories predominantly had the form of small technological enhancements, essential maintenance and the streamlining of production processes without considerable investment in modern machinery and equipment. This does not mean, however, that investment in new technology did not take place at all. The management of individual plants systematically substituted worn-out machinery with new devices and equipped the factories, according to financial capabilities, with new evaporators, diffusers, packing machines, etc.

As far as labor restructuring at individual state-owned sugar factories prior to their incorporation into *KSC* is concerned, reduction in employment occurred naturally at the plants as a result of the gradual automation and computerization of production processes. Neither group lay-offs nor voluntary redundancies took place.

Immediately after the establishment of *KSC* (holding) in August 2002, the company started to develop a strategic plan of action to be implemented systematically in the years 2003-2008. It was completed and accepted by the board of directors of *KSC* in August 2003.[345] The main purpose of the restructuring activities included in the plan is to transform *KSC* into a company able to generate profits and to compete successfully with foreign sugar producers operating in Poland.

One of the major components of the operational restructuring that had been implemented under the framework of the above strategic plan by the season 2004/05 was the cessation of beet processing at seven locations.

By the start of the campaign 2003/04, beet processing had been ceased in *Rejowiec*, *Pruszcz Gdański* and *Szczecin*. In 2004, *KSC* ceased beet processing at another four sugar factories: *Borowiczki*, *Sokołów*, *Żnin* and *Klemensów*. As a result of the developments, beet processing in the campaign 2004/05 took place at 20 out of the 27 sugar factories incorporated into/controlled by *KSC*.

The decision to close the above seven factories was made on the basis of comprehensive economic analyses. Some of the factors taken into account in the analyses include location of the raw material base of individual plants, their processing capacity and state of repair as well as their ability to take over the production quota and raw material base from other plants.

It is important to mention here that at the time of the formation of *KSC*, the sugar factories forming the company were all characterized by excessive capacity and an average campaign length that was much below the theoretical optimum (85-90 days). At the time of its establishment, *KSC* lagged behind foreign sugar producers operating in Poland with regard to this issue. Also, the average daily beet throughput and average sugar production were higher at factories privatized to foreigners than at the plants forming *KSC*. All this translated into higher unit

---

[345] The restructuring plan was developed by *KSC*, the Ministry of State Treasury and the consortium of consulting companies *Warszawska Grupa Konsultingowa Sp. z o. o./Pro-Invest International Sp. z o. o.* (See WGK/Pro-Invest International 2003).

production costs and lower competitiveness. The fact that consolidation of sugar factories was already in progress at all foreign companies constituted an additional, if not the main, stimulus for the launch of such process by *KSC*.

As well as the cessation of beet processing at several locations, operational restructuring implemented by *KSC* between the seasons 2002/03 and 2004/05 included a number of modernizing activities at selected plants. Their main purpose was an increase in the cost efficiency of operations as well as an improvement in the quality of manufactured products. The major investment projects implemented by *KSC* in the financial years 2003/04 and 2004/05 are listed in Table 48.

Table 48. Major investment projects at KSC factories, financial years 2003/04 and 2004/05

Brześć Kujawski: modernization of strike pans, installation of several pieces of machinery from other factories
Dobrzelin: installation of Diastar filter for defecation mud; modernization of magma III centrifuge (ACW 1350); installation of modernized slicing machines (TSM 2000) used since 2003 in Krasnystaw; modernization of strike pans and centrifuge station; modernization of sugar heating
Kluczewo: modernization of energy and heat economy (installation of two boilers (OR 32/80) and two turbo-genertors (AEG KANIS G-40))
Krasnystaw: modernization of the slicing station (purchase and installation of a new slicing machine (Putsch TSM 2200-22-600), transfer of a slicing machine (Putsch 2200-22-600) from the sugar factory in *Łapy*, redevelopment of sugarbeet bunker), modernization of strike pans [magma II and magma III] (exchange of heating chamber and equipment with mixers); introduction of dry reloading of beets + installation of new machinery for washing beets
Kruszwica: two new slicing machines (TSM 2200); modernization of strike pans, cascade magma III boiling; installation of seed magma I and III; installation of the digital system ABB Freelance 2000 (slicing machines, sugar end); new equipment for the measurement of sugar content in beet supplies
Lublin: standard syrup, modernization of fan coolers; new equipment for the measurement of sugar content in beet supplies
Łapy: modernization of the slicing station (purchase and installation of a new slicing machine (Maguin 200-600-60), transfer of a slicing machine (Maguin 2000-600-60) from the sugar factory in *Sokołów*, redevelopment of sugarbeet bunker; modernization of strike pans, installation of the digital system ABB Freelance 2000 (strike pans (magma II and III))
Nakło: modernization of sugarbeet slicing station (use of TSM 1600 slicing machines from Żnin and Dobrzelin); modernization of strike pans; installation of the digital system ABB Freelance 2000 (strike pans (magma I)); new equipment for the measurement of sugar content in beet supplies
Nowy Staw: expansion of thick juice filtration station and remelt tank; new equipment for the measurement of sugar content in beet supplies
Werbkowice: modernization of the slicing station (purchase and installation of a slicing machine (Putsch TSM 2200-22-600), redevelopment of sugarbeet bunker), modernization of strike pans station (magma I) (exchange of chambers and equipment with mixers, modernization of the sugar house), purchase and installation of a packing machine (ICA, 1 kg), modernization of coupling station (30/6 kV); introduction of dry reloading of beets + installation of new machinery for washing beets; new fluidized-bed type sugar dryer and sugar cooling machine

Source: KSC 2005, p. 14; KSC 2006, pp. 14-15.

The installation of *Egeria*, a management information system provided by *ComArch S.A.*, began at *KSC* in July 2003. The system facilitates communication and the transfer of data between the headquarters of *KSC* and its subsidiaries. The modules of *Egeria* installed at *KSC* support day-to-day activities and management processes in the fields of finance and accounting, controlling, materials management and sales and logistics.

As well as *Egeria*, *KSC* installed "*Plantacja SQL*" at around the same time. "*Plantacja SQL*" is a system that supports the coordination of the purchase and delivery of sugarbeets to individual factories in the national sugar corporation. The software also helps to calculate payments provided to beet growers.

At the end of 2003, the institution of the HACCP system was launched at all *KSC* plants where the system had not yet been instituted. In 2003 and 2004, HACCP was instituted at the following subsidiaries of *KSC*:

- *Krasnystaw* (HACCP certification granted in 2003 by TÜV Rheinland)
- *Werbkowice* (HACCP certification granted in 2003 by ISO QAR)
- *Lublin* (HACCP certification granted in 2003 by RW TÜV Essen)
- *Częstocice* (HACCP certification granted in 2003 by ISO QAR)

By the end of December 2005, the HACCP system had been instituted at (and the HACCP certification had been granted to) ten KSC factories: the above four as well as *Kruszwica*, *Kluczewo*, *Nowy Staw*, *Nakło*, *Łapy* and *Malbork* (KSC 2006, p. 15).

As well as the HACCP certificate, the sugar factory in *Lublin* was granted the ISO 9001:2001 certification (RW TÜV Essen) in 2003. By the end of December 2005, ISO 9001:2001 had been instituted at five *KSC* plants: *Kluczewo*, *Krasnystaw*, *Kruszwica*, *Lublin* and *Łapy* (ibid., p. 15).

In the coming years, *KSC* intends to continue the regional consolidation of sugar factories and to invest in the technological modernization of selected plants as well as in the improvement of the quality of manufactured products. In the medium to long term, the company strives to concentrate all sugar production in about eight to eleven factories that would be able to manufacture between 70,000 and 100,000 t of sugar.[346] The management of *KSC* has recently announced that by the campaign 2006/07, sugarbeet processing will have to be ceased at seven factories controlled by the corporation (*Janikowo* and *Opole* in 2005 and *Tuczno*, *Częstocice*, *Mała Wieś*, *Ostrowy* and *Wożuczyn* in 2006).

In spite of the cessation of beet processing at the above locations, a certain number of the factories' staff will still work at *KSC*. A number of workers are to be hired by plants where beet processing will be continued. Moreover, a limited number of workers will still have the possibility of working at closed sugar factories. Sugar produced and/or beets processed elsewhere will be stored at some of them, and other activities will take place. Factory workers who decide to leave their jobs on their own initiative will be provided with redundancy payments specified in a social package that was negotiated in 2003.

---

[346] *KSC* intends to invest a total of about PLN 200 million in the financial years 2004/2005 and 2005/2006.

Cessation of beet processing at selected factories is accompanied by the take-over of the production quotas and the raw material bases of the factories by other plants in *KSC*. This means that the closure of a given sugar factory does not have any serious consequences for the beet growers who deliver raw material to the plant. They continue to supply *KSC* with sugarbeets, delivering them to the plant that takes over the raw material base of the closed factory.

Let us now turn to the examination of the effects of operational restructuring implemented in the 1990-2004 time period at state-owned sugar factories in Poland.

Selected campaign data for 18 sugar factories owned/controlled by *KSC* is presented in Tables 49 and 50, out of the 20 plants where beet processing took place in the season 2004/05. Data from four processing campaigns was chosen to show the developments at individual plants between 1990 and 2004.

The main reason for the choice of the season 1995/96 as one of the seasons for which campaign results are presented here is that it is the time at which a comprehensive regulatory framework for the sugar sector in Poland was introduced. Previously, sugar producers in the country operated under a completely different regulatory environment (without production quotas or a minimal selling price for sugar, etc.). Another point in time for which selected campaign data for the 18 factories is presented is the season 2002/03. The rationale behind the choice of this season is obvious - it is the season when *KSC* (holding structure) was formed.

Data presented in Tables 49 and 50 shows that a number of positive developments took place at factories that presently form *KSC* between 1990 and 2004.

In the season 2002/03, the average sugar yield (in % of raw sugar value on beet) and the average extraction efficiency (recovery of sugar) at the factories were much higher than in 1990 and 1995. Between the campaigns 2002/03 and 2004/05, a further improvement in sugar yields and extraction efficiency took place at the factories forming *KSC*. Their performance in this field is currently similar to that achieved by other sugar producers operating in Poland. Nevertheless, it is also clearly visible that further structural changes within *KSC* are desperately needed. The average size (processing capacity) of the factories forming the company is still very small and the average campaign length at the plants (66 days in the season 2004/05 at the 18 factories included in Table 50) is far from the theoretical optimum. This is brought about by the fact that, given the total production quota allocated to *KSC*, the joint processing capacity of the factories in the company is too large to be fully utilized. In other words, *KSC* does not need 20 beet-processing plants to produce nearly 800,000 t of sugar.

It is important to mention at this point that the average campaign length of 87 days recorded in the sugar industry in Poland in the season 2004/05 has been achieved due to the group of factories privatized to foreign investors. Until the start of the campaign 2004/05, foreign sugar corporations operating in Poland consolidated 49 sugar factories taken over in the country into only 23 more scale-efficient plants. The campaign 2004/05 at the factories lasted on average 86-100 days.

Table 49. Selected campaign data, state-owned sugar factories, 1990/91 and 1995/96

	CAMPAIGN 1990/91					CAMPAIGN 1995/96				
	Campaign length (in days)	Average daily beet throughput (in tonnes)	White sugar production (in tonnes)	Sugar yield (in % of raw sugar value on beet)	Recovery of sugar (in%)	Campaign length (in days)	Average daily beet throughput (in tonnes)	White sugar production (in tonnes)	Sugar yield (in % of raw sugar value on beet)	Recovery of sugar (in%)
Brześć Kujawski	95	2,360	27,845	12.76	79.7	68	2,675	19,883	11.39	79.7
Częstocice	82	1,849	17,294	11.64	76.7	64	2,084	16,332	12.64	83.0
Dobrzelin	90	2,452	24,408	11.71	78.3	69	2,905	20,079	10.73	78.2
Gryfice	88	1,726	19,771	13.26	79.9	68	1,985	17,741	13.51	82.5
Janikowo	104	2,218	30,173	13.50	79.3	76	2,537	22,569	12.17	79.8
Kluczewo	102	2,801	35,081	12.66	79.0	54	3,975	25,554	12.25	79.9
Krasnystaw	93	5,520	62,187	12.61	80.2	64	6,405	48,524	12.47	80.6
Kruszwica	117	2,486	37,148	13.20	79.4	64	3,208	20,589	11.44	80.4
Leśmierz	107	1,975	23,811	11.72	76.7	68	2,567	19,966	11.88	83.4
Lublin	92	4,380	49,668	12.72	80.4	59	4,675	32,794	12.44	81.0
Łapy	76	4,479	38,437	11.84	77.3	41	4,806	21,896	11.65	80.4
Mała Wieś	74	2,225	18,688	11.90	78.6	70	2,309	16,763	10.86	77.9
Nowy Staw	117	1,555	21,568	12.16	76.9	74	2,151	20,157	13.02	83.2
Opole Lubelskie	95	1,750	20,302	12.60	80.4	66	1,920	14,661	12.02	80.5
Ostrowy	96	2,110	24,177	12.42	80.0	104	2,406	21,972	11.42	79.8
Tuczno	111	2,301	32,540	12.92	79.2	75	2,764	24,513	12.38	82.6
Werbkowice	91	4,182	49,401	13.05	80.5	78	4,691	44,163	12.33	78.9
Wożuczyn	95	2,728	33,195	13.07	81.6	72	3,151	28,228	12.62	81.2
Total			565,694					436,384		
Average	**96**	**2,728**	**31,427**	**12.54**	**79.1**	**69**	**3,179**	**24,244**	**12.07**	**80.7**

Source: IPC, STC (Several Issues); KSC 2005b.

In this situation, it is obvious that as long as *KSC* does not address the structural distortions which it currently faces, it will be extremely difficult for the company to keep up with other sugar companies operating in Poland.

As far as the use of major resources in the production of sugar is concerned, considerable cost savings were achieved in the 1990-2004 time period at the state-owned factories that currently form the *KSC*.

Between 1990 and 2002, total energy consumption per one tonne of manufactured sugar was reduced at this group of factories, on average, by 35% (from 4393 kWh to 2834 kWh). Between the seasons 2002/03 and 2004/05, the average energy consumption at the factories decreased by another 7% (to 2638 kWh/t of sugar). In sum, the total energy consumption at 18 out of 20 factories that currently form *KSC* was in the campaign 2004/05, on average, 40% lower than in the campaign 1990/91 (See Tables 51 and 52). At first, this seems to be a very good result.

Table 50. Selected campaign data, state-owned sugar factories, 2002/03 and 2004/05

	CAMPAIGN 2002/03					CAMPAIGN 2004/05				
	Campaign length (in days)	Average daily beet throughput (in tonnes)	White sugar production (in tonnes)	Sugar yield (in % of raw sugar value on beet)	Recovery of sugar (in%)	Campaign length (in days)	Average daily beet throughput (in tonnes)	White sugar production (in tonnes)	Sugar yield (in % of raw sugar value on beet)	Recovery of sugar (in%)
Brześć Kujawski	63	3,888	31,859	13.71	87.9	68	3,946	40,676	15.76	89.2
Częstocice	64 (a)	2,567	24,028	14.52	88.6	56	2,659	23,690	16.55	89.8
Dobrzelin	53	3,432	23,974	13.93	87.4	66	3,282	33,198	15.81	87.7
Gryfice	59	2,631	23,506	15.15	89.4	78	2,544	30,473	15.76	89.9
Janikowo	76	2,809	30,708	14.72	88.5	75	2,863	32,387	15.59	89.5
Kluczewo	58	5,004	42,663	15.20	90.1	75	5,241	60,724	15.84	90.3
Krasnystaw	77	6,614	65,789	13.51	85.0	60	7,084	65,933	16.08	90.4
Kruszwica	73	3,520	36,249	14.39	88.8	71	3,944	42,911	15.69	89.3
Leśmierz	54	3,112	22,812	14.18	87.4	57	3,209	28,147	16.08	88.5
Lublin	53	6,148	46,929	15.00	90.2	71	6,163	70,833	16.80	90.6
Łapy	50	5,257	37,442	14.72	90.1	64	5,635	52,687	14.75	88.9
Mała Wieś	64	2,476	21,024	14.10	87.7	73	2,592	29,584	16.09	89.3
Nowy Staw	64	2,654	24,562	14.90	88.5	76	2,811	30,954	14.79	87.9
Opole Lubelskie	65	1,964	18,678	15.15	90.0	52	2,019	17,163	16.93	90.7
Ostrowy	58	3,045	23,688	14.25	88.7	60	3,255	29,455	16.20	89.6
Tuczno	78	2,681	30,873	15.05	88.9	73	3,244	36,181	15.76	89.2
Werbkowice	58 (a)	5,417	46,589	14.80	89.6	64	6,036	59,529	16.06	90.2
Wożuczyn	54	3,405	26,016	14.17	88.0	58	3,416	30,445	15.97	89.8
Total			577,389					714,970		
Average	**62**	**3,701**	**32,077**	**14.53**	**88.6**	**66**	**3,886**	**39,721**	**15.92**	**89.5**

a) Days of beet slicing.

Source: IPC, STC (Several Issues); KSC 2005b.

Nonetheless, if one compares energy consumption at state-owned and privately-owned factories in the campaign 2004/05, it becomes clear that the former lag far behind the latter. The lowest energy consumption in the campaign 2004/05 was recorded at the factories of *Pfeifer & Langen Polska*. It amounted on average to only 1629 kWh/t of sugar. The average energy consumption at other foreign sugar companies operating in Poland was slightly higher but in all cases it was much lower than at the factories that form *KSC*. This means that apart from the need for further structural changes within the national sugar corporation, a lot remains to be done with regard to the energy systems of individual factories since energy consumption has a significant impact on total sugar production costs and, therefore, on the competitiveness of sugar producers. As can be seen in Table 52, total energy consumption at a number of factories that form *KSC* is close to or higher than 3000 kWh/t of sugar.

Table 51. Use of major resources, state-owned sugar factories, 1990/91 and 1995/96

	CAMPAIGN 1990/91						CAMPAIGN 1995/96					
	Total energy consumption (kWh/t of sugar)	Electric energy consumption (kWh/t of beet)	Use of coal (in % on beet)	Use of coke (in% on beet)	Use of limestone (in % on beet)	Use of fresh water (in % on beet)	Total energy consumption (kWh/t of sugar)	Electric energy consumption (kWh/t of beet)	Use of coal (in % on beet)	Use of coke (in% on beet)	Use of limestone (in % on beet)	Use of fresh water (in % on beet)
Brześć Kujawski	4222	27.5	6.28	0.55	5.16	155	3792	27.3	4.97	0.52	3.55	5
Częstocice	5207	30.5	7.07	0.52	5.94	n.a.	4491	28.0	6.63	0.55	5.81	75
Dobrzelin	5303	23.4	7.34	0.61	6.02	105	3786	21.2	4.73	0.41	5.57	72
Gryfice	3754	25.6	5.80	0.45	5.86	423	3474	23.2	5.48	0.56	6.35	276
Janikowo	4649	25.2	7.40	0.50	5.77	n.a.	4354	30.9	6.13	0.37	5.37	147
Kluczewo	4996	30.0	7.40	0.51	6.42	484	3182	24.3	4.49	0.39	5.21	47
Krasnystaw	3656	27.1	5.33	0.58	6.74	110	3132	25.1	4.49	0.39	4.98	109
Kruszwica	5817	27.0	9.10	0.70	7.25	142	4563	27.1	6.08	0.42	5.02	58
Leśmierz	4621	32.8	6.25	0.58	7.07	n.a.	4030	24.5	5.58	0.33	4.38	85
Lublin	2644	21.2	3.87	0.56	5.52	116	2791	20.7	4.01	0.32	4.74	63
Łapy	3648	35.5	4.87	0.64	6.80	111	3968	34.1	5.26	0.64	7.61	46
Mała Wieś	5427	27.1	7.60	0.71	6.83	241	3785	18.7	4.82	0.46	4.98	93
Nowy Staw	4387	28.7	6.20	0.51	5.58	194	3358	26.9	5.04	0.40	5.39	34
Opole Lubelskie	4142	27.7	6.07	0.55	6.63	110	n.a.	25.7	n.a.	0.51	5.69	43
Ostrowy	4631	25.7	6.75	0.45	6.01	171	3694	27.0	4.85	0.43	4.62	17
Tuczno	3923	21.7	5.96	0.54	6.32	223	4430	28.2	6.39	0.49	4.95	80
Werbkowice	4114	34.6	6.17	0.65	5.97	124	3345	27.4	4.73	0.44	4.72	169
Wożuczyn	3927	24.8	6.00	0.50	5.60	149	3441	28.8	4.98	0.34	3.98	68
Average	**4393**	**27.6**	**6.41**	**0.56**	**6.19**	**191**	**3742**	**26.0**	**5.22**	**0.44**	**5.16**	**83**

Source: IPC, STC (Several Issues); KSC 2005b; calculations by the author.

A considerable reduction in energy consumption at state-owned sugar factories between 1990 and 2004 was accompanied by an appreciable drop in the use of coal (-25%) and coke (-41%) in % on beet. The use of limestone and fresh water at this group of factories decreased at the same time by 34% and 88%, respectively. The only resource of which average consumption at state-owned plants increased, after their incorporation into *KSC*, is coal. In the campaign 2004/05, its average use (in % on beet) at the factories was 22% higher than in the campaign 2002/03.

Table 52. Use of major resources, state-owned sugar factories, 2002/03 and 2004/05

	CAMPAIGN 2002/03						CAMPAIGN 2004/05					
	Total energy consumption (kWh/t of sugar)	Electric energy consumption (kWh/t of beet)	Use of coal (in % on beet)	Use of coke (in% on beet)	Use of limestone (in % on beet)	Use of fresh water (in % on beet)	Total energy consumption (kWh/t of sugar)	Electric energy consumption (kWh/t of beet)	Use of coal (in % on beet)	Use of coke (in% on beet)	Use of limestone (in % on beet)	Use of fresh water (in % on beet)
Brześć Kujawski	2828	23.2	3.71	0.34	4.12	2	2577	24.3	4.69	0.30	3.59	1
Częstocice	3051	25.0	4.37	n.a.	n.a.	14	2639	26.5	5.04	0.42	4.94	15
Dobrzelin	2293	26.9	3.14	0.39	4.23	27	2321	29.1	4.15	0.36	4.09	37
Gryfice	3136	26.0	4.93	0.28	4.88	64	3288	27.4	6.03	0.34	4.27	61
Janikowo	3219	29.9	5.33	0.37	5.63	119	2867	28.5	5.14	0.45	4.57	32
Kluczewo	2064	29.0	2.69	0.28	4.80	n.a.	2139	26.2	3.84	0.24	3.26	2
Krasnystaw	2563	30.7	2.93	0.38	4.86	74	2468	31.3	4.49	0.31	3.92	46
Kruszwica	3724	28.7	4.65	0.44	5.47	49	2752	25.5	4.99	0.37	4.46	41
Leśmierz	2492	24.7	2.99	0.34	4.45	6	2280	23.1	4.22	0.37	4.31	11
Lublin	2468	22.9	3.60	0.34	4.61	40	2349	25.0	4.54	0.30	4.78	28
Łapy	n.a.	n.a.	n.a.	0.44	5.11	34	3065	27.9	5.21	0.36	4.62	30
Mała Wieś	2761	27.0	3.84	0.30	4.18	5	2777	26.8	5.16	0.31	4.12	n.a.
Nowy Staw	2845	32.5	4.14	0.38	4.47	11	3080	28.2	5.25	0.30	3.99	5
Opole Lubelskie	3172	30.8	4.32	0.29	4.29	37	2732	27.1	5.35	0.29	3.66	32
Ostrowy	2430	24.5	3.64	0.30	3.92	3	2216	24.4	4.11	0.28	3.68	6
Tuczno	3299	33.2	4.82	0.48	6.06	3	2677	27.0	4.85	0.29	3.67	8
Werbkowice	2628	27.3	3.19	n.a.	n.a.	52	2480	23.8	4.60	0.35	3.84	33
Wożuczyn	3203	27.7	4.79	0.32	4.72	29	2786	28.9	5.11	0.29	3.85	15
Average	**2834**	**27.6**	**3.95**	**0.35**	**4.74**	**33**	**2638**	**26.7**	**4.82**	**0.33**	**4.09**	**24**

Source: IPC, STC (Several Issues); KSC 2005b; Own calculations.

As previously mentioned, until the formation of *KSC*, reduction in employment at state-owned sugar factories in Poland occurred naturally, mainly as a result of technological modernization of individual plants. As of September 30, 2002, the total number of regular workers at factories incorporated into/controlled by *KSC* amounted to 6,853 (253 per factory). The restructuring program implemented by *KSC* since the establishment of the company includes large-scale labor restructuring. Due to the cessation of beet processing at selected factories, the employment level at *KSC* was reduced considerably. The main tools of labor restructuring used by *KSC* were voluntary redundancy programs and group lay-offs. Labor restructuring was also carried out by *KSC* at the remaining factories in order to optimize the employment level at the plants. Changes in employment in the time period September 30, 2002-January 1, 2004 at individual factories incorporated into/controlled by *KSC* are presented in Tables 53 and 54. As can be seen, the number of regular workers employed at the plants was reduced within the above time period by 21% (from 6,853 to 5,343).

Table 53. Employment level at state-owned sugar factories in Poland, September 30, 2002-September 30, 2003

Factory	Number of employees (as of 30.09.2002)	Number of employees (as of 30.09.2003)			
	regular	regular	seasonal	civil contracts	Total
Borowiczki	172	63	0	1	64
Brześć Kujawski	176	173	21	0	194
Częstocice	229	179	5	0	184
Dobrzelin	229	214	8	11	233
Gryfice	176	164	51	0	215
Janikowo	232	200	7	6	213
Klemensów	262	211	0	0	211
Kluczewo	225	181	8	5	194
Krasnystaw	556	499	2	0	501
Kruszwica	214	195	3	0	198
Leśmierz	206	188	6	1	195
Lublin (factory)	495	287	1	6	294
Lublin (bees)		136	0	0	136
Łapy	320	297	4	7	308
Malbork	220	214	388	6	608
Mała Wieś	223	149	0	5	154
Nakło	247	223	0	4	227
Nowy Staw	188	158	191	0	349
Opole	204	181	0	0	181
Ostrowy	211	161	36	1	198
Pruszcz Gdański	191	69	15	0	84
Rejowiec	173	96	0	5	101
Sokołów	238	203	6	8	217
Szczecin	192	177	0	0	177
Tuczno	236	193	23	0	216
Werbkowice	509	315	30	0	345
Wożuczyn	333	239	0	0	239
Żnin	196	183	18	0	201
Total	**6,853**	**5,548**	**823**	**66**	**6,437**

Source: KSC 2003, p. 93; KSC 2004, p. 35.

In 2004, 346 workers in factories owned/controlled by *KSC* accepted voluntary redundancies and left their jobs. It was already the second edition of a program of voluntary redundancies introduced at the national sugar corporation. The first edition, launched on June 10, 2003 and concluded in the end of December 2003, led to a reduction in employment at *KSC* plants of 502 persons (KSC 2004, p. 38). In 2004, group lay-offs took place in *Sokołów* and *Klemensów* after the cessation of beet processing at the local factories. 221 of the laid-off plant workers were provided with redundancy payments negotiated earlier in a social package.[347] The same method of labor restructuring was used by *KSC* with regard to the employees of the sugar factory in *Żnin* where beet processing also ceased. Employment contracts with 41 employees of *Żnin* were terminated by mutual agreement.

Table 54. Employment level at state-owned sugar factories in Poland, December 31, 2003-January 1, 2004

Factory	Number of employees (as of 31.12.2003)				Number of employees (as of 1.01.2004)			
	regular	seasonal	civil contracts	Total	regular	seasonal	civil contracts	Total
Borowiczki	66	1	0	67	66	0	0	66
Brześć Kuj.	166	3	0	169	166	2	0	168
Częstocice	175	0	0	175	174	0	0	174
Dobrzelin	211	0	2	213	211	0	2	213
Gryfice	162	1	2	165	162	1	2	165
Janikowo	186	2	1	189	186	0	0	186
Klemensów	206	0	0	206	204	0	0	204
Kluczewo	175	4	5	184	174	4	5	183
Krasnystaw	484	217	0	701	478	210	0	688
Kruszwica	193	66	0	259	192	7	0	199
Leśmierz	184	0	6	190	184	0	5	189
Lublin (factory)	231	25	2	258	225	0	2	227
Lublin (bees)	187	0	0	187	186	0	0	186
Łapy	293	0	2	295	293	0	2	295
Malbork	211	46	2	259	210	12	1	223
Mała Wieś	145	0	0	145	145	0	0	145
Nakło	204	1	0	205	203	0	0	203
Nowy Staw	155	58	1	214	154	36	1	191
Opole	173	0	0	173	170	0	0	170
Ostrowy	158	0	2	160	158	0	0	158
Pruszcz Gd.	63	0	0	63	60	0	0	60
Rejowiec	86	2	1	89	84	0	1	85
Sokołów	199	1	2	202	197	1	2	200
Szczecin	177	0	0	177	175	0	0	175
Tuczno	179	2	0	181	179	1	0	180
Werbkowice	307	285	0	592	302	24	0	326
Wożuczyn	231	196	0	427	230	146	0	376
Żnin	179	83	0	262	175	68	0	243
Total	**5,386**	**993**	**28**	**6,407**	**5,343**	**512**	**23**	**5,878**

Source: KSC 2003, p. 93; KSC 2004, p. 35.

[347] On December 30, 2003, the employees of *KSC* plants were provided with an employment guarantee of 36 months (starting on September 27, 2003). This guarantee embraces all workers who, on September 27, 2003 were employed at individual factories incorporated into *KSC* on the basis of open-ended contracts and had been working in the sugar industry for a period of at least three years within the last five years. In the event of termination of employment contracts by the employer before the end of the guaranteed employment period, the employer is obliged to provide the workers with redundancy payments on conditions specified in the social package provided to the workers (KSC 2004, p. 39).

As of September 30, 2004, 4,123 regular workers were employed at 20 working sugar factories owned/controlled by *KSC* (206 workers per sugar factory). The average number of campaign workers employed at the 20 plants during the campaign 2004/05 amounted to about 4,600 (230 per factory).[348] It means that the overall employment at the factories totaled about 8,723 people (436 per factory). This is a lot, not only by European standards but also if one looks at the sugar industry in Poland as a whole.

As was shown in other case studies that form the empirical part of the present research, the average employment level at factories owned by sugar companies competing with *KSC* in the Polish market is considerably lower than at the national sugar corporation. Only at factories owned/controlled by *BSO Polska* was the average employment level during the campaign 2004/05 similar to that recorded at *KSC* plants. 413 workers per factory were employed at BSO plants in Poland in the campaign 2004/05. Nevertheless, the average number of regular workers employed at the plants (152) was much lower than at *KSC* factories.

It must be pointed out, however, that not all *KSC* plants are seriously overstaffed. In *Kluczewo*, one of the largest sugar factories (in terms of total sugar production) forming *KSC*, regular staff in the campaign 2004/05 amounted to 175 workers. The campaign workforce totaled 160 people (335 in total). This is not optimal but acceptable. As of January 1, 2004, the level of overmanning among *KSC* plants was highest in *Krasnystaw*, *Werbkowice*, *Łapy* and *Wożuczyn* (See Table 54).

In the campaign 2004/05, total sugar production at factories owned/controlled by *KSC* amounted to 800,271 t (Rybski 2005, p. 48). This means that the average labor productivity within the company amounted to 92 t of sugar per worker. If one only takes into account regular staff, it emerges that the average labor productivity at *KSC* plants in the campaign 2004/05 amounted to 194 t per employee. In both cases it is a much poorer performance than that recorded at other sugar companies operating in Poland. It can be improved through further amalgamation of sugar factories and an increase in the automation level of production processes at strategic locations.

Labor restructuring at *KSC* has been accompanied by restructuring of the company's fixed assets. This has taken, *inter alia*, the form of a sale/rent of unnecessary real estate (buildings, machinery) to external investors (who 'take over', at the same time, a number of factory workers) as well as the formation of employee partnerships which will use these assets.[349]

Selected real estate has been/is to be transformed into sugar storehouses and/or warehouses. Furthermore, the restructuring of fixed assets within the *KSC* includes

[348] Information provided by the press spokesman of *KSC*.

[349] 134 real estates were sold by KSC in the financial year 2004/05 for PLN 7,475,026 (in total). In the same financial year, unnecessary machinery was sold by the company for the total amount of PLN 3,409,470 (KSC 2006, p. 16).

the relocation of certain assets from factories destined for closure to plants remaining in operation. A proportion of fixed assets, such as worn-out machinery and old buildings, are being scrapped and/or pulled down.

Table 55. Quality of sugar produced at state-owned factories in Poland, campaign 2004/05

	CAMPAIGN 2004/05									
	Color in solution (ICUMSA units)	Color type	Ash content (in %)	Non-soluble substances	Points for color in solution	Points for color type	Points for ash content	Total number of points	EU category	Amount of sugar in a given category (in t)
Brześć Kujawski	19.56	1.23	0.012	21.00	2.63	2.46	6.73	11.82	2	40,676
Częstocice	23.12	1.30	0.015	16.18	3.08	2.60	8.33	14.01	2	23,480
Częstocice	63.70	4.00	0.029	57.80	8.49	8.00	16.10	32.59	3	160
Częstocice								0	4	50
Dobrzelin	28.80	1.60	0.014	25.30	3.84	3.20	7.78	14.82	2	33,198
Gryfice	25.21	2.13	0.011	14.60	3.36	4.26	6.11	13.73	2	30,473
Janikowo	28.30	1.80	0.009	14.80	3.77	3.60	5.00	12.37	2	32,387
Kluczewo	19.10	0.97	0.007	10.40	2.55	1.94	3.61	8.10	2	60,724
Krasnystaw	16.58	0.16	0.005	4.97	2.21	0.32	2.49	5.02	1	9,431
Krasnystaw	28.16	0.98	0.012	8.84	3.75	1.95	6.67	12.37	2	56,502
Kruszwica	21.48	1.90	0.014	53.00	2.90	3.80	7.80	14.50	2	42,830
Kruszwica		6.00				12.00		12.00	3	81
Leśmierz	25.40	1.87	0.016	25.90	3.39	3.74	8.33	15.46	2	28,147
Lublin	12.70	0.53	0.008	5.70	1.69	1.06	4.56	7.31	1	70,833
Łapy	27.07	1.40	0.012	12.33	3.61	2.74	6.46	12.81	2	52,687
Mała Wieś	24.97	1.28	0.012		3.57	2.56	6.67	12.80	2	29,584
Nowy Staw	12.36	0.39	0.009	9.37	1.65	0.78	5.00	7.43	1	19,444
Nowy Staw	20.50	1.10	0.010	10.39	2.73	2.20	5.56	10.49	2	11,464
Nowy Staw	77.40	4.36	0.017	38.00	10.32	8.72	9.44	28.48	3	46
Opole Lubelskie	24.90	1.20	0.014	13.32	3.32	2.40	7.61	13.33	2	17,118
Opole Lubelskie	39.20	2.50	0.023		5.23	5.00	12.78	23.01	3	45
Ostrowy	24.70	1.00	0.015	16.21	3.30	1.94	8.34	13.58	2	29,455
Tuczno	25.20	1.19	0.013		3.36	2.38	7.22	12.96	2	36,181
Werbkowice	10.80	0.27	0.002	3.70	1.44	0.54	1.16	3.14	1	9,425
Werbkowice	17.88	0.62	0.007	7.50	2.38	1.24	3.88	7.50	1	40,276
Werbkowice	22.50	1.00	0.007	7.50	3.00	2.00	3.88	8.88	2	9,766
Werbkowice									3	62
Wożuczyn	24.98	1.77	0.015	23.60	3.33	3.54	8.33	15.20	2	30,445
Average	**26.58**	**1.64**	**0.012**	**18.20**	**3.56**	**3.27**	**6.79**	**11.85**		

Source: KSC 2005b, p. 9.

As far as the quality of sugar manufactured at factories owned/controlled currently by *KSC* is concerned, all of the plants already produced "white sugar of standard quality" (EU-category II) at the time of the establishment of the national sugar corporation. The sugar factory in *Werbkowice* produced, in the campaign 2002/03, extra white sugar (EU-category I).[350]

Between the seasons 2002/03 and 2004/05, the quality parameters on the basis of which sugar is classified into a given EU category improved at virtually all of the factories incorporated into *KSC*. At the present time, several *KSC* plants manufacture "extra white sugar" but "white sugar of standard quality" makes up 80% of the total sugar production within *KSC* (See Table 55).

As regards the assortment of products offered by the sugar factories that currently form *KSC*, it consisted, throughout most of the 1990s, of white sugar packed in 50kg and 1kg bags. In the season 2004/05, potential and existing customers of *KSC* were offered white sugar in 50kg, 30kg, 25kg, 5kg and 1kg bags as well as in sachets (5g). Other products currently in the product range of *KSC* include powdered sugar in various size bags as well as in bulk, lump sugar and refined sugar. Industrial buyers are offered sugar in bulk and in big bags (1000kg). All these products are marketed under the brand name *Polski Cukier* (Polish Sugar). As well as its core activity, i.e. production and sale of sugar, *KSC* also sells molasses, beet pulp and defecation lime.

15.5.2 Organizational Restructuring

As we learned in previous sections of this study, until the formation of the four sugar holdings in Poland and the establishment of *KSC*, state-owned sugar factories in the country functioned, since 1990, as independent economic units (owned by the state). Throughout the second half of the 1990s, these plants were systematically transformed into joint-stock companies. Until then, they were run by management boards consisting of a chief director and three departmental deputies (responsible for raw material management, technical maintenance and trade). Below this level, there were a number of functional managers at every factory. After the transformation of individual factories into joint-stock companies, the chief directors of the plants became chairmen of the board of directors and the departmental deputies became members of the boards. When the four sugar holdings were established in Poland, the number of persons sitting on the boards of directors of individual plants was reduced to two in order to facilitate decision making. The work of the management boards/boards of directors of individual plants was supervised by supervisory boards consisting, until the establishment of the four sugar holdings, of seven persons. From then on, the number of those sitting on the boards was reduced to five. The five-person supervisory boards were composed of two representatives of the State Treasury, one representative of a given sugar holding, one representative of the employees

[350] See IPC 2003, pp. 52-54.

of the given factory and one representative of the beet growers. In this situation, the State Treasury had a majority vote since the sugar holdings were completely owned by the state. At the top of the organizational structure of individual factories was the General Assembly of Shareholders.

During the time when individual state-owned sugar factories functioned as independent economic units, their management systematically introduced changes to the internal organizational structure in order to cut costs and streamline day-to-day operations. These sometimes took the form of a reduction in the number of functional managers through the amalgamation of two or more managerial posts. In order to streamline the transfer and storage of information, an increasing number of activities and databases were computerized (e.g. accounting, human resources management, etc.). The pace at which these processes were introduced at individual factories differed from location to location. Regarding the sale and distribution of sugar manufactured at state-owned sugar factories, the management of each plant managed this individually, meaning that each state-owned sugar factory competed for customers with all the other sugar producers in Poland.

After the decision to establish *KSC*, the first stage of the organizational restructuring embracing the state-owned sugar factories in Poland was the merger of three sugar holdings possessing majority stakes in the plants: *Mazowiecko-Kujawska Spółka Cukrowa S.A.*, *Poznańsko-Pomorska Spółka Cukrowa S.A.* and *Lubelsko-Małopolska Spółka Cukrowa S.A.* On August 26, 2002, the Minister of State Treasury, vested with the powers of the General Assembly of *Mazowiecko-Kujawska Spółka Cukrowa S.A.*, passed a resolution to change the name of the holding to *Krajowa Spółka Cukrowa S.A.* and to increase its capital through a contribution of the shares of *Poznańsko-Pomorska Spółka Cukrowa S.A.* and *Lubelsko-Małopolska Spółka Cukrowa S.A.*[351]

Krajowa Spółka Cukrowa S.A. launched its activity on September 13, 2002. On September 30, 2003, the District Court in Toruń made a ruling about the merger of *Krajowa Spółka Cukrowa S.A.*, headquartered in Toruń, and 22 state-owned sugar factories into one sugar corporation. The assets of individual plants as well as all their rights and obligations (including liabilities) were taken over by *Krajowa Spółka Cukrowa S.A.* By May 2005, another four state-owned plants had been incorporated into KSC.[352] At the present time, the company consists of

[351] The factors that decided about the choice of *Mazowiecko-Kujawska Spółka Cukrowa S.A.* as the holding that takes over the other two include, *inter alia*, a relatively good financial and economic condition of sugar factories forming the holding and most favorable geographical location (center of the country).

[352] As we learned in section 13 of the present study, at the time of the establishment of *KSC* three state-owned sugar factories (*Kluczewo*, *Gryfice* and *Pruszcz Gdański*) could not be incorporated into the company since they were the subject of litigation between *Nordzucker AG* and *KSC*. Incorporation of the sugar factory in *Szczecin* into *KSC* had to wait until the transformation of the company into a joint-stock company.

26 factories and the head office in Toruń. The only state-owned sugar factory in Poland that has not been incorporated into *KSC* so far (although it is controlled by the company) is the plant in *Leśmierz*.

The incorporation of individual sugar factories into *KSC* meant that the plants were no longer legal entities. They became subsidiaries of the national sugar corporation, which entailed, among other things, the liquidation of the boards of directors at individual factories. The plants are currently administered by subsidiary directors (in most cases, the former chairmen of the boards of directors that were liquidated).

After the incorporation of individual factories into *KSC*, the powers and the freedom of action of the management of the plants were severely restricted. Its role is limited to the coordination of day-to-day operations and the execution of policies dictated by the board of *KSC*. All strategic decisions concerning individual factories/subsidiaries (major investments, etc.) are made at the *KSC* headquarters. The subsidiaries' directors are entitled to a one-off expenditure of up to PLN 10,000 without the necessity of consulting with the head office of *KSC* in Toruń.

In December 2003, the following six departments were formed at the headquarters of *KSC*: Department of Organization and Management; Department for Production and Technical Matters; Raw Material Department; Restructuring Department; Sales Department; and Financial and Economic Department. The organizational structure of *KSC* is presented Appendix 2.

In January 2004, the sale of sugar manufactured at the subsidiaries of *KSC* was centralized. It is coordinated by the Sales Department of *KSC*. The main rationale behind the introduction of this change was to remove competition between individual subsidiaries of the national sugar corporation. Moreover, it is meant to strengthen the bargaining power of *KSC* and to increase the assortment of products offered.

As a result of the above activities, a noticeable change in the sales structure took place at *KSC* between January 2003 and September 2004. Where wholesalers first constituted the major distribution channel through which sugar manufactured at *KSC* plants was marketed, a gradual shift saw the initiation of direct sales to industrial buyers as well as chains/retail outlets. In September 2004, this form of sales accounted for more than 70% of *KSC*'s total sales, a development consistent with an objective set by *KSC* in its strategic plans, of gradually switching to direct sales (See Figure 144).

Apart from managing the sale of sugar manufactured at individual subsidiaries of *KSC*, the Sales Department of the corporation makes strategic decisions with regard to the pricing policy and the analysis of sale transactions. Moreover, the department negotiates and signs sale contracts with domestic and foreign customers. The implementation of individual transactions is the responsibility of the subsidiaries of *KSC*.

Figure 144. Structure of sales, KSC, January 2003-September 2004

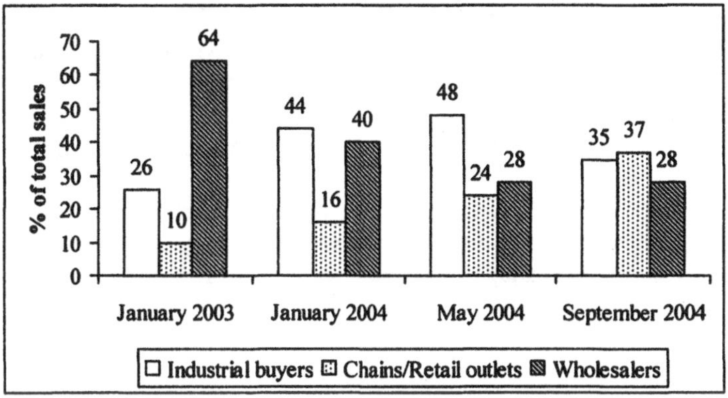

Source: KSC 2005, p. 13.

The centralization of sales management within *KSC* was accompanied by the centralization of logistics management. This refers to the transportation of sales, sugarbeet deliveries and other supplies. The head office of *KSC* negotiates conditions with freight companies commissioned for the delivery of products manufactured at individual *KSC* subsidiaries/factories, as well as the delivery of sugarbeets to the factories. *KSC* is seeking to withdraw gradually from cooperation with a large number of small freight companies and to put the entire logistics into the hands of a few large providers.

A significant organizational change introduced after the transformation of *KSC* from a holding into a sugar company is the change in liquidity management. As long as *KSC* functioned as a holding, individual sugar factories implemented their own financial policies aimed primarily at the maintenance of short-term liquidity. From the point of time when individual factories lost their status as legal entities and became subsidiaries of *KSC*, the responsibility for financing their operations shifted fully onto the shoulders of the national sugar corporation. This gave the management of *KSC* the possibility to plan and control financial flows within the company. It is expected that this will result in considerable cost savings and the stabilization of *KSC*'s liquidity.

As was mentioned earlier, *Egeria*, an integrated management information system was installed at *KSC* shortly after the establishment of the company. The system is expected to facilitate transmission of data and access to information, and to streamline management processes. The installation of *Egeria* was accompanied by the introduction of a uniform budgeting and accounting system as well as a uniform system of property valuation and calculation of production costs at all subsidiaries of *KSC*. This allows the easy comparison of production costs at individual subsidiaries and therefore facilitates adjustment to ever-changing circumstances.

As well as *Egeria*, an information system named *Plantacja SQL* (Plantation SQL) was installed at *KSC* at around the same time. The task of the system is to support raw-material management within the company. This includes, *inter alia*, contracting of beet deliveries, agricultural counseling, statistical analyses, purchase of raw material and managing beet growers' accounts. The institution of *Plantacja SQL* at *KSC* is expected to considerably reduce the costs of raw-material management.

Other management systems installed and/or to be installed in the near future at *KSC* include: a system of electronic circulation and storage of documents, a system of environmental care management and a system of managing electrical energy usage.

15.5.3 Raw Material/Agricultural Management

The raw material base of state-owned sugar factories currently forming *KSC* is the area where the most significant changes took place between 1990 and the formation of four sugar holdings and, subsequently, the national sugar corporation. Individual factories systematically introduced a wide range of activities aimed at the improvement of the productivity and quality of the beet harvest. This included, for instance, the use of better sugarbeet seeds, and better fertilizers and plant protection products. In cooperation with firms producing and/or selling these products, individual factories organized training courses for beet growers on all aspects of beet growing. After 1990, the management of many factories took the opportunity to visit such firms, as well as sugar companies, in Western Europe, e.g. in Germany and the UK. The know-how absorbed during such visits was then put into practice at home. Moreover, the mechanization of field work and schemes for paying farmers based on the sugar content in supplied raw material were gradually introduced. All this resulted in a systematic improvement in the quality of raw material processed at individual factories and an increase in the productivity of the harvest.

As shown in Tables 56 and 57, in the seasons 1990/91 and 1995/96 the average polarization of cossettes at 18 out of 20 factories forming *KSC* was much lower than in the campaign 2002/03, i.e. the point of time of the establishment of *KSC* (holding structure). In the campaign 2003/04, the average polarization of cossettes at the same group of plants exceeded 18%, which constitutes a remarkable achievement. A similar, albeit slightly lower, percentage was achieved at the factories in the campaign 2004/05—the average polarization of cossettes at the plants amounted to 17.79%.

Also, the sugar and sugarbeet yields per hectare improved considerably at the above factories by 2003/04. In the campaigns 2002/03 and 2003/04, the average sugar yield per hectare at the 18 plants was 31% and 56% higher, respectively, than in the campaign 1990/91 (See Tables 56 and 57).

The average sugar yield of 7.5 t per hectare, recorded at *KSC* plants in the season 2003/04 was higher than the industry average (6.9 t). Moreover, it was only slightly lower than the results achieved by sugar producers/beet growers in countries in the former EU-15. The EU-15 2003/04 average amounted to 8.4 t/ha (CEFS online database).

In the campaign 2003/04, the average sugarbeet yield per hectare at the raw material base of the 18 factories listed in Table 57 amounted to 47.2 t and was 22% higher than in the season 1990/91. In the campaign 2002/03, it amounted to 43.2 t and was 12% higher than in the season 1990/91. The industry average in the seasons 2002/03 and 2003/04 amounted to 45.5 t and 40.6 t, respectively (see Figure 28). In the season 2003/04, the sugarbeet yield per hectare in the former EU-15 averaged 54.3 t (CEFS online database).

Table 56. Raw material base of state-owned sugar factories in Poland, 1990/91 and 1995/96

	CAMPAIGN 1990/91						CAMPAIGN 1995/96					
	Polarization of cossettes (in %)	Sugar yield (in tonnes per hectare)	Sugarbeet yield (in tonnes per hectare)	Beet-procurement area (in ha)	Number of beet growers	Average size of beet plantations (in ha)	Polarization of cossettes (in %)	Sugar yield (in tonnes per hectare)	Sugarbeet yield (in tonnes per hectare)	Beet-procurement area (in ha)	Number of beet growers	Average size of beet plantations (in ha)
Brześć Kuj.	16.02	4.7	36.8	6,055	3,887	1.56	14.29	4.1	35.5	5,084	3,168	1.60
Częstocice	15.18	4.7	40.0	4,073	4,808	0.85	15.2	4.2	33.0	3,923	3,914	1.00
Dobrzelin	14.96	4.0	33.7	6,300	6,515	0.97	13.7	4.0	37.1	4,960	4,785	1.04
Gryfice	16.60	4.8	36.3	4,117	1,474	2.79	16.4	4.0	29.6	4,565	998	4.57
Janikowo	17.02	5.1	37.4	6,071	2,820	2.15	15.3	4.0	32.5	5,802	2,562	2.26
Kluczewo	16.02	5.4	43.0	6,582	2,410	2.73	15.3	4.7	38.0	5,660	1,482	0.74
Krasnystaw	15.72	4.9	39.1	12,736	18,484	0.69	15.5	3.9	31.4	12,500	14,743	0.85
Kruszwica	16.63	4.7	35.8	8,080	5,283	1.53	14.2	3.5	30.2	6,025	3,691	1.63
Leśmierz	15.28	4.6	38.9	5,613	5,667	0.99	14.2	4.6	38.7	4,698	3,993	1.18
Lublin	15.82	5.1	40.2	9,827	13,614	0.72	15.4	3.8	30.7	8,672	10,314	0.84
Łapy	15.32	3.9	32.9	8,240	8,983	0.92	14.5	4.0	34.0	4,678	3,881	1.21
Mała Wieś	15.15	4.1	34.6	4,614	4,558	1.01	13.9	3.7	33.6	4,557	4,001	1.14
Nowy Staw	15.82	5.7	46.9	3,964	2,142	1.85	15.6	5.0	38.6	4,080	1,482	2.75
Opole Lub.	15.67	4.8	38.0	4,396	9,533	0.46	14.9	4.1	33.7	3,640	6,128	0.59
Ostrowy	15.53	4.3	34.6	5,927	5,433	1.09	14.3	4.3	37.6	5,350	3,966	1.35
Tuczno	16.31	4.9	38.1	6,882	4,268	1.61	15	3.8	30.8	6,880	3,680	1.87
Werbkowice	16.20	5.7	43.7	8,752	7,737	1.13	15.6	4.7	37.9	9,799	6,294	1.56
Wożuczyn	16.01	5.8	44.5	5,756	5,645	1.02	15.5	4.7	36.9	6,498	4,248	1.53
Total				117,985	113,261					107,371	83,330	
Average	**15.85**	**4.8**	**38.6**	**6,555**	**6,292**	**1.04**	**14.94**	**4.2**	**34.4**	**5,965**	**4,629**	**1.29**

Source: IPC (Several Issues).

Table 57. Raw material base of state-owned sugar factories in Poland, 2002/03 and 2003/04

	CAMPAIGN 2002/03						CAMPAIGN 2003/04					
	Polarization of cossettes (in %)	Sugar yield (in tonnes per hectare)	Sugarbeet yield (in tonnes per hectare)	Beet-procurement area (in ha)	Number of beet growers	Average size of beet plantations (in ha)	Polarization of cossettes (in %)	Sugar yield (in tonnes per hectare)	Sugarbeet yield (in tonnes per hectare)	Beet-procurement area (in ha)	Number of beet growers	Average size of beet plantations (in ha)
Brześć Kuj.	15.60	5.8	42.5	5,547	2,020	2.75	17.30	7.6	47.8	5,382	1,869	2.88
Częstocice	16.39	6.1	41.7	3,967	2,228	1.78	18.44	6.8	41.3	3,466	1,914	1.81
Dobrzelin	15.94	5.2	37.4	4,477	2,439	1.84	17.54	7.1	44.6	4,711	2,326	2.04
Gryfice	16.94	6.7	44.1	3,529	274	12.9	17.74	6.5	41.0	4,715	297	15.88
Janikowo	16.64	6.8	46.2	4,581	1,293	3.54	18.64	7.4	46.9	4,406	1,223	3.60
Kluczewo	16.87	5.8	38.2	7,354	567	13	17.62	6.8	42.8	8,953	619	14.40
Krasnystaw	15.90	5.7	42.4	9,317	4,963	1.88	18.47	6.5	40.5	10,104	4,697	2.15
Kruszwica	16.20	6.8	47.5	5,378	1,127	4.77	17.89	8.7	55.1	4,928	1,083	4.55
Leśmierz	16.23	5.4	37.9	4,277	2,358	1.81	18.05	6.6	40.9	4,277	2,238	1.92
Lublin	16.64	6.7	44.3	7,059	4,266	1.65	18.72	11.0	65.2	6,457	3,556	1.81
Łapy	16.34	5.6	38.3	6,652	2,009	3.31	16.54	7.9	53.5	6,674	1,880	3.55
Mała Wieś	16.11	6.6	46.9	3,195	1,358	2.35	17.78	5.6	34.6	5,300	656	8.08
Nowy Staw	16.84	7.3	49.1	3,376	544	6.21	17.53	8.6	57.9	3,612	537	6.73
Opole Lub.	16.84	7.1	46.6	2,657	1,508	1.76	18.32	7.0	41.4	2,445	1,298	1.88
Ostrowy	16.06	5.2	36.8	4,273	1,652	2.59	18.10	6.9	42.7	4,272	1,616	2.64
Tuczno	16.93	6.9	46.0	4,526	1,018	4.45	18.47	8.6	54.6	4,200	988	4.25
Werbkowice	16.52	7.2	48.3	6,546	2,414	2.71	18.94	8.6	53.2	6,924	2,294	3.02
Wożuczyn	16.11	6.3	44.2	4,170	1,714	2.43	18.80	7.4	46.4	4,102	1,455	2.94
Total				90,881	33,752					94,928	30,546	
Average	**16.39**	**6.3**	**43.2**	**5,049**	**1,875**	**2.69**	**18.05**	**7.5**	**47.2**	**5,274**	**1,697**	**3.11**

Source: IPC (Several Issues).

Apart from a considerable improvement in agricultural yields, significant structural changes took place between 1990 and 2004 at the raw material base of factories currently forming *KSC*. In 1990, the beet-procurement area of the 18 plants included in Tables 56 and 57 was 20% larger than in 2003. The average size of beet plantations forming the beet-procurement area rose at the same time by almost 200% (from 1.04 ha to 3.11 ha). Information about the size of the beet-procurement area of the 18 factories in the campaign 2004/05 is not available. According to information provided in IERiGŻ (12/2005, p. 12), in 2004 the beet-procurement area of all working plants incorporated into/controlled by *KSC* totaled 123,900 ha. The plantations forming this raw material base had an average size of 3.34 ha (ibid., p. 12).

The number of beet growers delivering raw material to the 18 factories listed in Table 56 decreased between the campaigns 1990/91 and 2002/03 by 70% (from 113,261 to 33,752). In the season 2003/04, the number of growers delivering beet to the factories fell by another 9% and amounted to 30,546 growers. The corresponding number for the season 2004/05 is not available. According to information provided in IERiGŻ (ibid., p. 12), in 2004, the total number of beet growers delivering raw material to all working factories incorporated into/controlled by *KSC* amounted to 37,100.

The above structural changes materialized partly naturally, due to a systematic increase in the productivity and quality of the beet harvest, and partly as result of actions taken by sugar factories. Up to the point of time when beet growers in Poland were allocated beet growing and delivery rights (2002), the management of factories currently forming *KSC* made use of various permitted practices to influence desirable structural changes at their raw material base (increase in the average size of beet plantations and reduction in the average distance of the plantations from a given factory). The practices included, *inter alia*, contracting of raw material deliveries only with farmers growing beets on an area exceeding a certain threshold and/or burdening beet growers with the costs of transporting raw material to factories. In this way, individual factories gradually withdrew from cooperation with farmers situated far from beet-processing plants and those with very small beet plantations. Since the allocation of the "beet growing and delivery rights" to beet growers in Poland, the use of the aforementioned procedures by sugar producers is prohibited.

Despite the appreciable positive structural changes that took place between 1990 and 2004 at the entire raw material base of factories forming *KSC*, significant differences exist between individual plants with regard to this issue. As can be seen in Table 57, there are factories where the make-up of the raw material base is more or less optimized (e.g. *Kluczewo*, *Gryfice*) and there also those where the number of beet growers is still enormously high and the average size of beet plantations ludicrously small (e.g. *Krasnystaw, Lublin*). It is not difficult to imagine the scale of the costs of raw material management in *Krasnystaw*, *Lublin*, *Dobrzelin* and a number of other locations.

After the incorporation of individual state-owned plants into *KSC*, a number of significant organizational changes and restructuring measures were introduced with regard to their raw material base. The supply of beet growers with sugarbeet seeds, fertilizers and plant protection products has been centralized. A uniform system of contracting and purchasing raw material supplies as well as managing farmers' accounts was introduced. This includes the gradual introduction at all factories of a scheme for paying farmers individually on the basis of sugar content in the raw material supplied. In 2004, the number of *KSC* factories using such a scheme rose from three to eleven. In the campaign 2005/06, the scheme is to be used at all working *KSC* plants. The above processes are supported by aforementioned management software, *Plantacja SQL*.

Furthermore, a scheme to minimize freight costs has been in operation within *KSC*, seeking to redirect beet deliveries from individual plantations to the closest working sugar factory owned/controlled by *KSC*. This has been accompanied by gradual reduction in the number of regional sugarbeet-purchasing centers. In the seasons 2002/03, 2003/04 and 2004/05, their total number within *KSC* amounted to 162, 106 and 78, respectively (Wróblewski 2005, p. 30; Sypka et al. 2006).

At the same time, the amount of sugarbeets delivered directly to sugar factories increased from 29% in 2002 to 52% in 2004 (Sypka et al. 2006). The process of exchanging "beet growing and delivery rights" between farmers delivering raw material to *KSC* plants has also been used to minimize freight costs.

Since the raw material base of individual *KSC* factories/subsidiaries interpenetrates the raw material base of other sugar companies at a number of locations, *KSC* has sought an exchange of a part of its raw material base with that of other sugar producers. Nevertheless, this requires the fulfillment of two conditions: reaching an agreement with another sugar company and getting the approval of beet growers affected by the transaction. The latter can be a very difficult task and poses the main obstacle to an exchange of the raw material base between sugar producers.

15.5.4 Financial Restructuring

As was already mentioned at several points in the present study, sugar producers in Poland, both state-owned and private, generated losses in most years between 1990 and 2004, due to serious flaws in the regulation of the local sugar market and the resultant low market price of sugar. For this reason, the principal goal of financial restructuring carried out by individual sugar producers within this period was to maintain short-term liquidity. As far as state-owned plants are concerned, their financial surpluses were spent almost entirely on the repayment of debts and/or bank loans. Of course, asset engineering was conducted on a certain scale in order to reduce costs, taking the form of the outsourcing of various activities and the off-loading of non-productive assets.

At the time of the establishment of *KSC*, the financial and economic condition of the vast majority of sugar factories that later became subsidiaries of the national sugar corporation varied between bad and critical, with many of them on the brink of bankruptcy. In the financial year 2002/03, to September 30, 2003, the cumulative net loss of the economic units owned/controlled by *KSC* amounted to PLN 82.8 million. Six out of 27 units generated net profits totaling PLN 3.4 million. The financial results of the remaining 21 units were negative and amounted in total to PLN 86.2 million (See Table 58). The liquidity of most units was very low, which had an adverse effect on the promptness of the repayment of debts and their credit rating with banks. At the end of the financial year 2002/03, the average indebtedness of the 27 economic units listed in Table 58 came to 75% of their net asset value. In five cases, indebtedness exceeded this level. After the incorporation of individual units into *KSC*, responsibility for their debts was shifted onto the national sugar corporation, which made the credit rating of *KSC* at time of its establishment quite poor indeed.

Table 58. Financial results achieved by KSC plants in the financial year 2002/03

Sugar factory	Net loss (in PLN thousands)	Sugar factory	Net profit (in PLN thousands)
Borowiczki	-7078	Cukrownie Toruńskie	1292
Brześć Kujawski	-1734	Dobrzelin	984
Częstocice	-1325	Leśmierz	187
Gryfice	-1531	Nowy Staw	147
Janikowo	-4821	Ostrowy	470
Klemensów	-897	Sokołów	314
Kluczewo	-2925		
Krasnystaw	-8915		
Kruszwica	-13604		
Lublin	-289		
Łapy	-1697		
Malbork	-534		
Mała Wieś	-664		
Nakło	-7394		
Opole	-1823		
Pruszcz Gdański	-1254		
Rejowiec	-8854		
Tuczno	-2938		
Werbkowice	-7683		
Wożuczyn	-5853		
Żnin	-4408		
Sum	**-86220**	**Sum**	**3393**

Source: KSC 2004, p. 9.

Among the 22 sugar factories incorporated into *KSC* on September 30, 2003, only two, *Częstocice* and *Mała Wieś* did not have at that time any credit obligations. The lowest levels of indebtedness were at the following six plants: *Borowiczki* (PLN 1.1 million), *Sokołów* (PLN 1.4 million), *Ostrowy* (PLN 1.5 million), *Nowy Staw* (PLN 1.6 million), *Janikowo* (PLN 2.0 million) and *Klemensów* (PLN 2.3 million). The highest levels were recorded at the following factories: *Krasnystaw* (PLN 47.0 million), *Żnin* (PLN 29.9 million), *Werbkowice* (PLN 24.2 million), *Nakło* (PLN 19.8 million), *Łapy* (PLN 18.6 million) and *Wożuczyn* (PLN 15.2 million).

Financial restructuring was started by *KSC* at individual factories before their incorporation into the company. *KSC* provided some plants with loans which were to be liquidated after their incorporation into the company as a result of the settlement of bilateral financial obligations. As of September 30, 2003 such loans had been provided to the following factories: *Kluczewo* (PLN 15.0 million), *Klemensów* (PLN 13.1 million), *Rejowiec* (PLN 12.4 million), *Opole* (PLN 10.0

million), *Tuczno* (PLN 10.0 million), *Sokołów* (PLN 10.0 million), *Kruszwica* (PLN 8.1 million), *Wożuczyn* (PLN 5.6 million), *Pruszcz Gdański* (PLN 5.5 million) and *Gryfice* (PLN 3.8 million).

After the incorporation of individual factories into *KSC*, the company filed requests to banks to spread out the repayment of the factories' debts over a period of three years. The aggregate value of credit obligations to be repaid by *KSC* during the financial year 2003/04 amounted to PLN 156 million. At the same time, it was quite certain that the generation of an annual surplus by *KSC* units, which would allow for the full repayment of the debts was impossible.

As of September 30, 2003, credit debts of factories incorporated into/controlled by *KSC* had a total value of PLN 217 million. By the end of 2003, 12% of this sum (PLN 26 million) had been repaid.

KSC also inherited other liabilities from factories incorporated into the company. At the end of 2003, *KSC*'s financial obligations resulting from supplies and services amounted to PLN 539 million. About 60% of this sum (PLN 320 million) was made up of financial obligations towards beet growers. They were reduced by about PLN 60 million after the deduction of charges for sugarbeet seeds, plant protection products, etc. The remaining non-credit liabilities were payments for the supplies of various materials, as well as for campaign services. According to information provided in the restructuring plan of *KSC*, the settlement of financial obligations towards beet growers is to be financed to a large extent from credits taken out for the purchase of beets. Other debts are to be repaid gradually with the use of financial resources coming from sugar sales. Moreover, state support in the clearance of debts is anticipated in *KSC*'s restructuring plan.

In the financial years 2003/04 and 2004/05 (October 1-September 30), *KSC* had a turnover of PLN 1.557 billion and 1.769 billion, respectively (KSC Annual Report 2004/05, p. 12). In 2003/04, the company generated a net profit of PLN 52.9 million. The corresponding figure for 2004/05 is PLN 7.4 million (ibid., p. 20). The General Assembly of Shareholders of *KSC* decided to add the entire surpluses generated in 2003/04 and 2004/05 to the reserve capital of the company, which is to be used mainly for the repayment of debts from previous years. It is clear that these funds are insufficient to put the financial situation of *KSC* in order and to finance the restructuring process of the company.

In May 2004, the Polish government decided to transfer 64.6% of the share capital of *Kopex S.A.*, a state-owned company, into *KSC*. In August 2004, the General Assembly of Shareholders of *KSC* increased the share capital of the company by PLN 60 million through a new share issue. These shares were taken over by the State Treasury, which in exchange transferred *Kopex*'s shares into *KSC*. [353] The management of *KSC* declared shortly afterwards that the shares

[353] Prior to the above transaction, the Polish State Treasury owned 75% of the share capital of *Kopex*. The company was established in 1961, and functioned for over 30 years under the name "*Przedsiębiorstwo Budowy Zakładów Górniczych za Granicą - KOPEX*" (Overseas

would be sold in the near future to raise funds needed for further restructuring.[354]

The asset engineering carried out by *KSC* includes the outsourcing of certain activities, the sale of non-productive assets, the sale of minority stakes in several sugar factories privatized to foreign investors, and the transfer to third parties of ownership of buildings and of perpetual usufruct of plots.

15.5.5 Conclusions

The above analyses show that a number of positive developments took place in many areas at the group of state-owned sugar factories in Poland between 1990 and 2002. Probably the greatest progress was achieved with regard to the raw material base of individual plants. The productivity and quality of the beet harvest increased considerably. This was accompanied by desirable structural changes. A noticeable decrease in the number of beet growers and an appreciable increase in the average size of beet plantations was observed. Also the overall production efficiency of state-owned sugar factories improved considerably. The automation and computerization of operations was introduced systematically at individual plants. Shortly after the formation of *KSC*, a comprehensive restructuring plan of the national sugar corporation was developed for the years 2003-08. Restructuring activities implemented under the framework of the plan are similar to those introduced at other sugar companies operating in Poland, i.e. gradual consolidation of sugar factories, and investment in technological modernization, quality control and modern agriculture methods. As a result of these measures, between 2002 and 2004 the overall efficiency in both sugarbeet and sugar production increased at *KSC* factories .

In spite of these positive changes, the restructuring process at the group of state-owned sugar factories is in several aspects much less advanced than at plants privatized to foreign companies. The same can be said about productive efficiency. Whereas three out of four foreign sugar companies operating in Poland have concluded largely the amalgamation of sugar factories taken over in the country and have brought the campaign length at strategic locations to the theoretical

---

Mine Construction Company – KOPEX), with its headquarters in Katowice. In 1994, the company was transformed into a joint-stock company and changed its name for *Kopex S.A.* In 1998, it made its debut on the Warsaw Stock Exchange. *Kopex S.A.* specializes in the export of mining machinery as well as coal, coke and other raw materials, and provides various services for the mining industry (e.g. construction services, execution of industrial projects, modernization and development of mining operations, power plants, and other structures). For more details, see www.kopex.com.pl.

354 After the end of the financial year 2004/05, the process of the sale of *Kopex's* shares by *KSC* to *Zabrzańskie Zakłady Mechaniczne S.A.* (Zabrzańskie Mechanical Works Joint-Stock Company) was started. The investor was chosen by tender.

optimum, a lot remains to be done with regard to this issue within *KSC*. Moreover, the consumption of energy and other resources at factories forming the national sugar corporation is much higher than at privatized plants. Finally, many state-owned plants are seriously overstaffed. All this translates into low competitiveness in relation to foreign sugar companies operating in Poland. By the same token, the continuation of strategic restructuring processes within *KSC* is vital. It seems, however, that this will not be easy. The major obstacle standing in the way of *KSC*'s ambitious restructuring plan is the financial and economic condition of the company. Moreover, the financial results achieved by *KSC* so far, as well as those anticipated in the coming years, have been and will be insufficient for the self-financing of restructuring activities allowing *KSC* to fight off competition from foreign firms. At the same time, there is no doubt that providing *KSC* with state aid (*Kopex's* shares, loans) is not the correct way to maintain the company's competitiveness. And once the EU competition policy rules become binding in Poland, the option of bailing an enterprise out will become much more problematic.

In sum, it can be said that although the restructuring process of *KSC* is in progress and although it is heading in the right direction, for the time being the company has still not fully found its feet.

16 Conclusions

The main goal of the present study was to explore and evaluate how privatization with foreign involvement has influenced the restructuring process of the sugar industry in Poland up to the season 2004/05. Analyses carried out in the empirical part of this study lead to the following general conclusions:

Firstly, foreign investors who took over a number of sugar factories in Poland saved many of them from bankruptcy. Owing to a considerable injection of capital, and financial restructuring, they secured the survival of numerous plants and created conditions for their long-term functioning, thus securing the incomes of thousands of sugarbeet growers.

Secondly, the privatization of (a part of) the Polish sugar industry with foreign participation has contributed greatly to the realization of much needed structural changes in the sector. The consolidation of small and often ill-located plants into more scale-efficient units has taken place mainly among factories privatized to foreigners.

Furthermore, sugar factories selected by individual foreign investors as the strategic locations of the future have been thoroughly modernized. Many of them were utterly transformed in terms of productive efficiency. Operational restructuring carried out by individual investors at selected plants led to a considerable reduction in the use of resources. This, in turn, resulted in an increase in the cost efficiency of sugar production and, by the same token, the competitiveness of individual factories.

The capital strength and know-how of the sugar companies that established operations in Poland allowed a significant reduction in (over)employment in the domestic sugar industry without any major social disturbances. Since reduction in employment was not accompanied by a decrease in sugar production, a noticeable increase in labor productivity has taken place. This development is a proof that individual companies replace workers with new technology to boost productivity and reduce costs. Therefore, the significant drop in employment in the sugar industry in Poland within the last 14 years should be seen, contrary to the residual belief, as a positive event.

The privatization of sugar factories in Poland to foreign sugar corporations was followed by a considerable transfer of other types of know-how, rather than solely that used in labor restructuring. Individual investors pioneered the use of various modern practices in the cultivation, harvest and processing of sugarbeets. They introduced new quality, work safety and management standards as well as numerous innovations in the collection and logistics of beet supplies. This was accompanied by organizational changes streamlining management processes.

In the face of the above facts, a positive answer can be given to all three hypotheses formulated in the beginning of this study. It refers to all four foreign sugar companies operating currently in Poland.

The types of restructuring activities implemented by individual investors in order to increase the overall efficiency of operations are similar, so many common themes emerge in the case studies included in the empirical part of this study. A very important element is that post-privatization restructuring processes at factories taken over by foreign companies have been carried out at a swift pace. Until 2004, this pace was much more rapid than at the group of state-owned plants. In consequence, sugar factories privatized to foreigners systematically gained an ever increasing advantage in a number of fields (structural and organizational changes, campaign length, use of resources, overall efficiency) over factories controlled by the state.

After the formation of a national sugar corporation (*KSC*) from all state-owned factories, a comprehensive restructuring program of the company was started in order to catch up with the competitors. Restructuring activities introduced under the framework of the program are similar to those carried out by foreign sugar producers operating in Poland (consolidation of sugar factories, rationalization measures, investment in quality, technology and agriculture). Nevertheless, the management of the company has had to confront two major obstacles in the implementation of strategic restructuring processes. The capital strength of *KSC* is much less than that of foreign sugar companies. This puts the national corporation at a considerable disadvantage. The state provides the company with financial support (e. g. *Kopex*'s shares) but this is not a good method of maintaining the company's competitiveness. More importantly, the restructuring process of *KSC* is strongly politicized. In this situation, the consolidation of sugar factories meets with strong opposition and is hard to implement within a short period of time. It seems, however, that sooner or later the pressure of competition will enforce far-reaching structural changes within *KSC*.

One of the major general conclusions stemming from this research is that privatization of the Polish sugar industry with foreign participation was necessary for an effective restructuring of the sector and for the development of its competitiveness. The very slow pace of privatization, as well as flawed regulation of the sugar market in Poland, between 1995 and 2002 led to an unnecessary delay in the restructuring of the domestic sugar industry.

Certainly, it would be good to examine at some point of time in the future the restructuring efficiency of individual sugar companies operating in Poland. The implementation of the restructuring program of *KSC* is at an early stage. The same can be said about the restructuring process of a large group of Silesian sugar factories taken over by *Südzucker*. For this reason, a similar research project to the present one, carried out in about five years, would provide an answer to a number of questions that cannot be definitely answered at the present time. Nevertheless, the collection of the necessary data may prove extremely difficult. For some time now, individual sugar companies have been increasingly reluctant to provide detailed information on the campaign results. This is presumably a consequence of the fierce competition between the companies. The results of the 2004/05 campaign at individual working sugar factories in Poland (use of resources, agricultural yields, quality of manufactured sugar) were not published anywhere for the first time in nearly 50 years. Maybe this will change in the future but for the time being, the only way of obtaining such information is to turn directly to the sugar producers.

How will the restructuring process of the sugar industry in Poland develop in the future? It is obvious that there is still a lot to be done. The major indicators of productivity and efficiency in both sugarbeet growing and processing increased considerably on the industry level within the last 14 years. Nevertheless, most of them are still much lower than the results achieved in Western Europe. There is no doubt that further structural changes are highly desirable. The number of working sugar factories in Poland and their average size are far from the theoretical optimum. The same can be said about sugarbeet plantations.

The sugar market in Poland is divided among five companies which have to compete for customers. Four of them happen to be multinational sugar corporations with great experience and know-how. The restructuring activities implemented by the companies in Poland so far show that they have a long-term commitment to do business in the country. They have invested considerable sums of money in consolidation, modernization and the increase in competitiveness of local plants. In doing so, they force competitors to do the same in order to survive.

In sum, the current ownership structure in the sugar industry in Poland and the hitherto course of the restructuring process of the sector allow one to expect that the competitiveness of sugar producers in the country will continue to increase at a rapid pace. This will be favored by Poland's EU membership and the resultant adoption of rules and regulations forming the common organization of the markets in the sugar sector.

The pending reform of the EU sugar regime puts pressure on sugar producers in Poland to continually reduce the costs of operations and to increase productivity in both beet production and beet processing. This is likely to result in further amalgamation of sugar factories and the concentration of sugar production in areas where the conditions for sugarbeet growing and processing are most favorable. Moreover, a gradual fall in the number of sugarbeet growers and an increase in the average size of sugarbeet plantations can be expected.

References

Amsden, A., J. Kochanowicz, and L. Taylor (1994): The Market Meets Its Match: Restructuring the Economies of Eastern Europe, Cambridge, MA, Harvard University Press.

Andrzejewski, R. and M. Baranowski (1993) (eds.): State of Environment in Poland Report, electronic version, Global Resource Information Database, Warsaw Center (URL: http:// www.gridw.pl /raport_p/raport97/index.htm, downloaded on January 5, 2005).

Antkowiak, J. (1995): SUGARPOL- dla rolnictwa, in: Gazeta Cukrownicza 1/1995, Wydawnictwo SIGMA-NOT, pp. 18-20.

Bain & Company (2003): Management Tools 2003 (URL: http://www.bain.com/management _tools/strategy_brief.pdf, downloaded on May 15, 2004).

Balcerowicz, L. (1997): Socjalizm, Kapitalizm, Transformacja. Szkice z Przełomu Epok, Wydawnictwo Naukowe PWN, Warszawa 1997.

Balcerowicz, L. (1998): Determinants, Structure, and Impact of Privatization: Poland in Comparative Perspective, in: Samonis, V. (ed.) (1998): Enterprise Restructuring and Foreign Investment in the Transforming East: The Impact of Privatization, International Business Press, Binghamton, pp. 177-185.

Bałtowski, M. (1998): Prywatyzacja przedsiębiorstw państwowych: Przebieg i ocena, Wydawnictwo Naukowe PWN, Warszawa.

Bałtowski, M. and T. Mickiewicz (2000): Privatization in Poland: Ten Years After, in: Post-Communist Economies, Vol.12, No.4, 2000, pp. 425-443.

Bałtowski (2002) (ed.): Przedsiębiorstwa sprywatyzowane w gospodarce polskiej, Wydawnictwo Naukowe PWN, Wydanie drugie, Warszawa 2002..

Bałtowski, M. (2002a): Przekształcenia własnościowe przedsiębiorstw państwowych w Polsce, Wydawnictwo Naukowe PWN, Warszawa 2002.

Bałtowski, M. (2002b): Analiza przedsiębiorstw sprywatyzowanych na podstawie danych GUS i MSP, in: Bałtowski (2002) (ed.): Przedsiębiorstwa sprywatyzowane w gospodarce polskiej, Wydawnictwo Naukowe PWN, Wydanie drugie, Warszawa, 2002, pp. 52-87.

Barney, J. (2002): Gaining and Sustaining Competitive Advantage, Second Edition, Prentice Hall.

Barry, F. (2002): EU Accession and FDI flows to CEE countries: Lessons from the Irish experience University College Dublin, February 2002.

Barry, F. (2003): Irish Economic Development over Three Decades of EU Membership, August 2003 (URL: http://www.ucd.ie/economic/staff/barry/papers/Finance%20a%20Uver. pdf, downloaded on September 16, 2004).

Bavorova, M. (2002): Entwicklung des Tschechischen Zuckersektors seit 1989, Institut für Agrarentwicklung in Mittel- und Osteuropa, Discussion Paper No. 41.

Bevan, A. A. and Estrin, S. (2000): The Determinants of Foreign Direct Investment in Transition Economies, Centre for Economic Policy Research, Discussion Paper No. 2638, December 2000, London.

Białasiewicz, M. (2001): Raport: Polska w Unii- Jakość polskiej żywności, BOSS Informacje Ekonomiczne Sp. z o. o.

Blanchard, O., R. Dornbusch, P. Krugman, R. Layard and L. Summers (1991): Reform in Eastern Europe, Cambridge, MA: MIT Press.

Blattner (2002): Foreign Direct Investment in Transition, Seminar paper, Freie Universität Berlin (URL: http://www.wiwiss.fu-berlin.de/w3/w3tomann/tomann/SeminarWS0203/ Seminararbeiten/Blattner.pdf, downloaded on January 16, 2004).

Blomström, M. and A. Kokko (1997): Regional Integration and Foreign Direct Investment: A Conceptual Framework and Three Cases, Policy Research Working Paper 1750, World Bank, Washington, DC, April 1997 (URL: http://www.worldbank.org/research/trade/pdf/wp1750.pdf, downloaded on September 22, 2004).

Blume, C., N. Strand, E. Färnstrand (2002): Sweet Fifteen: The Competition on the EU Sugar Market, Swedish Competition Authority Report, December 2002, ISSN-nr 1401-8438.

Bogdziewicz, S. (2005): Restrukturyzacja zatrudnienia w grupie Pfeifer & Langen ze wsparciem outplacementowym, in: *Gazeta Cukrownicza* 4/2005, Wydawnictwo SIGMA-NOT, pp. 98-99.

Bornstein, M. (1999): Framework Issues in the Privatization Strategies of the Czech Republic, Hungary and Poland, Post-Communist Economies, 11:1, pp. 47-77.

Bornstein, M. (2001): Post-privatisation Enterprise Restructuring, in: Post-Communist Economies, Vol. 13, No. 2, 2001, pp. 189-203.

Brada, J. (1996): Privatization is Transition—Or is it?, *Journal of Economic Perspectives*, 10, pp. 67-86.

Branicki, J. (2003): Grupa British Sugar (Overseas), Kampania 2002/03, in: Gazeta Cukrownicza 3/2003, Wydawnictwo SIGMA-NOT, pp. 80-86.

Branicki, J. and M. Dziadowiec (2005): Kampania 2004/05 w cukrowniach Grupy BSO, in: Gazeta Cukrownicza 3/2005, Wydawnictwo SIGMA-NOT, pp. 66-68.

Bruhns, G. (1997): 250 Jahre Rübenzucker 1747-1997. Was Marggrafs Entdeckung bewirkte und veränderte, Zucker-Museum Berlin, Verlag Dr. Albert Bartens KG, Berlin, Germany.

Bruhns, G. (2000): Vergessene Pioniere: Erinnerungen an die Urheber der Rübenzuckerindustrie", in: Zuckerindustrie 125 (2000) Nr. 6, Verlag Dr. Albert Bartens KG, Berlin, Germany, pp. 399-403.

Brzeziński, M. (2002): Stan i perspektywy rozwoju przemysłu cukrowniczego w województwie zachodniopomorskim, Poznań, February 2002 (unpublished).

Buckley, P. J. and M. Casson (1976): The Future of the Multinational Enterprise, Macmillan, London.

Buckley, A. (2002): Inwestycje zagraniczne: Składniki wartości i ocena, Wydawnictwo Naukowe PWN, Warszawa 2002.

Buckley, P. J. (2004): Regional Integration and Foreign Direct Investment in a Globalised World Economy, in: Oxelheim, L. and P. N. Ghauri (2004) (eds.): European Union and the Race for Foreign Direct Investment in Europe, ELSEVIER, pp. 35-58.

Burak Cukrowy (2004): Nowe życie Cukrowni Gosławice, in: Burak Cukrowy 1/2004, p. 4.

Business Consulting Center (2004): Case Study: Nordzucker Polska Group, SAP system implementation (URL: http://www.english.bcc.com.pl/pad_files/aw_files/13_EN_CS_ Nordzucker_SAP_20041110-ang.pdf, downloaded on August 17, 2005).

Busse, M. and F. Jerosch (2006): Reform of the EU Sugar Market, in: Intereconomics, March/April 2006 (URL: http://www.hwwa.de/Forschung/Publikationen/Intereconomics/2006/ie_docs2006/ie0602-busse_jerosch.pdf, downloaded on April 25, 2006).

Bücherl, N. (2004): Bericht über die Kampagne 2003 in den polnischen Zuckerfabriken der Südzucker-Gruppe, in: Zuckerindustrie 129 (2004) Nr. 5, pp. 327-330.

Bücherl, N. (2005): Bericht über die Kampagne 2004 in den polnischen Zuckerfabriken der Südzucker-Gruppe, in: Zuckerindustrie 133 (2005) Nr. 4, pp. 311-314.

Carlin, W., J. Van Reenen, T. Wolfe (1995): Enterprise restructuring in early transition: the case study evidence from Central and Eastern Europe, in: *Economics of Transition*, Volume 3(4), 1995, pp. 427-458.

Carlin, W., and M. Landesmann (1997): From theory into practice? Restructuring and dynamism in transition economies, Oxford Review of Economic Policy, Vol.13, No.2.

Carstensen, K. and F. Toubal (2003): Foreign direct investment in Central and Eastern European countries: a dynamic panel analysis, in: Journal of Comparative Economics 32 (1), 2004, pp. 3-22.

Centrum Badania Opinii Społecznej (2005): Opinie o Prywatyzacji. Komunikat z Badań (BS/26/2005), Warszawa, Luty 2005.

Chandler, A. (1962): Strategy and Structure, MIT Press, Cambridge, MA 1962.

Chen, Edward K. Y. (1994): Introduction: Transnational Corporations and Technology Transfer to Developing Countries, in: Chen, Edward K. Y. (1994) (ed.): Transnational Corporations and Technology Transfer to Developing Countries, United Nations Library on Transnational Corporations, Volume 18, London, New York, pp. 1-35.

Chen, M. (1996): Managing International Technology Transfer, International Thomson Business Press.

Chen, M. (1999): BPR Methodologies: Methods and Tools, in: Elzinga, J.D., T.R. Gulledge and Ch.-Y. Lee (ed.) (1999): Business Process Engineering: Advancing the State of the Art, Kluwer Academic Publishers, Norwell, Massachusetts, USA.

Chudoba, Ł. (1991): Skuteczność oddziaływania instrumentów ekonomicznych w sterowaniu postępem naukowo-technicznym w przemyśle cukrowniczym, Warszawa 1991 (Studia i monografie Instytutu Ekonomiki Rolnictwa i Gospodarki Żywnościowej).

Chudoba, Ł. (1999): Koszty produkcji cukru w kampanii 1998/99, in: Rynek Cukru: Stan i perspektywy, Instytut Ekonomiki Rolnictwa i Gospodarki Żywnościowej, Warszawa, kwiecień 1999, pp. 37-40.

Chudoba, Ł. (2000): Koszty produkcji cukru w kampanii 1999/2000, in: Rynek Cukru: Stan i perspektywy, Instytut Ekonomiki Rolnictwa i Gospodarki Żywnościowej, Warszawa, maj 2000, pp. 39-42.

Chudoba, Ł. (2001): Koszty produkcji cukru w kampanii 2000/01, in: Rynek Cukru: Stan i perspektywy, Instytut Ekonomiki Rolnictwa i Gospodarki Żywnościowej, Warszawa, maj 2001, pp. 39-42.

Chudoba, Ł. (2002): Koszty produkcji cukru w kampanii 2001/2002, in: Rynek Cukru: Stan i perspektywy, Instytut Ekonomiki Rolnictwa i Gospodarki Żywnościowej, Warszawa, maj 2001, pp. 39-42.

Chudoba, Ł. (2003): Konkurencyjność polskiego przemysłu cukrowniczego, in: Nowe Cukrownictwo 2/2003, BMP Sp. z o. o., pp. 45-47.

Chudoba, Ł. (2004): Rynek cukru w Polsce obecnie i po integracji z Unią Europejską, in: *Gazeta Cukrownicza* 5/2004, Wydawnictwo SIGMA-NOT, pp. 125-129.

Chudoba, Ł. (2004a): Regulacje handlu cukrem w Polsce, kwiecień 2004 (URL: http://www.agro-info.org.pl/index/?id=9431c87f273e507e6040fcb07dcb4509, downloaded on November 4, 2004).

Chudoba, Ł. (2004b): Przemysł cukrowniczy, Fundusz Współpracy, Warszawa, kwiecień 2004.

Chudoba, Ł. (2004c): Tendencje spożycia cukru i ceny na rynku krajowym, kwiecień 2004 (URL: http://www.agro-info.org.pl/index/?id=9a96876e2f8f3dc4f3cf45f02c61c0c1, downloaded on November 4, 2004).

Chudoba, Ł. (2004d): Produkcja buraków cukrowych, Fundusz Współpracy, kwiecień 2004.

Chudoba, Ł. (2004e): Aspekty ekonomiczne funkcjonowania polskiego sektora cukrowniczego po integracji z Unią Europejską, in: Katalog: XII Wiosenne Spotkanie Cukrowników Cukier 2004, BMP Sp. z o. o., pp. 18-19.

Chudoba (2005): Produkcja Buraków Cukrowych-Informacja dla Plantatorów, Seria: Polska wieś w Europie, Fundacja Fundusz Współpracy, Warszawa, Kwiecień 2005 (URL: http://www.agro-info.org.pl/files/?id_plik=604, downloaded on June 8, 2005).

Commander, S., M. Dutz, N. Stern (1999): Restructuring in Transition Economies: Ownership, Competition and Regulation, Paper prepared for the Annual World Bank Conference on Development Economics, Washington, D.C., April 28-30, 1999 (URL: http://www.worldbank.org/research/abcde/washington_11/pdfs/stern.pdf, downloaded on December 16, 2003).

Court of Auditors (2001): Special Report No. 20/2000 concerning the management of the common organisation of the market for sugar, together with the Commission's replies, Official Journal of the European Communities, C50, Volume 44, 15 February 2001.

CSF Polska (2004): Implementation of Axapta in Südzucker completed, http://www.csf.com.pl/en/sw/n200504_sudzucker.html, downloaded on May 24, 2005.

Cukier i Skrobia, Wydawnictwo Bartens, Słubice, Poland, Several Issues.

Daniels, J. D. And L. H. Radebaugh (2001): International Business: Environments and Operations, 9th edition, Prentice-Hall, Inc., Upper Saddle River, New Jersey, 07458.

Davenport, T. H., J. E. Short (1990): The New Industrial Engineering: Information Technology and Business Process Redesign, in: Sloan Management Review, Summer 1990, pp. 11-27.

Davis, N. (1981), "God's Playground: A History of Poland", Volume II: 1795 To The Present, Oxford University Press, Oxford.

Djankov, S. and P. Murrell (2000): The Determinants of Enterprise Restructuring in Transition, World Bank, Washington D.C.

Djankov, S. and P. Murrell (2002): Enterprise Restructuring in Transition: A Quantitative Survey, Centre for Economic Policy Research, Discussion Paper No. 3319, April 2002.

Dmitrzak, A. (1981): Two Hundred Years of Sugar Industry in the Territories of Poland, 1774-1975, in: Łuczak, Cz. (ed.) (1981): Dzieje cukrownictwa w Polsce, Uniwersytet im. Adama Mickiewicza w Poznaniu, Poznań 1981, pp. 353-359.

Dobrinsky, R. (1996): Enterprise Restructuring and adjustment in the transition to market economy: lessons from the experience of Central and Eastern Europe, *Economics of Transition,* Volume 4 (2), 1996, pp. 389-410.

Dobrowolski, M. (2005): Kampania 2004/05 w grupie polskich cukrowni Suedzucker (URL: http://www.stc.pl/dload.php?co=suedzucker_kamp_2004.pdf, downloaded on May 30, 2005).

Dolata, M. (2000): Opinia: Potencjalne skutki zahamowania prywatyzacji Cukrowni Grupy Kalisko-Konińskiej, Poznań, 14.12.2000 (unpublished).

Domadenik, P., J. Prasnikar, J. Svejnar (2002): Defensive and Strategic Restructuring of Firms During the Transition to a Market Economy, William Davidson Working Paper Number 541, The William Davidson Institute at the University of Michigan, February 2003 (URL: http://eres.bus.umich.edu/docs/workpap-dav/wp541.pdf, downloaded on May 10, 2003).

Dunning, J. H. (1977): Trade, Location of Economic Activity and the MNE: A Search for an Eclectic Approach, in: Ohlin, B., P. O. Hesselborn and P. M. Wijkman (1977) (eds.): The International Allocation of Economic Activity, London, Macmillan.

Dunning, J. H. (1980): Toward an Eclectic Theory of International Production, *Journal of International Business Studies*, 1980, Vol. 11.

Dunning, J. H. (1988): The Eclectic Paradigm of International Production: A Restatement of Some Possible Extensions, Journal of International Business Studies, Vol. 19, pp. 1-31.

Dunning, J. H. (1988b): Multinationals, Technology and Competitiveness, Unwin Hyman Ltd., London.
Dunning, J. H. (2001): Assessing the Costs and Benefits of Foreign Direct Investment; Some Theoretical Considerations, in Maksimenko, P. and Rojec, M. (eds.): Foreign Investment and Privatization in Eastern Europe, PALGRAVE, New York, 2001, pp. 34-81.
Dunning, J. H. (2003): Relational assets, networks and international business activity, in: Dunning, J. H. and G. Boyd (2003) (eds.): Alliance Capitalism and Corporate Management: Entrepreneurial Cooperation in Knowledge Based Economies, Edward Elgar Publishing, pp. 1-23.
Du Pont, M. (2000): Foreign Direct Investment in Transitional Economies: A Case Study of China and Poland, St. Martin's Press, LLC., New York.
Earle, John S., R. Frydman, and A. Rapaczynski (eds.) (1993): Privatization in the Transition to a Market Economy. Budapest, Central European University Press.
EBRD (1999): Transition Report 1999: Ten years of transition, European Bank for Reconstruction and Development, London.
EBRD (2000): How do foreign investors assess the quality of labour in transition economies? Results from a postal survey, EBRD Working Paper, 2000 (URL: http://www.ebrd.com/pubs/tr/00/survey.pdf, downloaded on September 22, 2004).
EBRD (2005): Transition Report 2005: Business in transition, European Bank for Reconstruction and Development, London.
Edmondson G. and A. Bonnet (2004): Nowa droga Toyoty w Europie, *Business Week*, Edycja Polska, no. 11 (152), 8-21 lipca 2004, pp. 26-27.
Ernst, M., M. Alexeev, P. Marer (1996): Transforming the Core. Restructuring Industrial Enterprises in Russia and Central Europe, Westview Press.
Estrin, S., J.C. Brada, A. Gelb, I. Singh (1995): Restructuring and Privatization in Central Eastern Europe: Case Studies of Firms in Transition, M.E. Sharpe, Inc., New York.
European Commission (2003): Sugar, International Analysis: Production structures within the EU (22/09/03) (URL: http://www.europa.eu.int/comm/agriculture/markets/sugar/reports/rep_en.pdf, downloaded on February 15, 2005).
European Commission (2004): A Description of the Common Organisation of the Market in Sugar, European Commission, Agriculture Directorate-General, September 2004 (URL: http://www.europa.eu.int/comm/agriculture/markets/sugar/reports/descri_en.pdf, downloaded on October 4, 2004).
European Commission (2004a): Accomplishing a sustainable agricultural model for Europe through the reformed CAP- sugar sector reform, COM(2004) 499 final, Brussels, 14.7.2004 (URL: http://europa.eu.int/comm/agriculture/capreform/sugarprop_en.pdf).
European Commission (2004b): Commission appeals against WTO sugar ruling, Brussels, 15 October 2004 (URL: http://trade-info.cec.eu.int/doclib/html/119652.htm, downloaded on December 16, 2004).
European Commission (2004c): EU sugar sector: Facts and figures, MEMO/04/177, Brussels, July 14, 2004 (URL: http://www.europa.eu.int/rapid/pressReleasesAction.do?reference=MEMO/04/177&format=DOC&aged=1&language=EN&guiLanguage=en, downloaded on February 4, 2005.
European Commission (2005): The Commission outlines its support to ACP Sugar Protocol countries, Press release IP/05/85, Brussels, 24 January 2005 (URL: http://www.europa.eu.int/rapid/pressReleasesAction.do?reference=IP/05/85&format=DOC&aged=0&language=EN&guiLanguage=en, downloaded on January 28, 2005.

European Commission (2005a): Commission extends deadline for elimination of surplus sugar stocks in five new Member States, Press release IP/05/459, Brussels, 20 April 2005 (URL: http://www.europa.eu.int/rapid/pressReleasesAction.do?reference=IP/05/459&format=PDF &aged=0&language=EN&guiLanguage=en, downloaded on May 4, 2005).

European Commission (2005b): European Commission regrets attack on EU sugar regime, but will abide by WTO Appellate Body ruling, Press release IP/05/506, Brussels, 28 April 2005 (URL: http://www.europa.eu.int/rapid/pressReleasesAction.do?reference=IP/05/506& format=PDF&aged=0&language=EN&guiLanguage=en, downloaded on 4 May 2005).

European Commission (2005c): Proposal for a Council Regulation on the common organization of the markets in the sugar sector, URL: http://www.europa.eu.int/comm/ agriculture/capreform/sugar/prop_en.pdf, downloaded on June 22, 2005).

European Commission (2005d): Reforming the European Union's sugar policy, Update of impact assessment [SEC(2003) 1022], URL: http://www.europa.eu.int/comm/agriculture/ capreform/sugar/impact_en.pdf, downloaded on June 29, 2005).

European Commission (2005e): Sugar Reform will offer EU producers long-term competitive future, Press release IP/05/776, Brussels, 22 June 2005 (URL: http://www.europa.eu.int/ rapid/pressReleasesAction.do?reference=IP/05/776&format=PDF&aged=0&language=EN& guiLanguage=en, downloaded on June 29, 2005).

European Commission (2005f): The European Sugar Sector: Its importance and its future, June 2005, URL: http://www.europa.eu.int/comm/agriculture/capreform/sugar/infopack_ en.pdf, downloaded on June 29, 2005).

European Commission (2005g): EU radically reforms its sugar sector to give producers long-term competitive future, Press release IP/05/1473, Brussels, 24 November 2005 (URL: http://www.europa.eu.int/rapid/pressReleasesAction.do?reference=IP/05/1473&format=PD F&aged=0&language=EN&guiLanguage=en, downloaded on November 25, 2005).

Eurostat (2004): Agricultural income in EU-25 in 2004: +3.3% in real terms, Statistics in focus, Agriculture and Fisheries, 38/2004.

Farrow, B., P.D. Robbins and A.J.N. Warnes (1993): SugarPol (Toruń) Sp. z o. o., British Sugar's Joint Venture in Poland, in: International Sugar Journal 1993, Vol. 95, No. 1135B, pp. 255-258, 291-292.

Fischer Boel, M. (2005): Reform of the EU Sugar Regime, Speech delivered during European Parliament Plenary on March 10, 2005, SPEECH/05/162 (URL: http://www.europa.eu.int/ rapid/pressReleasesAction.do?reference=SPEECH/05/162&format=DOC&aged=0&language=EN&guiLanguage=en, downloaded on April 13, 2005).

Fischer Boel, M. (2005a): Sugar Reform: Giving the sector a viable long-term future, Presentation of the Proposal of the Sugar Reform, European Parliament, June 22, 2005, SPEECH/05/375, URL: http://www.europa.eu.int/rapid/pressReleasesAction.do?reference =SPEECH/ 05/375&format=PDF&aged=0&language=EN&guiLanguage=en, downloaded on June 29, 2005).

Flejterski, S. (1984): Istota i mierzenie konkurencyjności międzynarodowej, *Gospodarka Planowa*, nr 9, 1984.

F.O. Licht's World Sugar Statistics (Several Issues), supplement to F.O. Licht's International Economic Yearbook and Directory, F.O. Licht GmbH, Ratzeburg.

Foundation for the Development of Polish Agriculture (2004): Polska wieś po wejściu do Unii Europejskiej, Warszawa 2004.

Frankfurter Allgemeine Zeitung (2004): Milliardenkosten durch Reform des EU-Zuckermarktes, August 5, 2004, Nr. 180, p. 13.

Frankfurter Allgemeine Zeitung (2004a): Heftige Kritik an der Reform des EU-Zuckermarktes, July 15, 2004, Nr. 162, p. 10.
Frankfurter Allgemeine Zeitung (2004b): Wirtschaftsverbände streiten über Zuckerreform, November 11, 2004, Nr. 264, p. 15.
Frankfurter Allgemeine Zeitung (2004c): EU-Kommission streitet über Zuckerreform, July 12, 2004, Nr. 159, p. 11.
Frederick, R. (1994): Enterprise Restructuring in the Context of Privatization: An Overview of the Issues, in: Zecchini, S. (1994) (ed.): Trends and Policies in Privatization, Paris: OECD.
Frydman, R., A. Rapaczyński and J.S. Earle (1993): The Privatization Process in Central Europe: Economic Environment, Legal and Ownership Structure, Institutions for State Regulation, Overview of Privatization Programs, Initial Transformation of Enterprises. Budapest, New York: Central European University Press.
Frydman, R., C. W. Gray, M. Hessel, and A. Rapaczynski (1997): Private Ownership and Corporate Performance: Evidence from Transition Economies, EBRD Working Paper No. 26, European Bank for Reconstruction and Development, London.
Galli, G. and J. Pelkmans (ed.) (2000): Regulatory Reform and Competitiveness in Europe, II, Edward Elgar Publishing Limited.
Gazeta Cukrownicza (2005): Coroczna pokampanijna konferencja techniczno-promocyjna 2004/2005—część 2, in: Gazeta Cukrownicza 7/2005, Wydawnictwo SIGMA-NOT, pp. 209-217.
Gazeta Wyborcza (2004): Rolnik potrafi liczyć (Interview with Prof. Krzysztof Gorlach), Gazeta Wyborcza 30.11.2004, p. 2.
Gazeta Wyborcza (2005): MAN-y z Niepołomic, in: Gazeta Wyborcza, 17.08.2005, p. 17.
Gąsowski, Z. (1998): Developments in the Polish sugar industry, in: International Sugar Journal, 1998, Vol. 100, No. 1198, pp. 484-486.
Gąsowski, Z. (2004): Daleka od pierwowzoru, in: Cukrowniczy Przegląd Informacyjny BSO Polska, nr 3/2004, pp.18-19.
Giddy, I. H. (1978): The demise of the product cycle model in international business theory, *Columbia Journal of World Business*, Book 13, No. 1, pp. 90-97.
Gierszewski, S. (2001): Cukrownictwo polskie w zarysie historycznym, in: 175 lat Polskiego Przemysłu Cukrowniczego, Stowarzyszenie Techników Cukrowników, Dom Wydawniczy „Verbum", Warszawa 2001, pp. 23-35.
Gierszewski, S. (2002): Znaczenie przemysłowej produkcji cukru dla rozwoju gospodarczego regionu i kraju, in: Gazeta Cukrownicza 11/2002, Wydawnictwo SIGMA-NOT, pp. 312-318.
Główny Urząd Statystyczny (2003): Uprawy Rolne 2002, Warszawa, wrzesień 2003 (URL: http://sp.stat.gov.pl/spis/uprawy_rolne/publik.pdf, downloaded on February 15, 2004).
Główny Urząd Statystyczny (2005): Średnie zatrudnienie w klasie PKD 15.83 – produkcja cukru w latach 1994-2004.
Grabbe, H. (2001): Profiting from EU enlargement, Centre for European Reform (URL: http://www.cer.org.uk/pdf/p254_enlargement.pdf, downloaded on September 13, 2004).
Graham, Edward M. (1978): Transatlantic Investment by Multinational Firms: A Rivalistic Phenomenon, *Journal of Post Keynesian Economics* 1, pp. 82-89.
Graham, Edward M. (1985): Intra-Industry Direct Investment, Market Structure, Firm Rivalry, and Technological Performance, in Erdilek, A. (ed.): Multinationals as Mutual Invaders, Intra-Industry Direct Foreign Investment, London, Croom-Helm.

Greenspan, A. (2001): Globalization vs. Protectionism, Address delivered to the Committee on Finance, U.S. Senate, Washington, D.C., April 4, 2001, publ. in *Vital Speeches of the Day*, April 15, 2001, pp. 386-388.

Grosfeld, I. and G. Roland (1995): Defensive and Strategic Restructuring in Central European Enterprises, Centre for Economic Policy Research, Discussion Paper No. 1135, March 1995.

Gruszczyńska, J. (2004): OHSAS 18001 w Grupie BSO, in: Cukrowniczy Przegląd Informacyjny BSO Polska 2/2004, pp. 6-7.

Gruszecka, H. (2000): Krajowy przemysł cukrowniczy wobec wymagań jakościowych Unii Europejskiej, in: Gazeta Cukrownicza 6/2000, Wydawnictwo SIGMA-NOT, pp. 106-110.

Hagelüken, A. (2004): Süße Macht, in: Süddeutsche Zeitung Nr. 160, Mittwoch, 14. Juli 2004, Seite 61.

Hammer, M. (1990): Reengineering Work: Don't Automate, Obliterate, *Harvard Business Review*, July-August 1990, pp. 104-112.

Hammer, M and J. Champy (1993): Reengineering the Corporation: A Manifesto for Business Revolution, HarperCollins Publishers, Inc., New York.

Hare, P. G. (2003): Social Aspects of Industrial Restructuring and Their Financing, Discussion Paper 2003/05, Centre for Economic Reform and Transformation, Heriot-Watt University, Edinburgh (URL: http://www.sml.hw.ac.uk/cert/wpa/2003/dp0305.pdf, downloaded on May 26, 2004).

Hausner, J. (2004): Polskie strachy, polskie drogi, in: *Gazeta Wyborcza*, 24-25 kwietnia 2004, pp. 12-14.

Hill, Charles W. L. (2002): International Business: Competing in the Marketplace (Postscript 2002), 3rd edition, Mcgraw-Hill.

Hollensen, S. (2001): Global Marketing: A market-responsive approach, Second edition, Prentice Hall.

Hollowell, B. (1995): Polish Agriculture: An Improving Picture, in: British Sugar Beet Review, Volume 63, No. 1, pp. 39-41.

Hradesky, J.L. (1995): Total Quality Management Handbook, McGraw-Hill, Inc., New York.

Hymer, S. H. (1976): The International Operations of National Firms: A Study of Direct Foreign Investment, Cambridge, Massachusetts, MIT Press.

Instytut Ekonomiki Rolnictwa i Gospodarki Żywnościowej (IERiGŻ): Rynek cukru: Stan i perspektywy, Warszawa, Several Issues.

Instytut Przemysłu Cukrowniczego (IPC): Informacja o wynikach produkcyjnych i danych techniczno-technologicznych przemysłu cukrowniczego, Warszawa, Several Issues.

International Institute for Beet Research (2005): Sugarbeet in Europe- an environmentally friendly crop for sustainable plant production systems- Part 1, in: *Zuckerindustrie* 130 (2005) Nr. 2, pp. 89-95.

International Monetary Fund (1993): *Balance of Payments Manual*, Fifth Edition, Washington, D.C.

International Organization for Standardization (2002): ISO in brief (URL: http://www.iso.org/iso/en/prods-services/otherpubs/pdf/inbrief2002-en.pdf, downloaded on July 8, 2004).

International Sugar Organization, Sugar Year Book, London, Several Issues.

Janz, C.U. (2002): Unternehmenszusammenschlüsse in der Milch- und Zuckerindustrie unter wettbewerbsrechtlichen und ökonomischen Gesichtspunkten, Electronic Edition, Niedersächsische Staats- und Universitätsbibliothek, Göttingen (URL: http://webdoc.sub.gwdg.de/diss/2003/janz/janz.pdf, downloaded on March 19, 2004).

Jarosz, M. (ed.) (1997): Foreign Owners and Polish Employees of Privatized Enterprises, Institute of Political Studies, Polish Academy of Sciences, 1997.
Jaworowski, T. (1995): Polski Przemysł Cukrowniczy w Świetle Liczb i Ocen. Od zarania po 1995 rok, Stowarzyszenie Techników Cukrowników, Warszawa 1995.
Jaworowski, T. (2001): Polski przemysł cukrowniczy w świetle liczb i ocen. Od zarania po 2000 rok, in: 175 lat Polskiego Przemysłu Cukrowniczego, Stowarzyszenie Techników Cukrowników, Dom Wydawniczy „Verbum", Warszawa 2001, pp. 125-173.
Jensen, C. (2000), "The impact of foreign direct investment for technological change in transition: the case of Poland", University of Southern Denmark, Odense.
Johanson, J. and L. G. Mattson (1988): Internationalization in industrial systems, in: Hood, N. and J. E. Vahlne (eds.): Strategies in Global Competition, Croom Helm, Beckenham, United Kingdom.
Johansson, H.J., P. McHugh, A.J. Pendlebury, W.A. Wheller III (1993): Business Process Reengineering: Breakpoint Strategies for Market Dominance, Wiley, Chichister, New York, 1993.
Johnson, S. and G. W. Loveman (1995): Starting Over in Eastern Europe: Entrepreneurship and Economic Renewal, Harvard Business School Press, Boston, Massachusetts.
Jórdeczka, S. (2005): Kampania 2004 w Pfeifer & Langen Polska, in: *Gazeta Cukrownicza* 4/2005, Wydawnictwo SIGMA-NOT, p. 99.
Jórdeczka, S. and P. Małkowski (2004): Kampania 2003/04 w cukrowniach Pfeifer & Langen Polska, in: *Gazeta Cukrownicza* 4/2004, Wydawnictwo SIGMA-NOT, pp. 86-88.
Kamieniarz, J. (2004): Porozumienie branżowe- ważny dokument dla plantatorów i cukrowników w Polsce, in: Burak Cukrowy 4/2004, Wydawnictwo Bartens Sp. z o. o., p. 7.
Kamiński, B. and B. Smarzyńska (2001): Foreign Direct Investment and Integration into Global Production and Distribution Networks: The Case of Poland, World Bank, July 2001.
Karaszewski, W. (2001): Przedsiębiorstwa z udziałem kapitału zagranicznego w Polsce w latach 1990-1999, Wydawnictwo Uniwersytetu Mikołaja Kopernika w Toruniu, Toruń 2001.
Kirchberg, T. (2003): Rübenanbau und Zuckerwirtschaft in Polen, in *Deutsche Zuckerrübenzeitschrift* (online version), September 2003.
Kleta, K. (2003): Nowe życie Cukrowni Gosławice, in Nowe Cukrownictwo 3/2003, BMP Sp. Z o. o., pp. 5-6.
Klimaszewski, J. And A. Branicki (2004): Kampania 2003/04 w cukrowniach Grupy BSO, in: Gazeta Cukrownicza 4/2004, Wydawnictwo SIGMA-NOT, pp. 89-91.
Knapp, R. and P. Talks (2004): Sugar and the European Union: Implication of WTO Findings, and Reform, Foreign Agricultural Service, United States Department of Agriculture (URL:
http://www.fas.usda.gov/htp/sugar/2004/internet%20article%20on%20wto%20and%20reform%20rev1.pdf, downloaded on March 13, 2005).
Knickerbocker, F.T. (1973): Oligopolistic Reaction and Multinational Enterprise, Boston, Massachusetts, Harvard University Press.
Kobza, K. (1999): Aktualna sytuacja i perspektywy rozwoju uprawy buraka cukrowego w Polsce na najbliższe lata, in: Gazeta Cukrownicza 12/1999, Wydawnictwo SIGMA-NOT, pp. 231-233.
Kohnke, J. (2005): Pfeifer & Langen 1870-2004, in: *Zuckerindustrie* 130 (2005) Nr. 1, pp. 41-45.
Kojima, K. and Ozawa, T. (1984): Micro and Macro Economic Models of Foreign Direct Investment: Towards a Synthesis, *Hitotsubashi Journal of Economics*, Vol. 25, No. 2.

Kokocińska, M. (2002): Sytuacja koniunkturalna a konkurencyjność, in: Skawińska, E. (ed.) (2002): Konkurencyjność przedsiębiorstw: nowe podejście, Wydawnictwo Naukowe PWN, Warszawa-Poznań 2002, pp. 113-144.

Konarska-Gębala, W. (2004): Nowy żywy serwis, in: Cukrowniczy Przegląd Informacyjny BSO Polska 3/2004, p. 7.

Kondrakiewicz, T. (2000): Holdingi w przemyśle cukrowniczym. Procesy dostosowawcze do integracji z Unią Europejską, Wydawnictwo Uniwersytetu Marii Curie-Skłodowskiej, Lublin 2000.

Konieczka, T. (2002): Pozycja ekonomiczno-finansowa cukrowni w Polsce ze względu na wartość majątku ogółem w latach 1996-2000, in: Gazeta Cukrownicza 10/2002, Wydawnictwo SIGMA-NOT, pp. 293-297.

Konings, J. (2000): The Effects of Foreign Direct Investment on Domestic Firms: Evidence from Firm Level Panel Data in Emerging Economies, Centre for Economic Policy Research, Discussion Paper No. 2586, October 2000.

Kornai, J. (1998): The Place of Soft Budget Constraint Syndrome in Economic Theory, Journal of Comparative Economics 26 (1).

Kornai, J. (2000): Ten Years After The Road To A Free Market Economy: The Author's Self-Evaluation, Paper for the World Bank 'Annual Bank Conference on Development Economics- ABCDE', April 18-20, 2000, Washington D.C (URL: http://www.worldbank.org/research/inequality/pdf/kornai.pdf, downloaded on September 20, 2004).

Kotler, P. and G. Armstrong (2001): Principles of Marketing, 9th edition, Prentice-Hall, Inc., Upper Saddle River, New Jersey 07458.

Kotler, P. and F. Bliemel (2001): Marketing-Management: Analyse, Planung und Verwirklichung, 10., überarbeitete und aktualisierte Auflage, Schäfer-Poeschel Verlag, Stuttgart.

Kowalewski, Z. (1992): Początki cukrownictwa buraczanego w Europie i na ziemiach polskich, in: Gazeta Cukrownicza 4/1992, Wydawnictwo SIGMA-NOT, pp. 75-77.

Kozińska, K. (2005): Producenci ustawią się w kolejce, in: *Puls Biznesu*, 2 czerwca 2005, p. 11.

Kozmana, M. (2005): Polski cukier zasypał Europę, in: *Rzeczpospolita*, 8.02.2005, p. B3.

Krajowa Spółka Cukrowa (2004): Plan restrukturyzacji Krajowej Spółki Cukrowej na lata 2003-2005, Toruń, styczeń 2004.

Krajowa Spółka Cukrowa (2005): Raport Roczny 2003/04 (Annual Report 2003/04)

Krajowa Spółka Cukrowa (2005b): Wyniki kampanijne 2004/05, Krajowa Spółka Cukrowa S.A.

Krajowa Spółka Cukrowa (2006): Raport Roczny 2004/05 (Annual Report 2004/05)

Krick, A. (2000): Die Kozentration in der europäischen Zuckerindustrie, in: Zuckerindustrie 125 (2000) Nr. 6, Verlag Dr. Albert Bartens KG, Berlin, Germany, pp. 424-430.

Krkoska, L. (2001): Foreign direct investment financing of capital formation in Central and Eastern Europe, EBRD Working paper No. 67, December 2001.

Krugman, P. R. (1994): Competitiveness, a dangerous obsession, *Foreign Affairs*, Vol. 73, No. 2, March-April 1994.

Krupa, K. (2005): Unia widziana ze wsi, in Puls Biznesu, 27-29.05.2005, p. 2.

Kublik, A. (2004): Auta nas omijają, in: *Gazeta Wyborcza* 4-5.12.2004, p. 27.

Kublik, A. and L. Kostrzewski (2005): Straciliśmy 190 mln euro, in: *Gazeta Wyborcza* 10.05.2005, p. 28.

Kuczyński, M. (2005): Kampania po zmianach na przykładzie Cukrowni „Wróblin" S.A., in: Burak Cukrowy 1/2005 (ŚSC Edition), p. 8

Kuźmicz, M. (2003): Biedni mają głos, in: *Gazeta Wyborcza* 13-14 grudnia 2003, p. 32.

Lavigne, M. (1999): The Economics of Transition: From Socialist Economy to Market Economy, Second Edition, St. Martin's Press, New York 1999.
Leśniak, H. (2004): Dni Buraka Cukrowego w grupie Nordzucker Polska w 2004r., in: Burak Cukrowy 4/2004 (Nordzucker Polska Edition), Wydawnictwo Bartens, Słubice, p. 8.
Lipowski, A. (2001): Procesy Restrukturyzacji w Przedsiębiorstwach Przemysłowych Okresu Transformacji Systemowej, in: Mączyńska (2001) (ed.): Restrukturyzacja Przedsiębiorstw w Procesie Transformacji Gospodarki Polskiej, Tom I, Wydawnictwo DiG, Warszawa, pp. 50-60.
Lipton, D. and J. Sachs (1990): The Strategy of Transition, in: Creating a Market Economy in Eastern Europe: The Case of Poland, Brookings Papers on Economic Activity, Vol. I, 1990.
Lipton, D., and Jeffrey D. Sachs (1990a): Privatization in Eastern Europe: The Case of Poland, Brookings Papers on Economic Activity 20(2): 293–341.
Łękawski, W. (2001): Współczesna technologia cukrownicza, doświadczenia i perspektywy, in: 175 lat Polskiego Przemysłu Cukrowniczego, Stowarzyszenie Techników Cukrowników, Dom Wydawniczy „Verbum", Warszawa 2001, pp. 101-114.
Łuczak, Cz. (ed.) (1981): Dzieje cukrownictwa w Polsce, Uniwersytet im. Adama Mickiewicza w Poznaniu, Poznań 1981.
Machan, Tibor R. (2002): The Right to Private Property, Hoover Institution, Essays in Public Policy No. 109, Stanford University.
Mahler, P. (1991): Effizienzverluste in der deutschen Zuckerwirtschaft durch struktur-konservierende Wirkungen der EG-Zuckermarktordnung, Peter Lang Verlag, Frankfurt am Main 1991.
Malec, J. (2002): Stan aktualny i strategia uprawy buraków w Polsce, in: Gazeta Cukrownicza 8/2002, Wydawnictwo SIGMA-NOT, pp. 229-231.
Malec, J. (2005): Wyniki kampanii cukrowniczej 2004/05, in: Burak Cukrowy 2/2005, Wydawnictwo Bartens, Słubice, p. 1.
Malhotra, Y. (1998): Business Process Redesign: An Overview, IEEE Engineering Management Review, vol. 26, no. 3, Fall 1998 (URL: http://www.brint.com/papers/bpr.htm, downloaded on May 17, 2004).
Marinov, M.A., Trifonova Marinova, S., Watts, G. (1998): Privatization and Company Restructuring in Eastern Europe, in Samonis, V. (ed.) (1998): Enterprise Restructuring and Foreign Investment in the Transforming East: The Impact of Privatization, International Business Press, Binghamton, New York, pp. 29-46.
Marjankowska, B. (2002): Dzień dobry Panie Prezesie, in: Gazeta Cukrownicza 9/2002, Wydawnictwo SIGMA-NOT, pp. 250-252.
Marjankowska, B. (2003): Perła w koronie, in: Gazeta Cukrownicza 10/2003, Wydawnictwo SIGMA-NOT, pp. 292-294.
Marjankowska, B. (2004): Bezpieczeństwo i zadowolenie konsumenta, in: Gazeta Cukrownicza 1/2004, Wydawnictwo SIGMA-NOT, pp. 8-9.
Markiewicz, W. (2004): Lepsza kosa niż kasa, in: Polityka, nr 26 (2458), 26 czerwca 2004.
McDonald, Kevin R. (1993): Why Privatization is Not Enough, Reprint of an article published in the Harvard Business Review, May-June 1993.
Megginson, W. E. and J. M. Netter (2001): From State to Market: A Survey of Empirical Studies on Privatization, *Journal of Economic Literature* 39(2): 321–89.
Megyery, K. and F. Sader (1996): Facilitating Foreign Participation in Privatization, Foreign Investment Advisory Service Occasional Paper No.8, The International Finance Corporation and the World Bank, Washington D.C.

Meyer, K. (1997): Enterprise Transformation and Foreign Investment in Eastern Europe, Copenhagen Business School, Working Paper No. 7, June 1997.

Meyer, K. (1998a): Enterprise Restructuring and Investment (Foreign and Domestic): Frontiers of Transitions from Plan to Markets on the Eve of the 21st Century", in: Samonis, V. (ed.) (1998): Enterprise Restructuring and Foreign Investment in the Transforming East: The Impact of Privatization", International Business Press, Binghamton, pp. 7-27.

Meyer, K. (1998b): Direct Investment in Economies of Transition, Edward Elgar Publishing Limited, Cheltenham, United Kingdom.

Meyer, K. and S. Estrin (1998c): Entry Mode Choice in Emerging Markets: Greenfield, Acquisition, and Brownfield, Working Paper No. 18, Center for East European Studies, Copenhagen Business School, February 2002 (URL: http://web.cbs.dk/centres/cees/ publications/cees_wp_98/wp18.pdf, downloaded on September 13, 2004).

Meyer, K. (2002): Management Challenges in Privatization Acquisitions in Transition Economies, (URL: http://web.cbs.dk/staff/meyer/papers/JWB-privatization-acquisition.pdf, downloaded on May 27, 2004).

Microsoft (2004): Grupa Südzucker wybrała Microsoft Business Solutions—Axapta, URL: http://download.microsoft.com/download/c/5/1/c51fb0ae-013b-4e09-b5fb-e3b4beb057aa/Axapta%2520w%2520Sudzucker.doc&e=10313, downloaded on May 24, 2005.

Miedziak, S. (2003): Przesłanki ekonomiczne rozwoju polskiego przemysłu cukrowniczego po integracji z UE, in: Gazeta Cukrownicza 2/2003, Wydawnictwo SIGMA-NOT, pp. 49-58.

Ministry of Agriculture and Rural Development (2005): Wymiana handlowa artykułami rolno-spożywczymi Polski z innymi krajami w 2004r. (dane wstępne) (URL: http:// bip.minrol.gov.pl/DesktopModules/Announcement/ViewAnnouncement.aspx?ModuleID=1175&TabOrgID=1467&LangId=0&AnnouncementId=3044&ModulePositionId=1614).

Ministry of State Treasury (2001): Report on Ownership Transformations (1990-1999), Part II, Ministry of the Treasury, Republic of Poland, Warszawa 2001, pp. 64-77.

Ministry of State Treasury (2002): Krajowa Spółka Cukrowa S.A. powołana 26 sierpnia 2002, Biuletyn Ministerstwa Skarbu Państwa, sierpień/wrzesień 2002, pp. 12-15.

Ministry of State Treasury (2002b): Informacje o udziale inwestorów zagranicznych w procesie prywatyzacji polskiej gospodarki w latach 1990-2002 (URL: http://www.mst.gov.pl/ dokumenty/raport_inwestorzy_pl.pdf, downloaded on September 24, 2004).

Ministry of State Treasury (2002c), "Informacje o udziale inwestorów zagranicznych w procesie prywatyzacji polskiej gospodarki w latach 1990-2002", www.mst.gov.pl.

Ministry of State Treasury (2005): Wybrane procesy prywatyzacyjne z udziałem inwestorów zagranicznych (URL: http://www.msp.gov.pl/download.php?s=2&id=199, downloaded on November 14, 2005).

Moore, J. (1992): British Privatization- Taking Capitalism to the People, *Harvard Business Review*, January-February 1992, pp. 115-124.

Moosa, I. A. (2002): Foreign Direct Investment: Theory, Evidence and Practice, PALGRAVE, New York.

Najwyższa Izba Kontroli (2000): Informacja o wynikach kontroli realizacji ustawy z dnia 26 sierpnia 1994 o regulacji rynku cukru i przekształceniach własnościowych w przemyśle cukrowniczym, Departament Rolnictwa i Gospodarki Żywnościowej, Warszawa, wrzesień 2000.

Naszkowska, K. (2005): Zalewamy UE żywnością, in: *Gazeta Wyborcza*, 24.03.2005, p. 20.

Naszkowska, K. (2003): Cukier dla Francuzów, in: *Gazeta Wyborcza*, 27.03.2003, p. 21.

National Bank of Poland (2005): Kursy walut (URL: http://www.nbp.pl/kursy/archiwum/ internet.xls, downloaded on March 23, 2005).
Navaretti, G. B., J. I. Haaland and A. Venables (2002): Multinational Corporations and Global Production Networks: The Implications for Trade Policy, Centre for Economic Policy Research (URL: http://www.cepr.org/pubs/fdi_report.pdf, downloaded on July 1, 2004).
Nawrocki, I. (1989): Kapitał zagraniczny w polskiej gospodarce w latach 1976-1989, *Handel Zagraniczny* 1989, Nr. 4-5.
Nikiel, S (1999): Przemiany własnościowe, organizacyjne i techniczne Cukrowni Glinojeck, in: Gazeta Cukrownicza 2/1999, Wydawnictwo SIGMA-NOT, pp. 32-33.
Nowak, J. (2003): Wpływ przystąpienia Polski do Unii Europejskiej na dochody plantatorów, in: Burak Cukrowy 3/2003, Wydawnictwo Bartens, Słubice, p. 1.
Nöhle, U. (2004): The sugar market and trade agreements of the European Union, in: Zuckerindustrie 129 (2004) Nr. 10, Verlag Dr. Albert Bartens KG, Berlin, Germany, pp. 703-712.
OECD (2002): Global Industrial Restructuring, Business and Industry Policy Forum Report, (URL: http://www.oecd.org/dataoecd/59/47/1947035.pdf, downloaded on November 8, 2003).
OECD (2003): Agricultural Policies in OECD Countries: Monitoring and Evaluation.
OECD (2004): OECD Agricultural Outlook 2004-2013, Highlights (URL: http://www.oecd.org /dataoecd/63/28/32037536.pdf, downloaded on February 11, 2005).
Official Journal of the European Communities (2001): Council Regulation (EC) No. 1260/2001 of June 19, 2001 on the common organisation of the markets in the sugar sector, Official Journal of the European Communities 30.06.2001 L 178, p.1).
Official Journal of the European Communities (2004): Commission Regulation (EC) No. 1291/2004 of July 14, 2004, Official Journal of the European Communities 15.7.2004 L243/21.
Olesiński, Z. (2000): Proces prywatyzacji w Polsce, Wydawnictwo "Książka i Wiedza", Warszawa.
Opielewicz, T. (2005): Ocena skupu buraków na zawartość cukru w Wielkopolskim Cukrze S.A.- widziana oczami plantatorów, in: Burak Cukrowy 1/2005 (Nordzucker Polska edition), Wydawnictwo Bartens, Słubice, p. 4.
Oxfam International (2004): Dumping on the world: How EU sugar policies hurt poor countries, Oxfam Briefing Paper 61, Oxfam International, March 2004 (URL: http://www.oxfam.org.uk/what_we_do/issues/trade/downloads/bp61_sugar_dumping.pdf).
Oxfam International (2004a): An End to EU Sugar Dumping? Implications of the Interim WTO Panel Ruling in the dispute against EU sugar policies brought by Brazil, Thailand, and Australia, Oxfam Briefing Note, August 6, 2004.
Oxfam International (2005): EU sugar deal 'scandalous betrayal' of poor countries, Oxfam Press Release- 24 November 2005 (URL: http://www.oxfam.org.uk/press/releases/ trade_eu241105.htm, downloaded on December 4, 2005).
Ozawa, T. (1992): Foreign Direct Investment and Economic Development, *Transnational Corporations,* 1992, Vol. 1, No. 1, pp. 27-54.
Paluch, M. (2005): Dochodowość uprawy buraków cukrowych, in: *Burak Cukrowy* 2/2005, Wydawnictwo Bartens Sp. z o. o., Słubice, p. 9.
Pawełek, M. (2004): Reorganizacja bazy surowcowej Śląskiej Spółki Cukrowej, in: *Burak Cukrowy* 1/2004 (ŚSC Edition), Wydawnictwo Bartens Sp. z o. o., Słubice, p. 5.
Pawłowska, H. (2004): Obsługa odbioru buraków w Cukrowniach Śląskiej Spółki Cukrowej, in: Burak Cukrowy 4/2004 (ŚSC edition), p. 5.

Pełka, B. (1994): Restrukturyzacja przedsiębiorstwa przemysłowego, Wydawnictwo "ORGMASZ", Warszawa 1994.

Pierwszy Portal Rolny (2005): Dopłaty nas kuszą, (URL: http://www.ppr.pl/artykul.php?id=125119, downloaded on 27 May 2005).

Pinto, B., M. Belka and S. Krajewski (1993): Transforming State Enterprises in Poland: Evidence on Adjustment by Manufacturing Firms, Brookings Papers Econ. Act., pp. 213-261.

Pohl, G., R. E. Anderson, S. Claessens, S. Djankov (1997): Privatization and Restructuring in Central and Eastern Europe: Evidence and Policy Options, World Bank Technical Paper No. 368, The World Bank, Washington, D.C.

Polskie Wydawnictwo Ekonomiczne (1998): Leksykon Prywatyzacji, Wydanie II rozszerzone, PWE, Warszawa 1998.

Porter, M. E. (1998): The Competitive Advantage of Nations, MACMILLAN PRESS LTD, London 1998.

Porter, M. E. (1998a): Clusters and the new economics of competition, Harvard Business Review, November-December 1998, pp. 77-90.

Powaga, J. (2004): Nie tylko wypadki, in: Cukrowniczy Przegląd Informacyjny BSO Polska 3/2004, pp. 14-15.

Pro-Invest International Sp. z o.o. (2001): Analiza formalno-prawnych i ekonomiczno-finansowych warunków powołania Spółki „Polski Cukier", Warszawa 2001, (unpublished).

Prusek, T. (2005): Słodko-gorzki rok, in: *Gazeta Wyborcza*, 26.01.2005, p. 20.

Radosevic, S. (1999): International Technology Transfer and Catch-up in Economic Development, Edward Elgar Publishing.

Render, H. (1989): Ein Strukturkonzept zur Verbesserung der Wettbewerbsstellung der norddeutschen Zuckerwirtschaft, Peter Lang Verlag, Frankfurt am Main.

Roland, G. (1994): On the Speed and Sequencing of Privatization and Restructuring, *Economic Journal* 104(426): 1158–68.

Roland, G. (2000): Transition and Economics: Politics, Markets and Firms, Cambridge, Massachusetts, MIT Press.

Roland Berger Strategy Consultants (2002): Seven strategic priorities for outperformers, URL: http://www.rolandberger.de (date of download: October 16, 2002).

Rudestam, K.E. and R.R. Newton (2001): Surviving Your Dissertation: A Comprehensive Guide to Content and Process, Sage Publications, Inc., Thousand Oaks, London, New Delhi.

Rugman, A. M. (1981): Inside the Multinationals: The Economics of Internal Markets, New York, Columbia University Press.

Rugman, A. M. (1985): Internationalisation is Still a General Theory of Foreign Direct Investment, *Weltwirtschaftliches Archiv*, 1985, Nr. 3.

Rybski, J. (2005): Stan i perspektywy rozwoju branży cukrowniczej w Polsce, in: Gazeta Cukrownicza 2/2005, Wydawnictwo SIGMA-NOT, pp. 48-55.

Rygielski, R. (2003): Dokąd zmierza polskie cukrownictwo, in: Nowe Cukrownictwo 2/2003 (229), Branżowy Magazyn Przemysłowy (BMP).

Rząpała, T. (2005): System sterowania silosem na cukier i stacją segregacji cukru w Chełmży, in: Gazeta Cukrownicza 1/2005, Wydawnictwo SIGMA-NOT, pp. 13-15.

Sachs, J. (1993): Poland's Jump to the Market Economy, MIT Press, Second paperback edition.

Savas, E. S. (2000): Privatization and Public-Private Partnerships, Seven Bridges Press, LLC, New York.

Schmidt, K. and M. Schnitzer (1993): Privatization and Management Incentives in the Transition Period in Eastern Europe, Journal of Comparative Economics, 17, 264-287.

Schnepp, O., M. von Glinow and A. Bhambri (1990): United States-China Technology Transfer, Englewood Cliffs, New York, Prentice-Hall.

Schnetzer, R. (1999): Business Process Reengineering kompakt und verständlich, Verlag Vieweg, Braunschweig/Wiesbaden, 1999.

Schröder, D. (1998): Costs of sugar production, in: Poel van der, P.W., H. Schiweck, T. Schwartz (1998): Sugar Technology: Beet and Cane Sugar Manufacture, Verlag Dr. Albert Bartens KG, Berlin 1998, pp. 1067-1083.

Schultes, Karl A. (1994): Die Zuckerindustrie in den Reformländern am Beispiel Ungarn, in Zuckerindustrie 119 (1994), Nr. 8, pp. 687-690.

Skawińska, E. (ed.) (2002): Konkurencyjność przedsiębiorstw: nowe podejście, Wydawnictwo Naukowe PWN, Warszawa-Poznań 2002.

Skwierz, M. (2005): Ścisłe doświadczenia polowe grupy Südzucker, in: Burak Cukrowy 1/2005 (Śląska Spółka Cukrowa edition), Wydawnictwo Bartens Sp. z o. o., Słubice, pp. 4-5.

Smart, P.A., S.J. Childe, R.S. Maull (1999): Supporting Business Reengineering in Industry: Towards a Methodology, in: Elzinga, J.D., T.R. Gulledge and Ch.-Y. Lee (ed.) (1999): Business Process Engineering: Advancing the State of the Art, Kluwer Academic Publishers, Norwell, Massachusetts, USA.

Smoleński, Z. (2004): Prognoza cen na rynku krajowym (URL: http://www.ierigz.waw.pl/prognozy/doc/ceny_cukru.doc, downloaded on November 29, 2004).

Solska, J. (1999): Monopolka, in: Polityka, Numer 43/1999 (2216).

Sommer, U. (2005): Der Markt für Zucker 2004, in: *Zuckerindustrie*, 130 (54) January 2005, Bartens, Berlin.

Sommer, U. (2006): Der Markt für Zucker 2005, in: *Zuckerindustrie*, 131 (2006), No. 1, Bartens, Berlin, pp. 45-51.

Sołtyk, R. (2004): Zarobić jak rolnik na Unii, in: Gazeta Wyborcza, 18-19 grudnia 2004, p. 29.

Spetch, A., P. Kończalski and D. Grzenkowitz (1996): A letter from Poland, in: British Sugar Beet Review, Volume 64, No. 1996, pp. 34-36.

Stankiewicz, D. (1999): Stan polskiej branży cukrowniczej, Kancelaria Sejmu, Biuro Studiów i Ekspertyz, Informacja nr 691, Październik 1999.

Stankiewicz, M. J. (2002): Konkurencyjność Przedsiębiorstwa: Budowanie konkurencyjności przedsiębiorstwa w warunkach globalizacji, Wydanie I, Towarzystwo Naukowe Organizacji i Kierownictwa, Stowarzyszenie Wyższej Użyteczności „Dom Organizatora", Toruń 2002.

Stowarzyszenie Techników Cukrowników: Informator Kampania w Świetle Liczb, Several Issues.

Sugar Economy Europe, Verlag Dr. Albert Bartens, Berlin, Germany, Several Issues.

Surdykowska, S. T. (1997): Prywatyzacja, Wydawnictwo Naukowe PWN, Warszawa 1997.

Suszyński, C. (1999): Restrukturyzacja Przedsiębiorstw. Proces zarządzania zmianami, Polskie Wydawnictwo Ekonomiczne, Warszawa 1999.

Suszyński, C. (2003): Restrukturyzacja, konsolidacja, globalizacja przedsiębiorstw, Polskie Wydawnictwo Ekonomiczne, Warszawa 2003.

Südzucker (2004): The Südzucker Group. Profile 2004, June 2004 (URL: http://www.suedzucker.de/en/downloads/profile/)

Sypka, A., J. Marcinkiewicz and S. Matyaszczyk (2006): Przebieg kampanii 2005/2006 w cukrowniach Krajowej Spółki Cukrowej S.A. (URL: http://www.stc.pl/dhttp.php?co=ksc_ds.ppt, downloaded on February 27, 2006).

Szacki, W. (2004): Chłop potęgą jest, in: *Gazeta Wyborcza* 26.10.2004, p. 4.
Szymaniak, A. (2001): Kapitał zagraniczny w Polsce: Uwarunkowania napływu i działalności, Wydawnictwo Naukowe Instytutu Nauk Politycznych i Dziennikarstwa Uniwersytetu im. A. Mickiewicza w Poznaniu, Poznań 2001.
Świetlicki, S. (2004): Informacja o aktualnej sytuacji przemysłu cukrowniczego w Polsce, in: Gazeta Cukrownicza 2-3/2004, Wydawnictwo SIGMA-NOT, pp. 34-41.
Świetlicki, S. (2005): Wyniki techniczno-produkcyjne polskich cukrowni w latach 1990-2004, in: Gazeta Cukrownicza 2/2005, Wydawnictwo SIGMA-NOT, pp. 34-47.
Tirole, J. (1991): Privatization in Eastern Europe: Incentives and the Economics of Transition, NBER Macroeconomic Annuals, 221-259.
Tittenbrun, J. (1995), "Ekonomiczny sens prywatyzacji", Wydawnictwo Fundacji Humaniora, Poznań 1995.
Toyota Europe (2005): Toyota Achieves 8th Record Year of Sales in Europe (URL: http://www.toyota-europe.com/about_toyota/news/recordyearofsales041.html, downloaded on 11 May 2005).
Toyota Europe (2005a): Toyota Achieves 7th Record Year of Sales in Europe (URL: http://www.toyota-europe.com/about_toyota/news/toyota_year_end.html, downloaded on 11 May 2005).
Tygodnik Ciechanowski (2004): Cukrownia po przejściach, in: Tygodnik Ciechanowski Nr.7, 17-02-2004.
UNCTAD (1994): *World Investment Report 1994: Transnational Corporations, Employment and the Workplace*, United Nations Conference on Trade and Development, New York and Geneva.
UNCTAD (1999): Foreign Direct Investment and Development, Issues Paper, UNCTAD/ ITE/IIT/10 (vol. I), United Nations Conference on Trade and Development, New York and Geneva, 1999 (URL: http://www.unctad.org/en/docs//psiteiitd10v1.en.pdf, downloaded on October 1, 2004).
UNCTAD (2000): *World Investment Report 2000: FDI and the Challenge of Development*, United Nations Conference on Trade and Development, New York and Geneva.
UNCTAD (2001): *World Investment Report 2001: Promoting Linkages*, United Nations Conference on Trade and Development, New York and Geneva.
Upton, D. M. (1995): What Really Makes Factories Flexible?, Harvard Business Review, July-August 1995, pp. 74-84.
Urban, R., P. Szajner and A. Staszczak (2005): Analiza wpływu reformy cukru w UE na polskich producentów żywności, Instytut Ekonomiki Rolnictwa i Gospodarki Żywnościowej, Warszawa, styczeń 2005.
USDA (1997): Hazard Analysis and Critical Control Point Principles and Application Guidelines, National Advisory Committee on Microbiological Criteria for Foods, U.S. Food and Drug Administration, U. S. Department of Agriculture (URL: http://www.cfsan.fda.gov/~comm/nacmcfp.html, downloaded on July 12, 2004).
USDA (1999): Agriculture in Poland & Hungary: Preparing for EU Accession, Agricultural Outlook, December 1999, Economic Research Service/USDA.
USDA (2005): EU-25 Agricultural Situation: EU 2005 Agriculture Budget, GAIN Report E35005, USDA Foreign Agricultural Service, December 23, 2004.
Verband Süddeutscher Zuckerrübenanbauer (2002): *Zuckermarkt*, Zuckerrüben-Magazin, Beilage zur dzz- Die Zuckerrüben Zeitung, Nr. 32, September 2002 (URL: http:// www.zuckerwirtschaft.de/pdf/Broschuere_ZMO.pdf, downloaded on October 1, 2004).

Verband Süddeutscher Zuckerrübenanbauer (2005): Reform fordert Opfer, war aber unausweichlich, Pressemitteilung, Würzburg, 25.11.2005 (URL: http://www.vsz.de/news/2005/VSZ-%20Pressemitteilung-25-11-2005.pdf, downloaded on December 4, 2005).

Wagener, H.-J. (1994): Transformation as a Political-Economic Process, in: Wagener, H.-J. (ed.) (1994): The Political Economy of Transformation, Physica-Verlag, Heidelberg 1994, pp. 3-22.

Wagener, H-J. (1997): Privateigentum und Unternehmenskontrolle in Transformationswirtschaften, Discussion Papers 1/1997, Frankfurter Institut für Transformationsstudien (URL: http://fit.euv-frankfurt-o.de/veroeffentlichungen/discussion%20papers/pdf-format/ 97-1-Wagener.pdf, downloaded on October 2, 2003).

Wagener, H.-J., F. Bönker, E. F. Rosenbaum (2000): Privatization in Context: an Introduction, in: Wagener, H.-J., F. Bönker, E. F. Rosenbaum (ed.) (2000): Privatization, Corporate Governance and the Emergence of Markets, MACMILLAN PRESS LTD, London, pp. 1-13.

Waleriańczyk, E. W. (1993): Relacja z wizyty w British Sugar, in: Gazeta Cukrownicza 5/1993, Wydawnictwo SIGMA-NOT, pp. 91-95.

Waleriańczyk, E. W. (2001): Wybrane problemy przemysłu cukrowniczego w okresie 175-lecia (1826-2001), in: 175 lat Polskiego Przemysłu Cukrowniczego, Stowarzyszenie Techników Cukrowników, Dom Wydawniczy „Verbum", Warszawa 2001, pp. 37-66.

Walkenhorst, P. (1998): Restructuring the sugar industry in Poland: Transition from state socialism to the Common Agricultural Policy, Verlag Dr. Albert Bartens KG, Berlin, Germany.

Walkenhorst, P. (2001): Sugar sector restructuring in Poland: some benefits and costs of EU accession, in: *European Review of Agricultural Economics*, Vol. 28 (1) (2001), pp. 57-78.

Warnes, A.J.N and P.D. Thompson (1993): Zmniejszenie zużycia energii w cukrowniach British Sugar, in: Gazeta Cukrownicza 12/1993, Wydawnictwo SIGMA-NOT, pp. 243-244, 255.

Warszawska Grupa Konsultingowa (WGK) and Pro-Invest International (2003): Krajowa Spółka Cukrowa S.A.: Program restrukturyzacji i biznesplan na lata 2003-2008, Toruń-Warszawa, 4 lipca 2003 (unpublished).

Wawro, P. and W. Küster (2004): Die Privatisierung der polnischen Zuckerindustrie, in: Zuckerindustrie 129 (2004) Nr. 7, pp. 493-497.

Wawro, P. (2004a): Kampania 2003/04 w Grupie Nordzucker, in: Gazeta Cukrownicza 4/2004, Wydawnictwo SIGMA-NOT, pp. 93-95.

Wawro, P. (2005): Kampania 2004 w grupie Nordzucker, in: Gazeta Cukrownicza 4/2005, Wydawnictwo SIGMA-NOT, pp. 100-102.

Wesołowska, E., J. Olechowski, M. Rabij (2004): Wielka metamorfoza, in: Newsweek (Polish edition), 20.06.2004, pp. 54-55.

Węgrzynowski, Z. (2003): Modernizacja zakładu Cukrowni Gosławice, in Nowe Cukrownictwo 3/2003, BMP Sp. Z o. o., pp. 7-8.

Wężowska, M. (2004): Zombi rządzi. Haiti: 200 lat trudnej wolności i samotności, in: Polityka Nr 4 (2436), 24 stycznia 2004, pp. 43-45.

White, B. (2000): Dissertation Skills for Business and Management Students, Continuum, London, New York.

Williamson, O. E. (1985): The Economic Institutions of Capitalism, New York, Free Press.

Wilk, A. (2002): Franz Carl Achard i Ziemia Wołowska, in: Gazeta Cukrownicza 11/2002, Wydawnictwo SIGMA-NOT, pp. 314-316.

Winiecki, J. (2001): The role of the new, entrepreneurial private sector in transition and economic performance in light of the successes in Poland, the Czech Republic and Hungary, Bank of Finland Institute for Economies in Transition, Discussion Paper No.12, 2001.
Winiecki, J. (2002): Transition Economies and Foreign Trade, Routledge Studies of Societies in Transition, London 2002.
Wojnarowska, A. and A. Igras (2004): Ropczyce- jedna z piętnastu, in: Nowe Cukrownictwo 3/2004, pp. 11-13.
World Trade Organization (2005): European Communities-Export Subsidies on Sugar, Report of the Appellate Body, AB-2005-2, 28 April 2005 (URL: http://www.wto.org/english/tratop_e/dispu_e/265_266_283abr_e.pdf, downloaded on 4 May 2005).
Wróblewski, Ł. (2004): KSC u progu kampanii, in: Gazeta Cukrownicza 10/2004, Wydawnictwo SIGMA-NOT, pp. 274-275.
Wróblewski, Ł. (2005): Dłużej i efektywniej. Podsumowanie kampanii w KSC, in: Gazeta Cukrownicza 1/2005, Wydawnictwo SIGMA-NOT, p. 30.
Wykrętowicz, S. (1997): Najnowsze dzieje cukrownictwa w Polsce 1944-1989, Muzeum Narodowe Rolnictwa i Przemysłu Rolno-Spożywczego w Szereniawie, Poznań 1997.
Wysokińska, Z. (1998): Wpływ bezpośrednich inwestycji zagranicznych na dostosowania strukturalne w gospodarce, in: Olesiński, Z. (ed.): Bezpośrednie inwestycje zagraniczne w Polsce, Polskie Wydawnictwo Ekonomiczne, Warszawa 1998, pp. 113-135.
Wziątek-Kubiak (2003): Konkurencyjność polskiego przemysłu, Instytut Nauk Ekonomicznych PAN, Dom Wydawniczy Bellona, Warszawa 2003.
Zalewski, R. I. (2002): Rola jakości w budowie konkurencyjności firmy, in: Skawińska, E. (ed.) (2002): Konkurencyjność przedsiębiorstw: nowe podejście, Wydawnictwo Naukowe PWN, Warszawa-Poznań 2002, pp. 145-206.
Zieliński, M (2004): Inwestycja w Skansen, in: Wprost, 13 czerwca 2004, pp. 40-42.
Zink, K. J. (1997): Total Quality Management as a Holistic Management Concept, Springer-Verlag.
Zonis, M. and Semler, D. (1992): The East European Opportunity, John Wiley and Sons, Inc., New York.
Zuckerindustrie, Verlag Dr. Albert Bartens KG, Berlin, Germany, Several Issues.
Zuckerwirtschaft, Verlag Dr. Albert Bartens KG, Berlin, Germany, Several Issues.
Związek Plantatorów Buraka Cukrowego (Pomorski Cukier S.A. w Chełmży) (2005): Przebieg kampanii 2004 w Pomorskim Cukrze z perspektywy Związku Plantatorów Buraka Cukrowego, in: Burak Cukrowy 1/2005 (Nordzucker Polska edition), Wydawnictwo Bartens, Słubice, p. 8.
Żagiel, S. (n. a.): Wokół kryształu, in: Tygodnik Ciechanowski (online edition) (URL: http://www.tc.ciechanow.pl/arch/010925/cukier.htm, downloaded on September 9, 2005).
Żukowska-Gagelmann, K. (2001), "Productivity Spillovers from Foreign Direct Investment: The Case of Poland", European University Studies, Series V, Economics and Management, Lang Verlag, Frankfurt am Main 2001
Żurawska, M. (2005): Jak Plantatorzy oceniają współpracę z Cukrownią?, in: Burak Cukrowy 1/2003 (Nordzucker edition), Wydawnictwo Bartens, Słubice, p. 8.

Interviews

Stanisław Iwan (Managing Director of the sugar factory in Gryfice, Chairman of the Board of Directors of *Poznańsko-Pomorska Spółka Cukrowa* in the years 1998-2001), Gryfice, June 9, 2003; Gryfice, February 6, 2004; Słubice, March 3, 2004; Gryfice, March 20, 2004.

Dr. Adam Koziołek (Representative of Nordzucker AG in Poland, Member of the Board of Directors at the sugar factory in Opalenica), Przeźmierowo, January 12, 2004; Several phone interviews.

Jarosław Kamieniarz (Manager, Raw Material Management, Nordzucker Polska Sp. z. o. o.), January 30, 2004 (phone interview).

Stanisław Barnaś (President of the National Association of Sugarbeet Growers in Poland), January 30, 2004 (phone interview).

Dr. Łucja Chudoba (Institute of Agricultural and Food Economics in Warsaw), Pułtusk, March 11, 2004; Several phone interviews.

Rafał Wereszczaka (Corporate Communications Manager, Cukrownia Glinojeck S.A.), Pułtusk, March 10, 2004, Mrzeżyno, August 8, 2004; Warszawa, January 24, 2005.

Andrzej Zarzycki (Managing Director of the sugar factory in Glinojeck), Pułtusk, March 10, 2004.

Prof. Zygmunt Smoleński (Institute of Agricultural and Food Economics in Warsaw), Pułtusk, March 11, 2004.

Piotr Kończalski (Vice-director, Raw Material Management, sugar factory in Glinojeck), Pułtusk, March 11, 2004.

Dr. Stanisław Z. Dziedzic (Business Development Director, British Sugar Overseas Polska), Pułtusk, March 11, 2004; Warszawa, January 24, 2005.

Dariusz Zawadzki (Shift Superintendent, sugar factory in Unisław), Pułtusk, March 11, 2004.

Janusz Pierun (Representative of Pfeifer & Langen in Poland), Poznań, September 7, 2004; Poznań, October 13, 2004; Środa Wielkopolska, March 17, 2005.

Dr. Marian Brzeziński (Staff member of the Faculty of Economics at the Adam Mickiewicz University in Poznań; economic advisor to numerous sugar factories in Poland since 1991; co-author of the restructuring program of the national sugar corporation *Krajowa Spółka Cukrowa "Polski Cukier"*, main architect of the consolidation of sugar factories taken over by Nordzucker in Poland), Poznań, October 7, 2004.

Dr. Thomas Kirchberg (Chairmen of the Board of Directors of Südzucker Polska), Wrocław, October 25, 2004; Wrocław, May 18, 2005.

Dr. Gerd Jung (Chairman of the Board of Directors of Nordzucker Polska), Interview questions were sent to the interviewee by e-mail. The interviewee subsequently provided detailed answers in writing.

Maria Gothan (Chairman of the Board of Directors of *Wydawnictwo Bartens Sp. z o. o.* (Polish branch office of *Bartens* publishing house, headquartered in Berlin), editor of the periodical *Burak Cukrowy* (Sugarbeet) and the statistical booklet *Cukier i Skrobia* (Sugar and Starch) Słubice, Interviewed on several occasions.

Beata Szumniak (Communication and Administration Director, British Sugar Overseas Polska), Warszawa, January 24, 2005.

Michał Żero (Instytut Przemysłu Cukrowniczego, Leszno), March 1, 2005 (phone interview).

Tomasz Miara (Human Resource Manager, Pfeifer & Langen Polska), Środa Wielkopolska, March 17, 2004.

Piotr Szajner (Institute of Agricultural and Food Economics in Warsaw), Several phone interviews.

Matthias Neubert (Südzucker Polska), Wrocław, May 18, 2005; Several phone interviews.

Łukasz Wróblewski (Press Spokesman of *Krajowa Spółka Cukrowa*), Several phone interviews.

Kazimierz Kobza (Assosiation of Sugarbeet Growers in Poland), Interview questions were sent to the interviewee by e-mail. The interviewee subsequently provided answers in writing.

Appendix 1: Organizational structure of the Polish sugar industry (1989).

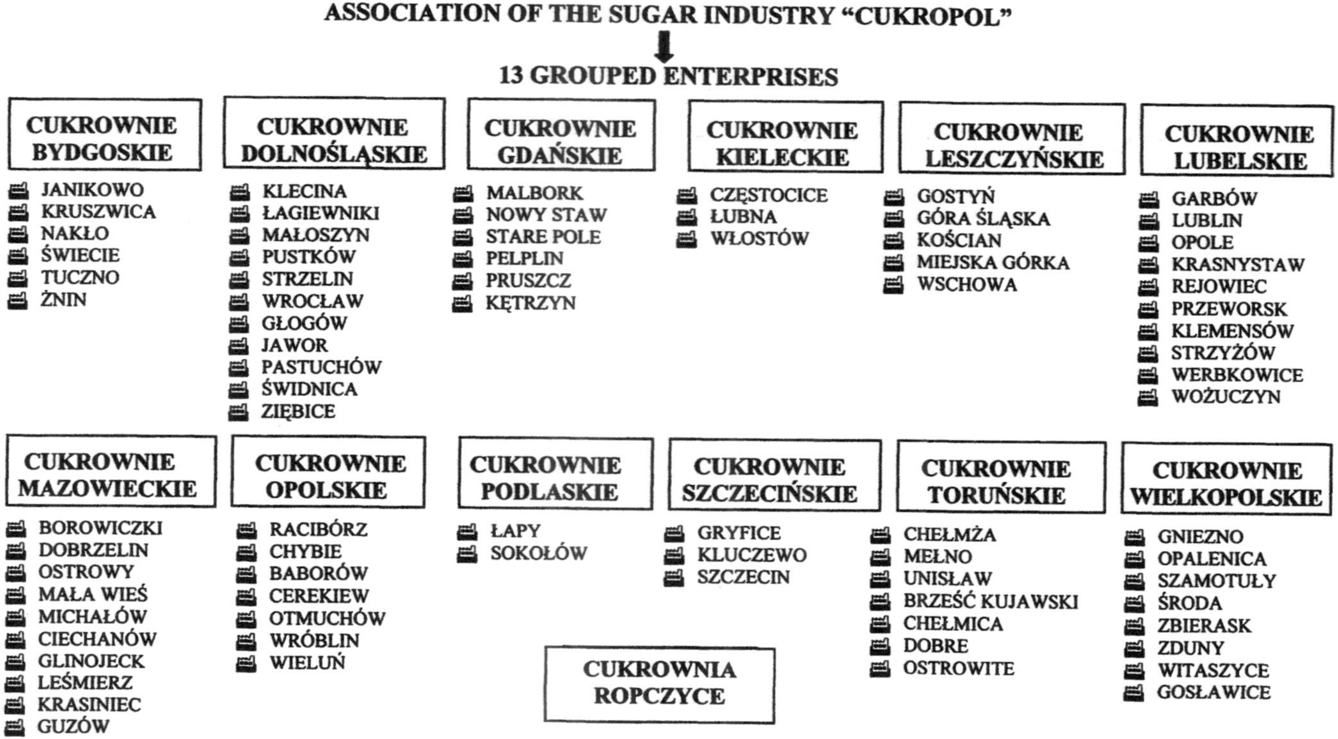

Source: Own illustration based on Wykrętowicz 1997, p. 85.

Appendix 2: Organizational Structure of KSC S.A. (2005)

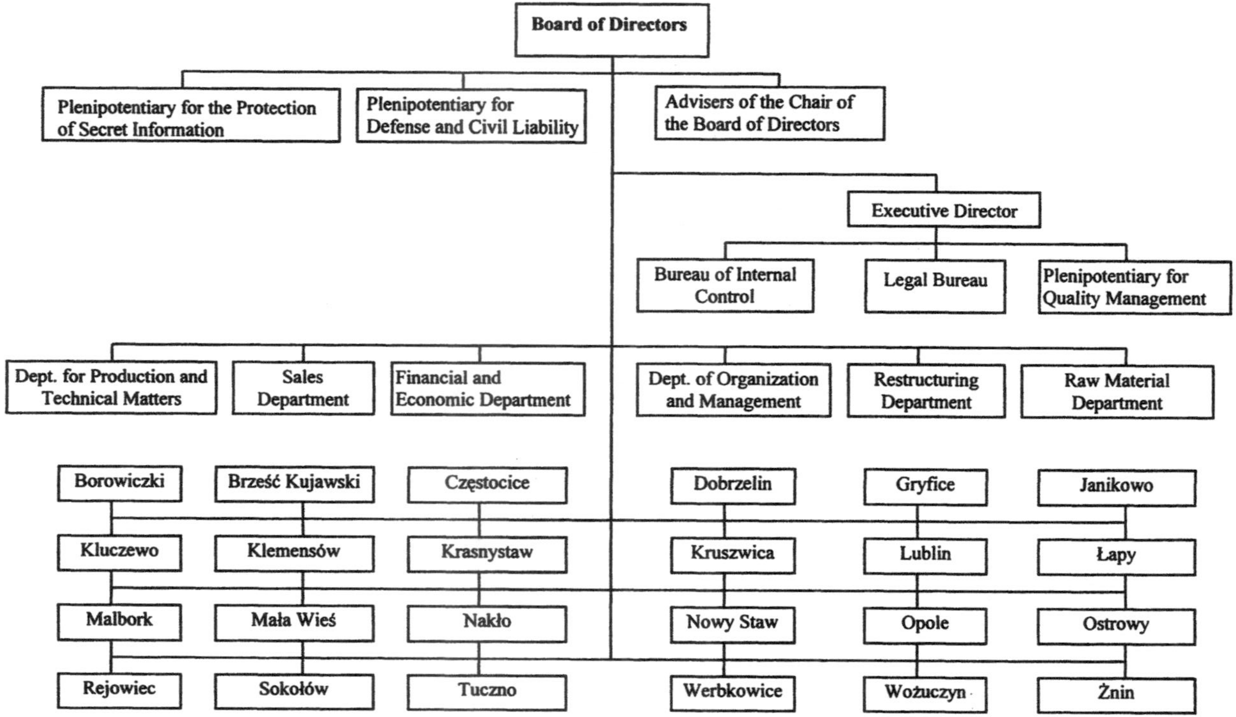

Source: KSC.

Joanna Długosz / Marcin Witkowski (Hrsg./eds.)

Perspektiven für Europa – eine neue Öffnung? Perspectives of Europe – The New Opening?

Frankfurt am Main, Berlin, Bern, Bruxelles, New York, Oxford, Wien, 2006.
293 S., zahlr. Abb., Tab. und Graf.
ISBN 3-631-54674-2 / US-ISBN 0-8204-9862-9 · br. € 42.–*

Die Beiträge dieses Sammelbandes verbindet das Ziel, Grundfragen der europäischen Integration zu erörtern sowie vielfältige Perspektiven für die Zusammenarbeit auf der europäischen Ebene aufzuzeigen. Behandelt werden folgende Bereiche: Perspektiven der europäischen politischen Zusammenarbeit, der Entwicklung der europäischen rechtlichen Standards, der europäischen wirtschaftlichen Integration, der Bekämpfung der Armut in der Europäischen Union, des freien Personenverkehrs in der Europäischen Union sowie der Bildung europäischer regionaler Initiativen. Dieses Buch intendiert die Begründung gemeinsamer europäischer Perspektiven für alle Mitgliedstaaten der Europäischen Union. Ferner wird die Frage behandelt, inwieweit die allgemein positive Bewertung der EU-Erweiterung in der europäischen politischen, rechtlichen, wirtschaftlichen und gesellschaftlichen Realität zum Ausdruck kommt.

The articles in this publication seek to explain some of the fundamental matters connected with the European integration process and will cast light upon several perspectives of European cooperation. The following themes have been examined most closely: perspectives of European political cooperation, development of European legal standards, European economic integration, fighting poverty in the European Union and the free movement of people within the European Union and creation of European local initiatives. The authors also attempt to discuss the question of how the generally positive evaluation of the European Union enlargement reflects the political, legal, economic and social reality in Europe.

Kolibri 360 GmbH
Ferdinand-Jühlke-Straße 7
99095 Erfurt, Deutschland
produktsicherheit@kolibri360.de

Druck:
CPI Druckdienstleistungen GmbH
im Auftrag der
Kolibri 360 GmbH
Ferdinand-Jühlke-Str. 7
99095 Erfurt